PARKER SCHOOL STUDIES
IN FOREIGN AND COMPARATIVE LAW

THE SOVIET LEGAL SYSTEM

Third Edition
Fundamental Principles and Historical Commentary

by
JOHN N. HAZARD
WILLIAM E. BUTLER
PETER B. MAGGS

Published for the
PARKER SCHOOL OF FOREIGN AND COMPARATIVE LAW
COLUMBIA UNIVERSITY IN THE CITY OF NEW YORK

BY

OCEANA PUBLICATIONS, INC.
DOBBS FERRY, NEW YORK
1977

Library of Congress Cataloging in Publication Data

Hazard, John Newbold, 1909-
   The Soviet legal system.

   (Parker School studies in foreign and comparative law)
   Bibliography: p.
   Includes indexes.
   1. Law—Russia. I. Butler, William Elliott,
1939-   joint author. II. Maggs, Peter B., joint
author. III. Title. IV. Series: Columbia University.
Parker School of Foreign and Comparative Law. Parker
School studies in foreign and comparative law.
Law   340'.0947   77-24349
ISBN 0-379-00790-8

© Copyright 1977 by Parker School of Foreign and Comparative Law

All rights reserved. No part of this publication may be reproduced or transmitted in any form or by any means, electronic or mechanical, including photocopy, recording, xerography, or any information storage and retrieval system, without permission in writing from the publisher.

Manufactured in the United States of America

To
Susan, Darlene, and Barbara

THE PARKER SCHOOL OF FOREIGN AND COMPARATIVE LAW

The Parker School of Foreign and Comparative Law is dedicated exclusively to the study and teaching of foreign and comparative law. The School owes its existence to the beneficence of Judge Edwin B. Parker, who left the bulk of his estate for the founding and support of a school which would prepare young persons "to render practical service of a high order to the government of the United States in its foreign relations or to financial and industrial institutions engaged in foreign trade or commerce."

The present mission of the Parker School is threefold. The School is required by the University Statutes to provide "the educational needs of the School of Law and the School of International Affairs with respect to instruction in the laws of foreign countries." To this end, the School offers five courses and five seminars. The School also has a research and publication program of its own and to date has published more than a dozen books on various aspects of foreign law. Lastly, the School offers each June a concentrated four weeks program in foreign law for lawyers interested in international problems. To date, more than five hundred lawyers have attended the program. They have come from all of the United States, and from Canada, Latin America, Western Europe, Japan and the Middle East.

In 1977 the School marked its forty-sixth year of affiliation with Columbia University in the City of New York.

TABLE OF CONTENTS

Preface xv

Part I: The Soviet State and its Citizens

Foreword 3

I. The Claim of Legality 5

    A. The Communist Party states Goals and prescribes Methods 8

    B. The Philosophers explain the Nature and Tasks of Law 11

    C. The Legislators define Law's Functions 14

II. Preparing Communist Self-Administration 15

    A. The Aim of Public Self-Administration 17

    B. The Voluntary People's Guards 19

    C. The Comrades' Courts 22

    D. Third-party Umpires 30

    E. Peoples' Control 31

    F. Social Prosecutors and Defenders 32

    G. Mass Legal Education 34

III. Soviet Federalism 35

    A. The Philosophical Novelty of Soviet Federation 38

    B. The Constitutional Structure of Federation 41

    C. Federal and Republic Relationship to Local Government .. 43

    D. Regulation of Conflict of Laws within the Federation 44

IV. Sources and Hierarchy of Law	47
A. The Theoretical Approach to Sources of Law	50
B. Protection of Constitutional Supremacy	53
C. Amendment of the Constitution	54
D. The Legislative Process	55
E. Judicial Interpretation and Legislative Initiative	55
V. The Instruments of Public Order	56
A. Structure and Jurisdiction of Courts	59
B. Extraneous Influences on Judges	67
C. The Notariat as a Control over Legality	69
D. The Registrar of Vital Statistics	71
E. The Procuracy as Control over Legality	72
F. State Security Agencies	75
G. Agencies of Public Order	76
H. The Bar	77
VI. Civil Rights and Socialism	81
A. Socialism's Rights and Duties	86
B. The Right to Representation	88
C. The Right to Religious Worship	90
D. The Right to Freedom of Movement	94
E. The Right to Freedom of Expression	96
F. The Right to Emigrate	104

VII. Procedural Due Process of Law 106

    A. The Constitution and the Codes 110

    B. Arrest 112

    C. The Preliminary Investigation 114

    D. Expert Opinion 118

    E. Presumption of Innocence 119

    F. The Right to Counsel 121

    G. Fair Trial 124

    H. Review by a Court 127

    I. The Extra-legal Review Function of the Press 129

    J. Modernization of Correctional Procedures 130

    K. Procedural Problems of Amnesty 131

VIII. Due Process for Civil Parties 132

    A. The Place of Civil Procedure in Contrast to
       Social Procedures 136

    B. Fundamental Principles 137

    C. The Role of the Court in Civil Cases 140

    D. Res Judicata 142

    E. Fair Trial 143

    F. The Procuracy in Civil Cases 145

IX. Criminal Law in the Preservation of Public Order 146

    A. Criminal Jurisprudence 150

B.	Punishment	151
C.	The Causes of Crime	159
D.	Intent	162
E.	Negligence	169
F.	Insanity	171
G.	Aggravating and Mitigating Circumstances	173
H.	Self-defense	175
I.	Immunity	176
J.	Approaching Contemporary Problems: Drug Abuse	177

Part II: Administering Soviet Socialism

	Foreword	181
X.	Delineation of the Public and Private Sectors	183
	A. State vs. Private Ownership	186
	B. Taxation	192
XI.	Use of the Land	193
	A. General Principles	195
	B. Allocation and Use of Land	198
	C. Payment for Use or Taking of Land	205
	1. Land Rent	205
	2. Land Taking	206
XII.	The Directing and Planning Agencies	209
	A. The Organizational Structure	212

	B. Plan Enforcement	213
	C. Production Quality Control	216
XIII.	The Operating Agencies	218
	A. Organizational Types	221
	B. Enterprise Powers	224
	C. Fraud	231
	D. Mismanagement	234
	E. Liquidation	239
XIV.	Law as an Instrument of Administrative Order	241
	A. Agencies for Adjudication of Contract Disputes	244
	B. Plan and Contract	247
	C. Fault	252
	D. Damages	263
	E. Unplanned Contracts	269
	F. Contracts between State Enterprises and Private Citizens	271
	G. The Economic Law Dispute	274
XV.	The Cooperatives as Supplementary Agencies	278
	A. The Collective Farm and its Members	281
	B. Plan and Contract on the Collective Farm	285
	C. The Farm of the Future	288
	D. Housing Construction Cooperatives	288
	E. Other Types of Cooperatives	291

XVI. Labor Relations and Public Enterprise 297

    A. Basic Guarantees of Workers' Rights 299

    B. Collective Agreements 304

    C. Individual Contract 308

    D. Resolution of Labor Disputes 310

    E. The Duty to Work 324

XVII. Encouragement of Inspiration 327

    A. Rewards for Writers 343

    B. Rewards for Scientists, Inventors and Innovators 345

Part III: Private Legal Rights and Obligations of Soviet Citizens

Foreword 359

XVIII. Personal Property Rights and Their Scope 361

    A. Socialist Theory and the Nature of Personal Property 363

    B. Nature and Scope of Personal Property Rights 365

    C. Restrictions on Personal Property Rights 374

    D. Loss of Rights of Personal Ownership 382

XIX. Inheritance and Socialism 389

    A. Fundamental Principles of Inheritance under Socialism... 392

    B. Inheritance by Will 397

    C. Inheritance by Operation of Law 402

    D. Inheritance in the Collective Farm Household 405

    E. Probate and Estate Administration 408

    F. Inheritance of Copyright 413

XX. Private Contracts 414

    A. Concept and Purpose of Contracts under Socialism 415

    B. Basic Formalities Relating to Conclusion of Contracts 417

    C. Invalidity, Illegality and Their Consequences 430

    D. Remedies for Breach of Contract 430

XXI. Torts and Social Insurance 436

    A. General Principles of Tort Liability 440

    B. Strict Liability Arising Out of
Extra-Hazardous Activities 450

    C. Employment-Related Injuries 459

    D. Liability for Injuries to Rescuers 466

XXII. Marriage and Divorce 469

    A. Fundamental Concepts of Family, Marriage
and Divorce 472

    B. Marriage 480

    C. Abortion 491

    D. Dissolution of Marriage 493

    E. Maintenance and Alimony 499

    F. Custody of Children 508

    G. Rules Applicable to Citizenship, Foreign Law
and International Treaties 509

XXIII. The Minor: His Rights and Responsibilities 512

A. Children Born Out of Wedlock 513

B. The Right of Support 520

C. Adoption 525

D. Parental Rights and Guardianship 532

E. The Minor as Employee 536

F. Legal Capacity and Civil Liability of Minors 538

G. Treatment of the Youthful Offender 541

Appendix — Legal Forms 553

Bibliography 561

Annotation to 1977 Draft Constitution 599

Index to Principal Texts 609

Index 613

PREFACE

Debate has raged for more than fifty years over the system of public order maintained within the U.S.S.R. Is it a legal system, and if so, is it unique, deserving to be classed with the common law, the civil law, Islamic and Hindu law as one of the principal legal systems of the world? The purpose of these volumes is to permit American readers to judge for themselves by examining the sources: communist party rules and directives, legislation, judicial opinions and the views of Soviet law professors.

There were few in the west at the time of the Russian revolution who thought the Bolsheviks legally minded. Yet, as the fervor of 1917 fades into history, those identifying the Soviet public order system with the negation of law are no longer many. The trend of legal philosophers in the west has been toward classification of the rules by which Soviet citizens live within the framework of one or the other of the two primary schools of legal thought. This diversity of view has been made possible by tendencies evidenced during the evolution of the Soviet state. The situation is no longer what it was in 1917.

John C.H. Wu, writing in the Catholic Encyclopedia,[1] has concluded that "this is positivism pushed to its logical end. The will of the dominant class becomes the essence of law, and reason becomes the handmaiden of will." For him as a proponent of natural law, the Soviet system is but an application of the positivist approach, to be accepted or rejected as a legal system, in accordance with the examiner's acceptance, or rejection, of positivism generally.

In contrast to Professor Wu's conclusion, Hans Kelsen, perhaps the most widely read positivist of the twentieth century, finds in Soviet legal philosophy as it has evolved since its third decade an element of the natural law approach. He declares, "What is most amazing in this theory of the bolshevik Vyshinsky is that it is exactly of the same type as the bourgeois theory which the Soviet writers have derided and ridiculed more than any other theory: the natural law doctrine. . .which precisely in accordance with Vyshinsky's recipe, works out, or pretends to work out principles 'from life,' that is, from nature in general and from the nature of

---

[1] John C. H. Wu, "Law," The Catholic Encyclopedia, Sixth Section Supplement II (1955), 13, column 1.

society, or, what amounts to the same, from the social relationships in particular; with the only difference that these principles are the ideal norms of capitalist law."[2]

The issue is joined as to whether roots of Soviet law are positivist or consonant with natural law thinking, but it is evident that eminent proponents of both approaches to public order systems have called the Soviet system "law." If the reader, after examination of the materials that follow, concludes that these philosophers are right, the second question is posed, namely is the Soviet legal system unique? Professor René David of the University of Paris finds the Soviet legal system one of the five principal legal systems of the world, unique because of the socialist structure of the society to which it is applied.[3] The late Baron Nolde, a Russian jurist of the Imperial period, who passed his mature years in France, declared the Soviet system "an original and autonomous system" even though it borrowed rules from the German and Swiss codes.[4]

Oxford University's Professor Emeritus of Comparative Law, F.H. Lawson, has quite the contrary view on uniqueness. He concludes that the Soviet legal system is but a variation of the civil law system, and that the Marxist political philosophy that infuses it has not changed its character.[5] In his mind the civil law system received from Rome provides the trunk of the tree. The Soviet legal system is but a branch, among the many branches representing the modern public order systems of France, Italy, Germany, Greece, Brazil and the many other countries following the pattern conceived originally by the Roman jurists.

Soviet legal philosophers have set Marxist inspired tasks for their legal system, but they have used familiar terms from the past and familiar formulae. To Lawson, as an Englishman, concerned as Englishmen have been traditionally with forms of action and legal remedies rather than with philosophical premises, the Soviet system cannot claim for itself a special chamber in the house of the law. It matters not to Lawson that Soviet philosophers think their political and economic goals to have caused a metamorphosis in their system of law justifying their claim to uniqueness.

As an innovation in this third edition, the work has been expanded into two volumes. The first contains brief historical notes as each chapter is introduced together with excerpts from statutes, academic treatises and court decisions designed to give the reader a sense of Soviet law as a public order system. The first volume has been prepared with teaching in mind, although casual readers and legal practitioners seeking a key to a system becoming of increasing importance in commercial relations between East and West should find it helpful as an introduction to more detailed study of a given subject. The second volume contains full texts of statutes, sometimes excerpted in the first volume, which are designed for those requiring the

---

[2]Hans Kelsen, The Communist Theory of Law (New York, 1955) 120.
[3]René David, Traité élémentaire de droit civil comparé (Paris, 1950) 224.
[4]Pierre Arminjon, Boris Nolde, and Martin Wolff, Traité de droit comparé (Paris, 1950), 1, 51.
[5]F. H. Lawson, book review, University of Chicago Law Review, XXI (1953-1954), 780-781. See also Harold J. Berman, Justice in Russia: An Interpretation of Soviet Law (Cambridge, Mass., 1951) 3.

full texts in their research. The focus is the present time, although some documents are taken from earlier periods. The reason for their inclusion is that they are still in force, or in the case of treatises and judicial decisions represent attitudes still held.

These two volumes are also a prologue, for the Soviet public order system is in constant flux. Two factors contend for domination. On the one hand there is the achievement of sixty years, most notable in the stabilization of society; in the general acceptance of a way of life. This has had profound influence outside the U.S.S.R., giving some specialists reason to believe that a convergence is approaching between the Soviet public order system as it moves into its seventh decade and the systems of the West, especially where the need to press toward a "welfare state" structure has been felt to meet the rising expectations of peoples. On the other hand there is the desire to retain the socialist core of the early years of militant communism when courts were popular and procedures simple. There is strong sentiment against any convergence with the West, and the legal structures are designed to prevent it. Marxist political philosophy still plays a role in the making of decisions in Moscow, although it is not entirely the same as the philosophy that motivated the revolutionaries of 1917.

Just what the two competing factors may do to the development of the Soviet legal system has yet to be appraised. Will institutional stabilization become more evident? Will the Marxist philosophical factor fade away as stabilization occurs, or will it be reasserted? The material in the two volumes is designed to facilitate the formulation of opinions on these questions. The search for answers acquires even greater interest as the Soviet model is taken up by leaders of developing countries in Africa and Asia. Each group seems to be searching for a system which represents in some measure the tradition of the lands they lead, but many say that the Eastern European model provides some part of their inspiration.

W.E.B.
J.N.H.
P.B.M.

February, 1977

THE SOVIET LEGAL SYSTEM

Contemporary Documentation and Historical Commentary

PART I

THE SOVIET STATE AND ITS CITIZENS

FOREWORD

Joseph Stalin died in 1953. For nearly thirty years he had increasingly influenced the course of Soviet law, bringing relationships between the Soviet state and its citizens to such a pass that his successors quickly expressed their determination to change radically the Soviet public order system. Nikita Khrushchev began the denunciation of Stalin's public order concepts at the 1956 Congress of the Communist Party, and his denunciation still stands, although muted at times.

A return to "socialist legality" as originally conceived by Lenin became the pledge of new leaders. Soviet legal scholars were directed to draft new laws to implement the political program of change. Just what was required to achieve a goal of stability of law and to put emphasis upon citizens' rights within a framework of Marxist thinking was unclear, but those who directed the technical work turned their attention to broad reform. They called for new measures to protect citizens from bureaucrats, to increase popular participation in the administrative work of government, to revise law controlling crime, to improve procedures to determine truth in trials, to bring practice into conformity with guidelines.[1]

Those who read the record set forth in Part I will have reason to ask, in the light of post-Stalin expressions of determination to restore Lenin's emphasis, whether a major turning point in Soviet law has been reached; whether Khrushchev's innovations have faded since his ouster in 1964; whether stability has replaced the flexibility favored by Stalin; whether the oft-stated goal of the "withering away of the state and law" guides contemporary policy makers.

---

[1] see V.M. Tchkhikvadze, L'évolution de la science juridique soviétique, 20 Revue Internationale de Droit Comparé 19 (1968) and V. Kudriavtsev, "Legal Science and Social Progress," 27 Current Digest of the Soviet Press, No. 27, pp. 4-5 (1975), translated from Izvestiia, July 8, 1975, p. 5.

CHAPTER I

The Claim of Legality

"A law is a political measure, it is politics."[1] With these words V.I. Lenin epitomized in 1916 his thinking on legal systems. The judges and administrators brought to office after the Russian revolution were frequently to cite these words as justification for application of measures dictated by their consciences, even though they had no support for such action in the document in their hand with its inscription, "law," "decree" or "instruction."

The attitude of mind that policy directives in the form of law were to be read for guidance but were not binding was encouraged by the events of the first months following the revolution. Since the Bolsheviks had seized power in November 1917 without a fully developed plan for the legal system they expected to install, they authorized the men and women chosen to preserve order and settle disputes to utilize their social consciences, and such laws of the dethroned Tsar as they might think still suitable as guidance.[2] Only a few key matters were made the subject of immediate legislation. Codes of law did not emerge for five years. It was a time for experimentation, guided in some measure by the Ministry of Justice, but one in which judges and administrators felt themselves essentially free to behave as they wished.

Some of them also thought that the legal system would soon fall into disuse as the state "withered away" in accordance with the prophecy of Marx and Engels. Under such circumstances it was hardly necessary to adhere strictly to rules set in formal documents expected soon to be pushed aside as irrelevant to the communist society of the Bolsheviks' dreams.

When the chaos resulting from the civil war of 1919-1920 made it clear that economic recovery was impossible without restoration of a form of controlled capitalism, Lenin began a strategic retreat, part of which was a more formal attitude

---

[1] V. I. Lenin. "Concerning a caricature of Marxism and concerning imperialist economism," 23 Sochineniia [Collected Works] (4th ed., Moscow, 1949) 36.
[2] Decree No. 1 on the Courts, November 27, 1917, [1917] I. Sob. Uzak. RSFSR. No. 4. item 50.

toward the rules of public order. In 1922 these were codified, and judges and administrators were ordered to abide by them, but still there was offered considerable latitude. In the criminal code a provision once found in Tsarist codes but abandoned in 1903, fourteen years before the revolution, was reintroduced, namely the principle of "analogy."[3] Under this principle a judge who considered a given individual "socially dangerous" might convict him of crime even though he had not violated any specific article of the criminal code. He supported his view by finding the action of the accused analogous to some different but relatively similar action that had been defined as crime by the code. Likewise, in the civil code, the judge was permitted to reject application of a rule of the code if he thought that in the given situation its application would result in a decision that was out of keeping with the aims of the new society.[4]

Not only were there escape clauses written into the codes, but the attitude of many of the draftsmen was that the codes were themselves to be temporary, made necessary solely as concessions to the effective functioning of neo-capitalism, and to be abandoned or at least simplified when the benefits of capitalist incentive had restored the economy sufficiently to make possible a new start in the direction of socialism. Beginning with 1927 new simple codes of procedure and of criminal law were printed and circulated widely for consideration as replacements for the codes of 1922.[5] In these codes judges were again to have broad powers to make up their own minds as to what was desired in each case.

Such individualization of the public order process did not meet Stalin's needs. He could not govern if he could not command and be certain of rigid compliance with his laws. He attacked the mounting popularity of the simplifiers at its very base, namely in the concept that as the economy moved toward socialism the state would begin to wither away. He declared in 1930[6] that while he held as a Marxist to the belief that the state would be unnecessary in a communist society as an apparatus of

---

[3]Art. 10, Criminal Code, RSFSR, effective June 1, 1922, [1922] I Sob. Uzak. RSFSR. No. 15, item 153, retained as Art. 16 of Criminal Code RSFSR, Decree of November 22, 1926, effective January 1, 1927, [1926] I Sob. Uzak. RSFSR, No. 80, item 600. For English translation see The Penal Code of the Russian Federal Soviet Republic (London, 1934). For the history of the analogy principle in Russian Imperial laws see N.S. Timasheff, "The Impact of the Penal Law of Imperial Russia in Soviet Penal Law," 12 American Slavic and East European Review 441 (1953). The analogy article was eliminated from the Criminal Code RSFSR, effective January 1, 1961. For text see Sovestskaia Iustitsiia, No. 17 pp. 5-32 (1961)

[4]Art. 1, Civil Code, RSFSR, Decree of October 31, 1922, effective January 1, 1923, [1922] I Sob Uzak. RSFSR, No. 7, item 904. For English translation see 2 V. Gsovski, Soviet Civil Law (Ann Arbor, Mich., 1949) 16.

[5]See Proekt Novogo Ugolovnogo Kodeksa RSFSR so Vstupitel'noi Stat'ei N.V. Krylenko [Draft of a New Criminal Code of the RSFSR with an introductory article by N.V. Krylenko (Moscow, 1930) and Gosudarstvennyi Institut po Izucheniiu Prestupnosti i Prestupnika, Proekt Osnovnykh Nachal Ugolovnogo Kodeksa RSFSR [Draft of the Fundamental Bases of the Criminal Code of the RSFSR] (Moscow, 1930).

[6]J.V. Stalin, "Political Report of the Central (Party) Committee to the XVI Congress" 1930. Eng. tran. of pertinent passage, Soviet Legal Philosophy (trans. by Hugh W. Babb) (Cambridge, Mass., 1951) 235.

compulsion, it could not wither by degrees. It must remain as a strong entity, the strongest the world had ever known, right up to the time that society passed into the communist epoch. This he declared to be the application of the dialectical method preached by Marxist philosophers. Having taken this philosophical position, he turned to the practical task of ridding himself of the legal technicians who had circulated the draft codes embodying their concepts. He arrested the Minister of Justice and the principal legal philosopher of the time as a part of the purges in 1937 and executed them a year later. He gave his principal supporter from among those who understood the techniques of law, namely Andrei Y. Vyshinsky, the task of revising legal philosophy and creating respect for Stalin's rules of public order among those who had to administer them.

Vyshinsky turned his facile pen to interpretation of Lenin's familiar phrase. He put Stalin's thought into these words, "To prate of Soviet law as a mere form of policy is to intimate that in Soviet statutes, in Soviet justice, and in the activity of Soviet courts, the force of a statute and the force of law are made to depend upon the political demands of the state. We repeat that law is, of course, a political category. At the foundation of Soviet law lie the political and economic interests of workers and peasants. These Soviet law was called to safeguard. To defend them is the basic task of Soviet law. Nevertheless law can no more be reduced simply to policy than can cause be identified with effect."[7]

Stalin called for strict observance of the law, but this did not mean to him that he was to be held personally to any humanistic standard. He drew a line between his own freedom to determine policy without regard to rules, other than those created by economics and natural science, and the freedom that he denied to subordinates to depart from the rules that he established for them to administer. It was this that caused him to say in 1936 when proposing adoption of a new constitution, "And we need stability of laws now more than ever."[8] He spoke on the eve of his purges, and he was soon to demonstrate that when policy was in issue, he would accept no concept of law as restraint, even against falsification of evidence when he thought that a given individual constituted a barrier to achievement of his aims.

Three years after Stalin's death his political heirs, led by Nikita S. Khrushchev, declared their intention never to repeat his dictatorial rule.[9] They affirmed their strict adherence to law, and said that it was binding on all, no matter how highly

---

[7] A.Y. Vyshinsky, "The Fundamental Tasks of Soviet Law" 1938. Eng. trans. in Soviet Legal Philosophy (trans. by Hugh W. Babb) (Cambridge, Mass., 1951). 303 at 329.

[8] Joseph Stalin, "On the Draft Constitution of the U.S.S.R., 1936," Leninism: Selected Writings (New York 1942) 402.

[9] N.S. Khrushchev, Unpublished speech to XX Congress of the Communist Party, February 25, 1956. Disclosed on June 4, 1956 by the United States Department of State. For translation, see L. Gruliow, ed. Current Soviet Policies II (New York 1957) 172; Prior to the speech criticism had been levelled only at Stalin's appointees in the Ministry of Internal Affairs. See editorial "Soviet Socialist Law is Inviolable," Pravda, April 6, 1953. For English translation, see Leo Gruliow, Current Soviet Policies (New York 1953) 259. At the XXII Communist Party Congress in 1961 Stalin was denounced openly and his embalmed body ordered removed from the mausoleum where it had been placed beside Lenin in 1953.

placed. Then they set out to draft a new program for the Communist Party to replace that of 1919 drafted under Lenin's guidance and long outdated. For the lawyers the program when it was adopted in 1961 introduced an innovation in political theory which was to have profound repercussions. It declared the dictatorship of the proletariat at an end, and found that there had come into existence a "state of all the people" in the U.S.S.R. Under this new banner there was begun a campaign of liberalization in law.

Khrushchev did not survive for more than a decade as "first among equals," for his many changes in policy, especially in the structure of the Communist Party and of the Soviet administrative apparatus, made enemies among the conservatives. He was ousted in October, 1964, for what were called his "hare-brained schemes," but also because he was found to have violated the principles of socialist legality. With his departure, a new emphasis began to emerge, but it did not lead to formal revision of his formula of a state of all the people. That remained a primary principle of the post-Stalin era, but the philosophers had to cope with it as the pendulum swung back in some measure to severity in the treatment of citizens.[10] The readings in this chapter will indicate the elements of theory and practice that are being woven together to create a basis for the law of the 1970s."[11]

A. *The Communist Party states goals and prescribes methods*

PROGRAM OF THE COMMUNIST PARTY OF THE SOVIET UNION.
October 31, 1961. Part II, section III and III (1).

The socialist state has entered a new period of its development. The state has begun to grow into a nation-wide organization of the working people of socialist society. Proletarian democracy is becoming more and more a socialist democracy of the people as a whole.

The working class is the only class in history that does not aim to perpetuate its power. Having brought about the complete and final victory of socialism- the first phase of communism- and the transition of society to the full scale construction of communism, the dictatorship of the proletariat has fulfilled its historic mission and has ceased to be indispensable in the U.S.S.R. from the point of view of the tasks of internal development. The state, which arose as a state of the dictatorship of the proletariat, has become, in the new contemporary period, a state of all the people, an organ expressing the interests and will of the people as a whole.

The further promotion of socialist law and order and the improvement of the legal rules governing economic organization, cultural and educational work and con-

---

[10] For a western analysis of the retreat from the language and, perhaps, also from the concept of the 1961 program, see Roger E. Kanet, The Rise and Fall of the 'All-People's State': Recent Changes in the Soviet Theory of the State, 20 Soviet Studies 81 (1968).

[11] For a selection of translations of Soviet legal philosophers who wrote between 1917 and 1961, see Michael Jaworsky, Soviet Political Thought (Baltimore, Md. 1967).

tributing to the accomplishment of the tasks of communist construction and to all-round development of the individual are very important.

The transition to communism means the fullest extension of personal freedom and rights to Soviet citizens. Socialism has granted the working people the broadest guaranteed rights and freedoms. Communism will bring the working people further great rights and opportunities.

The Party calls for enforcing strict observance of socialist legality, for eradication of all violations of law and order, for the abolition of crime and the removal of all causes of crime.

Higher standards of living and culture, and greater social consciousness of the people will pave the way to the abolition of crime and ultimate replacement of judicial punishment by measures of public influence and education. Under socialism, any one who has strayed from the path of the working man can return to useful activity.

The whole system of government and social organizations educates the people in the spirit of voluntary and conscientious fulfillment of their duties and leads to natural fusion of rights and duties to form the integral rules of communist society.

L.I. Brezhnev, REPORT OF THE CPSU CENTRAL COMMITTEE TO THE 25TH PARTY CONGRESS, February 24, 1976. Part 3. (White Plains, N.Y.: Compass Publications, Inc. 1976) 110-113.

Comrades, an important line of our whole work in communist construction is the all-around development of the political system of Soviet society. This means improvement of the Soviet state system, further development of socialist democracy, consolidation of the juridical basis of the life of the state and society, and invigoration of the activity of social organizations.

In carrying out this work, the Party and the Central Committee have always started from the premise that developed socialist society has already been built in our country and is gradually growing into a communist society, from the premise that our state is a state of the whole people, expressing the interests and the will of the whole people. We have always started from the premise that we now have a fully shaped new historical community, the Soviet people, which is based on the solid alliance of the working class, the peasantry and the intelligentsia, with the working class playing the leading role, and on the friendship of all the nations, large and small, of our country. We have sought to promote the all-around development of the activity of state agencies and social organizations stimulating their activity in every way.

In the sphere of state construction, the Party devotes special attention to the work of the Soviets. . .You will recall that some time ago laws were adopted on the initiative of the Political Bureau to extend the rights and material capabilities of rural, village, district and city Soviets. The experience gained in the period under review shows that to do so was correct. We might say that the work of the local Soviets has now acquired a new dimension. . .

Another matter we have constantly dealt with is improvement of our legislation and consolidation of the socialist legal order. The framing by Party and Government organs and the adoption by the U.S.S.R. Supreme Soviet and the Supreme Soviets of the republics of laws on some of the key problems of our life are of major sociopolitical importance. A considerable role in this effort was also played by the standing commissions of the U.S.S.R. Supreme Soviet, whose activity has in general been markedly invigorated in recent years.

We have adjusted our juridical rules to the new level to which our society has risen. Bills have been drafted to cover spheres of life which earlier had remained outside the framework of legal regulation, such as protection of the environment, including bodies of water, the subsoil, the air, and so on. It is a very good thing that we now have well-substantiated juridical rules making it possible to carry on purposeful work in the protection of nature.

The Political Bureau recently instructed the appropriate agencies to prepare proposals for further improving labor and administrative law and certain other laws in order to take account of the new phenomena in the life of our society.

Much also remains to be done to improve the legal regulation of economic activity. Our laws in this sphere should more effectively secure the solving of problems connected with improving output quality and enforcing greater economy in the use of resources. They should be made more effective in countering cases of defrauding the state, doctoring accounts, theft of socialist property, undue zeal in giving priority to local interests, etc.

The time has clearly come to issue a (uniform) code of laws of the Soviet state. This will help to enhance the stability of our whole legal order. It will make our laws more accessible to all Soviet citizens.

It is only natural, comrades, that we should have been devoting, and will continue to devote, undiminished attention to improving the activity of the militia, the procurator's office, the courts and the judicial agencies, which guard Soviet legality, the interests of Soviet society and the rights of Soviet citizens. The Party and the state highly respect the difficult work done by the men and women in these institutions, and have shown concern to provide them with well-trained and fitting cadres.

The state security organs have reliably safeguarded Soviet society from the subversive activity of the intelligence services of the imperialist states, of all types of foreign anti-Soviet centers and other hostile elements. The activity of these organs is geared to the requirements stemming from the international situation and the development of Soviet society. Our CHEKA men cherish and carry on the traditions initiated by Felix Dzerzhinsky, that noble soldier of the revolution.

The state security organs carry on all their work which takes place under the guidance and unflagging control of the Party, on the basis of the interests of the people and the state, with the support of the broad masses of working people, and with the strict observance of constitutional rules and socialist legality. That is the main source of their strength, and the main earnest of the successful exercise of their functions. . .

Comrades, social organizations are an integral part of the Soviet political system. Altogether they involve nearly the whole of the country's adult population, which in itself is a noteworthy fact. Out social organizations are one of the important channels through which citizens are able to participate in running the affairs of society.

Consider the trade unions, our most massive social organization, with a membership of over 107 million. The work of the trade unions is directly instrumental in securing the exercise of democracy in production, the basic sphere in which man's creative efforts are applied. . .

Many kind words have been and are being said about the Leninist Young Communist League, the Komsomol. And this, comrades, is indeed justified. The 35 million strong army of the YCL members is a reliable aide of the Party and its direct and militant reserve. Whatever the tasks the Party sets, the YCL always tackles them with the enthusiasm of youth. . .

RULES OF THE COMMUNIST PARTY OF THE SOVIET UNION, as adopted by the Twenty-second Communist Party Congress, October 31, 1961. Izvestiia, November 3, 1961.

Art. 67. At congresses, conferences, and meetings called by soviet, labor union, cooperative and other mass organizations where there are not less than three Party members, Party groups shall be formed. The tasks of these groups is to strengthen the influence of the Party in every way and to carry out its policy among the non-Party people, to strengthen the Party and state discipline, to combat bureaucracy, and to verify fulfillment of Party and Soviet directives.

B. *The philosophers explain the nature and task of law.*

A.I. Korolev, "SOCIETY, STATE, LAW." Sovetskoe Gosudarstvo i Pravo, 1976, No. 4, p. 23 (Excerpt.)

The historical necessity of the socialist state and law, their role in society. In replacement of the exploiting state and law come the socialist state and law, differing fundamentally from them. The necessity for their existance as the principal tools for constructing communism is convincingly proved by the Marxist-Leninist classics and confirmed by practice.

The definitive factor of social development, objectively creating the necessity for the existence of a state and law of the socialist type is the fact that in the transition from capitalism to communism, even though there occurs a fundamental change in the class structure of countries undergoing such a transistion, nevertheless the division of society into classes continues. Moreover, until socialism is established in those countries the remnants of the exploiting classes are preserved. Along with the class differences in a society, whether in the process of creating or having already created socialism, there are also other factors which have a definite influence on the organizational form of class society. Among these the first that must be indicated is ethnic (national) differences, bearing in mind that one of the fundamental principles of Marxist-Leninist ethnic (national) policy is the right of the nation to self-determination, which "cannot have any other meaning from the historical-economic point of view than political self-determination, state independence, the formation of a national state." (Marx and Engels, Vol. 20, Russian ed. pp. 291-2.) Apart from the social-economic factors of internal development, external factors also exert great influence on the organizational form of a class society during the transition from capitalism to communism. Further, two more points need to be mentioned in speaking of the historical necessity of the socialist state and law. Firstly, the differing times at which the socialist revolution is victorious in different countries: this was stated theoretically by V.I. Lenin and then proven in the practice of world social development. Its consequence is the coexistence of countries already on the road to socialist transformation with countries in which the exploiting structure is still preserved. The fundamental principle of mutual relations between capitalist and socialist countries emerges as peaceful coexistence, which, although excluding the possibility of armed conflict between countries of opposing social systems, does not terminate between them political and ideological struggle, taking the specific form of class struggle. The primary tool of both the capitalist and socialist countries is the state. Secondly, the victory of socialist revolutions in different countries leads to the emergence within them of national or multinational independent socialist states with their respective legal systems in which is manifested the sovereignty of peoples on their way to the construction of socialism and communism and to the realization of their right to free self-determination. Under such conditions the relationships between socialist countries is conducted as inter-state relationships.

Thus, in the transition from capitalism to communism, the state is not only objectively necessary, but the only possible form in which to organize society, and law is the regulator of social relationships. One must not conclude from what has been said that the socialist state and law do not differ in their nature and content from the types of state and law which have preceded them in history. While the exploiting state and law emerged and still exist to assure in some form or other the exploitation of man by man, the socialist state and law are called upon to assure that the exploitation of man by man is rooted out. In other words, the socialist state and law emerge and exist for purposes quite contrary to those that link the origin and existance of the exploiting state and law. Because of this the characterization of the socialist state by the classics of Marxism-Leninism is not "in the true sense of the word" a state, but rather a "quasi-state." (V.I. Lenin, Collected Works, Russian edition. Vol. 33, pp. 66, 18.) The same position must be taken with regard to socialist law.

Moreover, the exploiting state and law have always been and remain specific manifestations of class society, whose existence is linked first and foremost with the presence within society of antagonistic contradictions. The socialist state and law have a certain link with antagonistic contradictions within society only during the transition from capitalism to socialism, when the socialist state and law show themselves as instruments for suppressing their class enemies. Further, in contrast to the exploiting state and law, the socialist state and law appear as instruments for the suppression of the exploiting minority in the interests of the toiling majority. When socialism has been constructed and the antagonistic contradictions have faded away in society the socialist state and law will lose their characteristic feature as instruments of class repression.

Finally, while the exploiting state and law have always been in one way or another linked to the political rulership of a single exploiting class, the socialist state and law are instruments of political rule of a single class, the proletariat, only during the period of transition from capitalism to communism. To this end the proletariat exercises its political rule in alliance with the non-proletarian toiling masses, and first of all with the peasantry. When socialism has been constructed, the dictatorship of the proletariat will have performed its historical mission, and the process will begin of transforming the state of the proletarian dictatorship into a state of all the people, while proletarian law will become the law of all the people. With the construction of a developed socialist society those who wield state authority will become all the toiling classes and strata of society existing in the developed socialist society, and these will be guided by the working class. Correspondingly law will also reflect and strengthen the will of all the people with the working class at their head. This comes about by virtue of the fact that under conditions of developed socialism the working class continues to remain as the guiding force in society, although the forms of state guidance of society by the working class as it performs its historic mission are different.

The Communist Party constantly gives attention to the strengthening of the socialist state in every way, and to the development of socialist democracy. In developed socialist society the Soviet state stands forth as a state of all the people under the guiding role of the working class. The accomplishment of a program of constructing communism is impossible without guidance of the many faceted processes of social life by a vigorous and powerful state, precisely and effectively operating its mechanism. "The state as an organization of all the people will be preserved until the complete vistory of communism." So states the Program of the Communist Party.

The root difference between the exploiting state and law and the socialist state and law is predestined by the very differences in their historical fonts. While the exploiting state and law are being destroyed, the socialist state and law are growing into communist social self-administration and the system of social norms which correspond to it.

C. *The legislators define law's function.*

FUNDAMENTAL PRINCIPLES OF CRIMINAL LEGISLATION OF THE U.S.S.R. AND OF THE UNION REPUBLICS, December 25, 1958. [1959] Vedomosti Verkhovnogo Soveta SSSR, No. 1, item 6.

Art. 1. *The tasks of Soviet criminal legislation.*

Criminal legislation of the U.S.S.R. and of the Union Republics has the task of protecting the structure of soviet society and of the state, socialist property, the individual and rights of the citizen and the whole socialist legal order from criminal infringement.

To perform this task the criminal legislation of the U.S.S.R. and of the Union Republics defines the socially dangerous acts that are crimes and establishes the punishments to be applied to persons committing crimes.

FUNDAMENTAL PRINCIPLES OF CIVIL LEGISLATION OF THE U.S.S.R. AND OF THE UNION REPUBLICS, December 8, 1961 effective May 1, 1962. [1961] Vedomosti Verkhovnogo Soveta SSSR, No. 50, item 525.

Art. 1. *The tasks of Soviet civil legislation.*

Soviet civil legislation regulates property relationships and personal non-property relationships linked to them for the purpose of creating the material and technical bases of communism and of increasingly satisfying more fully the material and spiritual needs of citizens. In the circumstances provided by law civil legislation also regulates other personal non-property relationships.

The foundation of property relationships in Soviet society is the socialist system of economy and social property in the tools and means of production. The economic life of the U.S.S.R. shall be defined and directed by the state national economic plan.

FUNDAMENTAL PRINCIPLES OF LEGISLATION OF THE U.S.S.R. AND OF THE UNION REPUBLICS ON MARRIAGE AND THE FAMILY. June 27, 1968 effective October 1, 1968. [1968] Vedomosti Verkhovnogo Soveta SSSR, No. 27, item 241.

Art. 1. *The tasks of Soviet legislation on marriage and the family.*

Soviet legislation on marriage and the family has the following tasks: the further strengthening of the Soviet family, based upon the principles of communist morality;

the structuring of family relationships upon the base of a voluntary union in marriage of a man and a woman and on sentiments of mutual love, friendship and respect, free from property considerations, among all members of the family;

The rearing of children by the family in combination organically with public instilling of a spirit of devotion to the homeland, a communist attitude toward labor and the preparation of children for active participation in the making of a communist society;

the safeguarding in every way of the interests of mothers and children and the guarantee of a joyous childhood for every child;

the elimination once and for all of harmful relics and customs of the past from family relations;

the inculcation of a sense of responsibility to the family.

FUNDAMENTAL PRINCIPLES OF LEGISLATION OF THE U.S.S.R. AND OF THE UNION REPUBLICS ON LABOR. July 15, 1970 effective January 1, 1971. [1970] Vedomosti Verkhovnogo Soveta SSSR, No. 29, item 265.

Art. 1. *The tasks of Soviet legislation on labor.*

Soviet legislation on labor regulates the labor relationships of all workmen and clerks, contributing to the increase in labor productivity, increasing the effectiveness of social production and the rise as a result in the material and cultural living standard of toilers, strengthening labor discipline and by degrees transforming labor for the welfare of society into the paramount life need of every able bodied person.

Legislation on labor establishes a high level of labor conditions and protection by all means possible of the toiling rights of workmen and clerks.

CHAPTER II

Preparing Communist Self-Administration

Although the 1961 program of the Communisty party and the philosophers who interpreted it had laid the base for development of institutions representing a society advancing toward communism, practical steps were necessary to create these institutions. One of the most puzzling problems was to create institutions for preserving public order which would not be those of the state. Communist party leaders, whether believers in their task or cynical manipulators to retain power, needed to create forms which might conceivably lead to communist self-administration when the state would have withered away. Both doctrine and the practical necessity of enthusing the people in development of a unique system of public order totally unlike that of the bourgeois society they had been taught to despise required innovation.

The task was not wholly new, for the men around Lenin in 1917 had believed passionately in the early, if not immediate, withering away of the state once private ownership of means of production had been abolished. One of the institutional manifestations of this belief was the creation of comrades' courts, in which citizens working together in the army, the factory, on the farm or in the newly nationalized apartment houses might unite to create a new sense of social discipline through social pressures for conformity to principles of a new communist morality.[1]

Under this stimulus, the comrades' courts thrived, being of particular advantage in the large apartment houses where crowding was extreme and hot tempers flared.[2] Also, they served in some measure to create a new sense of discipline among factory workmen who revelled in the early years in a sense of liberation from the duty to respond without question to the orders of the factory manager or the gang foreman.

Even within the newly created general courts, there was experimentation with prosecution and defense. The Tsarist institutions were abolished, and in their place the community was asked to undertake both functions. Social organizations were expected to prosecute, and members of the family or friends of the accused were expected to help him present his defense.

While much of this experimentation proved that the complete replacement of state institutions by those of an aroused community was wholly impractical, the idea of an early withering away of the state flourished until the late 1920s. Then Stalin entered the argument to put an end to experimentation. He told the Communist Party Congress in 1930 that although the state must eventually wither away, it must do so in accordance with a dialectical process.[3] This he defined as requiring that the state first become the strongest instrument known to history so as to prepare for its eventual withering. The comrades' courts continued to function for yet a few years, but with the advent of the first of Stalin's purges in 1935, they ceased to assemble and their statute became a dead letter. The community as prosecutor had long since faded out of the courtroom scene, for a formal office of prosecutor had been established in 1922[4] after some experiments with half-way measures looking toward professionalization.

Nikita S. Khrushchev reversed the situation, attacking first Stalin's speech of 1930. At the 20th Communist Party Congress of 1956 he called Stalin's formula for withering absurd and denounced it as the basis for creation of Stalin's dictatorship, which was called "the cult of the individual."[5] He asked for immediate steps to begin the withering process. To implement his idea, he demanded return to the comrades' courts, the development of a Voluntary People's Guard and establishment of an entirely new concept, the "social assembly," which would bring to-

---

[1] Introduced first into the Red Army by decree of December 3, 1917. [1917] Sob. Uzak. RSFSR, No. 5, item 87. Rules in [1918] *Ibid.*, No. 55, item 613. Extended in 1919 to factories. See Kazimierz Grzybowski, Soviet Legal Institutions (Ann Arbor, Mich. 1962) 250.
[2] Cases have been analyzed in John N. Hazard. Soviet Housing Law (New Haven, Conn. 1939) 113-118.
[3] See Hugh W. Babb translation in Soviet Legal Philosophy (Cambridge, Mass. 1951) 235
[4] For history of the steps leading to it, see John N. Hazard, Settling Disputes in Soviet Society (New York, 1960) 217-230.
[5] For Eng. tr., see Leo Gruliow, ed., Current Soviet Policies II (New York, 1957) 172 at 177.

gether all of the workers in a factory, a farm, or a living area to sit in mass judgment upon a fellow who was conducting himself or herself as a "parasite."[6]

Khrushchev's enthusiasm for populist agencies to enforce order as harbingers of communism has not survived him. Some of his creations, notably the "social assembly," have passed from the scene to be replaced by orders of Executive Committees of local soviets or criminal proceedings before people's courts against vagrants. Party leaders seem to have accepted the arguments of the Soviet professional lawyers that this populist institution with its right to banish citizens from the community on the basis of a mass vote was out of keeping with the post-Stalin emphasis upon formal procedures to determine fact. The Voluntary People's Guards have been related more closely to state agencies than when they reflected Khrushchev's ideas. Even the comrades' courts are undergoing study because of incidents when solid citizens have been pilloried on the basis of apartment dwellers' incompatability.

In spite of these developments which suggest retreat from Khrushchev's espousal of populist institutions as the wave of the future, some of them continue to have the support of Communist Party leadership. Whether this support rests on a lingering thought that they are somehow related to communist ideology, as Khrushchev claimed, or on a sense that they have proved their pragmatic value in filling gaps in the work of state agencies engaged in the governing process is for the reader to determine. The material in this chapter is designed to etch the rough outlines of the points that need to be considered in reaching a conclusion.

A. *The aim of public self-administration.*

M. Malkov, Procurator of Moscow. "THE FOUNDATIONS OF LEGAL ORDER." Izvestiia, January 25, 1976, p. 4. (Excerpt)

The toilers of the capital are struggling to make real a noble task - turning Moscow into a model communist city.

What concrete meaning lies in the concept of a "model communist city"? General Secretary of the Central Committee of the Communist Party of the Soviet Union, L.I. Brezhnev, in speaking to the voters of the Bauman precinct of the capital said, "Moscow residents are called upon to set a high standard for emulation, not only in solving the problems of municipal construction but also in human relationships. A model communist city is one in which live people with a high level of culture, or awareness, a city of model social order."

The struggle of the capital's toilers to turn Moscow into a model communist city is headed by the city Party organization. The development of Moscow is plotted in a broad program. . . . , in which along with the successful fulfillment of the tasks

---

[6]For a summary of the various forms of decrees establishing the social assemblies, see R. Beerman, The Parasites Law, 13 Soviet Studies 191-205 (1961) For their practice see Harold J. Berman, Justice in the U.S.S.R. (2nd ed., Cambridge, Mass.) 84-86.

of the economy, the municipal works, the cultural institutions and the conditions of life, an important place is occupied by questions of the communist rearing of the toilers.

The primary role in assuring creation of a model system of order in the city is, of course, played by the Soviets of toilers' deputies. Their importance has risen greatly since the 24th Communist Party Congress (1971). Strengthening of state and labor discipline, the protection of the rights of citizens and of those of their interests protected by law - these matters have often been on the agenda of sessions of the borough soviets, and of their Executive Committees and permanent commissions. A decision "On the work of Executive Committees of borough Soviets in assuring the application of socialist legality and legal order" has been adopted by the Moscow Soviet.

Statistics demonstrate the sharp reduction in violations of law in our city, but we have taken account of the fact that much remains to be done to reduce them even further. To achieve this the major task is prevention; in the prophylactics of violation of law. Under the guidance of Party organizations the trade unions, the Komsomols, and administrative organs are conducting this work. Experience has proved that the most important role both in tracing the lines of the new man and in the struggle with many relics of the past in the minds of people is played first of all by collective workers on the job. It is there, where educational work is well organized, where high demands are placed on members of the collective, that there pervades an atmosphere of intolerance of drunkenness, absence from work, of falling away from the moral code. . .

Introduction of a model system of legal order is a task for the whole city, for all of society. It is well known how actively the people's guards work in our city - there are more than 300,000 of them; comrades' courts have great influence. In recent times still one more form of public participation in preserving order has been born; I have in mind the support points established by public organizations and the militia to prevent violations of law. The councils of these support points coordinate the prophylactic work of the district inspectors, the comrades' courts, the voluntary people's guards, the housing committees, the guards of the children's playrooms, etc. Together with the offices of the deputies to the Soviets, the cultural institutions and the sporting institutions they organize educational and mass-cultural work among the population. . .

In recent years the coordination of the activities of the militia, the procurators' office and the courts has improved in the prophylactics of violation of law; the links with public organizations have been strengthened. Investigators, procurators, militia workers often give lectures to the collectives of workmen on the job on the results of investigations of criminal cases, on violations of legality. . .

B. *The voluntary people's guards.*

"THE VOLUNTARY PEOPLE'S GUARDS, A NEW CHARTER," Izvestiia, June 4, 1974. p. 5.

Not long ago the Central Committee of the Communist Party of the Soviet Union and the U.S.S.R. Council of Ministers approved a new model charter, and the Pressidium of the U.S.S.R. Supreme Soviet issued an edict "On the fundamental duties and rights of the voluntary people's guards in protecting social law and order."

The edict and charter define the tasks and functions of the voluntary people's guards who must participate in upholding social law and order, in defending the rights and legal interests of citizens, in protecting socialist property, in preventing violations of law in the spirit of respect for the laws and regulations of socialist communal life. Furthermore, according to the new charter, the people's guards will participate in protecting nature and natural wealth, in succoring people and saving their property at times of natural disaster and of other exceptional circumstances, in tendering urgent assistance to persons suffering from accidents and violations of law or found in public places in a helpless condition. In border zones the people's guards must aid in protecting the state borders of the U.S.S.R.

The charter makes precise the role and place of the voluntary people's guards within the general system of activities of state and public agencies in the protection of legal order. Guards must act in contact with the collectives of workers on the job and with the agencies charged with maintaining order - the militia, the procurators' office and the courts.

There are a number of new regulations in the charter. Adult citizens of the U.S.S.R. are accepted into the guards if they express a wish to participate in protecting public order and are capable by virtue of their regular activities and their moral-political quality to carry out successfully the tasks put before the guards. Every guardsman takes an oath before the general assembly to carry out faithfully and truly his duty. . .

The charter requires every people's guard to be registered in the Executive Committee of the borough, city, village or hamlet Soviet of toilers' deputies. This registration is evidence of conformity to the rules established for the organization of guards. At the time of registration the guard receives from the Soviet authorization to perform his functions in the protection of public order and in the struggle against violations of law. . . Local Soviets and their Executive Committees guide the work of the guards stationed on the territory of the Soviet. .They may hear reports and communications from the commanders, and also reports on the work of the guards from directors of enterprises, institutions and public organizations regardless of their chain of command. . .[1]

---

[1]The edict is printed in Russian in [1974] Vedomosti Verkhovnogo Soveta SSSR, No. 2, item 326, and the Charter in [1974] Vedomosti Verkhovnogo Soveta RSFSR, No. 21, item 114.

INFORMATION, Chelovek i Zakon, 1973, No. 5, p. 98.

The Director of the Mogilev trolleybus administration issued an edict which admitted to membership in the voluntary people's guards thirty employees.

The Procurator of the Oktyabr borough of the city of Mogilev protested this edict as violating the Charter of the voluntary people's guards for the preservation of public order, which Charter was approved by decree of the Central Committee of the Communist Party of Bielorussia and the Council of People's Commissars of the Bielorussian S.S.R. on July 15, 1961. The Charter establishes that the voluntary people's guards are created at a founders' meeting composed of persons who have expressed a desire to enter the guards, and not by a decree of the directors of enterprises, public organizations or institutions.

The protest was examined and the illegal edict revoked.

CASE OF MARTYNENKO, Biulleten' Verkhovnogo Suda RSFSR, 1966, No. 9, p. 9

Martynenko was found guilty of permitting himself to exceed his authority as chief of the Komsomol operational detachment's staff of the Lenin ward of the city of Ulianovsk in beating under the following circumstances Gorin, who had been detained.

A group of students of the senior classes of middle schools Nos. 35 and 52 of the city of Ulianovsk, having drunk wine at a food shop began to push each other around on Karl Marx street. Goncharenko fell back from Gorin's blow on Ippolitov, and a dispute broke out between them because of this. The dispute was ended on the intervention of a bystander. Lipkhen asked Ippolitov's pardon on behalf of Gorin, and the whole group moved along the street.

Ippolitov, having been a pupil of the Komsomol operational detachment of Lenin ward, met members of this detachment on the street and told them that the students were violating the public order. In consequence, Gorin, Tykaev, Mikhailov and Lipkhen were detained and taken to the detachment's headquarters. The Commander of the detachment, Martynenko, without investigating the circumstances, struck Gorin two blows on the face with his fist. He struck Ippolitov once. Gorin was caused medium serious bodily injury by the blows, a double fracture of the jaw.

In the [Deputy Procurator's] protest [against the trial court's sentence and its affirmance on appeal] it was stated that Martynenko as a Commander of the staff of a Komsomol operational detachment could not be held responsible for crime defined in par. 2 of Art. 171 of the Criminal Code of the RSFSR [exceeding authority or official powers if accompanied by force, use of weapons, torment or insult]. He was not a responsible official. The protest raised the question of reclassification of the events under par. 1 of Art. 109 [intentional infliction of bodily injury not dangerous to life].

Having reviewed the record, the Judicial Division found no basis for satisfying the protest. It was evident from the evidence that Martynenko was chief of a model district Komsomol detachment of the operational group for struggle with violators of public order; members of the operational group had appropriate identification and when on patrol carried armbands.

Thus, Martynenko in performing his duties as Commander of the detachment exercised the functions of a representative of authority. As a representative of authority he was a responsible official.

Martynenko exceeded his authority in striking the detained Gorin twice in the face with his hand, causing a double fracture of the jaw.

Persons performing official duties on the basis of a public organization's operational rules may be called to account as for the commission of a crime by a responsible official when committing intentionally acts clearly going beyond the bounds of the rights and authority granted them by law.

Acting upon the basis of what has been set forth, the Judicial Division for Criminal Cases of the Supreme Court of the RSFSR in its decision of March 12, 1966, left unsatisfied the protest requesting reclassification of the offense under par. 1 of Art. 109 of the Criminal Code of the RSFSR.

CASE OF VASIL'EV AND LUKASHIN, Biulleten' Verkhovnogo Suda RSFSR, 1971, No. 4, p. 13

. . .Vasil'ev was found guilty by the Moscow City Court of accepting bribes from tradesmen while serving as a non-staff aid to the militia at the Moscow-Kazan railroad station together with his acquaintance Lukashin, who performed the function of inspector when control purchases were made.

Both convicted persons appealed the conviction on the ground that they were not responsible officials under par. 2 Art. 173 of the Criminal Code of the RSFSR, [receipt of a bribe as a responsible official] but that their acts should have been classified under par. 2 Art. 147 [repeated swindling or after prior group agreement].

The judgment was affirmed and the appeal dismissed for the following reasons:

The receipt by Vasil'ev and Lukashin of money from tradesmen after making control purchases was confessed by the convicted persons and confirmed by witnesses questioned by the court. Witnesses testified that after disclosing that the purchases had been for control purposes Vasil'ev and Lukashin would then say that they had received short weights and measures and would demand payment of money, threatening unfortunate consequences if they were not paid. Thus, they obtained bribes through extortion.

On becoming a non-staff aid of the militia, Vasil'ev performed as a public volunteer the functions of an employee of the militia and acquired the rights established by the regulations on non-staff workers, including the right to participate as a representative of the militia in conducting inspections and making checks. Therefore, Vasil'ev as a non-staff worker of the militia was a responsible official and can be the subject of the crime prescribed by Art. 173. . .

In representing himself while making control purchases to be a worker of the militia he acted like a responsible official and used his position as such. Therefore, Vasil'ev's acts were properly classified under par. 2 Art. 173, since he frequently took bribes by means of extortion. Lukashin served as Vassil'ev's assistant and together with him extorted and frequently took bribes. Under such circumstances his acts were properly classified under par. 2 Art. 173.

C. *The comrades' courts.*

STATUTE ON COMRADES' COURTS, July 3, 1961, as amended March 3, 1962, October 23, 1963 and January 16, 1965. Pub. in amended form in POLOZHENIE O TOVARISHCHIKH SUDAKH (Moscow, 1967).

Tasks of Comrades' Courts and Procedure for their Organization.

Art. 1. Comrades' courts are elected public organs charged with actively contributing to the rearing of citizens in the spirit of a communist attitude toward work, toward socialist property, toward preservation of the rules of socialist society, toward the development in soviet people of a sense of collectivism and comradely mutual assistance, toward respect for the dignity and honor of citizens. Of primary importance in the work of comrades' courts is the prevention of violations of law and of misdemeanors, detrimental to society, rearing of people through conviction and social influence, creating conditions of intolerance to any antisocial acts. Comrades' courts are invested with the trust of the collective, express its will and are responsible to it.

Art. 2. Comrades' courts in enterprises, institutions, organizations, higher and specialized secondary schools shall be established by decision of the general meeting of workers, employees or students.

Comrades' courts in collective farms, in apartment houses managed by housing management bureaus, housing administrations or combined in street committee managements, as well as in rural populated places and settlements shall be established by decision of a general meeting of the members of a collective farm, of apartment house occupants or of citizens of a village, or settlement with the consent of the respective executive committees of soviets of working people's deputies. . .

Cases Heard by Comrades' Courts.

Art. 5. Comrades' courts shall hear cases involving:
1) violations of labor discipline, including: absence from work without valid reason; tardiness in arriving at work or early leaving; poor quality work or idling as the result of an unconscientious attitude of the worker to his duties; failure to observe the technical safety regulations or other regulations concerning protection of labor, except in those cases where criminal responsibility is prescribed; of destruction, loss or damage to inventory, instruments, raw materials or other state or public property as a result of unconscientious relations of a person to his duties, if none of these cause notable damage:

1a) unauthorized use for personal reasons of means of transport, agricultural instruments, machine tools, instruments, raw materials and other property belonging to a state enterprise, institution, organization, collective farm or other cooperative or public organization, if these uses did not cause the said enterprises, institutions or organizations substantial harm;

2) petty theft of state or public property, first time commission of petty rowdyism, petty speculation, and also a first theft of consumer goods and personal possessions of small value which are the personal property of citizens in the event that the guilty party and the victim are members of the same collective.

NOTE. Cases listed in the present article shall be forwarded to the comrades' courts by the organs of the militia, the procurator's office and the court, but cases of petty theft of state or public property shall also be forwarded by the administration of enterprises, institutions, organizations, and collective farm administrations with notice to the office of procurator.

In the absence of a comrades' court at the place of work or dwelling of the offender, and also if the information as to the personality of the offender and the circumstances of the case suggest the futility of hearing the case in a comrades' court, the case shall be tried in the district (city) people's court in the manner established by law. No cases concerning persons who have been brought twice before the comrades' court for petty theft shall be heard by a comrades' court.

2) appearance in an intoxicated condition or other unworthy conduct in public places or at work; distilling of moonshine liquor and other strong alcoholic drinks, when committed the first time and without the intention of sale and in small quantity;

3) unworthy behavior toward women, failure to perform duties related to the rearing of children, unworthy behavior toward parents;

4) abusive language, circulating slander against members of the collective, beatings, light bodily injury not causing an upset to health, if such activities occur for the first time, foul language;

5) the damaging of trees and other greenery;

6) the damaging of dwelling and non-dwelling premises and other equipment of a service character, if no notable damage is caused; failure to observe the fire safety rules;

7) violation of the regulations for communal living within apartments and dormitories; disputes of tenants over use of subsidiary premises, and of facilities of the house, or over payment of charges for communal services, over payment of costs of running repairs of places in common use, and over establishing procedures for the use of green plots between coowners of a dwelling;

8) property disputes between citizens for amounts up to 50 rubles, if the disputing parties agree to hearing of the case in a comrades' court;

8a) disputes over procedure for using structures which are the common property of two or more citizens, over division of the communally owned property of a peasant household and over apportioning of a collective farmer's share, over division of property between spouses, in the event that the disputing parties agree to the hearing of the case in a comrades' court.

9) other antisocial acts not entailing criminal responsibility;

10) administrative violations if the agencies or responsible officials with the right of exacting penalties without court hearing think it necessary to transfer the case for hearing to a comrades' court;

taking the law into one's own hands, failure to give aid to a sick person, illegal medical treatment, acquisition of property by clearly criminal means and other criminal activities if they do not represent great social danger and the organs of the militia, the procurator or the court think it necessary to transfer the case for hearing to a comrades' court.

Procedure for the Hearing of Cases in Comrades' Courts.

[Six articles: opening of a case on charges brought by trade unions, people's militia, street or apartment house committees, public organizations, assemblies of citizens, individual citizens, executive committees of soviets or other committees or agencies of a soviet, managements of enterprises, institutions and collective farms, the court, procurator or investigating organs, and on the initiative of the comrades' court itself; prompt hearing within 15 or 7 days, depending on the charge; preparation of the case by the court which has the right to demand presentation of evidence and to compel the appearance of witnesses; public hearings in non-working hours and with a bench of at least three members of the court with right in the accused to request removal of a member as personally interested in the case, this to be decided by the other members of the court; observers may put questions or make statements; a record is kept; the accused must be present, unless summoned twice without appearance and for no good reason; return of a case to procurator, court, or investigating organ if it came from them and the accused fails to appear on two summonses; decision on majority vote of members of court participating, signed by all.]

Measures of Public Influence to be applied by Comrades' Courts.

Art. 14. A comrades' court in hearing a case and reaching a decision shall be guided by legislation in force, by the present Statute and its sense of public duty.

Art. 15. A comrades' court may apply to the accused the following measures of influence:

1) require the offender to apologize publicly to the victim or the collective;

2) announce a comradely warning;

3) announce public censure;

4) announce a public reprimand with or without publication in the press;

5) levy a money fine up to 10 rubles if the offense is not related to a violation of labor discipline, but in cases of petty theft of state or public property a fine up to 30 rubles, and on repetition of petty theft—up to 50 rubles;

6) propose to the management of an enterprise, institution, or organization application of one of the following measures in conformity with labor legislation in force: transfer of the offender to a lower-paid job or demotion;

6a) propose to the management of an enterprise, institution or organization dismissal in accordance with established procedures of any person performing work related to the education of minors or youths, or work related to the distribution or custody of articles of value if the comrades' court concludes, after taking into consideration the character of the offenses committed by the offender that it is impossible to trust him at this work in the future;

6b) propose to the management of an enterprise, institution or organization transfer to unskilled physical labor in the same enterprise, institution or organization for a period up to 15 days with payment at the rate established for unskilled work when the person has committed petty rowdyism, petty speculation, petty theft of state or public property, theft of low value items of personal use and enjoyment, beating, and light bodily injury;

7) raise the question of evicting the offender from his apartment if he is unable to get along with other occupants or if he exhibits a predatory attitude toward the housing facilities;

8) a comrades' court in addition to the application of measures of influence stipulated in paragraphs 1-7 of this article may require the offender to compensate the victim for losses up to 50 rubles from illegal acts. In hearing a case of petty speculation a comrades' court shall order delivery of the item which was the subject of the speculation to the state treasury. In cases of theft of state or public property a comrades' court must in every case require the offender to make full restitution of the harm caused.

Direction of the Comrades' Court.

Art. 21. Direction of comrades' courts in enterprises, institutions, organizations, higher and middle schools shall be in the factory, plant and local labor union committees. Comrades' courts in collective farms, in apartment houses managed by housing management bureaus, housing administrations, or managed in combination with others through street committee managements, as well as in rural populated places and settlements shall function under the guidance of executive committees of the local soviets of toilers' deputies.

Art. 22. Technical services of comrades' courts shall be supplied by the respective administrations of enterprises, institutions, organizations, housing management bureaus and housing administrations or by the collective farm managements or executive committees of the village or rural settlement soviets of working people's deputies.

L. Mikhailovskaia, "BEFORE ONE'S COMRADES," Pravda, August 7, 1970. Eng. trans. in 22 CDSP, No. 32, p. 4 (1970). (Excerpt).

Dear Editors of Pravda! Our comrades' court recently received material from the borough militia division concerning disorderly conduct by Citizen Yeremina. . .The material is sent to us so that we could take appropriate measures. This raises the question as to what measures the comrades' court can take when Yeremina has already been told what she is threatened with if she continues her improper behavior. We considered Yeremina's case and gave her a comradely warning. But still we had doubts: Weren't our court's actions an unnecessary formality. The militia and the people's court have the power to take sterner measures. . . .

The editors passed this letter on to me, along with a request to reply to it. . . .Are comrades' courts necessary if the courts and the militia have sterner measures at their disposal?

The state agencies carrying on the struggle against crime and violations of the law - the courts, the procurator's office and the militia - usually deal with people after they have broken the law. . .The comrades' court knows the offender as a member of its own collective; it knows him from various angles and often over a long period of time. Consequently it is easier for this kind of court to find an individualized approach that will make the person change his way of thinking and return to the right path. Finally, the upbringing work done by the comrades' court is not limited to the hearing of the case. A correct decision can fail to achieve its aim only if the future behavior of the offender is left unsupervised by the public. . . .

The decision of a comrades' court is a legal document and must be made in strict conformity with the law; the facts established in the document must be true. No state agency or official has the right to impose its or his point of view on a comrades' court or to predetermine the essence of the decision it will read. . . .

Since most of the members of the comrades' court are not professional jurists, it is very important to organize their training correctly and to familiarize them with the existing legislation and the basic principles of various branches of law.

It seems to us that individual difficulties in the work of comrades' courts are related to certain imperfections in the law. . .it says nothing about the maximum size of the collectives in which the courts may be elected. However, a comrades' court in an enterprise with thousands of workers cannot be a real court of comrades and cannot work with people individually. In our view it would be advisable to revise the procedure for elections to the comrades' courts in large collectives.

A. Aleksandrova and Ye. Rozanova, "NO, THIS IS NOT A COMRADES' COURT." Izvestiia, August 1, 1970, p. 5. Eng. trans. in 22 CDSP. No. 32, p. 1 (1970). (Excerpts).

While walking in the street one day, the Tveretinov's saw an injured puppy. They picked it up and brought it home. Their only neighbor, Grishina, did not object. . .Two year's later Grishina suddenly declared, "I don't want that dog around here! Get rid of it." The apartment house committee immediately ruled that the dog had to be removed within three days. They did not care where. When the Tveretinovs did not obey, the case went to a comrades' court. . .

The Tveretinovs were given no peace. Day after day they were visitied by people who are active in public affairs. They came in two's and three's, from the apartment house committee and from the comrades' court. Tveretinov's mother was very ill at the time; in fact she was dying. . .They shamelessly came on the fourth day after the funeral. What amazing callousness! . . .

The Tveretinovs were not allowed to speak at the court session; they were rudely interrupted. The representatives of Tveretinov's fellow workers at the plant were given a hostile reception. The same thing was true for the representatives of the Society for the Protection of Nature. . .

Whereas under normal conditions the judge may disagree with the investigator's conclusions, reject witnesses' testimony or refuse to heed the arguments of the defense or the prosecution, nothing of the sort happened here, nor could it have. At every stage, the inquiry was conducted by the same people. The Tveretinovs could not very well complain about the witness Obukhova, who had visited them before the court session, to Obukhova in her capacity as a member of the court. . .The judges themselves appeared as witnesses. They also conducted the investigation and they tried the case. . .

When the comrades' courts were established it was assumed that they would conduct a comradely inquiry. . .things will work themselves out, since everything is simple among comrades. We see what this leads to. . .

A form that is democratic in nature does not in and of itself determine content as well. . .A public hearing that cannot rise above the level of bickering teaches bad lessons. . . Every one understood that the dog was only a pretext. But what would happen, we reflected, if a deeper and more acute conflict were to fall into their hands?

Here are the final moments of the court session:

Shablin (judge) "Tveretinov, answer to the point: Do you want a reconciliation?" Tveretinov: "Yes."

Shablin: "Grishina! Do you want to make peace with him, Granny?"

Grishina: "No. Why should I?"

Shablin. "So you don't want the dog to remain in the apartment?"

Grishina: "No, I don't."

Tveretinov: "I ask that Comrade Grishina tell us why she doesn't and what she wants."

Grishina: "I've already told you: I don't need that dog. What good is it?"

Shablin: "Everything is clear! Well, that's all."

The decision was made: the dog must be removed. This decision was illegal: the comrades' courts have no such authority. . .The Tveretinovs were publicly reprimanded "For having insulted and slandered the members of the comrades' court and even for having written a letter to superior organizations." And afterwards, after the decision had been made public the judges wrote up a different one. Strange as it may seem no one has the right to annul a decision by a comrades' court (The borough Executive Committee can only return the case for a new hearing.) Not even the people's courts have this privilege. . . .

The comrades' courts are currently the subject of a serious discussion. . .After all, there are about 200,000 of them throughout the country. A thorough analysis of our 10 years of experience with the comrades' courts will undoubtedly provide an opportunity to correct their present defects. . .

CASE OF KOCHUGOVA. Sbornik postanovlenii prezidiuma i opredelenii subenoi kollegii po ugolovnym delam Verkhnovnogo Suda RSFSR 1964-1972 (Moscow, 1974) p. 445.

Kochugova was convicted by the Sherinskii county people's court under par. 2 of

Art. 144 of the Criminal Code RSFSR [repeated theft].

The Judicial Division for criminal cases of the Khakass Provincial Court terminated the case for lack of action constituting a crime. The presidium of the same court rejected the procurator's protest in which he had proposed setting aside the judgment of the people's court and the ruling of the Judicial Division of the Provincial Court and referral of the file of the case for additional investigation.

The Deputy procurator of the RSFSR forwarded a protest to the Judicial Division for Criminal Cases of the Supreme Court of the RSFSR proposing setting aside the ruling and decree of the Presidium of the Provincial Court and referral of the file to a new cassational review.

The Judicial Division accepted the protest.

Kochugova was convicted of having stolen in January 1965 from Kriukova's apartment a woman's watch "Zaria" and 6 rubles; in March 1965 she stole 80 rubles from Kuznetsova, and in April of the same year she stole 10 rubles from the apartment of Sartakova.

The Judicial Division's and the presidium of the Provincial Court's conclusion that the case should be terminated for lack of action constituting crime is incorrect since it is contrary to the evidence in the case. It is evident from the file that the facts of theft of the watch and money from Kriukova and also the money from Kuznetsova in addition to having been personally admitted by Kochugova are confirmed by the testimony of the victims and of witnesses. The theft of money from Sartakova's apartment by Kochugova is confirmed by testimony of the victim.

The Provincial Court's conclusion is groundless to the effect that in the first two thefts there is an unrevoked decision of the police investigators to send the material without initiation of criminal proceedings to an agency for the application of social pressure, and that, consequently, criminal proceedings cannot be initiated on those facts. In accordance with Art. 10 of the Code of Criminal Procedure of the RSFSR the transmission by the police investigators of materials concerning persons who have committed crimes for trial by a comrades' court is permitted only with the consent of a procurator. No such consent of the procurator is found in the record. Therefore, the reference of the Judicial Division and of the Presidium of the Provincial Court to this decision as a circumstance providing a basis for terminating the case with regard to Kochugova cannot be held to be justified.

Furthermore, it is not evident from the case that the material on commission of theft by Kochugova was in fact transmitted to a comrade's court by the police investigators. And even further, could one classify as of minor importance the crime committed by Kochugova; as not constituting great social danger? That is the type of crime to which Art. 10 of the Code of Criminal Procedure of the RSFSR applies.

On new cassational review of the case the judgment remained unchanged.

CASE OF TSIGANOK, Radiansk'e Pravo, 1972, No. 10, p. 107.

. . .The people's court of Iampil's'kii District in its decision of July 15, 1970 refused to open a criminal case against Tsiganok under par. 1 Art. 106 [inflicting light bodily injury] of the Criminal Code of the Ukrainian SSR, but referred the materials to a comrades' court for consideration, noting the fact that Tsiganok had committed an insignificant offense for the first time and could be set straight with the help of application of measures of social influence.

[After protests of procurators and decisions of intervening courts, during which process the victim informed the court of his reconciliation with the accused, the matter reached the Plenum of the Supreme Court of the Ukrainian SSR which supported the original decision of the people's court to refer the matter to a comrades' court, saying:]

The Judicial Division for Criminal Cases of the Supreme Court of the Ukrainian SSR in quashing the decision of the people's court and the decision of the Presidium of the Sums'skii Provincial Court relied on the fact that par. 4 Art. 5 of the Statute on Comrades' Courts of the Ukrainian SSR contains an exhaustive list of offenses against the person which may be considered by comrades' courts. Since the aforementioned Statute does not include cases concerning the infliction of light bodily harm without injury to health, in the opinion of the Judicial Division the people's judge had no right to transfer to the comrades' court a case involving light bodily harm causing injury to health, since the offense was covered by par. 1 Art. 106 of the Criminal Code of the Ukrainian SSR. This decision was reached without consideration of the rule of par. 9 of the same article and also without consideration of the norms of the Criminal Code and Code of Criminal Procedure of the Ukrainian SSR which regulate the given questions.

Comrades' courts themselves on their own initiative have the right to take for consideration cases of light bodily harm without injury to health under par. 4 Art. 5 of the aforementioned Statute, as well as cases transferred to them under par. 2 Art. 106, but they are not authorized to take under consideration cases involving acts covered under par. 1 Art. 106, since such cases are not included in the list that is contained in the Statute. In contrast with this situation, par. 9 Art. 5 of the Statute on Comrades' Courts allots to the competency of comrades' courts the offenses of taking the law into one's own hands, acquisition of property knowingly obtained by criminal means and other criminal activities if they are not of great social danger and the agencies of Internal Affairs or the Procuracy or the judge find it necessary to transfer such matters for consideration to comrades' courts.

This norm of the Statute on Comrades' Courts is in complete conformity with Art. 51 of the Criminal Code of the Ukrainian SSR and Art. 8 of the Code of Criminal Procedure under which the instigation of a criminal prosecution for a minor offense committed for the first time can be refused, or a case may be closed at any stage in the proceedings, or transferred for consideration to a comrades' court, if a court, a judge, or a Procurator and also the investigating agencies of the militia or other agency of investigation with the consent of the Procurator decide that because of the character of the case and the person of the accused he can be corrected with the help of social pressures. Except for this the law does not include any restrictions on types of offenses.

Thus, in accordance with par. 9 Art. 5 of the Statute on Comrades' Courts of the Ukrainian SSR, Art. 51 of the Criminal Code, and Art. 8 of the Code of Criminal Procedure, the judge, if he finds it necessary, has the right without instigating a criminal case for a minor offense committed for the first time, even when there was intent to commit light bodily harm and when temporary injury to health occurred, to transfer to the comrades' courts the file on the case. Such a decision should be taken in each instance after consideration of the concrete circumstances of the offense, the personality of the accused, and also the opinion of the victim. The rights of the accused and of the victim must be considered, and the latter must be informed of the decision and of his right to appeal. . .

As is apparent from the record of the given case, and the statement submitted by the victim requesting that Tsiganok not be prosecuted, the people's judge properly refused to instigate proceedings. . .and transferred the case to a comrades' court for application to the guilty party of measures of social influence. . .

D. *Third-party umpires.*

V. Volozhanin, "MORE ATTENTION TO THIRD PARTY UMPIRES,"
Sovetskaia Iustitsiia, 1968, No. 5, p. 11.

With the aid of third-party umpires the parties may regulate conflicts arising between them without turning to the agencies of justice. Unfortunately up to this time third party trial of cases with the participation of citizens has not come into wide use. This is explained in some measure by the simplicity and easy access of courts in defense of the working people. Nevertheless, both the well known failure to evaluate highly this form of legal defense and the inadequate education provided as to its use are also responsible.

Under Arts. 141 and 155 of the Code of Civil Procedure of the RSFSR and corresponding articles in the other Union Republics, the Soviet court is given the direct duty of explaining to litigants their rights to take their case to a third party umpire. If this duty were properly performed, it would make court trial unnecessary.

In the law reviews the view has been expressed that the existence of comrades' courts makes superfluous trial by third party umpires. It is impossible to agree with this position, since the competence of the third party umpire and of the comrades' court differ. Notably, the former may hear disputes between citizens without limit in amount (Art. 1 of the Statute on Third Party Umpires). In practice a third party umpire court may be set up in any place, while comrades' courts are not everywhere. Trial of the case by a third party umpire facilitates the creation of an atmosphere with less appearance of compulsion.

The third party umpire courts are usually considered to be a form of social trial of civil cases. Nevertheless, speaking strictly, they are not social organizations, since they are chosen by the parties and not by the collective; they do not try their cases in public and their judgments do not reflect the opinion of the collective etc.

But, third party umpire courts must not be considered to be state agencies. It is a form of legal defense *sui generis,* permitted to function within the limits established by legislation. The agreement to take a matter to a third party umpire is in content procedurally an agreement between all interested parties. A *compromis,* concluded without the consent of the creditors and debtors, may not be applied to them. In departure from previous legislation on the subject the *compromis* does not require notarial certification. The preliminary consent of the umpire to participate is not required. Nevertheless, his refusal to participate voids the agreement (Art. 11 of the Statute). The parties have the right to denounce the *compromis* only in the event that it is discovered after conclusion of the agreement that the umpire is interested in the outcome (Art. 6).

Conclusion of a *compromis* deprives the parties of their right to go to a people's court (Arts. 129 and 219 of the Code of Civil Procedure of the RSFSR). Nevertheless it would have been desirable to specify in the law that the agreement might be terminated in the event of the mutual desire of the parties to do so. Under Art. 219 of the Code of Civil Procedure of the RSFSR a *compromis* is reason to terminate people's court proceedings in the case. Nevertheless, if the parties void the agreement, they regain their rights to people's court examination.

E. *Peoples' Control*

ORDER ON PEOPLES' CONTROL, December 19, 1968. Sotsialistichekaia Zakonnost', 1969, No. 5, p. 83.

By order of the Central Committee of the Communist Party of the Soviet Union and the USSR Council of Ministers of December 19, 1968 the Statute on Agencies of Peoples' Control was approved. Excerpts are published below:

1. The most important activity of the agencies of Peoples' Control is rendering aid to Party and State agencies in the systematic verification of the execution of Party and State directives by Soviet, economic and other organizations in further achievement of guidance in building communism, in the struggle to improve economic performance, to strengthen State discipline and maintain socialist legality.

9. The foundation of the system of Peoples' Control is the groups and posts of Peoples' Control...

10. Groups and posts of Peoples' Control, when necessary, conduct verification, raids, inspections in enterprises, collective farms, administrative offices and organizations, participate in verification and audit of their production and financial-economic activities ordered by superior organs, have the right to inform themselves of documents and evidence bearing on matters investigated, hear reports and explanations of persons guilty of disrupting plans and assigned tasks, of permitting violations of state discipline, of bureaucratic approaches and of red tape, uneconomic activity and abuse of authority, censure guilty persons, require them to stand before their fellow workers to report on measures taken to eliminate shortcomings, transfer cases to be heard by comrades' courts.

Groups and posts of Peoples' Control put before administrations, Party and other social organizations of the collective being investigated matters which emerge as a result of their verification, especially suggestions that employees guilty of permitting some inadequacy or other be held responsible. . .

F. *Social prosecutors and defenders.*

A. Basov, Rostov Province Deputy Procurator. "THE PUBLIC REPRESENTATIVE IN COURT." Izvestiia, October 20, 1972. Eng. trans. in 24 CDSP, No. 42. p. 17 (1972) (Excerpts)

P. Pashkevich. . .quite validly criticizes instances wherein collectives unfortunately appoint public representatives for the defense in the interest of persons who have committed serious crimes, and who, by their past actions or way of life, do not deserve public support. . .He suggests that the legally established procedure. . . orients representatives toward a one-sided approach to a case and turns them into assistants of the prosecutor or the defense attorney. Consequently, P. Pashkevich suggests the public should select its representative without giving him a definite assignment to conduct defense or accusation. He suggests that the existing law should be changed in this respect. . .

The institution of public representatives for prosecution and defense has proven itself in practice. The public representatives express the opinion of their comrades; they are granted the rights of independent participants in the proceedings and are not assistants to the prosecutor or the defense attorney. It is important, in our opinion, to strive for a situation in which the public representative expresses the opinion of the public in court, an opinion based on universally acknowledged moral principles, and this opinion is taken by the collective as an expression of the collective's will and conscience.

M. Kachalov, Procurator of the Novolian County of Gomel Province, Bielorussian SSR., Chelovek i Zakon, No. 10, 1971, p. 67.

During the morning in conspicuous places there were posted notices that in the village club of the village of Kirov there would be held a circuit session of the people's court with the participation of social and state prosecutors. Long before the beginning of the proceedings the room was overfull. Many workmen and clerks of the Kirov state farm and inhabitants of the village were present. The criminal case against V. Baranovskii was to be heard in which he was accused of attacking two citizens with a knife while drunk. One received serious wounds, the other light ones.

Hundreds of those present listened to the case in tense silence. They met with approval the speech of the social accuser, who was president of the workers' committee of the labor union of the Kirov State farm, A. Otchenash. He demanded in the name of the collective that the criminal be punished severely.

These circuit sessions of the people's court have been conducted in the Zavoitian village club, in the inter-collective farm confectionary organization, in the confectionary factory "Red Mozyrianin," and elsewhere. In only the first half of this year the circuit sessions have heard more than 50% of the criminal cases, each with participation by state and social accusers.

As a rule, the social accusation is presented by the secretary of the Communist Party organization, by members of local labor union committees, or the best workers - people who have authority and are shown respect, those to whose opinion the public in the collective listens.

The circuit sessions of the people's court and the participation in them of social accusers has great educational value; they help to inform people of our laws better than other sessions; they make clear the inevitability of punishment for crime, and convince the public of the fairness and well founded nature of the sentence. In the last analysis this tells favorably on the strengthening of socialist legality and law and order in the county, on reduction in crime.

CASE OF KOZLOBAEV AND NOVIKOV, Biulletin' Verkhovnogo Suda RSFSR, 1968, No. 1, p. 12.

Kozlobaev and Novikov were convicted of conspiring with Deriabina, who was convicted on Sept. 3, 1966, of theft from the fields of a state farm of 740 kilograms of millet. The stolen grain was recovered and returned to the state farm.

The workers' and clerks' collective of the central administration of the state farm voted at a general meeting to send a request to the Supreme Court of the R.S.F.S.R. asking that the convicted persons be bound over to it for social parole.

The presidium of the provincial court in its ruling stated that the public and the leadership of the state farm had taken an incorrect and unprincipled position with regard to the thieves of the state farm's wealth. Instead of severe censure of the guilty persons, they had defended them.

The ruling of the presidium of the provincial court is without foundation and must be revoked. Under Art. 52 of the Criminal Code of the RSFSR social organizations and working people's collectives may request transfer to them for purposes of social parole of persons who have committed crimes not representing great social danger, when the deeds did not cause serious consequences.

Considering the concrete circumstances of the case and the family situation of the guilty persons, the state farm's collective sent a petition to the Supreme Court of the R.S.F.S.R. asking for transfer of the convicted persons to social parole.

The court may accept or reject the petition of the collective. However, the ruling issued by the provincial court on the subject was not sufficiently supported with reasons. From the above, the Judicial Division for Criminal Cases of the Supreme Court of the RSFSR by its decree of June 30, 1967 revoked the ruling in the case of Kozlobaev and Novikov.

G. *Mass legal education.*

SPREADING INFORMATION ON LEGISLATION: AN IMPORTANT TASK OF COMMUNIST REARING OF SOVIET CITIZENS. Sovetskoe Gosudarstvo i Pravo. 1973. No. 1, p. 3.

On September 21, 1972 there occurred in the Kremlin a joint meeting of the legislative proposals committees of the Council of the Union and the Council of Nationalities of the Supreme Soviet of the U.S.S.R. They discussed the matter of spreading information on legislation among the population. The meeting was conducted by the two committee chairmen, V. Kapitonov and I.G. Kebin. . .

I.G. Kebin. .in his opening speech remarked that in the resolutions of the 24th Congress of the Communist Party of the Soviet Union and in the decrees of the Party's Central Committee there are repeated declarations on the necessity of continually strengthening socialist legislation and law and order in our country. The successful accomplishment of the tasks set by the 24th Congress is possible only if there is developed a high social consciousness and sense of discipline among the toilers and strick application by all citizens of Soviet laws. But, in order to apply laws, one has to know what they are. Consequently, spreading information on legislation among the population is an effective means of strengthening legality and law and order.

A. Elivanov, OUR PEOPLE'S UNIVERSITY OF LEGAL KNOWLEDGE. Sovetskaia Iustitsiia, 1966, No. 18, p. 1.

The People's University of Legal Knowledge of the Lenin Ward of Kazan has opened its doors for the sixth year, wide and hospitably. . . . About 500 persons attend, drawn on a strictly voluntary basis. . . . Thanks to the attention given by party and public organizations of the ward, the University has been able to gather a collective of teachers-enthusiasts, giving their time and knowledge to the people in response to recognition of their obligations to society.

The choice of subjects is made to permit the students not only to obtain in the two year program the necessary minimum of legal knowledge, but also to apply it in their practice and their social work. . . . Classes meet twice a month for two hours. As examples of the courses, the faculty of labor and civil law, which instructs primarily clerks in the state apparatus of the soviets; directors and inspectors of the personnel departments and of the wage and work departments of enterprises and organizations; and also labor union activists, has a study plan taking into consideration what they know, their interests and the specifics of their work.

For those attending the faculty of people's assessors, the lectures concern the basic questions of criminal, criminal procedural, civil, and civil procedural law, placing emphasis on the most important questions necessary to the accomplishment of justice. For those who attend the faculty of chairmen of comrades' courts more attention is given to practice sessions concerning the handling of a case, the writing of a decision and of the court record and conduct of comrades' court sessions. But matters of theory are not forgotten. Together with study of the Statute on Comrades' Courts, lectures are given to them on the concept of crime, on the principles of evidence, and some on selected questions of civil law necessary to the decision in comrades' courts of specific categories of civil cases.

In the faculty of the voluntary people's militia the fundamentals of administrative law on the protection of public order are studied, together with matters concerning the protection of the person in criminal law and questions of criminology.

Much time is spent on doing practical work, exchanging experience of commanders and chiefs of staffs of the voluntary people's militia for the prevention of crime.

CHAPTER III

Soviet Federalism

Like all federal structures, that of the U.S.S.R. was a political accommodation, but its proponents believe it unique. Socialism is credited with making the relationship between the component parts quite different from what they are in the United States, Switzerland, Germany or Mexico. The pattern of government is conceived to be a complex created in response both to necessity and to the dictates of political theory.

The necessity was great at the time of formation at the end of 1922. Long years of resistance to Russification within the Tsarist Empire, where centralization under Moscow was the fundamental principle of administration, had left its mark on the mentality of the many peoples who were less numerous than the great Russians.[1] Psychologically, they were hardened in their opposition by the requirement that they speak Russian in government offices, the courts and elsewhere, if they hoped for political and social advancement. Lenin played upon this hostility to garner support for his revolution against Tsarist authority. When the revolution was won, he had to pay the price in permitting the minority peoples to withdraw from what was called the "prison of peoples" and create their own independent states.

It was Lenin who signed the decree setting the Grand Duchy of Finland free, and permitting even the Ukraine and Bielorussia which had long been incorporated completely within the Imperial centralized structure to withdraw. He revealed his

---

[1]For a history of the Soviet federation, see Richard Pipes. The Formation of the Soviet Union: Communism and Nationalism, 1917-1922 (Cambridge, Mass. 1955).

motives, however, in his arrangements for the lesser peoples who, because of small numbers and very limited economic and cultural development, seemed to him incapable of resisting continued direction from Moscow. For them he devised a status within the new Russian Republic which gave them cultural autonomy in the form of the right to use their own language in public offices, courts and schools but kept them tied economically and politically to the center. To dramatize the relationship, he called the Russian Republic a "federation," but it had none of the usual political forms, such as a second chamber of its legislature to represent all component parts equally.

While freeing the ethnic groups to go their own way as independent states, Lenin continued to hold one strong card, namely the influence of the Communist Party in each. This Party was not permitted to create ethnic units within a federal structure. It was held to a unitary form, with the aid of which Lenin hoped to bring the independent states back together, once their nationalistic fervor had cooled and they were shown the economic, military and political advantages of working together.[2] This he succeeded in doing in 1922, although not with Finland or the Baltic states. His new federation of the Union of Soviet Socialist Republics was said to be "socialist in substance, national in form." It was looser than the federation within the Russian Republic, which he continued to maintain in its more centralized form. The component parts of the new state were called "federated republics," and, as such, were given equality of representation in one of the chambers created in the new bi-cameral legislature. In the division of powers between center and republic, the center reserved in the legislative field only the right to establish the fundamental principles. When economic planning was in issue, however, the center governed. Here was the "socialist" imprint not found in other federations.

After Lenin's death Stalin developed the system, emphasizing constantly the centralized features, even at the expense of the powers assigned to the republics. By 1935 he was ready with the draft of a new constitution which provided for further centralization, in that the codification of law was to become the sole right of the central government, and this he was able to establish as the "Stalin" Constitution on December 5, 1936.

The 1936 Constitution was centralist in that it provided for legal codification by the federal legislature and also for increased federal administrative authority, but it retained one of the centrifugal features from the first Constitution, namely the right of secession. Perhaps the aim was to pacify the remaining although waning opposition to centralism still evident in some of the republics; perhaps there was expectation that peoples of neighboring states could be persuaded to revolt and bring their new states into union with the U.S.S.R. if there seemed to be the possibility of withdrawing in the event of disillusion. Communist Party members could have had no illusion as to the meaning of such a clause, for Stalin on various occasions had

---

[2]For an account of the debates on a federal structure for the Communist Party, see Leonard Schapiro, The Communist Party of the Soviet Union (New York, 1960).

THE SOVIET STATE AND ITS CITIZENS 37

declared that Communists could not support an ethnic minority's campaign for secession if the result would be a step backward on the ladder of time to capitalist structures.[3]

Centralization was fostered by Stalin during the second world war because he thought military and economic efficiency required it, but the All-Union codes of law which he had promised and provided for in the 1936 Constitution remained in the drafting stage. The leisure and the personnel were evidently not available in wartime to permit completion, nor was wartime suitable to a major change in the relationships between the center and the republics. In Stalin's declining years of the late 1940's and early 1950's the federal structure remained unchanged, but after his death debate began. In 1957 a Constitutional amendment restored to the republics the right they had lost in 1936, namely the right to draft their own codes of law, albeit subject to federal fundamental principles to be enacted by the federal legislators under Communist Party guidance.

The 1957 reversal of the trend toward centralism was not to last, for there emerged in the late 1960's doctrinal emphasis upon phasing out structures designed to pacify ethnic minorities. Attention was focussed on creation of a new Soviet man, reflective of the line in the Communist Manifesto of 1848 saying that workers knew no fatherland. Party ideologues began to write of the merger of various ethnic cultures into one common Soviet culture. What this meant for the federal structure was debated in preparation for drafting a third federal constitution. Some believed that the slow movement toward completion of the draft, which drew L.I. Brezhnev's comments in 1976, was caused by the indecision of the Communist Party's Politburo on how the republics should be related to the center, and whether the preservation of a semblance of ethnic purity and political autonomy within a republic should take precedence in drafting economic plans over boundaries that would be logical economically.

The debate over ethnic autonomy did not affect the concept of decentralization in administration, as far as the authority of local government was concerned. The local Soviets were still respected for what they could contribute to economic efficiency. Indeed, under Khrushchev's leadership local government was made the basis for restructuring the vast industrial administrative mechanism of the U.S.S.R. After his ouster a more conventional approach to administration was reinstituted. The details of this mechanism will be set forth in Part II of this volume, but the materials in this chapter will permit the reader to consider the possibility that over the next decade increasing separation of ethnic from economic boundaries will occur.

The 1977 draft of the third federal constitution suggests that the federal structure has survived the debate with no change in form. Arts. 72 and 75 set forth the new wording to be compared with old Art. 14. Changes are primarily verbal.

---

[3]See Stalin's message of 1913 to his colleagues in the Social Democratic Parties of Europe and his report to the VII All-Russian Congress of his party in 1917. Eng. tr. in J.V. Stalin, Marxism and the National Question (Moscow, 1935) 19 and 62.

The appendix to this volume carries the new text.

A. *The philosophical novelty of soviet federation.*

M.G. Kirichenko, THE PROBLEM OF DELIMITING CONSTITUTIONAL LAW OF THE UNION AND OF THE REPUBLICS, Sovetskoe Gosudarsvo i Pravo, 1967, No. 11, p. 53.

The activity of agencies of the U.S.S.R. and of the Union Republics in the field of legislation expanded actively after the XXth Congress of the Communist Party of the Soviet Union [1956] when the Communist Party adopted the important decisions directed toward further broadening of the rights of Union Republics in all fields of state, economic and socio-cultural construction. The first important act was the law of the Supreme Soviet of the U.S.S.R. of February 1957 proposed by the Legislative Drafting Committees of the Council of the Union and Council of Nationalities to transfer to the competence of the Union Republics the legislation for the structure of the Union Republic courts, as well as for civil, criminal and procedural codes, while retaining in the U.S.S.R. the right to establish only fundamentals for these matters.

With the broadening of the Union Republics' rights in the field of economic and socio-cultural construction, the norm making activity of the supreme executive agencies of the Republics is also activated. The Councils of Ministers of the Union Republics were given the right independently to decide many economic and other questions which previously were decided in a centralized way by the all-union agencies of state administration.

All of this proves that the problem of delimiting the competence of the U.S.S.R. and of the Republics in the legislative sphere was formerly and remains one of the most important problems in the construction of the Soviet Union state system. The question of what fields of legislation, and in what measure, ought to be the exclusive competence of the union agencies, has always been closely bound together with the question of the limits on the sovereign rights of the Union Republics. Consequently the decision of these questions cannot be arbitrary; it requires taking into consideration the opinion and interests of the Union Republics at whose wish the Union was formed. On the other hand, these decisions in all cases must contribute to the strengthening of the power and might of the Union state which is the guarantee and bulwark of the successful national-state development of each Union Republic.

In view of the community of interests between the socio-economic structure of the Union Republics there can be no disagreement in principle and no discord between all-union and republic legislation. For this very reason the Republics themselves often have raised the question of unification of different branches of legislation.

The further development of democratic forms of legislative activity, in our view, requires solution of a number of constitutional questions, concerning delimitation of the legislative competence of the U.S.S.R. and of the Union Republics. The following variants are possible: 1) all matters relating only to the Union may be specified in a new all-union Constitution whether implied or stipulated directly, while all other questions pertain to the Union Republics; 2) a listing of all matters or fields concerning the competence of the Union Republics may be placed in the U.S.S.R. Constitution, assuming that all other matters shall be decided by the Union; 3) one can delimit precisely in the all-union Constitution the competencies of both the Union and Union Republics, giving a complete list of all matters of all-union and republic competency; 4) one could give a list by way of example of the most important matters to be decided by the Union and Republics, having in view the possibility of swift changes in events and conditions of life of socialist society. In our view the last variant ought to be adopted.

Legislative practice recognizes other means of deciding these matters as well. There are certain fields of state activity in which both agencies of the Union and of the Union Republics have to exercise their competence in some degree. For example, the functions of drawing up, reviewing, approving and executing the state budget is performed both by the Union and the Republics, of course within the appropriate limits and quantities. It is not by chance therefore that legislation on budget rights is clearly divided into union and republican. It is also known that there existed in the past and currently exists an all-union budget law.

Consequently, some branches of state activity are subjects of joint competency of the Union and of the Republics. But this "jointness" must not be considered in the literal meaning of the word. It is not a matter of duplication of Union and Republic agencies, nor of repetition of one and the same act by each. What has happened is that within one and the same field of state activity, delegated to the Union and to the Republics for execution, there is and cannot fail to be an elementary limitation of spheres of competence. While the Union agencies establish general principles of legislation in a given sphere, the Republic agencies in their legislation develop and provide details of these principles appropriate to the specific conditions of the given republic.

There have existed and now exist in nature no single or absolutely precise criteria for delimiting the competence of the U.S.S.R. and of the Union Republics in the field of legislation. The criteria, approaches and methods of deciding these problems differ; they are not of permanent "magnitude." Their content is conditioned on the concrete historical conditions of life of the Soviet federated state, on the needs of the successful building of communism in our multi-national country. They must be flexible, mobile, capable of alteration every time that the Party thinks a given set of social circumstances at a given moment is more or less important.

Moreover, the practice of state construction in many cases requires approval of unified principles of legislative work developed, in the main, similarly at different stages of the existence of the Soviet state, and required in like manner both for the U.S.S.R. agencies and those of the Union Republics.

All these matters have importance in theory and practice.

M.Ia. Shafir, KOMPETENTSIIA SSSR I SOIUZNOI RESPUBLIKI [The Competency of the USSR and of the Union Republics] (Moscow, 1968) 4-5.

It is completely obvious that the proper functioning of such a large federal state as the USSR, numbering within itself more than 100 different nations and ethnic groups, inescapably presupposes a precise drawing of lines between the competency of the USSR and of the union republics, and also a means of assuring the necessary coordination of the activities of their state agencies. This is especially important under current conditions in the development of communism, when the further drawing together of ethnic groups is occurring, when the centralized apparatus of plan guidance is being strengthened and when at the same time the wide potentials of all union republics are being utilized in solving problems arising in the creation of a material-technical base of communism, in transforming socialist social relationships into those of communism and also in rearing the new man.

The establishment of precise, scientifically based demarcation lines between the competencies of the USSR and of the union republics encompasses a whole complex of questions, linked with the development of ethnic relationships, and with perfecting the legislative and administrative process.

(1) Such demarcation is necessary to facilitate the further strengthening of fraternal collaboration and the mutual assistance of all Soviet nations and ethnic groups within the framework of a federal state, and to resolve successfully the political, economic and cultural tasks, standing before the USSR and before each union republic during the period of developing communism.

(2) It also has decisive importance in establishing the competencies of supreme agencies of state authority and administration and also of the central specialized agencies of the USSR and of the union republics; it facilitates the working out of scientific principles for state administration and prevents the emergence of subjectivism and voluntarism in constructing the state apparatus.

(3) It is closely linked to the rights of the toilers guaranteed in the Constitution; to the development in all possible ways of the freedom of the person and to the strengthening of the regime of socialist legality.

. . . Nevertheless, the theoretical side of this problem, and also the forms in which the competencies of the USSR and of the union republics are to be constitutionally strengthened still remain insufficiently clarified, and they still require analysis from every angle. . .

L.I. Brezhnev, REPORT OF THE CPSU CENTRAL COMMITTEE TO THE 25TH PARTY CONGRESS, February 14, 1976, Part 3. (White Plains, N.Y.: Compass Publications, Inc. 1976) 117-118.

I repeat, a great deal has been done. And the time has now come to sum up what has been accomplished. That is our premise in preparing the Draft of a new Constitution of the U.S.S.R. This work is being done thoroughly, without haste, so as to consider every problem that arises with the greatest possible precision, and then to throw the draft open for discussion by the whole people. But here, at the Congress, I should like to say a few words about some of the important points by which we are guided in this work.

The Draft of the new Constitution should quite evidently reflect the great victories of socialism and formally put on record not only the general principles of the socialist system, expressing the class substance of our state but also the basic features of a developed socialist society and its political organization.

The nature of the tasks connected with the building of the material and technical basis of communism makes it necessary to give a more detailed description in the Constitution of the principles governing the management of the national economy. At the same time, it is also advisable to reflect the role of the state in the spiritual life of the society and in insuring the conditions for the development of science, public education and culture. In this way we shall emphasize the humanistic character of the socialist state, a state which sets itself the goal of building communism in the interests of the working man, the interests of the people as a whole.

One of the basic features of the draft of the new Constitution will be the further consolidation and development of socialist democracy.

The idea is to establish a stricter system of accountability by all executive agencies to the elected organs of power. Furthermore it is envisaged that draft all-union laws are to be submitted for discussion by the whole people, such discussion is already our practice, but now it is to be given legal expression.

Of course, this is an enumeration of only some of the basic points, but I think that what has been said provides an idea of the lines along which the work is being carried on.

We started from the premise that the new Constitution should establish and define in precise terms the supreme goal of our state. And this supreme goal is to build a communist society.

B. *The constitutional structure of federation.*

CONSTITUTION OF THE U.S.S.R., December 5, 1936, as amended (Eng. tr., Moscow, 1972).

Art. 13. The Union of Soviet Socialist Republics shall be a federal state, formed on the basis of a voluntary union of the following Soviet Socialist Republics, enjoying equal rights:
Russian Soviet Federative Socialist Republic,
Ukrainian Soviet Socialist Republic,
Bielorussian Soviet Socialist Republic,
Uzbek Soviet Socialist Republic,
Kazakh Soviet Socialist Republic,
Georgian Soviet Socialist Republic,
Azerbaidjan Soviet Socialist Republic,
Lithuanian Soviet Socialist Republic,

Moldavian Soviet Socialist Republic,
Latvian Soviet Socialist Republic,
Kirghiz Soviet Socialist Republic,
Tajik Soviet Socialist Republic,
Armenian Soviet Socialist Republic,
Turkmen Soviet Socialist Republic,
Estonian Soviet Socialist Republic.

Art 14. The jurisdiction of the Union of Soviet Socialist Republics, as represented by its higher organs of state power and organs of state administration, shall extend to:

(IV) control over the observance of the Constitution of the U.S.S.R., and ensuring conformity of the Constitution and the Union Republics with the Constitution of the U.S.S.R.;

(XVII) definition of the basic principles of land tenure and of the use of mineral wealth, forests and waters;

(XX) definition of the fundamentals of labor legislation;

(XXI) definition of the fundamentals of legislation on the judicial system and judicial procedure and the fundamentals of civil, criminal and corrective labor legislation;

(XXII) legislation on Union citizenship; legislation on rights of foreign nationals;

(XXIII) definition of the fundamentals of legislation on marriage and the family;

(XXIV) promulgation of all-Union acts of amnesty,

Art. 15. The sovereignty of the Union Republics shall be limited only in the spheres defined in Article 14 of the Constitution of the U.S.S.R. Outside of these spheres each Union Republic shall exercise state authority independently. The U.S.S.R. shall protect the sovereign powers of the Union Republics.

Art. 16. Each Union Republic shall have its own Constitution with due account for the specific features of the Republic and drawn up in full conformity with the Constitution of the U.S.S.R.

Art. 17. Every Union Republic shall have the right freely to secede from the U.S.S.R.

Art. 19. The laws of the U.S.S.R. shall have the same force within the territory of every Union Republic.

Art. 20. In the event of any discrepancy between a law of a Union Republic and a law of the Union, the Union law shall prevail.

PROCURATOR'S PROTEST OF ILLEGALITY OF ADMINISTRATIVE REGULATION, Sotsialisticheskaia Zakonnost', 1971, No. 6, p. 86

The Procurator of the Azerbaidjan SSR protested the regulation, issued by the Deputy Minister of Agriculture of the Republic on September 17, 1970, No. 13-7/

645, saying that the Deputy Minister by his regulation issued in response to an inquiry of the chief of Masallin county agricultural administration for explanation of a procedure to be followed in removing from use for individual garden plots of workers of the State Farm "Odessa," 3 hectars of land allocated to the State Farm for its agricultural needs, proposed that the removal be conducted in accordance with the rules then in effect in the republic, namely on the basis of an order from the director of the State Farm and a decision of the county Soviet's Executive Committee.

This regulation was illegal for the following reason: In accordance with Art. 26 of the Fundamental Principles of Land Legislation of the USSR and of the union republics ". . .in the event of inadequate land to establish individual garden plots to meet the needs of workers and clerks, the amount of land made available for individual garden plots may be increased on petition of the directors of the economic enterprised concerned with the consent, . . . in republics not divided into provinces by the Council of Ministers of the union republic." Thus, the amount of land for individual garden plots of the State Farm "Odessa," in Masallin county may be increased at the expense of land assigned to the State Farm for its agricultural needs only with the consent of the Council of Ministers of the Azerbaidjan SSR.

In accordance with Art. 5 of the edict of the Presidium of the USSR Supreme Soviet of June 19, 1958, USSR laws are in force throughout the entire territory of the USSR from the moment they are declared in force. By Art. 1 of the edict of the Presidium of the USSR Supreme Soviet of June 4, 1969 "On the procedure for entry into force of the Fundamental Principles of Land Legislation" it is established that until the land legislation of the USSR and of the union republics is brought into conformity with the Fundamental Principles, the laws in force on land legislation of the USSR and of the union republics shall be applied so long as they do not conflict with the Fundamental Principles.

Being guided by Art. 13 of the Statute on Procurator's Supervision in the USSR, the Procurator of the Republic requested that the regulation of the Deputy Minister of Agriculture be annulled as being contrary to law. The protest was satisfied.

C. *Federal and Republic relationship to local government.*

CONSTITUTION OF THE U.S.S.R., December 5, 1936, as amended.

Art. 94. Soviets of Working People's Deputies shall be the organs of state power in Territories, Provinces, Autonomous Provinces, National Areas, counties, towns and rural localities (stanitsas, villages, hamlets, kishlaks, auls).

Art. 95. Soviets of Working People's Deputies. . .shall be elected for a term of two years by the working people of the respective Territories. . . .

Art. 96. The rate of representation in Soviets of Working People's Deputies shall be determined by the Constitutions of the Union Republics.

Art. 99. The Executive Committees elected by Soviets of Working People's Deputies and consisting of a Chairman, Vice Chairmen, a Secretary and members shall be executive and administrative organs of the Soviets of Working People's Deputies of Territories. . . .

MODEL STATUTE OF A CITY OR BOROUGH SOVIET OF WORKING PEOPLE'S DEPUTIES, approved by Edict of the Presidium of the USSR Supreme Soviet, March 19, 1971. [1971] Vedomosti Verkhovnogo Soveta SSSR, No. 12, item 134.

Art. 1. A City, or borough Soviet of Working People's Deputies is an organ of state authority in a city and a borough and decides, within the limits established by law, all questions of local concern, arising from general state interests and from the interests of the working people of the city.

The City Soviet of Working People's Deputies participates in discussion of questions of district, provincial, territorial, Republic and All-Union concern. The City Soviet of Working People's Deputies of a city which is subordinate to a county, and a borough Soviet within a city also participate in discussion of questions of concern to the respective county and city.

D. *Regulation of conflict of laws within the federation.*

FUNDAMENTAL PRINCIPLES OF CIVIL LEGISLATION OF THE U.S.S.R. AND OF THE UNION REPUBLICS. December 8, 1961, effective May 1, 1962. [1961] Vedomosti Verkhovnogo Soveta SSSR, No. 50 item 525.

Art. 18. The civil law of one Union Republic shall be applied in another Union Republic in accordance with the following rules:

1) to relationships arising from the right of ownership, the law of the situs of the property shall apply;

2) in the event of conclusion of an agreement, legal and physical capacity to act shall be determined in accordance with the law of the place of conclusion of the agreement;

3) the law of the place of conclusion of the agreement shall be applied to the form of the agreement. The same rule shall be applied to obligations arising from agreement, if by law or by agreement of the parties it is not provided otherwise;

4) the law of the forum shall be applied to obligations arising out of the causing of injury, but on request of the injured party, the law of the place where the injury was caused shall be applied;

5) the law of the place of opening of an inheritance shall be applied to inheritance relationships;

6) matters of limitations of time on the bringing of actions shall be determined by the law of the union republic by whose legislation the given relationship is governed.

THE SOVIET STATE AND ITS CITIZENS

FUNDAMENTAL PRINCIPLES OF LEGISLATION OF THE U.S.S.R. AND OF THE UNION REPUBLICS ON MARRIAGE AND THE FAMILY. June 27, 1968. [1968] Vedomosti Verkhovnogo Soveta SSSR, No. 27, item 241.

Article 8. *Application of Union-Republic Legislation on Marriage and the Family.* The contracting of marriage; the relations between spouses and between parents and children; adoption; the establishment of paternity; the collection of alimony; guardianship and wardship; the dissolution of marriage; and the registration of documents pertaining to civil status shall all be regulated by legislation of the Union Republic whose agency performs or registers the respective act or settles a dispute that has arisen.

The validity of marriage or of an adoption, the establishment of guardianship or wardship and the validity of documents pertaining to these shall be regulated by the legislation of the Republic on whose territory the marriage was concluded, the adoption effected, the guardianship or wardship concluded or the act of civil status registered.

FUNDAMENTAL PRINCIPLES OF CRIMINAL LEGISLATION OF THE U.S.S.R. AND OF THE UNION REPUBLICS, December 25, 1958. [1959] Vedomosti Verkhovnogo Soveta SSSR, No. 1, Item 6.

Art. 4. *The Functioning of the Criminal Laws of the U.S.S.R. and of the Union Republics with Respect to Acts Committed on the Territory of the U.S.S.R.*

All persons committing criminal acts on the territory of the U.S.S.R. are held responsible in accordance with the laws in effect at the scene of the crime.

CODE OF CRIMINAL PROCEDURE, RSFSR, October 27, 1960. [1960] Vedomosti Verkhovnogo Soveta RSFSR, No. 40, item 592.

Art. 1. *Legislation on Criminal Procedure.*

Regardless of the place of commission of a crime, the procedure in criminal cases on the territory of the RSFSR shall be conducted in all cases in accordance with the Code of Criminal Procedure of the RSFSR.

COMMENTARY TO THE CODE OF CRIMINAL PROCEDURE OF THE RSFSR 1960 (Leningrad, 1962) 134.

4. In performing any act of investigation on the territory of another Union Republic the investigator shall be guided by the norms of the Code of Criminal Procedure of that Union Republic.

CASE OF ZOBNOVA AND SHPAKOV, Biulletn' Verkhovnogo Suda SSSR, 1973, No. 1, p. 16.

A.A. Zobnova and M.V. Shpakov were found guilty on May 11, 1971 by the peoples' court of the Leningrad borough of Ashkhabad of violation of Arts. 17 and 154, par. 2 of the Criminal Code of the Ukrainian SSR and Arts. 15 and 171, par. 2 of the Criminal Code of the Turkmen SSR. Shpakov was found guilty additionally under Art. 171, par. 1 of the Criminal Code of the Turkmen SSR. The former was sentenced to 7 and the latter to 3 years of deprivation of freedom. The judgment was upheld on appeal by the Supreme Court of the Turkmen SSR on June 15, 1971.

Zobnova and Shpakov were found guilty of conspiring during October, 1970 to purchase on the territory of the Ukrainian SSR for the purpose of turning an illegal profit a number of manufactured goods, which they transported to the Turkmen SSR for resale. They were arrested near the airport of Ashkhabad. Shpakov was also found guilty of speculating [blackmarketing] in manufactured goods in Ashkhabad.

The Deputy Procurator of the Turkmen SSR protested the judgment, proposing that the accusation of Zobnova and Shpakov under Arts. 15 and 171, par. 2 of the Criminal Code of the Turkmen SSR be withdrawn, but his protest was rejected by the Presidium of the Turkmen SSR Supreme Court. The protest was filed again with the Plenum of the same court, but rejected on June 22, 1972. The USSR Procurator General then protested the judgment to the Plenum of the USSR Supreme Court, proposing that there be dropped from the judgment conviction of Zobnova and Shpakov under the Criminal Code of the Ukrainian SSR. The Plenum of the USSR Supreme Court satisfied the protest for the following reasons:

Zobnova's and Shpakov's guilt of attempted speculation reflected in their purchase on the territory of the Ukrainian SSR of manufactured goods for subsequent resale in the Turkmen SSR for the purpose of making a profit was proved by evidence in the record, and their acts were properly classified under Arts. 15 and 171, par. 2 of the Criminal Code of the Turkmen SSR. The conviction of Shpakov under Art. 171, par. 1 of the Criminal Code of the Turkmen SSR for speculation in Ashkabad was also well founded in fact.

The classification of Zobnova's and Shpakov's acts, however, under Arts. 17 and 154, par. 2 of the Criminal Code of the Ukrainian SSR, which also provide for attempted speculation, cannot be recognized as correct. It is evident from the record that Zobnova and Shpakov, having purchased goods on the territory of the Ukrainian SSR transported them for resale to Ashkhabad. They were arrested at that place, and they were unable to carry out their intended plan. Thus, the convicted persons, having begun to commit the crime in one place, continued with it as an attempt in another place, where it was cut short. These acts, since they were committed at the place of arrest, constituting the further realization of the same criminal intent, must be classified under the law of the union republic on whose territory they were cut short.

The fact that the crime was commenced on the territory of the Ukrainian SSR provides no reason for a supplementary classification under the law of that republic, since the first steps do not constitute the elements of any separate crime and are part of the acts directed toward execution of a criminal intention which was cut short by the state authorities on the territory of the Turkmen SSR. . . . .

[The conviction under the Ukrainian SSR Criminal Code was eliminated from the judgment.]

CHAPTER IV

Sources and Hierarchy of Law

Although determined to sever all ties with the substantive law of the Russian Empire, the lawyers designated to develop the new Soviet legal system soon exhibited conformity in most ways to traditional attitudes toward sources and hierarchy of law. Their inheritance was a system favoring written law, emanating from a central source. Althought the Tsar of the Russian Empire had permitted the peasants to govern their own social relationships under ancient peasant customary law, and the indigenous peoples of central Asia and Siberia to live by tribal custom, the primary source of law in the Empire had been statutes and codes. Judicial decisions had been given no force of stare decisis. When the Tsar had been compelled to share the legislative process with a parliament after the riots of 1905, he had taken the precaution to include in the Constitution an escape clause permitting decree law in an emergency, except with regard to the electoral law. Even this exception he ignored later when he feared for the life of the dynasty. Such was the Imperial heritage.[1]

Practice of the Bolsheviks after the revolution conformed in appearance to old attitudes in all but centralization, but the reasons were different. Bolsheviks argued that customary law, other than that of the peasants, should be rejected because it could not but incorporate the customs of bourgeois society or of the backward tribes of the East. Judge-made law was also rejected on the ground that judges would for a time be influenced by the bourgeois society in which they had been reared, and they were in any event too inexperienced and legally unprepared to be permitted to decide matters of policy, except during a short transitional period while the statutes were being drafted. Codes and statutes alone were desired as sources of the new law since they could provide the most authentic and the most speedily effective instrument with which to alter the community.

The priority of statutes as a source of law remained unchallenged for over twenty years, but in the 1940s an objection to the policy of preference for legislation as a source of law was voiced for the first time. The objection provided the first real test

---

[1] See Samuel Kucherov, Courts, Lawyers and Trials under the Last Three Tsars (New York, 1953).

of motives since the rejection of most custom and of judge made law at the outset of the regime. Two distinguished professors, while holding to the view that the Soviet legal system could not accept court precedent as a source of law, found it possible to warn in 1940, "To deny court precedent as a source of law does not mean the denial of all guiding significance to court practice."[2]

The issue had been broached, and in 1943 a more junior Soviet author was emboldened to argue that while Marxists must look with suspicion on courts in bourgeois societies as barriers to socialism, Soviet society of the 1940s could countenance no conflict between court and legislature. Court practice was to him in a position from which it could develop within the framework of socialist law in the step-by-step transition to communist society. He argued that there was good reason to accept court practice as one of the sources of Soviet law, albeit of lower rank than legislation.

To western minds trying to imagine the credibility of the argument to men with Marxist background the 1943 author's argument would seem acceptable. Nevertheless it was rejected. The Soviet court of the 1940s was held by a congress of jurists, called to consider the matter, to have no law-making power, except what little it might exercise under guise of the limited authority given the Plenum of the Supreme Court by the Judiciary Act of 1938 "To give interpretations of the laws of the U.S.S.R." In effect the Soviet jurists were reaffirming the traditional position of jurists within the Romanist systems of Continental Europe.

While the role of legislation as the sole source of law was uncontroverted, the hierarchy of law within the category of legislation was not so clear. Bolshevik attitudes on this subject emerge in examination of the role of the constitution in the Soviet legal system. The first constitution of the Russian Republic, promulgated in 1918, was conceived as a statement of lofty aims, of ultimate goals, rather than as a set of rules to which even policy makers would be held unless they took the trouble to seek the will of the people in amendment.[3] Although appearing to favor a conventional hierarchy of law, with the constitution ranking superior to all other forms of legislative action, the draftsmen made no provision for protection of this supremacy. The legislature was to be its own judge of the constitutionality of its actions. This principle was retained in the two successor federal constitutions promulgated in 1923 and 1936, although the Supreme Court of the U.S.S.R. was given the authority by the 1923 constitution to respond to requests of the legislature for an opinion as to conformity with the constitution of legislation of a constituent republic. Even this limited form of judicial review was, however, removed from the 1936 constitution.

No provisions for amendment were included in the Russian Republic's constitution of 1918 nor in the first federal constitution. Still, amendments were introduced

---

[2] For the arguments and stages of discussion, see John N. Hazard, "The Soviet Court as a Source of Law," 24 Washington Law Review 80 (1949).

[3] For English translation of the various Soviet constitutions, see Jan F. Triska (ed.) Constitutions of the Communist Party States. (The Hoover Institution of War, Revolution and Peace, Stanford University, 1968), 2-76.

by the legislature with no more formality than that attendant upon enactment of any law. An amending procedure requiring two thirds majority vote of each chamber of the legislature for constitutional amendment in contrast to a simple majority for a law was introduced in the second federal constitution, but it was soon ignored in practice, for it became customary for the Presidium of the Supreme Soviet to take provisional measures through decree action and to request amendment of the constitution only after the decrees had long been in effect.[4]

The emergence of this practice of decree law, in some cases violative of express provisions of the constitutions, was the more remarkable in view of Stalin's recognition of the undesirability of such action. Speaking at the constitutional convention of 1936 he took note of the practice of earlier days under which even the executive had issued orders with the force of law. He declared, "It is time we put an end to a situation in which not one but a number of bodies legislate."[5] Some thought that only the Supreme Soviet would legislate thereafter and that its interim body, the Presidium, would take only technical emergency measures, leaving matters of wide social concern for enactment by the Supreme Soviet as required by the constitution. No one seems to have anticipated that a decree would be put into force if it contravened a provision of the Constitution and that constitutional amendment would be sought only after proclamation of the decree.

In spite of the provisions of the 1936 constitution and his own explanation that legislation would issue only from one body, Stalin proved himself unable or unwilling to abide by the restrictions he had created. Almost immediately the Presidium, as the interim policy making body sitting in the long intervals between the brief meetings of the Supreme Soviet, began enacting provisional legislation, sometimes revising provisions of the constitution on the structure of the Council of Ministers. Only months after the changes had been put into effect was ratification sought from the Supreme Soviet. This irregular procedure reached the extreme in 1946 of a decree altering the Constitutional age requirement for deputies to the Supreme Soviet. Before seeking ratification from the Supreme Soviet new elections were held in conformity with the new age minimum, and ratification was sought only after the deputies elected under the new rule had been seated in the Supreme Soviet. Subsequently, fees were introduced for higher education in violation of the article of the constitution guaranteeing free education. Not for seven years was the constitution's article on education brought into conformity with the provisions of the routine law. To western oriented constitutional lawyers, A.Y. Vyshinsky's 1947 speech to the Supreme Soviet explaining the proposal of his constitutional editing committee to amend the consitution to conform to already existing laws makes unfamiliar reading.[6]

---

[4]See John N. Hazard, "Constitutional Problems in the U.S.S.R.," in James Kerr Pollock, ed., Change and Crisis in European Government (New York, 1947) 3 at 12-13.
[5]See Joseph Stalin, Leninism: Selected Writings (New York, 1942), 402.
[6]Zasedaniia Verkhovnogo Soveta SSSR (Tret'ia Sessiia), 20-25 Fevralia 1947 g. Stenograficheskii Otchet (Moscow, 1947), 307.

The conclusion is inescapable that although the constitution was declared supreme in the hierarchy of Soviet sources of law, there was no adherence to the hierarchy in Stalin's time. Further it has been seen that the state agency that legislated and even amended the Constitution was not always the Supreme Soviet as was required by the constitution. On the contrary, practice established the Presidium of the Supreme Soviet as most frequently the source of law, and the Supreme Soviet was asked to approve months or even years later what the Presidium had done.

Even a decade after Stalin's death and more than two years after Nikita Khrushchev's ouster from power the attitude toward the constitution's place in the hierarchy of laws remained unchanged. In 1966 the constitution was amended again in the manner of 1946 when the Presidium of the Supreme Soviet decreed an increase in the number of deputies to be seated from each of the Union Republics. This was more than a simple increase in numbers, for it changed the relationship between Union and Autonomous Republics since the latter were given no increase in representation. In spite of the important nature of the change, it was not submitted to the Supreme Soviet for approval until after the conduct of elections under the new system. Then, when the deputies elected in the number provided for by the Presidium had gathered in their Kremlin palace for the first sitting of the Supreme Soviet in its new form, they ratified the act under which they had been elected.

Soviet jurists during the discussion preceding publication of the draft of the third federal constitution questioned the efficacy of existing measures to assure recognition of the supremacy of the Constitution in the hierarchy of laws. Their proposals for change went unheeded, however, for the 1977 draft showed no institutional change. Readers of this chapter may determine from the materials what issues were before the draftsmen and what attitudes may be expected to guide Soviet policy makers as they move into the post-1977 era.

A. The theoretical approach to sources of law.

A.F. Shebanov, "Sources of Law," ENTSIKLOPEDICHESKII SLOVAR' PRAVOVYKH ZNANII [Encyclopedia of Legal Knowledge] (Moscow, 1965) 171.

The term "sources of law" is used in legal science to designate various acts of state agencies establishing norms of law or sanctioning norms which already have emerged in society.

Every historical type of state and law recognizes its own sources of law; consequently their significance is not identical in different states, even when they are of the same type, in different periods of development. Thus, in the exploitive state during different periods of its development the most widely distributed source of law was customary law (i.e. rules which came to be established in the consciousness of man as the result of long usage and a multiplicity of repetitions in practice) conformity to which was sustained by the compulsory process of judicial decision, administrative order and legislation. In England, the USA and other so-called

Anglo-Saxon countries this concept of source of law is widely diffused as judicial precedent. When the absolute monarchy was established, the ruling source of law in exploitive society became the normative act published by agencies of the state, especially legislative acts. In slaveholding and feudal law the legislation was generally a written statement of legal customs and precedents. In bourgeois law during the earliest stage of its evolution there was proclaimed the principle of supremacy of legislation enacted by parliament over all other sources of law. In the period of imperialism, however, a constantly more evident place among sources of law was given to administrative orders, first among which were orders of the executive, of the chief of state and of the head of the government. Simultaneously, the state upheld conservative customs and utilized precedents widely.

In socialist states normative acts issued by the authorized state agencies or adopted by public organizations of working people and sanctioned by the state predominate among sources of law. . . .In the U.S.S.R. the first rank among sources of law in held by legislation. But sources of law also include edicts of the Presidium of the Supreme Soviet of the U.S.S.R. and of the Presidiums of the Supreme Soviets of the Union and Autonomous Republics when their purpose is to create norms; normative decrees and directives of the Council of Ministers of the U.S.S.R. and of the Councils of Ministers of the Union and Autonomous Republics. . .; normative orders and instructions of Ministries of the U.S.S.R. and of Union and Autonomous Republics and of chairmen of state committees; normative decisions and orders of local soviets of working peoples' deputies and of their executive committees. A place of constantly increasing importance among sources of law is held by those acts of public organizations (for example, decisions of the All-union Central Council of Labor Unions) sanctioned by the state, as well as their charters (for example, the charter of the agricultural artels), and collective agreements concluded by factory labor union committees with the administrations of enterprises and state offices.

The term "sources of law" is also used in legal science in the sense of a source for discovery of law in legislation, edicts, literary relics, and archeological materials permitting study of the nature and content of law in differing historical epochs.

M.E. Farber, V.A. Rzhevskii, VOPROSY TEORII SOVETSKOGO KONSTITUT-
SIONNOGO PRAVA [Questions of the Theory of Soviet Constitutional Law] (Moscow, 1967) 36.

In what lies the purpose or function of the constitution as the fundamental law of the socialist state?

First: to fix in law the factual authority and sovereignty of classes, of ethnic groups, of the people in the socialist state; to define the forms by which this authority and sovereignty are to be exercised.

Second: to establish a system of state agencies, superior and inferior, and to define in accordance with functions given them the line of subordination and their competency, utilizing as a guide in so doing the Leninist principles of the working peoples' participation in administration, of democratic centralism, of the subordination of the civil service to politics, of the guiding role of the Communist Party in the political system.

Third: to define the principles of regulation by law, setting forth in detail the rules of the legislative process so that they conform to the requirements of socialist democracy and legality.

Fourth: to guarantee the complete freedom of the individual as it has emerged in socialist states; to define in law the constitutional foundations of that freedom, the mutual relations between state and individual.

The practical purpose of the constitution is to give to the norms of constitutional law a special nature in distinction from other social norms (moral, organizational, and others) and from many norms of civil, criminal and other branches of law.

The peculiar legal nature of the norms of constitutional law are their 1) normative character, 2) constituent character, 3) programmatic character and 4) force as supreme law.

K.A. Mokicheva, editor, TEORIIA GOSUDARSTVA I PRAVA [Theory of State and Law] (Moscow, 2nd ed. 1970) 449-451.

Law differs from other norms of socialist society by virtue of the fact that it is in a certain form. The forms of socialist law are specific. It is primarily composed of official actions of state agencies. Other legal forms (precedent, legal custom, norm creating agreements) are either in general excluded, or have under socialism extremely reduced diffusion.

The matter of the form of socialist law has not only theoretical but also practical importance, since the legal force and other elements related to the effect and application of norms of law depend on the form in which law is expressed.

The normative-legal act is the specific form of socialist law. It is first of all an action of State character, published directly by the State and its agencies, and in specifically defined circumstances by social organizations, but acting independently without the specifically granted authority of the State.

Further, it is an act which gives rise to some sort of legal consequences. Not all State acts may be considered to be forms of law. Acts of moral-political importance such as addresses, appeals, declarations, statements are issued by the socialist State with the purpose of explaining domestic and foreign policy and of mobilizing the toilers to put it into effect. These are not law creating acts. Thus, only actions having legal meaning, may be viewed as forms of socialist law. . .

Normative-legal acts must be distinguished from legal acts having no normative character. In the course of their activity organs of the socialist State adopt decisions and issue regulations relating personally to specific organizations and persons. Such are, for example, planning directives, decisions in the assignment of housing, on the award of pensions, judicial decisions, judgments, etc. These are legal actions since they bear legal consequences, but they do not create and do not formulate legal norms. Similar legal documents are issued when the State's competent organs apply norms of law to concrete situations, deciding a practical matter on the basis of and in execution of legal prescriptions. Such an act is a decision relating to a concrete specifically indicated person. Therefore, in contrast to normative acts, these legal actions are called personally-defined or individual acts. Individual legal documents are issued by all State agencies, while the circle of agencies endowed with authority to issue normative acts is strictly circumscribed. . .

An important attribute of normative legal acts of socialist states is their strict hierarchy, i.e. the system of subordination, the rank order on which the legal force of one or another normative act depends.

In the system of normative-legal acts of the socialist State, the leading place belongs to the law (legislation). The principle of the supremacy of legislation to all other acts is one of the primary features of socialist democracy and socialist legality. Other normative acts are issued on the basis of, in accordance with, and in execution of legislation, i.e. they have a sub-law character. These normative acts may be classified in accordance with their legal force as legislative and sub-legislative. A law, however, must not be seen apart from other normative acts, since it is thanks to the latter that the prescriptions of a legislative act are put into force.

B. *Protection of constitutional supremacy.*

"FROM THE PROCURATOR'S AUDITING PRACTICE," Sotsialisticheskaia zakonnost', 1966, No. 7, p. 85.

A decision issued in violation of the Ukrainian SSR Constitution: The Executive Committee of the Menchichensk village soviet. . .confirmed as secretary of the village soviet Babak, who was not a deputy of the soviet. This decision is illegal for the following reasons: Under Art. 58 of the constitution of the Ukrainian SSR and Art. 33 of the Statute on the village soviet of working peoples' deputies of the Ukrainian SSR an executive committee shall be elected by the soviet from its members and shall comprise a chairman, his deputy, a secretary and executive committee members. Consequently, the executive committee of the village soviet elected the secretary illegally, since a secretary of a village soviet may be only a deputy.

The decision of the village soviet, being in violation of the legislation in force is annulled in accordance with the protest of the county procurator.

S.I. Rusinova i V.A. Rianzhin, editors. SOVETSKOE KONSTITUTSIONNOE PRAVO. [Soviet Constitutional Law] (Leningrad, 1975) 60-61.

The U.S.S.R. Constitution of 1936 provided no special method for protecting the constitution. The Communist Party of the Soviet Union in recent years has disclosed an active struggle with subjectivism and voluntarism in matters relating to state guidance of society. On the basis of resolutions of the October and November (1964) and of the March and September (1965) Plenary Sessions of the Central Committee of the C.P.S.U. and on the basis of decisions of the XXIII Congress of the Party there were corrected many errors of this tendency permitted during preceding years. Subjectivism and voluntarism in their very nature are enemies of the spirit of constitutional legality. Therefore, it would be expedient to establish in the U.S.S.R., and also in each of the union republics, a constitutional council as an organ of supreme supervision over all, even including the supreme, legislative agencies to maintain adherence to the constitution.

C. *Amendment of the constitution.*

CONSTITUTION OF THE U.S.S.R., December 5, 1936.
Art. 146. Amendments to the Constitution of the U.S.S.R. shall be adopted by a majority of not less than two-thirds of the votes in each of the Chambers of the Supreme Soviet of the U.S.S.R.

F.M. Kalinychev, "THE PRINCIPAL DISTINCTIVE CHARACTERISTICS OF THE SOVIET SOCIALIST CONSTITUTION," Sovetskoe Gosudarstvo i Pravo, 1967, No. 11, p. 48.

Historical experience gives evidence that a Soviet constitution cannot be in some manner created once and for all time as a fixed and unchangeable document. The strength of Soviet constitutions lies in the fact that they reflect correctly things as they are, and at the same time they are a powerful factor in forward movement. Consequently, the development of the Soviet constitutions has been indissolubly linked with the history of Soviet society, with the struggle of the soviet people, guided by the Communist Party, to create socialism and communism.

V.I. Lenin emphasized at the VII All-Russian congress that "We have never looked upon our activity generally, nor our constitution in particular as a model of perfection. The question of amending the constitution is raised at this congress. We agree to amendment, and let us look at the proposal, but we shall not fix the amendment in the law 'for all eternity.' "

The present constitution of the U.S.S.R. was adopted more than 30 years ago. During that interval there have occurred deep transformations in the economic, political, and cultural life of our country, and also in its international position. The essence of these changes is to be found in the fact that socialism has won a complete and final victory in our country. The Soviet Union has entered into a new period in its development—the period of building communism. The Soviet socialist state, which emerged as a state of the dictatorship of the proletariat, has developed into a state of all the people, reflecting the will and interests of all strata of our country's population and becoming the instrument of all of society, of all the people. During that interval the U.S.S.R. has come out of the capitalist encirclement in which it long found itself. There has been created a world-wide socialist system - the great commonwealth of socialist states. . . .

D. *The legislative process.*

CONSTITUTION OF THE U.S.S.R., December 5, 1936
Article 32. The legislative power of the U.S.S.R. is exercised exclusively by the Supreme Soviet of the U.S.S.R.
Article 48. The Supreme Soviet of the U.S.S.R. at a joint sitting elects the Presidium of the Supreme Soviet of the U.S.S.R.
The Presidium of the Supreme Soviet of the U.S.S.R. is accountable to the Supreme Soviet of the U.S.S.R. for all its activities.
Article 49. The Presidium of the Supreme Soviet of the U.S.S.R.:
b) Issues edicts;
c) Gives interpretations of the laws of the U.S.S.R. in operation.

E. *Judicial interpretation and legislative initiative.*

CONSTITUTION OF THE U.S.S.R., December 5, 1936.
Art. 104. The Supreme Court of the U.S.S.R. is the highest judicial agency. The Supreme Court of the U.S.S.R. is charged with the supervision of the judicial activities of all the judicial bodies of the U.S.S.R. and of the Union Republics within the limits established by law.
Art. 112. Judges are independent and subject only to the law.

STATUTE OF THE SUPREME COURT OF THE U.S.S.R., February 12, 1957, as amended September 30, 1967. [1957] Vedomosti Verkhovnogo Soveta SSSR, No. 4, item 85 and [1967] *Ibid.*, No. 40, item 526.
Art. 1. In conformity with Art. 104 of the U.S.S.R. constitution, the Supreme Court of the U.S.S.R. is the supreme judicial organ of the U.S.S.R.
The duties laid upon the Supreme Court of the U.S.S.R. are audit of the judicial activity of the judicial agencies of the U.S.S.R., as well as of the judicial agencies of the Union Republics within the limits set by the present statute. The Supreme Court of the U.S.S.R. verifies the application by the courts of the Union Republics of All-union legislation, and also the execution of the decrees of the Plenum of the Supreme Court of the U.S.S.R.
The Supreme Court of the U.S.S.R. under the circumstances and in conformity with the procedure established by law decides questions arising out of treaties of judicial assistance concluded by the U.S.S.R. with other states. The Supreme Court of the U.S.S.R. has the right of legislative initiative.
Art. 9. The Plenum of the Supreme Court of the U.S.S.R.
c) reviews materials generalizing on judicial practice and judicial statistics and issues guiding instructions to courts on questions of application of legislation in court proceedings.
d) presents to the Presidium of the Supreme Soviet of the U.S.S.R. proposals on matters to be resolved by legislation regarding interpretation of the laws of the U.S.S.R.

CHAPTER V

The Instruments of Public Order

The Bolsheviks entered upon the task of governing the new Russia with determination to simplify the process of adjudication. In this they were supported by the masses of the people, disgruntled as is the lay public in most lands with what seems to be the complexity of courts, the accusatory bias of prosecutors, the sometimes money-grubbing practice of lawyers, and the frequent brutality of the professional police.

The Bolsheviks promised change. They would introduce a simple tribunal to be presided over by a wise elder of the community or a communist oriented younger person. Disputes would be heard without the aid of prosecutors or members of the bar. Even the police would be abolished as an institution, and in its place would be created a people's militia, distinguished by its close link with the masses. Its members would be recruited from the common people, and control would be in the hands of the local soviet and not the central government.

The instruments of public order in Soviet society were to be restored to a simplicity mindful of the primitiveness of tribunals in tribal society, and when conditions of abundance and wide-spread education in social duties had created the prerequisites for communism, even these primitive tribunals were to wither away. In their stead would rise the citizen's inner voice of social conscience, prompted when necessary by a reminder from neighbors and friends who sensed that guidance was needed to develop attitudes appropriate to the communist society.

The first decree on the courts[1] put the new plan into effect. Prosecutors and bar were abolished, and the single "people's court" under the guidance of a wise man, flanked by part-time lay judges or "assessors," sitting in rotation, was established to hear disputes, listen to accusations from aggrieved parties and defense from relatives and friends, take whatever measures seemed necessary to learn the facts, and finally issue a decision that would be subject to appellate review, not by a perma-

---

[1] November 24, 1917. [1917-1918] I Sob. Uzak. RSFSR, No. 4, item 50.

nent higher court but by a "congress" of the local people's judges gathered together at intervals for this purpose within each county. Even then, there could be no appeal unless the sentence exceeded seven days detention or required payment of more than 300 rubles in satisfaction of civil claims.

By 1921 most of this simplicity of structure had been lost under the pressure of necessity. Judges had complained that they had no time to ascertain facts without the help of prosecutors and bar. Lenin himself had complained to his Commissar of Justice of the inadequacy of a system that provided no means of unifying practice through a procedure of review on a national scale. The increasing number and complexity of problems facing the judges had required establishment as early as 1920 of a "special session" of the people's court, and had resulted in 1919 in expansion of the political courts of the revolution, the "revolutionary tribunals," into a specialized system of three courts hearing matters relating to discipline in the army, protection of transportation, and attempts to overthrow the regime. An investigating commission had been established in 1918 to prepare cases before submission to court, and the central government had coordinated the people's militia in 1920 into a single national system of professional keepers of order. At the top of the court hierarchy was established in March, 1921, a department of the People's Commissariat of Justice to serve as a supreme court, to parallel the Supreme Revolutionary Tribunal created earlier to hear appeals from the lower tribunals and to try cases of extreme political importance. Dreams of simplification of the instruments of public order had faded.

Into this increasingly complex situation came Lenin's New Economic Policy in 1921 for the purpose of utilizing the incentives of the private enterprise system to restore an economy devastated by years of civil war. The Commissar of Justice told his colleagues that the new conditions required revision of legal institutions and adoption of precise codes of law. From the drafting commissions there emerged the fundamentals of a bifurcated complex three stepped court structure, flanked by professional prosecutors and professional bar. There was thus brought into being a system that was to remain throughout Stalin's life, with such changes, however, as became necessary in 1923 to adapt it to the federal structure established at the very end of 1922. These included a Supreme Court of the U.S.S.R. to rule over the judicial systems of the republics, and the transfer to the federal level of the specialized courts dealing with matters of the army, transportation and political crime. By this move they became inferior federal courts, subordinate to the new federal Supreme Court.

In 1934[2] Stalin expanded the jurisdiction of the security police to create Special Boards within the Commissariat of Internal Affairs released of any obligations to follow the code of criminal procedure and subject to no Supreme Court review, thus adding to the then existing system of federal and republic courts, yet another sys-

---

[2] Decree of November 5, 1934, [1935] I Sob. Zak. SSSR, No. 11, item 84.

tem, albeit secret in its operation and administrative in its subordination.

This was the inheritance of Stalin's political heirs. One of their first acts was abolition of the Special Boards, though they seem to have feared disorder in relaxing Stalin's terror, for they did not publish the repeal of the 1934 statute, and only months later let the news be known to the general public in legal articles.[3] By their extensive reforms of 1958 they left only one system of inferior federal courts, the military tribunals, and limited its jurisdiction over civilians to crimes of espionage. The burden of judicial review was restored to the republic Supreme Courts to reverse a practice under which the federal Supreme Court had assumed jurisdiction to such an extent that it was unable to hear the large number of cases brought to it. This element of the reform proved, however, to have been premature, for in 1967 the Supreme Court was again given many powers of review over lower court activities to assure uniformity of practice and conformity to policy directives.

The revulsion from Stalin's practices led to structural reform. The Procurator's Office was reinforced by enactment of a new statute, emphasizing its role as scourge of illegalities in administration;[4] the prestige of the bar became the concern of high policy makers, leading to new republic statutes;[5] the Ministry of Internal Affairs was renamed as a Ministry for the Protection of Public Order in an attempt to escape the bad name acquired by Stalin's security police during his purges;[6] and the Ministries of Justice in the federal government and in the republics were abolished because they had acquired a reputation of meddling in the adjudicative functions of the courts.[7] Their administrative duties were transferred to the Supreme Courts and their legislative drafting placed in the hands of a special committee of the Council of Ministers.

By degrees, however, in subsequent years, some of the former names and structural patterns were restored. The Ministry for the Protection of Public Order reverted to its traditional name as the Ministry of Internal Affairs,[8] and the federal and republic Ministries of Justice were recreated, although deprived of their previous authority to audit the judicial work of the courts.[9] It was explained, in justification of the move, that the courts had found burdensome the administrative functions of the Ministries which had been thrust upon them with the prior reform.

The courts became increasingly professional with the passing of the turbulent revolutionary years, and they were aided by the no-less-professional procurators, investigators, militia and bar. The non-professional agencies discussed in Chapter 2 remained at their side but always in a supplementary rather than an alternative role.

The materials in this chapter are designed to permit the reader to estimate the

---

[3]See Harold J. Berman, Law Reform in the Soviet Union, 15 Am. Slavic and East European Review 183-185 (1956).
[4]Statute of May 24, 1955, [1955] Vedomosti Verkhovnogo Soveta SSSR, No. 9, item 222.
[5]Statute of July 25, 1962, [1962] Vedomosti Verkhovnogo Soveta RSFSR, No. 29, item 450.
[6]Edict of July 26, 1966, [1966] Vedomosti Verkhovnogo Soveta SSSR, No. 30, item 594.
[7]Edict of April 13, 1963, [1963] Vedomosti Verkhovnogo Soveta RSFSR, No. 15, item 299.
[8]Edict of November 25, 1968, [1968] Vedomosti Verkhovnogo Soveta SSSR, No. 48, item 467.
[9]Edict of August 31, 1970, [1970] Vedomosti Verkhovnogo Soveta SSSR, No. 36, item 361.

extent to which the legal structures of the era being called that of "developed socialism" have retained the flexibility and simplicity of the formative years of Soviet legal development, and in what degree there has been preparation for eventual withering away of the state apparatus as the era of developed socialism merges into subsequent eras designed to lead to pure communism.

A. *Structure and jurisdiction of courts.*

S. Bannikov, Vice President of the USSR Supreme Court, "THE MISSION OF THE JUDGE," Izvestiia, February 6, 1975, p. 6 (Excerpt).

It is widely known what an important educational influence the activity of our court has. Whatever subject the court investigates always touches the interests of citizens, the state, and society. Only a court is given the right to announce its judgment in the name of the State, and this gives special importance to its acts. Having the force of law, the court judgments are compulsory for all organizations, responsible officials, and citizens, and they must be executed throughout the whole country.

Legislative norms, which serve as guides to our courts are the firm foundation for the issuance of just well grounded judgments. Nevertheless, much depends also upon the judges, on their skills and ability to put law into life, since, as A.F. Koni said correctly in his time, "No matter how good the rules for action are, they can lose their effectiveness and meaning in inexperienced, uncouth or unscrupulous hands."

The court accomplishes justice through collegial examination of civil and criminal cases. This activity of the court is strictly regulated by law. All procedural demands of legislation must be observed without fail. Nothing is inconsequential here; there is no division of legislative norms into important and second level norms, since violation of any one of them at any stage in the proceedings is incompatible with the principles of justice. . .

N.A. Lokhov, "SOME QUESTIONS ON THE JUDICIAL SYSTEM OF THE U.S.S.R., OF THE UNION AND OF THE AUTONOMOUS REPUBLICS," pub. in S.A. Golunskii, editor, Voprosy sudoproizvodstva i sudoustroistva v novom zakonodatel'stve Soiuza SSR [Questions of court procedure and the judicial system in the new legislation of the U.S.S.R.] (Moscow, 1959) 381-391.

Our country has entered upon the epoch of full construction of a communist society. The great achievements in economy and culture of our state, with which it approached the XXI congress of the Communist Party of the Soviet Union provide clear evidence of this fact.

N.S. Khrushchev said in his report to the XXI congress, "To make the transition to communism we must have not only development of the material-technical base, but a high level of awareness in every citizen of society.". . .The educational work must be conducted primarily by methods of persuasion. The consciousness of a part of our population is still prisoner to prejudices, backward notions, ideas having their roots deep in the past. . . .To struggle with violators of law, measures of state compulsion must be applied along with other means of influencing people.

One of the agencies of state compulsion is the soviet court, charged with strengthening decisively the struggle with criminal assaults on the soviet public and state structure, on law and order, on socialist property. The soviet court must suppress decisively every assault on the political, labor, housing and other personal and property rights and interests of citizens of the U.S.S.R., on the rights and interests protected by law of state agencies, enterprises, collective farms, cooperatives and other public organizations. But a soviet court is not solely an organ of state compulsion. In all of its activity it educates citizens in the spirit of devotion to their socialist Motherland and to the business of communism, in the spirit of strict and unwavering execution of soviet laws, of honest relationship to state and public duty, of careful relationship to socialist property, respect for the rights, honor and achievements of citizens, for the rules of socialist intercourse (Art. 3 of the Fundamental principles of the legislation on the judicial system).

For the purpose of further democratization of the soviet court in execution of the decisions of the XX congress of the Party and of the sixth session of the Supreme Soviet of the U.S.S.R., fourth convocation, on the broadening of the powers of the Union Republics in the sphere of legislation, changes became necessary in the legislation on the judicial system. At the 2nd session of the Supreme Soviet, fifth convocation, on December 25, 1958, there were adopted the Fundamental principles of legislation on the judicial system of the U.S.S.R., of the Union and Autonomous Republics.

The Fundamental principles. . .are an important legal act of our state characterizing the further democratic organization and activity of the soviet court. The new Fundamentals include within them most of the propositions contained in the Law on the judicial system of the U.S.S.R., of the Union and Autonomous Republics of 1938. These have already shown their living character and have been proved sound during the entire period of existence of the Soviet state. Still, together with these propositions, there are incorporated in the Fundamental principles of the judicial system of 1958 a number of new propositions, making necessary some changes in the organization and activity of our judicial system.

At the present time the building of a communist society in our country has required still more democratization of the entire state apparatus, including the court, and still closer link with the broad toiling masses. . . . The Fundamental principles establish a single system of general courts, providing only for one type of special court—the military tribunals to hear cases of crimes committed by military personnel.

The principal link in the soviet judicial system has been and remains the people's court, destined to hear the preponderant majority of criminal and civil cases. Before adoption of the Fundamentals the people's court was split into several precincts in a county, that is there existed the precinct system of people's courts. The number of precincts of the people's courts was determined by the density of population, by the geographical limits of the territory of the county (city), by the number of cases brought to trial. With the adoption of the Fundamental principles there has been established a single county (city) court, that is within each county or city, not divided into boroughs, there will be a single people's court. This reorganization is a substantial novelty. . . .It will permit establishment of the closest ties between court and local soviet and party organs, public organizations, and will permit improvement in the propaganda for law.

According to the Fundamental principles the county (city) people's court, being the principal link in the soviet judicial system, will be elected by citizens of the county for five years instead of for the three year term provided by the law on the judicial system of 1938. . . .Lengthening of the term. . .will permit a judge to learn better the conditions and special characteristics of the county, and better to conduct the propaganda for law designed to prevent and stamp out crime.

The new legislation introduces some changes in the method of election of people's judges. Although the people's judges will as before be elected by the citizens of the county (city) on the basis of general, equal and direct elections with secret ballot, the people's assessors will be elected at general meetings of factory and office workers and peasants at their places of work or residence, and of military personnel in their units, for a two year term.

The former method of election of people's assessors in groups of from 50 to 75 persons at one time gave no opportunity to the electors to know each candidate put forward for election by the public organizations. The new method of election will permit electors to know personally their candidate who works with them in the same group. Further, under this system the assessor will be linked to his group and may conduct within it concrete work in making propaganda for soviet law.

The Fundamentals. . .anticipate creation of plenums within the Supreme Courts of the Union Republics. This is related to the broadening of rights of the union republics in the legislative field, and especially with the granting to the Union Republics of the right to enact criminal, civil and procedural codes as well as laws on the judicial system. . . . The establishment of plenums . . . will give them the opportunity to center in their hands the generalization of court practice and to issue guiding instructions to the courts of the union republic.

The Fundamentals give to the Union Republics the right to keep the presidiums of the Supreme Courts of the Union Republics or to abolish them. . . . We think that the existence of presidiums of Supreme Courts of the Union Republics will provide the opportunity for quick correction of such errors as have been permitted, will give the opportunity to examine in timely fashion protests by way of audit made against sentences, judgments, orders and rulings of lower courts. The same may be said also of the presidiums of the territorial, provincial and other courts corresponding to these.

FUNDAMENTALS OF LEGISLATION ON THE JUDICIAL SYSTEM OF THE U.S.S.R. AND OF THE UNION AND AUTONOMOUS REPUBLICS, December 25, 1958. [1959] Vedomosti Verkhovnogo Soveta SSSR, No. 1, item 12.

Art. 1. *The Judicial System*

In accordance with Article 102 of the Constitution of the U.S.S.R., justice in the Soviet Union is administered by the Supreme Court of the U.S.S.R., the Supreme Courts of the Union Republics, the Supreme Courts of the Autonomous Republics, provincial, territorial and city courts, the courts of autonomous regions and national areas, county (city) people's courts and also by military tribunals.

Art. 8 *The Collective Examination of Cases in All Courts.*

Cases are examined collectively in all courts. Cases are examined in courts of original jurisdiction by a judge and two people's assessors. Appeals and protests are examined in the judicial college of a higher court by three of its members.

Cases of protest against court judgments, sentences, orders and rulings that have already come into force are examined by the judicial divisions of the Supreme Court of the U.S.S.R. and the Supreme Courts of the Union Republics by three members of the division concerned.

The presidium of a court examines cases with the majority of the members of the presidium present.

The plenum of a court examines cases with no less than two thirds of its membership present.

Art. 16. *The Courts of the U.S.S.R. and the Union-Republics.*

Courts of the U.S.S.R. and courts of the Union Republics function in the Union of Soviet Socialist Republics.

Art. 17. *Courts of the U.S.S.R.*

The Supreme Court of the U.S.S.R. and the military tribunals are courts of the U.S.S.R.

Art. 18. *Courts of the Union Republics.*

Courts of the Union Republics are: the Supreme Court of the Union Republic, the Supreme Courts of the Autonomous Republics, provincial, territorial and city courts, the courts of autonomous regions and national areas and the county (city) people's courts.

Art. 19. *The Electoral System for County (City) People's Courts.*

The people's judges of the county (city) people's courts are elected by citizens of the county (city) on the basis of universal, equal and direct suffrage by secret ballot for a term of five years.

The people's assessors of the county (city) people's courts are elected at general meetings of factory or office workers and peasants at their place of work or residence, and at meetings of members of the armed services in their units for a term of two years.

Regulations for the election of people's judges and people's assessors are provided in the legislation of the union republics.

Art. 20. *The Electoral System for Provincial, Territorial and City Courts and for Courts of the Autonomous Regions and national Areas.*

Provincial, territorial and city courts, the courts of autonomous regions and national areas are elected by the soviets of toilers' deputies concerned for a term of five years.

Art. 21. *The Composition of a Provincial, Territorial or City Court and of the Court of an Autonomous Region or National Area.*

A provincial, territorial or city court or the court of an autonomous region or national area consists of a chairman, deputy chairmen, the members and the people's assessors and functions as the following bodies:

(a) the judicial division for civil cases;
(b) the judicial division for criminal cases;
(c) the court presidium.

Art. 24. *The Electoral System and Competency of the Supreme Court of a Union Republic.*

The highest judicial body of a Union Republic is the Supreme Court of the Union Republic.

The Supreme Court of a Union Republic is charged with the supervision of the judicial activities of all court bodies in the Union Republic as laid down in the legislation of the U.S.S.R. and the Union Republics.

The Supreme Court of a Union Republic is elected by the Supreme Soviet of the Union Republic for a term of five years.

Art. 25. *The Composition of the Supreme Court of a Union Republic.*

The Supreme Court of a Union Republic consists of a chairman, deputy chairmen, the members of the Supreme Court and the people's assessors and functions as the following bodies:

(a) the judicial division for civil cases;
(b) the judicial division for criminal cases;
(c) the plenary session of the Supreme Court.

A presidium of the Supreme Court of a Union Republic may be established where provision is made for it in the legislation of the Union Republic.

The competency of presidiums and plenary sessions of the Supreme Courts of Union Republics is laid down in the legislation of the Union Republic.

Art. 26. *The Electoral System and Competency of the Supreme Court of the U.S.S.R.*

The Supreme Court of the U.S.S.R. is the highest judicial body of the Union of Soviet Socialist Republics.

The Supreme Court of the U.S.S.R. is charged with the supervision of the judicial activities of the court bodies of the U.S.S.R. and also the court bodies of the Union Republics within the limits established by the Regulations for the Supreme Court of the U.S.S.R.

The Supreme Court of the U.S.S.R. is elected by the Supreme Soviet of the U.S.S.R. for a term of five years.

Art. 27. *Composition of the Supreme Court of the U.S.S.R.*

The Supreme Court of the U.S.S.R. consists of the chairman, deputy chairmen, members of the Supreme Court of the U.S.S.R., and people's assessors, elected by the Supreme Soviet of the U.S.S.R., and also representatives of the Supreme Courts of the Union Republics who hold the office of members of the Supreme Court of the U.S.S.R.

The Supreme Court of the U.S.S.R. functions as the following bodies:
 (a) the judicial division for civil cases;
 (b) the judicial division for criminal cases;
 (c) the military division
 (d) the plenary session of the Supreme Court of the U.S.S.R.

Art. 29. *Requirements for Candidacy as Judge and People's Assessor.*

Any citizen of the U.S.S.R. who enjoys the right to vote and has attained the age of 25 years by election day may be elected judge or people's assessor.

Art. 30. *Equal Rights of People's Assessors and Judges in the Administration of Justice.*

When discharging their duties in court people's assessors enjoy the same rights as the judge.

Art. 31. *Period for Which People's Assessors are Empanelled to Serve in Court.*

People's assessors are empanelled according to roster for not more than two weeks a year with the exception of those cases when a longer period is required to complete the hearing of a case begun with their participation.

Art. 33. *The People's Judges Report to Their Electors.*

People's judges report back systematically to their electors on their own work and the work of the people's court.

Art. 35. *Recall of Judges and People's Assessors Before Their Term of Service Has Elapsed.*

Judges and people's assessors may be recalled and deprived of authority before their term of service has elapsed only by their electors or by the body electing them or by force of a court sentence passed on them.

Art. 37. *Disciplinary Responsibility of Judges.*

Judges are responsible for discipline in accordance with the regulations prescribed by the legislation of the U.S.S.R. for judges of courts of the U.S.S.R. and by the legislation of the Union Republics for judges of courts of Union Republics.

Art. 38. *The Execution of Court Decisions, Rulings and Orders.*

Judgments, rulings and orders in civil cases and sentences, rulings and orders in criminal cases insofar as they concern property exactions are executed by the sheriffs attached to the court.

The demands presented by sheriffs in pursuance of court sentences, judgements, rulings and orders are obligatory for all persons in office and for all citizens.

STATUTE ON THE SUPREME COURT OF THE U.S.S.R., approved February 12, 1957. [1957] Vedomosti Verkhovnogo Soveta SSSR, No. 4, item 85, as amended September 30, 1967.

Art. 11. The judicial division for civilian cases and the judicial division for criminal cases of the Suprene Court of the U.S.S.R.:

(a) examine as a court of original jurisdiction respectively civil and criminal cases of exceptional significance referred by law to their jurisdiction;

(b) examine by way of court audit protests of the Chairman of the Supreme Court of the U.S.S.R. and of the Procurator General of the U.S.S.R. and of their deputies against judgments and sentences of the Supreme Courts of the union republics in civil and criminal cases if these judgments and sentences are in conflict with all-union legislation or violate the interests of other union republics.

Art. 12. The military division of the Supreme Court of the U.S.S.R.

(a) examines as a court of first instance criminal cases of exceptional significance referred by law to its jurisdiction;

(b) examines appeals and special rulings and protests against sentences, judgments and rulings of military tribunals of the Armed Forces, of Military Districts, Army groups, Fleets, and individual armies in circumstances provided by law;

(c) examines by way of court audit protests of the Chairman of the Supreme Court of the U.S.S.R., of the Procurator General of the U.S.S.R. or their deputies, and also protests of the Chairman of the Military Division of the Supreme Court of the U.S.S.R. and of the Chief Military Procurator against sentences and rulings of the military tribunals of the Armed Forces, of Military Districts, Army groups, fleets, and individual armies of districts and fleets.

Art. 13. Divisions of the Supreme Court of the U.S.S.R. examine cases as a court of original jurisdiction with a bench of a chairman who shall be a member of the Supreme Court of the U.S.S.R. and two people's assessors.

Appeals and protests and also protests by way of court audit of the division are examined with a bench of three members of the Supreme Court of the U.S.S.R.

CODE OF CRIMINAL PROCEDURE RSFSR, effective January 1, 1961, as amended.

Art. 35. A county (city) people's court has jurisdiction over all cases, except those subject to the jurisdiction of higher courts or to military tribunals.

Art. 36. Territorial, provincial, city courts, courts of autonomous provinces and of national districts have jurisdiction over crimes proscribed by Arts. [there follows a list of code articles concerning crimes against the state (with the omission of espionage, smuggling, evasion of military service in peacetime, evasion of compulsory civilian service or taxes in wartime, illegal exit abroad or entry, violation of transport rules with small consequences, violation of currency regulations when not conducted as a business), failure to report most serious crimes; crimes against socialist ownership on an especially large scale; homicide under aggravating circumstances; rape by groups or recidivists resulting in grave consequences; issuing of poor quality non-standard or incomplete products repeatedly or on large scale; acceptance of bribes by an official previously convicted or repeatedly accepting bribes; illegal institution of proceedings against persons known to be innocent; illegal arrest; unjust sentencing; and infringing the life of a policeman or people's guard.]

Art. 37. The Supreme Court of an autonomous republic has jurisdiction of the cases set forth in Art. 36 of this Code.

Art. 38. The Supreme Court of the RSFSR has jurisdiction over all cases of special complexity or of special social meaning, and may take jurisdiction on its own initiative or on the initiative of the Procurator of the R.S.F.S.R.

Art. 40. A higher court has the right to assume jurisdiction as a court of original jurisdiction over any case within the jurisdiction of a lower court.

STATUTE ON MILITARY TRIBUNALS, December 25, 1958. [1959] Vedomosti Verkhovnogo Soveta SSSR, No. 1, item 14.

Art. 1. In accordance with Art. 102 of the Constitution of the U.S.S.R. military tribunals are courts of the U.S.S.R. and are within the single judicial system of the U.S.S.R.

Art. 9. Military tribunals have jurisdiction over:

   (a) all crimes committed by those in military service as well as by those subject to military obligations during the period they are proceeding with training preparations;

   (b) all crimes committed by persons of the officer, non-commissioned officer and enlisted staffs of the organs of state security;

   (c) all cases of espionage.

Art. 10. In localities where because of exceptional circumstances the general courts are not functioning, military tribunals examine all criminal and civil cases.

Art. 11. Military tribunals examine together with criminal matters civil suits of military units (departments), state and public enterprises, offices and organizations, and also of individual citizens for the recovery of damages for injury caused to them by the crimes.

Art. 19. The Supreme Court of the U.S.S.R. excercises audit over the judicial activity of military tribunals.

Art. 22. The structure and personnel of military tribunals are established by the Chairman of the military division of the Supreme Court of the U.S.S.R. together with the Minister of Defense of the U.S.S.R.

The personnel of the military tribunals and of the Military Division of the Supreme Court of the U.S.S.R. are part of the personnel of the Armed Forces of the U.S.S.R. and enjoy all of the same privileges on an equal basis with the personnel of military units and of departments of the Ministry of Defense of the U.S.S.R.

V. Zaichuk, Ukrainian SSR Minister of Justice, "AN INDIVIDUAL OPINION," Izvestiia, May 22, 1975, p. 5 (Excerpt).

. . . We do not know what debates there were and how they went in the judges' chambers. In all likelihood they were stormy because the lay assessor Ivanova did not agree with the other two judges. She set forth her view in writing, and it was attached to the record (an individual opinion is not read when the judgment is announced in court).

What perplexed the lay assessor? She was in agreement on the finding of guilt. But she was against the sentence (3 years deprivation of liberty) meted out to one of the persons before the court, namely Shchebliuk. Although Shchebliuk surely participated in the criminal group, he resold at higher prices only a very small quantity of steel. Moreover, Shchebliuk is a model worker, an active participant in collective farm construction, his personal reference from his place of work was affirmative, he was often commended. In Ivanova's view the court did not take into account these mitigating circumstances.

As you can see, there were weighty arguments in the opinion of the lay assessor. E.D. Ivanova was a person with broad experience in life, a petroleum engineer at the refinery "Friendship," guiding herself by her personal undertertanding of her duty to justice, considering the personality of the person before the court. She defended her view methodically and with principles. And Soviet legislation gives a lay assessor the right (as it gives it also to the professional judge if the latter is in the minority). Of course, a higher court does not have to agree with an individual opinion, but it must examine it.

In this case the Lvov Provincial Court considered the conclusion of the President of the Court well founded and reduced the punishment of Shchebliuk.

B. *Extraneous influences upon judges.*

V.P. Rad'kov, SOTSIALISTICHESKAIA ZAKONNOST' V SOVETSKOM UGOLOVNOM PROTSESSE [Socialist Legality in Soviet Criminal Procedure] (Moscow, 1959) 152.

The Party agencies mobilize and direct judges to consistent realization of the demands of the law. However good the laws may be, they can provide nothing by themselves. Without the extensive organizational work of the C.P.S.U. they would remain unenforced.

The Party is the guiding core of all state agencies. With its leadership it provides tangible conditions for subjection to law of the activity of all court organs. Judges who fail to meet this demand are subjected to public influences.

In exercising Party guidance over courts, the agencies and organizations of the C.P.S.U. stop all activity violating the independence of judges in deciding concrete cases.

The Central Committee of the C.P.S.U. in its order on the facts of interference by some local Party organs in the decision of court cases (1954) declared that local

Party agencies are required to provide political guidance and control over the activities of the judicial and procuratorial agencies.

The Central Committee of the C.P.S.U. condemned the practice of illegal interference of the Zarechinsk ward committee of the C.P.S.U. of Tula with the activity of the people's court of the 3rd precinct in examining concrete criminal and civil cases. . . . The Central Committee declared that extensive illegal interference in the work of the court on the part of local Party agencies "undermines the authority of the court, disorganizes the judges and pushes them into giving illegal decisions, violates the principle established by the U.S.S.R. constitution on independence of judges and their subjection solely to law, deprives the procuratorial and judicial agencies of independence and plants in them irresponsibility."

S. Bannikov, Vice President of USSR Supreme Court, "THE MISSION OF A JUDGE," Izvestiia, February 6, 1975, p. 6 (Excerpt).

The primary task of preserving the independence of judges lies, of course, upon the judges. But sometimes they need support, including that of our press. It is no secret that now and then as a result of hurried and one-sided information reaching the public about the circumstances of some case, a faulty impression is formed around it, and the judges are subjected to one-sided pressures. Under such circumstances it is very important to defend them from any preconceived approach, bearing in mind that such interference more likely fosters not the prevention of judicial errors but their stimulation, sowing doubt as to the objectivity of the judgments issued by the court.

EDICT OF AUGUST 12, 1971 ON CREATION OF A U.S.S.R. MINISTRY OF JUSTICE, [1971] Vedomosti Verkhovnogo Soveta SSSR, No. 33, item 332.

The Presidium of the USSR Supreme Soviet decrees:

1. The Union-Republic Ministry of Justice of the USSR shall have the following functions:

Organized guidance of the judicial organs of the union republics and military tribunals, guidance of the bar, of the State Notary, and other agencies of justice;

Systematization and preparation of drafts of law codes;

Execution of other functions in accordance with legislation of the USSR and of the union republics.

STATUTE ON DISCIPLINARY RESPONSIBILITY OF JUDGES OF THE COURTS OF THE RSFSR, June 12, 1965. Sovetskaia Iustitsiia, 1965, No. 14, p. 31.*

2. Judges . . . shall be disciplined a) for violation of labor and state discipline,

---

*By amendment of May 26, 1976 a College on disciplinary affairs replaces the Presidium of each court as the competent disciplinary body and authorizes local Soviets and Ministers of Justice to initiate proceedings.

b) for shortcomings in judicial work as the result of negligence or lack of discipline of the judge, c) for commission of acts unworthy of a soviet judge.

3. Cases involving charges of the commission of disciplinary offenses shall be heard by the Presidium of the Supreme Court of the RSFSR, the Presidiums of the Supreme Courts of the Autonomous Republics, of territorial, provincial and city courts, of courts of autonomous provinces and of national districts.

5. The right to instigate disciplinary proceedings belongs to: the presidents of the Supreme Courts of the Autonomous Republics and of territorial, provincial, city courts, of courts of autonomous provinces and of national districts with regard to members of these courts and to presidents of county (city) peoples' courts and to peoples' judges; the president of the Supreme Court of the RSFSR and his vice presidents with regard to all judges of RSFSR courts.

6. The circumstances of the disciplinary offense shall be verified by the persons listed in paragraph 5, and written explanations shall be demanded of judges held to a disciplinary accounting, and on the basis of these materials an order to open a disciplinary proceeding shall issue.

7. Judges may be charged on a disciplinary proceeding not later than one month from the day on which the fact of the commission of the offense becomes established.

8. A disciplinary proceeding shall be conducted at a public sitting of the Presidium in the presence of the judge charged. A special order shall be issued on the subject of the penalty.

9. The Presidium may exact the following disciplinary penalties: a) a formal taking notice of the offense, b) a reprimand, c) a severe reprimand. If the presidium finds no basis for exacting a disciplinary penalty when it has completed the hearing, it shall terminate the proceeding.

10. If the Presidium concludes that the judge is unsuited to the post he holds, it shall raise in the manner provided by law the question of his removal before the expiration of his term.

If there are elements of crime in the judge's acts, the Presidium shall raise the question of instigating criminal proceedings against him in the manner established by law. . . . The Supreme Court must be informed of [either] proposal.

C. *The Notary as a control over legality.*

STATUTE ON THE OFFICE OF STATE NOTARY, [1973] Vedomosti Verkhovnogo Soveta SSSR, No. 30, item 393.

Part I. *General Propositions.*
Art. 1. The duties of the Office of State Notary are the protection of socialist property, of the rights and interests of citizens, of State administrative offices, economic enterprises and organizations, collective farms and other cooperative and social organizations; to strengthen socialist legality, and justice; to prevent violation of law

through correct and timely certification of contracts and other agreements; the formal recognition of rights to inheritance; the execution of levies upon property and other notarial acts.

DUTY TO DETERMINE DECEDENT'S ESTATE, Sovetskaia iustitsiia, 1976, No. 13, p. 34.

The heir of a decedent requested the Norilsk State Notarial Office of Krasnoiarsk Territory to ascertain from the Savings Bank of the City of Kalinin whether a bank account was held in the name of his father, who had lived in Norilsk and to determine whether the Bank had instructions as to its disposition on death. The State Notary recommended to the heir that he make the request of the Savings Bank himself.

The RSFSR Ministry of Justice's Notarial Bureau explained that if the heirs file a formal request for issuance of a certificate of inheritance and present evidence of death and other documents confirming their right, the Notary is required on their request in accordance with Art. 56 of the RSFSR Statute on the Office of State Notary to ask the Savings Banks named by them whether they have bank deposits. Information on the dispository instructions may be communicated only to the person to whose benefit they are issued.

CERTIFICATION OF A LAST WILL AND TESTAMENT, Sovetskaia iustitsiia, 1976, No. 8, p. 32.

The Notary of the Novonnin State Notarial Office of Volgograd Province certified a last will and testament signed by two persons as spouses. The Legal Department of the Volgograd Provincial Soviet of Working People's Deputies instructed the Notary that a single last will and testament signed by two persons may not be certified, even when both spouses request certification. The legality of the Legal Department's instruction is confirmed by Art. 79 of the Instruction on the method of performing Notarial acts by the State Notarial Offices of the RSFSR, dated January 31, 1975.

CERTIFICATION OF LEASE, Sovetskaia iustitsiia, 1976, No. 18, p. 33.

The question has arisen in Notarial practice whether a Notary may certify a lease of a dwelling constructed without permission. The RSFSR Ministry of Justice's Notarial Bureau has explained that since a dwelling constructed without permission cannot be an object of a property interest, a citizen who has constructed the dwelling without permission has no right to dispose of it, especially by lease, and the State Notaries have no right to certify such contracts.

CERTIFICATION OF A COPY OF A DIPLOMA, Sovetskaia iustitsiia, 1976, No. 5, p. 34.

In the practice of the State Notarial Offices in Amur Province, the question has been raised whether the State Notary may certify the authenticity of a duplicate copy of a diploma issued on completion of University study and signed by the President of the State Examining Commission functioning at the time of issuance but not at the moment of completion of the study. The RSFSR Ministry of Justice's Notarial Bureau has explained that in accordance with the Instruction on the preparation, completion and issuance of diplomas to persons completing study in a USSR University, approved by the USSR Ministry of Higher and Specialized Education, No. 9, dated January 11, 1961, as amended, a diploma or duplicate diploma shall be signed by the President of the State Examining Commission functioning at the time of issuing the document. Therefore, the State Notary has the right to certify the authenticity of the copy of the duplicate University diploma signed by the President of the State Examining Committee functioning in the year of issuance of the document.

D. *The Registrar of Vital Statistics.*

STATUTE ON ZAGS (BUREAU FOR REGISTRATION OF ACTS OF CIVIL STATUS). June 19, 1974. [1974] Sobranie Postanovlenii Pravitelstva RSFSR, No. 17, item 94.

1. The Department (bureau) for registration of acts of civil status of the Executive Committee of a county Soviet of Working People's Deputies shall be established by the county Soviet of Working People's Deputies in accordance with legislation of the RSFSR, and shall be subordinate as regards its activity to both the county Soviet and its Executive Committee and to the Department for registration of acts of civil status of the Executive Committee of the superior Soviet of Working People's Deputies.

2. The principal tasks of the Department (bureau). . .shall be:

-registration of acts of civil status in precise conformity with existing legislation on marriage and the family in the interests of the state and society, and also to protect the personal and property rights of citizens;

-inculcate in the culture of new civil rituals the solemn registration of marriages and births.

Iu. Gusev, "A BETTER DEPARTMENT (BUREAU) OF ZAGS. Sovetskaia iustitsiia, 1976, No. 14, p. 23 (excerpt).

. . .working relationships have been established between the ZAGS and agencies of law, the courts, the organs of internal affairs, public health, social security, as the result of which fewer errors are being made in application of legislation on marriage and the family, in the preparation and issuance to citizens of documents needed to obtain passports of the new model and the registration of acts of civil status is occurring on time and in complete fashion. . .

More attention is being given to work with youth planning to marry. The practice is widening of conducting a betrothal ceremony for persons filing a request to register a marriage. . . The effectiveness of conferences with spouses filing for divorce has increased. Thus, in the Kaluga City ZAGS 136 couples were reconciled by the ZAGS staff out of 321 filing for divorce. . .

The registration of all births and 80.5% of marriages in the Morshansk ZAGS were conducted ceremonially. The Zags bureau chief, Z.T. Sabel'kina, has directed the work of the evening university for young people for three years. She has delivered 24 lectures and published 10 articles in the local paper. . .But, the ceremonial registration of marriages is still poorly organized in some ZAGS. . . The Departments of ZAGS in . . . are studying carefully and from every side the reasons for the inadequacies that have been disclosed. . .

E. *The Procuracy as a control over legality.*

A.L. Rivlin, ORGANIZATSIIA SUDA I PROKURATORY V SSSR [Organization of the Court and Prosecutor's Office in the USSR] (Kharkov, 2nd ed., 1968) 22-23 (Excerpts).

The Procurator's Office performs no administrative or economic activity, its only task being the duty to supervise, to make certain that the laws are observed by other state organs. The Procurator's Office does not interfere in their economic or administrative activity, limiting itself to verification of conformity to law of this acitivity. . . .

The Procurator's and judicial organs are closely linked in their activities. This linkage is reflected first of all in the fact that both exercise the function of the Soviet State of preserving the law. In this relationship, the tasks performed by the Procurator's Office are identical in considerable measure to those performed by the courts.

STATUTE ON PROCURATOR'S AUDIT IN THE U.S.S.R., May 24, 1955.
[1955] Vedomosti Verkhovnogo Soveta SSSR, No. 9, item 222.
Art. 5. The organs of the procurator's office of the U.S.S.R. constitute a single centralized system, headed by the Procurator General of the U.S.S.R. with subordination of lower procurators to higher.
Art. 6. On the basis of Art. 117 of the Constitution of the U.S.S.R. the organs of the procurator's office perform their functions independently of any local organs, being subordinate only to the Procurator General of the U.S.S.R.
Art. 7. The Procurator General of the U.S.S.R. is responsible to the Supreme Soviet of the U.S.S.R. and is subordinate to it, but in the period between sessions of the Supreme Soviet of the U.S.S.R., he is subordinate to the Presidium of the Supreme Soviet of the U.S.S.R.
Art. 9. The Procurator General of the U.S.S.R. may present to the Presidium of the Supreme Soviet of the U.S.S.R. a proposal on questions requiring solution through legislation, or requiring interpretation of a law in accordance with the procedure set forth in subsection (c) of Art. 49 of the Constitution of the U.S.S.R.
Art. 17. The Procurator General of the U.S.S.R. and procurators subordinate to

him, in conducting the audit of the precise execution of the laws in the organs of militia inquiry and preliminary investigation, are required: (1) to prosecute persons guilty of committing crime, to take measures so that not a single crime shall remain undisclosed, nor a single criminal escape responsibility; (2) follow matters strictly so that not a single citizen is subjected to illegal or unfounded prosecution or to any other illegal limitation of rights; (3) see to the unvarying observance by militia inquiry and preliminary investigation agencies of the rules of procedure established by law for investigating crimes.

Art. 23. The Procurator General of the U.S.S.R. and the procurators subordinate to him: (1) participate in the preliminary sittings of a court to determine procedures to be followed; (2) participate in the examination of criminal and civil cases in court sessions and give opinions as to questions arising during the trial; (3) support the state's accusation in court when criminal cases are examined; (4) bring suit in civil proceedings or as a civil suit joined to a criminal prosecution, and support suits in court if this is required in protection of state or social interests or the rights and legal interests of citizens; (5) file protests in the manner established by law against illegal or unfounded sentences, civil judgments, decisions and rulings of court organs; (6) give opinions on criminal and civil cases reviewed by higher courts on appeals or protests; (7) provide an audit over the execution of court sentences.

Art. 24. The Procurator General of the U.S.S.R. and all procurators subordinate to him have the right within the limits of his authority, to demand any civil or criminal case from the court organs for verification in accordance with auditing procedures.

"DECISION OF COUNTY EXECUTIVE COMMITTEE INFRINGING THE STATUTE ON PROCURATOR'S AUDIT IN THE USSR," Sotsialisticheskaia zakonnost', 965, No. 11, p. 89.

The Executive Committee of the Ilishevsk county soviet of working peoples' deputies of the Bashkir ASSR named the county procurator chairman of the county committee to verify the conformity of collective farm charters in the county to law.

The decision was taken in violation of the law. According to Art. 117 of the constitution of the U.S.S.R. and Art. 6 of the Statute on Procurator's Audit in the U.S.S.R. the agencies of the procuracy perform their functions independently of any local agencies, being subordinate only to the Procurator General of the U.S.S.R. Therefore, the Executive Committee had no right to place upon the procurator any duty not established by law.

On the basis of the county procurator's protest the decision is annulled.

CASE OF MAL'TSEV, FEDOROV, OSTASHKIN AND MALYKH, Biulletin' Verkhovnogo Suda RSFSR, 1967, No. 2, p. 16.

Mal'tsev, Fedorov, Ostashkin and Malykh were convicted under part 2 of Art. 145 of the Criminal Code of the RSFSR [open theft by a group in conspiracy] by judgment of the Melekin city people's court of Ulianov province. M., F., O., and

M. were found guilty of attacking Markelov, Shishkin and others not identified on April 16, 1966. While threatening with children's toy pistols they took from the victims two watches with trademarks "Zim" and "Uran," a cigarette lighter and other small items.

The investigating agencies classified the criminal acts as violation of paragraphs "a" and "b" of part 2 of Art. 146 of the Criminal Code of the RSFSR [assault with intent to rob when committed with weapons or articles used as weapons].

The defense lawyers asked the people's court to reclassify the crime under part 2 of Art. 145. The procurator also joined in the request at the court hearing. The people's court concluded that the convicts had committed assault with intent to rob, thus agreeing with the procurator's and defense lawyers' position.

On appellate review the lawyers held to their opinion expressed at the trial. The Judicial Division for Criminal Cases of the Ulianov Provincial Court found the position of the lawyers and procurator on classification of the crimes a violation of the decree of the plenum of the Supreme Court of the RSFSR of March 22, 1966 "On judicial practice in cases of assault with intent to rob and banditry." Consequently, the Judicial Chamber issued a special ruling, presenting the question to the presidium of the college of advocates and to the procuracy of the county as to whether appropriate measures should be instituted against the procurator and the defense lawyers who had participated in the trial.

The president of the Ulianovsk Provincial Court issued a protest to the Presidium of his court, asking it to set aside the special ruling of its Judicial Division. On reviewing the protest the Presidium decided that the special ruling . . . was not based on the law; in particular, it infringed the procedural standing of a defense attorney and a procurator in a criminal trial, as established by Arts. 248 and 249 of the Code of Criminal Procedure of the RSFSR. In Art. 248 it is provided that a procurator shall present to the court his thoughts on the application of the criminal law and measures of punishment for the prisoner, guiding himself by the requirements of the law and by his inner conviction, based upon his review of all circumstances of the case.

Pursuant to Art. 249 the defense attorney shall inform the court of his conclusions on the substance of the charge, with regard to circumstances mitigating responsibility, and concerning measures of punishment.

Thus, the procurator and lawyer are free to inform the court of their conclusions and cannot be held liable because their views did not correspond with those in the court's judgment.

Based upon the above the Presidium of the Ulianovsk Provincial Court revoked the special ruling of the Judicial Division for Criminal Cases as it related to the procurator and the lawyers.

LIPETSK PROVINCIAL SOCIAL INSURANCE DEPARTMENT VS. RADOSH,
Biulletn' Verkhovnogo Suda RSFSR, 1969, No. 2, p. 8.

The Lipetsk Provincial Social Insurance Department brought suit by way of subrogation against Radosh to recover 285 rubles on the ground that because of defendant's fault as operator of a motorcycle, he caused an accident from which Citizen Dourechenski suffered bodily injuries and was classified as an invalid in Group II. From January 19, 1966 to January 19, 1967 the victim was paid a pension in the amount of 158 rubles, which sum the plaintiff sought to recover from Radosh.

At the trial the plaintiff's representative declared that taking into consideration the concrete circumstances of the case and the financial situation of the defendant the Social Insurance Department withdrew the claim. The Judicial Division of the Lipetsk Provincial Court then terminated the proceedings.

Having reviewed the case on the protest of the Lipetsk Provincial Procurator, the Judicial Division for Civil Cases of the RSFSR Supreme Court set aside the decision of the Lipetsk Provincial Court's Judicial Division and remanded the case for trial on the merits, saying in its ruling of November 28, 1968 the following:

Under Art. 34 of the Code of Civil Procedure RSFSR a plaintiff has the right to amend his claim as to its legal rationale or subject, to raise or lower the amount claimed, or to withdraw the claim. In this article, however, it is stated that the court shall not accept the withdrawal of suit or an acknowledgement of liability and shall not agree to reconciliation if such acts are contrary to law or violate the rights of some one and interests protected by law.

In the given concrete case the plaintiff's withdrawal is not in accord with the State's interest. Under Art. 463 of the Civil Code RSFSR an organization or citizen responsible for causing injury is required on suit by way of subrogation brought by a state social insurance or social security agency to repay the sum paid out as compensation or as a pension to the victim.

Under such circumstances the court was required to try the case on its merits and in taking into consideration the concrete circumstances of the case, the degree of defendant's fault, and his financial situation to decide the case.

F. *State security agencies.*

A.E. Lunev, ed., ADMINISTRATIVNOE PRAVO [Administrative Law] (Moscow, 1970) 505-506.

To take measures assuring the day by day protection of state security, there functions a system of agencies and troops of state security, and also border guards. Under the USSR Constitution and the constitutions of the Union and Autonomous Republics the system of agencies of state security of the USSR comprises the Comittee of State Security [K.G.B.] under the USSR Council of Ministers, the Committees of State Security under the Councils of Ministers of the Union and Autonomous Republics, and the State Security Administrations of the Union Republics in the Provinces and Territories and large cities, and also organs commanding the border guards. . .

Political vigilance, legality and a close link to the people are the most important bases for activity of the agencies of State Security, or their employees in the struggle with enemies of our State and people.

G. *Agencies of public order.*

A.E. Lunev, ed., ADMINISTRATIVNOE PRAVO [Administrative Law] (Moscow, 1970) 518-519.

The Union-Republic Ministry of Internal Affairs of the USSR is the central departmental agency in the field of protection of public order; its primary tasks being: assuring the existence of public order, prevention, suppression and full disclosure of crimes; correction and reeducation of convicts held in correctional labor institutions; protection against fire of state, public and personal property of citizens; assuring the safety of movement of automobile transportation, city electrified transportation and pedestrians.

The Ministry of Internal Affairs directs various services of the militia (criminal investigations, struggle with theft of state property and speculation, administrative services, passport work, etc.), the activities of correctional labor agencies, internal guards; it organizes the fire departments throughout the country, and maintains in its work the closest link with public organizations and the broad masses of working peoples. . .

Ministries of Internal Affairs are organized in the Union and Autonomous Republics. In the Provinces and Territories there function administrations of internal affairs of the Executive Committees of the respective Soviets. In the cities and counties there are departments of internal affairs of the city and county Soviets' Executive Committees.

EDICT ON AUTHORIZATION TO THE AGENCIES OF PUBLIC ORDER TO CONDUCT PRELIMINARY INVESTIGATIONS, April 6, 1963. [1963] Vedomosti Verkhovnogo Soveta SSSR, No. 16, item 181.

To fortify the struggle with crime, the further strengthening of legality and the broadening of the democratic foundations of Soviet criminal judicial proceedings the Presidium of the Supreme Soviet of the U.S.S.R. decrees:

1. There shall be established, alongside the investigating agencies of the procuracy and of state security, investigating agencies for the protection of public order. Investigators . . . shall be guided by the norms of legislation on criminal procedure concerning preliminary investigations.

2. In consequence of Art. 1 of this edict Art. 28, part 1 of the Fundamental Principles of Criminal Procedure of the U.S.S.R. and of the Union Republics shall be put in the following form:

"The preliminary investigation of criminal cases shall be conducted by the investigators of the procuracy, and also by investigators of the agencies of public order in cases of crime listed in legislation of the U.S.S.R. and of the Union Republics, and by agencies of State Security in cases provided by the following articles: 1 (treason), 2 (espionage), 3 (terrorist act), 4 (terrorist act against a representative of a foreign state), 5 (sabotage), 6 (wrecking), 7 (anti-soviet agitation and propaganda), 9 (organizational activity directed toward the commission of especially dangerous state crimes, and also participation in an anti-soviet organization), 10 (especially dangerous state crimes, committed against another state of the working people), 12 (disclosure of state secrets), 13 (loss of documents containing state secrets), 15 (smuggling), 16 (mass disorders), 20 (illegal exit abroad or illegal entry into the USSR), 21 (violation of the rules of international aviation), 25 (violation of the rules on foreign exchange operations), 26 (those paragraphs concerning failure to inform on state crimes, provided for by Arts 1-6 and 9), 27 (those paragraphs concerning concealment of state crimes provided for by Arts. 1-6, 9, 15 and 25) of the Law on Criminal Reponsibility for State Crimes and subsections 'a', 'b' and 'c' of Art. 23 (disclosure of military secrets or the loss of documents containing military secrets) of the Law on Criminal Liability for Military Crimes."

H. *The Bar*.

U.S.S.R. MINISTRY OF JUSTICE'S ORDER ON "IMPROVING GUIDELINES FOR ACTIVITIES OF THE BAR, December 25, 1972. Biulletin' Normativnykh Aktov Ministerstv i Vedomostv SSSR, 1973, No. 6, p. 144.

Par. 3. Ministries of Justice of the Union and Autonomous Republics, Legal Departments of the Executive Committees of Territorial, Provincial and City Soviets of Working People's Deputies shall improve the organization of their verification of the conformity to the Statute on the Bar by the Presidiums of the Colleges of Lawyers, the maintenance of democratic principles in the organization and activity of lawyers, the preparation for and timely assembly of general meetings, the election of guiding organs, etc.

STATUTE ON THE INSTITUTION OF ADVOCATES IN THE RSFSR, July 25, 1962. [1962] Vedomosti Verkhovnogo Soveta RSFSR, No. 29, item 450.

Part I. *General Provisions:* Art. 1. In conformity with Art. 23 of the law on the Judicial System of the RSFSR Colleges of Advocates shall function in Republics (Autonomous Republics), territories, provinces and cities (in the cities of Moscow and Leningrad) for the purpose of making available defense attorneys at the preliminary investigation and in court and representation in civil cases in court and in state arbitration tribunals and also to provide other legal assistance to citizens, public enterprises, state offices, organizations and collective farms within the RSFSR.

Colleges of Advocates are voluntary associations of persons performing the lawyer's function and operating on the basis of this Statute.

Art. 3. The Colleges of Advocates perform the tasks entrusted to them by: a) consulting on legal matters, giving advice, giving explanations and answering questions on legislation; b) drafting applications, complaints and other documents of a legal character at the request of citizens, public enterprises, state offices, organizations and collective farms; c) sending lawyers to preliminary investigations and court proceedings as defense counsel for the accused, as representatives of victims, of civil plaintiffs and civil defendants; d) participating in judicial examination of civil cases as representatives of plaintiffs, defendants and of other persons participating in the case; e) representing public enterprises, state offices, organizations and collective farms in court and before state arbitration tribunals under powers of attorney and providing them with other legal assistance.

Art. 4. Only a person who is a member of a College of Advocates may practice law.

Art. 5. Organization, guidance and control over activities of the Colleges of Advocates are provided by the Council of Ministers of the Autonomous Republics, executive committees of territorial, provincial and the Moscow and Leningrad city soviets of working peoples' deputies.

General guidance of the Colleges of Advocates of the RSFSR and control over their activity is performed by the Juridical Commission of the Council of Ministers of the RSFSR.

Art. 6. The fees to be charged for legal assistance and also the procedure for providing free legal assistance shall be prescribed by instructions of the Juridical Commission of the Council of Ministers of the RSFSR.

Art. 11. Admission to membership in a College of Advocates shall be effected by the presidium of the College of Advocates. Application for admission to membership shall be examined within not more than one month of receipt, as a rule in the presence of the applicant. Each admission shall be communicated to the Council of Ministers of the Autonomous Republic, or the executive committee of the territorial, provincial, Moscow or Leningrad city soviet of working peoples' deputies. The [same agency] shall have the right to oust the new member within one month of being informed of his admission.

Art. 12. Any member of a College of Advocates may withdraw from the College at any time and on his own volition. Lawyers who withdraw to fill elective office must be readmitted on their request on termination of their duties.

Art. 13. Expulsion from a College of Advocates shall be effected by the presidium of the College and also by the Council of Ministers of the Autonomous Republic or by the executive committee of the territorial, provincial, Moscow or Leningrad city soviet of working peoples' deputies and by the Juridical Commission of the Council of Ministers of the RSFSR in the event of a) demonstrated lack of fitness for performance of a lawyer's duties, b) systematic violation of the regulations of the College of Advocates and unconscientious performance of their duties, c) acceptance of compensation for services other than legal consultation, d) commission of offenses degrading the calling of a Soviet lawyer, e) commission of a crime.

MATTER OF RADCHENKO, Radians'ke pravo, 1967, No. 6, p. 94.

The Judicial Division for Criminal Cases of the Supreme Court of the Ukrainian SSR considered a criminal case at a judicial session on the protest of the Deputy President of the Supreme Court of the Ukrainian SSR against a special ruling of the Judicial Division for Criminal Cases of the Poltava Provincial Court dated August 23, 1966, in which the Division called the attention of the appropriate agencies to the improper conduct of the lawyer Radchenko at the trial of the criminal case involving Koval' and Pavlov. The protest raised the question of vacating this special ruling.

The protest should be satisfied. The Judicial Division for Criminal Cases of the Poltava Provincial Court, in considering, by way of cassation, on August 23, 1966, the case of Koval' and Pavlov, who had been convicted by the Kremenchuk people's court on July 23, 1966 under Art. 206, para. 2 of the Criminal Code of the Ukrainian SSR, rejected the appeals of the lawyers, affirmed the decision, and entered a special ruling with respect to the lawyer Radchenko.

In this ruling the Division stated that the lawyer Radchenko, in conducting Pavlov's defense, "ignoring the undoubted guilt of Pavlov, both at the trial and in the cassational appeal raised the question of his aquittal for lack of proof that he had commited a crime. Instead of using legal means and methods of protecting the interests of the defendant, the lawyer Radchenko, ignoring indisputible proof and evidence, in fact started to shield Pavlov and thus was defending a crime." Further the Division stated that the position taken by the lawyer "did not help in the search for objective truth and the rendering of a lawful decision."

However there was no basis for the entering of such a special ruling. It appears from the materials of the case that Pavlov and Koval' were convicted on the ground that they, on May 25, 1966, from hooligan motives, inflicted upon Klosev bodily injuries of medium severity. The convicted party Pavlov neither at the stage of the preliminary investigation nor at the trial admitted that he was guilty. The accusation of hooliganism against Pavlov was based upon the testimony of the victim Klosev and the witness Iatsin. The lawyer considered that their testimony was insufficient for a finding that Pavlov was guilty and so at the trial of the case, both in the court of first instance and by way of cassation, raised the question of the lack of proof of Pavlov's guilt. The record contains nothing to the effect that the lawyer Radchenko used illegal methods of defense. Standing alone, the disagreement of the lawyer with the conclusions of the investigative agencies and the court cannot be the basis for the raising of the question of his responsibility in a disciplinary or other proceeding.

The Judicial Division terminated the special ruling with respect to the lawyer Radchenko that had been entered on August 23, 1966 by the Judicial Division for Criminal Cases of the Poltava Provincial Court.

MURZIN VS. CHITIN PROVINCIAL COLLEGE OF LAWYERS, Biulleten' Verkhovnogo Suda RSFSR, 1970, No. 5, p. 13.

Murzin sued the Chitin Provincial College of Lawyers to recover fees in the amount of 100 rubles due him for the conduct of cases while working as a lawyer in the Chitin Provincial College of Lawyers, from which he was expelled on June 6, 1966. He argued that this sum of money was due him for work done up to the time of suit and stood to his credit on the books of the College. On April 17, 1969 the books of the College showed 100 rubles, but the Presidium of the College and the general meeting of members refused to pay him.

A member of the College argued before the court that jurisdiction was lacking over the dispute. The Judicial Division for Civil Cases of the RSFSR Supreme Court, having reviewed the case on the appeal of Murzin, rejected his appeal, saying in its ruling of December 2, 1969:

In accordance with the Statute on the Institution of the Bar, RSFSR, the College is a voluntary association of persons, engaged in the practice of law. Lawyers work in legal consultation offices, not under an employment contract with the College, but their rights and duties related to their activity as lawyers spring from their membership in the College. The procedures and conditions for admission and expulsion from the College, for claiming and receiving payment for their work are regulated by the said Statute. Disputes over the matters indicated, including payment of fees are decided by the Presidium of the College, and also by the Executive Committee of the Provincial (Territorial) Soviet of Working People's Deputies or by the Council of Ministers of the Autonomous Republic, which supervises the activity of a given College. Since the investigation of the disputes is not within the jurisdiction of courts, the members of the Chitin Provincial Court correctly refused, in accordance with par. 1 Art. 129 of the Code of Civil Procedure RSFSR, to accept the claim for trial.

D. Fiolevskii, Director of Legal Consultation Office, "THE USEFUL ADVICE OF A JURIST," Izvestiia, July 22, 1975. p. 5.

Not long ago in checking up on the work of a lawyer for a state enterprise, I asked the enterprise director whether he was content with his collaboration with his legal adviser. "Our lawyer," the half joking - half serious director replied, "is worth his salt, not less than 1,500 rubles a month."

The comment was really unnecessary, for during the year since the lawyer came to the enterprise its previously unchanging debtor position running to thousands of rubles was ended; the lawyer brought under control the contractual obligations of the supplier; the work of suing on claims was booming; they began to collect fines for delayed deliveries. It would not be an exaggeration to say that the financial affairs of the enterprise had changed substantially for the better. How could one fail to note the services of the lawyer-adviser?

E.A. Malex and M.M. Skliarskii, "The activity of lawyers in representing the personal and property rights of citizens," in A.I. Sukharev, ed., ROL' I ZADACHI SOVETSKOI ADVOKATURY [The Role and Tasks of the Bar] (Moscow, 1972) 15.

. . .The activity of lawyers in representing personal and property rights of citizens cannot be conducted solely in court. Lawyers represent citizens' interests also before administrative agencies. It is a fact that more than 90% of those seeking aid in legal consultation offices are interested in and receive aid in matters of civil law.

The lawyer's activity in the defense of personal and property rights of citizens in the preponderant majority of legal aid cases never reaches court. Thousands of citizens enter legal consultation offices daily for advice and explanations, for the preparation of legal documents.

The heightened role of lawyers is the result not only of the ever-increasing demands to maintain the rights and legal interests of toilers in settling their labor, housing, marriage-family, and other disputes, but in ever more complex social relationships of citizens regulated by law. In the Moscow City College alone about 400,000 persons asked for legal aid in matters of civil law during 1971. . .

CHAPTER VI

Civil Rights and Socialism

Partisanship is characteristic of revolutions. Those who have been ousted by the mob storming the palace lose their heads, and lesser officials are denied full participation in the new order. Discrimination is widespread, both in law and in social relationships. The Russian revolution followed the historic pattern, but it introduced a difference. For many who stormed the winter palace or the manor house of their landlord, desire for revenge and for a place in the sun differed not a bit from the motives of the mob in other lands on such occasions, but for those who participated as communists there was a new element.[1] They believed that they were acting in the stream of history, not blindly but in application of laws of social development understood at last and harnessed to the benefit of man. Discrimination there would be, but it would be "scientific." Those whom Marx and Engels had categorized as the "bourgeoisie" were not to share equally in political life with the working clas-

---

[1]See E.H. Carr, The Bolshevik Revolution 1917-1923 (New York, 1950) 70-101.

ses because they were presumed to wish to block the road to socialism. Civil rights were to be restricted on Marxist class lines. This was made clear by the first constitution of the new Russian Republic, adopted in 1918. No one could vote or hold office who employed labor for profit, who lived on income not derived from his own labor; who was a private trader or middleman, or monk, priest, policeman of the former regime or member of the former Royal Family.[2] Not until 1936 was this form of political discrimination abandoned.

The law on the franchise set the pattern for the enjoyment of other civil rights. Speech, association, assembly: all were guaranteed by the first constitution but with restrictions conforming to the political philosophy of the Bolsheviks. The first bill of rights opened with an article declaring, "The basic task placed during the present transitional moment on the constitution of the R.S.F.S.R. is the establishment of the dictatorship of the city and village proletariat and of the poorest peasantry in the form of a powerful all-Russian Soviet authority with the objective of complete suppression of the bourgeoisie, the exploitation of man by man and the installation of socialism, under which there will be neither division into classes nor a State authority."[3] The bill closed with a pointed statement, "Guiding itself by the interests of the working class as a whole, the R.S.F.S.R. deprives of political rights those individuals and specific groups who use these rights to the detriment of the interests of the communist revolution."[4]

The pattern of discrimination set by the constitution was carried into a host of laws. Preference was given in University admissions to those who could vote. The same was true in the allocation of housing, and non-voters were denied the right to join housing cooperatives. On every employment application the question was asked as to "social origin," and prosecution followed for those young men and women who falsified their record to say that they came from the working or peasant classes in order to overcome the discriminatory rule.

While political discrimination was fostered to assure retention of political power, discrimination was condemned when it rested on other grounds. Thus, the new constitution declared equality regardless of race or sex, and guaranteed freedom of conscience, although in the latter case the Marxist position that religion was the opiate of the people found expression in a specific guarantee of the right to disbelieve and to propagate atheism.

The draftsmen of the first constitution had their eyes on public opinion abroad as well as at home in preparing their bill of rights. One admitted candidly that guarantee of the right of association in any form for any purpose amounted to commission of a crime against one's self, "since no State can make an unlimited promise."[5] Yet the promise was made to win friends.

When the U.S.S.R. was established and its constitution promulgated in 1923,

---

[2] Art. 65.
[3] Art. 9.
[4] Art. 23.
[5] P. Gurvich. Istoriia Sovetskoi Konstitutsii [A History of the Soviet Constitution] (1923).

there was not a word on civil rights. The guarantees of the constitutions of the various Soviet Socialist Republics forming the union were considered adequate. Some cases reached the republic courts on prosecution for counter-revolutionary agitation. A pattern of thought emerged in the judicial decisions, for the judges in each case sought to determine whether the hostile words had been spoken for the purpose of attempting to overthrow the Soviet regime or in unthinking and suddenly aroused anger. A measure of intent was found in the class background of the speaker. If he was a worker, he was presumed innocent of evil intent. Thus a man who spoke out in the village soviet against plans for the sowing season was successful in obtaining the quashing of his conviction by the lower court because the Russian Republic's Supreme Court found that "from the record it is apparent that the accused was a workman, that he had been at the front in the civil war, that he was an invalid and that he was not a class enemy."[6]

By 1936 times had changed. The ravages of the first world war and of the civil war that followed were beginning to be overcome. Unemployment was said to have been eliminated. The private employer of labor and the private merchant were to be found in only very limited form, for the New Economic Policy which Lenin had introduced as a temporary retreat to capitalism in order to restore the economy had come to an end. The communist party called for a new constitution to reflect the new social condition. When it was published for discussion, it presented a novelty for it had a bill of rights, as its predecessor of 1923 had not. This bill differed from that of the 1918 constitution of the Russian Republic because it contained in addition to the previously stated political rights a new category of economic rights, the most vaunted being the "right to work." From that moment emphasis upon the relative importance of the various human rights was changed. Throughout the U.S.S.R. and abroad the economic rights to work, rest, leisure and social security were widely advertised. When the second world war had been terminated and the United Nations began preparation of a Universal Declaration of Human Rights, it was these rights that the Soviet delegate pressed most vigorously.[7]

When the United Nations later published its yearbook of human rights, the section contributed annually by the U.S.S.R., in contrast to the politically oriented chapters submitted by governments of other states, contained a report on the extent to which the economy had improved under the program of the Five Year Plans. The justification was that socialism's unique contribution to the subject of human rights had been establishment of conditions under which for the first time an individual could enjoy complete fulfillment of himself, for only under conditions of state ownership of the means of production could an individual be sure of employment, and of food, clothes, and housing in return for his toil. Since the economic rights relate primarily to economic administration and labor law, they will be treated in Part II of this study. Attention will be focused in Part I on political rights since they have been traditionally related to public law. This chapter will consider the political

---

[6]Case No. 22,627, Sud. Prak. RSFSR, 1931, No. 4, p. 9.
[7]John N. Hazard, The Soviet Union and a World Bill of Rights, 47 Columbia L. Rev. 1095 (1947).

rights of franchise, equality, speech, assembly, association, and the subsequent chapters on due process of law will consider criminal and civil procedure.

In the political realm, discrimination was removed by the 1936 constitution from the franchise, but there was introduced in the form of constitutional guarantee what had become a convention under the earlier consitution, namely that political activity could be guided by only a single political party. Further, there was created an electoral procedure which in practice, though not by virtue of any provision of law, limited the number of candidates presented for each office to one. The name of the sole candidate might be and was sometimes scratched, by sufficient numbers of voters in some districts when local Soviets were being formed, to require a second election, but no one had the opportunity of running for office unless he had been approved by the Communist Party. By no means all candidates belonged to the Party, but all had its cachet.

Speech, assembly, and association continued to be guaranteed by the 1936 constitution, but again with limitation to exercise in the interest of socialism.[8] In a wartime case the Supreme Court of the U.S.S.R. repeated its early position on the implication of intent. A military official engaged in training recruits seems to have uttered some unprintable words which violated the constitution, probably because they slurred a soldier's ethnic or racial origin. In acquitting the accused of the crime of anti-soviet agitation, the court referred to the man's impeccable revolutionary background; as a soldier in the Red Army during the civil war of 1919, as a prisoner of a White commander, as a member of the Communist Party for 23 years; and concluded that his opinions were evoked not by any orientation against Soviet authority but to strengthen military discipline.[9]

Stalin was ruthless in suppression of his critics in the years from the great purge of the late 1930s until his death in 1953. For millions the route to Siberian prison or death was the secret conviction by the Special Boards of the Ministry of Internal Affairs. Explanation of this attitude has been found in early statements of Stalin's and Lenin's attitudes toward the individual. As a young man in 1906 Stalin had written, "The keystone of Marxism is the mass, whose liberation, in its opinion, is the basic prerequisite for the liberation of the individual. This means that in the opinion of Marxism the liberation of the individual is impossible until the mass has been liberated. Hence, its slogan, 'Everything for the mass.' "[10]

Lenin had created the basis for such views within the U.S.S.R. by saying during the stormy days when the fate of the Russian revolution hung in the balance, "I have discussed soberly and categorically which is better, to put in prison several tens or hundreds of instigators, guilty or not guilty or to lose thousands of Red Army men and workers? The first is better. And let me be accused of any mortal

---

[8]For the official Soviet view on these provisions, see A.Y. Vyshinsky, The Law of the Soviet State (New York, 1948) Chap. IX.
[9]Case of K, Sud. Prak. Verkh. Suda SSSR, 1944, Vol. III(IX), p. 9.
[10]J.V. Stalin, "Anarchism or Socialism," I Sochineniia [Collected Works] (Moscow, 1946) 295-296.

sin whatever and of violating freedom—I admit myself guilty, but the interests of the workers will win out."[11]

Stalin built upon these principles, adding his distinctive features in two ways. What was for Lenin admissible to save his social order came for Stalin to be admissible to force citizens to trod the path he prescribed to increase production, as when he ordered the liquidation of the kulaks as a class in 1930 to facilitate collectivization of agriculture. Still later, sacrifice of the individual became admissible to preserve Stalin's personal power, without which he feared Soviet society would revert to capitalism. Some believe that he became psychopathic, and that his fears drove him even to accept as plausible acts of state security what seemed to be only acts of revenge against his opponents of the early years of Party history.

Whatever the cause of Stalin's actions, freedom of expression suffered in spite of constitutional guarantees. Criticism on any ground other than on improving methods of economic development became dangerous to the critic, and even the critics of economic features had to take care lest they be thought to have masked political criticism in economic terms. The record of Stalin's declining years is being disclosed as years pass since his death.[12] At the time the courts showed no evidence of what was happening because enemies were accused in secret before the Special Boards. Also pre-publication censorship and licensing of meetings reduced the chances of criticism for which prosecution would subsequently follow. There were only the public demonstrations of Stalin's wrath when he closed a play or banned a book after it had passed the censors. Books were even withdrawn from University library shelves, and their authors arrested in the great purge of 1935-1937.

Stalin's death came as such a relief to his critics that in the first flush of excitement during what Ilia Ehrenburg called "The Thaw" much was published. Some authors even circulated still-doubtful literature away from the eyes of the continuing censorship in the form of clandestine books. Some even smuggled their manuscripts abroad for publication. For a time this activity was left unmolested, but with Nikita S. Khruschchev's ouster the fears expressed within the Communist Party by members of Stalinist mentality reemerged. After debate within the Central Committee of the Party, prosecutions were initiated. Some of the documents resulting from the trials are reproduced in this chapter.

The mid-1970's became years of reassessment of attitudes on rights of citizens. The U.S.S.R. Supreme Soviet ratified in 1973 the two United Nations Covenants on Human Rights, one devoted to political rights and one to economic rights.[13]

---

[11]V.I. Lenin, 24 Sochineniia [Collected Works] 3rd ed.,(Moscow, 1935) 241.

[12]Since Stalin's death various persons executed on Stalin's orders after secret hearings have been declared innocent posthumously. Noted examples among the lawyers are Stalin's Minister of Justice, N.V. Krylenko, and his legal theoretician, E.B. Pashukanis. See records of memorial meetings for them. Sovetskoe Gosudarstvo i Pravo (1960). No. 9, p. 30, and *Ibid.* (1968) No. 8, p. 150.

[13]See D.A. Loeber, "The Soviet Procuracy and the Rights of the Individual Against the State," I J. of the Internat. Commiss. of Jurists 59-105 (1957).

[13]Edict of September 18, 1973, [1973] Vedomosti Verkhovnogo Soveta SSSR, No. 40, item 564.

Lawyers of the Soviet Ministry of Foreign Affairs were directed to review the U.S.S.R.'s Constitution of 1936 to determine what was required to bring its Bill of Rights into conformity with the newly assumed international obligations. The draft of a third federal constitution reflects the review. Its provisions are printed in the appendix to this volume.

The so-called "Helsinki Agreement" of 1975 has also raised issues of civil rights for the U.S.S.R. Its 3rd section reasserts the rights of inter-communication between citizens of participating states and raises the question of the extent to which emigration must be permitted. Soviet policies in the latter area were brought into wide discussion in many countries.

Unquestionably the restraints of the Stalin era are being relaxed, but there seems to be some reluctance on the part of Soviet leadership to move fast toward liberalization of policies. Outsiders can only speculate as to whether this reluctance is the product of fear for the security of the Soviet state, or whether it reflects the intolerance of dissidents among doctrinaire communists who have nothing but contempt for those who will not accept the goals and the methods which Communist Party leaders prescribe as necessary to the era of what they call "developed socialism."

The materials in this chapter are indicative of what is available to outsiders attempting to assess current Soviet trends of thought. The reader may be able to discern the direction of future law reform in this area of key concern to Western-trained constitutionalists.

A. *Socialism's Rights and Duties*

L.I. Brezhnev, REPORT OF THE CPSU CENTRAL COMMITTEE TO THE 25TH PARTY CONGRESS, February 14, 1976. Part 3. (White Plains, N.Y.: Compass Publications, Inc. 1976) 116-117.

Comrades, critics abroad frequently seek to distort the meaning of the measures taken by the Soviet state for the purpose of consolidating our legality and legal order. Any reference to the need to tighten discipline and enhance the responsibility of citizens to society is depicted over there as a violation of democracy. What can one say about this?

Indeed, in our concern for the all-round development of the individual and for the rights of citizens, we have also given due attention to the problems of strengthening social discipline and fulfillment by all citizens of their duties to society. After all, democracy is inconceivable without discipline and a sound social order. Indeed, it is the responsible approach of every citizen to his duties and to the people's interests that constitutes the only reliable basis for the full embodiment of the principles of socialist democracy and true freedom for the individual.

Let us recall Lenin's saying that in our society, what is moral is that which serves the interests of communist construction. Similarly, we can say that for us the democratic is that which serves the people's interests of communist construction.

We reject everything that runs counter to these interests, and nothing can persuade us that this is the wrong approach. We know exactly where we are going as we improve our political system. We are fully convinced that the course we have chosen is the right one.

Today, we know not only on the basis of theory but also from long years of practice that genuine democracy is impossible without socialism, and that socialism is impossible without a steady development of democracy. We see the improvement of our socialist democracy as consisting above all in a steady effort to ensure ever fuller participation by the working people in running all the affairs of society, in further developing the democratic principles of our state system, and in creating the conditions for the all-around development of the individual. This is the direction in which the Party has worked and will continue to work in the future.

Comrades, socialism is a dynamically developing society. We have not marked time for one single day, we have been constantly advancing. That is why the work done to improve the political system of our society has a profound social meaning and significance.

FUNDAMENTAL RIGHTS AND DUTIES OF CITIZENS, Constitution U.S.S.R., December 5, 1936.

Art. 122. Women in the U.S.S.R. are accorded equal rights with men in all spheres of economic, government, cultural, political and other public activity.

The possibility of exercising these rights is ensured by women being accorded an equal right with men to work, payment for work, rest and leisure, social insurance and education, and by state protection of the interests of mother and child, state aid to mothers of large families and unmarried mothers, maternity leave with full pay, and the provision of a wide network of maternity homes, nurseries and kindergartens.

Art. 123. Equality of rights of citizens of the U.S.S.R., irrespective of their nationality or race, in all spheres of economic, government, cultural, political and other public activity is an indefeasible law.

Any direct or indirect restriction of the rights of, or, conversely, the establishment of any direct or indirect privileges for, citizens on account of their race or nationality, as well as any advocacy of racial or national exclusiveness or hatred and contempt, is punishable by law.

Art. 124. In order to ensure to citizens freedom of conscience, the church in the U.S.S.R. is separated from the state, and the school from the church. Freedom of religious worship and freedom of anti-religious propaganda is recognized for all citizens.

Art. 125. In conformity with the interests of the working people, and in order to strengthen the socialist system, the citizens of the U.S.S.R. are guaranteed by law: (a) freedom of speech; (b) freedom of the press; (c) freedom of assembly, including the holding of mass meetings; (d) freedom of street processions and demonstrations.

These civil rights are ensured by placing at the disposal of the working people and their organizations printing presses, stocks of paper, public buildings, the streets, communications facilities and other material requisites for the exercise of these rights.

Art. 126. In conformity with the interests of the working people, and in order to develop the organizational initiative and political activity of the masses of the people, citizens of the U.S.S.R. are guaranteed the right to unite in public organizations; trade unions, cooperative societies, youth organizations, sport and defense organizations, cultural, technical and scientific societies; and the most active and politically-conscious citizens in the ranks of the working class, working peasant and working intelligentsia voluntarily unite in the Communist Party of the Soviet Union, which is the vanguard of the working people in their struggle to build communist society and is the leading core of all organizations of the working people, both public and state.

Art. 128. The inviolability of homes of citizens and privacy of correspondence are protected by law.

Art. 134. Members of all Soviets of toiling people's deputies. . .are chosen by the electors on the basis of universal, equal and direct suffrage by secret ballot.

Art. 135. Elections of deputies are universal: all citizens of the U.S.S.R. who have reached the age of 18, irrespective of race or nationality, sex, religion, education, domicile, social origin, property status or past activities, have the right to vote in the election of deputies, with the exception of persons recognized as insane in accordance with the procedure established by law.

B. *The right to representation.*

CRIMINAL CODE OF THE RSFSR, effective January 1, 1961 as amended.

Art. 132. Hindering the exercise of electoral rights by a citizen of the U.S.S.R. by means of force, fraud, threat or bribery—shall be punished by deprivation of freedom for a term of up to two years or correctional labor for a term of up to one year.

Art. 133. Forgery of electoral documents or knowingly miscounting votes, and also violation of the secrecy of voting, by a member of the electoral commission or by other responsible persons—shall be punished by deprivation of freedom for a term of up to three years or correctional labor for a term of up to one year.

STATUTE ON ELECTIONS TO THE SUPREME SOVIET OF THE USSR, January 9, 1950. [1950] Vedomosti Verkhovnogo Soveta SSSR, No. 2 (617) p. 1.

Art. 1. On the basis of Art. 134 of the Constitution of the USSR elections for deputies to the Supreme Soviet of the U.S.S.R. will be conducted by the voters in accordance with the principle of universal, equal and direct suffrage by secret ballot.

Art. 2. On the basis of Article 135 of the Constitution of the U.S.S.R. elections of deputies are universal: all citizens of the U.S.S.R. who have reached the age of 18, irrespective of race or nationality, sex, religion, education, domicile, social origin, property status or past activities have the right to vote in elections of deputies to the Supreme Soviet of the U.S.S.R., with the exception of persons recognized as insane in accordance with the procedure established by law.

Art. 9. Persons, resident on the territory of the USSR and not citizens of the U.S.S.R., but being citizens or subjects of foreign states have no right to participate in elections or to be elected to the Supreme Soviet of the U.S.S.R.

Art. 12. On the lists of voters shall be included all citizens having the right to vote and dwelling (permanently or temporarily) at the moment of preparation of the lists on the territory of a given soviet, if they shall have reached 18 on election day.

Art. 18. Thirty days before elections the executive committee of the soviet of toilers' deputies shall post the list of voters for general inspection or provide the voters with an opportunity to familiarize themselves with these lists within the building of the soviet or of the electoral precinct.

Art. 20. In the event of transfer of a voter's place of residence in the period between posting of the list of electors and election day, the appropriate executive committee of the soviet of toilers' deputies shall issue to him a form, established by the presidium of the Supreme Soviet of the U.S.S.R., 'Certificate of Right to Vote,' and an entry shall be made on the voting list 'departed'; at his new residence (permanent or temporary) the voter is entered on the list of voters on presentation of his 'Certificate of Right to Vote' and on proof of his identity.

Art. 71. Elections to the Supreme Soviet occur on one day which shall be the same for the entire U.S.S.R.

Art. 76. In the polling place there shall be prepared special rooms, or a separate booth shall be furnished for the marking of the ballot by the voter. No one may enter, including members of the electoral commission, except the voter during the marking of the ballot.

Art. 77. Every voter shall vote in person, coming for this purpose to the polling place. The votes shall be made by depositing the ballot in the ballot box.

A.M. Kim, SOVETSKOE IZBIRATEL'NOE PRAVO [Soviet Electoral Law] (Moscow, 1965) 185.

A preliminary discussion of candidacy with participation of the public helps the electors to express their wishes freely under the circumstances of secret voting; aids in forming fully representative agencies of state authority. In the noted decree of the Central Committee of the C.P.S.U. of January 22, 1957 "On improving the activity of soviets of working peoples' deputies and strengthening their links with the masses," it is said that in putting forward candidates for the position of deputy, there must be no haste, and they must first be discussed at meetings of workers in shops, and at meetings of collective farmers in their brigades. There must be preliminary conversations during which the general view must be brought out. Only after this shall a single candidate be named at the general meeting.

Soviet electoral law sets no limits to the number of candidates for each electoral district, and in practice in a majority of the electoral districts several candidates for the position of deputy are put forward. Nevertheless, during wide and free discussion by the electors themselves the candidates are distilled down to a single one for each electoral district, and it is his name that is placed on the ballot for secret voting.

Consequently, it is not the electoral law that limits the number of candidates for deputy in the district to one person, but the free will of the electors themselves. This has deep socialist meaning, since in our society, where long ago struggles for power among competing political forces ended, there also cannot be competing candidates at the elections.

COMMUNICATIONS ON ELECTION RESULTS: Izvestiia, June 19, 1974, and *Ibid.* June 21, 1975.

U.S.S.R. Supreme Soviet elections, June 18, 1974. 161,724,222 electors were placed on the electoral lists. 161,689,612 voted or 99.98%. To conduct the elections for the Council of the Union there were organized on the territory of the U.S.S.R. 767 electoral districts, elections being held in all of them. 161,355,959 voters, i.e. 99.79% voted for the candidates. 332,664 voters voted against them. 750 electoral districts were organized to conduct the elections to the Council of Nationalities. In the Union Republics, 161,443,605 voters voted for the candidates (99.85%), and 245,750 against; in the Autonomous Republics, 12,146,943 voted for the candidates (99.68%) and 38,661 against; in the autonomous provinces 1,187,822 voted for the candidates (99.72%) and 3,293 against; in the national districts 667,085 voters voted for the candidates (99.72%) and 1,892 against.

Local elections, June 1975. 2,210,824 deputies of local soviets were elected. Of these there were 1,147,190 men (51.9%), 1,063,634 women (48.1%), 967,906 members or candidates of the Communist Party (43.8%), 1,242,918 non-party members (56.2%), 896,374 workmen (40.5%), 600,636 collective farmers (27.2%). Among the deputies to local soviets 664,833 persons were under 30 years of age (30.1%), of whom 413,356 (18.7%) were members of the Komsomols. In 68 electoral districts the candidates on the ballot did not obtain an absolute majority of the votes and were not elected deputies. In 37 electoral districts there were no elections because there was no candidate. In 3 electoral districts the elections were declared void for violation of the electoral law. In all of these districts new elections will be held.

C. *The right to religious worship.*

CRIMINAL CODE OF THE R.S.F.S.R., effective January 1, 1961, as amended.

Art. 142. The violations of laws on the separation of church and state and of school and church shall be punished by correctional labor for a term of up to one year of by a fine of up to fifty rubles.

The same acts, when committed by a person previously convicted of violating the laws on separation of church and state and school from church, as well as organized activity directed to the commission of such acts, shall be punished by deprivation of freedom for a term of up to three years.

Art. 143. Hindering the performance of religious rites, so long as they do not interfere with public order and are not accompanied by encroachment upon the rights of citizens shall be punished by correctional labor for a term of up to six months or public censure.

Art. 227. Organizing or directing a group, whose activity, although carried on with the appearance of preaching religious beliefs and performing religious ceremonies, is related to causing harm to the health of citizens or with any other infringements of the person or rights of citizens, or with inducing citizens to refuse calls to social activity or performance of civic duties, or with inducing minors to enter such a group, shall be punished by deprivation of freedom for a term of up to five years or by exile for a similar term with or without confiscation of property.

EDICT OF MARCH 18, 1966 ON APPLICATION OF ART. 142, [1966] Vedomosti Verkhovnogo Soveta RSFSR, No. 12, item 221.

The Presidium of the Supreme Soviet of the RSFSR decrees on the basis of section "c" of Art. 33 of the RSFSR constitution, in clarification of questions raised in practice on application of Art. 142 of the Criminal Code of the RSFSR that; the following activities shall incur criminal liability under Art. 142 as violation of the laws on separation of church and state:

Compulsory collection of taxes and contributions for the use of religious organizations and clergy, preparation for the purpose of mass distribution, or mass distribution, of appeals, letters, leaflets and other documents exhorting refusal to observe legislation on religious denominations; commission of fraudulent acts for the purpose of arousing religious superstitions in the masses of the population; organization and conduct of religious meetings, processions and other ceremonies of the denomination, violating public order; organization and systematic conduct of classes to teach religion to minors in violation of the regulations established by law; refusal to hire or to accept in a school, dismissal from work or from a school, and deprivation of privileges or priorities of citizens because of their attitude toward religion.

EDICT OF MARCH 18, 1966 ON ADMINISTRATIVE LIABILITY FOR VIOLATION OF LEGISLATION ON RELIGIOUS DENOMINATIONS [1966] Vedomosti Verkhovnogo Soveta RSFSR, No. 12, item 219.

The Presidium of the Supreme Soviet of the RSFSR decrees that the following activities shall constitute violation of the legislation on religious denominations:

Refusal of religious organizations to register the organization in state agencies; violation of the regulations established by law for the organization and conduct of religious meetings, processions and other ceremonies of the denomination; organization and conduct by clergy of the denomination and by members of religious organizations of special meetings of children and of youths, and also of work, literary and other circles or groups, having no relationship to the performance of functions of the denomination.

These acts shall incur a fine of up to 50 rubles, levied by the administrative commission of the executive committee of the county and city soviets of working peoples' deputies.

EDICT ON AMENDMENTS TO DECREE OF APRIL 8, 1929 "ON RELIGIOUS ASSOCIATIONS," JUNE 23, 1975. [1975] Vedomosti Verkhovnogo Soveta RSFSR, No. 27, item 572.

4. A religious association of a group of believers may enter upon activity only after the Council on Religious Affairs of the USSR Council of Ministers has taken a decision to register the association or group of believers. . .

5. In order to register a religious association its organizers, being not less than 20 persons, file a petition to register a religious association and to open a prayer house (church, Roman Catholic church, temple, mosque, synagogue, etc.) with the Executive Committee of a county or city Soviet of working people's deputies.

[the petition is transmitted up the hierarchy of Soviets with the comments of the transmitting Soviet's Executive Committee to the Council on Religious Affairs which is given the right to accept or reject the petition without need of stating reasons]

10. To satisfy religious needs the believers constituting the religious association may receive on the decision of the Council of Religious Affairs. . .for rent-free use a special prayer house under the conditions and in accordance with the procedures provided for in the contract concluded between the religious association and the agent of the Executive Committee of the county or city Soviet of working people's deputies. Each religious association or group of believers may use only one prayer house.

12. General meetings of the religious association or group of believers (except for prayer services) may be held only with the consent of the Executive Committee of the county, or city Soviet of toilers' deputies.

18. The teaching of any religious doctrine in schools is forbidden. The teaching of religious doctrine may be permitted only in ecclesiastical educational institutions, opened in the manner established by law.

33. The buildings of a religious cult must be insured at the expense of the persons executing the contract, the beneficiary being the Executive Committee of the Soviet of working people's deputies on whose territory the building stands.

The proceeds of insurance in the event of fire shall be used as is decided by the Council of Ministers of the Autonomous Republic, or the Executive Committee of the Provincial, city (Moscow and Leningrad) Soviet of working people's deputies decides, in agreement with the Council of Religious Affairs. . .to rebuild the burned prayer house or to meet the cultural needs of the county or city in which the prayer house stood.

36. The transfer of the building of a cult, being used by believers, to other purposes (closing of the prayer house) is permitted solely on decision of the Council on Religious Affairs on motion of the Council of Ministers of the Autonomous Republic or the executive Committee of provincial, city (Moscow and Leningrad) Soviet of working people's deputies if that building is necessary for the State or public needs. The believers, constituting the religious association shall be informed of such a decision.

45. The construction of new prayer houses at the expense of believers is permitted in individual cases at the request of religious associations with the consent of the Council on Religious Affairs. . .

54. Religious associations and members of groups of believers have the right to take up collections and accept voluntary gifts in the prayer house among the members of the given religious association but only for the purpose of maintaining the building, of obtaining property for the cult, or paying the wages of those who serve the cult and the expenses of the executive organs.

M. Vorotynova, "UNDER THE MASK OF THE MEEK AND HUMBLE," Kazakhstanskaia Pravda, August 18, 1967, p. 4.

Alma Ata. A so-called "Sunday School" for children has been organized by Klassen, Bondar and Telegin, members of the Evangelical Baptist Society. The three of them sat in the prisoners' dock, their heads bowed. They seemed completely respectable in appearance, but only in appearance. Experienced wolves lurked behind their masks of meekness and humility. They were members of the illegal reactionary organization called the "Initiators," and were being tried for violation of Soviet legislation on religious denominations. The defendants and also some of the witnesses who were members of the same organization attempted to prove during the trial that they were only guilty of devotion to their faith.

Was this really true? The facts belied their hypocritical claims, ripping the mask of meekness and humility from these "Godly" characters. Even their membership in the "Initiators" demonstrated their deliberate intention of violating Soviet laws, for the "Initiators" are well-known for their demand that Soviet laws on religious cults be repealed. Their slogan calls for unrestricted religious propaganda.

Returning to the children to whom the preachers were forceably teaching the Gospel. We do not know by what means the children were compelled to attend prayer meetings of the fanatics, to bow their heads and learn God's word, but we know that the "men of God" made progress in their efforts to confuse the children's minds and corrupt their souls.

Several teen-agers who had attended the "Sunday School" came before the court, mostly students of secondary schools Nos. 17, 71, 78 and 101. They looked outwardly like any of their fellows . . . but this was only outwardly. They could be distinguished immediately from other children by their wary, alienated, introverted looks, by the withdrawn look in their faces. Irina Kibernik, a 16 year old, appeared in court as a witness. She was asked whether she believed in God, whether she attended prayer meetings, went to Sunday School and what she intended to be when she grew up. Irina answered none of these questions. She fixed her eyes inscrutibly on the judges and kept stubbornly silent. Her friend, the 8th grade student, Liza Penner, told the court defiantly, "I will not tell you anything. What's the good?"

"We have but one law and we obey it, the law of God." This was the answer given on behalf of the children by their adult "brethren," Borodyk, Telegin and others.

This was the heart of the evil caused by the group of fanatics. By poisoning the minds and souls of the children with religious hatred, they were educating them in a spirit of disobedience to Soviet laws. They were depriving them, as it were, of the right to be full fledged citizens of our country as well as robbing them of the joy of learning and the happiness of childhood.

What did they offer in exchange? "Blessed are the poor in heart, for theirs is the kingdom of heaven."

The defendants were also charged with printing and disseminating, in addition to their religious literature, a mass of "writings" slandering Soviet power . . . distorting our reality. A poem said that faith in God was persecuted in our country, that for religious believers nothing had changed in the last ten years.

The "compositions" for parents counselled rearing children in a religious spirit, counterposing religious upbringing to upbringing in school and impressing upon parents the fact that religion has no future without the children.

Whatever is said by the defendants in justification, this is not religion, but unlimited slander of Soviet authority, the same authority that gave these very "brethren" in Christ the opportunity to lead a secure life, to work, receive a pension in old age and enjoy the benefits of civilization.

D. *The right to freedom of movement.*

CRIMINAL CODE OF THE R.S.F.S.R., effective January 1, 1961, as amended.

Art. 198. The malicious violation of passport regulations in communities where special regulations on residence and registration have been put into effect, if such violation takes the form of residence without a passport or without registration, and if the offender has already twice previously been subjected to an administrative penalty for such a violation, shall be punished by deprivation of liberty for a term of up to one year, or by assignment to compulsory correctional work for the same term or by fine of up to 50 rubles.

EDICT ON FINES FOR VIOLATION OF PASSPORT REGULATIONS IN MOSCOW AND MOSCOW PROVINCE, May 8, 1963. [1963] Vedomosti Verkhovnogo Soveta SSSR, No. 20, item 222.

The Presidium of the Supreme Soviet of the U.S.S.R. decrees:

That in extension of Art. 13 of the edict . . . of June 21, 1961 . . . there shall be extended to agencies of the militia the right to levy fines directly as an administrative act without referral to the administrative commissions of the executive committees of the county and city soviets of working peoples' deputies for violation of passport regulations in Moscow and Moscow Province. [Extended to Leningrad, January 15, 1976.]

STATUTE ON PASSPORT SYSTEM IN U.S.S.R., AUGUST 28, 1974. [1974]
Vedomosti Verkhovnogo Soveta SSSR, No. 19, item 109.

1. The passport of a citizen of the USSR is the basic document establishing a Soviet citizen's identity. Every USSR citizen of 16 years of age must have a USSR passport.

2. The following information on the identity of a citizen shall be entered in the passport: Name, date and place of birth, ethnic origin. The entry on ethnic origin in the passport shall be made on the basis of the ethnic origin of the parents. If the parents have different ethnic origins, then on issuance of the first passport the ethnic origin of either the father or the mother shall be entered, depending on the wish of the recipient of the passport. The entry cannot be changed at a later time. The passport shall also contain the following information on children: name, date, place of birth. This entry shall be made by the Agency for Registering Acts of Civil Status.

4. Notations shall be placed in the passports of citizens: on marriage and divorce, by the Agencies for Registering Acts of Civil Status; on military service by the military commissariats; on registration or deregistration of domicile by the agencies of internal affairs and persons authorized to do so by the Executive Committee of village and hamlet Soviets of working people's deputies.

22. Citizens shall be registered at their place of residence. . .

23. Citizens changing their place of residence, and also leaving for another place for temporary residence for more than one and a half months, except those leaving on an official business trip, on vacation, for recreational occupancy of a cottage, for rest or a health cure, must register before leaving. Citizens who do not have in their passports or in other documents provided for in Art. 2 of the present Statute a notice of registration for departure may not be registered on arrival elsewhere.

CASE OF FIL'KIN, Biulleten' Verkhovnogo Suda RSFSR, 1975, No. 2, p. 11.
. . .Filkin was found guilty of the following: On October 23, 1972 he was released from a correctional labor colony, having served his term; he went to Petrozavodsk where he took up residence without registration; he got no job; he lived an anti-social, parasitic way of life. On two occasions, December 18, 1972 and April 12, 1973 Fil'kin was fined by an administrative tribunal for violation of the passport regulations.

Moreover, Fil'kin engaged in vagrancy, wandering around among the cities of Karelia and the Provinces bordering them. . .He was frequently detained by the militia for vagrancy and warned to stop wandering and to get a job. He was convicted by the Petrozavodsk city peoples' court for vagrancy, and the conviction was affirmed.

The Deputy Procurator General of the RSFSR protested the sentence for lack of elements of a crime. The protest was satisfied on July 14, 1974 by the Judicial Division for Criminal Cases of the RSFSR Supreme Court for the following reasons:

The court held Fil'kin guilty of malicious violation of the passport regulations, basing its opinion on the fact that he had twice been fined administratively on December 18, 1972 and April 12, 1973 for residing in Petrozavodsk without registration. However, under Art. 198 of the Criminal Code of the RSFSR, criminal responsibility for malicious violation of the passport regulations arises in the event of residence of a person without registration under conditions that he had twice been fined administratively for an analagous violation.

As is evident from the record, Fil'kin after April 12, 1973 could not violate the passport regulations, since on April 11, 1973 to May 8, 1973 he was detained in a reception-distribution center of the Ministry of Internal Affairs, and on May 8, 1973 he was formally arrested in the present case. Consequently, there were no elements of a crime, as defined in Art. 198 of the Criminal Code in the acts of Fil'kin.

E. *The right to freedom of expression.*

LAW ON CRIMINAL RESPONSIBILITY FOR STATE CRIMES, December 25, 1958. [1958] Vedomosti Verkhovnogo Soveta SSSR, No. 1, item 8, as amended, [1961] *Ibid.* No. 21, item 222.

Art. 7. Agitation or propaganda conducted for the purpose of overthrowing or weakening Soviet authority or for the commission of single especially dangerous state crimes; the distribution for these same purposes of slanderous inventions defaming the Soviet state and public structure, and also the distribution or preparation of or possession for these same purposes of literature having such a content—shall be punished by deprivation of freedom for a term of from six months to seven years or exile for a term of from two to five years.

The same acts committed by a person previously sentenced for especially dangerous state crimes, and also if committed in wartime—shall be punished by deprivation of freedom for a term of from three to ten years and with exile for a term of from two to five years, or without exile.

Art. 8. Propaganda for war, in whatever form it is put—shall be punished by deprivation of freedom for a term of three to eight years and with exile for a term of from two to five years, or without exile.

Art. 9. Organizational activity directed to preparation for or commission of especially dangerous state crimes, to the setting up of an organization having as its purpose the commission of such crimes, and likewise participation in anti-soviet organizations—shall be punished in accordance with Arts. 1-8 of this law.

Art. 11. Propaganda or agitation for the purpose of stirring up race or ethnic hostility or discord. and also direct or indirect limitations of rights or the creation of direct or indirect privileges of citizens on the basis of their race or ethnic group— shall be punished by deprivation of liberty for a term of from six months to three years or exile for a term of from two to five years.

Art. 16. Organization of mass disorders, accompanied by pogroms, destruction, arson and such other acts, as well as indirect commission of such acts by participants in the above mentioned crimes or the presentation by them of armed opposition to authority—shall be punished by deprivation of freedom for a term of from two to fifteen years.

EDICT AMENDING CRIMINAL CODE OF THE RSFSR, September 16, 1966.
[1966] Vedomosti Verkhovnogo Soveta RSFSR, No. 38, item 1038.

Art. 190(1). The systematic distribution in oral form of deliberately false fabrications harming the Soviet state and social structure, and also the preparation or distribution in written, printed or other form of productions of such content shall be punished by deprivation of freedom for a term of up to three years or by corrective labor without deprivation of freedom for a term of up to one year or by fine of up to 100 rubles.

Art. 190(3). The organization or active participation in group activity seriously violating public order or accompanied by clearly illegally insubordinate demands on representatives of authority or entailing disruption of the functioning of transport, state or public agencies and enterprises shall be punished by deprivation of freedom for a term of up to one year, or corrective labor without deprivation of freedom for a term of up to one year, or by fine up to 100 rubles.

"FROM THE COURTROOM—HERE THE LAW RULES," Izvestiia, February 11, 1966, p. 4 and February 16, 1964, p. 4.

Our readers are already familiar with the activities of these two persons who now sit in the prisoners' box, Siniavskii, with a diploma as candidate of philosophical sciences and senior scientific associate of the Institute of World Literature of the U.S.S.R. Academy of Sciences, and Daniel, a member of the Writers' Union, a translator of poems. Both of them in their works glorified our Motherland, wrote of the high moral countenance of the Soviet man, criticized (in utmost degree Siniavskii) those of their colleagues who seemed to them insufficiently patriotic. This was in their works which appeared in Soviet publications.

Simultaneously, for several years they penned anti-soviet libels and sent them abroad to bourgeois publishers. These published them eagerly . . . printing them in many languages, provided them with anti-soviet prefaces and distributed them widely. They even sent them into the U.S.S.R. Both authors wrote their works under pseudonyms.

The indictment reads that the prisoners were accused of crimes defined in Art. 70 of the Criminal Code of the RSFSR. Our law establishes that anti-soviet literature is literature containing calls to harm or weaken Soviet authority. These men before the court called directly for a struggle against our social structure, against our moral system.

In the anti-communist propaganda of recent years, a noted place was given to the anti-Soviet false productions, "The Court is in Session," "What is Socialist Realism," "The Lovers," published in the West under the pseudonym Abram Terts and also "Moscow is Speaking," "Hands," and others written under the pseudonym of Nikolai Arzhak.

In the indictment a large quantity of material is systematically set forth disclosing the personalities of Siniavskii and Daniel. . . .Here is one excerpt, far from the most trenchant but clearly characterizing the full infamy of the accuseds' varied countenances. It is to be found in Siniavskii's writing (from "The Court is in Session").

It is known that in the process of the birth of man one stage is like that of a fish. Why let these fish resources of the country die? In the beautiful future they will utilize the dear little fishes. They will extract them carefully from the mother's womb and place them in special ponds to grow, teaching them to live independently. Let them grow scales and fins under state protection. Thus alongside the abortion clinics there will be a fish hatchery, and canning plants in great number. Some will be sardines and some will be little eels, according to their ethnic characteristics. Everything will occur with the blessing of Marxism."

Of course, they say that although this is very indecent, still it is not anti-Soviet. The Western press evaluates this story somewhat differently. 'The Court is in Session' is the most direct and open reflection of the complete dissatisfaction with the Soviet system." . . . TIME Magazine in its issue of October 29, 1965 calls Siniavskii "an angry enemy of communism."

After the speeches of the defense attorneys, the prisoners presented their final pleas. Siniavskii gave the impression, as he had before, that he can in no way descend from his "literary-esthetic clouds." Daniel once again tried to deny the anti-Soviet content of his works. Nevertheless, he acknowledged that he sent them abroad illegally and thereby created the opportunity for our enemies to use them against the Soviet country, causing it harm and striking a blow against it.

The trial had lasted four days. The evidence introduced by the accusation, by the testimony of the prisoners, of witnesses, of experts, of the documents introduced proved irrefutably that Siniavskii and Daniel had slandered the socialist Motherland and its people and had put into the hands of the enemy an ideological weapon to be used in the struggle against the Soviet state.

The court sentenced Siniavskii, A.D. to seven years of imprisonment in a corrective labor colony of the most severe category and Daniel, Iu. M. to five years imprisonment in the same.

N.N. Iakovlev, THE MERCENARY, Literaturnaia Gazeta, 1974, No. 8, p. 14.

We find in our work on American studies and the theory and history of international relations increasingly frequent filthy footprints of a wretched band of persons whom the West calls dissidents. Or, to be more exact, we meet the consequences of their activities as they appear in the spoken and printed word, magnified a thousand times by the propaganda of imperialists, and turned into the steoretypes of Western thinking about the USSR in accordance with the rules of psychological warfare.

The malicious hissing of renegades, amplified enormously by technical means: radio and television, simply deafens some people abroad and brings them to incorrect and dangerous conclusions regarding our country. Finally, this error complicates international relations, because it serves as a continuing source of fuel for the dying bonfire of the cold war.

TASS AGENCY COMMUNIQUE, Izvestiia, February 15, 1974, p. 4.

For the systematic commission of acts incompatible with being a citizen of the USSR and harmful to the USSR A.I. Solzhenitsyn has been deprived of USSR citizenship by decree of the Presidium of the USSR Supreme Soviet and expelled from the Soviet Union as of February 13, 1974. His family may join him when they think it necessary.

CASE OF TESHAEV, Biulleten' Verkhovnogo Suda SSSR, 1971, No. 1, p. 30.

X. Teshaev was convicted on August 7, 1970 by the Judicial Division for Criminal Cases of the Tadzhik SSR Supreme Court of a variety of crimes: Art. 71 (violation of the principle of ethnic and racial equality), 203[1] (distribution in oral form of deliberately false fabrications harming the Soviet State) [identical to Art. 190 (1) of RSFSR Criminal Code, *supra*], and Art. 220, par. 2 (malicious hooliganism) of the Criminal Code of the Tadzhik SSR.

Teshaev was found guilty of distributing systematically among the factory workers and some citizens of the city views intended to excite ethnic hostility, of distributing false fabrications harming the Soviet State and social structure, of committing hooligan acts with exceptional cynicism in content and impertinence, gravely violating the social structure and exhibiting clear lack of respect for society; all of this while working at the factory "Tadzhik Tekstilmash" in the city of Dushanbe during 1968-1969.

Having reviewed the case on the protest of the USSR Deputy Procurator General, the Judicial Division changed the judgment for the following reasons:

Teshaev, as the witnesses testified in court, thinking himself offended, quarrelled with the factory workers with or without reason, uttering on these occasions unprintable words and permitting incorrect expressions with regard to persons of other ethnic origin living in Tadzhikistan. The court found in these acts of Teshaev the evil intent of "stimulating ethnic hostility," and it classified these acts under Art. 71 of the Criminal Code of the Tadzhik SSR, which establishes responsibility for violation of ethnic and racial equality.

However, conviction of Teshaev for commission of crimes set forth above is not supported by the record.

The definition of the crime in Art. 71. . .establishes responsibility for propaganda or agitation, having as its aim the stimulation of racial or ethnic enmity or differences, and also the direct or indirect limitation of rights, or establishing direct or indirect privileges of citizens, depending on their racial or ethnic status.

Thus, the law establishes that under Art. 71. . . .a person is responsible who distributes among a more or less wide circle of persons certain views, or among a comparatively narrow circle of persons views, ideas, which stimulate or can stimulate these persons to scornful or hostile relations with any ethnic group or race.

From the testimony of witnesses and of Teshaev himself, however, it is seen that the latter during the period when he was annoyed maintained hooligan relations with respect to some persons working in the factory; threatened them with brutality; lowered their sense of dignity and achievement. Often these acts of Teshaev were linked with the ethnic origin of a number of persons.

There is no evidence in the record indicating that these actions bore the character of agitation or propaganda directed toward violation of the ethnic equality of Soviet citizens.

The court also should have considered facts concerning the health of Teshaev. Holding that Teshaev so far as his health was concerned could hold himself to account for his acts and guide them, the forensic psychiatric expert among other things noted that he "detected influences remaining from childhood of an organic disease of the central nervous system which had retarded the mental development at the stage of mild congenital mental retardation."

Teshaev's commission of insolent and cyncial acts in public places, including those intended to lower the honor and dignity of individual citizens contains the elements of malicious hooliganism and must be classified under par. 2 Art. 220 of the Criminal Code of the Tadzhik SSR.

Teshaev was without foundation convicted also under Art. 203^1, providing responsibility for distributing deliberately false fabrications, harming the Soviet state and social structure. The witnesses questioned by the court had not found Teshaev systematically distributing in oral form deliberately false fabrications, harming the Soviet state and social structure. It must also be remarked that the accusation on this score set forth in the indictment and the court's judgment does not correspond to the dispositive provisions of that article. In the documents it is said that Teshaev "distributed deliberately false fabrications," "distributed slanderous fabrications," "intentionally distributed slanderous rumors," while by law responsibility under Art. 203^1 is established for systematic distribution in oral form of deliberately false fabrications harming the Soviet State and social structure and also the preparation or distribution in written, printed or other form of productions with such content.

The elements set forth above were not established in Teshaev's case.

The Judicial Division, being in agreement with the protest, quashed the judgment of the Judicial Division for Criminal Cases of the Tadzhik SSR Supreme Court with regard to X. Teshaev, excluding from it the conviction for violation of Arts. 71 and 203^1 of the Criminal Code of the Tadzhik SSR, and terminated the case with regard to those charges for lack of events constituting such a crime.

THE SOVIET STATE AND ITS CITIZENS

DECREE OF JUNE 6, 1931. CENSORSHIP [1931] Sob. Uzak. RSFSR, No. 31, item 273.

1. For the purpose of putting into effect all types of political ideological, military, and economic control over items prepared for preparation or distribution in the press, over manuscripts, pictures, drawing, etc., and also over radio announcements, lectures and exhibitions, there shall be organized under the People's Commissariat of Education of the RSFSR a Chief Administration for Matters of Literature and Publishing Houses (GLAVLIT).

2. In order to carry out the tasks placed upon it, GLAVLIT shall be permitted to forbid printing, publication, and distribution of productions which:

(a) contain agitation or propaganda against Soviet authority and the dictatorship of the proletariat;

(b) reveal state secrets;

(c) stir up ethnic and religious fanaticism;

(d) have a pornographic character;

[Subsequent sections ommitted.]

DECREE OF JUNE 26, 1932, [1932] Sob. Uzak. RSFSR, No. 64, item 288.

The Council of People's Commissars decrees that:

1. Printing enterprises (typographic, lithographic, zincographic, metal engraving, etc.), enterprises producing and selling typewriters, letter presses, multigraphing apparatuses (rotating reproducers, glass engraving, shapirographs, etc.) and their accessories and also shops for casting stereotypes and for the preparation of stereotype blocks may be opened on the territory of the RSFSR by state agencies, cooperatives and other public organizations only on receipt of permission granted by the militia administrations of Autonomous Republics, territories and provinces with the concurrence of local committees for press matters.

5. Duplicating apparatuses and their accessories may be acquired by offices and organizations only with special permission granted by city and county militia administrations.

9. Violation of the regulations established by the present decree and instructions issued thereunder shall subject the offender to a fine of 100 rubles or correctional labor without deprivation of freedom for a term of up to one month and in appropriate cases to criminal liability.

STATUTE ON ARTISAN-HANDICRAFT BUSINESSES, May 3, 1976, [1976] Sob. Post. SSSR, no. 7, item 39 (excerpt).

3. Throughout the entire territory of the USSR citizens are forbidden to engage in the following types of artisan-handicraft businesses:

(c) the manufacture of multigraph and copying machines, all types of rubber stamps, stamping machines, printing presses, fonts of type, reproduction of all types of printed matter and photographic products, the multiplication of grammophone records, moving picture films and magnetic tapes;

10. If a violation of the established procedure for engaging in artisan-handicraft businesses is discovered, and also on discovery of persons engaged in forbidden business, the official of the finance agency or internal affairs agency conducting the verification is required to withdraw from the violator the registration certificate (if one is in his possession), to determine the identity of the offender from his passport (or the document issued in lieu of it), and to prepare a formal record of the violation.

The formal record must be transmitted to the administrative commission attached to the executive committee of the county (city) soviet or working people's deputies to initiate action against the citizen committing the violation, in accordance with the legislation of the union republic.

In circumstances when engaging in the forbidden business incurs criminal responsibility under existing legislation, the relevant documents are transmitted to the investigating agencies.

STATUTE ON THE STATE COMMITTEE OF THE RSFSR COUNCIL OF MINISTERS FOR AFFAIRS OF PUBLISHING HOUSES, POLYGRAPHIC ESTABLISHMENTS AND THE BOOK TRADE, August 28, 1974. [1974] Vedomosti Verkhovnogo Soveta RSFSR, No. 23, item 128.

. . .The State Committee of the RSFSR Council of Ministers for Affairs of Publishing Houses, Polygraphic Establishments and the Book Trade of the RSFSR shall provide guidance in publishing, polygraphic production and the book trade in the RSFSR, and also exercise a review function throughout the republic on the thematic trends and content of published literature in all its forms.

The State Committee . . . shall be held responsible for the condition and further elevation of the ideological political level of publications, for the quality of production of the polygraphic industry and for the most complete satisfaction of the republic's need for it, for the scientific-technical progress and technical level of polygraphic production and for the condition of the book trade in the RSFSR.

DECREE OF MAY 15, 1935 ON LICENSING OF MEETINGS, [1936] Sob. Zak. SSSR, No. 26, item 209.

The Council of People's Commissars of the U.S.S.R. decrees:

1. The calling of Congresses, as well as of conferences and meetings in which representatives of local agencies participate, by state agencies of the U.S.S.R. and by All-Union cooperative and public organizations shall be permitted only with the consent of the Council of People's Commissars of the U.S.S.R., while calling of meetings within an agency concerning various departments of work shall require the consent of a People's Commissar or of the director of the central administration of the U.S.S.R. under whose jurisdiction the work lies.

2. The calling of Congresses, conferences and meetings in which local representatives participate, when these concern agencies of the republics shall be permitted

with the consent of the Council of People's Commissars of the corresponding union republic.

DECREE OF APRIL 7, 1960 ON RESPONSIBILITY FOR ILLEGAL CONSTRUCTION AND USE OF RADIO TRANSMITTERS, Sotsialisticheskaia zakonnost', 1960, No. 6, p. 85.

In a decree of the Presidium of the Supreme Soviet of the RSFSR of April 7, 1960 it is provided:

1. It is established that the construction and use of radio transmission equipment without the required permission incurs application of measures of public influence or measures of administrative influence in the form of a fine in the amount of 500 rubles with confiscation of the radio apparatus that has been used.

On second construction and use of radio transmission equipment without the required permission, committed after application of the measures of influence indicated, the guilty person shall be fined at three times the amount.

2. Evidence of illegal construction and use of radio transmission equipment shall be examined by a people's judge sitting alone within 72 hours after its receipt from the organs of the militia with summons of the person committing the violation, and in the necessary circumstances with witnesses.

The order of the people's judge levying the fine shall be executed immediately, and there shall be no appeal.

3. The order of the people's judge establishing responsibility for illegal construction and use of radio transmission equipment may be changed or withdrawn on protest of the procurator to the people's judge himself, as well as to the chairman of the appropriate district (national district), provincial, territorial court, court of an autonomous province or of the Supreme Court of an autonomous republic.

EDICT ON FINES FOR VIOLATION OF REGULATIONS ON RADIO-ELECTRONIC COMMUNICATING EQUIPMENT, Sotsialisticheskaia zakonnost', 1973, No. 1, p. 73.

The Presidium of the USSR Supreme Soviet on August 10, 1972 decrees:

There is conferred upon the organs of State inspection of the electrocommunications system of the USSR Ministry of Communications the right to levy fines on responsible officials of enterprises, offices and organizations guilty of violating the regulations on acquisition, installing, construction and use of radio frequencies, the norms for radio broadcasting and for permitted industrial interference with radio reception, without reference to the administrative commission [the principal agencies authorized to levy fines]

YOUR TELEPHONE, Izvestiia, March 29, 1975, p. 5

The USSR Ministry of Communications on June 28, 1974 approved, effective January 1, 1975, new regulations for the use of the city telephone circuits. The editors have received many letters asking for explanations of these regulations. The

Honored Jurist of the RSFSR, K. Budaeva, responds:
Q. May the Telephone Station disconnest the telephone?
A. The subscriber must pay his local and long distance charges on time; must not permit unauthorized installation or transfer of installation of telephones; must protect the telephone apparatus and equipment installed in his quarters from damage and keep them in good condition. The telephone may not be used for purposes contrary to the interests of the State and social structure. In the event that the subscriber violates these conditions the communications enterprise has the right to disconnect the telephone and remove it.

F. *The right to emigrate.*

AMENDMENT TO THE EDICT OF APRIL 29, 1942 "ON THE RATES FOR STATE FEES." Sotsialisticheskaia zakonnost', 1971, No. 2, p. 86.

On September 22, 1970 the USSR Council of Ministers decreed:

1. For issuance to USSR citizens of proof that relatives and friends abroad have issued invitations to emigrate, and when issued with a certification that the invitations have been received from persons living in capitalist countries, a state fee shall be charged as follows:

(a) for issuance of proof of the invitation - 5 rubles.

(b) for certification that the invitation has been recieved from persons living in capitalist countries - 15 rubles.

2. A fee of 1 ruble shall be charged for issuance of a passport for use abroad by persons departing the country for private reasons.

3. Arts. 9,10,17,18 and 19 of the Edict of April 29, 1942. . .shall read as follows:

9. For the issuance to USSR citizens, foreigners and stateless persons resident permanently within the USSR (except for political emigrants) of documents authorizing departure from the USSR (except for diplomatic passports):

(a) to socialist countries for temporary or permanent residence - 30 rubles.

(b) to other countries for temporary or permanent residence - 400 rubles.

19. For certification of withdrawal from USSR citizenship:

(a) to persons resident abroad - 50 rubles.

(b) to persons resident within the USSR and having the intention to depart subsequently for socialist countries - 50 rubles.

(c) to persons living within the USSR and having the intention to depart subsequently for capitalist countries - 500 rubles.

EDICT ON REPAYMENT BY USSR CITIZENS, EMIGRATING PERMANENTLY, OF STATE EXPENDITURES FOR EDUCATION, August 3, 1972. [1972] Vedomosti Verkhovnogo Soveta SSSR, No. 52, item 519.

The Presidium of the USSR Supreme Soviet decrees:

Citizens of the USSR, emigrating permanently abroad (except those emigrating to

THE SOVIET STATE AND ITS CITIZENS 105

socialist countries) shall be required to repay state expenditures for study in higher educational institutions, in graduate schools, in computer programming schools, in adjunct teaching positions, and for receipt of corresponding academic degrees.

The amounts and conditions of repayment of said expenditures shall be determined in accordance with procedures established by the USSR Council of Ministers.

INSTRUCTION ON REPAYMENT OF STATE EXPENDITURES, August 3, 1972. [1972] Vedomosti Verkhovnogo Soveta SSSR, No. 1, item 4.

1. USSR citizens, emigrating permanently abroad, shall repay State expenditures for study in higher educational institutions in the following amounts:

In 1,000 rubles:	Completed course	If studied for: 1 yr.	2 yrs.	3 yrs.	4 yrs.	5 yrs.
Moscow State Univ.	12.2	2.4	4.9	7.3	9.8	-
Other Univs.	6.0	1.2	2.4	3.6	4.8	-
Engineering & Higher Military Schools	7.7	1.5	3.1	4.6	6.1	-
Agr. & Forestry Schs.	5.6	1.1	2.3	3.4	4.5	-
Medical, pharmaceutical, Dental, Physical Training	8.3	1.4	2.8	4.2	5.6	7.0
Economic, Law, Pedagogical, Archival-historical & institutes of culture	4.5	0.9	1.8	2.7	3.6	-
Foreign Language Faculties	6.8	1.4	2.8	4.1	5.5	-
Art Institutes (conservatories, theater, beauxarts, literary)	9.6	1.9	3.8	5.7	7.7	-

2. Additional payments to repay State expenditures shall be made by persons who have studied in graduate schools, in computer programming schools in adjunct teaching positions, and for receipt of corresponding academic degrees.
    (a) from persons studying in graduate schools [etc.] 1,700 rubles for every year of study.
    (b) from persons who have received the academic degree of candidate of science - 5,400 rubles.
    (c) from persons who have received the academic degree of doctor of science (in addition to the sum specified in paragraph "b" of this article) - 7, 200 rubles.

3. [This paragraph established exceptions to the repayment requirement for persons whose health or age permitted them to cease work under Soviet labor law, and also

under certain other conditions such as marriage with a foreigner before August 2, 1972. There is a 70% reduction in payment for emigrants to a developing country and an 80% reduction if the emigrant has married a citizen of a developing country]

CHAPTER VII

Procedural Due Process of Law

To the layman of many lands no obvious criminal should be set free because of violation of procedural requirements at his trial. Procedure is often criticized for standing in the way of justice and protection of society. With such a commonly held view among laymen even in Western countries it is no surprise that the Russian revolutionaries adopted the same attitude when they set about devising their own court procedure. Judges were given no procedural guidance by the first decree on the courts,[1] and even the second decree[2] establishing a district court to clear away the cases held over from pre-revolutionary times instructed the judges to apply the old Imperial code of 1864 only to the extent that it had not been revoked by the new government and did not conflict with the concept of justice of the toiling classes.

Necessity soon compelled departure from the rule of absolute simplicity. By July, 1918 the Commissar of Justice had issued a first instruction on court procedure for the local people's courts relating both to criminal and civil procedure.[3] This was not a long and complex code but a simple guide telling the judge how to facilitate his work, and including such maxims as an instruction to acquaint oneself with the file on the case before the trial to determine whether the accusation is properly formulated and supported by sufficient evidence to merit trial. He was told how to summon parties, and what questions to ask and in what order after the trial opened. He was advised that he should permit the parties to call witnesses, but could exclude those that had information that was not pertinent.

Hostility to formality, even as it was creeping in through the new rules, appeared openly in the paragraph on evidence. The judge was told, "In hearing both criminal and civil cases, the local people's court is not cramped by any formal considerations, and is permitted to admit any evidence it wishes under the circumstances of

---

[1] November 24, 1917. [1917-1918] I Sob. Uzak. RSFSR. No. 4, item 50.
[2] February 15, 1918. *Ibid.*, No. 28, item 366.
[3] July 23, 1918. Ibid., No. 53, item 597.

THE SOVIET STATE AND ITS CITIZENS

the case, and to demand it of persons who have it."

Emphasis in the July rules was upon proceedings before trial, and in this emphasis the draftsmen showed the influence upon them of the old tsarist procedure and of that generally in use in the Romanist systems of Continental Europe. Unlike the common law system, where the full examination of the case begins only at the trial, and where the preliminary proceedings before a grand jury determine only whether the prosecutor has a prima facie case, the civil law system provides for a full review of both sides of the case by an examining magistrate who then prepares a full record and conclusion on the basis of which the indictment is drawn.[4] The trial itself becomes in considerable measure under this system a verification of the record prepared by the examining magistrate, although there can be the introduction of surprises at the trial by able counsel who know how to introduce them without being charged with having concealed evidence during the preliminary investigation. The July rules provided for just such a preliminary investigation of all sides of the case before the indictment was drawn, and authorized the creation of an Investigating Commission to conduct it in those cases where the complexity of the materials prevented the judge from reaching the heart of the matter in a brief examination.

Hostility to formality was further revealed in the very month that the first rules of procedure appeared, for the Third Decree on the Courts of July 20, 1918[5] told the judges that they were never to let formalities stand in the way of a just decision. Review of the work of the local people's courts had been established by the first decree of 1917 to hear appeals by parties sentenced to more than seven days imprisonment or required to pay a judgment of more than three hundred rubles, but reviews were to be of substantial matters, not of procedural violations. To be sure there could not have been appeal from procedural violations at the time of the first decree, for there was as yet no prescribed procedure. Even in the summer of 1918 when such rules were already in effect, the third decree made no provision for reversal if there were violation.

The first general statute on the courts, called the People's Court Act of November 30, 1918[6] enlarged upon the July rules to provide much more detailed procedure, but the judge was still authorized to manage the case. He was not to sit back and wait for the prosecution and defense to bring the materials before him. He had no duty to follow any rules on burden of proof if he thought the peace of the community required his intervention on behalf of a side unable to further its own interests. The draftsmen noted their increasing concern for procedure, however, for they inserted a new clause permitting the setting aside of the decision of a people's court on appeal "in the event that there are found substantial violations or incorrect application of decrees, especially violation of the forms of court procedure, and also

---

[4]See David and DeVries, The French Legal System: An Introduction to Civil Law Systems (New York, 1958).
[5][1917-1918] I Sob. Uzak. RSFSR, No. 52, item 589.
[6]*Ibid.*, No. 85, item 889.

in the event that the investigation has been incomplete." Here was the first specific mention of reversal for procedural violation, and it signalled a change in attitude.

Yet, what the draftsmen wanted could not be guaranteed in practice. Courts continued to search for the substance and to ignore procedural provisions, and they could be almost certain that they would not be reversed on appeal. This was especially true during the period when civil war ravaged the land from 1919 to 1920, for war is not conducive to maintenance of procedural niceties when a presumed enemy stands before the bench. This was admitted in 1922 when the first code of criminal procedure was introduced for discussion. In support of its adoption, one author pleaded, "Now that the objective conditions of civil war are changing, there are no obstacles to realizing in Soviet Russia in the very near future the complete protection of the individual in court."[7] Another author revealed that simplicity had created real problems, for "the means of investigating the case, the technique of court procedure, had been reduced to a primitive explanation of the matter to the persons before the court, which in the majority of cases decided the matter at that very first sitting."[8]

Opposition to procedural reform in 1922 with the introduction of the New Economic Policy was still so great when the subject came before a congress of jurists called to consider it, that the legislature's chairman, Mikhail Kalinin, found it necessary to ridicule those who thought a plea for return to legality meant a return to the bourgeois point of view.[9] He even pointed to English respect for procedure to demonstrate that a court that observed the rules strengthened its position in the eyes of the masses. In short, he was saying that the new Russia could profit from the English view, but he hastened to try to take the cynicism out of his remarks by claiming that what the English bourgeoisie did to delude the masses, the Soviet court would do for the real good of the masses, for it was an instrument of the proletariat with the interests of the masses at heart.

The 1922 code of criminal procedure, and in 1923 the code of civil procedure, and a revised code of criminal procedure established the rules that remained with only slight change to the decade of the 1960s. Part I of the Code of Criminal Procedure established a procedural bill of rights: no one could be deprived of freedom or imprisoned except in the situation defined in the law and in accordance with the procedure established by law. Every judge and prosecutor who found within his jurisdiction some one imprisoned without proper authority or in excess of the period permitted by law was to release that person immediately. A judge or prosecutor who learned that some one within his jurisdiction was imprisoned in an improper place or under improper conditions was to take measures to see that the requirements of the law were adhered to. A preexisting civil judgment in a case was to have effect in a criminal action only to establish an event, and not the guilt of the

---

[7]I. Slavin, Ezh. Sov. Iust., No. 1 (January 1, 1922) pp. 6-7.
[8]See Grig. Ryndziunskii, Ezh. Sov. Iust. No. 7 (February 12, 1922) p. 5.
[9]Ezh. Sov. Iust., No. 5 (January 29, 1922) p. 6.

accused. All court hearings were to be public, except when military, diplomatic, or state secrets required closing of the doors, or in cases involving sex crimes. Even when the case was heard in camera, the sentence had to be announced publicly. An accused individual was to have the right to an interpreter and to receive the indictment and other documents in the trial in his own language. A record was required at all stages of the procedure, including a statement of the substance of any testimony, signed by the witness concerned. Within three days after preparation of the record the parties who participated had the right to file their comments on its completeness and truth, and the court was required to decide the merits of the objection.

The experience of the past was utilized in establishing the procedural stages of a criminal action. Seven stages, reminiscent of those in any court of Continental Europe, were created: (1) initiation of proceedings, (2) short inquest by the militia or other organs of detention, (3) preliminary investigation, (4) transfer to court, (5) trial, (6) judicial review, and (7) execution of the sentence.

Upon federation, the central government enacted in 1924[10] general principles of criminal procedure incorporating the system as it had evolved in the Republics and taken form in their first extensive codes. Here was reaffirmation at the highest level of the major elements that constituted in Soviet eyes the essentials of a fair trial and communism's bid for a place in the hearts of those men the world around who yearned for a society in which only the guilty would be punished for violation of society's rules.

Stalin was to intrude his concept of rule by terror in the years that followed, for after the assassination of his Leningrad communist party chief under mysterious circumstances now hinted to have been planned by Stalin, the codes of the republics were ordered amended in 1934[11] to deny to a "terrorist" an attorney at the trial, the right to be present in person and the right to appeal. In 1937 at the height of Stalin's purges an amendment changed the rules for counterrevolutionary "diversionists and wreckers," so that they were to receive their indictment twenty-four hours before trial, could not appeal, and were to be executed immediately if their plea for mercy was denied.[12] Not until 1956 in revulsion against the excesses of Stalin's time and after Nikita Khrushchev had exposed Stalin's complete disregard for the provisions of the code of criminal procedure were these exceptional decrees repealed.[13] A new campaign of legality was begun, flowering in the adoption of new general principles of criminal procedure, followed by enactment of codes of criminal procedure in the various republics, putting the general principles into a framework familiar to the Soviet jurists who had worked with the first codes.

The selections that follow will suggest the extent to which procedural matters now concern the Soviet jurist and form a part of his concept of socialist legality.

---

[10]October 31, 1924. [1924] I. Sob. Zak. SSSR, No. 24, item 204.
[11]December 1, 1934 [1934] *Ibid.*, No. 64, item 459.
[12]September 14, 1937. [1937] *Ibid.*, No. 61, item 266.
[13]April 19, 1956. [1956] Vedomosti Verkhovnogo Soveta SSSR, No. 9, item 193.

A. *The constitution and codes.*

CONSTITUTION OF THE U.S.S.R., December 5, 1936.
Art. 103. In all Courts cases are tried with the participation of people's assessors, except in cases specially provided for by law.
Art. 110. Judicial proceedings are conducted in the language of the union republic, autonomous republic or autonomous province, persons not knowing this language being guaranteed the opportunity of fully acquainting themselves with the material of the case through an interpreter and likewise the right to use their own language in court.
Art. 111. In all Courts of the U.S.S.R. cases are heard in public, unless otherwise provided for by law, and the accused is guaranteed the right to defense.
Art. 127. Citizens of the U.S.S.R. are guaranteed inviolability of the person. No person may be placed under arrest except by decision of a court or with the sanction of a procurator.

FUNDAMENTALS OF SOVIET CRIMINAL PROCEDURE, December 25, 1958.
[1959] Vedomosti Verkhovnogo Soveta SSSR, No. 1 (933), item 15.
Art. 32. The organ conducting the inquest or the investigator has the right to detain a person suspected of having committed a crime punishable by deprivation of liberty only on one of the following grounds: (1) when the person is caught in the act of committing the crime or immediately after its commission; (2) when eyewitnesses, including also the victim, point directly to a given person as having committed the crime; (3) when, on the person of the suspect, or on his clothing, in his possession or in his dwelling, obvious traces of the crime have been discovered.

When there are other facts giving reason to suspect a person of having committed a crime, he may be detained only in the case of attempted flight, or if he has no permanent place of residence or when his identity has not been established.

A person detained on suspicion of having committed a crime has the right to appeal against the action of the person conducting the inquest, the investigator or the prosecutor, and may make a statement and submit petitions.

In every case of detention of a person suspected of having committed a crime the organ of inquest or the investigator must draw up a statement showing the grounds and reasons for the detention and must report it to the procurator within 24 hours. Within 48 hours from the moment he receives information of the detention of a person the procurator is required either to give his sanction for detention or remand or release the detained persons.

CODE OF CRIMINAL PROCEDURE, R.S.F.S.R., effective January 1, 1961 as amended.
Art. 11. No one may be placed under arrest except on court order or with the sanction of the procurator.

The procurator is required immediately to free every one illegally deprived of freedom or held under guard in excess of the period provided by law or by a court sentence.

Art. 13. Justice in criminal cases is administered only by a court. No one may be found guilty of committing a crime and suffer punishment except by court sentence.

Art. 96. Detention under guard as a means of restraint shall be employed in conformity with the requirements of Art. 11 of the present code only for crimes for which the punishment of deprivation of freedom is provided by law.

For persons accused of committing crimes provided for by Arts. [here follows a list including state crimes, crimes against socialist ownership, serious offenses against life and health, serious offenses against personally owned property, speculation, bribe giving and taking, malicious giving of false incriminating testimony, torture by investigators, issuance knowingly of unjust sentences having grave consequences, resisting arrest with force or threat of force, infringing the life of a policeman, and military crimes] detention under guard as a means of restraint may be employed only on grounds of the danger of the crime. .

Art. 122. Militia agencies have the right to detain a person suspected of having committed a crime for which deprivation of freedom may be prescribed as punishment only in the following circumstances:

(1) when this person was caught in the act of committing the crime or immediately after its commission;

(2) when eyewitnesses, including also the victim, point directly to a given person as having committed the crime;

(3) when on the person of the suspect, or on his clothing, or in his possession or in his dwelling obvious traces of the crime have been discovered;

When there are other facts giving reason to suspect a person of having committed a crime, he may be detained only in the case of attempted flight or if he has no permanent place of residence, or when his identity has not been established.

In every case of detention of a person suspected of having committed a crime, the militia is required to prepare a statement stating the grounds and motives, and within 24 hours, to inform the procurator of it. Within 48 hours after receipt of the notice of detention the procurator must give his sanction to detain under guard or free the detained person.

CRIMINAL CODE, RSFSR, effective January 1, 1961 as amended.

Art. 176. Knowingly moving an innocent person in the direction of criminal responsibility when committed by a person conducting an inquest, by a preliminary investigator or a procurator—shall be punished by deprivation of freedom for a term of up to three years.

The same acts, when linked with accusation of an especially dangerous state or other grave crime or with the falsification of accusatory evidence—shall be punished by deprivation of freedom for a term of from three to ten years.

Art. 177. Issuance by judges knowingly of an unjust sentence, judgment, order or ruling—shall be punished by deprivation of freedom for a term of up to three years.

The same acts, entailing grave consequences—shall be punished by deprivation of freedom for a term of from three to ten years.

Art. 178. A knowingly illegal arrest—shall be punished by deprivation of freedom for a period of up to one year.

Knowingly illegal detention—shall be punished by correctional labor for a term of up to one year or dismissal from office.

Art. 179. Compulsion to give testimony by means of threat or other illegal acts on the part of a person conducting the inquest or preliminary investigation—shall be punished by deprivation of freedom for a term of up to three years.

The same acts if linked with the application of force or with mockery of the person being questioned—shall be punished by deprivation of freedom for a term of from three to ten years.

Art. 180. Knowingly giving false denunciation on the commission of a crime—shall be punished by deprivation of freedom for a term of up to two years or correctional labor for a term of up to one year.

The same acts, linked with accusation of especially dangerous state or other grave crime or with forgery of evidence of guilt, and also if committed with motives of self-interest—shall be punished with deprivation of freedom for a term of from two to seven years.

B. *Arrest*

CASE OF BORTKEVICH, Biulleten' Verkhovnogo Suda SSSR, 1968, No. 4, p. 26.

A.V. Bortkevich was found guilty of refusing to submit to a militia worker, of refusing to present documents and of resisting arrest on October 30, 1966 while intoxicated on one of Kiev's streets. The President of the Supreme Court of the U.S.S.R. filed a protest with the Plenum of his court in which he proposed that proceedings be terminated for want of a crime in Bortkevich's actions. The Plenum finds the protest well founded.

Art. 188-1 of the Criminal Code of the Ukrainian SSR under which B.'s acts fall provides for liability for opposing a militiaman in the performance of his duty of protecting public order. In furtherance of the intent of the article in order to accuse a person of the crime proscribed it is necessary to establish that the guilty person opposed the legal activity of the militia worker (or of a voluntary people's militiaman), who was performing his official duty in keeping with his authority and in pursuance of the established legal procedures.

The record discloses that the actions leading to the charge were committed under the following circumstances. On October 30, 1966 the senior sergeant Bortkevich was discharged from his unit for city leave for a period of up to 24 hours. He spent some time at his Mother's and in the evening, having changed to civilian clothes, went with his brother to be the guest of a friend at a party on the occasion of the latter's call to military service. Since the friend's house was next door, they went out without overcoats or hats.

After 10 p.m. Bortkevich and his brother Arkadii Serediuk went out into the street to return home. Both were intoxicated but they did not violate public order. They met near the house the militia workers Ivanushkin and Zanud'ko who were on patrol duty. Noting B. and S. the militia workers, seeing the men without coats, asked them to show their documents. B. replied he was a soldier and that his documents were in an apartment in the house next door. The militia workers could have verified the documents in the apartment and thus establish identities, but they proposed to B. and S. that they follow them into the next street to the militia office. B. and S. categorically refused to go.

As is evident from the above B. and S. committed no violation of law, and there was no reason to arrest them, using the severest measures. Nevertheless the militia workers and also a militia sergeant who had come up twisted their arms and tried to force them to enter the office. Bortkevich resisted and Serediuk escaped and went home, from which there soon came out their mother, citizeness Serediuk. The latter tried to explain to the militia workers what had happened but they paid her no attention, and with the application of force they put Bortkevich in the militia office.

It is evident from the above that the acts of the militia workers were not called for by considerations of public order. There was no basis for detaining Bortkevich or for charging him with crime.

Under Art. 32 of the Fundamental Principles of Criminal Procedure of the U.S.S.R. and of the Union Republics the arrest of a person suspected of committing a crime is permitted only if he is apprehended in commission of the crime or immediately thereafter, or when eyewitnesses identify him directly as the person who has committed a crime, or when there is found on the person or in the house of the suspect clear evidence of the crime. If such circumstances exist, giving reason to suspect a person, he can be detained only if he has attempted to flee or if he has no place of permanent residence or when his identity has not been established.

None of these reasons for arresting Bortkevich were present, and his identity, as has been said above, could have been established easily.

In ignoring the provisions which have been set forth and in concluding that Bortkevich was guilty, the judicial agencies who heard the case did not take into consideration that the arrest of a man is a very serious measure of compulsion which ought to be applied not arbitrarily but only when sufficient reason is found and in strict conformity to the requirements of socialist legislation. . . .[All court judgments and orders were vacated and proceedings terminated.]

In addition, the Plenum issued a special ruling concerning the incorrect actions of the militia workers and sent it to the Ministry for Protection of Public Order.

C. *The preliminary investigation.*

CASE OF KARAKASHIANTS AND OTHERS, Biulleten' Verkhovnogo Suda SSSR, 1973, No. 2, p. 34

The Judicial Division of the Azerbaidjan SSR's Supreme Court convicted Karakashiants, E A., Mamedov, V.A. and Barkar, A.I. on March 14, 1972 under par. 1 Art. 94 and par. 3 Art. 145 of the Criminal Code of the Azerbaidjan SSR of group assault with intent to rob and of intentional manslaughter. . .

. . .During the preliminary investigation and the trial several violations of procedural law were permitted. Under Art. 151 of the Code of Criminal Procdure of the Azerbaidjan SSR in the order instituting criminal proceedings there must be set forth the crime of which the accused is charged and the time, place and other circumstances of the crime. Under Art. 226 of the Code of Criminal Procedure there must be set forth in the indictment: the facts of of the crime as established by the preliminary investigation, the place, time, means, motives, and consequences of the crime committed by each of the accused, and also the evidence which confirms both the facts constituting the crime and also the investigator's conclusion as to the guilt of each of the accused.

However, the organs of preliminary investigation did not state in the accusation or in the indictment concretely what part Karakashiants and Barkar played in the homicide. In the indictment there is no reference to the evidence confirming Karakashiants and Barkar's guilt in the killing of Goncharenko. This fact limited the possibilities for the accused of exercising their right to defense.

The court thought it proven that Karakashiants in handing the pistol to Mamedov said to him that he should shoot Goncharenko, and that Mamedov complied. Thus, Karakashiants was found guilty of instigating Mamedov to kill. . . but this conclusion of the court was based on the insufficiently verified testimony of the witness Chukhachev. At the trial Chukhachev testified, "When I asked Goncharenko, 'what has happened to you?' "he replied that three unknown fellows had attacked him and that one of the criminals in a white shirt had said to another who had a pistol in his hand, "Shoot, what are you looking at?" And then he shot him in the stomach.

Nevertheless, at the preliminary investigation this witness had given different testimony. Nothing was written in the record of September 17, 1971 of this conversation with Goncharenko, and at the interrogation of January 31, 1972 (the transcript is signed by his own hand), he testified, "When I came to the place of the events, I heard some one talking; I heard a curse and a dispute; then there were some threats, and after that some one cried out, 'Shoot, what are you looking at?' After that there were shots, and the criminals ran off somewhere."

From this testimony of Chukhashev, it follows that he knew nothing of the conversation of the criminals either from the victim, Goncharenko, or from persons who were on the spot. At the trial Chukhashev declared that Goncharenko told him of this conversation at the place of the events, and in the ambulance on the way to the hospital. Moreover, none of the witnesses who were present when Goncharenko was given first aid at the place of the events confirmed this conversation, and the witness Kasynova, who accompanied Goncharenko in the ambulance to the hospital testified that the victim during the trip was unconscious.

In not clarifying the circumstances of Chukhashev's testimony and not comparing the testimony with other evidence gathered in the case, the court reached the conclusion without sufficient basis that Goncharenko was killed by Mamedov upon the instigation of Karakashiants. As to Barkar, nothing was said in the judgment as to which of his acts had to be viewed as proof that he had taken part in the homicide. This violated Art. 334 of the Code of Criminal Procedure. . .

[The case was remanded for a new investigation, after further discussion of the inadequate verification of testimony]

CASE OF KEBULADZE AND OTHERS, Biulleten' Verkhovnogo Suda SSSR, 1971, No. 1, p. 40.

By a ruling of the Military Tribunal of the Pribaltic Military District on August 28, 1970, the criminal case of Kebuladze, G. and K. was remanded for supplementary examination. The tribunal stated the following:

At the trial the accused Kebuladze declared that he spoke Russian poorly; therefore on acquainting himself with the evidence in the record on termination of the preliminary investigation, which had been conducted without an interpreter, he had not understood half of what was there. During the trial the Military Tribunal became convinced that Kebuladze really did speak Russian poorly.

In the record there are the minutes recounting the moment when Kebuladze was informed of the termination of the preliminary investigation and the presentation to him of the materials of the case, in which it was said that Kebuladze had refused the services of an interpreter. Nevertheless, the interpreter Agladze who was called to the trial declared that he had not translated the aforementioned minutes into Georgian, and the accused Kebuladze declares that he did not understand the substance of the minutes. In particular, he did not understand that it stated that his right to acquaint himself with the materials with the participation of a lawyer had been explained. The interpreter Agladze declared at the trial that he did not remember whether the preliminary investigator had explained to the accused, Kebuladze, that he had the right to acquaint himself with the materials in the case with the participation of a lawyer.

Under the circumstances set forth the Pribaltic Military Tribunal found it to be true that the investigating organs had not met the requirements of Arts. 16 and 204 of the Code of Criminal Procedure of the Latvian SSR. The Military Procurator of the Pribaltic Military District filed a protest requesting that the District's Tribunal's ruling be set aside, saying that the Tribunal had taken into consideration in ordering review only the oral declaration of the accused Kebuladze that he had spoken Russian poorly and had not been informed of his right to a lawyer to acquaint himself with the record of the preliminary investigation.

The Procurator argued that, as was evident in the record, the accused had been interrogated by several employees of the Military Procurator's Office, and on every interrogation, after it had been explained to him that he had a right to testify in his native Georgian, he declared that he spoke Russian and needed no interpreter.

When Kebuladze was informed of the termination of the preliminary investigation in the investigation isolation cell where he was being detained, the interpreter Agladze was summoned, but Kebuladze refused his services, as was indicated in the minutes at the time when he acquainted himself with the record. The interpreter confirmed this fact in court.

The accused, G., testified at the trial that he served with Kebuladze in a military unit, and they always spoke only in Russian. After the reading in court of the indictment, written in Russian, Kebuladze said that he understood the indictment but would not plead guilty.

Thus, the conclusion was reached in the Procurator's protest that Kebuladze's frequent refusal of the services of an interpreter, the content of his testimony given in Russian on what occurred and his part in it, and also his notation in Russian on the minutes of the preliminary investigation provide reason to conclude that he speaks Russian and understood all of his rights as they were explained to him.

It was also argued in the protest that Kebuladze at the preliminary investigation had pleaded guilty to the accusation brought against him, and that, therefore, his rejection of the services of an interpreter on acquainting himself with the evidence was explained logically. On receiving the indictment Kebuladze made no objection and did not protest that no lawyer or interpreter had been named for him. The Procurator thought that Kebuladze's lack of desire for a lawyer was also evidenced by the fact that the agreement with the lawyer Malov to defend his interests at the trial was concluded not with the accused himself but with his parents.

[For all of these reasons the Procurator concluded that the Military Tribunal's remand was groundless and should be set aside]

It is evident from the record that in the conduct of the first preliminary investigation it was not determined whether Kebuladze really knew Russian. At the preliminary inquest he said he did, but at the same time he said he did not know the meaning of some words. In view of this, it was necessary to clarify in what measure this reflected on his understanding of what transpired as a whole. However, this was not done, and all of the investigation that followed with Kebuladze was conducted without an interpreter.

[the court then reviewed the evidence in detail]

Under such circumstances the court's conclusion that Kebuladze did not know sufficiently the Russian language and that he needed an interpreter to acquaint himself with all of the materials in the case was well founded. This fact was recognized by the Procurator at the trial for he proposed a recess during the trial for several days so that the indictment might be translated into Georgian, that it be given to Kebuladze, and that he be given an opportunity to acquaint hiself with the record with the participation of a lawyer.

Nevertheless, the Procurator's proposal was not accepted, since if Kebuladze had agreed to it, he would in fact have been denied the right granted to him by Art. 203 of the Code of Criminal Procedure to appeal points raised during the preliminary investigation.

CASE OF BORISOV AND IL'INA, Biulleten' Verkhovnogo Suda SSSR, 1971, No. 2, p. 41.

The Military Tribunal of the Leningrad Garrison issued a special ruling when pronouncing judgment in the case of Borisov and Il'in to the effect that there had been violations of the Code of Criminal Procedure RSFSR during the preliminary investigation. . . .these being that the preliminary investigator in an attempt to eliminate conflicts in the testimony of witnesses, disclosed to them what other witnesses had said after their own testimony had been recorded. [the instances were set forth in detail].

The Military Tribunal rejected the Procurator's protest, holding that the investigator's acts violated Arts. 158, 162 and 163 of the Code of Criminal Procedure, which prescribe the procedure to be used in eye to eye confrontation of witnesses in the event of substantial contradictions.

[the decision was again protested to the Military Division of the USSR Supreme Court on the ground that the interrogations had not commenced with revelation of what other witnesses had said, but that each interrogation had commenced, as required by Art. 158, with a request to the witness tell everthing he knew of the events on which he had been summoned to testify, although there had been supplementary questions after the variances had been disclosed. The USSR Supreme Court's Military Division then declared:]

The law of criminal procedure provides for a specific procedure to be used in the preliminary investigation and places on the investigator the responsibility for conducting the investigation in accordance with the law (Arts. 127, 129 Code of Criminal Procedure). The interrogation of witnesses, like any other activity in the investigation, is conducted in accordance with procedural rules, whose purpose is to obtain truthful and full testimony. The disclosure of testimony as part of the proceedings is provided for by the Code of Criminal Procedure. However, both at the preliminary investigation and at the trial, it is permitted only in exceptional cases, strictly limited by law.

During the preliminary investigation the law provides only for disclosure of the testimony of participants through confrontation eye to eye, when the testimony is already in the record of preceding interrogations and when the contradictions are substantial, and even then only when the testimony is given in eye to eye confrontation and is recorded in the record (par. 3 Art. 163 Code of Criminal Procedure). These limitations are designed to prevent the possibility of one person's testimony influencing another's. For this purpose the law requires the investigator to interrorgate witnesses summoned in the same case separately while other witnesses are absent. Measures must also be taken to prevent the witnesses from associating with each other (par. 1 Art. 158).

The investigator's actions while questioning a witness must have no elements of suggestion. The disclosure to a witness of the testimony of other witnesses may encourage him to trim his replies to fit those already entered in the case. The impermissibility of such action springs from the requirement in the law that the interrogation of a witness must commence with his account of the events known to him (par. 5, Art. 158). Only after this is the investigator permitted to pose questions to the witness. But they must be formulated and presented in such a way that the witness cannot extract from them any information to guide his own answer. For this reason the law prohibits leading questions (Arts. 158, 163).

In view of the circumstances of this case, it follows that the conclusion in the special ruling that the disclosure of testimony of other persons is equivalent to asking leading questions must be held to be correct. For the reasons indicated it is impossible to agree with the protest's argument that the law does not prohibit disclosure by the investigator during his investigation of the testimony of other persons interrogated in the case. That position is contrary to law.

D. *Expert opinion.*

CASE OF KAFAROV, Biulleten' Verkhovnogo Suda SSSR, 1971, No. 5, p. 34.

. . .To support its conclusion that Rzaev's death resulted from asphyxiation caused by strangling with hands the court relied on the conclusion of a forensic-medical expert, given during the preliminary investigation and also on the testimony of B. Mamedov, Kurban, Gabibov, Aliev and G. Mamedov, and others. This conclusion of the court cannot be accepted as well founded. None of the witnesses questioned at the trial confirmed that Kafarov, as was stated in the judgment, "grabbed Rzaev by the throat with both hands and choked him to death." Moreover, a number of eyewitnesses on whom the court relied in the judgment gave testimony at the trial, putting in serious doubt the court's conclusion as to the reason for Rzaev's death.

The eye-witness B. Mamedov testified in court, "After Kafarov choked Tair, the latter rose and moved off about 10-12 meters, tottered and fell." The witness Gabibov testified, "Tair, after getting up, began to fall, tottered, and then fell." The witness Kurban gave the court testimony which is reproduced in the judgment, "Kafarov threw Tair Rzaev to the ground, began to choke him. Rzaev resisted. The teacher Babib (Mamedov) rushed over with a grape vine and hit Kafirov several times. Rzaev rose, went off from 5 to 6 meters, fell to the ground and never rose again."

The court gave no evaluation in the judgment of the testimony, even though it conflicted with the conclusions of the forensic-medical expert as to the cause of Rzaev's death. Moreover, the court paid no attention to the testimony of the witness B. Mamedov and Gabibov to the fact that when they took Rzaev on a motorcycle to the village hospital the doctor was able to feel the victim's pulse and gave an injection, after which Rzaev was taken in an ambulance to the city hospital in Sumgait, where the doctor reported on arrival that it was already too late.

In spite of this conflicting testimony the court not only did not demand a new expert examination but even did not interrogate the doctors who examined Rzaev at the village and city hospitals; did not summon and did not interrogate the forensic-medical expert to determine whether he would reaffirm his conclusion on taking into account the circumstances set forth above. The presentation of a second forensic-medical expert report of examination at the trial was necessary also because the conclusion given at the preliminary investigation by the expert suffers from serious inadequacies. As is evident from the conclusion, the autopsy of Rzaev was incomplete in particular; the skull was not opened, although its condition had substantial importance in establishing the reasons for death.

In the conclusion it was stated that in Rzaev's autopsy the sublingual bone and cartilage of the throat were found to be unbroken. The expert reached his conclusion that Rzaev's death occurred because of strangulation with hands on the basis of discovery during examination of a haemmorrhage at the upper rear of the soft tissues of the neck, organs which are damaged also when there is slight pleurasy. On a new forensic-medial examination it must be clarified whether these indications are characteristic of strangulation. . .

In agreeing with the protest the Judicial Division quashed the judgment as it relates to Kafarov and remanded the case for new examination from the stage of the trial.

E. *Presumption of innocence.*

M. Baliev and V. Savitskii, LEGALITY AND JUSTICE. Izvestiia, September 19, 1975. p. 5.

. . .Among the most important democratic principles of Soviet criminal procedure is the presumption of innocence and the right of the accused to a lawyer. The practical importance of the presumption of innocence is in the fact that since the accused is presumed to be not guilty, in order to convict and punish him there is required uncontested, undoubted evidence. If such does not exist, the accused must be acquitted. This is so regardless of whether he is able or unable to present evidence of his innocence.

Those who have followed the discussion that has continued for so many years around the presumption of innocence know how many difficulties it has been necessary to overcome to preserve in our criminal procedure this priceless idea, filled with deep legal and political meaning. M. S. Strogovich has performed enormous service to this end. In all of his works he has clearly enunciated the leit motif: struggle with criminality with every means available, but never transgress the law one iota; accuse the guilty decisively, but do not fall into an accusatory bias. He has always stood for clarity and simplicity of procedural form, but he has never compromised with attempts to bring about procedural vulgarization.

CASE OF SHESTOPEROV, Biulleten' Verkhovnogo Suda SSSR, 1970, No. 1, p. 35.

...Shestoperov was found guilty of raping on January 8, 1965 the minor girl D., born August 12, 1955. The court found that Shestoperov's act was committed in the following circumstances:

On the evening of January 8 Shestoperov entered the yard of the house where D. lived and tricked her into going into the fields, where he raped her.

The court stated in the judgment that Shestoperov's guilt was confirmed by the subsequent testimony of the victim, who in her first statement and during subsequent interrogations at the preliminary investigation and at the trial declared that a man whom she remembered well had raped her, and that Shestoperov was that very man. In describing the appearance and clothes of the man, she said she had seen him in her courtyard.

The court referred in the judgment to the testimony of defendant's parents and an employee in the children's department of the militia, Akhvishvili, to the effect that they had taken D. after the event to public places, parks, stadiums, movie houses, and had shown her suspicious men and a large number of photographs, but the victim declared that she remembered the rapist well and he was not among the people shown to her.

A year and 2 months later D., while playing in the courtyard of her home with a boy, saw Shestoperov walking by and said to the boy that he was the uncle who "hurt her." The children told the parents, and they reported to the militia, and Shestoperov was arrested. He categorically denied the charge, saying the girl might have erred and taken him for some one else, especially since, at the time when the crime was committed according to the girl's testimony he did not wear glasses nor the cap which he was wearing when arrested. Further, he had accompanied Khitsishvili to the village Asoreti on January 8.

The trial court found Shestoperov's explanation not in accordance with the facts and refuted by the testimony of other witnesses [the contradictions were then stated].

The judgment against Shetoperov must be quashed and the case terminated for the following reasons:

Shestoperov pleaded innocent at both the preliminary investigation and the trial. He declared that D., in identifying him in the street, had made a mistake...

The basis for accusing Shestoperov...is solely the testimony of the minor victim to the effect that on March 24 she saw Shestoperov and recognized him as the criminal who had raped her more than a year earlier. The identification of Shestoperov by the victim raises doubts as to its truth. Shestoperov's identification by the victim violated the rules of Arts. 162-164 of the Code of Criminal Procedure of the Georgian SSR: He was placed before the victim alone and not in a group as the law requires...

It must also be kept in mind that the victim was nine and a half years old at the time of the rape. The events occurred after 7 P.M. when it was already dark. The 9 year old girl, seeing the criminal for a short time and as a rapist, who according to her own testimony blindfolded her, beat her and hurt her, naturally was frightened and shaken by what happened to her.

From the record it is evident that D. from the age of 4 had suffered from brain disease, meningo-encephalitis, as a result of which she had progressively lost her hearing and suffered an impediment in her speech. . .The forensic expert psychiatrist declared that her testimony might be taken into consideration like the testimony of other children, that is, taking into consideration the mental condition of those of her age. However, it was necessary to take into consideration what was evident from the expert-psychiatrist's conclusion, that after what happened to her D. became nervous, irritable, her sleep was confused, she had nighmares.

[the court then set forth other reasons to doubt D's testimony]

Taking what has been said above into consideration, and bearing in mind that under Art. 43 of the Fundamental Principles of Criminal Procedure. . .a conviction cannot be based on conjecture and that all doubts concerning proof of guilt, if it is impossible to resolve them, must be interpreted in favor of the accused, the Judicial Division finds that the testimony of the minor victim, given a year and two months after having been raped and her identification of the rapist as Shestoperov, who happened to be passing by, being unsupported by any other objective evidence, cannot constitute a foundation for an accusatory judgment against Shestoperov who categorically denied his guilt.

[The judgment was set aside, and the prosecution terminated for lack of proof of crime].

F. *The right to counsel.*

CASE OF KONDRATEV, Biulleten' Verkhovnogo Suda SSSR, 1973, No. 3, p. 25.

Kondratev, R.G. was convicted of raping K., born on June 5, 1954 (a minor) by the Judicial Division of the Esthonian SSR Supreme Court on May 26, 1971.

[The case was remanded by the Judicial Division for Criminal Cases of the USSR for retrial after review on a protest. Violation of Art. 22 of the Fundamental Principles of Criminal Procedure of the USSR and the union republics, and par. 5, part 1, Art. 38 of the Esthonian SSR Code of Criminal Procedure was found for the following reasons]

At the trial the lawyer Villik was named to participate as Kondratev's lawyer. Kondratev declared to the court that he refused to be represented by this lawyer because "the lawyer's position did not correspond to his position." The court, nevertheless, did not release the lawyer from participation in the case, motivating its refusal by saying that "the sanctions of the article under which Kondratev was prosecuted provided for the death penalty."

During the trial after the interrogation of the victim, Kondratev again declared his refusal to have this lawyer. The lawyer Villik also asked to be relieved from further participation in the proceedings, since "his point of view did in fact differ." Only after that did the court, after consultation by the judges among themselves while on the bench, release the lawyer Villik, and the proceedings continued without the presence of a lawyer.

It must be noted that Kondratev did not refuse a lawyer, but he refused to permit the lawyer Villik to perform his duties. The lawyer also refused to defend Kondratev. In permitting the trial to continue without a lawyer under these conditions, the court violated Art. 35 of the Esthonian SSR Code of Criminal Procedure on the right of an accused to a lawyer. There also participated in the case both public and state accusers, who requested that the exceptional penalty be applied to the prisoner, and Kondratev did not plead guilty.

CASE OF SHUMKO, CHERKASOV, FURMANOV, MARGARITTO, Biulleten' Verkhovnogo Suda RSFSR, 1976, No. 2 p. 9.

The minors Shumko, Cherkasov, Furmanov, Margaritto were convicted by the Magadan Provincial Court unders pars. 'b', 'g', 'z' of Art. 102 of the Criminal Code RSFSR of intentional homicide against Pukhov and Bormotin. The crime was inspired by hooligan tendencies and committed with extreme brutality.

The Judicial Division for Criminal Cases of the RSFSR Supreme Court quashed the judgment on October 3, 1975 after review on cassation and remanded for retrial for the following reasons:

The investigating organs and the court permitted violation of the accused's right to a lawyer. Under Art. 47 of the Code of Criminal Procedure the same person may not be the lawyer for two accused persons, if the interests of one of them conflict with the interests of another. As is evidenced from the record Shumko denied at the preliminary investigation that he had tramped on the victim. However, the accused Margaritto and Furmanov at the interrogation during the preliminary investigation accused him of this.

In view of the conflict of testimony between Shumko and Margaritto there was a confontation eye to eye. In the interrogation as an accused person Margaritto responded to the lawyer's question, "Who was most active in committing the crime?" by saying that Shumko was, but Shumko in his testimony denied it.

In spite of such conflict in the interests of these accused minors, their defense at the preliminary investigation was carried on by a single lawyer, Sh. The court in spite of par. 5, Art. 222 of the Code of Criminal Procedure, paid no attention to the violation of the right to a lawyer but transferred the case to court and set a day for trial.

The court itself violated the right of the accused Furmanov to a lawyer. As is evident from the record of the trial, after the announcement to those present of the names of the judges, the accused Furmanov refused the lawyer Sh. as his counsel. Instead of asking the accused whether he would like to invite another lawyer and, if so, which one, the court retired to chambers to discuss Furmanov's declaration and issued a ruling denying Furmanov's objection. It should be noted that the current

Code of Criminal Procedure RSFSR has no provision concerning objection to a lawyer. Therefore, the court had to examine the accused Furmanov's declaration in accordance with the procedure provided by Art. 50 of the Code of Criminal Procedure, as a rejection of defense, which it was not.

It is evident from the record of the trial that the lawyer Sh. asked not one question during the trial, not even of Furmanov whom he was defending. He did not even file an appeal, even though the minor, Furmanov, appealed the judgment. Under such circumstances it must be recognized that Furmanov was in fact deprived of defense, which under Art. 345 of the Code of Criminal Procedure is a substantial violation of the Code of Criminal Procedure, requiring quashing of the judgment.

CASE OF GULOV, Biulleten' Verkhovnogo Suda SSSR, 1972, No. 1, p. 25.

. . .Gulov did not plead guilty [to theft of cooperative property] After the case went to court Gulov. . .asked that he be given the opportunity through his relative Sadullaev to invite a lawyer. There is no evidence in the record of what the court decided in response to this request, but on the first day of the trial, September 16, 1970, Gulov did not object to participation in the case of the lawyer Sulaimanov, who was named to defend him but without knowledge of the case. The following day, he rejected the services of this lawyer and requested the court to replace him, naming three lawyers, any one of whom he would like to have as counsel.

It is stated in the record of the trial that on September 18, 1970, having heard with regard to Gulov's request the opinion of the procurator and the lawyer participating in the case, the court rejected without giving reaons Gulov's request. . .

It must be noted that the existing criminal procedure (Art. 50 Code of Criminal Procedure Tadjik SSR) provides for a personal invitation of counsel by an accused person and also of other persons at the request of or with the consent of the accused person. Therefore the court had no right to prevent Gulov from inviting counsel of his choice on the ground that there was already in the case a lawyer named by the court. In deciding the question the court did not take into consideration that under par. 3 Art. 51 of the Tadjik SSR Code of Criminal Procedure, the court is required to assure the presence of a lawyer in the case only when none is called by the accused himself, or by his legal representative or by other persons commissioned to do so. . . .

[The case was remanded for retrial in the same court but with a different bench of judges]

CASE OF KUDRIAVTSEV, Biulleten' Verkhovnogo Suda RSFSR, 1970, No. 5, p. 9.

. . .After the judgment had been quashed by the Supreme Court by way of supervision, the trial court in considering the case a second time did not inform in sufficient time the Presidium of the College of Lawyers of the day of the hearing, and thus did not fulfill the requirements of Art. 238 of the Code of Criminal Procedure RSFSR. Consequently, a lawyer was named to defend Kudriavtsev only on the day of the hearing. He needed, moreover, some time to travel to the court house, and he was deprived of any opportunity to familiarize himself with the record in any detail. Any opportunity to present additional evidence in accordance with the requirements of Art. 236 of the Code of Criminal Procedure was denied.

During the consideration of the case by the District People's Court in its preparatory session Kudriavtsev requested as his lawyer the lawyer who had defended his interests during the proceedings by way of supervision, and he expressed lack of confidence in the lawyer named by the court for the retrial. The court refused to satisfy Kudriavtsev's request on the ground that it lacked sufficient basis.

The circumstances indicate that the participation of the lawyer named by the court was purely formal in character, and Kudriavtsev was in fact deprived of the right to counsel. This violation of the criminal procedural law is substantial, and requires without question the quashing of the judgment.

G. *Fair trial*.

CASE OF SOLDATENKOV, Biulleten' Verkhovnogo Suda RSFSR, 1971, No. 5, p. 10.

. . .Soldatenkov was accused of raping the minor I., taking advantage of her helpless condition, and thereafter he systematically had sexual intercourse with her under conditions of compulsion.

The Judicial Division for Criminal Cases of the Bashkir ASSR Supreme Court remanded the case for supplementary investigation of the victim's testimony at the trial that in addition to Soldatenkov, one Baev, whom she identified in court, had tried to commit a sexual act with her during the summer of 1968 at the children's camp.

Under Art. 26 of the Code of Criminal Procedure RSFSR there may be joined in a single proceeding only charges against several persons of complicity in the commission of one or of several crimes; charges against a single person for commission of several crimes, and also charges of concealment of said crimes or failure to report them even when the failure to report was not promised to the actor in advance.

In this case, as the record indicates, the question of Baev's guilt is irrelevant to the crime charged against Soldatenkov. Since Baev was not an accomplice to the crime charged against Soldatenkov, the court had no reason to remand the case for supplementary investigation. Investigation of Baev may, and if grounds are found, must be conducted by the investigating organs independently of the trial of the case against Soldatenkov.

CASE OF GAPOV, Biullenetn' Verkhovnogo Suda RSFSR, 1969, No. 2, p. 27.

. . .Under Art. 42 of the Fundamental Principles of Court Procedure of the USSR and of the union republics, investigation of a case in court shall occur only with regard to the accused and only with relation to the accusation for which he was brought to court. A change in the accusation at the trial is permitted only if it does not worsen the prisoner's situation. In the present case these requirements were not met.

In the decree instigating proceedings against Gapov it was charged that "On June 21, 1958 under authorization No. 119 and invoice No. 1014 he received from the Shakhrizausk State Farm Vineyard No. 2 190.60 decaliters of pure alcohol (or 200 decaliters of spirits by volume) of which he stole 92.91 decaliters of a value of 107,032 rubles 32 kopecks (in pre-revaluation rubles)." In the indictment the same charge was made.

In the judgment it was held that "On June 21, 1958 Gapov received authorization No. 119 to obtain from the Sh. State Farm vineyard No. 2 for delivery to Kuliabsk State Farm Vineyard No. 4 800 decaliters of spirits. On the basis of this authorization on June 21, 1958 the bookkeeping office of State Farm Vineyard No. 2 issued invoice No. 1014 of June 21 for 800 decaliters of spirits. Gapov received on this invoice on the same day from the manager of the warehouse, Grigoli, 200 decaliters of spirits by volume or 190.60 decaliters of pure alcohol. With Grigoli's complicity Gapov poured the spirits into metal containers which Grigoli had in the warehouse and took them at night from the warehouse and with the help of a person not identified at the investigation put them on truck No. GAZ 09-76, driven by Levitskii, and delivered the stolen wine to the house of the prisoner Vangiev."

...Thus the court found that Gapov had stolen 200 decaliters.

Consequently, the court in finding Gapov guilty of stealing 200 decaliters of spirits went beyond the limits charged in the indictment, even though it gave judgment against him for 107,032 rubles, which was the sum to be recovered according to the indictment. On the basis of the above the Judicial Division, being guided by Art. 11 of the Statute on the Supreme Court of the USSR decreed:

The judgment of the Judicial Division for Criminal Cases of the Tadjik SSR Supreme Court with regard to Gapov, I.A., is altered to exclude from the judgment the statement that 200 decaliters was stolen by him, and he is considered convicted of misappropriating 92.91 decaliters of spirits with a value of 10,703 rubles (at the new rates for rubles).

CASE OF KRAVTSEVICH, Biulleten' Verkhovnogo Suda RSFSR, 1971, No. 4, p. 15.

Kravtsevich was convicted under par. 3 Art. 117 of the Criminal Code RSFSR by judgment of the Vladimir Provincial Court and sentenced to 15 years deprivation of freedom in a correctional labor colony of strict regime. Kravtsevich was convicted of raping A. under the following circumstances:

After being released from a place of imprisonment, he went to the City of Karabanovo in Vladimir Province, where he took up residence in A.'s apartment. On February 26, 1970 Kravtsevich came home late at night in a drunken condition, and taking advantage of the absence of others forcefully undressed A., threw her on the bed, and raped her.

Kravtsevich appealed, requesting that the judgment be quashed since the court heard the case in his absence and found him guilty of rape without sufficient reason. The Judicial Division for Criminal Cases of the RSFSR Supreme Court by its ruling of November 5, 1970 quashed the judgment for the following reasons:

As is evident from the record Kravtsevich refused to appear at the trial, giving as his reason that a number of witnesses had not been questioned [at the preliminary investigation]. The court, taking no measures to secure the prisoner's appearance, heard the case in his absence, which under the circumstances was a serious violation of criminal procedural law, requiring under par. 3 Art. 345 of the Code of Criminal Procedure RSFSR unconditional quashing of the judgment.

Under Art. 246 of the Code of Criminal Procedure RSFSR examination of a case in the absence of the prisoner may be permitted only in two cases: (a) when he is beyond the frontiers of the USSR and refuses to appear in court, and (b) if he may not be sentenced for the crime charged to deprivation of freedom, and he asks that the investigation proceed in his absence.

In this case Kravtsevich, as is evident from the record, was held under guard in the investigation isolation cell, and, therefore, the court had the opportunity to make him appear in court, but it did not do so. Under these circumstances the hearing in the absence of the prisoner was contrary to law and, therefore, the accusatory judgment must be quashed. . .

CASE OF OSKANOV, Biulleten' Verkhovnogo Suda RSFSR, 1970, No. 3, p. 9.

. . .In accordance with Art. 301 of the Code of Criminal Procedure RSFSR a court is to base its judgment only on evidence examined at the trial. In spite of this requirement the court in the case of Oskanov based its judgment on the testimony of witnesses and of the victim given by them during the stage of preliminary investigation. These persons were not brought to court in spite of the fact that at the trial it was thought necessary to interrogate the witnesses Khantygova, Khantygov, and Murzabekov.

In spite of this, these witnesses were not interrogated in court. The court, however, in support of its finding of guilt of Osman Oskanov, referred to the testimony they gave at the preliminary investigation and trial of Mohamed Oskanov, his son.

Under Art. 286 of the Code of Criminal Procedure RSFSR, disclosure at the trial of testimony given by a witness during the preliminary investigation may take place in the absence of the witness for reasons preventing his appearance at the trial, or if the said witness evades the court. Otherwise, the court must bring a witness into court and question him.

In the trial of Osman Oskanov, who pleaded not guilty to beating Khantygov and Mostoev, he declared that he went on June 12 in the morning to the hamlet of Kalinin and spent the night at Barkinkhoev's and on June 13 learned of the homicide of Mostoev. Barkinkhoev confirmed these circumstances at the trial.

Batyr Oskanov, son of the prisoner, and the witness Kostoev were also questioned and they told of the circumstances under which Batyr Oskanov was beaten by Khantygov and Mostaev.

[This was the event that stimulated the father and another son to fight with Mostoev, during which he was killed].

Thus, the charge against Oskanov is not confirmed by the examination at the trial. Persons named in the indictment were not interrogated in court, although their testimony has substantial importance to a correct decision in the case.

[The case was remanded for retrial from the stage of preliminary investigation]

CASE OF ORTENBERG, Sotsialisticheskaia zakonnost', 1968, No. 3, p. 83.

Ortenberg was found guilty of stealing oil worth 143,254 rubles from the varnish and paint shop of the Odessa factory for the outfitting of retail shops.

The First Deputy Procurator General of the U.S.S.R. filed a protest with the Presidium of the Odessa Provincial Court stating that the indictment had been approved by N. Meshkev, acting procurator of the Odessa province, and the appeal had been reviewed by his wife, serving at the time as a member of the provincial court. This violated Art. 54 of the Code of Criminal Procedure of the Ukrainian SSR, and without question is cause for vacating the court's judgment.

H. *Review by a court.*

CASE OF VYSOKIKH, Biulleten' Verkhovnogo Suda RSFSR, 1972, No. 12, p. 8.

Vysokikh was convicted under par. 3, Art. 92 of the Criminal Code RSFSR [systematic theft of state property by an official, causing severe loss] by judgment of the Krivosheinsk District people's court of Tomsk Province on July 16, 1971 and sentenced to 5 years deprivation of freedom with confiscation of property and deprivation of the right to occupy a position related to the distribution of money and materials of value. The judgment was affirmed by the Judicial Division for Criminal Cases of the Tomsk Provincial Court. . .

The Presidium of the Tomsk Provincial Court on March 29, 1972 altered the judgment and affirmance, reclassifying Vysokikh's acts under par. 2, Art. 92 [systematic theft by official without severe loss] but left the rest of the judgment and affirmance in force.

The Judicial Division for Criminal Cases of the RSFSR Supreme Court, on reviewing the case on the protest of the Deputy President of the RSFSR Supreme Court against the supplementary punishment [confiscating property and forbidding future employment of the same type], satisfied the protest and said the following:

Vysokikh was found guilty of maliciously using her official position when she was President of the Kozhevnikov District Council of the All-Russian Voluntary Fireman's Society to misappropriate systematically the Association's funds to the total amount of 2,065 rubles. Her guilt was proven, not only by her own confession, but by the auditing reports, the testimony of witnesses, by documents and by other evidence.

Her acts were properly reclassified by the court under par. 2, Art. 92 of the

Criminal Code because of the amount appropriated. Nevertheless, the Presidium of the Provincial Court, in changing the classification of Vysokikh's acts did not discuss the punishment. The supplementary measures of punishment applied by the court to Vysokikh must be excluded from the judgment and subsequent court decisions since they were established by the court in violation of Art. 353 of the Code of Criminal Procedure RSFSR [a case shall be considered in the usual manner after the vacating of an original judgment].

As is evident from the record, the first judgment of the people's court with respect to Vysokikh [prior to the judgment of July 16, 1971 here under review], under which she was convicted of violating par. 3, Art. 92 of the Criminal Code RSFSR and sentenced to deprivation of freedom without application of supplementary measures of punishment [confiscation of property, etc.] had been quashed by the Provincial Court on appeal by the lawyer defending the convicted person's interests because of violation of Art. 254 Code of Criminal Procedure [accused to be examined only on the basis of the accusation on which he has been brought to trial] and the decree of the RSFSR Supreme Court's Plenum "On the judicial sentence."

On the second hearing of the case [the July 16, 1971 judgment here under review] the court had no right to increase the measure of punishment of Vysokikh. The Presidium of the Provincial Court in reclassifying Vysokikh's crime under par. 2, Art. 92, did not exclude from the judgment the order to confiscate property, even though this supplementary measure of punishment was not provided for as a sanction under par. 2, Art. 92, nor did it exclude the punishment of deprivation of the right to occupy a position having property responsibilities, since they had not been included in the first judgment [the one prior to July 16, 1971].

Taking the aforementioned into consideration, the Judicial Divison for Criminal Cases of the RSFSR Supreme Court, by its decree of August 22, 1972 altered the judgment of the people's court and the decision and decree of the Presidium of the Provincial Court, excluding from the judgment and the subsequent court decisions the order to confiscate property and the supplementary measure of punishment in the form of deprivation of the right to occupy a position related to the distribution of money and materials of value. The rest of the judgment, the decision and the decree were left in force by the Presidium.

CASE OF ISHIGENOV AND LABUTIN, Biulleten' Verkhovnogo Suda RSFSR, 1972, No. 8, p. 13.

Ishigenov and Labutin were convicted on March 27, 1972 under pars. 'b' and 'z', Art. 102 of the Criminal Code RSFSR to 15 and 10 years' deprivation of freedom respectively. They were found guilty of intentional homicide of Suvorov and Zamiatin while behaving in a hooligan manner.

In his cassational appeal the lawyer declared that the judgment regarding Labutin violated Art. 353 of the Code of Criminal Procedure RSFSR [see case of Vysokikh above], since the first judgment [October 29, 1970] under which Labutin was convicted of violating par. 3, Art. 206 of the Criminal Code RSFSR had been quashed, not on the protest of the Procurator and not on complaint of the victim, but on discovery of new circumstances evidencing commission of a more serious crime than had been established in the case.

The Judicial Chamber for Criminal Cases of the RSFSR Supreme Court, reviewing the case on cassation, left the judgment of March 27, 1972 in force for the following reason:

It is evident from the record that Labutin was first convicted of hooliganism and sentenced by the judgment of October 29, 1970 under par. 3, Art. 206 of the Criminal Code RSFSR to 6 years' deprivation of freedom [the case was later sent back by the Supreme Court's Judicial Division for Criminal Cases for a more penetrating examination of the circumstances of the homicide, and on that examination the investigating organs established that Labutin aided in the homicide, and at a subsequent trial he was convicted and sentenced to the more severe sentence permitted for that offense. When the case was reviewed on the lawyer's appeal, the court said:]

Since on a new investigation of the case after the quashing of the judgment it was established that there were circumstances indicating that Labutin had committed not hooliganism but had participated in an intentional homicide, i.e. in a more serious crime, on the new trial in the trial court, the court properly applied Art. 353 of the Code of Criminal Procedure on increasing the sentence on finding a more serious crime. Thus no violation of law was permitted on rehearing of Labutin's case.

I. *The extra-legal review function of the press.*

M. Maliakov, Deputy Procurator General of the U.S.S.R., GUARDING THE LAW, Literaturnaia Gazeta, April 21, 1976, p. 12.

Some time ago the newspaper "Literaturnaia Gazeta" published an article by its correspondent to the effect that in Alma Ata a group of youths had been arrested for hooliganism by the organs of the Procurator, but without sufficient reason. The Procurator's Office of the USSR reacted operationally to the signal. It was established by the Procurator that the guilt of the arrested persons was not substantiated, and they were released. On the Procuracy's order the persons guilty of poor quality investigation of the case were punished. . .

Can one draw from this case or any other like it the far-reaching conclusions drawn by an Italian newspaper out of ignorance. . .that "Literaturnaia Gazeta took its protest (?!) directly to the Procurator's Office of the USSR, which recognized the published account to be substantially correct." Well, what follows from this? It is only the most normal democratic phenomenon when the Procurator's Office recognizes the press's publication to be correct. But, here is the conclusion of the Italian newspaper: "They say that the Soviet press often publishes articles against individual cases of abuse of power, but it is usually a matter of criticism of various faults of enterprises or scientific research institutes, or an article written to improve the living conditions. A frontal conflict between the press and the militia or judicial organs is of new and deserved importance."

Where does the author find a frontal conflict? How should the Procuracy react to fair criticism? With silence? Resting on the honor of the uniform? Or honestly and without regard to persons protect the law, performing its most important functions conferred on it by the USSR Constitution? . . .

In December, 1975, in the newspaper Pravda there was published an article under the title, "They sewed with white thread." The article cast doubt on the ruling of the people's court in the case of a henhouse keeper accused of stealing chicken feed. The newspaper's signal was immediately investigated, the facts confirmed, and the unfounded ruling set aside on the Procurator's protest. The people's court judge was punished by the disciplinary committee for carelessly investigating the case. . .

In recent times the Soviet press has been taking a larger part in preventing violations of law. On the pages of the newspapers and magazines there are ever more frequently being published articles, notes, feulletons, in which are disclosed the circumstances facilitating commission of crimes and other violations of law. The tenor and significance of these articles is to mobilize public opinion in the struggle with similar situations and the reasons why they occur. Such materials arouse a wide response. . . The XXV Congress of the Communist Party of the Soviet Union gave great attention to the further strengthening and development of socialist democracy and to making our legislation effective; to strengthening socialist law and order. . .

J. *Modernization of correctional procedures.*

CASE OF DIATLOV, Biulleten' Verkhovnogo Suda RSFSR, 1974, No. 3, p. 12.

Diatlov was convicted on February 15, 1972 under Art. 186 of the Criminal Code RSFSR and sentenced to one year's deprivation of freedom for escape from a curative labor prophylactorium, with application to him of a compulsory cure for alcoholism on the basis of Art. 62 of the Criminal Code RSFSR.

On October 6, 1972 the medical commission of the establishment in which Diatlov was undergoing his compulsory cure issued its conclusion that after he had served his term, his care should be continued in an establishment of special curative and labor regime. On the basis of this conclusion the Solikam City people's court of Perm Province on October 30, 1972 issued a decree extending Diatlov's cure after completion of his term of compulsory cure for alcoholism in a curative-labor prophylactorium for one year.

On the protest of the Procurator of Perm Province, the Presidium of the Provincial Court changed the decree, excluding from it the extension of Diatlov's compulsory cure for the specific period of one year. The RSFSR Deputy Procurator General filed a protest in the Judicial Division for Criminal Cases of the RSFSR Supreme Court, asking that the decree of the Provincial Court be quashed on the ground that under Art. 62 of the Criminal Code and Art. 58 of the RSFSR Correctional Labor Code, the court must, in prolonging a period of compulsory cure, state the concrete period for which the compulsory cure has been extended.

The Judicial Division. .in its decision of November 27, 1973 refused to satisfy the protest, stating that when a crime has been committed by an alcoholic and a compulsory cure has been ordered for him under Art. 62 of the Criminal Code, and also when the term of the compulsory cure has been extended after release of such a person from a place of deprivation of freedom, the court does not set a concrete period of compulsory cure.

On extending the compulsory cure for alcoholism under Art. 62 of the Criminal Code persons undergo the cure in institutions with special curative and labor regimes. The Solikam City people's court extended Diatlov's compulsory cure in a curative-labor prophylactorium, and this was incorrect, since persons are sent for cure in a curative-labor prophylactorium under the procedure established by the edict of the Presidium of the RSFSR Supreme Soviet of April 8, 1967 and not under the procedure established by Art. 62 of the Criminal Code

[The Judicial Division then changed this part of the ruling of the people's court].

K. *Procedural problems of amnesty.*

CASE OF BALASHOVA, Biulleten' Verkhovnogo Suda RSFSR, 1968, No. 6, p. 18.

The criminal prosecution of Balashova was terminated by ruling of the preliminary sitting of the October District people's court of Rostov-on-Don on the basis of par. 'b' Art. 2 of the Edict of the Presidium of the USSR Supreme Soviet of October 31, 1967 "On amnesty in connection with the 50th anniversary of the Great October Socialist Revolution." The President of the Rostov Provincial Court filed a protest with the Presidium of the Court, in which he proposed revocation of the ruling of the People's court.

Having acquainted itself with the case, the Presidium of the Rostov Provincial Court stated:

Balashova was accused under par. 1 Art. 89 of the Criminal Code RSFSR of stealing systematically when she was working as a nurse in the Children's Hospital No. 3 children's linen and bedclothes belonging to the hospital and having a value in excess of 500 rubles.

As is evident from the record Balashova pleaded guilty in part, but because of the amnesty she was not called to the review of the case in the preliminary sitting; she was not notified of the day of the sitting, nor was her consent to termination of the proceedings ascertained. Balashova informed the court of her categorical opposition to termination of the case and asked that it be heard on the merits with her participation.

The court had no right to terminate proceedings under the Edict on Amnesty, not having received the accused's consent. In view of the aforesaid, the Presidium of the Rostov Provincial Court in its decree of February 21, 1968 revoked the court's ruling and remanded the case for retrial beginning with the stage of transfer to court.

CHAPTER VIII

Due Process for Civil Parties

For the Russian revolutionaries of 1917 tsarist civil procedure had provided the principal avenue of what they called their "exploitation." Through the civil suits of tsarist times the capitalists had enforced their money claims against their debtors, and these debtors were the workmen and peasants. If the new social order were to be patterned for the good of the masses, it would not let property owners use the courts to the detriment of the poor.

Civil suits were to come before the same people's courts as the criminal prosecutions, and there was to be the same informality in determining the facts and deciding what was fair. The judge was left to his own resources as to the law he would apply and the steps he would take to determine the facts. This was the rule of the first decree on the courts, of 1917. Still, the business of the past needed sorting and reasoned decision, and for this reason the second decree on the courts of 1918 created the "district courts" to hear the civil as well as the criminal cases pending from before the revolution, and established a bench of judges who had legal education and permitted the appearance of lawyers to plead the claim and the defense. The civil procedure of tsarist times was to be followed in these courts to the extent that it had not been repealed or did not conflict with the concept of justice of the toiling masses.

When the "district courts" had completed their work, they were abolished and matters returned to the single people's court, but even this court had by that time been given some procedural guide in the form of the July rules of 1918, and then by the November 18, 1918 general statute on the courts. The fate of the working man was kept in mind, for the judge was instructed not to sit back and wait for the parties before him to protect themselves, but he was to be active in searching out the facts. This was required not only in criminal cases but in civil cases as well. It was a time of militant communism when capitalists were being driven from their factories and homes following nationalization, private banks were being absorbed in the state bank, and when such civil suits as were to come before the courts would

THE SOVIET STATE AND ITS CITIZENS 133

be primarily requests for the settlement of disputes over ownership of workers' and peasants' property.[1] Courts were not faced with the claims of usurious loan sharks, but the simple quarrels of citizens comparable to those of children in the same family. The judge as the wise elder would determine the facts out of the tumult and vituperation of the charges and counter charges, and would take a firm line as fair as seemed possible and designed to keep order in the new society.

Perhaps to the surprise of the policy makers of the time, the number of civil suits was not inconsiderable. Though in later years Soviet authors have been wont to belittle the work of the early courts in the civil law field, statistics published at the time show that civil suits increased by leaps and bounds once the courts were opened and receptive to them.[2] By April, 1918, the civil cases had increased from the 276 decided in January, 1918, to 3,339, or 31 per cent of the work of the courts reporting their statistics, and the Commissariat of Justice announced that the civil cases were increasing at a rate much faster than the criminal. This required enlarging the staffs of the people's courts. By June the civil cases had increased six times over those filed in January, while the criminal cases had only doubled in number. The great bulk had to do with contract and tort, these being about 60 per cent of the total, while the rest were divided between suits for divorce and for maintenance.

The severe test of attitudes toward civil procedure came with the introduction of neo-capitalism under the New Economic Policy. While disputes for the years 1917-1921 had been limited in the main to persons who were of the working classes, now it could be anticipated that the new bourgeoisie would become the principal litigants. Should they be permitted to use the courts to enforce payment of loans and contract purchase prices? Was the Soviet court to be turned into an instrument of the tolerated but evil bourgeoisie? These were the questions placed before the draftsmen of 1922 when they considered civil procedure. To be sure the office of prosecutor was being established as a watchman eyeing the new bourgeoisie to make sure that they did not use their newly granted economic rights to subvert soviet power, but some of the jurists wondered if this was enough.

The government's spokesman in introducing the draft code of civil procedure to the legislature took pains to declare that the new code had the proletariat at heart.[3] It was short with only 317 articles in contrast to five times that number under the Tsar. There was to be no reliance on custom, for that, in the official view, had been created by the bourgeoisie, and the five years of Soviet society had been too short to develop a new proletarian custom. While the familiar rule of other societies that the state's concern with civil matters was only to provide a forum for the settlement of disputes and to await the bringing of the action by one of the parties sufficiently incensed to come to court, the Soviet court was not to be allowed to

---

[1] See John N. Hazard, Law and Social Change in the USSR (1953) Chap. 1.
[2] D. Kurskil, Report, Prol. Rev. 1 Pravo, No. 1 (August 1, 1918) p. 40.
[3] Ia. Brandenburgskii, Vtoraia Sessiia, V.TS.I.K., X Sozyva, zasedanie vtoroe. pp. 38-47.

stop there. The prosecutor was given the right not only to intervene in a civil suit once it had been filed, but even to instigate proceedings if he thought the interests of the state or of the toiling masses required.[4] This would protect a party who feared to sue because of his dependence upon the wrongdoer or for some other reason.

The Soviet judge was not to follow the rule of Art. 367 of the Tsarist code which had denied to the judge the right on his own initiative to demand that one or the other party produce evidence. "We require the judge to take an active part in civil procedure. . . . We have structured our procedure so that the workers and peasants who turn to a court with whatever civil claim may be confident in advance that they will find in the judge himself defense and protection of their interests." These were the comforting words the government spokesman used to allay the fears of the deputies scrutinizing the draft.

Five parts were provided by the new code: (1) general principles including rules regulating representation in court, jurisdiction, fees, fines, limitations of time, and summonses; (2) steps in presenting a suit and trying it; (3) special proceedings relating to the administration of decedent's estates, enforcement of arbitral awards, deposits, court orders issued in conformity with documents requiring no trial, divorce, release from compulsory military service because of religious conviction, and complaints against the actions of state notaries; (4) appeal and review of decisions; and (5) execution of judgments and decisions.

The rules themselves were closely patterned on those of the Romanist codes of civil procedure in Continental Europe. Emphasis was upon documentation. Thus, the rules of evidence were not as permissive as were those in criminal procedure. To enforce the formal requirements set by the civil code for certain legal transactions, the code of civil procedure required that documents prepared in the required form be presented to substantiate a claim, and parole evidence in proof of an obligation was inadmissible.[5]

Class attitudes soon intruded themselves, however, for an author later summarized practice by saying, "The approach of the court to evidence must be based upon the social-class analysis of the role and testimony of the witnesses, on the analysis of the true class relationships under which the given case arose. Thus, the evaluation of the evidence in Soviet civil procedure is characterized by the following elements: (1) in a class approach to evidence, (2) a dialictic method of evaluation, (3) an objective character of evaluation as a counterweight to bourgeois subjectivism."[6] He was writing fifteen years after the enactment of the code and reflecting the contempt for the NEPmen which had increased as the Soviet economy had been strengthened and as state planning had been introduced, to be followed by the final liquidation of all but a fringe area of private enterprise.

---

[4]Art. 2.
[5]Art. 128.
[6]A.F. Kleinman, Grazhdanskii Protsess (1934) p. 37.

While a class approach was encouraged in the acceptance or rejection of the testimony of witnesses to a civil suit, it was not to be the basis for acceptance or rejection of specific provisions of law. The Supreme Court of the Russian Republic made this clear in 1926 in denouncing decisions in which judges had sought to utilize an article of the procedural code authorizing the filling of gaps in the law to create their own law for a case before them.[7] This instruction from the Supreme Court had been made necessary by a widely disseminated view of the principal draftsman of the civil code to the effect that "If, in examining a concrete case, the court sees that the general normative laws when applied in practice to the given case would lead to a result violative of proletarian politics, he cannot apply existing laws but must lift himself up to the general well-springs of proletarian politics."

By the Supreme Court's instruction of 1926 there was brought into focus a concept that was to become of increasing importance as time passed. By 1928 the NEP was being taxed out of existence, and by 1930 the private production of goods with large staffs of employed labor was no more. By 1932 the conduct of the profession of merchant was made a crime. The source of consumers' goods was the state store, or the cooperative's booth in the local market, and in a few cases the pile of twig brooms or baskets set up by an individual artisan on the pavement of the market place. Parties to civil suits would no longer include a NEPman on one side and a member of the working class on the other. Both parties now would be wage earners, or one might be a cooperative, and these associations of peasants or workmen were in a favored category as forms transitional to socialism. One party might also be a state agency. Society was moving into the first stage of its final form. Its further development required stability and social order, and this the procedural code provided.

The transition had been complete from the time when civil procedure was considered to be the weapon of the artful and evil bourgeoisie to the new conditions of stable socialist society. There was no longer reason to speak of the discrimination made desirable by the class approach. The class approach now required no discrimination. It required strict observance of the procedure established and maintained by a state which fostered social stability in the interest of what had come to be called the toiling masses, united in what Marxists termed a "classless" society.

Civil procedure has provided an increasingly stable and important element in the system of Soviet socialist legality as years have passed. Stalin's encouragement of production through use of property incentives has augmented the quantity of property privately owned, and legal problems have multiplied. As has been indicated in the material on the Soviet Bar, the work of the lawyers has increased, as indicated by the fact that in Moscow in the 1970's over 400,000 persons called upon lawyers annually to consult on civil law matters. The Fundamental Principles of Civil Procedure, adopted in 1961, and the republic codes based on them, have retained the main features of the system developed during the 1920's for civil litigants, although

---

[7]Instruction No. 1 of 1926, Shornik Deistv, Raz. Verkh. Suda RSFSR (1930) p. 166.

flexible procedures for the solution of minor disputes remain in the Comrades' Courts, as has been indicated in Chapter II.

The materials in this Chapter are designed to permit readers to determine the extent to which procedural formality has replaced the flexible system of conflict resolution in use during the formative years of Soviet law when revolutionary sentiment was strong.

A. *The place of civil procedure in contrast to social procedures.*

D.M. Chechot, "JUDICIAL PROTECTION OF SUBJECTIVE RIGHTS AND INTERESTS," Sovetskoe Gosudarstvo i Pravo, 1967, No. 8, p. 44.

The right to judicial protection of subjective civil rights or of interests protected by law is guaranteed by law to every interested person. A waiver of the right to go to court is void (Art. 3 of the Code of Civil Procedure of the RSFSR).

Existing Soviet legislation provides three general forms for the defense of civil rights: by a court; by an arbitration tribunal (state and Ministerial arbitration); and social (commission for labor disputes, Labor Union Committee, comradely courts and third party umpires). In certain cases citizens may protect themselves through an administrative office, but this is not an exception from the general regulations.

The court and agencies of public defense of rights: Broadening of the social forms of protection of rights is closely linked with the process of transformation of socialist state activity into communist public self-administration. This process will be gradual and lengthy. Recently a considerable number of civil cases have been transferred to the jurisdiction of social organizations. But, in broadening the sphere of application of social forms for protecting rights, the legislature guarantees at the same time, as a rule, to the interested parties that they may utilize the judicial form as the highest form for the protection of rights.

In the process of developing social forms for the protection of rights there have appeared along with the affirmative trends some which in our view are negative. Can one really approve the attempt to transfer a maximum number of civil cases to the jurisdiction of social organizations?. . . . Such proposals have been presented. Thus, for example, it has been proposed to transfer suits for alimony to the Labor Union Committees; to broaden the jurisdiction of comrades' courts to hear civil law disputes concerning property; and it has been said that in the not-distant future all judicial functions in the hearing of civil law disputes will be transferred to social courts, established on the principles of comrades' courts or of third party umpires. We must say that such proposals are first of all out of step with real-life practice and, secondly, that they spring from erroneous theoretical assumptions.

The period of full construction of communism is far from meaning that the foundations of the state will shrivel. On the contrary, the task of strengthening and elevating the role of state activity (including that of justice) still prevail over tasks of preparing for the withering away of the state.

With regard to practice, experience shows that in spite of attempts to activate a system of third party umpires, such resolution of disputes between citizens has not occurred generally, and even such resolution of disputes between socialist organizations is rarely encountered. Review of property disputes by comradely courts has not occurred widely. During 1966 comrades' courts in the housing bureau of Leningrad heard 13,178 cases and of these only 222 cases (1.5%) concerned property.

Judicial protection is not by chance the leading form of protection of rights. It is the form which is the most democratic, the most universal, the most capable of determining truth. . . . Even though of recent times the number of civil cases in the courts has been reduced the judicial form for protecting rights is still used relatively frequently. The growth of the material well-being of citizens, the development and expansion of trade turnover, the growing complexity of legal relations cannot but have influence in increasing the number of civil cases. Also, one must take into consideration that not all civil cases have to do with violation of law (special proceedings to establish death, etc.), and in not all civil cases may the conduct of the parties be found subject to reproach (strict liability without fault, some divorces, etc.)

B. *Fundamental principles*

FUNDAMENTAL PRINCIPLES OF CIVIL PROCEDURE OF THE U.S.S.R. AND OF THE UNION REPULBICS, December 8, 1961, effective May 1, 1962. [1961] Vedomosti Verkhovnogo Soveta SSSR, No. 50 (1085), item 526.

Art. 5. Every interested person has the right in accordance with the procedure established by law to proceed to court for defense of violated or disputed rights or of an interest protected by law. Denial of the right to proceed to court shall be without effect.

Art. 6. A court shall commence examination of a civil case (1) on complaint of a person seeking defense of his rights or of an interest protected by law; (2) on request of a procurator; and (3) on request of an organ of state administration, labor unions, state offices or enterprises, collective farms or other cooperative and public organizations or of individual citizens when by law they may bring suit in court for the protection of the rights and interests of other persons.

Art. 16. A court is required, without limiting itself to the evidence and explanations that have been introduced to take all measures provided by law to clarify from all sides, completely and objectively the real circumstances of a case, the rights and duties of the parties. A court must explain to the persons participating in the case their rights and duties, warning them of the consequences of committing or not committing procedural acts and must provide them assistance in defending their rights.

Art. 17. Evidence in a civil case shall be any factual materials on the basis of which the court in accordance with the procedure established by law determines the presence or absence of circumstances supporting the claim or defense of the parties, and other circumstances having importance for the correct decision of the case.

These facts shall be established by the following means: explanations of the parties and of third persons, the testimony of witnesses, written documents, material evidence and the conclusions of experts.

The circumstances of the case requiring confirmation by specific types of evidence may not be proved by any other types of evidence.

Art. 18. Every party must prove the circumstances on which he relies to support his complaint or defense.

Evidence shall be presented by the parties and by other persons participating in the case. If the evidence presented is insufficient, the court shall propose to the parties and to the other persons participating in the case that they present supplementary evidence, or it shall gather such evidence on its own initiative.

Art. 19. The court shall assess evidence on the basis of its inner conviction, basing this upon full, comprehensive and objective examination at the trial of all of the circumstances of the case in their totality, being guided by the law and a socialist concept of justice.

No evidence shall have predetermined weight for the court.

Art. 21. A criminal sentence, that has become final, is binding on a court examining the civil law consequences of the acts of a person with regard to whom the court sentence was issued, but only as to establishment of the fact of the acts and their commission by a given person.

Art. 24. Every citizen, as well as state offices, enterprises, collective farms and other cooperative and public organizations having the right of juridicial and other cooperative and public organizations having the right of juridical personage may be parties to a civil proceeding, as plaintiff and defendant.

Parties have equal procedural rights. Parties have the right to familiarize themselves with the materials of the case, to request removal of judges, to present evidence, to participate in the examination of evidence, to appeal rulings, to give oral and written explanations to the court, to present their conclusions and considerations, to oppose appeals against rulings and the conclusions and considerations of the other party, to appeal the judgments and decisions of courts, to demand the compulsory execution of a court judgment, to be present during the activity of the sheriff in executing the judgment and also to exercise other procedural rights given by law.

Persons taking part in cases arising from administrative legal relations and in cases subject to the rules for special proceedings shall enjoy the rights and assume the duties of parties, except for the exemptions established by law.

Parties are required to use all procedural rights granted to them with good faith.

The plaintiff may change the grounds or demand set forth in his complaint, raise or lower the amount requested or withdraw his complaint. The defendant shall have the right to admit his liability. The parties may terminate the case by conciliation.

The court shall not accept a withdrawal from suit and shall not approve a conciliation of the parties if those activities violate the law or violate any one's right and interests protected by law.

Art. 28. Citizens may conduct a case in court personally or through a representative. Cases of persons lacking physical capacity shall be conducted by their legal representatives.

Cases of juridical persons shall be conducted by their agencies or their representatives.

Art. 29. The procurator shall have the right to bring a civil suit or to enter a civil case at any moment in the proceedings, if protection of state or social interests or the rights and interests of citizens protected by law so requires.

Participation of the procurator in examination of civil cases is compulsory in those circumstances when it is directly provided for by law or when the necessity of participation of the procurator in a given case is recognized by the court.

The procurator participating in a case shall have the right to familiarize himself with the evidence, to request the removal of judges, to present evidence to participate in the investigation of evidence, to protest rulings, to give conclusions on questions arising during the conduct of the trial or relating to the substance of the case as a whole, and also to exercise any other procedural rights given him by law.

Art. 30. In the circumstances provided by law organs of state administration, labor unions, state offices and enterprises, collective farms and other cooperative and public organizations or individual citizens may bring suit to defend the rights and interests of other persons protected by law. Organs of state administration in the circumstances provided by law may be invited by a court to participate in the proceedings, or they may enter on their own initiative to give conclusions in the case for the purpose of performing the duties placed upon them and to protect the rights of citizens and the interests of the state.

Organs of state administration, offices, enterprises and organizations in the person of their representative, and individual citizens named in the present article may familiarize themselves with the evidence in the case, request the removal of judges, give explanations, present evidence, participate in the examination of evidence, protest rulings and use other procedural rights given them by law.

Art. 33. After accepting the complaint a judge shall conduct a preliminary preparation of the case for examination in court, with the aim of prompt and correct examination of the case.

Art. 35. The court of original jurisdiction in hearing a case must examine the evidence in the case directly; listen to the explanation of persons participating in the case and to the testimony of witnesses and the conclusions of experts; familiarize itself with the written evidence; and look at the material evidence. Exceptions to the present rules shall be permitted only in the circumstances established by the legislation of the Union Republics.

Examination of a case shall be conducted orally and with a bench of judges that remains the same throughout the trial. In the event that one of the judges is replaced during the trial, the examination must be recommenced from the beginning.

Court sittings in every case must be without interruption, except for rest periods. Before termination of a case that has been initiated or before termination of the hearing a court shall have no right to examine other cases.

Art. 37. The judgment of the court must be in accord with the law and be grounded in fact.

The court shall rest judgment only on that evidence that has been heard during the trial. There must be a statement in the judgment in every case: of the circumstances of the case as established by the court, of the evidence on which the conclusions of the court rest and of the reasons why the court rejects any evidence, of the laws on which the court has relied, of the conclusions of the court as to satisfaction of the complaint or rejection in whole or in part, of the period for appeal and of the procedure for appealing.

Depending upon the circumstances of the case as they have been disclosed the court may exceed the limits of the plaintiff's complaint if this is necessary to protect the rights and interests of state offices, enterprises, collective farms and of other cooperative and public organizations or of citizens protected by law.

The court's judgment shall be reached by a majority vote, and shall be set forth in writing and signed by all of the judges. A judge who finds himself in the minority shall have the right to set forth in writing his own view, and this shall be included in the file.

C. *The role of the court in civil cases.*

STATE FARM 'MOLODINSKII' vs. KARPACHEVA, Biulleten' Verkhovnogo Suda RSFSR, 1975, No. 1, p. 11.

The State Farm 'Molodinskii' brought suit against Karpacheva to recover 4,855 rubles damages, claiming that because of the defandant's fault a shortage of 49,305 kilograms of potatoes had occurred. The State Farm had suffered a loss in the sum claimed.

The Chekhov City people's court in Moscow Province on January 29, 1973 terminated proceedings when the State Farm withdrew its complaint. The court's decision was not appealed by way of cassation. The Presidium of the Moscow Provincial Court on the protest of its President set aside the ruling and remanded the case for retrial for the following reasons:

Under Art. 165 of the Code of Civil Procedure RSFSR before permitting a plaintiff to withdraw his claim, a court must clarify the causes of the situation. In the present case, as is evident from the record of the court sitting, the court did not make clear to the parties the consequences of this procedural act; did not determine the motives of the State Farm's withdrawal of suit.

In the course of the proceedings on revision the President of the State Farm declared that he had no intent to abandon the suit entirely; he had requested that the case be terminated in order to clarify the details of some of the circumstances.

The court found the withdrawal of the suit by the State Farm to be a violation of the interests of the State, since, in accordance with Art. 34 of the Code of Civil Procedure RSFSR, a court will not permit withdrawal of a suit if this act conflicts with law or transgresses some rights and interests protected by law.

REFELD vs. SHAPOSHNIKOV, Biulleten' Verkhovnogo Suda RSFSR, 1968, No. 7, p. 4.

By decision of the Printzlerberg District Court of Berlin Shaposhnikov was declared father of the child of Beata Refeld. Maintenance payments of 75 DM monthly were awarded Beata Refeld for the child, beginning with birth and continuing until the age of 13. Payments would then be 85 DM monthly until the child was able to support himself. Beata Refeld and the Berlin City Court filed a petition under Arts. 44-47 of the Treaty of Judicial Assistance in Civil, Family and Criminal Cases between the USSR and the German Democratic Republic, which entered into force on June 12, 1958, asking for execution of the judgment on the territory of the RSFSR

[The Voronezh Provincial Court executed the judgment]

Shaposhnikov requested that the Provincial Court's ruling be vacated, objecting to the suit, arguing that the Provincial Court had given him no opportunity during a month to present his opposition to recognition of the Berlin judgment.

In verifying the record the Judicial Division for Civil Cases of the RSFSR Supreme Court affirmed the ruling of the Voronezh Provincial Court and rejected Shaposhnikov's complaint in its ruling of February 13, 1968, saying:

Under Art. 26 of the Treaty. . .the legal relationships between a child born to unmarried parents and its mother on the one hand and to its father on the other are governed by the legislation of the contracting state of which the child is a citizen. In the present case the child is a citizen of the German Democratic Republic, and, consequently, the legal relationships between him and his parents must be determined by the legislation of the GDR. The decision of the Berlin District Court must be executed under Arts. 45-47 of the Treaty. . .on USSR territory.

The petition for execution is in proper form, has the necessary requisition and is accompanied by the official documents required by the Treaty. In view of this the court had no grounds to refuse the petition to execute the judgment of the Berlin District Court on the territory of the USSR . . . Shaposhnikov's objection to the substance of the suit, in particular his claim that he is not the father of the Refeld child, may not be the object of investigation and verification in examination of a case concerning the execution of a foreign judgment. These objections (if they have any foundation) may be cause for review of the judgment of the Berlin District Court in accordance with the procedures provided for such review.

NIKITINA vs. VIKULOV, Biulleten' Verkhovnogo Suda RSFSR, 1975, No. 1, p. 12.

Naumov has a family of 3 persons: By order of September 14, 1973 he, his son and Nikitina with whom he was living without registration of marriage were assigned an apartment of 17.9 square meters. In another apartment in the same building there lived the family of Virkulov (4 persons). In October 1973 Naumov and the Virkulovs exchanged apartments, voluntarily without a formal exchange authorization and without notice to the local Soviet of working people's deputies.

Nikitina brought suit against Virkulov to have the exchange declared void and to evict them from the apartment, declaring that the exchange was made without her knowledge at a time when she was temporarily absent from the apartment because Naumov was systematically misusing alcohol.

The Chistopolskii peoples' court of the Tatar ASSR terminated the case on the ground of lack of jurisdiction, saying in its ruling that the defendants may be evicted from the disputed apartment under the administrative procedure available with the Procurator's consent. The Judicial Division for Civil Cases of the Tatar SSR Supreme Court vacated this ruling and returned the case to the same people's court for decision on the merits. The Presidium of the Tatar SSR Supreme Court, in reviewing the protest of the Deputy President of the RSFSR Supreme Court by its decree of April 11, 1974 vacated the ruling of the Judicial Division and restored the judgment of the peoples' court for the following reasons:

Under Art. 327 of the Civil Code RSFSR the procedure for exchange of living quarters is established by the Ministry of Communal Economy of the RSFSR. In accordance with the instruction on the exchange of living quarters, approved by the Ministry on January 9, 1967, the exchange of living quarters in buildings of State, cooperative and social organizations is permitted only with the consent of the lessor and must be formulated by an exchange order of the executive committee of the local Soviet. This is the only legal basis for the occupancy of quarters received by way of exchange.

Citizens who exchange their living quarters voluntarily without exchange orders, under Art. 338 Civil Code may be evicted from their quarters through an administrative proceeding with the consent of the Procurator. Since Naumov and the Virkulovs exchanged apartments voluntarily without the consent of the Soviet's Executive Committee and without an exchange order, eviction of them from the apartments occupied by them may proceed not through judicial proceedings but through administrative proceedings with the consent of the Procurator. . .

D. *Res judicata.*

T. ABRAMENKO vs. RAMENSK REGISTRATION BUREAU, Sotsialisticheskaia zakonnost', 1970, No. 1, p. 90.

House No. 63 on Sovetskii Street in the village of Il'inskoe of Moscow Province was owned by A. Sul'e? In 1951 his daughter, L. Abramenko, filed suit for recognition of her property right in one third of the house. Judgment was given for her on March 29, 1951 by the Ramensk District peoples' court, and her right was registered in the Ramensk Office of Technical Inventories.

A. Sul'e appealed by way of cassation to the Judicial Division for Civil Cases of the Moscow Provincial Court, which quashed the judgment on July 19, 1954 and remanded the case to the peoples' court for retrial. Later L. Abramenko requested that the case be terminated, and this was done by the peoples' court on August 5, 1954. In spite of this decision no change was made in the registration of L. Abramenko's ownership of one third of the house.

In February 1965 L. Abramenko died, and on August 2, 1965 her husband, T. Abramenko, obtained from the Notary a certificate of inheritance to his deceased wife's Savings Bank account and to a one third interest in the house in the village of Il'inskoe. The Ramensk Registration Bureau, on the basis of the ruling of the peoples' court of August 5, 1954, refused registration to T. Abramenko of one third onwership of the disputed house, which it had registered on October 11, 1965 as entirely the property of A. Sul'e.

T. Abramenko brought suit to require the Registration Bureau to annul the registration of October 11, 1965 and to recognize his right to ownership of one third of the house. The case was terminated by a ruling of the Ramensk City peoples' court on the ground that there was a judgment of the peoples' court entered in the very same case on August 5, 1954.

[The USSR Deputy Procurator General protested the decision. The Judicial Division for Civil Cases of the USSR Supreme Court satisfied the protest, saying:]

Under par. 3 Art. 219 of the Code of Civil Procedure RSFSR a court shall terminate proceedings if there is in force a judgment or ruling of a court issued in a conflict between the very same parties on the same subject and on the same grounds rejecting the suit.

In comparing the documents it is evident that the parties as well as the basis for suit have changed. In 1951 L. Abramenko brought suit against A. Sul'e for recognition of her property right in one third of the house on the ground that they had bought it together. In 1967 T. Abramenko brought suit. His claim rests in substance upon the fact that he is heir after the death of L. Abramenko, although in form it was brought to annul registration of a property right and was directed to the City Soviet's Executive Committee. Under such circumstances the court had no reason to refuse to accept suit or to terminate the case. The court must examine the details of the complaint, bearing in mind that the dispute is between citizens and the Soviet's Executive Committee, and its appropriate agency may be joined as a third party. The court must also take into consideration that the defendant, A. Sul'e, had let pass the period established by Art. 345 of the Code of Civil Procedure RSFSR to present an executory document for execution. Moreover, she in general had not received the executory document under the judgment of the peoples' court dated August 5, 1954 and had not filed a request to have the statute of limitations waived. As a result a third of the house from 1957 to 1967 belonged to L. Abramenko who is now the deceased owner who has passed it to her heir.

E. *Fair trial.*

O. TOKARSKII vs. V. TOKARSKII, Biulleten' Verkhovnogo Suda RSFSR, 1971, No. 8, p. 3.

O. Tokarskii sued V. Tokarskii to void a will and a contract of gift and to divide an estate on inheritance, claiming that her father D. Tokarskii, who died on July 20, 1967, was seriously ill and unable to understand the meaning of his act on January 20, 1964 when he executed his will bequeathing all his property to his second wife, V. Tokarskii, and his minor daughter, O. Tokarskii, and when he executed a contract of gift on December 24, 1966 transferring his dwelling to V. Tokarskii. The Moscow City Court gave judgment for O. Tokarskii.

The judgement was quashed by the RSFSR Supreme Court's Judicial Division for Civil Cases and remanded for new trial for the following reasons:

O. Tokarskii at the moment of trial had come of age and under Art. 32 of the RSFSR Code of Civil Procedure acquired the capacity to exercise her rights in court personally or through a representative. In view of that fact she was joined as a defendant in the case by the court. However, the court in violation of Art. 106 of the Code of Civii Procedure did not notify her of the day of the hearing and reviewed the case without her, depriving her of the right to defend her interests in court.

Under Art. 308 of the Code of Civil Procedure the court's judgment must be quashed if a case is heard by a court in the absence of any one of the persons participating in the case who was not informed of the time and place of the hearing.

A. LEUSHKIN vs. V. LEUSHKIN, Biulleten' Verkhovnogo Suda RSFSR, 1972, No. 1, p. 13.

A.D. Leushkin sued his son V.A. Leushkin and daughter-in-law to recover 2,760 rubles on the ground that under a contract of August 12, 1968 he had performed for the defendant work in constructing a house having a value in the amount sought, but that the money had not been paid him up to the present.

In the peoples' court the plaintiff amended the complaint to include as defendant only his son, excluding the daughter-in-law, and the son acknowledged his obligation fully. The Altyr District peoples' court gave judgment for plaintiff. There was no appeal. The President of the Chuvash ASSR Supreme Court protested the judgment to the Presidium of his court and asked that it be quashed and a new trial held. The Presidium satisfied the protest for the following reasons:

Under Art. 34 of the RSFSR Code of Civil Procedure the court is required to determine the reason why the plaintiffs did not join the daughter-in-law as a defendant and to verify whether the defendant's rights and interests protected by law were not violated thereby. It is not evident from the record why the daugher-in-law was not summoned to court and why the case was tried in her absence.

In a petition for revision the daughter-in-law Leushkina declared that the contract of August 12, 1968 was fictitious and was executed to reduce her share in the community property whose division was the subject of suit by V. Leushkin after termination of their life together.

The court, in hearing the case without joining the daughter-in-law, Leushkina, as a defendant or as an interested party denied her the opportunity to verify her explanation of the suit and this substantially reduced her right as a property owner in the disputed house.

MOZYR KOMBINAT vs. K., Sotsialisticheskaia zakonnost', 1971, No. 2, p. 90.

. . .Agreeing with the protest, the Presidium of the Provincial Court satisfied it for the following reason:

Under par. 7 Art. 284 of the Code of Civil Procedure of the Bielorussian SSR a court judgment must always be quashed if it is issued by judges other than those who presided at the trial. As is evident from the record of the trial, the judges present were Germanov, Lipovich, and Alferov, while those who signed the judgement were Germanov, Lipovich and Afanas'ev. This violation is without question reason to quash the judgment. . .

TARKHOV vs. ISKOIANTS, Biulleten' Verkhovnogo Suda RSFSR, 1974, No. 8, p. 6.

. . . Tarkhanov in his cassation complaint asked that the judgement be quashed as having been decided in violation of the rules of procedural and substantive law. The Judicial Division for Civil Cases of the RSFSR Supreme Court, having reviewed the case on September 6, 1973, quashed the judgment, saying:

The court rejected Takharov's claim for the reason that he and Iskoiants had concluded a contract for sale of an automobile, and the fact that it was not formulated in the manner prescribed by law could not raise doubts as to its existence, since it was executed. The court relied as the basis for its conclusion on the testimony of Iskoian, Gondarenko and Dangulov during the preliminary investigation of the criminal case. The testimony of these persons, except for that of Iskoiants was not heard at the trial: the court did not explore this testimony, and the parties gave no explanation of it. Only the representatives of the parties were questioned at the trial.

Such simplification in examination of a case led to grievous violation of the requirements of Art. 192 RSFSR Code of Civil Procedure, under which a court may base its judgment only on the evidence that was investigated at the trial, and Art. 14 Code of Civil Procedure requires the court to take all measures prescribed by law for a full and objective explanation of the true circumstances of the case; of the rights and duties of the parties.

On retrial the court must take into consideration the aforementioned and must verify minutely the circumstances of the case and issue the appropriate decision.

F. *The Procuracy in civil cases.*

SHUROV vs. SHUROVA, Biulleten' Verkhovnogo Suda RSFSR, 1966, No. 7, p. 7.

The procurator of the Shumiachskii county brought an action on behalf of Shurov against Shurova to declare invalid a marriage registered on June 28, 1962. At the court session the procurator disavowed the suit and the court terminated the proceedings. The Presidium of the Smolensk Provincial Court left unsatisfied a protest of the Smolensk provincial procurator requesting that the judgment of the people's court be vacated.

Having examined the case on the protest of the Deputy Procurator of the RSFSR the Judicial Division for Civil Cases of the Supreme Court of the RSFSR revoked the decisions of the people's court and the ruling of the Presidium of the Provincial Court, stating the following in its ruling of March 14, 1966.

Under Art. 41 of the Code of Civil Procedure of the RSFSR a procurator has the right to bring an action or to enter a proceeding at any stage in the procedure if this is required for the protection of the state or public interests or of the rights and interests of citizens protected by law.

As it appears from the record the procurator of Shumiachskii county brought suit in the interests of Shurov. Shurov was brought into the case. The procurator's disavowal of the suit he had brought did not deprive the person in defense of whose interests the suit had been brought of the right to demand that the case be heard on its merits. Shurov insisted on continuation of the hearing and objected to its termination. Under such circumstances the court was required to hear the case, and not to terminate proceedings.

CHAPTER IX

Criminal Law in the Preservation of Public Order

Societies reflect their philosophies, goals, prejudices and problems in what they punish as crime. The Soviet legal system is the product of all of these forces. Its Marxist philosophy has given the criminal law a class flavor, in that the enemies of society have been presumed to be those who had been in tsarist times landlords, factory owners and their estate and factory managers, and also in the expectation that as capitalist elements were rooted out of the economy, the major threats to communism, requiring suppression through criminal law, would become less intense, and criminal law would, like other branches of law, wither away. But the criminal statutes had another function springing from this very concept of ultimate withering. They were not only to eliminate class enemies but to prepare the way for achievement of ultimate goals. They were to provide the outlines of a new society, defined in terms of the actions it would not permit, and also a system of penalties that would be effective not only as a deterrent to the prospective wrongdoer but also, as a means of rehabilitation; of education in the ways of the hoped-for new world.

Although such elements of reasoned social engineering have been prominent in soviet criminal law since 1917, there have also been elements in short term thinking, and even of unreasoned prejudice. Hot headed reaction to a given surge of a particular type of offense, such as rape or gang warfare, have resulted in a sudden increase in penalties and instructions to judges to show no mercy, and the maintenance of the penalty of death for a wide variety of offenses has suggested emotional prejudice stronger than the reasoned expectation that most criminals can be rehabilitated if given a chance to learn of their opportunities in a fully employed and satiated society such as a socialist economy is supposed to provide.

Not until 1922 were the Soviet penologists prepared to draft a criminal code. By the earliest decrees on the courts, the judges were left free to define as criminal whatever their consciences suggested, as guided by Marxist political thought and a residue of the imperial criminal code not found disconsonant with the new life. Only in a few critical areas were there specific statutes defining crime, those of 1918 being concerned specifically with instigation to treason, counterrevolutionary activity, refusal to answer a call to military service, bribery of state officials, refusal to till the land in accordance with orders from local authorities, violation of the rules relating to the use or distribution of metals, trade in state monopolized goods and refusal to report surplus grain. There were no statutes on murder, bodily injury, rape or robbery. These offenses were expected to be so patently contrary to social order as to fall within the group requiring punishment in application of the judge's social consciousness.

By 1919 the Commissariat of Justice felt the need of clarification of those details of criminal law that could be expected to be confusing to the inexperienced men and women charged for the first time with the application of criminal penalties. A "Basic aid"[1] was issued to define the function of Soviet criminal law, and to be specific on such matters as what should be considered in determining an appropriate punishment; the exemption of minors, the insane and those who acted in self-defense from criminal responsibility; the seriousness to be attributed to attempts, preparation for crime and complicity; the function of the suspended sentence; and the territorial jurisdiction of the laws of the RSFSR.

With the introduction of the New Economic Policy, the codifiers prepared in 1922 for the RSFSR,[2] a full conventional Continental-type criminal code in two parts, the general part repeating and expanding upon the general principles that had first appeared in the "basic aid" of 1919, and the second part being a long catalogue of specific crimes, prominent among which were to be found offenses against the state, but also including the full gamut of the usual crimes against the person. The other republics formed in the Soviet model soon followed suit. These codes included articles stating the general range of permissible punishments, leading up to shooting as an exceptional measure, and including such unusual penalties as exile from the country and "correctional labor" which was the creation of an obligation to continue to work wherever one was for a given period and to pay a share of

---

[1] December 12, 1919 [1919] I Sob. Uzak. RSFSR, No. 66, item 590.
[2] Effective June 1, 1922, [1922] I Sob. Uzak. RSFSR, No. 15, item 153.

one's wages into the state treasury. The former was later to sink into unimportance as Soviet leaders learned to their sorrow that to exile was but to create an enemy abroad who could and often did intrigue against the Soviet regime, and in 1958 it was removed from the new Fundamentals of criminal law. "Correctional labor," however, grew to such importance that it was hailed as the most frequently used penalty, peculiar to the Soviet system and of great value in reeducating the minor offender. Some Soviet authors doubted this evaluation and held it to be no more than an installment fine, at least during the period from 1940 to 1956 when all citizens were prevented[3] from leaving their jobs without the state manager's permission unless suffering from ill health or unless chosen to prepare for assumption of greater responsibilities.

The 1922 code was a step in the direction of precision in definition of crime, but it was not a complete departure from the concept of punishment in accordance with the dictates of the social consciousness of the judge. Laying hold of an old tsarist code provision that had been in effect from 1864 to 1903[4] known by the term "analogy," the Soviet draftsmen inserted an article permitting a judge to consider the social danger of an individual even when he had committed no act defined as a crime in the specialized part of the code. He was to be guided by analogizing the dangerous act to some act defined as crime, but at the outset the analogies were not always apparent, as when a husband was executed for the sadistic murder of a wife, followed by dissection of her torso and shipment in a trunk to a remote railway station, the court arguing that the crime was analagous to banditry. At the time of this decision the code permitted the death penalty for banditry but not for murder without political motives or very serious social consequences.

Federation caused enactment of Fundamental principles of criminal law in 1924.[5] These were in the main those that had been introduced in the criminal codes of the various republics in 1922, although limited to the concerns of the general parts of those codes.

The 1922 code was replaced in the RSFSR in 1926 by a second version,[6] keeping to the same general lines, but later amended on frequent occasions, sometimes to mark the rise or fall in the social danger accredited an offense such as rape or sadistic murder; sometimes to reflect the economic changes occurring in the country as when with the end of the period of the New Economic policy the conduct of a commercial business of purchase and sale for a profit was made criminal; and sometimes to incorporate new forms of activity conceived by Stalin to be threats to his personal power. It was these latter additions to the chapter on crimes against the state that increased the indefiniteness inherent in the "analogy" article by defining

---

[3]Decree of June 26, 1940, [1940] Ved. Verkh. Sov. SSSR, No. 20.
[4]See N.S. Timasheff, The Impact of the Penal Law of Imperial Russia on Soviet Penal Law, 12 American Slavic and East European Review 441 (1953).
[5]Decree of October 31, 1924, [1924] I Sob. Zak. SSSR, No. 24, item 204.
[6]Decree of November 22, 1926, [1926] I Sob. Uzak. RSFSR, No. 80, item 600.

such crimes as "counter-revolutionary sabotage" or "the undermining of state economic entities for counterrevolutionary purposes" by misusing state entities or even hampering their normal activities.

It was against the indefiniteness encouraged by Stalin that his heirs rebelled after his death, and the 1958 Fundamental principles of criminal law were designed to usher in a more clearly defined concept of social danger. As with the other fields of law the Fundamentals had to be followed by detailed criminal codes in each of the republics before the full sweep of the reform could be determined, and this occurred only in 1960 and thereafter. Since the state and military crimes were still defined solely by the federal government, the codes of the republics merely incorporated in their entirety the 1958 statutes on those subjects, but the specifications of other offenses and the penalties to be applied were left to the local leaders, guided, as usual, by the Communist Party members among them who saw to the preservation of considerable but not complete uniformity.

Within two years after adoption of the Fundamentals, criminal policies veered again toward the more severe. As campaigns were conducted to eradicate various types of crime, amendments to the Criminal Code were introduced to increase flexibility by offering a wider range of punishments.

Soviet criminal law has proven itself to be in constant flux between increase and relaxation of severity. One of the elements of the dynamic is failure fully to come to grips with the sociology of crime. So long as authorities were content to explain it in terms of continuing capitalist elements, whether in the form of saboteurs sent through Soviet border guards or misguided minds influenced by foreign broadcasts or as yet uneradicated capitalist motivation to aggrandize one's property at the expense of others, the science of Soviet penology has been hampered. In theory socialism provides employment for all, an abundance of the good things in life, and contentment devoid of desire for social protest. In practice, desire for comforts has increased as their availability has increased, and waves of theft from state institutions have engulfed even high officials who have built and furnished comfortable homes out of state resources. Also second generation youths, devoid of the revolutionary fervor of their parents and often without their guidance due to over-full schedules of political activity, have fallen into the same paths of juvenile delinquency as have youths in other lands. The problem of understanding why bored youths become drunkards, thieves and customers of peddlers who cater to their tastes in jazz, clothing and even sex is worrying Soviet penologists who speak now really of investigating the causes of crime.

The specialists in Soviet criminal law in the 1970s must choose between a new scientific approach based upon the increasingly important research of Soviet penologists, or a continuation of the practice of "campaigns" based upon intuitive decisions by those responsible for the administration of the Soviet public order system.

The chapters on civil rights and due process have already disclosed a considerable number of definitions of crime and the forms of penalties thought suitable to their eradication. This chapter will focus on the more technical problems originally presented by the 1919 "basic aid," namely, self defense, accessories, attempts and mistakes; the range of penalties devised to cope with crime in a socialist society; and those offenses that may be said to have acquired special meaning in a society that produces primarily with state-owned property and distributes without the intervention of private middlemen.

The reader may ask whether the record suggests whether official tempers are rising, or whether since Khrushchev's ouster there is emerging greater expectation that milder penalties together with education and a salutary experience with correctional labor will reduce the incidence of crime.

A. *Criminal jurisprudence.*

N.I. Zagordnikov, "THE PRINCIPLES OF SOVIET SOCIALIST CRIMINAL LAW," Sovetskoe Gosudarstvo i Pravo, 1966, No. 5, p. 65.

The principles of Soviet criminal law may be divided into two groups according to content: a) general principles which permeate socialist law as a whole and which acquire notable specificity only when examined as principles of Soviet criminal law, and b) special principles inherent in criminal law alone, disclosing its specific features, underpinning its foundations, constituting the characteristic elements of that very branch of law.

The general principles are those of socialist democracy, socialist legality, socialist humanism and socialist internationalism.

The principle of socialist democracy in Soviet criminal law is reflected first of all in the fact that it protects the most democratic social and state structure in the world. . . . The most important criminal laws are adopted after wide discussion. . . . They echo the needs and longings of the Soviet people; they are directed toward creating an influence on the building of communism ever better and more effectively. . . . They are applied to all in the same way.

The principle of socialist legality is primarily reflected in the fact that the norms of Soviet criminal law are compulsory for all citizens, orgnizations and officials . . . . Only persons guilty of committing a defined crime are punished. . . . The violations of socialist legality during the cult of the personality did not change the social nature of Soviet criminal law and its fundamental principles.

The norms of criminal law on analogy and on the possibility of application of punishment to persons who have not committed concrete crimes but who were dangerous because of previous activity were temporary in character. They were dictated by special historical conditions, violent class warfare, and as these conditions disappeared, they were replaced by other laws reflecting the new relationships of class forces, the moral-political unity of the Soviet people.

The principle of socialist humanism comes forward as a grouping of the characteristic fundamental principles of Soviet criminal law: compassion, attentive and sympathetic relationship to the individual, reflected both in the content of the institutions of Soviet criminal law and in the application of its norms. The humanism of Soviet criminal law is manifest in the fact that criminal law is called upon to protect the most important achievement of mankind—workers' power. Criminal law protects the working people's socialist state, the policy of peace and the prevention of war, the most important conditions assuring the building of communism in our country. Humanism is in the fact that the norms of criminal law in the last analysis serve the purpose of protecting and defending the rights and interests of the individual.

The principle of socialist internationalism is found in the fact that Soviet criminal law protects the social, economic and political interests of free sovereign peoples, progressing along the road of socialism and communism, the interests of the whole world system of socialism.

The special principles are the principle of decisive, partisan and multifaceted protection of the political, economic, national achievements of the working people, which make feasible the building of communist society under the leadership of the C.P.S.U. It reflects most clearly the class features, the purposeful direction of Soviet socialist law and the fundamental contrast to bourgeois exploitive criminal law. Second, the principle of participation of the people in application of the norms of criminal law and the execution of penalties and other measures substituted for them. Third, the principle of prevention of crime. . . . Fourth, the principle of the concurrence of prohibitory criminal law and moral evaluation of actions recognized as criminal. . . . And, fifth, the individualization of responsibility.

Scientific elaboration of these principles permits better understanding of Soviet criminal law as a whole and of each of its norms in particular.

B. *Punishment*

FUNDAMENTAL PRINCIPLES OF CRIMINAL LAW OF THE U.S.S.R. AND OF THE UNION AND AUTONOMOUS REPUBLICS, December 25, 1958, as amended.

Art. 21. *Types of punishment.*

Persons found guily of crime may be sentenced to the following basic penalties:

1) deprivation of liberty;
2) exile;
3) banishment;
4) correctional labor without deprivation of liberty;
5) deprivation of the right to occupy a certain post or to engage in certain activity;
6) fines;
7) social censure.

Members of the armed forces on regular service may also be penalized by dispatch to a disciplinary battalion.

In addition to these basic penalties the following supplementary penalties may be

included in the sentence;
   confiscation of property;
   deprivation of military or other special rank.
   Banishment and exile, deprivation of the right to occupy a certain post or engage in a certain activity and fines may be applied as supplementary as well as basic penalties.
   Other penalties than those listed in this article may be fixed by the legislation of the union republics in accordance with the principles and general provisions contained in the present Fundamentals.
   Art. 22. *An exceptional measure of punishment—the death penalty.*
   A sentence of death by shooting may be applied as an exceptional measure of punishment until such time as it has been fully abolished, in cases of state crime provided for by the U.S.S.R. Law on "Criminal Responsibility for Crimes against the State," for intentional homicide under the aggravating circumstances indicated in the articles of the criminal laws of the U.S.S.R. and of the Union Republics, establishing responsibility for intentional homicide, and in special cases provided for by legislation of the U.S.S.R., and also for some other especially dangerous crimes.
   The death penalty may not be applied to persons who have not reached the age of eighteen at the time of committing the crime. The death penalty may not be applied to women who are pregnant at the time of execution of the sentence.
   Art. 23. *Deprivation of freedom.*
   Deprivation of freedom may not be for a term longer than ten years, but for especially severe crimes and for especially dangerous recidivists, as provided by legislation of the U.S.S.R., it may be extended for a term not to exceed fifteen years.
   Art. 24. *Exile and Banishment.*
   Exile is defined as the removal of a convicted person from his place of residence and his obligatory settlement in a prescribed area.
   Banishment is defined as the removal of a convicted person from his place of residence with prohibition to live in certain places.
   Exile and banishment may not be inflicted on persons who have not reached the age of 18 at the time the crime is committed. Exile is not applicable to pregnant women and women with dependent children under the age of eight years.
   Art. 25. *Correctional labor without deprivation of liberty.*
   Correctional labor without deprivation of liberty is applicable for periods up to one year, and the sentence is served either at the convicted person's place of work or at some other place in the vicinity of his residence. Deductions from the earnings of a person sentenced to correctional labor without deprivation of liberty are made for the benefit of the state to an amount fixed by the sentence but not exceeding 20% of the earnings.

CORRECTIONAL LABOR CODE RSFSR, [1972] Vedomosti Verkhovnogo Soveta RSFSR, No. 51, item 1220.
Art. 1. The correctional Labor Code of the RSFSR has as its task assuring the execution of criminal penalties in such a way that it will be not only chastisement for committing a crime but also will correct and reeducate convicted persons in the spirit of an honest relationship to labor, precise conformity to laws, and respect for the rules of a socialist way of life, and will prevent the commission of new crimes not only by the convicted person but also by other persons and will facilitate the eradication of crime.

The execution of penalties does not have as its purpose physical suffering or lessening of a man's dignity.

AMENDMENT ON CONDITIONAL SENTENCE, April 11, 1974, [1974] Vedomosti Verkhovnogo Soveta SSSR, No. 16, item 245.
In further perfection of Criminal Legislation the Presidium of the USSR Supreme Soviet decrees:

1. Art. 23 of the Fundamental Principles of Criminal Legislation of the USSR and of the union republics of December 25, 1958. . .shall be amended after par. 9 to add new paragraphs with the following text:

"In prescribing punishment to an adult able bodied person convicted for the first time to deprivation of freedom for a term of from one to three years, taking into consideration the nature and the degree of social danger represented by the crime that has been committed, the personality of the guilty person and other circumstances of the case, and also the possibility of his correction and reeducation without isolation from society, but under circumstances of public supervision over him, a court may decree the conditional sentencing of the person to deprivation of freedom with the obligation to perform labor for the term indicated in places defined by the agencies charged with execution of the sentence, and with a statement in the judgment of the motives for such a decision. . .

ON DEPRIVATION OF USSR CITIZENSHIP. Vedomosti Verkhovnogo Soveta SSSR, 1970, No. 1, p. 10.
In accordance with the USSR Law of August 19, 1938 "On USSR Citizenship," the Presidium of the USSR Supreme Soviet by its Edict of December 19, 1969 has deprived of USSR citizenship for offenses defaming the dignity of a citizen of the USSR Svetlana Iosifovna Allilueva, born in 1924, a native of Moscow, now living in the U.S.A.

CASE OF ALIEV. Biulleten' Verkhovnogo Suda SSSR, 1973, No. 6, p. 28
Aliev, A.A. was sentenced to death by shooting under Art. 94, par. 9 [intentional homicide] of the Criminal Code of the Azerbaidjan SSR by the Judicial Chamber of the Supreme Court of the Azerbaidjan SSR on 28 April 1973. He was found guilty of having killed Mamedov, E.K. on October 12, 1972 under circumstances of spe-

cial brutality. The crime was committed under the following circumstances:

Aliev in 1969, while studying at the Baku professional technical school met Mamedov, a student at the same school, establishing good relationships. After graduation Aliev remained in Baku to work and lived in a dormitory, but Mamedov left to work in Saatly. They continued to maintain friendly relations.

On October 12, 1972 Mamedov returned to Baku and went to the dormitory where Aliev lived to visit his acquaintances. At about 8 P.M. he dropped in to Aliev's room and suggested that they go out together on the next day. Then Mamedov entered room no. 135 to see his former fellow students, Nagiev, Ragimov and Dunemaliev. About midnight Aliev entered the room and asked Mamedov to step into the corridor. When he did so, Aliev asked why he thought poorly of a girl whom Aliev was dating. A dispute ensued over this subject, and it grew into a fight during which Aliev struck Mamedov 13 blows with a penknife, wounding him in various parts of the body. Mamedov died in a few hours in a hospital.

The Judicial Division of Criminal Cases of the USSR Supreme Court, reversing the decision on the protest of its Vice President, satisfied the protest for the following reasons:

Aliev was proved guilty of intentional homicide of Mamedov, and his actions were properly classified under the Code. However, Aliev's sentence failed to take into consideration the concrete circumstances and his personality. Under Art. 22 of the Fundamental Principles of Criminal Legislation. . .the death penalty is an exceptional punishment. The USSR Supreme Court's Plenum in its decree of June 30, 1969 "On the judicial sentence" explained that courts in deciding whether to apply the death penalty must be guided by the rule that the penalty can be applied only when the need to apply it is indicated by special circumstances aggravating responsibility and where there is exceptional danger to society in the person committing the crime.

Aliev was 21 years old when he committed the crime; had graduated from the professional-technical school; was working as a painter-plasterer; performed his work on construction projects faithfully, completing his assignments on time; and had no prior court record. Taking these facts relating to his personality into consideration and also the concrete circumstances of the case the Judicial Division for Criminal Cases of the USSR Supreme Court reached the conclusion that sentencing of Aliev to the exceptional measure of punishment was unnecessary. [All prior decisions were set aside, and the death penalty was reduced to 15 years deprivation of freedom in a correctional labor colony of strict regime.]

PLUNDERERS' PUNISHMENT. Baku Rabochy, December 25, 1975, p. 4. Eng. trans. in 27 CDSP No. 52, p. 7 (1976).

The Azerbaidjan Supreme Court has examined a criminal case involving especially large thefts of socialist property at the Lenkoran Vegetable Grading and Packing Factory and on a number of fishing collectives in Lenkoran District. . .The trial showed that in the fisheries the people's property had been squandered in an organized manner over a long period of time and that vast sums of state money had been plundered and misappropriated by criminal elements holding executive posts at the factory and in the fishing collectives. The losses . . .totalled about 9 million rubles.

During the court hearing 64 persons were convicted; two directors of the vegetable factory who had worked there at different times; 11 managers of receiving stations; 8 commodity appraisers; 4 chairmen and 4 chief bookkeepers of fishing collectives; 3 agronomists and others. All were given severe penalties. The ringleaders [5 names] were sentenced to the extreme penalty, execution by a firing squad. Large amounts of jewelry, 9 passenger cars and several houses built with unearned income were confiscated from the convicted persons.

CASE OF VETOSHKIN, Biulleten' Verkhovnogo Suda RSFSR, 1969, No. 5, p. 11.

Vetoshkin was sentenced under Art. 206, par. 2 [malicious hooliganism] of the RSFSR Criminal Code by the Suktyvkarst city people's court to 2 years deprivation of freedom. An unserved suspended sentence of September 7, 1967 - one year's deprivation of freedom- was cumulated under Art. 41 of the Criminal Code to the present sentence to make a total of 3 years' deprivation of freedom in a labor colony for minors.

[On appeal the Komi ASSR Supreme Court altered the sentence to remove the one year cumulation on the ground that Vetoshkin had benefitted as to that first sentence from the amnesty of October 31, 1967. The Procurator protested, and his protest was satisfied by the Judicial Division of the RSFSR Supreme Court, which said:]

Vitoshkin was found guilty of malicious hooliganism while drunk; shouting unprintable words; starting a fight with Osipov; paying no attention to the warnings of Osipov's parents; striking Osipov in the face with his fists causing light bodily injury; and then while upsetting a table, he threatened the citizens with a screwdriver and broke the glass in a window.

The Komi ASSR's Supreme Court's Judicial Division applied the amnesty decree of October 31, 1967 to the convict and freed him from punishment because his first conviction preceded publication of the decree. The Judicial Division did not, however, take into consideration the negative facts characterizing the person of the convict. From the record it is evident that Vitoshkin systematically violated public order; was often drunk; did not work anywhere; had been fined for petty hooliganism and finally committed the crime for which he was convicted on September 7, 1967 under Art. 206, par. 1. . .and was given a suspended sentence of one year's deprivation of freedom. After that he did not reform himself, but committed more serious crimes during his probationary period. The amnesty, as stated in the Edict of October 3, 1967 applies to persons not presenting great social danger and who have demonstrated by exemplary conduct and a conscientious relationship to their work that they have reformed. Such circumstances have not been established in this case. [The decision was held to be unfounded and the case returned for new cassational review]

CASE OF IL'IN, Biulleten' Verkhovnogo Suda RSFSR, 1968, No. 11, p. 13.

Il'in was declared to be an especially dangerous recidivist by judgment of the Tuva ASSR Supreme Court of August 25, 1967 and convicted under Art. 102, par. b of the RSFSR Criminal Code [intentional homicide from motives of hooliganism] The RSFSR Supreme Court's Judicial Division left the judgment unchanged. . . .The Vice President of the RSFSR Supreme Court protested, arguing for exclusion from the judgment of the finding of especially dangerous recidivist and proposed sentence to a correctional labor colony on the ground that Il'in's former conviction under Art. 142, par. 1 of the RSFSR Criminal Code of 1926 [intentional severe bodily injury] had been expunged by passage of the period of the statute of limitations.

After reviewing the record, the Presidium of the RSFSR Supreme Court satisfied the protest, saying:

As is evident from the copy of the people's court's judgment of January 9, 1957 Il'in was convicted under Art. 142, par. 1 of the 1926 Criminal Code of the RSFSR to 6 years' deprivation of freedom. When the judgment was issued, he was placed under guard.Thus the period of the punishment began January 9, 1957. On January 31, 1961 Il'in was freed conditionally, having served 4 years 21 days of his sentence. In order to expunge the conviction under Art. 51, par. 6 of the RSFSR Criminal Code Il'in needed a 5 year period of freedom. The period when his record of conviction expired must be reckoned from the moment he was freed, i.e. from January 31, 1961 and not from the day of termination of the unserved portion of the sentence.

Il'in committed a new crime 6 years 4 months and 23 days after having been freed from punishment under the former judgment. During that period his former conviction had been expunged by running of the statute of limitations. Therefore, the prior judgment cannot be used as the basis for declaring Il'in to be an especially dangerous recidivist. [All prior orders were changed to eliminate the declaration of especially dangerous recidivist: the rest of the judgment was left in force.]

CASE OF GUDKOV, Biulleten' Verkhovnogo Suda SSSR, 1971, No. 5, p. 19.

Iu.V. Gudkov was convicted under Art. 208, par. 2 and Art. 92, par. 2 of the RSFSR Criminal Code [repeated theft of state property by abuse of official position and acquisition or marketing of property known to have been acquired criminally]. The court ordered forfeited to the state, as the means used to commit a crime, the following items: a Moskvich automobile, a Northern-3 refrigerator, a Festival radio receiving set, a gold watch, etc. The judgment was affirmed by the Judicial Division for Criminal Cases of the Moscow City Court.

Gudkov was found guilty of utilizing his position as engineer of the All-uion research and experimental construction institute of food machinery to steel systematically from the institute radio parts during 1961 and for 3 months of 1962. During this period he stole parts of a value of 504 rubles 35 kopecks, selling a part of them in the autumn of 1961 to an employee of the Department Store "Pioneer" for 80 rubles and keeping a part of them at his home. Gudkov stole 6 volumes of a service manual, "The elements of radiotechnical and electronic instruments," having a value of 38 rubles 70 kopecks. Gudkov was also found guilty of acquiring during 1960 from some one, not identified by the investigation, of radio parts known to have been stolen, these having a value of 80 rubles.

[On appeal the conviction under Art. 92 was set aside as unproved, but that under Art. 208, par. 2 was sustained. Then the President of the USSR Supreme Court protested that part of the judgment confiscating Gudkov's property, and the USSR Supreme Court Plenum satisfied the protest for the following reasons:]

According to the judgment the inventoried property (automobile, refrigerator, etc.) was confiscated as means of committing the crime . . . under Art. 86 RSFSR Code of Criminal Procedure. Yet, apart from the fact that there is not enough evidence to conclude that the aforementioned property was used to commit the crime, the court on hearing the case did not take into consideration that confiscation of money or property from a convict is permitted by law only if it was material evidence. From the record it is evident that the aforementioned items were not found to be material evidence, and they were not marked as such or investigated either by the investigating organs or the court. It was also not established that Gudkov acquired the inventoried property with money acquired by a criminal act.

Ignoring the aforementioned rule of law, the court arbitrarily applied confiscation of property as a supplementary measure of punishment when neither the sanctions under Art. 208, par. 2 for violation of which Gudkov was convicted, nor under Art. 92, par. 2 for violation of which he was initially found guilty included such a penalty. [The sanction of confiscation was ordered excluded from the judgment, but the rest of the sentence was left in effect]

CASE OF BOLGOV, Biulleten' Verkhovnogo Suda RSFSR, 1971, No. 2, p. 6.

Bolgov was sentenced to 4 years' deprivation of freedom in a correctional labor colony of general regime by Shchebelin county people's court under Art. 211, par. 3 of the RSFSR Criminal Code [violation of transport operating rules resulting in multiple deaths]. The Gomo-Altai autonomous provincial court affirmed the sentence. The RSFSR Deputy Procurator protested the sentence to the RSFSR Supreme Court's Judicial Division for Criminal Cases on the ground that the sentence did not correspond to the seriousness of the crime nor to the personality of the convict. He asked that the case be remanded for new investigation. The Judicial Division satisfied the protest, saying:

Bolgov has been found guilty of violating the safety rules for automobile transport as the result of which several persons died. The circumstances were the following: On December 11, 1970 Bolgov was driving a trailer truck ZIL-130 from Busk to Tashkent. At the 148 kilometer post in overtaking automobile GAZ-51 in violation of Art. 36, and Art. 49, par. "v" of the Regulations for traffic on streets of cities, population centers and highways of the USSR, he failed to give a timely signal and cut in before the overtaken vehicle within from 10 to 15 meters. The truck driven by him locked onto the left side of automobile GAZ-51, striking it with the trailer, as a result of which the trailer became uncoupled and overturned. As a result of the accident 3 persons died and 6 were injured.

If one considers that the aforementioned serious consequences occurred because of Bolgov's guilt, the punishment meted out..., 4 years' deprivation of freedom, clearly does not correspond to the seriousness of the crime. On a new judicial examination the court must investigate carefully the factual circumstances of what happened and verify more thoroughly the reasons for the accident. Also it must determine more carefully which of the injuries suffered by the 6 victims resulted from the accident since the hospital doctor's conclusion as an expert has a substantial inadequacy: he speaks of "severe" bodily injuries; the light bodily injuries are not limited to the consequences flowing from these. The conclusion is in no way explained.

If on retrial it is established that Bolgov permitted violations of the road regulations, and as a result of this the consequences indicated followed, the court must decide whether more severe punishment should not be applied to him. Moreover, the court must decide whether in accordance with the sanctions of Art. 211, par. 3 of the RSFSR Criminal Code [deprivation of freedom for a term of from 3 to 15 years with or without deprivation of the right to drive transport vehicles for a term not exceeding 5 years] the accused should be deprived of his driver's license.

Considering the complexity of the case it is expedient to remand it for trial in the provincial court of the Gomo-Altai autonomous province.

CASE OF ALFEROV, Biulleten' Verkhovnogo Suda RSFSR, 1974, No. 8, pp. 7-8.

Alferov was sentenced by the Kursk provincial court under Art. 173, par. 2 of the RSFSR Criminal Code [repeated acceptance of bribes while in an official position.] to 8 years' deprivation of freedom in a correctional labor colony of severe regime with confiscation of his bank accounts in the amount of 6,000 rubles, a 3% state loan bond in the face amount of 1,000 rubles and cash in the amount of 610 rubles found during a search of his apartment. Furthermore, Alferov was shorn of his academic degrees as a "candidate of philosophical sciences." The judgment was not appealed.

The Judicial Division for Criminal Cases of the RSFSR Supreme Court, in reviewing the case on the protest of the RSFSR Deputy Procurator against depriving Alferov of his academic degree, satisfied the protest and stated the following:

Alferov was found guilty of accepting bribes regularly from students in 1971 while serving as a teacher of philosophy at the Kurst scientific-consultation bureau of the extramural institute of Soviet trade to give passing grades in philosophy on tests and examinations. Alferov's guilt was established and his act was correctly classified under Art. 173, par. 2...Nevertheless, the judgment in violation of Art. 36 of the RSFSR Criminal Code [deprivation of military and other ranks and of orders, medals and honorary titles] deprived Alferov of his academic degree. Art. 36...does not provide for deprivation of academic degrees and titles. This is provided for by an instruction on the procedure for awarding academic degrees and naming of teaching titles, approved by the Supreme Attesting Committee of the Ministry of Supreme and Middle Specialized Education of the USSR, dated June 23, 1972.

Under paragraph 67 of this instruction, scientific teaching personnel committing amoral, antipatriotic and other offenses incompatible with the title of a Soviet scientist may be deprived of their academic degrees (doctor of science and candidate of science) and of their title (professor, dotsent, senior scientific assistant, assistant, and junior scientific assistant) on petition of the scientific councils of supreme scientific schools and scientific research institutes by the Supreme Attesting Committee. Courts must inform the Supreme Attesting Committee of persons with acadeemic degrees and titles who have been convicted. [The protest was satisfied and the Supreme Attesting Committee was notified of Alferov's conviction so that it might decide the question of depriving him of his degree and title].

C. *Causes of crime.*

A.A. Gertsenzen, UGOLOVNOE PRAVO I SOTSIOLOGIIA [Criminal Law and Sociology] (Moscow, 1970) 30, 34-35.

Soviet literature on criminal law in the 1920's was characterized by attempts to find a way to combine the legal and sociological aspects of investigation...In recent years the sociological element has disappeared from criminal law textbooks. The question may be posed - why? ... There are many reasons...As is well known, during a certain period sociological research was generally neglected, during which period, instead of studying the broad field of social problems on a really factual basis, discussion was limited to dogmatic commentary on various propositions of historical materialism.

An important part was played by the widely dispersed view that sociological problems were beyond the boundaries of criminal law, and the circulation of this view undoubtedly had an influence more or less on the normative approach to research in the field of criminal law... We often notice how in studies devoted to research in criminal law the usual formal legal commentary on individual criminal legal norms of law is the methodology in use. This kind of research can be conducted in complete separation from the reality of society, and authors in comparing criminal legal norms can polemicize with other authors over their interpretation, adding their commentaries to tens of others of the same type previously published.

One must also note the widely used method in criminal law literature of using certain examples from investigatory or judicial practice to strengthen an author's position and assertions. Even though this method has no probative or scientific force, and even though it violates V.I. Lenin's famous comments on the impermissibility in scientific research of relying upon isolated facts, it is widely used in our criminal law literature as a substitute for sociological research. It only looks like scientific research and does not come near to recognition of the nature of the matter studied... It is time to give the "right of citizenship" in the Soviet science of criminal law to the sociological aspect along with and in common with the purely legal aspect.

BOOK REVIEW OF GERTSENZON, Sotsialisticheskaia zakonnost'. 1970, No. 12, p. 82.

... It is very valuable that Prof. A. Gertsenzon for the first time has brought the sociological study of institutions of the general part of the criminal law into our legal literature. On the basis of sociological study of 100 criminal cases of homicide or inflicting bodily injury when exceeding the limits of necessary self-defense, the author demonstrated that similar study would permit disclosure of the most typical errors of investigating agencies and courts in applying Art. 13 of the Fundamental Principles of Criminal Legislation [necessary defense]. Thus, it seems that in the preliminary investigation, 81% of the cases of intentional homicide and severe bodily injury were classed as having been committed without exceeding the limits of necessary self defense; 19% . . . with exceeding the limits. . .

The people's courts in these same cases qualified them differently. In 22% they found no exceeding of limits. . . i.e. four times less, and in 77% (instead of 19%) they found that there had been use of force exceeding the limits of self defense. The picture is even more developed after looking at cases in cassational courts. Here there was not even one case in which severe crime was found without the presence of acts which exceeded the limits of necessary self defense. 91% of the cases were found to have been those in which the limits of necessary self defense had been exceeded, while 9% were terminated for lack of the elements of crime because the limits of necessary self defense had not been exceeded. This example, in our view, demonstrates convincingly the great practical value of sociological research into the institutions of the general and special parts of criminal law. . .

Iu. Solopanov and vs. Kvaskis, "RECIDIVISM AND RECIDIVISTS," Sovetskaia iustitsiia, 1972, No. 7, p. 9

We conducted a statistical analysis in 1969-70 of data gathered on criminal repeaters after release from correctional institutions. . . Our findings were that the same crimes were repeated as follows: 47% of those convicted of crimes against personal property; 43% of those convicted of vagrancy, and 59% of those convicted of hooliganism. Murder, rape and serious bodily injury were repeated by only 14% of the persons previously convicted of such crimes, although 49.8% of this group was convicted subsequently of hooliganism. . .

Recidivism is at a much higher rate among those with a large number of convictions. The effectiveness of the various regimes of corrective labor colonies also affects the rate of recidivism. New crimes are less likely from those released from strict regime colonies than from general regime colonies. The average detention in general regime colonies is only 33% to 40% of the detention in strict regime colonies. . .

I.I. Karpets, "ON THE NATURE AND CAUSES OF CRIME," Sovetskoe Gosudarstvo i Pravo, 1966, No. 4, p. 82

To study social trends, including study of crime, its causes and the conditions that facilitate it, one must approach methodologically from a Marxist position. . .Crime is by nature a complex social phenomenon. To lay it to biological causes, in whatever manner this is attempted, would be to conceal its real nature, its social content, and would, therefore, conflict with Marxist-Leninist science. . .

At a United Nations Congress. . .bourgeois scientists stressed the growth of cities (urbanization) and technical progress, taking the position that social progress of itself and its various manifestations - the growth of cities and industrialization - are causes of crime. . .But the experience of the Soviet Union and of other socialist countries demonstrates that industrialization alone need not give rise to crime. . .

. . .It is often asked whether it can be concluded that since crime exists in socialist society, socialism as a social structure is giving rise to crime. To answer this question we must recall Lenin's proposition that during the first phase of communism society will do away at the outset with that injustice created by the fact that the means of production have been appropriated by individuals, but it is not in a position to do away immediately with the further injustice which rests on the distribution of consumer goods in accordance with "work" rather than need.

Under socialism the materio-technical base is more weakly developed than under communism. The growth of material security, of the cultural level, of the social consciousness of the members of society is still not high enough. There still exist some factors of historical development, such as the difference between city and country and other non-antagonistic contradictions during the first phase of communism. Consequently, conditions for the liquidation of crime and its causes have not yet been completely established in our society which is building communism. . .

Of course, one must emphasize two imporant points - First, in our society there are no primary rudimentary reasons such as the exploitation of man by man, unemployment, impoverishment and other social vices which grow out of exploitative society. . .Secondly, the social causes of crime in the U.S.S.R. are being overcome in the process of creating communism.

In explaining the causes of crime as a social phenomenon one must begin with the formula of the relics of the past and the activities of the imperialist camp. . .Research projects. . .have demonstrated that the form and intensity of this influence depends upon a number of circumstances. . .especially on the character and intensity of the information coming out of imperialist states, on the character of links with persons living in capitalist countries (relatives, acquaintances, etc.) or persons who are in our country as temporary visitors. . . .

As to the other aspect of the formula- the relics of the past. . . They are many . . .learned from parents, acquaintances, and from the milieu. . .Drunkenness of parents, petty bourgeois views, etc.: these are relics which a young person can see often.

. . .The principle of distribution according to work does not and cannot give rise to the desire to commit crime. Every understanding Soviet man recognizes the justice of this principle. . .but in isolated cases the improper evaluation of work can create the desire to commit crime.

MEASURES TO INTENSIFY THE STRUGGLE WITH DRUNKENNESS AND ALCOHOLISM. Decree of the Council of Ministers USSR, May 16, 1972.
Sbornik partiinogo rabotnika, Vypusk 13 (1973) 183.

The Council of Ministers decrees:

1. In order to reduce the level of consumption of alcoholic drinks in the country, it is deemed necessary:

—to introduce measures to reduce the production of vodka and strong distilled products in 1972-75;

—to increase markedly the production of non-alcoholic drinks so as to meet completely the demands of the population for these drinks;

—to instruct the State Planning Commission USSR, the Ministry of the Food Industry and the Council of Ministers of the Union Republics to include in their annual plans:

[here follow paragraphs devoted to reduction of production of strong liquors; increase in production of wines and beer; allocation of capital resources to create productive capacity for vodka substitutes; the manufacture of equipment to make wines and beers; increase in the production of grapes and hops; and the manufacture of the necessary containers for such products].

D. *Intent.*

CASE OF RODINA, M.T. and RODINA, D.I., Biulleten' Verkhovnogo Suda SSSR, 1969, No. 6, p. 8.

M.T. Rodina was convicted by the people's court of Chilinzar borough of Tashkent on July 15, 1967 of violating Art. 88, par. "v" of the Uzbek SSR Criminal Code [intentional serious bodily injury causing death] and D.I. Rodina of violating Art. 17 and Art. 88, par. "v" [complicity in the same crime]. The criminal acts were committed by Rodin in the following circumstances:

During the evening of February 18, 1967 Rodin together with his wife, his mother and his wife's brother, Mikhail Shevchenko, took some drinks at their home. After Shevchenko left Rodin and his wife broke into a dispute; Rodin began to beat her and she, in fleeing, jumped out of a second story window. Below, under the window, stood a bed with metal rods protruding upward. In falling, Zinaida

Rodina struck a rod on the bed and received a serious concussion. . . Not stopping with what had already happened, Rodin also jumped out of the window, found Zinaida and continued to beat her. As a result of the fall and the beating, Zinaida Rodina suffered severe bodily injury from which she died the next day.

D.I. Rodina, the mother of M. Rodin, was found guilty of inciting her son to commit the aforementioned crime and of helping him to beat the victim.

On August 8, 1968 the Judicial Division for Criminal Cases of the Uzbek SSR Supreme Court, in reviewing the case by way of judicial supervision, classified Rodin's acts under Art. 87 of the Uzbek SSR Criminal Code [incitement to suicide]. D.I. Rodina's acts were qualified under Arts. 17 and 87 [complicity in incitement to suicide].

[The Republic Procurator and later the Procurator General of the USSR protested to the Republic Supreme Court and to the USSR Supreme Court].

The USSR Supreme Court's Plenum satisfied the protest for the following reason:

In classifying the acts of the convicts as incitement to suicide the Judicial Division for Criminal Cases relied on the fact that the death of the victim resulted from the severe concussion suffered when falling after jumping from the window of her apartment and not from the injuries inflicted by her husband. The Presidium and then the Plenum of the Uzbek SSR Supreme Court agreed with this.

The decision of the courts indicated cannot be accepted as well founded; first of all because this conclusion that there was present in the acts of the convicts the elements of the crime of incitement to suicide is incorrect. That crime supposes under the law intentional self-destruction of the victim incited to commit the act by the actions of the guilty person, as set forth in Art. 87 of the Uzbek SSR Criminal Code. In the present case it has been established that M.T. Rodin, incited by his mother, D.I. Rodina, in fact did beat his wife, but she, as the evidence in the record indicated, jumped from the window, trying to save herself from her husband's acts and not trying to end her life by suicide. The fact that in falling she struck the bed's metal rod protruding upward under the window and received a severe concussion consequently gives no reason to view what happened as an attempt to commit suicide. Proof of the absence of such an intention is seen in the fact that even though injured she nevertheless tried to flee from Rodin who was pursuing her, and she asked the neighbors for help.

From the record it is evident that Rodin, catching up with his wife in the courtyard, when she was already severely injured and in serious condition continued to beat her. From the testimony of witnesses, Iusupov, Kutliev, Raemin and Grebentsova, it can be concluded that Rodin as well as his mother, who hindered efforts of other persons to stop the beating, recognized the condition of the victim and the consequences with which she was threatened as a result of the beating. In accordance with the conclusions of the forensic-medical experts, the injuries caused by Rodin aggravated the generally serious condition of the victim Rodina and hastened her death.

Taking the above into consideration, it is necessary to conclude that bodily injuries caused Rodina by the further beating represented danger to the life of the victim and consequently must be considered as grave. Under these circumstances Rodin's act was properly classified by the court under Art. 88, par "v". . .as intentional bodily injury occasioning death. The crime of Rodina was also correctly classified as instigation of her son to commit the crime indicated. She persuaded him to proceed with these acts, knowing their character and danger.

[The judgment of the people's court was reinstated, and the rulings of the Uzbek Supreme Court set aside]

CASE OF BARENKO, Biulleten' Verkhovnogo Suda RSFSR, 1969, No. 8, p. 17

Barenko was convicted under RSFSR Criminal Code, Art. 102, par "b" [intentional homicide with a weapon dangerous to the lives of many]. Having received the case on appeal by the convict and his lawyer, the RSFSR Supreme Court's Judicial Division for Criminal Cases established:

Barenko was found guilty of intentional homicide under the following circumstances: During the evening of September 15, 1968 Bakemenko set forth a supper in the courtyard of his house and invited his neighbors, the Barenko couple and the Kamenev family. At 10 P.M. Barenko and Kamenev went off to Barenko's house for cigarettes. In the courtyard of Barenko's house a dog, escaping from Barenko's hands, bit Kamenev. On returning to the courtyard Kamenev told Bakemenko of what happened and added that Barenko had purposely let the dog go.

Barenko insisted that the dog had twisted himself out of his hands and that he did not set him on Kamenev. Nevertheless, Kamenev and Bakemenko shoved Barenko through the gate, causing him injury. When he reached home, Barenko seized a hunting gun, loaded it and returned to Bakemenko's house. Seeing Barenko coming, Bakemenko went to meet him. Barenko, having stopped at the courtyard gate, 8 to 9 meters away, shot and killed Bakemenko.

The Judicial Chamber found the judgment subject to modification, saying: Barenko's guilt was proved by his own testimony, by the testimony of Bakemenko's wife, and the witness Kamenev, and by the conclusion of the forensic-medical expert as to the cause of Bakemenko's death. Nevertheless, Barenko's criminal act was qualified under Art. 102, par. "d" incorrectly. When the court classified the acts of the convict as homicide committed with means endangering the lives of many, the court presumed that Barenko in shooting at Bakemenko knew of the presence of other people in the courtyard, and, therefore, foresaw the possibility that other people would also die from the shot.

Yet, to qualify intentional homicide committed with means endangering the lives of many it must be established that the guilty person, having the intent to kill a specific person chose a means of killing that he knew to be dangerous to the lives of many persons. Thus, the danger for other people must be real under the given concrete circumstances. In the instant case the view of the court that Barenko was conscious of the danger to the lives of others in what he did was not confirmed by the evidence. The record establishes that the people in the courtyard were not at table at the moment of shooting. The circumstances that Bakemenko's wife at the moment of shooting was right behind her husband also is no proof of the convicted person's realization of the danger to the lives of others from his acts. The convicted person testified that at the moment of shooting he did not see the victim's wife since it was dark. The wife herself confirmed this fact.

Taking the above into account, Barenko's acts should have been classified under RSFSR Criminal Code Art. 103 [intentional homicide without aggravating circumstances].

CASE OF MATIUSHKIN, Biulleten' Verkhovnogo Suda RSFSR, 1967, No. 3, p. 3.

The Deputy Procurator of the RSFSR filed a protest with the RSFSR's Supreme Court's Presidium raising the question of reclassification of Matiushkin's acts from RSFSR Criminal Code Art. 108, par. 2 [intentional infliction of grave bodily harm causing death] to Art. 106 [negligent homicide], and to fix his punishment at 3 years' deprivation of freedom [the trial court had sentenced him to 6 years].

Having examined the record the RSFSR's Supreme Court's Presidium ruled: Matiushkin was found guilty of inflicting severe bodily injury upon the seven year old boy, Nikolai Karchin, from which death resulted. Matiushkin on June 5, 1963 was escorting some autobuses loaded on railroad flatcars. On passing through the station of Kovylkino Matiushkin noticed a group of youngsters playing ball. Several stood near the roadbed and threw stones at the buses. Among this group was Nikolai Karchin, later the victim.

Being on one of the flatcars of the train, Matiushkin seized a metal pipe belonging to the coupling hose of the braking system of the car and a fragment of plank and threw them at the youths. The metal pipe fell on Nikolai Karchin's head, who died in the hospital on June 7, 1963 as a result of the traumatic injury to his skull and brain. Matiushkin denied his guilt, testifying that while escorting the freight he stood on the braking platform and threw nothing at the youths.

On the basis of the evidence in the record the court concluded that Matiushkin deliberately inflicted a serious bodily injury on Karchin with the metal pipe, causing death. The court's conclusion is disputed in the protest, and it is asserted that Matiushkin killed Karchin through negligence. As grounds for claiming that there was no intent to cause bodily injury to the victim the protest points to the fact that Matiushkin threw the metal pipe and the fragment of plank at the youths with no intent to cause any one harm but to prevent damage by stones to the autobuses on the flatcars. Therefore, he had not anticipated that harmful consequences could flow from his acts.

It is impossible to agree with such an assertion. The witnesses who were questioned in the case have confirmed that Matiushkin threw objects at the youths from a moving train at close range, and that among the objects thrown was a metal component of significant weight. Matiushkin acted deliberately, not negligently, in throwing the pipe, being aware that he might hurt some one, and he allowed this.

Under such circumstances Matiushkin must bear responsibility for his acts and the ensuing consequences. As is evident from the medical expert's testimony the injuries inflicted upon the victim fall in the category of grave ones causing death. . . [the judgment was affirmed].

CASE OF STARCHAK, Biulleten' Verkhovnogo Suda SSSR, 1972, No. 2, p. 11

V.N. Starchak was convicted under Ukrainian SSR Criminal Code Art. 117, par. 3 [rape of a minor] by the Lugansk Provincial Court on November 21, 1966. The conviction was affirmed by the Ukrainian SSR Supreme Court's Judicial Chamber on January 10, 1967. Starchuk was found guilty of raping a minor, A., born on July 24, 1949.

On August 21, 1966 Starchuk met A. at a dance in the park of the city of Ravenki. At about midnight he and his friend R. took A. and her neighbor B. to town. In the city center all four of them and one K. who joined them passed around a bottle of wine. K. then went home, and A. and B. entered on invitation the apartment of R.'s brother, who was absent at the time. Again they drank wine.

After that when R. and B. left the room to enter the kitchen, Starchuk who was drunk began to propose to A. sexual intercourse. When A. refused, Starchuk raped her and then told A. that he would stay with her until morning. Nevertheless, Starchuk did leave the room, and A., fearing that she would be raped again, fled to the balcony and jumped to the street from the second floor. On falling, A. suffered bodily injury of average severity.

[The classification of the crime was protested with a proposal that it be reclassified under Art. 117, par. 1. (i.e. rape without aggravating circumstances)]

The protest was satisfied for the following reason:

The court reached the conclusion on adequate evidence that Starchuk was guilty of the rape of A. This was supported by testimony of the victim, the witness B., R. and others; and also by the forensic-medical expert. Yet, the qualification of the act as rape of a minor cannot be accepted. Under Art. 117, par. 3 in order to accept this qualification of the crime, the guilty person must know or consider probable that he is committing a forced sexual act with a minor, or he could or should have foreseen the probability. It is evident from the record that the victim's appearance, her conduct, and other circumstances did not suggest her minority.

Starchuk cannot be held responsible under Art. 117, par. 2 [rape by a person who has previously committed rape]. It is true that this was not the first time he had been convicted of rape, but the first conviction had already been expunged at the time of the second. [The conviction was reclassified under Art. 117, par. 1].

CASE OF KUDELINSKII, Biulleten' Verkhovnogo Suda RSFSR, 1970, No. 6, p. 11.

Kudelinski was convicted under RSFSR Criminal Code Art. 211, par. 2 [violation of transport rules by driver of vehicle] and sentenced to 3 years' deprivation of freedom by the Kursk county people's court of Kursk Province. The sentence was affirmed by the Kursk provincial court. The Presidium of the Provincial Court changed the sentence to a conditional one and excluded from it a supplementary punishment - revocation of Kudelinskii's driving license.

Kudelinskii was convicted of violating the safety rules for motor transport, causing severe consequences under the following circumstances: During the evening of November 21, 1968, Kudelinskii, a driver for a collective farm of a loaded truck GA2-51 assigned to him, entered a dining hall in the village of Starkovo, where he met the drunken Kobelev and Zherdev. They asked him to drive them home to the village of Petrovo, but he refused, saying that the back of the truck was filled with freight. Nevertheless, when he went off to the store, Kobelev and Zherdev climbed into the back of the truck. When he came out of the store Kudelinskii asked Zherdev to get out of the truck, and he did so. Not knowing whether Kobelev had also left, Kudelinskii drove on toward the village. On the way Kobelev who was still drunk fell off the back of the truck and fell under a wheel, dying from the injury.

At the trial Kudelinskii explained that he had not seen Kobelev in the back of the truck; that he had seen only Zherdev whom he had asked to leave. [The RSFSR Deputy Procurator protested the conviction for lack of the elements of a crime]. The Judicial Chamber satisfied the protest in its ruling of February 9, 1970 for the following reasons:

As is evident from the record and as was found by the trial court Kovelev sat in the truck voluntarily and without Kudelinskii's knowledge, demonstrating grave carelessness and placing hiself in a dangerous position. Kudelinskii broke no rules of the road, and there is nothing in his actions that is criminally punishable. The accident occurred because of the gross carelessness of the victim himself. Since, under the circumstances, Kudelinskii did not know and could not know that Kobelev was in the back of the truck, he cannot be held criminally responsible for Kobelev's death which was the result of his own grave carelessness.

CASE OF A.G. IVANOV, Biulleten' Verkhovnogo Suda SSSR, 1972, No. 2, p. 16

A.G. Ivanov was convicted by a people's court of the Leningrad borough of Riga on October 22, 1970 of violating the Latvian SSR Criminal Code, Art. 211, par. 1 [systematic vagrancy], and was given a suspended sentence of one year's deprivation of freedom with a probationary period of 2 years. Ivanov was found guilty of malicious refusal to perform an order to work and to end his parasitic way of life. According to the judgment the crime was formulated as follows:

Ivanov was dismissed on July 25, 1967 from the Riga factory "Dinamo" for absence from work without acceptable reasons and for drinking, refraining from socially useful work and leading a parasitic life over a long period of time. The agencies of Internal Affairs warned Ivanov repeatedly, and then the record on him was sent to the District Procurator to decide whether to apply compulsory measures to make him work. The Executive Committee of the borough Soviet sent him to work at the factory "Rigasel'mash" by its decisions of June 10 and July 8, 1970. However, on August 18, 1970 he regained himself his former job at the factory "Dinamo" and did not obey the Executive Committee decision.

[The judgment was protested up to the USSR Supreme Court because of the absence of elements of a crime, and the USSR Supreme Court's Plenum satisfied the protest, saying:]

Under the provisions of the Latvian SSR's Criminal Code Art. 211 it is criminally actionable for a person conducting an anti-social type of life to refuse to obey an order of an Executive Committee of a county (city)Soviet. . .to work and to stop leading a parasitic way of life. It follows from this that criminal responsibility for this type of crime may be enforced if a citizen, in spite of the Executive Committee's order refuses to work and carries on his former way of life. In this case no such circumstances have been established.

Ivanov testified at his trial that after dismissal from the factory "Dinamo" he tried to find other work, applying to various organizations, but he was refused because of a derogatory entry in his labor record book. In March 1970 he was in a hospital for treatment. After the Executive Committee's order he could not get work immediately because he had lost his documents, and he was able to obtain a new passport and residency permit only at the factory "Dinamo" where he had worked formerly. At the factory "Rigasel'mash" to which the Executive Committee had sent him, he was not offered work on a shift. This explanation of Ivanov was confirmed by certificates included in the record.

The Judicial Chamber and the Presidium of the Latvian SSR Supreme Court. . .presumed that when a person ordered to perform socially useful work under compulsion finds work for himself in another enterprise, it is not irrefutable reason to free such person from criminal responsibility. This conclusion cannot be accepted as correct. The Edict of the Latvian SSR's Supreme Soviet's Presidium of April 30, 1970 had as its purpose establishment of criminal responsibility for the failure of a person, refusing for unacceptable reasons to engage in socially useful work, to obey an order to work. A number of measures are set forth in the Edict compelling such persons to put their feet on the path to an honest life of labor. Only when a person maliciously refuses to work and clearly does not wish to execute the Executive Committee's order is there a basis for criminal responsibility.

The circumstances that Ivanov got work not at the enterprise indicated in the order but at another one is no indication of commission of the crime defined by Art. 211. . . It is evident from the record that Ivanov himself took measures to get work but was unable to do so immediately upon receipt of the order because he had no passport. To obtain a new passport and residency permit took more than a month. In order to get the necessary documents he once again entered upon work at the factory "Dinamo," and this antedated the prosecution. The element of maliciousness is absent in this case [the case was dismissed for lack of the elements of a crime].

E. *Negligence*

CASE OF KARPOV, Biulleten' Verkhovnogo Suda RSFSR, 1970, No. 7, p. 9.

Karpov was convicted of violating RSFSR Criminal Code Art. 108 [intentional infliction of grave bodily injury] and Art. 218, par. 1 [illegal keeping of arms]. There was no appeal.

[protests were filed, and the case reached the RSFSR Supreme Court's Judicial Division for Criminal Cases, which stated the following]:

Karpov was found guilty of fabricating and keeping without a permit a homemade pistol and of inflicting intentionally bodily injury on Noskov, 18 years old, causing his death under the following circumstances:

Noskov was stuying in the beginning year at the Kursk polytechnic institute, where he had unsatisfactory grades in many subjects and finally stopped studying. In October 1968 Noskov petitioned the Institute's Dean to be transferred to an evening school, but he withdrew the petition later at his parents's request, although he did not wish to continue his Institute studies for the balance of 1968. So as not to be dismissed from the Institute, Noskov decided to injure himself, to go to a hospital, and to obtain academic leave from study in the Institute. For this purpose he asked the youth Aleksander Sokhin to shoot him with the homemade pistol which he and Karpov had fabricated. Sokhin refused. Then Noskin, in order to become ill, swam the Tuskar' River in November 1968 when the air's temperature was minus 5.4 centigrade. Since he did not become ill thereafter, he asked his friend Oleg Karpov to wound him with a pistol shot. Karpov consented, and on November 15, 1968 Noskov and Karpov prepared the home-made pistol, loaded it with sulphur scratched off of matches and placed a piece of metal wire in the barrel. Noskov wrote a note saying that Karpov would shoot him at his own request. Karpov tried to shoot Noskov that evening, but it did not explode. The next day Noskov, in order to lift suspicion from Karpov, spread a rumor among his friends that he was being shot at. On November 19, 1968 Noskov and Karpov took the loaded pistol and went to the Railroad Hospital's grounds where Karpov was to shoot and wound him. On seeing the watchman they changed their plans and took the electric trolley car to the stop "Perekal Square" and went toward the bridge across the Tuskar' River. Crossing the bridge and making sure that no strangers were present Karpov shot the pistol at 4 meters distance from Noskov and killed him.

The protest is not to be satisfied for the following reason: Karpov's guilt in committing the crime was proved, and he does not deny it himself. Classification of the crime under Art. 108, par. 2 is correct, since he, shooting at the victim from a firearm anticipated and consequently permitted the commission of intentional bodily harm. Karpov's acts were also correctly classified under Art. 218, par. 1. Under these circumstances the declaration in the protest that Karpov's guilt was expressed in the form of criminal self-confidence, and that his acts must be qualified as negligent homicide under Art. 106 is without foundation.

CASE OF RUSSOV, Sotsialisticheskaia Zakonnost', 1970, No. 11, p. 90.

Russov was convicted on September 2, 1967 by the Nikolaevsk Provincial Court of intentional homicide. On cassation, the Ukrainian SSR Supreme Court's Judicial Division for Criminal Cases amended the judgment, qualifying the crime as intentional severe bodily injury resulting in the death of the victim. The USSR Deputy Procurator General, thinking that Russov was guilty of negligent homicide, filed a protest, proposing reclassification. The Ukrainian SSR Supreme Court's Plenum did not agree, only reducing the penalty. The USSR Procurator General filed a protest on analagous grounds with the USSR Supreme Court's Plenum.

It was established that the crime was committed under the following circumstances: During the daytime of June 22, 1967 the students of Nikolaevsk Shipbuilding Institute, Sirenko and Serdiuk, entered a store and asked the salesgirl Zheregelia to join them at the movies that evening. She refused, since she hardly knew them, and, furthermore, both were drunk. Insisting that his invitation be accepted, Serdiuk seized Zheregelia's hand, and Sirenko took off her wristwatch, saying he would return it only at the movie theater. Both left after this. Soon after another group of students entered the store: Russov, Zakharov, Popov and Shestakov. Zheregelia told them the story and begged them to recover her watch. All four then overtook Serdiuk and Sirenko.

Finding that the latter had the watch, Russov demanded that Sirenko return the watch or take it back himself to Zheregelia. Sirenko refused. Then Russov struck him with the palm of his hand on the right and left sides of his jaw. Sirenko fell, lost consciousness and soon died of concussion of the brain and hemorrhage on the brain, as established by the forensic-medical expert.

Russov testified that he had struck the victim with the flat of his hand and had no idea that such serious consequences would follow. The nature of Russov's acts gave no evidence of an intent to cause the victim's death or serious bodily injury. Sirenko and Russov had not known each other previously, and, moreover, there were no circumstances which could have excited Russov to do this. In striking the blow the convict's only aim was to force Sirenko to return the watch.

There is no evidence that the blow was heavy. In the autopsy Sirenko was not found to have exterior blood stains, abrasions or other injuries evidencing a remarkably heavy blow. The forensic-medical expert testified in court that "blows on the jaw with the palm of a hand rarely cause death." Witnesses testified that when Sirenko fell and lost consciousness, Russov was frightened, tried to give him aid, and said that he had not anticipated such consequences; that he would go himself to the militia to tell all. Thus, Russov's acts and his conduct both before and after the events give no reason to believe that Russov wanted Sirenko's death or intended to cause him grave bodily harm.

Thus, Russov cannot be held responsible for intentional commission of grave bodily harm causing death. Although he did not anticipate but should have anticipated the possibility of causing severe consequences as a result of the blow he struck, his acts should have been classified as negligent homicide. The protest was satisfied by the USSR Supreme Court's Plenum and the crime reclassified under Ukrainian SSR Criminal Code Art. 93.

F. *Insanity.*

CASE OF TOSHIN, Biulleten' Verkhovnogo Suda RSFSR, 1971, No. 4, p. 16.
   The Vologod Provincial Court terminated proceedings in the criminal prosecution of Toshin under RSFSR Criminal Code Art. 102, "b" and "h" [intentional homicide of two or more with hooligan motives] and Art. 206, par. 2 [malicious hooloiganism] and ordered that he be treated in a psychiatric hospital of a special type. The case was remanded for new trial by the RSFSR Supreme Court's Judicial Division for Criminal Cases on the victim's personal appeal for the following reasons:
   The Provincial Court's ruling violated the requirements of the RSFSR Code of Criminal Procedure Art. 410 and RSFSR Criminal Code Arts. 58 and 59. Under Art. 410, when a court finds that a socially dangerous act has been committed by a person who was in an irresponsible condition, it shall issue a ruling not to hold the person guilty but to free him from criminal responsibility in accordance with RSFSR Criminal Code Art. 11 [nonimputability because the accused cannot realize the significance of his actions or control them because of a chronic mental illness, temporary mental derangement, mental deficiency or other condition of illness].
   The court did say in its ruling that Tochin's guilt in committing homicide in a manner dangerous to the lives of many persons, in attempting to kill two or more persons, and in committing malicious hooligan acts was fully confirmed by the evidence submitted, but that in view of the fact that Toshin was held to be irresponsible, the proceedings were terminated, and he was sent for compulsory treatment to a psychiatric hospital of a special type. Yet, in sending Toshin for compulsory treatment, the court at the same time terminated proceedings in his case-- that was incorrect.
   With regard to persons who have committed a crime in an irresponsible condition the proceedings may be terminated under RSFSR Code of Criminal Procedure Art. 410 only if the person because of the character of the acts committed and the conditions of his disease does not represent a social danger and needs no compulsory treatment. Toshin committed a serious crime, and, as is evident, from the expert psychiatrist's conclusion needs compulsory treatment in a psychiatric hospital of a special type. Under such circumstances the court was required in conformity with RSFSR Criminal Code Arts. 58 and 59 [commitment to a psychiatric hospital] to settle in its ruling the question of the type of psychiatric hospital to which Toshin must be sent for compulsory treatment.

CASE OF EKIMOV, Biulleten' Verkhovnogo Suda SSSR, 1973, No. 3, p. 25
   Ekimov was convicted by the Altai Territorial Court on March 10, 1970 under RSFSR Criminal Code Art. 171, par. 2 [exceeding authority if accompanied by use

of a weapon] to 6 years' deprivation of freedom and under Arts. 15 and 102, par. "e" [attempted homicide committed in a manner dangerous to many persons] and sentenced for all his crimes to 8 years deprivation of freedom in a correctional labor colony of severe regime. [the penalty was later reduced to 4 years by the RSFSR Supreme Court's Presidium]. . .

At about 5 P.M. on December 13, 1969 Ekimov drank some wine during working hours and went to a department store in the City of Biisk to meet his wife who was a saleswoman in the radio parts department. While talking with her, he was bumped by a customer, Dudukin, and Ekimov proposed they go to the street. On leaving the store Ekimov warned Dudukin that he was an employee of the militia. A dispute resulted and Ekimov and Dudukin entered a passageway between the store and the city Procurator's office. Dudkin struck Ekimov in the face with his hand. Instead of stopping Dudukin's incorrect acts, Ekimov, clearly exceeding his authority as defined in Arts 230-234 of the Regulations for patrol duties of the militia, used a weapon (a pistol of the Makarov model). Knowing that there were many people on Kirov Prospect he shot at Dudukin twice at a distance of about 1½ meters with the purpose of killing him, as was stated in the judgment. Dudukin was struck in the hand by the first shot and the fifteen-year old Antonova, who was walking along Kirov Prospect, was struck in the thigh. Afterwards, without any need, Ekimov shot the fleeing Dudukin in the back and caused him severe bodily injury dangerous to his life. Antonova suffered light bodily injury which harmed her health for a short time.

[the judgment was protested by the USSR Supreme Court's President on the ground that Ekimov had committed the crime while suffering from a sudden fit of mental agitation. The protest was satisfied by the USSR Supreme Court's Plenum for the following reasons]:

. . .the conclusion. . .was reached by the court without considering the factual circumstances of the crime. From the record it is clear that Dudukin, who was drunk and had often been convicted previously, began the quarrel. Ekimov explained that Dudukin had responded rudely to his remarks and had pulled him by the hand into the street. When Ekimov warned that he was a militia employee, Dudukin declared that nevertheless he would beat him and he called him "garbage." On coming out into the street and finding himself in a passageway between buildings, Dudukin cursed Ekimov with unprintable words and added, "I'll gnaw through your throat," and then, unexpectedly he hit Ekimov twice in the face and put his hand in his pocket in which something made a metallic sound. It was dark. Ekimov said to Dudukin, "Don't you come near me," and when the latter pulled his hand out of his pocket, Ekimov shot at him and then shot mechanically at him once again. He did not, however, want to kill him.

[the testimony of witnesses confirming the facts was reviewed]

The evidence taken all together provided grounds to conclude that Dudukin's blows excited in Ekimov severe mental agitation since the blow in the street was unexpected. Ekimov's acts were a direct reaction to the application of force to him. . . At the trial Ekimov in giving testimony about the shots explained that at the moment of the blow he fell back against the wall and lost consciousness for an instant: finding himself in such a situation he could not refrain from shooting. Further, Ekimov testified that while serving in the Army he had suffered a concussion of the brain which makes itself felt when he is severely upset. . .He declared, "Dudukin suddenly hit me in the teeth with his fist. I had to hold myself in so as not to fall down. . .Later everything was as if in a fog, and only when I regained my memory, I hazily remember that Dudukin jumped back and fell. . .I felt badly. My head whirled." In response to another question he said, "I was in such a condition that everything swam before my eyes; everything in my head was blurred. I felt nauseated. How I shot, I don't know." [Ekomov's Army discharge after hospitalization was proved by a certificate as to post-concussion encephilopathy].

All of these facts provide grounds for recognizing that Ekimov committed the crime stated in the judgment in a condition of suddenly emerging severe mental agitation brought on by Dudukin's blow. Under such circumstances the fact that Ekimov's acts presented a danger to those around him and that Antonova was lightly wounded cannot be accepted as the elements of the crime of intentional homicide. . . Ekimov's acts in shooting twice at Dudukin and causing him severe bodily injury dangerous to life must be qualified under Arts. 15 and 104 [attempted intentional homicide committed in a state of strong mental agitation]. As to the accusation under Art. 171, par. 2, it is well founded because he clearly exceeded the authority accorded him by law, using for the purpose a weapon entrusted to him to perform his official duties.

In setting punishment the USSR Supreme Court Plenum took into consideration that Ekimov had no previous court record; had favorable references from his job; had frequently been commended by his superiors for his success in combatting crime. A newspaper clipping in the file indicates that in 1969 he had saved the lives of 5 drowning children [all previous judgments were altered, and punishment was set at 3 years' deprivation of freedom].

G. *Aggravating and mitigating circumstances.*

CASE OF KURBATOVA, Biulleten' Verkhovnogo Suda RSFSR, 1970, No. 12, p. 11.

Kurbatova was convicted by the Makhachkalinin City Court under RSFSR Criminal Code, Art. 154, par. 2 [speculation on a large scale] and sentenced to 3 years' deprivation of freedom and confiscation of her personal property and the fruits of her black marketing. She was found guilty of buying and reselling goods in large quantities for the purpose of making a profit. She purchased 122 women's woolen, silk and satin dresses for 1010 rubles; 106.5 meters woolen, silk, satin and brocaded cloth for 1158 rubles; gold jewelry and other objects for 797 rubles 95 kopecks. Kurbanova took part of the purchased items to Magomedsaidova for subsequent sale.

The judgment was affirmed on appeal by the Dagestan ASSR Supreme Court's Judicial Chamber for Criminal Cases, but it and the cassational ruling were changed by the Dagestan ASSR Supreme Court's Presidium. Art. 44 [conditional nonapplication of punishment] was applied and the punishment reduced to 3 years probation. The confiscation of personal property was struck from the judgment.

[The RSFSR Deputy Procurator protested the change in the sentence. The protest was satisfied, the RSFSR Supreme Court Judicial Division for Criminal Cases, saying]:

The Presidium of the Dagestan ASSR Supreme Court, finding Kurbanova guilty of black marketing, applied Art. 44 because she had minor children. Nevertheless, the circumstances cannot in the given situation serve as sufficient grounds for a suspended sentence of Kurbanova. It was established by the record that she bought a remarkable quantity of manufactured goods, including gold jewelry to resell them, and she had already resold part of them at speculator's prices. In issuing the judgment the court took into consideration only that she had minor children and applied almost the minimum sanctions allowed by law.

CASE OF MONAKHOV, Biulleten' Verkhovnogo Suda SSSR, 1968, No. 4, p. 21

Monakhov was convicted by the Azerbaidjan SSR Supreme Court under Azerbaidjan SSR Criminal Code Art. 88-1 (theft of state property in especially large quantities) and sentenced to 10 years' deprivation of freedom with confiscation of his personal property and service of his sentence in a corrective labor camp of strenuous regime. At the same time the court ordered that judgment be given against Monakhov in favor of the Baku Transport Shipping Bureau in the sum of 2,195 rubles and against him and Allakhverdiev jointly in favor of the Baku Radio Factory in the sum of 1,050 rubles and against both of them and also Azmamedov jointly in the sum of 1,167 rubles in favor of the Baku Transport Shipping Bureau.

[The sentence was protested by the USSR Supreme Court's President, proposing a reduction in sentence in application of Art. 40 to 6 years' deprivation of freedom (milder punishment in light of circumstances and convict's personality)]

The Judicial College satisfied the protest for the following reasons: Monakhov confessed his guilt. . . [then follows a detailed account of repeated theft from containers which he was carrying on his truck] Evidence in the case established that he stole state property and especially large quantities. His acts were correctly qualified, but there were grounds before the court justifying a reduction in sentence under Art. 40. The Azerbaidjan SSR Criminal Code Art. 36 lists as circumstances mitigating responsibility on determination of a sentence: sincere repentance, giving oneself up, as well as actively facilitating the exposure of the crime. As the evidence before the investigating and court examinations indicates, Monakhov gave himself up, recounted at length the circumstances of the theft which made it possible to recover and return to the state 6,285 rubles and to apprehend other participants in the crime. One must also take into consideration that this was Monakhov's first offense, that he was engaged in socially useful work, and that he has a family. . . On the basis of what has been said, and in application of Art. 11 of the USSR Supreme Court's Statute, the Judicial College rules: that the sentence. . .be changed and the punishment be reduced to 6 years' deprivation of freedom with confiscation of his personal property and service of the sentence in a corrective labor camp of strenuous regime.

H. *Self defense*.

CASE OF BUBNOV, Biulleten' Verkhovnogo Suda RSFSR, 1970, No. 10, p. 6.

Bubnov was convicted under RSFSR Criminal Code Art. 112, par. 2 [intentional infliction of light bodily injury] and sentenced to 3 months deprivation of freedom by the Sudeslavskii people's court of the Kostromo Province, and additionally under Art. 108, par. 1 [intentional infliction of grave bodily injury]. For both crimes he was sentenced to one year's deprivation of freedom in a corrective labor camp of severe regime. Bubnov was found guilty . . . under the following circumstances:

On August 28, 1969 Bubnov took goods on a truck reserved for his use to a store in the village of Pervushino, and he remained to pass the night in Zhukov's house. During the night, hearing the noise of the truck's motor, he went out into the street and saw that the truck in which he had transported the goods had been taken by some one for a distance of about 15 meters from the house. Near it in a drunken condition stood persons unknown to him - Kuz'michev, Sobolev, Smirnov and Michurin. Bubnov started the motor, returned the truck to its former position and wanted to reenter the house, but Sobolev and Kuz'michev stopped him and asked him to bring out to them a glass and something to eat. Bubnov replied that he could not comply as he did not live in the house. Then Sobolev and Kuz'michev began to curse Bubnov, threatening to drive the truck away. Smirnov and Michurin at that moment got into the truck and Kuz'michev and Sobolev continued to curse Bubnov; and, moreover, Sobolev grabbed him by the collar of his jacket. Bubnov seized a heavy stick that stood by the fence and served as a bar to the door and struck first Sobolev and then Kuz'michev on their heads.

Reviewing the case on the protest of the RSFSR Supreme Court's Deputy President . . .proposing termination of the proceeding for lack of the elements of a crime, the RSFSR Supreme Court's Judicial Division for Criminal Cases in its ruling of June 3, 1970 satisfied the protest for the following reasons:

The people's court's conclusions that Bubnov intentionally caused bodily injury to Kuz'michev, and the conclusion of the Provincial Court's Presidium that he had caused it while exceeding necessary self-defense, conflicts with the evidence in the record. The record establishes that Kuz'michev, Michurin, Smirnov and Sobolev on August 28, 1969 drank liquor to celebrate Sobolev's return from confinement where he had served a sentence for malicious hooliganism, and, then, going to Zhukov's house, they tried to start the truck entrusted to Bubnov; they cursed him and threatened him with a beating; Sobolev seized Bubnov's jacket and Kuz'michev, as Bubnov testified, tried to strike him with his guitar.

The Provincial Court's Presidium, reviewing the file by way of judicial revision, correctly stated that Bubnov had reason to fear for his life and health, but, in conflict with their conclusion, noted in the ruling that Bubnov resorted to means of self-defense which he ought not to have used. Nevertheless, the Presidium did not say concretely in the ruling just how Bubnov exceeded the limits of necessary self-defense.

The Plenum of the USSR Supreme Court in its decree of October 23, 1956 "On errors in court practice in cases concerned with application of legislation on self-defense," declared that courts must not mechanically compare the means of defense with the means of attack, but must consider the degree and character of the danger threatening the defender, as well as his strength and the possibility of parrying the attack.

It is established by the record that real danger threatened Bubnov. He found himself at night alone facing several drunken citizens; to parry the attack he inflicted with a heavy stick bodily injuries on persons making an attempt on his life and health. These acts of Bubnov must be evaluated as having been committed in necessary self-defense without exceeding the limits.

I. *Immunity*.

CASE OF IUSUPOV, Biulleten' Verkhovnogo Suda RSFSR, 1971, No. 8, p. 9.

Iusupov was convicted by the Ichalkov county people's court of the Mordvinian ASSR under RSFSR Criminal Code Art. 211, par. 2 to 3 years' deprivation of freedom in a corrective labor colony of general regime. Iusupov was convicted because on September 23, 1970, being drunk, he placed in the back of an unloaded truck two passengers, also drunk, and drove them from the village of Maly Ichalk of Ichalkov county to the Kemaliansk forest preserve. Along the way the passenger Ruzavin fell off the truck and passed under the rear wheel and died from his injuries. Being convinced that Ruzavin was dead, Iusupov went into hiding and gave no information on what had happened.

> [The case reached the Judicial Division of the RSFSR Supreme Court on protests, the last of which was satisfied by the Judicial Division on February 19, 1971, which said in its ruling:]

The Judicial Chamber for Criminal Cases of the Mordvinian ASSR's Supreme Court quashed the judgment and remanded the case for retrial because the investigating organs had begun criminal proceedings against Usupov without the consent of the Aksenov Village Soviet, of which Usupov was a deputy. In the protest the question was raised of annulling the ruling of the Judicial Chamber and the Presidium's decree and remanding for new trial since Iusupov was prosecuted, not on the territory of the Soviet where he was a deputy, but in another county, where the crime was committed.

From the record it is evident that the Judicial Division in quashing the court's judgment used as its guide the Statute on the Village Soviet of 1957, which lost force in 1968. In accordance with Art. 68 of the RSFSR Law on Village and Hamlet Soviets of Toilers of the RSFSR, approved July 19, 1968 the consent of a village Soviet is required in the event of initiating criminal proceedings against a deputy on the territory of the Soviet where he is a deputy.

It was established in the case that Iusupov committed the crime on the territory of Ichalkov county where criminal proceedings were instigated against him, while he is a deputy of the Aksenov village Soviet of Liambir county.

J. *Approaching contemporary problems: drug abuse.*

DECREE ON AMENDMENT TO SOME LAWS OF THE RSFSR, July 15, 1974.
    [1974] Vedomosti Verkhovnogo Soveta RSFSR; No. 29, item 782.
    ... Art. 224. [Criminal Code] The illegal manufacture, acquisition custody, conveyance, or sale of narcotics:

The illegal manufacture, acquisition, custody, transportation or conveyance for the purpose of sale, and also the illegal sale of narcotics--

> shall be punished by deprivation of freedom for a term of ten years with or without confiscation of property.

The same acts committed repeatedly, or by preliminary agreement among a group of persons, or by a person previously having committed one of the crimes provided for by Arts. 224-1, 224-2, 225 and 226 [manufacturing narcotics, growing poppies, keeping of dens, and pandering] of the present Code or by an especially dangerous recidivist, and also if the subject of these acts was narcotics in large quantities.

> shall be punished by deprivation of freedom for a term of from 6 to 15 years with confiscation of property.

> [subsequent paragraphs omitted: concerning the same activities but without the purpose of sale. Milder penalties are prescribed]

THE SOVIET LEGAL SYSTEM

Contemporary Documentation and Historical Commentary

PART II
ADMINISTERING SOVIET SOCIALISM

FOREWORD

Societ socialism stands on its promise to produce abundantly. From this expectation all else in Soviet society flows. A people satiated with the goods of this world, and with time and opportunity to enjoy cultural values, can be expected to become a good society, an attractive model to be emulated by citizens of other lands.

Abundant production is expected to require order, not the order that results from the flow of private enterprise with its intricate network of voluntary associations, but rather the order created by a centrally directed national economy. Planners channel material resources as the common good seems to require, and they expect to eliminate duplication and waste, as the planning function is perfected.

While the ordering of goods has presented troubles, these have been small compared with those presented by the people of the Soviet Union. The ideal planned society requires social discipline if human resources are to be related to the allocation of materials. Yet, the masses who work in the planned economy are in a transitional stage. They move slowly away from familiar procedures and ways of thought, especially when the goals toward which they are being led seem remote or undesirable. This has encouraged Soviet leaders to dictate to the people, while making concessions to their historical prejudices when opposition to swift change has approached the point of rebellion.

The allocation of resources for maximum productive use and the stimulation of people to work these resources efficiently require massive regulation. This is the major current task of the Soviet legal system. After Stalin's death the task was broadened by Nikita Khrushchev's direction that administrators find a way to absorb the masses in their own regulation in what is called "public self-government." His successors have sought to speed the transition to abundance, by adapting the principles of business management of the most advanced foreign countries for application in the Soviet planned economy.

In many eyes Soviet administration of economic resources is creating the unique feature of the Soviet legal system. The study of this problem is the task of Part II.

CHAPTER X

Delineation of the Public and Private Sectors

Communist party chiefs from Lenin to the present have placed their faith in their ability to remain in power and ultimately to attract the adherence of peoples beyond the borders of the U.S.S.R. on economic planning. It is through the intricate detail of the prospective and annual plans that scarce resources are expected to contribute their maximum usefulness in the achievement of abundance. Common logic has seemed to the communist to require that no one produce what he cannot be sure of selling lest it be wasted, and that no one be permitted to produce what he can surely sell if the economic resources required for its manufacture could be used to the good of the greater number in some other way.

Yet, to the communists, man through history has shown himself avaricious, seeking always to benefit his own pockets and exhibiting little or no concern for the common good if the benefits to its promoters are not immediately apparent.[1] The common logic of community improvement is not apparent if minds are closed. Sacrifice for future generations has not seemed a popular prospect except in time of war or natural disaster, and even then there have been the profit seekers who have sought to exploit public misery for personal benefit.

How can public misery created by avarice be overcome? To Karl Marx and his colleague, Friedrich Engels, the evil had to be attacked at its source, and this they found to be the private ownership of productive resources. This became the theme of the Communist Manifesto of 1848: If the ownership of land, raw materials and factories could be taken from private hands and placed in an institution truly representative of the public, the road would lie open for a more productive society in which products would be distributed in accordance with need.

Marx and Engels left the matter with their analysis of what must be done to prepare the way. The agency to whom the productive property should be transferred was for others to define, and Lenin took it upon himself to name as that agency the

---

[1]Friedrich Engels, The Origin of the Family. Private Property and the State. (1884, Eng. Trans., New York, 1942)

Soviet state as the tool of the people and to draft the first decrees after the revolution to deprive private owners of their productive wealth and to transfer it to officers of the new state for administration. His expectation was that all productive wealth would be placed eventually in the Soviet state as the true representative of the people, but as a realist he saw the perils of immediate transfer. The state created by the Bolsheviks in 1917 had an inadequate apparatus to utilize the wealth productively. The transfer could be accomplished by a stroke of the pen, but efficient administration would have to wait until personnel could be trained. The administrators of privately owned wealth might be availed of for a time, but they could not be trusted fully, whether they had been owners or only stewards of owners, for it was presumed that both categories had been trained to think in terms of private gain and would hamper if not sabotage the Bolsheviks' efforts to remake the face of the social order.

The earliest decrees evidenced Lenin's plan.[2] He had his new legislature, the Congress of Soviets, nationalize the land in two steps, first landlords' estates, and in February 1918 all land, hoping by taking two steps to avoid creating an immediate opposition among the middle class and more successful peasants, who had only since the turn of the century begun to find real satisfaction in private farming, encouraged during the last days of the Tsar.

Banking as the key to modern economic life because of the necessity of credits to expand industry was made a state monopoly, as was its related source of credit, the insurance business. Industry came later on Lenin's schedule, for he had no skilled managers to direct expropriated plants. Yet, even in the face of a shortage of personnel he thought it politically necessary to expropriate some of the largest plants by name, and in some of the smaller he was forced to install individual public managers or permit continuing direction by the extemporaneous committees of workers who had assumed duties when the owners had been murdered, or had fled, or had been ousted by those who were suspicious of their loyalty to the concepts of the new regime. Not until November 29, 1920 was Lenin prepared to nationalize all industry, except plants with but a few workmen. With this decree he completed essentially the program of nationalization which he had initiated in 1917. Land, buildings, credit agencies, industries, transportation, merchant shipping, and distribution points were the property of the state, with exceptions for the property of individual fishermen, small homeowners, droshky coachmen, artisans and industrialists employing fewer than five men with machines or ten without.

The victory required by Marxist theory had been won, but Lenin decided almost immediately that he had moved too fast in a nation devastated by participation in the first world war, and by the civil war that had followed it, and still lacking in understanding of what he and his colleagues of the communist party were trying to

---

[2]For translation of many of the decrees, see James H. Meisel and Edward S. Kozera, editor. Materials for the Study of the Soviet System: State and Party Constitutions, Laws, Decrees, Decisions and Official Statements of Leaders in Translation. (2nd ed. Ann Arbor, Mich., 1953.)

do. Primarily to mollify the recalcitrant peasants, but also to utilize private initiative in industry for such time as it might be necessary to rehabilitate the limping economy, he reversed his policies in part, and introduced the New Economic Policy in the summer of 1921. He returned ownership of some small factories to original owners or others willing to risk their capital in hopes of recovery of their investment before a second wave of nationalization. He opened the markets to private trade, and returned decrepit dwellings to private landlords that they might be put in repair. In the flush of this activity he died in January, 1924.

His policy of limited capitalism was continued until such time as Stalin thought the most pressing needs of the economy had been met, and the Soviet state prepared with new personnel to provide the nucleus of a state apparatus of skilled technicians to assume for a second time administration of the total economy. At this point the cautious planning that Lenin had begun in 1920 with a plan for electrification was supplanted by full scale planning of the entire economy. With this act in 1928 the New Economic Policy was phased out of existence, and the problem of public administration became as large as the economy itself, for all but minimal productive resources had been taken from private hands.

By 1936 the process was declared complete, for the Constitution adopted that year hailed the achievement of socialism and forbade the further employment of private labor for productive purposes, banning in Marxist terms, "the exploitation of the labor of others."

The documents currently establishing state ownership as the legal foundation of the Soviet economy require little space. The many individual decrees of the early years nationalizing various types of productive property were replaced in 1936 by the few articles incorporated in the first chapter of the Constitution of the USSR. The 1977 draft Constitution made no change in these fundamental principles. Consequently a volume devoted to the contemporary scene need only reproduce these articles to include the legal foundation of current practice.

Still, there is a line below which the policy of nationalization has not stretched. While the basic issues of state ownership of any productive resource large enough to employ labor is settled, there is an unresolved issue. It is posed by the producers who employ no labor in such widely disparate occupations as writing poetry and shining shoes. Should these vestiges of private enterprise continue to have a place in Soviet socialism?

So that readers outside the Soviet Union may formulate their views as to what the future of such private enterprise may be, licensing and tax acts are included in this chapter together with pertinent provisions of the criminal law. Further materials on private productive activities appear in the chapter "The Cooperatives as Supplementary Agencies."

A. *State vs. Private ownership.*

CONSTITUTION OF THE USSR, December 5, 1936

Art. 4. The economic foundation of the USSR is the socialist system of economy and the socialist ownership of the instruments and means of production, firmly established as a result of the liquidation of the capitalist system of economy, the abolition of private ownership of the instruments and means of production, and the elimination of exploitation of man by man.

Art. 5. Socialist property in the USSR exists either in the form of state property (belonging to the whole people) or in the form of cooperative and collective farm property (property of individual collective farms, property of cooperative societies).

Art. 6. The land, its mineral wealth, waters, forests, mills, factories, mines, rail, water and air transport, banks, communications, large state-organized agricultural enterprises (state farms, machine and tractor stations and the like), as well as municipal enterprises and the bulk of the dwelling houses in the cities and industrial localities, are state property, that is belong to the whole people.

Art. 7. The common enterprises of collective farms and cooperative organizations, with their livestock and implements, the products of the collective farms and cooperative organizations as well as their common buildings, constitute the common, socialist property of the collective farms and cooperative organizations.

Every household in a collective farm, in addition to its basic income from the common, collective farm enterprise, has for its personal use a small plot of household land and, as its personal property, a subsidiary husbandry on the plot, a dwelling house, livestock, poultry and minor agricultural implements—in accordance with the rules of the agricultural artel.

Art. 9. Alongside the socialist system of economy, which is the predominant form of economy in the USSR, the law permits the small private economy of individual peasants and handicraftsmen based on their own labor and precluding the exploitation of labor of others.

Art. 10. The personal property right of citizens in their incomes and savings from work, in their dwelling houses and subsidiary home enterprises, in articles of domestic economy and use and articles of personal use and convenience, as well as the right of citizens to inherit personal property is protected by law.

FUNDAMENTAL PRINCIPLES OF CIVIL LAW OF THE U.S.S.R. AND OF THE UNION REPUBLICS,

December 8, 1961, effective May 1, 1962. [1962] Vedomosti Verkhovnogo Soveta SSSR, No. 50 (1085), item 525.

Art. 21. State Property

The state is sole owner of all state property.

State property assigned to state organizations shall be administered by these organizations, which shall exercise within the limits established by law, and in accordance with their organizational purpose, the tasks set by the plan and the designation of the property, the right to possess, use and dispose of the property.

State property is the land, its mineral wealth, waters, forests, mills, factories, mines, electric stations, water, air and automobile transport, banks, communications, state-organized agricultural, trading, municipal, and other enterprises, as well as the bulk of the dwelling houses in the cities and industrial localities. Any other property may be state owned.

The land, its mineral wealth, forests, waters are exclusively the property of the state and may be distributed only for use.

Art. 25. Personal property.

Property intended to satisfy citizens' material and cultural needs may be their personal property. Every citizen may have as his personal property his income and savings from work, his dwelling house (or a part thereof), and subsidiary home enterprises, articles of domestic economy and use, articles of personal use and convenience. Property that is the personal property of citizens may not be used to obtain unearned income.

STATUTE ON ARTISAN-HANDICRAFT BUSINESSES, May 3, 1976
[1976] Sob. Post. SSSR, no, 7, item 39 (Excerpt)

1. Artisan-handicraft businesses of citizens is defined as their activity in making manufactured articles for sale to the public, or to provide services for pay. Engaging in business with the employment of wage labor is forbidden.

2. Throughout the territory of the USSR engaging in all types of artisan-handicraft businesses is permitted, except for those businesses which are prohibited by the present Statute or by other legislation of the USSR and of the union republics.

3. Throughout the entire territory of the USSR citizens are forbidden to engage in the following types of artisan-handicraft businesses:

(a) processing agricultural or other food products purchased or donated, including the production from them of any edible products and all types of beverage (whether ready-to-consume or semi-manufactured);

(b) Manufacture or repair of any type of weapon, manufacture of military supplies, explosives and fireworks;

(c) [polygraphic instrumentalities: this paragraph appears in Chapter VI (E) of this volume]

(d) manufacture of bars and ribbons for exhibiting orders and medals, and also of badges and medals;

(e) manufacture of chemical and perfumery-cosmetic products;

(f) manufacture of poisonous and narcotic preparations, and also medicine of any kind and articles of medical technology;

(g) manufacture and dying of leather, sheep skins and furs, and also manufacture of items from pelts and also manufacture of items from pelts of valuable animals not bearing the state identification mark, if they are of the type which by law of the union republics must be delivered to the state;

(h) transportation of passengers and freight by any means of transport (except row boats, on horseback and on other animals when consent has been given by the executive committee of the Soviet of Working Peoples' Deputies);

(i) operation of boarding houses, dressing rooms, baths, gambling houses, all types of attractions and organizations for the showing of spectacles;

(j) manufacture of wares from precious and colored metals, precious stones and amber or wares incorporating such materials, and also the repair and reworking of the said wares with the incorporation therein of precious and colored metals, precious stones and amber owned by the artisan;

(k) manufacture of candles, ikons and church utensils.

The Council of Ministers of union republics may, in addition, forbid citizens to engage in other types of artisan-handicraft businesses if the development of them might do injury to society's interests.

4. Persons wishing to engage in permitted artisan-handicraft trade must obtain from the financial department of the county (city) Soviet of Working People's Deputies at his domicile a special certificate of registration indicating the period for which it is valid during a given calendar year. The certificate is issued to citizens who have reached the age of 18. The form of the registration certificate shall be established by the USSR Ministry of Finance.

The USSR Ministry of Finance is authorized to except certain categories of citizens engaged in artisan-handicraft businesses from the obligation to obtain registration certificates.

Issuance of a registration certificate at a place of temporary residence is permitted only to collective farmers engaged, with the permission of the collective farm administration, in artisan-handicraft businesses outside the county in which they have their domicile.

There shall be listed in the registration certificate issued to a citizen the names of the members of his family participating in the business.

Registration certificates may not be issued to two or more persons to engage in the same type of business in one and the same building.

5. A license fee of 5 rubles shall be collected for the issuance of a registration certificate.

[omitted paragraphs concern provisions for return of the registration certificate on termination of the business, on the localities where the goods may be sold, on presenting the certificate for verification by inspectors, and on periodic verification by authorities in conformity with regulations]

10. [penalty clause: this paragraph appears in Chap. VI (E) of this volume]

11. Citizens engaged in artisan-handicraft businesses shall pay a tax on income received from the activity in accordance with the procedure and in the amounts established by the laws in force.

EVENING MOSCOW, ADVERTISING SUPPLEMENT, March 31, 1976, p. 3.
Miscellaneous
I tune the piano. Tel. 252-31-. . . I translate from English. Tel. 245-08-. . .
I give lessons
Playing the guitar for all beginners, learning to read music, performing songs, ballads, and romances. Tel. 137-38-. . .

CASE OF FADEEV, Biulleten' Verkhovnogo Suda RSFSR, 1970, No. 10, p. 15.

By a decision of the Iadrin District People's Court of the Chuvash ASSR, Fadeev was sentenced under Part 1 of Art. 153 [Private Enterprise and Commerical Intermediary Activity] of the Criminal Code of the RSFSR with the application of Art. 43 [Application of a More Lenient Punishment than that Provided by Law] of the Criminal Code of the RSFSR, to one year of corrective labor tasks at his place of work with the withholding of 10% from his wages. At the same time 739 rubles and 71 kopecks were recovered from him for the income of the state.

Fadeev was found guilty of committing the following criminal acts.

Not having a registration certificate for the right to engage in a handicraft occupation (making wagon wheels), Fadeev from July through August 1968 made wagon wheels and sold them.

During this period he made 206 wheels and sold them to the Defense of the Country Collective Farm of Pil'nen District of Gorky Region for 37 rubles each as compared to the state retail price of 22 rubles, making a profit of 679 rubles 72 kopecks.

[On review the decision was reversed on the following grounds.]

As was established in the record and by the decision of the court, Fadeev, by occupation a wheelwright, in July and August 1968 made 206 wagon wheels at his own home for sale to the Defense of the Country Collective Farm, without having a registration certificate for doing this.

These actions by Fadeev were improperly evaluated by the agencies of preliminary investigation and the court as engaging in private enterprise activity.

In making wheels for the collective farm, Fadeev acted as a private person, not using state, cooperative, or other social forms, while the language of Part. 1 of Art. 153 of the Criminal Code of the RSFSR provides liability for engaging in private enterprise activity only if with the use of these forms.

Fadeev could have been subject to liability for engaging in a handicraft industry without a registration certificate under Art. 162 [Engaging in a Prohibited Occupation] if that type of occupation was forbidden.

In the Rules for Registration of Craftsmen and Artisans, approved by Decree of the Council of Ministers of the USSR of June 30, 1949, No. 2883, there is no prohibition of the issuance of registration certificates for this type of occupation.

Thus Fadeev was convicted under Part 1 of Art. 153 of the Criminal Code of the RSFSR without sufficient grounds therefore.

CASE OF SHORIN, Biulleten' Verkhovnogo Suda RSFSR, 1967, No. 2. p. 5.

Shorin was convicted by the Kalinin County People's Court under Art. 153. Par.

1 of the Criminal Code of the RSFSR.

He was found liable to pay 19,590 rubles to the state.

[Upon review this decision was reversed on the following grounds:]

By sentence of the court Shorin was found guilty of private entrepreneurial activity. He contracted with the collective farms "Dawn" and "Young Communist" to organize glass-blowing workshops for them. As head of these workshops, Shorin received 5% of the value of products sold for his work and the glassblower workers received 30%-35%. He himself recruited glass blowers for the work, who were hired upon his recommendation, he found raw materials; got purchasers for the products and established prices for it, making these prices significantly high so as to increase the pay. As a result, there was paid, from the moment of conclusion of the contract (in one case from 1960, in the other from 1963) 12,219 rubles to the glass blowing workers with 7372 rubles going to Shorin himself.

The accusation against Shorin of private entrepreneurial activity with the use of a social form is not confirmed by the evidence considered at the trial.

The text of Art. 153, par. 1, of the Criminal Code of the RSFSR provides liability for private entrepreneurial activity with the use of state or cooperative forms. From this it follows that one of the essential conditions of the elements of the crime is the use of one of the indicated forms for the organization of private entrepreneurial activity and the illegal extraction of profit.

However the fulfillment, under a labor contract with a collective farm, of tasks connected with the output of a given type of product still cannot by itself be regarded as private entrepreneurial activity and entail criminal liability.

In the present case it was established that Shorin was the manager of the glass-blowing workshops under a labor agreement concluded with the managers of the collective farms "Dawn" and "Young Communist" and conscientiously fulfilled the obligations placed upon him.

All monetary funds received from the sale of goods produced in the glassblowing worshops were paid to the account of the collective farms. The administrations of the collective farms themselves later paid Shorin the wages due him. In exercising management of the glass-blowing workshops, Shorin acted in the interests of the collective farms, on the basis of labor contracts concluded with them which cannot serve as a basis for a conclusion that his activity was criminal.

Under these circumstances, the people's court and the later judicial instances were mistaken in finding in Shorin's actions the elements of the crime provided in Art. 153, par. 1, of the Criminal Code of the RSFSR.

CASE OF UTEKESHEV, Biulleten' Verkhovnogo Suda RSFSR, 1968, No. 5, p. 4.

By a judgment of the Tselinnyi County People's Court, Utekeshev was sentenced under Art. 154, Par. 2, of the Criminal Code of the RSFSR to two years of deprivation of freedom, suspended with a probationary term lasting for two years.

The case was not reviewed by way of cassation.

The Deputy President of the Supreme Court of the RSFSR entered a protest before the Judicial Division for Criminal Cases of the Supreme Court of the RSFSR, seeking reversal of the judgment because of lightness of the measure of punishment.

Having examined the materials of the case the Judicial Division has satisfied the protest.

Utekeshev was found guilty in that he, during 1961-65, systematically, as a business, engaged in speculative activity, buying up automobiles and motorcycles and reselling them for a profit. In all, during this period, Utekeshev made an illegal profit of 1670 rubles.

The guilt of Utekeshev in committing speculative acts was proved by the materials of his case and his actions were correctly qualified. However the measure of punishment decreed for him is unjustifiably soft.

From the materials of the case it is apparent that while working as a senior herdsman, Utekeshev for a long time, and for the purpose of extracting unearned income, engaged in the form of a business, in the illegal buying up and resale of motorcycles and automobiles. In violation of the rules in force, Utekeshev did not register the motorcycles and automobiles which he bought. He bypassed the special stores and sold privately at elevated prices, making a profit.

Originally the people's court heard the case of Utekeshev at an extramural session at the place of work of the defendant, at the state farm "Lemon". In connection with the improper requalification of Utekeshev's action from Par. 2 to Par. 1 of Art. 154 of the Criminal Code of the RSFSR and the softness of the measure of punishment applied to him, the judgment was reversed on the protest of the President of the Supreme Court of Kalmyk ASSR and the case was remanded for a new trial.

At the second trial of the case, the people's court sentenced Utekeshev to an even lighter measure of punishment, applying a suspended sentence without the confiscation of the two motorcycles seized from him.

In deciding the question of the application of a suspended measure of punishment to Utekeshev, the court cited the fact that it was his first conviction, his family position, his positive character references, and the petition of the collective of the division of the state farm "Lemon" that the convict be transferred to it for reeducation.

However these circumstances were not a basis for the application of a suspended sentence to Utekeshev. It must be kept in mind that he committed a crime involving heightened social danger.

All these circumstances could have been considered by the court in sentencing Utekeshev to a term of punishment provided by the sanction provision of Art. 154, Par. 2 of the Criminal Code of the RSFSR.

Moreover, the people's court in violation of the decree of the Plenum of the Supreme Court of the RSFSR of October 29, 1963, "on Judicial Practice in Speculation Cases," did not consider the question of the confiscation from Utekeshev of the unjust enrichment gained through speculation.

On the basis of the aforesaid, the Judicial Division for Criminal Cases of the

Supreme Court of the RSFSR by a decision of Dec. 11, 1967, reversed the sentence with respect to Utekeshev and remanded his case for a new hearing in a different county people's court of the Kalmyk ASSR from the trial stage.

B. *Taxation*

RATES OF INCOME TAX AND TAX ON BACHELORS AND CITIZENS OF THE USSR WHO ARE SINGLE AND WHO HAVE SMALL FAMILIES, FOR WORKERS AND EMPLOYEES RECEIVING WAGES AT THEIR BASIC PLACE OF WORK OF 71 TO 90 RUBLES A MONTH, Appendix to the Decree of the Council of Ministers of the USSR of December 25, 1972, No. 882, Sob. Post. SSSR, 1973, No. 1, p. 6.

Monthly Earnings in Rubles	Monthly Amount of income tax without reduction for dependents (rubles-kopecks)	Monthly Amount of tax on bachelors and citizens of the USSR who are single or have small families (rubles-kopecks)
71	0-25	0-20
72	0-59	0-47
73	0-93	0-74
74	1-30	1-01
75	1-65	1-28
76	2-00	1-55
77	2-39	1-82
78	2-73	2-09
79	3-07	2-36
80	3-41	2-63
81	3-75	2-90
82	4-09	3-17
83	4-43	3-44
84	4-77	3-71
85	5-11	3-98
86	5-45	4-25
87	5-79	4-52
88	6-13	4-79
89	6-47	5-06
90	6-81	5-33

Note. The present rates also apply to military servicemen, students, and other citizens, assessed for income taxes on the same basis as workers and employees.

ON RAISING THE MINIMUM INCOMES NOT SUBJECT TO INCOME TAX FOR CITIZENS ENGAGED IN HANDICRAFT AND ARTISAN OCCUPATIONS, [1970] Vedomosti Verkhovnogo Soveta SSSR, No. 3, item 24.

The Presidium of the Supreme Court of the USSR decrees:

1. To increase the amount of the minimum incomes not subject to income tax for citizens from handicraft and artisan occupations to 720 rubles a year.

2. To lower by an average of 15.3% the existing rates of income tax for assess-

ment of the incomes of citizens from handicraft and artisan occupations.

3. In accordance with Articles 1 and 2 of the present edict to introduce in the Edict of the Presidium of the Supreme Soviet of the USSR the following changes and additions:

. . .

3) supplement the edict with Article 19-a with the following content:

From the incomes from handicraft and artisan occupations tax is collected at the following rates:

Amount of Annual Income	Amount of Tax
from 720 to 800 rubles	30% of the amount over 720 rubles
from 800 to 1200 rubles	24 rubles + 35% of the amount over 800 rubles
from 1200 to 1800 rubles	164 rubles + 40% of the amount over 1200 rubles
from 1800 to 3000 rubles	404 rubles + 50% of the amount over 1800 rubles
from 3000 to 5000 rubles	1004 rubles + 60% of the amount over 3000 rubles
from 5000 and above	2204 rubles + 65% of the amount over 5000 rubles

CHAPTER XI

Use of the Land

Land was the primary source of wealth in pre-revolutionary Russia. Although industrialization had spread rapidly in Russia in the twentieth Century, it lagged far behind Western Europe. Russia was essentially an agricultural country at the time of the revolution with an agricultural mentality not only among the great majority of the population, the peasantry, but also among the workmen who in most cases maintained links with their villages to which they returned during harvest seasons and in old age. It is not accident that a decree on the land was among the few drafts placed by Lenin before the Congress of Soviets after power had been seized.

"Land" meant farms to the Russians, and perhaps for this reason a separate decree concerning city plots was not issued until August 20, 1918[1] to nationalize urban land, and also, in cities of more than 10,000, the buildings upon it if they exceeded dimensions to be set by each local soviet.

How was land to be used? To avoid the chaos that would have resulted if there had

---

[1][1918] I Sob. Uzak, RSFSR, No. 62, item 674.

been no orderly distribution, definition of a procedure for allocation to users was made the first business of the new regime. Even with a prescribed procedure many peasants took the law into their own hands. The land decrees had placed the use in "the whole toiling population." Regulations had to follow to establish a procedure under which the local land committees would allocate this use, giving priority to those forms of tillage that would be communal, such as the "communes" and agricultural cooperatives. Some of the former estates that had been engaged in highly specialized agriculture requiring the preservation of centralized and skilled management for exploitation to fullest benefit were kept intact and declared to be state farms. Later they took the legal form of public corporations when industry was put in that form. The bulk of the land was distributed among the traditional peasant households to be tilled as the patriarchically organized families might wish. Some of these created loosely organized communal associations to pool resources to buy agricultural equipment or to market produce, and these became known as the TOZ.

Of the various systems of land use devised in the early years there remain today in the agricultural sphere only the agricultural artel, now generally known popularly as the "kolkhoz" or collective farm, the state farm or "sovkhoz" and some hundred thousand private homesteads, "edinolichniki," in remote regions operating as traditional peasant households.[2] The TOZ and communes are no more. For industrial, transportation, distribution and dwelling purposes, the land is placed in the hands, primarily of public corporations, although since the end of the second world war, and for much the same reason as at the end of the first world war, land use for the construction of private dwellings, summer cottages, and the development of fruit and vegetables gardens has been transferred to associations of city workmen and intellectuals, or in the case of small dwellings to individuals.

The literature suggests that there is a recurring fear lest use on a private basis or even in associations of city people degenerate into use to gain a private income in the form of rent charged by owners of tenants or as a result of profitable sales. Some fear that private property instincts may be developed with emergence among users of a selfish proprietary consciousness tending to override the publicly favored sense of obligation to the community. Even in the usage of collective farms there is the wind of change. Just before his death Stalin called in 1952 for the transformation of collective farm property into property of the whole people,[3] and Khrushchev later made this specific in pressing for a transition to state farms.

His successors announced an indefinite delay in this transition and reversed some of Khrushchev's restrictions on private land usage. They provided substantial capital for modernization of collective farms, but disappointing results have led to a call by the Party for organization of agro-industrial complexes which would attempt to bring to agriculture the more successful experience of soviet industrial organization. The details of what these developments will mean to social organizations will be

---

[2] J. A. Newth, Soviet Agriculture: The Private Sector, 1950-1959. 13 Soviet Studies 160-171 (1961).
[3] J. V. Stalin, Economic Problems of Socialism in the U.S.S.R. (Eng. trans., Moscow, 1952).

discussed in the chapter on cooperatives, but the fact of transition is having its effect on the use of the land.

Simple as the distribution of state-owned land might appear to be, it has called forth a vast body of regulations which create a complex pattern. The documents of this chapter include the core of the decrees, judicial decisions and explanations that clarify the situation. In the past, Soviet legal theorists have laid stress on the contention that the Soviet system of land use planning is far different and far better in results compared to land use elsewhere, even to that in countries where the land has been nationalized but without revolution on the Soviet model. However, recently, Soviet theorists have taken a more critical look at their land law and have found it wanting, in that two of its previously praised features, absence of rent and possibility of reallocation without payment, have actually hindered rather than helped rational planning. They have urged reforms to introduce a greater element of cost-consciousness into land use planning going well beyond those reforms which were partially incorporated in the Fundamental Principles of Land Legislation enacted in 1968.

A. *General Principles*

FUNDAMENTAL PRINCIPLES OF LAND LEGISLATION OF THE U.S.S.R. AND THE UNION REPUBLICS, [1968] Vedomosti Verkhovnogo Soveta SSSR, No. 51, item 485. Translated in full in CDSP, Vo. XXI, No. 1, p. 14 (Jan. 22, 1969).

The Great October Socialist Revolution destroyed the semiserfdom land structure of Tsarist Russia, which condemned the peasantry to poverty and retarded the development of the productive forces of the county. By the Decree on Land of the Second All-Russian Congress of Soviets of Workers', Soldiers', and Peasants' deputies of November 8 (October 26) 1917, private ownership of land was abolished forever and all land was transformed into common wealth and transferred free of charge to the working people for their use.

State ownership of land, which arose as a result of nationalization, is the basis of land relations in the U.S.S.R. Land, which in the conditions of private ownership served as a tool for the exploitation of man by man, is used in the U.S.S.R. for the development of the productive forces of the country in the interests of the whole people.

State ownership of land has played an immense role in the victory of socialism in the U.S.S.R. It made possible the most efficient possible placement of all branches of the national economy and was one of the most important conditions for the transfer to socialist forms of land use.

With the creation, in the course of the construction of socialism, of conditions for the mass collectivization of the separated individual farms, the peasantry, under the leadership of the Communist Party, with the allaround help and support of the working class, started on the road to socialism. As the result of the transformation into life of Lenin's cooperative plan and the victory of the collective farm system, the peasant question found its true solution.

State ownership of land helps the creation of the material and technological basis of communism in our country; the gradual transfer to communist social relations; and the liquidation of the difference between the city and the countryside.

Land in the U.S.S.R., the greatest wealth of Soviet society, is the chief means of production in agriculture and the spatial basis for the placement and development of the national economy. The scientific and rational use of all lands, their protection and the all-around enhancement of the fertility of the soil are tasks for all the people.

Part 1
GENERAL PROVISIONS

Art. 1. The tasks of Soviet land legislation.

The tasks of Soviet land legislation are the regulation of land regulations for the purposes of ensuring the rational use of land, the creation of conditions for the enhancement of their effectiveness, the protection of the rights of socialist organizations and citizens, and also the strengthening of legality in the area of land relations.

Art. 2. Land legislation of the Union of Soviet Socialist Republics and of the union republics.

Land relations in the U.S.S.R. shall be regulated by the present Fundamental Principles and by other acts of U.S.S.R. land legislation, by the land codes and other acts of land legislation of the union republics.

Mining, forest and water relations shall be regulated by special legislation of the U.S.S.R. and the union republics.

Art. 3. State ownership of land of the U.S.S.R.

In accordance with the Constitution of the U.S.S.R. the land in the Union of Soviet Socialist Republics is state property, i.e. common wealth.

The land in the U.S.S.R. shall remain in the exclusive ownership of the state and shall be made available only for use. Activities, which directly or covertly violate the right of state ownership of land are forbidden.

Art. 4. The single state land fund

All land in the U.S.S.R. constitutes a single state land fund, which in accordance with its basic assigned purpose consists of:

1) agricultural land, granted for use to collective farms, state farms and other land users for agricultural purposes;

2) land of populated centers (cities, urban type settlements and rural populated centers);

3) land for industry, transport, resort, reserve and other non-agricultural use;

4) land of the state forest fund;

5) the land of the state water fund;

6) the land of the state reserve.

The procedure for assignment of land to these categories and for transfer of land from one category to another is to be determined by U.S.S.R. and union republic legislation.

Art. 7. The land users

Land in the U.S.S.R. shall be granted for use: to collective and state farms and to other agricultural state, cooperative and social enterprises, organizations and institutions; to industrial, transport, and other non-agricultural state, cooperative, and social enterprises, organizations and institutions; to citizens of the U.S.S.R.

In instances provided by the legislation of the U.S.S.R. land may also be granted for use to other organizations and persons.

Art. 8. The granting of land for use without payment

Collective and state farms and other state, cooperative and social enterprises, organizations, and institutions, as well as workers' collectives and citizens of the U.S.S.R. shall be granted land for use without payment.

Article 24. Land for social use and auxiliary land of collective farms

Land presented to a collective farm by a state deed for indefinite (perpetural) use, shall consist of land for social use and auxiliary land. Auxiliary land shall be physically demarcated from land for social use.

In case of a shortage of auxiliary lands for the granting to collective farm households of plots of land in accordance with the norms provided by the charter of the collective farm, an increase shall be allowed in the area of the auxiliary fund from lands for social use by decision of the general meeting of the members or of a meeting of deputies, approved by the executive committee of the provincial (or territorial) soviet of working people's deputies, council of ministers of the autonomous republics not having provincial division, by the council of ministers of the union republic.

The use within the farms of land assigned to the collective farms shall be conducted on the basis of the charter of the collective farm in accordance with the pressent Fundamental Principles and also with other legislation of the Union of Soviet Socialist Republics and the Union Republics.

Art. 25. The right of the collective farm household to an auxiliary land plot.

Every collective farm household has the right to an auxiliary plot of land granted by the procedure and within the limits of the norms provided by the charter of the collective farm.

The same right shall be maintained for collective farm households in which the sole member of the household able to work has been drafted into the ranks of the Armed Forces of the U.S.S.R. for a period of active duty or occupies an elective position, has matriculated for study, temporarily transferred to other work with the consent of the collective farm or by the organized recruitment procedure, and also when only minors remain in the membership of the collective farm household.

The right of use of the auxiliary plot shall also be maintained for collective farm households, all members of which have lost their ability to work as the result of old age or invalidism.

Collective farm households shall be granted pasture for their cattle in accordance with the charter of the collective farm.

Art. 26. Auxiliary lands of state farms and other state agricultural enterprises, organizations and institutions

From the lands granted for use for agricultural needs to a state farm or other state agricultural enterprise, organization or institution, in accordance with the approved plan of internal land allocation, auxiliary lands shall be separated and physically demarcated, as designated for grants to workers and employees of auxiliary land plots within the limits of norms established by the legislation of the union republics.

B. *Allocation and Use of Land*

PROCURATOR'S PROTEST AGAINST ILLEGAL DECISIONS OF GENERAL MEETING OF COLLECTIVE FARM MEMBERS, Radians'ke pravo, 1968, No. 8, p. 95.

By decision of the general meeting of the collective farmers of the V. I. Lenin's Light Collective Farm of Kremenchug District of Poltava Region, lots were allocated from the collective farm supplemental fund for the construction of dachas for three citizens who did not live on the territory of the collective farm and were not collective farmers.

These decisions violate the Model Statute of the Agricultural Artel, and also party and government decrees on questions of collective farm construction. In particular, in the Decree of the Council of Ministers of the USSR and the Central Committee of the All-Union Communist Party (Bolsheviks) of September 19, 1946, "On Measures for the Liquidation of Violations of the Statute of the Agricultural Artel on Collective Farms," there is a sharp condemnation of the practice of debasing the common lands by means of the illegal allocation of lands of collective farms to various organizations and individuals in the form of the creation on collective farm lands of all sorts of subsidiary operations and individual gardens of workers and employees. The decree provides that the officials guilty of debasing public land must bear strict responsibility.

The decisions of the general meetings of the collective farm were rescinded on protest of the procurator.

MODEL CONTRACT FOR ASSIGNMENT OF A LOT FOR PERPETUAL USE FOR THE CONSTRUCTION OF AN INDIVIDUAL DWELLING HOUSE WITH THE RIGHT OF PERSONAL OWNERSHIP, Approved by order of the State Committee on Construction of the RSFSR and the Ministry of Municipal Services of the RSFSR on October 6, 1965, No. 67, M. S. Makarov (editor), *Spravochnik gosudarstvennogo notariusa* (State Notary's Handbook) (Moscow), 1972), p. 52.

19   , City (Village) of ....
1. The Department of Municipal Services of the Executive Committee of the ....Soviet of Working People's Deputies in the person of ....in accordance with a decision of the Executive Committee of the ....Soviet of Working People's Deputies of ....19. . . . Assigns to the builder ....with the right of perpetual use the lot denoted as No. ....on..........St. ....in ....city (village), having a frontage of.........meters, a back boundary of ....meters, a right boundary of ....meters, a left boundary of........meters, with an overall area of ....sq. meters, indicated on the plan attached to the contract for the construction of a (stone, wood, mixed) dwelling house of ....floors, with an area of ....sq. meters of useful space, including ....sq. meters of living space with outbuildings of ....sq. meters in full accordance with the approved plan of..........19. . ., No. . . .

Note. The land plan and building plan are an inseparable part of this contract.

2. The builder is obliged to begin construction not later than one year from the day of signing the present contract and to conduct the construction work at such a pace that all of the building will be completed in the course of not more than three years, i.e., by 19
3. Upon completiong of construction the structures erected on the lot may be put into use after the recognition by the acceptance commission of the local soviet of working people's deputies of the full readiness of the erected structure, formalized by a certificate of the commission.
4. If the erection of the structures is not finished on time by the builder for reasons not depending upon the builder, the term for finishing the structure may be extended for not more than one building season by the Department of Municipal Services.

   The builder is obliged to finish construction by the new deadline under penalty of the consequences provided by Par. 12 of the present contract.
5. In case of deviation from the conditions indicated in Par. 1, the builder is obliged at his own expense to make the corresponding changes and corrections in the structure according to the instructions of the architectural-construction inspection agency within the time-limits established by it.

   If the builder refuses to make the changes and corrections in the completed building, or fails to make them within the established time, and also in case of the erection of structures on the lot which are not provided for by the contract, on the decision of the executive committee of the city (or district) or

village soviet of working people's deputies, the builder must stop construction, and within one month, with his own efforts and at his own expense, remove all structures or parts of structures erected by him and put the lot in order.
6. The erection on the lot of dwelling structures without a decision of the executive committee of the city (or district) soviet of working people's deputies, and of non-dwelling structures without the permission of the Department of Municipal Services (or in cities where the position of chief city architect has been introduced—without the permission of the chief city architect) are not allowed.
7. In case of destruction of the building by fire or other natural calamities for builders in districts left in the general plan with individual buildings, the right for perpetual use of the lot is preserved on the condition of restoration or reconstruction on the lot of a new building according to an approved project during a term of not more than three years.

   The exact time limits for commencement of restoration and completion of restoration of the structures shall be established by a special agreement with the Department of Municipal Services.
8. The builder must make both regular and major repairs of the structures.
9. The builder is obliged to plant . . . percent of the area with greenery (including fruit trees and berry bushes) on instruction of the Department of Municipal Services within the term established by the latter and to keep and restore these plantings in the future.
10. The builder is responsible for: the condition of the lot, the construction of sidewalks within the boundaries of his lot, constant care and maintenance in proper order both of the lot and of the sidewalks and passageways adjacent to it in accordance with the rules established by decisions of the Executive Committee of the . . . . . . Soviet of Working People's Deputies.
11. The builder may use for construction and future household needs the construction materials found on the lot allocated to him and beneath its service, however the places of excavation of these materials must be properly developed (filling in pits, etc.) as they are used.

    Cutting or transplanting of trees suitable for lumber is allowed only with the permission of the Executive Committee of the . . . . . . Soviet of Working People's Deputies.
12. For violation of the time-limits for beginning and finishing construction established by the present contract, the Department of Municipal Services has the right to recover from the builder by a judicial proceeding a contractual sanction (not over 2 rubles and 50 kopecks) for each day of lateness.

    In case of a systematic (more than two-times) violation without compelling circumstances by the builder of the time-limits for construction established by the present contract or of the failure to erect structures on the lot within a term that has been extended by the Department of Municipal Services, or in case of deviation from the conditions indicated in Par. 1 of the contract and the refusal of the builder to make a correction, the lot, by decision of the executive committee of the city (or district) soviet of working people's deputies may be taken by a judicial procedure with an award for the use of the Department of Municipal Services of damages caused or of a contractual sanction.

In case of substantial deviations in construction from the approved house plan or of a gross violation of the basic construction norms and rules, the house, on decision of the city (or district) soviet of working people's deputies must be removed by the builder or shall be removed by a compulsory procedure at the cost of the builder, or be taken without compensation by judicial procedure and be registered in the housing fund of the local soviet of working people's deputies.

13. Until the completion of the house (Par. 3 of the contract) and its recognition by a commission of the local soviet of working people's deputies as ready for use, the builder does not have the right to sell the house or part of it to other persons or organizations without the permission of the Department of Municipal Services.
14. Legal Addresses: Department of Municipal Services ....
    ....Soviet of Working People's Deputies
    ....builder
    The builder must notify the Department of Municipal Services in writing within one week of any change of address.
15. All expenses for the conclusion of this contract are to be paid by the builder.
16. This contract under penalty of invalidity is subject to compulsory registation at a notarial office.
    Appendix: lot plan and building plan.
    Department of Municipal Services   (signature)
    Builder   (signature)

PROCURATOR'S PROTEST OF ILLEGAL SALE OF DACHA, Sotsialisticheskaia zahonnost', 1973, No. 3, p. 87.

The administration of the Buriat Consumers' Union adopted a decision to sell to B. Molonov, the director of its motor pool, a duplex dacha in connection with the economic inexpediency of keeping it on the books of the motor pool.

The procurator of the Buriat ASSR entered a protest against this decision on the following grounds. The Council of Ministers of the USSR, by decree of December 30, 1960, No. 1346, "On Individual Construction of Dachas" (citation omitted), forbade everywhere the assignment to citizens of lots for individual construction and found it necessary to stop the sale to citizens of dachas by state, cooperative, and public organizations. As was established by an inspection, the dacha was used for recreation by employees of the consumers' union, and moreover it underwent major repairs not long before the sale with the expenditure of over 1800 rubles.

The administration of the Buriat Consumers' Union considered the procurator's protest and rescinded the illegal decree.

PROCURATOR'S PROTEST OF ILLEGAL ASSIGNMENT OF STATE LAND, Sotsialisticheskaia zakonnost', 1973, No. 5, p. 85.

The Executive Committee of the Kharabalin District Soviet of Working-People's Deputies (Astrakhan Region) decided to assign a plot of land with an area of 30 hectares [74 acres] from the land of the state reserve to the Sevvodstroi Trust for the construction of dwelling houses.

The district procurator protested the decision on the following grounds: according to Art. 13 of the Land Code of the RSFSR (1970, citation omitted), the executive committees of district soviets of working peoples' deputies have the right to assign plots of land from the land of the state reserve with an area not greater than 10 hectares [25 acres].

The protest has been satisfied. The decision of the executive committee has been brought in exact accordance with the law.

EXECUTIVE COMMITTEE OF THE SHELKOVO CITY SOVIET OF WORKING PEOPLE'S DEPUTIES vs. SMIRNOVA, Biulleten' Verkhovnogo Suda RSFSR, 1975, No. 5, p. 15.

The Executive Committee of the Shelkovo City Soviet of Working People's Deputies brought an action against Smirnova to take without compensation, for inclusion in the local Soviet's stock of housing, a part of a house being maintained in a neglectful manner. The owners of the house in equal shares are Bychkova, Kurakina, and Smirnova. Smirnova, despite the warning of the town soviet of working people's deputies refused to start repairs. Bychkova and Kurakin agreed to repair the house.

The Shelkovo City People's Court of Moscow Region satisfied the claim, and decided to take without compensation from Smirnova the one-third part of the home which belonged to her and to transfer it to the stock of housing of the Zagorianskii Town Soviet of Working People's Deputies.

In satisfying the claim, the people's court relied on the position that according to Art. 141 [Neglectful Upkeep of a House] of the Civil Code of the RSFSR, if a citizen acted neglectfully with respect to a house belonging to him, allowing its disintegration, then the executive committee of the local soviet of working people's deputies could set a reasonable term for the owner to repair the house. If the citizen without compelling reasons failed to make the necessary repair, the court on an action by the executive committee of the local soviet of working people's deputies could take the neglectfully maintained home without compensation and transfer it to the stock of the local soviet of working people's deputies. By an expert examination it was established that the house in question needed major repair. Smirnova was warned twice of the necessity of making major repairs to the house, but did not begin repairing it, and put obstacles in the way of the owners in carrying out the repairs.

On protest of the Deputy President of the Supreme Court of the RSFSR, the Presidium of the Moscow Regional Court on November 6, 1974, reversed the decision of the people's court, and remanded the case for a new hearing on the following grounds.

From the explanations of the defendant it appears that on September 11, 1972 a contract was concluded between the owners of the house on the joint repair of the home, and in fulfillment of it she gave money to Bychkova for repair. Under these circumstances, the conclusion of the court that the defendant had refused to carry out the decision of the Zagorianskii Town Soviet on the repair of the house was made without proper verification of this circumstance.

Later a dispute arose between the owners on the use of the house. The defendant testified that Kurakina unwarrantedly took possession of the second floor of the house and that this was the reason that the part she occupied remained unrepaired. This is confirmed by the content of the decision of the Zagorianskii Town Soviet of Working People's Deputies. This is also mentioned in the decision of the court in the present case.

An explanation should have been made to the defendant that the existance of this conflict did not free her from participation in the repair of the house; that the dispute could be solved by bringing an appropriate action in court. There is nothing in the record to the effect that this situation was explained to Smirnova. At the judicial session the defendant asserted that she was ready to start repairing the house.

The court should verify what was the cause of the defendant's refusal to repair the house: unwillingness to take account of the decisions of the executive committee or the conflict which had arisen about the procedure for use of the house. This circumstance should be considered in decision of the action for the taking of the house without compensation from the owner on the bases of Art. 141 of the Civil Code of the RSFSR.

DISTRICT EXECUTIVE COMMITTEE vs. BASKAKOVA, Biulleten' Verkhovnogo Suda SSSR, 1975, No. 4.

In 1939, I. V. Baskakov bought a house consisting of one room measuring 20.33 sq. meters on a lot with an area of 459 sq. meters in the city of Tbilisi at 76 Kakbetskaia St. The house was constructed without permission, and therefore the proper formalization of the contract for purchase and sale of it was not made. On the same lot, before the start of the Second World War, I. V. Baskakov, his son, P. I. Baskakov, and the wife of his son, N. Ia. Baskakov, built without permission one more house consisting of two rooms with a general area of 32.2 sq. meters.

On October 4, 1967, after the death of I. V. Baskakov, the Executive Committee of the Council of Working People's Deputies of the Twenty-six Commissars District of the City of Tbilisi adopted a decision which legalized the construction of the one room house. The Bureau of Techinical Inventory made an appropriate legal registration of this house.

In November 1967, the district executive committee brought an action in court for the taking without compensation and transfer to the housing stock of the soviet of working people's deputies of the second house (with an area of 32.2 sq. meters) in which N. Ia. Baskakova was living on this lot.

On July 5, 1968, the People's Court of the October District of the City of Tbilisi dismissed this claim of the executive committee.

[After numerous judicial hearings at various levels, this decision was affirmed on the following grounds.]

It is established in this case that the dwelling house whose taking the plaintiff sought was constructed in 1939-40 by the defendant Baskakova, her husband and father-in-law. She and her family have been living in the house until the present time. Her husband went from this home to the battlefront in 1943 and was lost missing in action.

In 1956 by a normative act, the executive committees of city and district soviets of working people's deputies of the Georgian SSR were authorized to formalize in the appropriate manner the transfer of lots to those who had built major structures before the issuance of the act on the condition that these structures satisfy the urban building requirements. If the structures erected without permission by builders before the issuance of this normative act do not meet these requirements and must be removed, then the builders, as is provided in this act, must be assigned other lots and a time-limit must be set for removal of the structure erected without permission.

The plaintiff brought an action for the taking of a house from the defendant and for its transfer to the housing stock of the district soviet of working people's deputies, from which one could reach the conclusion that the structure was a major one and was suitable for use as housing. Thus, in this case according to the above-mentioned normative act, the executive committee of the district soviet could conduct a legal registration of the house as it did for the house earlier built on this lot. It should not have ordered its taking without compensation. Taking account of this normative act, it should be noted that the People's Court of the October District of the City of Tbilisi correctly decided this case on July 5, 1968, when it dismissed the claim of the executive committee for the taking of the house without compensation. The court also considered the concrete circumstances of this case. As was already noted, the house was constructed by P. I. Baskakov, the husband of the plaintiff. He lived in this house with his family and left for the front from this house. In this instance the plaintiff did not have any necessity for raising the question of taking the house of the family of a servicemen who perished at the front in World War II.

NOSKOVSKAIA vs. INZHKOOPTRANSTROI, Sovetskaia iustitsiia, 1961, No. 2, p. 29.

By decision of the general meeting of members of the Inzhkooptranstroi, Dacha Construction Cooperative Noskovskaia was expelled from membership for violation of the charter, in that she has not executed the decision of the administration of the cooperative on demolition of an illegally constructed second dwelling, and for obtaining non-labor income from a garden placed on a plot of land allotted for a cottage on which the work was performed by an employed person.

Noskovskaia being of the opinion that the decision of the general meeting of the cooperative expelling her was incorrect, brought suit for reinstatement: She claimed that the decision of the general meeting had been issued in violation of sec. 21 of the Model Charter of the Dacha Construction Cooperative, as approved by the Council of Ministers of the RSFSR on September 24, 1958, since the circumstances set forth in the decision may not serve as the basis for exclusion of her from membership in the cooperative.

The Moscow City Court gave judgment for the plaintiff, restoring Noskovskaia to membership.

The Civil Division of the Supreme Court of the RSFSR, in reviewing the case on the protest of the deputy chairman of the Supreme Court of the RSFSR, by its decision of November 11, 1960 set aside the judgment of the Moscow city court and remanded the case for new trial: on the ground that Noskovskaia, being a member of the Inzhkooptranstroi Dacha Construction Cooperative since 1937, was using a plot of land of 2635 square meters and a house composed of two rooms on the first floor and one room on the second floor and a porch. In 1948, taking advantage of the fact that her husband was a member of the administration of the cooperative, the plaintiff built a second dwelling illegally on the same plot of land.

In verification of the activity of the cooperative by the Moscow Building Administration and by special commissions of other agencies it was established that Noskovskaia had turned a cooperative dacha, designed for summer vacations into a winter dwelling, which for 12 years she had leased on a full year basis. The second building was also rented. From rentals of these buildings Noskovskaia received considerable non-labor income. In addition Noskovskaia had a large fruit orchard on her cottage plot as well as poultry, for the working of which she hired laborers. She sold the produce on the local market.

Under the circumstances set forth the conclusion of the Moscow city court that Noskovskaia was incorrectly excluded from membership in the cooperative on the ground that she had not violated the charter is found contrary to the evidence in the case. Exploitation of a dacha to obtain non-labor income is a grave violation of Sec. 20 of the Model Charter of the Dacha Construction Cooperatives, therefore, the general meeting of members of the cooperative had good grounds for excluding Noskovskaia from the cooperative for violation of the charter.

C. *Payment for Use or Taking of Land*

1. Land Rent

N. N. BEDENIN, RATIONAL USE OF THE LAND IS THE BASIS FOR IMPROVING THE EFFICIENCY OF AGRICULTURAL PRODUCTION, Sovetskoe gosudarstvo i pravo, 1972, No. 10, p. 64.

In the literature on questions of land law, there is a certain underevaluation of the role and significance of economic levers in the rational and most effective use of land resources. Often doubts are expressed as to the possibility of applying economic-value categories to the area of land relations. Statements of this type are groundless. They are confirmed neither by the experience of building socialisms in the USSR and the brother socialist countries, nor by the results of carrying out the economic reform.

. . .

Proposals for the introduction of direct rent payments that would aid the more effective and rational use of land assigned to a farm deserve attention and experimental testing. Payments of this type do not contradict in our view either the nationalization of land in the USSR nor the exclusive state ownership of it. On the contrary, the right of the state to take rent payments flows directly from nationalization and state ownership of land. . . . Even the Soviet state takes a differential rent, basicly through the system of purchase (delivery) prices for agricultural products. However this mechanism of taking a differential rent does not always "work out" and give the desired results, since the soil, climatic, and economic conditions of activity of farms are different not only for zones of the country, but also within them.

2. Land Taking

FUNDAMENTAL PRINCIPLES OF LAND LEGISLATION OF THE U.S.S.R. AND THE UNION REPUBLICS, [1968] Vedomosti Verkhovnogo Soveta SSSR, No. 51, item 485. Translated in full in C.D.S.P., Vol. XXI, No. 1, p. 14 (Jan 22, 1969).

Art. 16. Procedure for taking of land for state or social needs.

The taking of a parcel of land or part of it for state or social needs shall be effected on the basis of a decree of the Council of Ministers of a Union Republic or the Council of Ministers of an autonomous republic or by a decision of the executive committee of the appropriate soviet of workers' deputies in the manner established by the legislation of the U.S.S.R. and the union republics.

The taking of parcels from land which is being used by collective farms by state farms or other state agricultural enterprises, from lands occupied by reservoirs, protective forests and reserves or other land having cultural or scientific significance shall be permitted only in instances of particular necessity.

In exceptional cases, and only by a decree of the Council Ministers of the union republic, irrigated and drained land, arable land, land areas occupied by perennial fruit plantings may be taken for non-agricultural needs and also land occupied by water-protection, protective and other forests of the first group for use for purposes not connected with forestry.

The taking of parcels of land which are being used by collective farms may be conducted only with the consent of the general meetings of the members of the collective farms or the meetings of deputies, and from land which is being used by state farms or other state, cooperative or social enterprises, organizations or institutions of all-union or republican subordination by agreement with the land users and the respective ministries and departments of the U.S.S.R. or the union republics.

Art. 18. Compensation of land users for damages caused by the taking or temporary occupation of land

Damages caused to land users by the taking of parcels of land for state or social needs or by the temporary occupation of land parcels are subject to compensation.

Compensation for damages shall be conducted by the enterprises, organizations and institutions to whom the land parcels are transferred in accordance with a statute to be adopted by the Council of Ministers of the U.S.S.R.

Art. 19. Compensation for losses of agricultural production connected with the taking of land for non-agricultural needs.

Enterprises, organizations and institutions to which are transferred for construction and other non-agricultural needs parcels of land occupied with agricultural crops, shall be compensated for losses of agricultural production connected with the taking of these parcels (in addition to compensation for damages in accordance with Article 18 of the present Fundamental Principles).

The measures and procedure for determination of the losses of agricultural production subject to compensation and also the procedure for the use of such assets shall be established by the Council of Ministers of the U.S.S.R.

IVANOVA vs. HOUSING CONSTRUCTION COOPERATIVE AND DISTRICT EXECUTIVE COMMITTEE, Biulleten' Verkhovnogo Suda RSFSR, 1965, No. 3, p. 3.

Ivanova brought suit in court against a housing construction cooperative organization seeking to be provided with living space. In her statement the plaintiff affirmed that her sister Barmina had owned a home on Matrosov St. in the city of Saratov with 18.65 square meters of living space. In 1963 the sister died, leaving the house to her by will. The plaintiff accepted the inheritance, moved into the house, and relinquished the room in which she had been living to the housing administration. On May 30, 1964, the house belonging to her was removed by the housing construction cooperative. The housing construction cooperative refused to provide her with living space. Therefore she brought suit against the housing construction cooperative and the executive committee of the district soviet of working peoples' deputies seeking to be provided with living space.

The Saratov Provincial Court granted Ivanova's claim. The court required the executive committee to provide her with a separate apartment.

In its appeal the executive committee asked that this decision be reversed on the grounds that provision of living space should be made the responsibility of the organization for which the lot was taken for construction of an apartment house.

The Judical Division for Civil Cases of the Supreme Court of the RSFSR affirmed the decision of the Saratov Provincial Court and denied the appeal, stating the following in its decision of November 20, 1964.

It is true that the lot, on which the structure which belonged to Ivanova was located, was allotted to the organization for the construction of an apartment house. However later the executive committee canceled this decision and by a new decision transfered this lot to the housing construction cooperative.

Therefore the organization cannot be obligated to provide housing space to persons evicted from the houses that were removed.

Such an obligation also may not be placed upon the housing construction cooperative.

In accordance with para. 2 of the Decree of the Central Committee of the CPSU and the Council of Ministers of the USSR of Nov. 19, 1964, "On the Further Development of Cooperative Housing Construction," in case of taking for the cooperative with its consent of a lot on which there are structures which must be removed and belong to citizens by right of personal ownership, the housing construction cooperatives are freed from making compensation for the cost of the removed homes, structures and buildings and the cost of fruit and berry plantings and gardens located on the lot of land taken for the cooperative, and also from the provision of living space for persons resettled from these homes.

The payment to citizens of the cost of homes, structures, buildings, fruit and berry plantings and gardens and also the provision for them of living space is carried out by executive committees of soviets of working people's deputies according to the procedure established by the Decree of the Council of Ministers of the USSR of December 15, 1961.

In such cases only expenses connected with the dismantling of the building and the removal of trash are allocated to the cost of construction.

Thus, the decision of the court with respect to placing upon the executive committee the responsibility for presenting living space to Ivanova was correct.

WORKERS' SUPPLY DEPARTMENT vs. CONSTRUCTION DIVISION,
Sovetskaia iustitsiia, 1968, No. 1, inside back cover.

By decision of the Kirov Region Executive Committee there was transferred to the Construction Division of one of the Boards a plot of land on which there was located a store belonging to the Workers' Supply Department of the Kirov Division of the Gorky Railroad. In connection with the forthcoming construction on the site, the store had to be demolished. The Workers' Supply Division brought an action in State Arbitration Attached to the Kirov Region Executive Committee seeking to recover from the Construction Division 13,727 rubles, constituting the book value of the above mentioned structure.

State Arbitration attached to the Kirov Executive Committee, having considered the dispute which had arisen, found that the demand of the plaintiff should not be satisfied, since according to the Instruction of the People's Commissariat of Finances of the USSR, the People's Commissariat of Justice of the USSR and State Arbitration Attached to the Council of People's Commisars of the USSR of May 26, 1940, and the Instruction Letter of State Arbitration Attached to the Council of

Ministers of the USSR of December 11, 1953 (citations omitted) the transfer of enterprises, buildings and structures of state organizations to other state organizations in connection with the taking of plots of land on which they were erected must be conducted without compensation from balance-sheet to balance-sheet. The question of the transfer of the structure from the books of the Division of Workers' Supply to the books of the defendant must be decided not by State Arbitration but by the Ministries or departments of the parties, since by the Decree of the Council of People's Commissars of the USSR of February 15, 1936, "On the Procedure for the Transfer of State Enterprises, Buildings and Structures," as amended (citations omitted), it is provided that buildings and structures may be transferred from one organization of the USSR to another by order of the directors of both organizations.

For these reasons, State Arbitration attached to the Council of Ministers of the USSR, having considered on appeal of the plaintiff the decision in the present case, found it correct and did not find a basis for its reconsideration.

CHAPTER XII

The Directing and Planning Agencies

With the plan as their pride, Soviet theorists have focused their effort to improve the efficiency of industrial management on the mechanism that creates and directs execution of the plan. The dynamic has been the search for a balance between severe centralization on the one side and utilization of local initiative on the other. All modern socialists have dreamed of planning, and when in power they have tended to move in the direction of ever increasing centralization. The first contemporary Marxian socialist to see the peril of centralization was Marshal Tito of Yugoslavia. In an effort to overcome stultification of imaginative effort when all decisions are taken at headquarters, he reversed the process which he had inherited from Stalin, calling centralism the "cancer of socialism". Yugoslavia under the guidance of Tito's communists has moved far since 1948 in the direction of decentralization and reduction of centralized planning to a minimum statement of planning objectives in basic industrial areas.

Stalin proved himself to be a confirmed centralizer. At his death the national economic plan contained a multitude of details and was devised and directed by administrators sitting in Moscow, allowing little decision making at republic levels, and almost none locally, except for small industry operated by local soviets with locally obtained materials and serving local needs. Even locally directed production was coordinated in the national plan on the basis of recommendations from local administrators. But Stalin's centralism had not been built without interruption on the stage set by Lenin and his early plan for electrification.[1] There were periods when efforts were made to create institutions that would be responsible both locally and centrally. Some of these institutions survived all of Stalin's centralization, and proved that the institutional forms created to avoid stultifying centralism could be nullified in practice. Thus, the State Planning Commission[2] has been constructed ever since it began to function for more than study purposes, as a two-stepped agency so as to divide responsibility for preparation of the plan between the republics and the central government. The republic State Planning Commissions were legally required to report to the respective republic's Council of Ministers and to consider the special needs and desires of the distinctive ethnic group for whose government the republic was created. Still, the republic commission was also subordinate to the federal planning commission, and practice increased this subordination to the point that all matters of even slight importance were referred to Moscow for decision.

Stalin's budgetary procedures were also centralized in practice. While each republic nominally adopted its own budget, this occurred after the total income and expenitures for the republic had been set by the budget established for the federal government. There was in reality very little authority left to the republic agencies to decide how money should be spent. The federal government set the tax rates, collected the income and on appropriation by the Supreme Soviet of the USSR returned to the republics for investment in new construction and operation of existing industrial plants subject to republic jurisdiction the sums agreed upon through the planning mechanism as necessary to the national welfare. Major industries were not even nominally within the republics' budgets or the republics' plans, for they were directed from Moscow without the possibility of intervention by republic authorities through structures called All-Union Commissariats.

During Stalin's dictatorship he experimented with ministerial organization charts and the division of industries into their component parts to reduce the burdens of centralized direction through the creation of multiple ministries. He also developed the Union-Republic form of ministry, created in 1923 at the time of federation and designed to place the planning function in the federal government but to leave the operating function in the republic for those industries producing consumers' goods.

Stalin's trend was, however, toward centralization of planning authority and even direction of key industrial activity by federal offices. Operating decisions were left to the administration of the republics only in the mass consumption goods industries, and to provincial or city administrators only for those small scale brick yards, glass factories, musical instrument shops and the like which catered to special requirements of the province or produced construction supplies too heavy to ship great distances and requiring no allocation of supplies from outside the province.

---

[1]Resolution of December 29, 1920, [1921] I Sob. Uzak, RSFSR, No. 1, item 11.
[2]Created by decree of February 22, 1921, [1921]; Ibid. No. 17, item 106.

Nikita Khrushchev attacked Stalin's centralized system in the administrative reforms of 1957, introduced after discussion of his March theses calling for a radical departure from centralization. His scheme required elimination of all but a few of the All-Union Ministries, with transfer of their planning functions, albeit in less detailed form, to departments of what was renamed the State Planning Committee, and creation of new regional economic councils in relatively small economic districts with authority to plan and direct industry.

Khrushchev's successors rapidly removed key industries from the jurisdiction of regional economic councils and returned them to the centralized control of the specialized industrial ministries. Then in September 1965, it was announced that the regional economic councils were to be completely abolished and all major industry was to be placed under the jurisdiction of industrial ministries. In form, the new system seemed strikingly like that which had prevailed before 1957; however the Soviet leaders stated that this would be centralization with a difference. Before 1957, there were very significant limits on the legal power of the state enterprises subordinate to the various ministries; now, it was promised, the enterprises would be given much greater powers. In implementation of these promises, new legislation was passed defining the status of the enterprises and the ministries and the rules governing their relations with each other. In particular, economic reform legislation radically revised the treatment of enterprise income with the aim of substantially increasing the importance of profit incentives in the administration of the economy. Further reforms have created "industrial combines" and "production combines." These reforms are designed to reduce the number of intermediate administrative organizations and to put those that remain on a profit and loss basis.

The republics retain the somewhat greater budgetary powers which they had gained after Stalin's death. However, with the transfer of the most important branches of industrial activity back to all-union control, the new budgetary powers have lost some of their significance. The republics may retain a portion of the funds collected in taxes on state industry within the republic, and may extend it with greater budget autonomy in choice of projects than in Stalin's day. Still, the national budget contains the overall figures for each republic, and no money can be retained unless it is within the amount permitted as appropriations to investment and operation within the republic. The mechanism still permits use of tax money collected in the wealthier republics, such as the RSFSR or the Ukrainian SSR for transfer to investment in the less developed republics of central Asia.

A major new development of the 1970's has been the rapid creation of an "automated system of administration" which would provide for the maximum use of computers in the planning and administration of economic activity.

Today two schools of thought compete among Soviet theorists of economic planning. Some argue for a lessening of central control and an increased reliance upon market forces. Others call for expanded and more rational central control based upon the information gathering and analysis capabilities of the most modern electronic data processing systems. Through the early 1970's, the former school predominated, partly because few computers were available for civilian uses. However, centralism has long been ingrained in Soviet thinking, and the outsider can not but wonder if there will not be a swing back to it once the immediate potentials of profit-oriented reforms have been realized and computer control becomes more feasible.

A. *The organizational structure*

CONSTITUTION OF THE U.S.S.R., December 5, 1936, as amended:

Art. 64. The highest executive and administrative agency of state power of the Union of Soviet Socialist Republics is the Council of Ministers of the USSR.

Art. 65. The Council of Ministers is responsible and accountable to the Supreme Soviet of the USSR, or, in intervals between sessions of the Supreme Soviet, to the Presidium of the Supreme Soviet of the USSR.

Art. 66. The Council of Ministers of the USSR issues decrees and regulations on the basis of and in pursuance of the laws in force, and verifies their execution.

Art. 67. Decrees and regulations of the Council of Ministers of the USSR are binding throughout the territory of the USSR.

Art. 74. The Ministries of the USSR are either All-Union or Union-Republic Ministries.

Art. 75. Each all-Union Ministry directs the branch of state administration entrusted to it throughout the territory of the USSR either directly or through the bodies appointed by it.

Art. 76. The Union-Republic Ministries, as a rule, direct the branches of state administration entrusted to them through Ministries of the Union Republics with the same name; they administer directly only a definite and limited number of enterprises according to a list confirmed by the Presidium of the Supreme Soviet of the USSR.

Art 79. The highest executive and administrative body of state power of a Union Republic is the Council of Ministers of the Union Republic.

Art. 80. The Council of Ministers of a Union Republic is responsible and accountable to the Supreme Soviet of the Union Republic, or, in the intervals between sessions of the Supreme Soviet of the Union Republic, to the Presidium of the Supreme Soviet of the Union Republic.

Art. 84. The Ministers of a Union Republic direct the branches of state administration which come within the jurisdiction of the Union Republic.

Art. 86. The Ministries of a Union Republic are either Union-Republic or Republic Ministries.

Art. 87. Each Union-Republic Ministry directs the branch of state administration entrusted to it, and is subordinate both to the Council of Ministers of the Union Republic and to the corresponding Union-Republic Ministry of the USSR.

Art. 88. Each Republic Ministry directs the branch of state administration entrusted to it and is directly subordinate to the Council of Ministers of the Union Republic.

B. *Plan enforcement*

REINFORCED CONCRETE PRODUCTS PLANT No. 4 vs. SYTOV, GORDETSKII, ZAKHARENKOV, and SMEKALOVA, Biulleten' Verkhovnogo Suda RSFSR, 1972, No. 6, p. 1.

An audit of the activity of Reinforced Concrete Products Plant No. 4 of the Leningrad Main Administration of Construction Materials conducted by the Leningrad Inspection and Audit Board of the Ministry of Finances of the RSFSR revealed false additions in the reports of the plant on fulfillment of the plan for volume of goods sold. In particular the audit established that for 1969 the actual achievement of the plan for sales of products was 99.9%, while in the reports 101.6% was shown, and in the first quarter of 1970, 99.2% instead of the 100.2% of plan shown in the reports. As a result of exaggerating the percent of fulfillment of the sales plan, employees of the plant were illegally paid 36,000 rubles of bonuses, included 504 rubles and 60 kopecks to Sytov, the director of the factory; 503 rubles and 73 kopecks to Gordetskii, the chief engineer, 342 rubles and 78 kopecks to Zakharenkov, the chief accountant; and 316 rubles and 68 kopecks to Smekalova, head of the planning division.

In connection with the fact that these officials refused voluntarily to fulfill the demands of the Audit Board for return of the bonuses they had received, the Reinforced Concrete Products Plant No. 4, brought an action against them in court. By the time the case was decided, 100 rubles had been withheld from Sytov when he left his job, Zakharenkov had returned in full the 342 rubles and 78 kopecks which he had received earlier, and 18 rubles were withheld from Smekalova.

The Leningrad city court awarded 404 rubles and 60 kopecks from Sytov and 298 rubles and 68 kopecks from Smeliakova, and since the representative of the plaintiff renounced the case at the judicial hearing, directed that these amounts go into the income of the state.

In a cassational appeal, Sytov disputed the decision of the court, relying on the fact the reports on fulfillment of the plan for sales of products was compiled by the plant in exact correspondence with the Model Instruction approved by the Central Statistical Administration of the USSR as amended (citations omitted), that the factory correctly included in the volume of products sold the price of products paid for by customers but not removed from the warehouse. For these reasons Sytov asked that the decision of the court be reversed and the case be remanded for a new hearing.

For its part, the Barricade Production Combine (the legal successor of Reinforced Cement Products Plant No. 4) asked that the decision of the court be changed and the sum determined by the court be awarded not to the income of the state but to the use of the Barricade Combine. It indicated that the representative of the plant renounced the action without having the authority to do so, and the court in awarding the sum of damages not for the use of the Combine, but for income of the state violated property interests of the combine.

The Judicial Division for Civil Cases of the Supreme Court of the RSFSR, by a decision of November 30, 1971, satisfied the appeal of the combine, but left Sytov's appeal unsatisfied on the following grounds.

The intentional distortion by officials of Reinforced Concrete Products Plant No. 4, including its former director, Sytov, of report data on the fulfillment of the plan of sales of finished products by exaggerating the fulfillment, in connection with which Sytov illegally received 504 rubles 60 kopecks of bonuses has been established by the decision of the investigative agencies of February 24, 1971. The elements of the crime provided by Art. 152 [apparently a misprint for Art. 152-1 "False Additions and Other Distortions of Reports on Plan Fulfillment—translator's note] of the Criminal Code of the RSFSR have been established in the actions of Sytov and Zakharenkov and the case with respect to them has been dismissed only on the grounds that they both underwent disciplinary punishment and the damage they caused by the illegal payment and receipt of bonuses can be compensated by civil judicial proceedings.

These circumstances are attested by the audit certificate of the Leningrad Inspection and Audit Board of the Ministry of Finances of the USSR, where it is also indicated that the administrators of the plant for the purpose of exaggerating the volume of products sold in violation of current rules which forbade the inclusion in the amount of products sold the price of finished products that were in the enterprise warehouse, during the course of 1969 and the first quarter of 1970 included this type of products in the sales plan and thus artificially raised the indicators of the work of the plant. Audit by the Inspection and Audit Board and the agencies of investigation established that for the above-mentioned period, the indicators of the volume of sales of finished products was raised by 905,100 rubles. Part of the finished products that had been paid for by the customer (or purchaser) but in fact had not been shipped from the plant, for which the plant had issued warehouse receipts was included in the volume of products sold, but thereafter was shipped to other purchasers. Then, warehouse receipts were again issued for the same products to account for the credit in favor of the purchaser generated by the transactions.

Sytov's arguments that the Model Instruction of November 19, 1963 did not exclude the possibility of including in the amount of sales even those products which were paid for by customers but not removed from the warehouse of the enterprise (of the manufacturer) are unconvincing since, in the first place, in the instruction itself there is no indication that the volume of sales of products includes even that which is in fact located at the warehouse of the manufacturing plant and in the second place, in accordance with the explanation of the Central Statistical Administration of the USSR of January 16, 1970, such a possibility is allowed only in exceptional cases and on the condition that the production has been accepted by the customer and such acceptance is provided for by contract.

However it is established in the record that at Reinforced Contract Products Plant No. 4, the practice of including in the fulfillment of the plan the sales of those products which in fact were not sold was widespread and was not caused by exceptional circumstances. Moreover the products were transferred to other purchasers and again formalized with warehouse receipts.

In these circumstances the court properly held for the recovery from Sytov and Smekalova of the bonuses illegally received by them, and this decision does not contradict the law or the proofs which have been collected.

However, the award of the amount recovered not for the use of the plaintiff—Plant No. 4 (or its legal successor—the Barricade Combine), but to the income of the state was in error.

According to Article 34 of the Civil Procedure Code of the RSFSR, the plaintiff has the right to change the bases or object of an action to raise or lower the amount of the claims or to renounce the proceedings. However, if these actions contradict the law or violate anyone's rights and interests that are protected by law, the court should not accept this renunciation and should decide the dispute on the merits.

In the present case the court correctly did not take into account the statement of the representative of the plaintiff about the renunciation of the action, since he was not authorized for this, and his actions were contrary to the law and the interests of the plaintiff. However such a statement does not cause a replacement of the initial plaintiff by another person just as it also cannot serve as a ground for the entry of a decision not for the use of a party appearing as plaintiff in a case but for the use of other perons or for the award of the amount recovered to the income of the state.

The decision of the court in this respect was adopted contrary to the demands of Articles 34 and 36 of the Civil Procedure Code and violates the interests of the Barricade Combine.

CASE OF SHLEPIN AND FUFAEV, Sotsialisticheskaia zakonnost', 1970, No. 4, p. 88.

The procuracy of Gorky Region audited the progress of the Sormov Oil Depot in fulfilling the edict of the Presidium of the Supreme Soviet of the USSR of April 24, 1958, "On Liability for Non-Fulfillment of Plans and Tasks for Supply of Products."

On the basis of the results of the audit, a representation was made to the head of the Gorky Board of the Main Administration of Oil Supply of the RSFSR.

In the representation it was indicated that the administrators of the Sormov Oil Depot grossly violated the demands of the legislation on preferential supply of products to other union republics and for all-union needs. For the fulfillment of the supply plan for enterprises of the Kazakh SSR, it was necessary to ship 19 tons of cable grease. However, in February 1969, there was a failure to supply 1600 kilograms of it, and in March and June there were no shipments at all, as a result, the amount short for the first six months was 39,600 kilograms or 70% of the plan. Of the 26,000 kilograms of cable grease planned for enterprises of the Lithuanian SSR, only 8300 kilograms or 32 percent were shipped. The oil depot systematically violated the plans for shipment of cable grease to other users also. For the Perm Cable Factory there was a shortage in supply in January 1969 of 1400 kilograms, in

February of 38,000 kilograms, in May of 17,200 kilograms, and for the whole six months, 40,500 kilograms. The enterprises of Primorskii Province were supposed to receive 15,000 kilograms but their supply was interrupted. However neither in May nor in June was the shortage made up. During the first six months of 1969, 7600 kilograms less than was provided by plan was supplied to enterprises of Kaliningrad Region, 5000 kilograms less to enterprises of Staropol' Region, 6500 kilograms less to the Udmurt ASSR, 7000 less to Krasnodar Province, 8000 kilograms less to Vologda Region, etc.

The administrators of the oil depot, taking advantage of the poor quality of inspection by the dispatchers of the goods and transport division of the Gorky Board of the Main Administration of Oil Supply, not only acted carelessly toward their obligations for fulfillment of the state supply plan, but at times, abusing their official position, shipped products subject to allocation without delivery orders, and used for nonplan shipments transport facilities allocated for the fulfillment of the supply plan. In the plan of supply of products for April 1969, enterprises of Tiumen Region were not included, however 4100 kilograms were shipped to them; in May with a plan of 2300 kilograms, 6000 kilograms were shipped in all for the six-months period, 5800 kilograms were shipped above the plan. To enterprises of railroad transport, 8300 kilograms were shipped in May without a plan, and June another 7000 kilograms. A particularly large amount of products were shipped above the plan to enterprises of the Ukrainian SSR, in January—11,000 kilograms, in February 4300 kilograms, in March 30,200 kilograms, in May 9200 kilograms, and in June 12,800 kilograms.

The procuracy of Gorky Region, demanded that measures be taken for the elimination of the violations which had been revealed and raised the question of bringing Shelpin, the director of the oil depot, and Fufaev, the head of the goods and transport division of the Board to disciplinary responsibility.

The representation has been considered. By order of the head of the Gorky Board of the Main Administration of Oil Supply of the RSFSR, a reprimand has been issued against Shelpin for violation of State Discipline, and Fufaev has been placed upon probationary status because of the unsatisfactory quality of checking the fulfillment of plans for shipment of oil products. The order considered a number of measures for improvement of accounting and the guaranteeing of timely fulfillment of supply plans.

C. *Production Quality Control*

CASE OF THE SOLOTVINSKII WOODEN PACKING COMBINE, Sovetskaia iustitsiia, 1969, No. 7, p. 32.

An agent of the Committee of Standards, Measures, and Measuring Instruments for Ivano-Frankovo Region conducted an inspection of the application of State Standard 8777-67 for barrels for liquid and dry contents at the Solotvinskii Wooden

Packing Combine in May 1968. As a result of the inspection, 15 barrels of 162 that were at the combine on the day of the inspection were found to correspond to the above mentioned state standard.

The inspection report was sent to State Arbitration attached to the Ivano-Frankovo Region Executive Committee, which on its own initiative brought an action about the production by the Solotvinskii Wood Packing Combine of nonstandard goods. The amount of fine was determined by State Arbitration to be 43,500 rubles, which was 20% of the value of all production made by the combine in the period from February through July of 1968.

Having considered the case, State Arbitration found it possible to reduce the amount of the fine to 2 thousand rubles which was recovered for the income of the all-union budget.

The Solotvinskii Wood Packing Combine appealed to State Arbitration attached to the Council of Ministers of the USSR for reconsideration of the decision which had been adopted indicating that it had received no complaints from purchasers in connection with improper quality of barrels.

The decision of State Arbitration attached to the Ivano-Frankovo Region Executive Committee was found to be incorrect. The Statute on Supply of Goods for Production and Technological Use and the Decree of the Council of Ministers of the USSR of October 27, 1967, provide for the award for the use of a purchaser of a fine for the supply of products not of good quality. Existing law does not provide for the award of a fine for preparing the products not corresponding to standards.

In the present case the inspection of the quality of production was conducted by an agent of the Committee of Standards, Measures and Measuring Instruments at The Solotvinskii Wood Packing Combine in the process of the manufacture of goods and thus the fact of supply of goods of improper quality had not taken place. Under these circumstances, State Arbitration Attached to the Ivano-Frankovo Region Executive Committee did not have grounds for bringing an action on its own initiative, and certainly not for the exaction of a fine from the Solotvinskii Wood Packing Combine.

As a result of the aforesaid, the decision of State Arbitration was reversed and the action was dismissed.

CHAPTER XIII

The Operating Agencies

With nationalization of industry, transport and trade after the events of 1917, operation became a pressing problem for public administration. Lenin had the idea almost immediately of placing responsibility for operation of each state industry in one manager,[1] but he faced a political and practical problem. The political one arose because of the hostility to private management developed in the declining years of the Empire by many working men. They wanted to run their plants themselves through a process that seemed democratic to them. This suggested committees. The practical problem arose because there were almost no men trained to be responsible managers. Committee rule had to be accepted for lack of anything more efficient and popular.

Soviet operating agencies were also influenced at the time by the traditional approach of administration in many countries to the operation of state-owned railways, the post office, and military arsenals. These state activities were commonly run by Ministries of Railways, Post and Telegraph, and War, each conducting their economic activities as units within the ministerial bureaucracy, as departments of the whole, having no separate property responsibility and consequently no need to show a profit. Books of account were kept only to thwart embezzlement. Appropriations came from the national budget annually as their bureau chiefs justified the need, and they turned all of their receipts back to the state treasury without the right to identify those receipts later as their own if they needed funds. The national parks are conducted in this fashion in the United States by the Department of the Interior.

Soviet industry, followed this administrative pattern when it was brought into being. A Supreme Council of National Economy was created[2] to receive the various nationalized units of production, and this central operating authority delivered raw materials, financed investment, and took delivery of goods. No one knew what the costs were or whether they were being met from values delivered. Accounting was maintained to check on dishonesty in use of appropriations but not to determine

---

[1] Alexander Baykov, The development of the Soviet Economic System (New York 1947).
[2] December 5, 1917, [1917] I Sob. Uzak, RSFSR, No. 5, item 83.

efficiency of operation, through a comparison of costs and receipts as measured by a profit and loss statement.

Chaos and inflation resulted. Administrators had no thought of costs on the operating level. The situation was made worse by the Civil war, which required that priority be given to military requirements regardless of cost. It was against this system that Lenin moved when he introduced his scheme of the New Economic Policy in 1921. Although his primary targets were the peasant and return of peasant produce to city markets, his secondary target was industrial efficiency. In restoring limited capitalism, he not only hoped to avail himself of the historic desire of men to make profits for their own use through the small industries they were permitted to regain as owners, but he obtained a second and to him more important benefit. He reestablished the concept of measuring efficiency in terms of profit and loss. He told his state managers that they must operate in competition with the Private sector of the economy and produce at no greater cost, using as their yardstick whenever possible the market price of similar goods produced by capitalists.

To make such accounting possible, revision of the system of Ministerial operation through Ministerial departments or bureaus became imperative. The reorganization occurred in 1923 in what became known as the "First Decree on the Trusts,"[3] creating for each group of allied industry an accounting unit, taking the legal form of a public corporation. In structure the new unit would look much like its prototype in the private sector. It would have a charter defining its powers and duties; a capital and operating fund; and its principal controls would be in the form of those established by the bookkeeping department. It would be required to prepare and file with the Commissariat of Finance balance sheets showing the state of its assets, and profit and loss sheets showing how efficient it was.

To make these new public corporations responsible agencies Lenin's original concept of "one man management" was widened. This meant that the committees of workmen, where still existing, were to be dissolved and replaced by a single manager, responsible to his superior in the Supreme Council of National Economy, and expecting to be dismissed if he could not demonstrate his efficiency.

The scheme proved successful to such an extent that it was decided to create public corporations for the management of the various industrial units that were parts of the original trusts, and in 1927 there was published the "Second Decree on the Trusts,"[4] for this purpose. It remained, until replaced by a new statute in 1965, the backbone of the legislation relating to the legal structure of the operating agencies. The only question on which experimentation continued was the size of the unit required to show a profit. Near the end of Stalin's life, it was made very small, being each shop within a factory, but the trend since his death has been toward larger and larger units of industrial organization in attempt to match the efficiencies of the large corporations of the capitalist world.

---

[3] April 10, 1923, [1923] I Sob. Uzak. RSFSR, No. 29, item 336.
[4] June 29, 1927, [1927] I Sob. Uzak. RSFSR, No. 39, item 392.

All state economic activity of an operating kind is now directed by the public corporation, whether it be engaged in industry, transportation, trade, public housing, or in agriculture as a state farm. The corporate form is used regardless of whether the activity is under the planning supervision of a Ministry or a local soviet's executive committee. Nothing with major income from its operation is in any other form. Only Ministerial functions returning no income remain as bureaus, and some of them have charters to facilitate control.

The one-man management concept has also remained, as it had evolved under Stalin on the basis of Lenin's plans, but it has undergone changes in the measure of control exercised over the judgment of the manager. While the "committee of workers" is no more in the form assumed when it seemed necessary to supervise possibly disloyal managers or previous owners of a nationalized industry, there is a system of control that might be called its political heir. Under Stalin in the 1930's it had a form called the "triangle," in which management shared with the shop steward from the trade union and the communist party secretary for the cell functioning among the plant workers in establishing policies related to production. While the manager was without question "boss" of the enterprise, in that he would be held accountable for mismanagement, he had to seek political advice from the party secretary, and advice on his labor relations from the trade union shop steward. They could not veto his decisions, but they could complain to their superiors in their own hierarchy, and thus bring the matter to the attention of the Minister or other senior responsible official in the hierarchy to which the public corporation's manager reported.

Stalin abolished the "triangle" in 1937 due to his fear that it would impede bold decisions at a time when maximum production was necessary to meet Hitler's threat of war. Thereafter, the manager became a very powerful figure, subject only to the auditing controls of the Ministry of State Control and the security supervision of the Ministry of Internal Affairs and at various times its companion arm, the Ministry of State Security. The party's and the trade union's representatives remained in the factory, but they were muted and could have influence only through unofficial persuasion or through complaint to higher echelons. The result was the growth of nearly authoritarian managers, sometimes called members of a new managerial class—people who bore the brunt of criticism of such former communists as Milovan Djilas of Yugoslavia. Khrushchev thought it necessary to take action to redress the balance after Stalin's death.

Khrushchev's remedy was to restore the "triangle" in fact though not in name or formal standing. The trade unions were given increased authority in managerial decisions by law of July 9, 1958, while the communist party units in the factories were directed by communist party resolution of 1959 to create committees of their members to see that political decisions of the party were properly executed. The manager remained responsible, but the role he was to play created sufficient doubts in the minds of citizens to require publication of literature on the role of the manager under the new arrangements and reaffirmation of the concept of one-man management. The return to the ministerial system since 1965 probably increased the power of the manager vis-a-vis the trade union and the party unit, for the manager may now appeal to powerful officials in his ministry in Moscow to back up his decisions.

The issue of managerial authority can never be closed completely under the Soviet system, for the communist party is required by political theory to lead. It cannot leave the manager alone, and it seems unable to rely upon the fact that he is also a member of the party to exercise its leadership informally through that relationship. Further, experience has shown that managers sometimes make decisions in complete violation of the labor law on dismissals, as will be shown in the chapter on labor law. The pressure on them for efficiency and successful performance has to be countered by the intervention of an appropriate watchdog, and the trade union, as the agency closest to the workers' problems has seemed again and again in Soviet history the most suitable control mechanism even though by strengthening its hands the risk is taken of creating a political opposition. Today with the emphasis upon public self-government, the trade union as the representative of all who work outside the cooperative or as artisans is the obvious agency to be given a more vigorous role in the management of production. Traditionally trade unions smack of Democracy, and experience has shown that the people can be taught discipline with less resistance when those who do so are ostensibly on their side, rather than in the position of manager, who regardless of his status as the representative of their own state, represents for them authority not fully concerned with their special problems.

The documents chosen for presentation will provide the framework for the mechanism through which the forces and counter forces are at work.

A. *Organizational Types*

GENERAL OUTLINES FOR ADMINISTRATION OF BRANCHES OF INDUSTRY, Izvestiia, Sept. 6, 1974, p. 3, col. 1.

The government of the USSR, proceeding from the Directives of the Twenty-fourth Congress of the CPSU and in accordance with the Decree of the Central Committee of the CPSU and the Council of Ministers of the USSR of March 2, 1973, "On Certain Measures for the Further Improvement of the Administration of Industry," has approved general outlines for the administration of the coal, gas, and oil branches of industry.

The general outlines provide for the elimination of a multistage system for the administration of these branches of industry and the transfer to their administration by two and three link systems. Administration of basic production will be conducted: in the coal industry by a two-link system (Ministry of the Coal Industry of the USSR—production combine, enterprise) and by a three-link system (Ministry of the Coal Industry of the USSR—Ministry of the Coal Industry of the Ukrainian SSR—production combine, enterprise); in the gas industry, taking account of the specific nature of the development of this branch in separate regions of the country—by a two link system (Ministry—production combine, enterprise) and by a three link system (Ministry—all-union industrial combine—production combine, enterprise).

It is planned to create for the coal industry (for basic production), as the primary link, 47, in the gas industry 32, and in the oil industry 22 production combines. This will involve in the coal industry the elimination of about 1,600, in the gas industry of around 200, and in the oil industry of over 300 independent enterprises and organizations which will be included as production units in the structure of the corresponding production combines.

In the gas industry, as the intermediate link of administration there will be created 12 all-union industrial combines, including 8 all-union combines for the extraction of gas in different regions of the country.

The overall number of organizations which relate at present to the intermediate link of administration has been significantly decreased.

Simultaneously new structures have been created for the central staffs of the Ministry of the Coal Industry of the USSR, the Ministry of the Oil Industry, and the Ministry of the Gas industry. The Main Production Boards in the central structure of these ministries are being abolished.

The work for the improvement of administration in accordance with the approved general outlines is to be concluded in the gas industry in 1974, in the oil industry in 1975, and in the coal industry in 1976.

The full realization of these measures for the improvement of administration will allow the achievement of an economic effect in the coal industry in the amount of 120 to 130 million rubles, in the gas industry in the amount of 100 to 110 million rubles, and in the oil industry in the amount of 27 million rubles annually, and also significantly to reduce the number of employees of the administrative apparatus.

STATUTE ON THE RUSSIAN INDUSTRIAL COMBINE FOR THE PRODUCTION OF SYNTHETIC COTTON FABRICS (RUSPROMTEKHNOTKAN') OF THE MINISTRY OF THE TEXTILE INDUSTRY OF THE RSFSR, Approved by decree of the Council of Ministers of the RSFSR of November 6, 1975, Sob. Post. RSFSR, 1975, No. 22, Item 155.

1. The Russian Industrial Combine for the Production of Synthetic Cotton Fabrics (Rospromtekhnotkan') of the Ministry of the Textile Industry of the RSFSR is a single production-economic complex, consisting of production combines and enterprises for the production of synthetic cotton and silk fabrics, cotton and long-fiber yarn, batting, batting products, and non-woven materials. Organizations created by the established procedure may be included in the structure of Rospromtekhnotkan'.

The administration of Rospromtehknotkan', bears responsibility for the condition and development of the production and economic complex, for scientific and technical progress and the technical level of production, for the quality of output produced and for the fullest satisfaction of the needs of the national economy and the public for this output, for the effective use of capital investments, the timely opening and ultilization of productive capacities, the observance of projected cost of construction and financial discipline, and also for the fulfillment of the tasks of the state plan and obligations to the treasury.

2. Rospromtekhnotkan' is in direct subordination to the Ministry of the Textile Industry of the RSFSR.

3. The activity of Rospromtekhnotkan', is constructed on the basis of observance of the interests of the national economy, of the industrial combine, and of the production combines and enterprises included in its structure, with a proper combination of centralized planned management and economic independence and initiative of Rospromtehknotkan' and the production combines and enterprises.

Rospromtekhnotkan' acts on the basis of economic accountability, ensures the full recovery of expenditures for production of output, including expenditures for drafting, design, and scientific research work, for the mastery of new products and processes (except for scientific research, experimental design work and work for the mastery of new technology financed in the established manner with funds of the Ministry of the Textile Industry of the RSFSR), for the maintaining of the administrative staff, and also ensures receipt of the profits necessary for accounts with the treasury and the banks, for the development of Rospromtekhnotkan', for the formation of assets, reserves and for other purposes. The full covering of expenditures for the production of output and the receipt of profit must be ensured under strict observance of discipline in price formation.

The Ministry of the Textile Industry shall assign capital investments to Rospromtekhnotkan' by the established procedure.

STATUTE ON THE PRODUCTION COMBINE, approved by decree of the Council of Ministers of the USSR of March 27, 1974, Sob. Post. SSSR, 1974, No. 8, Item 38.

I. General Provisions

1. A production combine is a single production and economic complex whose structure includes factories, plants, scientific-research, design, drafting, and technical organizations and other production units.

The production units included in the structure of the production combine are not legal persons and the effect of the Statute on the Socialist State Production Enterprise does not extend to them.

The production combine is the basic (primary) link of industry; its activity is constructed on the combination of centralized management with the economic independence and initiative of the combine itself.

2. The production combine, using the state property assigned to its operational administration or use, carries out its activity through the efforts of the collective of the combine under the guidance of the superior agency in accordance with the national economic plan, on the basis of economic accountability; fulfills the obliga-

tions imposed upon it, and enjoys the rights connected with this activity; has an independant balance sheet; and is a juridical person.

STATUTE ON THE SOCIALIST STATE PRODUCTION ENTERPRISE, Ekonomicheskaia gazeta, Oct. 20, 1965, p. 24. Translated in full in CDSP, Vol. 17, No. 42, pp. 3-10 (Nov. 11, 1965).

I. GENERAL PROVISIONS

1. The socialist state production enterprise shall be the basic link in the national economy of the USSR. Its activity shall be based upon the combination of centralized guidance with economic independence and initiative of the enterprise.

2. The socialist state production enterprise, using the state property assigned to its operative administration or use, shall accomplish its economic and production activities (preparation of products, fulfillment of work, rendering of services) by the efforts of its collective, under the guidance of the superior agency, in accordance with the national economic plan, on the basis of economic accountability, shall fulfill the obligations and enjoy the rights connected with this activity, shall have a separate account and shall be a juridical person.

. . .

4. The administration of the enterprise shall be accomplished on the basis of one-man management. Non-governmental organizations and the whole collective of workers of the enterprise shall participate extensively in the discussion and accomplishment of measures for ensuring fulfillment of the state plan, for the development and improvement of the productive economic activity of the enterprise, for the improvement of the working and living conditions of its employees.

B. *Enterprise Powers*

PROCURATOR'S PROTEST OF VIOLATION OF LABOR LEGISLATION, Chelovek i zakon, 1972, No. 6, p. 115.

The executive committee of the Gur'ev City Soviet of Working People's Deputies adopted a decision which required of the directors of all enterprises, organizations and institutions that they stop accepting workers and employees at work unless they were assigned by the city bureau for public job placement.

The procurator protested this decision as contradicting labor legislation, and the Statute of the State Socialist Production Enterprise (citation omitted), in accordance with which the director of an enterprise, institution, or organization has the power to accept citizens for work independently in the manner provided by law.

The procurator's protest has been satisfied and the illegal decision reversed.

PROCURATOR'S PROTEST OF ILLEGAL ESTABLISHMENT OF AN ADMISSION CHARGE FOR A RESTAURANT, Radians'ke pravo, 1972, No. 2, p. 109.

The administration of the Nadvirnian District Consumers' Union of Ivano-

Frankovo Region established a charge of 20 kopecks for admission to the Hutsul'shchina Restaurant located in the Iaremcho Village, on the ground that it is a unique structure and has the value of a museum.

The procurator protested the decision of the administration of the consumers' union, but the protest was rejected by the management of the regional consumers' union, which stated that the admission charge of 20 kopecks for restaurant visitors was collected for a souvenir booklet for visiting a unique structure, which the restaurant was. For this payment a citizen had the right to listen without time limit to the concert program in the restaurant.

Relying on the fact that the legislation in force does not provide for payment for admission to restaurants, the procuracy of the Ukrainian SSR brought a protest to the administration of the Ukrainian Cooperative Union against the decision of the administration of the Nedvirnian District Consumers' Union.

The protest has been satisfied and the decision of the administration rescinded.

PURCHASE OF HOUSING BY STATE INSTITUTIONS AND ENTERPRISES,
Sovetskaia iustitsiia, 1968, No. 24, outside back cover.

Representatives of state enterprises and institutions often apply to state notarial offices in Khabarovsk Province for certification of contracts for the purchase and sale of houses belonging to citizens by right of individual ownership, simultaneously presenting letters of ministries and departments in which the specific state institution or enterprise is given permission to obtain a home belonging to a citizen by right of individual ownership at the expense of the enterprise fund, and at the expense of profits and funds for social and cultural measures and housing construction.

The question has arisen for the notaries as to whether or not they should certify contracts by which a state institution (or enterprise) buys a house from a citizen at the expense of funds for social and cultural measures and for housing construction, considering that the law gives state institutions and enterprises the right to obtain houses from citizens at the expense of the fund for capital investments.

The Division of Notary Offices of the Supreme Court of the RSFSR has explained to the Khabarovsk Province Court that the enterprise fund is a general fund which is created at the expense of transfers from profit received (or savings from cost reduction), realized on the condition of fulfillment or overfulfillment of the state plans approved for the enterprises by the established procedure.

The assets of the enterprise funds are expended for the assimilation of new technology, the expansion of production, housing, and the construction of employee facilities, for the repair of the housing stock, for individual bonuses, etc. Payments for capital investments are also made from the enterprise fund.

According to Art. 1 of the decree of the All-Russia Central Executive Committee and the Council of People's Commisars of the RSFSR of May 10, 1935, "On the Acquisition by State Institutions and Enterprises, Cooperative and Public Organizations of Structures from Private Persons," as amended (citations omitted), state institutions and enterprises may obtain houses belonging to citizens by right of individual ownership at the expense of the fund for capital investments. Therefore, the notaries may certify contracts in the cases mentioned above if in the permissions issued by the ministries and departments it is indicated that the purchase of houses from citizens may be made at the expense of the part of the enterprise fund designated for capital investment. This question has been agreed upon with the Republic offices of the State Bank and the Construction Bank.

CHARTER OF THE ALL-UNION COMBINE FOR THE IMPORT AND EXPORT OF FOOD PRODUCTS OF ANIMAL ORIGIN "PRODINTORG" (THE ALL-UNION COMBINE "PRODINTORG"), Vneshniaia torgovlia, 1966, No. 10, p. 54.

General Provisions

1. The All-Union Combine "Prodintorg" is an independent economic organization, having the rights of a juridical person and operating on the basis of economic accountability.

2. The All-Union Combine "Prodintorg" bears responsibility for its operations and obligations with its property within the limits of the property against which execution may be levied under the law in force in the USSR.

The state, its agencies and other organizations are not responsible for the operations and obligations of the All-Union Combine "Prodintorg".

The all-Union Combine Prodintorg is not responsible for claims against the state, its agencies and other organizations.

3. The All-Union Combine "Prodintorg" is located in Moscow.

4. The All-Union Combine "Prodintorg" shall have a circular seal with the words "All-Union Combine for Export and Import" going around the circle and in the center the word "Prodintorg" with the three letters "P", "I", and "T" located one above the other.

Functions

5. The All-Union Combine "Prodintorg"; (a) conducts operations for export from the USSR and sale on foreign markets and import into the USSR, in particular, of meat, meat products, meat by-products, canned meat, fresh and pressed caviar, canned crab and fish, seafood products, domestic fowl, eggs and egg products, wild game, milk, canned milk, milk products and cheese, fats and oils of animal and vegetable origin, pedigreed, draft and meat horses, pedigreed livestock and animals for zoos, sugar and raw sugar; (b) studies the supply and demand on foreign markets for goods of its types; (c) participates in exhibitions and fairs held both in the USSR and abroad; (d) organizes the advertising of goods of its types; (e) participates in the development and implementation of measures for increasing the export reserves of goods of its types; (g) participates in the development of measures for the improvement of the work of warehouse and transport organizations which engage in the storage, loading, unloading and transportation of export and import goods of the types of the combine.

Rights of the Combine

6. In order to carry out the functions indicated in Art. 5 of the present Statute, the All-Union Combine "Prodintorg" shall have the right, in the manner established by the legislation of the USSR, (a) to conclude all types of contracts, transactions and other legal acts, including credit and bills of exchange and banking operations with institutions, enterprises, corporations, partnerships and physical persons and to sue and defend in court and arbitration both within the USSR and abroad; (b) to acquire, alienate, construct, rent and rent out every type of movable and immovable property and also to found subsidiary enterprises for its activities both in the USSR and abroad; (c) to found, both within the USSR and abroad, in accordance with legislation in force, its departments, offices, bureaus, representatives and agencies, and also to participate in every type of combine, corporation, partnership and organization whose activity corresponds to the tasks of the Combine.

Assets

7. The charter capital of the All-Union Combine "Prodintorg" shall be established in the amount of seven million rubles.

Administration of the Combine

8. The Administration of the All-Union Combine "Prodintorg" shall be conducted by a President of the Combine and his deputies named in the established manner.

Duties shall be distributed among the President and his deputies by the President of the Combine.

9. The President of the Combine shall administer all the affairs and property of the Combine, make in the name of the Combine all types of transactions and other legal acts connected with the activity of the Combine, shall deal directly on all business of the Combine with all institutions, enterprises and physical persons, both on the territory of the USSR and abroad.

10. All foreign trade transactions executed by the All-Union Combine "Prodintorg" in Moscow must be signed by two persons, one of whom shall be the President of the Combine or his Deputy, and the other a person empowered to sign foreign trade transactions by a power of attorney signed by the President of the Combine.

Bills of exchange and other money obligations in foreign trade issued by the Combine in Moscow must bear the signature of the President or of his deputy and of the chief bookkeeper of the Combine.

All foreign trade transactions and documents relating to the acquisition, alienation or leasing of immovable property and also bills of exchange and other monetary obligations issued outside of Moscow (both on the territory of the USSR and abroad) must be signed by two persons of whom one shall be the President of the Combine or his deputy, and the other a person acting under a power of attorney issued by the Presiuent of the Combine, or by two persons who have received powers of attorney signed by the President of the combine giving the right to sign the aforementioned transactions and documents.

Accountability and Distribution of Profits

11. The fiscal year of the All-Union Combine "Prodintorg" shall be established to commence with January 1 and run until December 31 of each calendar year.

12. The accounts and balance sheets of the All-Union Combine "Prodintorg" shall be prepared and approved in the manner established by the laws and regulations in force in the USSR.

13. The procedure for distribution of the net profit of the All-Union Combine "Prodintorg" shall be determined by the laws and regulations in force in the USSR.

Liquidation

14. The procedure for liquidation of the All-Union Combine "Prodintorg" shall be determined by the laws and regulations in force in the USSR.

The Charter of the All-Union Combine "Prodintorg" published in the journal "Vneshniaia torgovlia," No. 1 for 1952 is no longer in force.

DECREE ON THE IMPROVEMENT OF PLANNING AND THE INTENSIFICATION OF THE ECONOMIC STIMULATION OF INDUSTRIAL PRODUCTION, Oct. 4, 1965. Spravochnik partiinogo robotnika, Vypusk shestoi [Party Worker's Handbook, Sixth Issue] (Moscow, 1966), p. 218.

II. ON THE INTENSIFICATION OF THE ECONOMIC STIMULATION OF ENTERPRISES AND THE STRENGTHENING OF ECONOMIC ACCOUNTABILITY

12. To recognize the necessity of intensifying the role of profit in the economic stimulation of enterprises and the enhancement of the material interest of collectives and individual employees of enterprises in the achievement of the best possible results of their work. The proportions of profit left at the disposition of enterprises must be dependent upon the improvement of the results of their financial and economic activity.

Profit must be the source for formation of the enterprise funds, for the financing of its own capital investments, for the growth of working assets, and for other expenses of the enterprise.

13. To establish that the following shall be established at the disposition of the enterprises from profits and other resources of their own: (a) a fund for material

reward; (b) a fund for cultural and social measures and housing construction; (c) a fund for development of production.

Unused remainders of these funds shall be transferred to the following year and shall not be subject to withdrawal.

21. For the purposes of heightening the interest of enterprises in the better use of basic production assets and working assets, to establish a payment by the enterprise to the treasury from profit in dependence upon the value of basic production assets and working assets—a payment for basic assets and working assets.

24. To establish the following procedure for distribution of the profit received by the enterprise; (a) from the profit, the enterprise first of all shall contribute to the treasury payment for basic assets and working assets and fixed payments and also shall pay interest on bank loans; (b) after the making of these payments the profit of the enterprise shall be directed to the formation of a fund for material reward, a fund for social and cultural measures and housing construction, and a fund for development of production. For application of the norms of payments to these funds profit is taken after the subtraction from it of payment for basic production assets and working assets, fixed payments, and interest on bank credit; (c) from the remaining portion of profit there is carried out the repayment of credits given for capital investment (except for credit repaid at the expense of the fund for development of production), the financing of centralized capital investments, the growth of its working assets and other expenditures within the limits of sums provided by the plan, and payments are also made to reserves for the rendering of financial assistance and for other purposes in accordance with the decisions of the government of the USSR. The difference between the general sum of profit and the above-mentioned payments and allotments, and also part of the profit used for the covering of planned expenses shall be sent to the treasury in the form of a deposit of the free remainder of profit.

27. The rate of payment from profit to the fund for material reward shall be determined by norms depending upon the increase of the volume of products sold (or of the amount of profit) and the level of profitability provided in the annual plan. Norms shall be established as a percentage of the wages fund: for every percent of increase of the volume of production sold in comparable prices (or of the amount of profit), provided in the plan for the given year, in comparison with the previous year; for every percentage point of profitablity provided in the annual plan.

The norms shall be stable for a series of years and shall be differentiated by branches (and where necessary by groups of enterprises within a branch). No limits for payments to the fund of material reward shall be established.

PROCURATOR'S PROTEST OF ILLEGAL ALLOCATION BY A LOCAL SOVIET OF HOUSING SPACE, Sotsialisticheskaia zakonnost', 1968, No. 6, p. 84.

The Executive Committee of the Grozno City Soviet of Working People's Deputies adopted a decision which obliged the oil industry administration to allocate five percent of housing space in a building constructed from transfers from above-plan profit.

This decision is illegal on the following grounds. According to the Decree of the Council of Ministers of the USSR of October 26, 1966, "On the Procedure for Allocation of Housing Space of Enterprises and Organizations" (citations omitted), all housing space of enterprises and organizations to which the Statute on the Socialist State Production Enterprise Applies and which is built from assets of above-plan profit and above-plan savings used in addition, above transfers to the fund of the enterprise (or organization), and also other assets of enterprises and organizations which in accordance with legislation may be used for housing construction, is to be allocated in the procedure provided for housing space constructed with assets of the fund of the enterprise (or organization). The Statute on the Socialist State Production Enterprise of 1965 (citation omitted), provides that housing space in buildings constructed at the expense of the enterprise fund and the consumption fund are to be allocated entirely to persons on a list approved by the joint decision of the administration of the enterprise and the factory, plant, or local committee of the trade union, with subsequent notification of the executive committee of the soviet of working people's deputies. These decrees do not provide for the allocation by local soviets of housing space constructed at the expense of the enterprise fund.

The illegal decision of the city executive committee was protested by the procurator of the Chechen-Ingush Autonomous Republic. The decision has been rescinded.

PROCURATOR'S PROTEST OF ILLEGAL ORDER INFRINGING UPON THE RIGHTS OF THE DIRECTOR OF AN ENTERPRISE, Sotsialisticheskaia zakonnost', 1970, No. 1, p. 89.

By an order concerning the Main Administration of the Chemical Photographic Industry of the Ministry of the Chemical Industry of the USSR of April 8, 1968, No. 17-K, a list of positions, appointments to which required the action of the Main Administration was approved. The list included assistant enterprise director for employee facilities, the division head and assistant chief engineer for safety. In addition, the order obliged directors of enterprises to coordinate with the Chief Administration the appointment (or dismissal) of heads of personnel divisions.

This order, not based upon the law, and in essence infringing upon the rights of the enterprise director was protested by the Deputy Procurator General of the USSR. According to Pars. 89 and 91 of the Statute on the Socialist State Production Enterprise (citation omitted), the superior agency appoints (and dismisses) the enterprise director and deputy directors, the chief accountant, and the head of the division of technical control. The enterprise director himself appoints (and dismisses) to other positions including the head of the personnel division, and coordination with the superior agency is not required.

The protest has been considered. The necessary changes have been made in the order.

PROCURATOR'S PROTEST OF VIOLATION OF LEGISLATION ON STANDARDS, Sotsialisticheskaia zakonnost', 1973, No. 12, p. 76.

R. Belostotskii, deputy chief of the local industry board of the executive committee of the Leningrad City Soviet of Working People's Deputies, by order No. 1-976 of March 28, 1973, allowed the Metalloposuda Combine to supply non-retail users with enamelware produced with deviation from the republic technical criteria (RTU-427-29).

The Procurator of Leningrad entered a protest against this order and raised the question of its rescission, since in accordance with the rules for observance of state standards, any changes in republic technical conditions are subject to obligatory consultation with the State Planning Committee of the RSFSR, to approval by it, and to state registration. Thus, R. Belostotskii exceeded his official powers by his order. The protest also called attention to the fact that legislation has established criminal responsibility for repeated or large scale release from an industrial enterprise of products not meeting standards or technical conditions.

The protest has been satisfied, the illegal order has been rescinded.

C. *Fraud*

SUPERVISION OF THE EXECUTION OF LAWS ON LIABILITY FOR DECEPTION OF THE STATE, FALSIFICATIONS, AND EXAGGERATIONS BY THE PROCURATOR OF ASTRAKHAN REGION, Sotsialisticheskaia zakonnost', 1970, No. 11, p. 89.

The Procuracy of Astrakhan Region verified how the decree "On Measures for Preventing Instances of Deception of the State and for Strengthening Checking of the Accuracy of Reports on Fulfillment of Plans and Obligations" (citations omitted) was being carried out in the Zelenginsk, Volodar, and Marfin state farms of Volodar District.

Facts of deception of the state were found. These were reflected in falsifications in the state report for 1969 of the production of milk, of the fulfillment of the plan and obligations for its sale to the state and of expenditures for food service. In addition the administrators of the Marfin State Farm in 1969 and in the first quarter of 1970 illegally received loans from the state, presenting fictitious balance sheets to the State Bank. At the end of December 1969 the directors and chief accountants of the state farms, with the purpose of achieving in 1969 the 1968 level of milk production, raised the indicators in the state reports of milk production by 387.6 hundred weight under fictitious invoices made out for the Marfin Butter and Cheese Factory. Likewise, Podsiorin, director of the Zelenginsk state farm and chief accountant Andreshev falsely added 82 hundredweight of milk to the report of sale for food service and 33 hundredweight under fictitious invoices to the butter and cheese factory; in all they made a fraudlent addition of 115 hundredweight of milk. Khalolev, director of the Volodar State Farm and chief accountant Mukhambetov raised the indicators for milk receipts in the state reports by 86.9 hundredweight including 30.9 hundredweight sold to the government and 56 hundredweight sold to workers and employees of the state farm. Kalinin, director of the Marfin State Farm and chief accountant Berkaliev falsely added 185.5 hundredweight of milk to the state report, puportedly made available for needs of employees of the state farm and 27.5 hundredweight of milk under fictitious invoices to the butter and cheese factory. In addition the director and chief accountant of this state farm, during 1969 and the first quarter of 1970 presented to the State Bank distorted report balance sheets, in which they hid unsecured lability on debts, and illegally received credits from the state. In the balance sheet reports of the state farm there was reflected each month a remainder of goods and material assets, giving the appearance of the existence of assets. In particular, in the accounts of the state farm for September, October, and November 1969 a profit and excess over working capital were shown, which gave the appearance of profitability of the state farm, but in fact the state farm finished the year 1969 with a loss of 245 thousand rubles and with a shortage of its own working funds of 135 thousand rubles. In March 1970 the administrators of the state farm once again, hiding the lack of assets for security, received a credit in the State Bank of 36,300 rubles. These violations of legality took place with the knowledge of Liubchenko, the former head of the Volodar District Agricultural Administration, and Dzhantureev, the chief bookkeeper.

The procurator of the region made a representation to the Astrakhan Region Administration of Agriculture in which according to the Statute on Procuratorial Supervision in the USSR he demanded the elimination of the noted violations of legality and the conditions making them possible and that the guilty officials be brought to strict disciplinary responsibility for the falsifications and distortions in state reporting.

The representation was considered by the Head of the Regional Administration of Agriculture who issued an order in which he defined measures for preventing violations of legality. The directors and chief accountants of the state farms, and Dzhantureev, the chief accountant of the district agricultural administration were strictly punished.

The procurator of the region took measures for punishment of the officials of the Marfin Butter and Cheese Factory who were guilty of falsifications and other distortitions in state reports and informed the regional committee of the party about the violations of legality which had been discovered.

CASE OF DIM AND LEBEDEVA, Biulleten' Verkhovnogo Suda RSFSR, 1975, No. 6, p. 10.

The Amur Region Court convicted Kim under Part 3 of Art. 92 [Theft of State or Social Property, Committed by Misappropriation or Embezzlement or by Means of Abuse of Official Position] and Art. 152-1 [Falsifications and other Distortions of Reports on Fulfillment of Plans] and Lebedeva under Part 3 of Art. 92 and Art. 152-1 of the Criminal Code of the RSFSR. (Other persons were also convicted in the case.)

Kim, the chairman of the Blagoveshenskii District Consumers' Union, and

Lebedeva, an economist, in a conspiracy lasting from 1971 through 1973 to give an appearance that all was well in the fulfillment of the merchandise turnover plan (the most important indicator of the work of the regional consumers' union) and to illegally receive bonus awards, presented to the Amur Region Consumers' Union knowingly exaggerated data on the fulfillment of the sales plan. In all for this period there were falsifications in report documents for 23 months for an overall sum of 335,500 rubles.

Committing systematic falsifications and knowing full well that bonuses are provided in case of fulfillment of the monthly plan of merchandise turnover, Kim and Lebedeva personally received bonuses and gave approval for illegal payment of bonuses to other employees of the district consumers' union, i.e. in this matter committed theft of the cooperative's assets. In all during the period 1971-1973 the amount stolen in connection with additions to reports of fulfillment of the plan of merchandise turnover by Kim and Lebedeva amounted to 3998 rubles and 98 kopecks, of which Kim personally received 293 rubles and 9 kopecks and Lebedeva got 175 rubles and 39 kopecks.

The Judicial Division for Criminal Cases of the Supreme Court of the RSFSR, having considered the case on February 28, 1975 on the cassational appeals of the convicted persons and their lawyers, indicated the following.

The guilt of Kim and Lebedeva in falsification and in theft of social monetary funds by illegal computation and payment in connection with it of bonuses is proved by the testimony of witnesses, by the statements of Udod, who has been convicted, by audit reports for 1971 though 1973, by Lebedeva's account books for merchandise turnover which are attached to the record, by reports and balance sheets for the above mentioned period, by payment orders and other documents, by other proofs considered in the judicial hearing, which were given the appropriate weight by the court, and also by the explanations of the accused themselves who did not deny the fact of presenting knowingly exaggerated data on the fulfillment of the plan of merchandise turnover to the superior organization.

The arguments of the appeals of the convicted defendants Kim and Lebedeva and their lawyers that in presenting knowingly incorrect reports on the fulfillment of the merchandise turnover plan, the defendants did not have the intent to steal public monetary funds paid in the form of illegally allocated bonuses is disproved by the record. For instance, in June 1973, the plan of merchandise turnover was established at 697,000 rubles and in fact was fulfilled to the extent of 691,800 rubles.

From the exerpts attached to the record from the Statute on Payment of Bonuses to Employees of Consumers' Societies transferred to the New System of Planning and Economic Incentives in 1972 and certificates of the Amur Regional Consumers' Union, it appears that the monthly bonus depends upon the fulfillment of the plan of merchandise turnover. Kim and Lebedeva know about that Statute, since they were guided by it in the calculation of bonuses.

The witness Sitkova testified in court that the employees of the district consumers' union initially received a bonus for January 1972 in the overall amount of 214 rubles and 97 kopecks, and for March, of 509 rubles and 2 kopecks. In connection with the fact that the district consumers' union changed to a new system of economic incentives, a recalculation of bonuses was made and additional bonuses were paid for January and March.

As appears from the record, for these months falsifications of plan fulfillment were made in a substantial amount: in January for 15,600 rubles and in March for 57,200 rubles. Knowing of the falsifications Kim did not conduct the recalculation in accordance with the New Statute on Bonuses and approved documents for the receipt of clearly illegal bonuses under the new system, personally receiving in so doing a bonus of 81 rubles and 40 kopecks.

All this data as a whole together with other materials in the record allowed the court to conclude that falsification of fulfillment of the plan of merchandise turnover made by Kim and Lebedeva were accompanied by the wilfull illegal calculation of receipt of bonuses for themselves and other members of the district consumers' union.

In accordance with the explanation contained in Par. 10 of the decree of the Plenum of the Supreme Court of the USSR of January 12, 1973, "On Judicial Practice of Cases of Falsifications and Other Distortions in Reporting on the Fulfillment of Plans," if the falsifications in state reporting or the presentation of other wilfully distorted report data was accompanied by the willful illegal receipt for one's own ownership or the ownership of other persons of material assets, the act must be qualified under the aggregate of the articles providing liability for theft and falsifications and other distoritions of reporting on fulfillment of plans.

Therefore, in qualifying the actions of Kim and Lebedeva connected with the illegal calculation and payment of bonuses as theft of public assets, the court proceeded from the demands of the law and was guided by the guiding explanations of the Plenum of the Supreme Court of the USSR.

D. *Mismanagement*

CASE OF BASKHANOV, NUNAEV, AND STEPANOVA, Biulleten' Verkhovnogo Suda RSFSR, 1974, No. 2, p. 9.

The Supreme Court of the Chechen-Ingush ASSR sentenced Baskhanov, Nunaev and Stepanova under Art. 152 [Release of Poor Quality, Nonstandard, or Incomplete Products] of the Criminal Code of the RSFSR.

They were found guilty in that while Nunaev was working as director of the factory, Stepanova as senior technician, and Baskhanov as chief engineer of the Gudermess Bread Factory, they repeatedly allowed the release of poor quality and nonstandard bread and bakery products, which were delivered to stores and restaurant enterprises of the City of Gudermess and Gudermess District of the Chechen-Ingush ASSR.

In violation of the state standard, the Gudermess Bread Factory repeatedly released loaves of wheat bread, buns, and rolls having a deviation in weight of 2.65

to 15%, instead of the plus or minus 2.5% of the norm permitted for this type of product.

For instance, on November 10, 1971, 176 loaves of nonstandard bread having a short weight for each loaf of 5 to 15% were released to the Dawn Store.

On the same day, 1168 kilograms of bread and roll products, including 784 kilograms of bread, 218 buns, and 168 kilograms of Yaroslavl rolls, having a short weight in each instance of 5 to 12% reached the shipping department of the bread factory.

On December 29, 1971, 784 loaves of which 384 (49%) had a short weight in each loaf of 3 to 10% reached the shipping department of the bread factory.

On May 12, 1972, 140 items of bread and rolls having a short weight in each item of up to 5% reached the shipping department of the bread factory.

On June 27, 1972, 224 loaves of bread having a short weight in each loaf of 2.65% were delivered to Store No. 21 from the bread factory.

On July 6, 1972, 336 loaves of low quality bread, having a short weight for each loaf of up to 11.65% were delivered to the same store.

On September 21, 1972, 252 loaves of bread with a 5.64% short weight reached Store No. 8; 392 loaves of bread with a short weight of 4.63% reached Store No. 2; 490 loaves with a short weight of 9.42% and 146 loaves with a short weight of 6.31% reached Store No. 5; 146 loaves with a short weight of 8.42% reached Store No. 6; and 56 and 70 loaves with a short weight of 7 and 2.25% in each loaf reached Cafeterias No. 6 and 2.

In addition, 1168 kilograms of bread and roll products which reached the shipping department of the bread factory on November 10, 1971, were not only nonstandard, but poor quality, in connection with which the representatives of State Retail Inspection forbade their loading.

In all, in this manner, the chief engineer, Baskhanov, together with the director of the factory, Nunaev, and the senior technician, Stepanova, allowed the release of nonstandard and poor quality bread in the amount of 3974 loaves.

In an appeal, Baskhanov, not considering himself to be guilty, stated that he had been convicted without justification, since he worked on problems of the operation of machines and apparatus, the technical supply of the factory, and the supply of the public with bread, while checking the quality of production was the obligation of the director of the factory and the senior technician. In addition, he had not had knowledge of any of the facts of release of poor quality products by the factory.

The Judicial Division for Criminal Cases of the Supreme Court of the RSFSR, having considered the case of August 6, 1973, by way of cassation, left the decision without change and stated the following.

The release by the factory of nonstandard bread products is confirmed by certificates of the state inspector of retailing quality of retail goods of November 10 and December 29, 1971, and May 12, 1972, the testimony of many witnesses, employees of stores where the bread was taken, certificates of checking of the weight of bread arriving at the store, invoices for bread, and other materials of the case.

Baskhanov's statement that he did not know about these facts with the exception of those discovered by the state inspector on December 29, 1971 and May 12, 1972, is without basis, since also after this the Gudermess District Consumers' Union gave both oral and written notice to the administration of the factory of instances of supply of nonstandard bread to the stores.

From the testimony of the witness Trufanov, the organization instructor of the District Consumers' Union, it appears that chief engineer Baskhanov was invited to a meeting of retail employees, where questions of the quality of bread and roll products were considered.

Under his job duties, Baskhanov was obliged to check the activity of the senior technician of the factory for the purpose of preventing occurances of the release of nonstandard and poor quality bread products, particularly since Baskhanov knew about them, since he had signed certificates of the state inspector reporting the release of nonstandard products.

Of itself the fact of release of nonstandard and low quality products and on a large scale is a basis for the liability under Art. 152 of the Criminal Code of the RSFSR of particular officials, including the chief engineer.

STORE No. 38 vs. KRATSBERG, Sotsialisticheskaia zakonnost', 1969, No. 12, p. 78.

Financially-independent Store No. 38 of the Kurgan City Food Market brought an action in court against Kratsberg for the recovery of 445 rubles of damage. The plaintiff claimed that on June 29, 1968, Kratsberg, director of Store No. 38, without the consent of the food manager, for the purpose of fulfilling the plan and receiving a bonus, instructed the stock room supervisor to get two tons of salami at the meat combine and to send part of it for sale at stands in the collective farm market which were not equipped with refrigeration apparatus. The stock room supervisor received 1540 kilograms of salami, 700 kilograms of which he transferred to the stands despite its refusal by the salespersons. Since the demand for salami was insignificant and it was being stored in poor conditions, on the following day the public health physican forbade its sale. As a result of the reprocessing of the salami into a lower grade, the store suffered losses of 445 rubles.

Kratsberg did not accept the claim and explained that he instructed Tverdov to get not two tons, but one ton of salami. However the latter got more of the product and without proof of its quality. Kratsberg stated that the salami was not fully processed by the supplier, began to spoil and was submitted for reprocessing.

In the court decision it was indicated that the manager of the store, giving instructions to obtain the product in a large quantity, incurred an ordinary production risk, and was without fault in the spoilage of the salami.

The Deputy Procurator General of the USSR protested the judicial decisions in the case, as rendered in violation of the demands of Articles 14 and 192 of the Civil Procedure Code of the RSFSR on insufficiently studied materials.

Salami, for attestation of quality, should be stored at a temperature of 0 to 6 degrees Celsius for not more than 48 hours. An inspection established that the salami was spoiled before the expiration of the time for selling it since it was in stands neither equipped nor adapted for the storage of perishable products (certificates of the public health physician). The defendant's statement about the receipt of poor quality salami without checking was not verified by the court. However if he had received poor quality products, the director of the store was obliged in accordance with the Instruction approved by State Arbitration attached to the Council of Ministers of the USSR of April 25, 1966, to inform immediately the supplier of this and to call upon his representative or to execute a certificate with the participation of the quality inspection agency. Kratsberg did not inform the meat combine of the supply of poor quality products and did not present the salami for examination by the quality inspection agency. The plaintiff's arguments about the receipt of a perishable item exceeding the limits of customer demand were also not verified. Previously he had never received a ton and a half of salami. This product was delivered in small amounts and was sold in stores equipped with refrigerators. In the first six months of 1968, according to the situation on June 26, 1968, only 122.6 kilograms of salami had been sold through the stands of the store. At the new hearing of the case the court should verify all these circumstances, question the head of the sales division of the meat combine with whom Kratsberg agreed about the quantity of products to be supplied, clarify the possibility of reprocessing spoiled products without lowering quality grade, and in accordance with Art. 83 of the Code of Laws on Labor and Art. 4 of the Instructions of the People's Commissariat of Labor of June 1, 1932, award damages from those at fault within the limits set by law.

The protest of the procurator was approved by the Judicial Division for Civil Cases of the Supreme Court of the RSFSR, and the case was remanded for a new hearing.

CASE of T., Biulleten' Verkhovnogo Suda RSFSR, 1974, No. 9. p. 6.

The Erikhit-Bulagat District People's Court of the Ust'-Ordin Buriat National Area sentenced T. under Art. 99-1 [Criminally Negligent Use of Storage of Agricultural Machinery] of the Criminal Code of the RSFSR with the recovery from him for the use of the Oloi State Farm of 901 Rubles. T. was found guilty in that working as the chief engineer of the Oloi State Farm and being responsible for the use of agricultural machinery, as a result of a careless attitude toward his obligations he did not ensure the proper storage of the agricultural machinery. As a result of his criminally negligent storage, two combines lost some of their parts which caused the Oloi state farm a 901 ruble loss.

At the court hearing T. admitted that he was guilty.

The Judicial Division for Criminal Cases of the Area Court left the decision without change. The Judicial Division for Criminal Cases of the Supreme Court of the RSFSR, having considered the case on the protest of the deputy Chairman of the Supreme Court of the RSFSR seeking the reduction of the amount of the civil claim, satisfied the protest and indicated the following.

T.'s guilt in carelessness and criminally negligent storage of agricultural machinery has been shown by the materials in the record. His actions were correctly qualified under Art. 99-1 of the Criminal Code of the RSFSR. However the question has properly been raised in the protest about altering the decision with respect to the Civil claim.

T. has not been convicted before, has admitted his guilt, has 5 young children as dependants, and has a good reference from his place of work.

As appears from certificates presented by the director of the state farm, T. obtained the parts for repair of the combines at his own expense and the combines have been repaired. As of July 20, 1972, his debt on the writ of execution was 246 rubles.

Considering the aforesaid and taking into consideration that the crime committed by T. was not that of personal gain, the Division, by a decision of November 28, 1973 found it possible to reduce the sum recovered from the convicted person in compensation for damages.

INSAR CENTRAL SAVINGS BANK NO. 4300 vs. SUDEIKIN, Biulleten' Verkhovnogo Suda RSFSR, 1970, No. 3, p. 15.

By a decision of the Insar District People's Court of September 19, 1968, Arkhangel'skii was reinstated at work as a guard at the Insar Central Savings Bank No. 4300 with payment to him of wages for 20 working days of involuntary layoff.

The Judicial Division of the Supreme Court of the Mordovian ASSR by a decision of October 15, 1968, left the decision of the People's Court without change. Since the administrator of the Insar Central Savings Bank No. 4300 did not carry out the decision of the People's Court, Arkhangel'skii applied to the same people's court in December 1968 with a claim for payment to him of wages for the time during which the decision was not carried out.

The Insar District People's Court awarded wages in the amount of 187 rubles from the Savings Bank for the use of Arkhangel'skii, and indicated that this amount should be recovered by a third-party action for the use of the savings bank from Sudeikin, the administrator of the savings bank.

The Presidium of the Supreme Court of the Mordovian ASSR, considering the case on the protest of the Deputy President of the Supreme Court of the RSFSR, altered the decision of the Insar District People's Court, lowering the amount recovered from Sudeikin for the use of the Insar Central Savings Bank to 40 rubles.

The Presidium indicated the following.

According to Art. 407 of the Civil Procedure Code of the RSFSR in case of the nonfulfillment by the administration of an enterprise, institution, or organization of a court decision on the reinstatement of an employee at work, the court shall issue a decision for the payment to that employee of wages for the whole time from the day of issuance of that decision until the day of its execution.

Damages caused by the payment to the employee of monetary sums as the result of nonfulfillment of the decision of a court may be recovered in an action by the enterprise, institution, or organization, or on the initiative of the court from the offical who is at fault in the nonfulfillment of the court decisions for reinstatement at work. The measure of the amount awarded in these cases is defined by the legislation on labor.

Since the administration of the savings bank did not execute the decision of the court for the reinstatement of Arkhangel'skii at work, the court correctly awarded him wages for the time of nonfulfillment of the decision.

As was established by the court, the party at fault in the nonexecution of the decision of the court was Sudeikin, the administrator of the savings bank, who did not deny before the court that the decision of the court was not indicated on his order, since he considered that the decision was incorrect.

In these circumstances the court correctly placed the obligation upon Sudeikin for compensating for the damages caused to the savings bank as the result of the nonexecution of the judicial decisions. However, the court entirely without foundation imposed full monetary liability upon him for the damage caused.

Within the limits of the full amount of the damage Sudeikin could bear monetary liability only in the cases indicated in Art. 83-1 of the Code of Laws on Labor. As appears from the record, there is no basis for imposing full monetary liability upon Sudeikin.

In these circumstances Sudeikin may bear monetary liability for damage caused to the savings bank in accordance with Art. 83 of the Code of Laws on Labor of the RSFSR within the limits of one third of one months wage or salary.

As appears from data in the record, Sudeikin's salary is 120 rubles a month.

Thus, 40 rubles is subject to recovery from Sudeikin for use of the savings bank.

E. *Liquidation*

ARZGIR DISTRICT PROCURATOR ex rel. RED OCTOBER COLLECTIVE FARM vs. CONSTRUCTION ADMINISTRATION OF THE CHOGRAISK RESERVOIR, Biulleten' Verkhovnogo Suda RSFSR, 1972, No. 9, p. 2.

The Procurator of Arzgir District of Stavropol' Province brought an action in court against the Construction Administration of the Chograisk Reservoir and Irrigation Systems of the Kalmyk ASSR to recover 31,415 rubles for the use of the Red October Collective Farm. As a basis for the action it was noted that arable lands of the farms in the Arzgir District, including 2642 hectares belonging to the Red October Collective Farm were taken for construction of the Chograisk Reservoir. The amount of expenditures of the collective farm were determined by a special commission as 82,777 rubles, which in accordance with current rules should have been reimbursed to the collective farm.

In May 1969, the Construction Administration of the Chograisk Reservoir paid the Collective Farm 52,362 rubles. The remaining amount remained unpaid. In January 1970, the Construction Administration of the Chograisk Reservoir was liquidated in connection with the completion of construction of the reservoir and subsequently the Construction Administration of the Iki-Burul' Agricultural Pipeline was organized.

The Procurator of Arzgir District, believing that the Administration of the Chograisk Reservoir had not compensated the collective farm in full for its unused expenditures incorporated in the plots of land that were taken, brought an action to recover 31,415 rubles against the Construction Administration of the Iki-Burul' Agricultural Pipeline and the Ministry of Land Improvement of the Kalmyk ASSR.

The Supreme Court of the Kalmyk ASSR dismissed the action.

Considering the case by way of cassation, the Judicial Division for Civil Cases of the Supreme Court of the RSFSR, by a decision of September 7, 1970, left the decision without change and the appeal unsatisfied on the following grounds.

In case of the discontinuance of a legal person by way of liquidation (Art. 37 of the Civil Code of the RSFSR), a liquidation commission conducts all accounts with creditors and debtors during a period established by the agency adopting the decision to discontinue the legal person.

Therefore, as is correctly indicated in the decision of the court, all claims had to be made by the collective farm before the end of the period of work of the liquidation commission, i.e. before February 5, 1970. The plaintiff made its demand only in April 1970, and moreover to organizations which were not the legal successors.

Also, the demands cannot be considered to be well founded in substance.

As is apparent from the materials of the case, the Chograisk Reservoir was under construction during four years and all that time the collective farm used the buildings and structures on the land which was taken. The depreciated value of all structures was defined in 1965 at 83,777 rubles approximately, without taking into account the fact that they would still be used by the collective farm for four years.

By an act of May 15, 1969, of the commission, which consisted of the director of construction of the Chograisk Reservoir, the Chairman of the Red October Collective Farm, and other persons, after a physical inspection of all the productive structures of the Red October Collective Farm falling in the zone of the Chograisk Reservoir and a verfication of their depreciated value on January 1, 1969, defined the value as 52,362 rubles. By this act the collective farm was obliged to free all productive structures falling in the zone to be flooded by June 1, 1969. This act and also the court testimony of the witness Tsipurov confirm the fact of the use by the collective farm of the buildings on the taken land during four years, which fact led to the reduction of the amount of the unused expenditures in comparison with the amount defined in 1965.

STATUTE ON THE PERMANENT PRODUCTION CONFERENCE, approved by the Council of Ministers of the USSR and the All-Union Central Council of Trade Unions, June 18, 1973, Sob. Post. SSSR, 1973, No. 15, Item 80.

The permanent production conference is an important form of socialist democracy, public supervision, and practical introduction of the working masses into management.

The permanent production conference aids the all-around development of the creative initiative of workers and employees and its use in the decision of the most important problems of enterprises and organization, ensuring the effectiveness of social production, strengthening the interest of employees in the results of their labor and the overall achievements of work, attracting working people into the supervision of production.

. . . .

3. The permanent production conference directs its work at ensuring the fulfillment of the tasks of the state plan for the enterprise, organization, shop, or other structural subdivision, discovery of reserves and possibilities for production for adoption of demanding plans and raising the effectiveness of production, and also for fulfilling the plan of social development of the collective, improving socialist competition, all-around raising of labor productivity on the basis of broader use of the latest achievements of science, technology, advanced experience, scientific organization of work and supervision of production.

CHAPTER XIV

Law as an Instrument of Administrative Order

The Soviet economy is guided by the economic plan, but experience has shown that not every detail of the production relationship between public corporations can be planned at headquarters. In the earliest days of nationalized industry direction from above had been attempted by the Supreme Council of National Economy. Its bureaus ordered an industry to deliver its products to another that would utilize them to make a completed object, and the workers' councils that ran each plant had no concern but to do the best they could in meeting the order from headquarters by producing, delivering and accepting the goods as the order dictated.

While such a system might have worked, had industry remained small, and had there been no New Economic Policy, it had no place after creation of the public corporations with general directions to compete successfully against the private sector of the economy in proof of efficiency. Directors of trusts had to reduce costs, and part of their success lay in obtaining raw materials at the lowest prices possible and selling their products at the highest prices that could be obtained. This called for resumption of the practice of making sales contracts and with this development came the application of the rules of the new civil code to contract performance and the settlement of disputes. Legal advisers of the public corporations prepared the documents and fought the cases when they reached the courts. The early 1920's were times when relations governed by the law of sales presented a picture that would have been entirely understandable to any lawyer trained in the continental system of civil law.

Then came radical change. The private enterprise sector was doomed and the state sector was pushed to the fore in performance of the newly conceived national economic plans. The year 1927 was a landmark with the second decree on trusts, and the inauguration of the concept of the plan as law. Relations in the productive process became for public corporations the steps necessary to perform the plan. Most of them were in fulfillment of directives from the ministries concerned with execution of that part of the plan sent to them by the State Planning Commission for completion. Voluntary selection of suppliers was now a rarity. For the massive equipment of heavy industry every detail of the relationship between the producing corporation and the consuming corporation was planned. For consumers' goods, there was still some permissiveness, as directors were allowed to seek out their counterparts in other corporations and make arrangements for supply of the materials needed to meet the requirements of the plan.

The question was raised early as to the desirable form of fully planned relations between state enterprises. Some lawyers denied that contract was a suitable form, since an essential element in their eyes was a voluntary meeting of the minds. The plan prevented any such voluntary relationship, and contracts for a time disappeared from practice. The planning orders were then the sole documents necessary to production and delivery, supplemented when necessary by agreement on minor details of specifications. By 1931 the necessity for a document of greater complexity had become felt, and the approach changed. Even when the planners had dictated that an electric equipment corporation deliver a turbine to an electric utility corporation, the numerous details of specifications, delivery dates, spare parts and payment required expert knowledge and time that the central planners could not have. A document drafted by the parties in fulfillment of the planned relationship became obligatory, and the decree of February 18, 1931[1] called it a "contract." To distinguish it from the ordinary sales contract, it was given the name of "contract of supply."

Having now a contract defining with precision the terms of the planned relationship, the parties could rely upon it when a dispute arose in performance, for the facts of the agreement were clear. During the New Economic Policy when the old sales contracts had been utilized, the regular courts had heard disputes, unless they arose between two trusts under the direction of the Supreme Council of National Economy. For such disputes the central body had created an arbitration department to settle arguments. But the scheme displeased the government and on March 4, 1931[2] a decree abolished the arbitration tribunals and put all disputes between pub-

---

[1] [1931] I Sob. Zak. SSSR, No. 10, item 109.
[2] [1931] *Ibid.*, No. 14, item 135.

lic corporations in the courts.

The result was chaos. Soviet writers now say that the courts proved completely inadequate. They took too long, and they did not understand production. Within two brief months there was a complete reversal of policy, for on May 3, 1931[3] there was created a novel system of administrative courts to be called "State Arbitration." Those who were to judge in the new tribunals would specialize in the relationships of public corporations, and administer rules that would have their inspiration in the civil code but would be applied with whatever flexibility was required to achieve the major purposes of the contract relationship—performance of the plan. To facilitate decision, the directors of the corporations who were parties to the dispute were to sit with a professional arbitrator so that in the congenial atmosphere of a group of persons standing not upon their legal rights but approaching the problem with a desire to get things done, the broken chain of relationships necessary for production might be restored in the event of late deliveries, and damages paid to recoup losses of the victim of the negligence, but these were secondary considerations. The primary concern was performance by means of any improvisation the directors could imagine. Only if they proved unimaginative, would the arbitrator step in. To assure that legalistic thinking would not enter the discussion of a solution, legal advisers to the corporations were banned. The directors alone were to be participants.

The system broke down. Directors were too busy to attend the many sessions required as supply relationships expanded and disputes multiplied. They sent their legal advisers to save time. These men thought in legal terms, and even the arbitrators in seeking a solution found the rules of the civil code convenient. Literature came to declare that the rules of the civil law were applicable to determination of disputes, and the law permitted the legal advisers to represent the corporation. Still, the position continued that this was a special relationship, and there was a distinction between what was called "economic law" or the law of relations between public corporations, and "civil law" or the law of the relations between private individuals.

Even this attitude emphasizing the distinguishing features of "economic law" suffered a harsh blow in 1937 when its major proponent and members of his school of thought were ousted and eventually purged as Stalin's enemies. They had been preaching the withering away of the law with the advent of socialism, and this meant above all else the introduction of considerations solely of expediency in the relationships on the economic front. Stalin put an end to this view of the role of law in the society he chose to dominate, for he required strict orderly conduct from his administrators to achieve maximum results and the discipline his system required. Not until his death was there a reevaluation, and it came with the drafting of a new set of fundamental principles for civil codes. The question was asked again whether it was not time to separate the rules relating to public corporations

---

[3][1931] *Ibid.*, No. 26, item 203.

from the civil code and to return to the discussion of an "economic law." Some of the most influential professors and administrators argued for this, and the matter went to the legislative drafting committee of the Council of Ministers, where high communist party members shared in the decision. When the draft was published in 1960 for discussion, it combined the law of public enterprise with that of private individuals, making some exceptions but including both types of relationships in the same document.

Opponents of the combination not only have not been silenced, but they have published for a discussion a draft economic code. They think the Fundamental Principles of Civil Legislation adopted in 1961 to be an absurd document, and they have not hesitated to say so. They agree that it is self-evident that the relations of the public corporations have a special character. For example, a private individual cannot go to court to require another individual to sell him something. The public corporation may do so, and pre-contract disputes are a significant part of the practice of the arbitration tribunals, for they bear relationship to performance of the plan.

A. *Agencies for Adjudication of Contract Disputes*

STATUTE ON STATE ARBITRATION ATTACHED TO THE COUNCIL OF MINISTERS OF THE USSR, approved by decree of the Council of Ministers of the USSR, January 17, 1974, No. 60, Sob. Post. SSSR, 1974, No. 4, Item 19.

1. State Arbitration attached to the Council of Ministers of the USSR (State Arbitration of the USSR) is a union-republic agency.

State Arbitration guides the agencies of state arbitration, ensures the uniform and correct application of legislation in the resolution of economic disputes by all state arbitration agencies and by the arbitration agencies of ministries and departments, and also supervision of the correctness of decisions of state arbitration agencies, decides the largest and most important disputes between state, cooperative and other public enterprises, organizations, and institutions, of all-union subordination or of different union republics in accordance with its established jurisdiction.

State Arbitration of the USSR bears responsibility for the organization, status, and improvement of the activity of agencies of State Arbitration.

2. The main tasks of State Arbitration of the USSR are: ensuring the protection of the property rights and legal interests of enterprises, organizations, and institutions in the decision of economic disputes; aiding the heightening of the effectiveness of social production, strengthening of economic accountability, development of rational economic ties between enterprises, organizations, and institutions, enhancing the role of contract in their relations and developing cooperation among them in the fulfillment of the national economic plan; actively influencing, in the resolution of economic disputes at enterprises, organizations, and institutions their observance of socialist legality and state discipline in the fulfillment of planned tasks and con-

tract obligations; fighting localism and departmentalism; guiding the agencies of state arbitration, ensuring the strict observance of socialist legality in their activity, the uniform and correct application of legislation in the resolution of economic disputes by all state arbitration agencies and the arbitration agencies of ministries and departments; the systematic study and generalization of arbitration practice and the development on this basis of proposals aimed at the improvement of economic relations and also for the elimination of shortcomings in the activity of enterprises, organizations, and institutions.

KOKAND SHOE FACTORY vs. "DZHAMBULKOZHOBUV" PRODUCTION COMBINE, Sovetskaia iustitsia, 1967, No. 7, p. 32.

According to Par. 15(a) of the Statute on State Arbitration attached to the Council of Ministers of the USSR and the corresponding paragraphs of the statutes on state arbitration in the union republics, disputes between enterprises and organizations of a single ministry, department or cooperative system are not subject to decision in state arbitration.

State Arbitration attached to the Council of Ministers of the USSR received a complaint by the Kokand Shoe Factory against the "Dzhambulkozhobuv" Production Combine. Since the parties to the dispute belong to the Ministry of Light Industry of the USSR, State Arbitration should have refused, in accordance with Par. 57 of the Rules of the Consideration of Economic Disputes by State Arbitration Tribunals, to take the claim under consideration. The claim however was taken under consideration by mistake. When it discovered at the hearing, that the Kokand Factory and the "Dzhbulkozhobuv" Combine were enterprises of the same ministry, State Arbitration, in accordance with Par. 82 of the Rules, terminated proceedings in the matter for lack of jurisdiction. In accordance with Sec. 36 of the Instruction of the Ministry of Finances of the USSR of April 26, 1965, "On the State Excise Tax," and Par. 40 of the Rules for Consideration of Economic Disputes, the claimant was refunded the state excise tax paid by him in filing the claim with State Arbitration.

LETTER OF THE DIVISION FOR GENERALIZATION OF PRACTICE AND ISSUANCE OF INSTRUCTIONS OF STATE ARBITRATION ATTACHED TO THE COUNCIL OF MINISTERS OF THE USSR OF APRIL 17, 1967, Sovetskaia iustitsiia, 1968, No. 3, p. 32.

The Shchekino Production Combine of Wood-Processing Enterprises reported that the Kishinev Furniture Factory, without having received the consent of the enterprise, transferred a dispute which had arisen between them for decision by a private arbitration tribunal, and so violated the principle of voluntary consent in the decision of the question of transferral of disputes by enterprises and organizations for consideration by private arbitration tribunals.

In connection with the query of the Shchekino Combine as to the legality of the creation in these circumstances of a private arbitration tribunal, the Division for

Generalization of Practice and Issuance of Instructions of State Arbitration attached to the Council of Ministers of the USSR stated that, in accordance with Par. 1 of the Temporary Rules for Consideration of Economic Disputes by a Private Arbitration Tribunal, individual disputes may be transferred for decision by such a tribunal by mutual consent of the parties. Therefore, in cases when the consent of the other party to transferral of the dispute to a private arbitration tribunal is lacking, such a tribunal is not to be formed.

If a communication of non-consent to a proposal for the consideration of a private arbitration tribunal is not received within the ten day term established by Par. 4 of the Temporary Rules, the proposal is considered to be accepted. In case of non-consent to such a proposal, notification of this should be so sent that the organization which proposed the transferral of the dispute for decision by a private arbitration tribunal will receive it before the expiration of a ten day term calculated from the date of receipt of the proposal.

In the event however that the notification of non-consent to the proposal to consider the case in a private arbitration tribunal arrives late, but the proceedings in the private arbitration tribunal have not already started, the dispute should not be transferred to a private arbitration tribunal, considering the voluntary nature of its formation. In a proceeding already started in the established manner, a refusal to consider the dispute in a private arbitration tribunal is not allowed.

CEMENT FACTORY vs. REGIONAL COMMITTEE OF THE TRADE UNION OF MACHINE BUILDING WORKERS, Sovetskaia iustitsiia, 1971, No. 10, outside back cover.

The administration of a cement factory brought an action in State Arbitration attached to the executive committee of the Kuibyshev Regional Soviet against the regional committee of the trade union of machine building workers for the recovery of 38,831 rubles and 18 kopecks for an obligation which arose as a result of the unilateral transfer of funds by the defendant for an obligation for insurance premiums.

In its complaint the plaintiff indicated that for the period from February 1 through September 1, 1969, it used funds it had transferred for social insurance to pay payment orders for pensions of pensioners working at the factory in the amount of the complaint.

On September 26, 1969, during an audit of the correctness of the payment of pensions, the regional committee of the trade union established that the orders under which the pensions were paid were not signed by the chairman of the factory committee of the trade union. At the time of the audit the certificates were signed by the chairman of the factory committee.

At the end of 1969 the factory submitted an annual report to the regional committee of the trade union; the orders for payment of pensions were taken into account and the regional committee made no complaints to the factory.

After almost a year following the audit, i.e. on August 5, 1970, the regional committee of the trade union by transfer authorization No. 1, recovered 38,831 rubles 18 kopecks from the bank account of the factory as owing for insurance premiums.

In considering the case State Arbitration supposed that a dispute has arisen between the parties, flowing not from the regulation of questions of social insurance but from the causing of damages to the factory by fault of the regional committee which in bad faith used its right to unilateral transfer of funds from the account of the factory.

State Arbitration awarded 38,831 rubles and 18 kopecks from the regional committee of the trade union. The trade union appealed to State Arbitration attached to the Council of Ministers of the USSR for reconsideration of the decision on the ground that the case was not subject to the jurisdiction of State Arbitration.

The question of the jurisdiction of the case was considered at a special session of State Arbitration attached to the Council of Ministers of the USSR. The decision of the session noted that according to Par. 9 of the decree of the Central Executive Committee and the Council of People's Commissars of the USSR of August 23, 1931, an underpayment of insurance premiums together with the penalties for it is recovered by an administrative non-adversary procedure in accordance with the procedure established for the recovery of taxes.

According to Par. 15(c) of the Statute on State Arbitration attached to the Council of Ministers of the USSR and the corresponding paragraphs of the statutes on state arbitration of the union republics disputes on taxes and non-tax payments recovered for the state budget in accordance with the Statute on the Recovery of Tax and Non-tax Payments are not subject to decision in State Arbitration.

Under these circumstances all disputes between insurers and trade union agencies concerning the recovery of debts and the nonacceptance into account as insurance premiums of expenditures for social insurance made by the enterprise are decided by the superior trade union agencies and are not subject to the jurisdiction of state arbitration.

In connection with the aforesaid, the decision of State Arbitration attached to the Executive Committee of the Kuibyshev Regional Soviet is reversed and the case is dismissed.

B. *Plan and Contract*

CONSTITUTION OF THE U.S.S.R., December 5, 1936

Art. 11. The economic life of the U.S.S.R. is determined and directed by the state national-economic plan, with the aim of increasing the social wealth, of steadily raising the material and cultural standards of the working people, of consolidating the independence of the U.S.S.R. and strengthening its defensive capacity.

FUNDAMENTAL PRINCIPLES OF CIVIL LAW OF THE U.S.S.R. AND OF THE UNION REPUBLICS, December 8, 1961, effective May 1, 1961 [1961] Vedomosti Verkhovnogo Soveta SSSR, No. 50. item 525. (Titles of articles omitted.)

Chapter 3. *Supply*

Art. 44. Under a contract of supply the supplying organization obligates itself to transfer to the purchasing organization (the buyer) within a given period of time or on a certain date ownership of, or, in accordance with the provisions of Arts. 21 and 30 of these Fundamental Principles, the right to dispose of a specific product in accordance with a planning order binding on both organizations and relating to distribution of the product concerned; the purchasing organization obligates itself to accept the product and to pay for it at the established prices. A supply contract is also an agreement concluded between organizations in exercise of their own judgment by which the supplier obligates itself to deliver to the buyer at a time that does not coincide with the moment of conclusion of the contract a product that is not distributed in accordance with a plan.

The supply of a product without conclusion of a contract shall occur only in those circumstances established by the Council of Ministers of the USSR or by the council of ministers of a union republic.

MODEL CONTRACT FOR THE SUPPLY OF GOODS WITH DIRECT LONG-TERM ECONOMIC LINKS, Biulleten' normativnykh aktov, 1974, No. 2, p. 42.

, 19

The . . . . .Enterprise, hereinafter called "Supplier," by. . . . . . .,acting on the basis of . . . ., and the . . . . .Enterprise, hereinafter called "Purchaser," by. . . . ., acting on the basis of . . . ., proceeding from the task of providing Purchaser with goods in the amount, assortment, and quality necessary to it, taking into consideration the interests of the national economic plan, and also for the purpose of organizing longterm cooperation for the fulfillment of planned tasks for the production and supply of goods, have concluded the present contract on the following:

1. In accordance with the plan for assignment of . . . . .on the basis of the present contract between Supplier and Purchaser direct long-term economic relations for supply of . . . . .shall be established for the period of effectiveness of the long-term plan of development of the national economy from 19   through 19

The effectiveness of the present contract shall extend (without further agreement, by agreement of the parties) for the period of effectiveness of the following long-term plan for the development of the national economy, until 19   inclusive, unless changes are made in the established procedure in the plan for assignment of the Purchaser to the Buyer.

. . .

(designation of goods)

KRASNODAR PROVINCE PROCUREMENT AND SALES BOARD v. CHERNIATINSK GLASS FACTORY, Sovetskaia iustitsiia, 1972, No. 14, inside back cover.

The Krasnodar Province Procurement and Sales Board brought an action in State Arbitration Attached to the Executive Committee of the Briansk Regional Council to compel the Cherniatinsk Glass Factory to conclude a contract for supply of goods in accordance with a delivery order which had been issued and for the recovery from it of a fine for refusal to conclude a contract. State Arbitration refused to satisfy the demands of the Board, since contractual relations for delivery of goods between the parties were established by means of acceptance of the delivery order for implementation (the delivery order contained all the necessary data for the supply) and within the ten day period after the receipt of the order neither of the parties demanded the formalization of the relations for supply of goods by the conclusion of a contract.

The Board requested that the decision of State Arbitration be reversed on the ground that according to Par. 24 of the Statute on Supply of Goods, despite the existance of a delivery order accepted by the parties for implementation, each of the parties could at any time demand the conclusion of a written contract and the other party did not have the right to refuse.

State Arbitration attached to the Council of Ministers of the RSFSR found the appeal of the Krasnodar Province Procurement and Sales Board to be ungrounded.

In accordance with Par. 19 of the Statute on Supply of Goods a contract may be concluded: by the composition of a single document signed by the parties, by the exchange of letters or telegrams, by the approval by the supplier of the order of the buyer, or by the acceptance by the parties of a delivery order for implementation in the circumstances provided by Art. 24 of the Statute. The delivery order is considered to be accepted for implementation and takes the force of a contract if within a ten-day period after the receipt of the delivery order the interested party does not propose to the other party agreement upon supplementary conditions of supply or does not inform the agency issuing the delivery order and the other party that it does not consent to the order.

Therefore, the demand for the formalization of the relations for the delivery of goods on the basis of a delivery order by the conclusion of a contract signed by the supplier and the buyer can be demanded by an interested party not at any time, but not later than ten days after the receipt of the order, i.e. before contractual relations are already established by the acceptance of the delivery order for execution.

CASE OF THE TIKHVIN ALUMINA PLANT, Sovetskaia iustitsiia, 1967, No. 20, p. 34.

In accordance with a contract dated March 5, 1966, the Tikhvin Alumina Plant was to ship to a buyer, in the course of the second, third and fourth quarters of 1966, 170 tons of polishing powder. In fulfillment of this contract, the supplier, up to August 1, had shipped 93.7 tons. The buyer refused to accept the remaining powder. In a telegram sent to the supplier he stated that his refusal of the goods was caused by a change in production technology, in connection with which the buyer had raised the question of withdrawal of the allocation permits for 1966. At the same time the buyer warned the supplier that the latter should stop shipping, otherwise the goods would not be paid for.

Since the buyer did not succeed in having the allocation permits changed, the Tikhvin Alumina Plant, considering the buyer's refusal of the goods to be groundless, filed a claim with State Arbitration attached to the Briansk Province Executive Committee for the award of the sanction provided by Par. 74 of the Statute on Supply of Goods for Production and Technical Use.

By a decision of December 9, 1966, State Arbitration denied the claim of the Plant, on the grounds that the claimant, despite the refusal of the buyer, was obliged to ship the goods to the buyer, since the buyer had not obtained a withdrawal of the allocation orders. The Tikhvin Alumina Plant applied to the chief arbitrator of State Arbitration attached to the Briansk Province Executive Committee with a request for the reconsideration of the decision rendered. In this request the Plant called the attention of the chief arbitrator to the contention that its actions were legal and the most expedient in the situation which had developed. If the Plant despite the refusal of the buyer had shipped the powder to it anyway, this would have led to great unproductive expenditures for unloading, storage of goods, demurrage of freight cars, and payment for goods not needed by the buyer.

The chief arbitrator rejected the arguments of the Tikhvin Alumina Plant and left the decision in force. In doing so he stated that a unilateral refusal to fulfill a contract and alteration of its conditions is not allowed. Therefore the Plant had the right to ship the powder and to present a bill for payment.

In connection with an appeal by the Plant to the Briansk Province Executive Committee, the latter, by an order of February 25, 1967, reversed the decision of State Arbitration and satisfied the claim of the Plant. Not being in agreement with the award of a sanction, the buyer raised the question of the reversal of the order of the Provincial Executive Committee.

State Arbitration Attached to the Council of Ministers of the RSFSR on delegation of the Council of Ministers of the RSFSR, considered the request of the buyer and noted that the conditions of the contract were violated not by the supplier but by the buyer, since the latter failed to present evidence of the withdrawal of the allocation order. The Refusal to receive the goods violated the plans of the supplier and complicated the sale of goods already produced for which breach, in accordance with Par. 74 of the Statute on Supply of Goods, the buyer was obliged to pay a sanction.

MOSCOW WHOLESALE WAREHOUSE OF ROSKHOZTORG vs. CHEMICAL PLANT; MOSCOW WHOLESALE WAREHOUSE OF ROSKHOZTORG VS. KHIMFOTO, Sovetskaia iustitsiia, 1966, No. 20, p. 32.

State Arbitration attached to the Council of Ministers of the RSFSR received for consideration an application by the Moscow Wholesale Warehouse of Roskhoztorg to compel a chemical factory to conclude a contract for supply in 1966 of products for an economic use of plastic, and a pre-contract dispute between this warehouse and the Moscow Factory "Khimfoto" on the amount of products of polyethylene film to be supplied in 1966.

During the consideration of these disputes, the suppliers, the chemical plant and the factory "Khimfoto," tried to avoid concluding contracts with the warehouse of Roskhoztorg or to reduce the amount of products to be supplied, relying upon the insufficiency of the supply of raw material established for their plans of production. The buyer, the warehouse of Roskhoztorg, insisted on the supply of the whole quantity of products for economic use provided by the production plans of the suppliers, for the reasons that these products enjoyed great demand with the public, were sold on forward contracts to a series of trade organizations and their value was included in the plan for trade turnover.

Since the amount of products made from plastic and polyethylene film allocated to the warehouse by the distribution plan corresponded to the production plans established for the suppliers, State Arbitration attached to the Council of Ministers of the RSFSR obliged the chemical plant and the factory to conclude contracts with the warehouse, adopted the specifications for the contract in the draft preferred by the warehouse, and explained that the question of the insufficiency of supply of raw material for the production plans could be considered in the decision of disputes over the exaction of sanctions for failure to supply fully the products, but not in the conclusion of contracts. At the same time State Arbitration made a proposal to the State Planning Committee of the RSFSR and the superior organizations of the chemical plant and the factory "Khimfoto" concerning the provision of the necessary supply for the production plans established for them, or, in the alternative for changing the plans and bringing them into accordance with the available supplies of raw material.

ENTERPRISE vs. BROAD COAL PIT, Sovetskaia iustitsiia, 1970, No. 22, outside back cover.

In accordance with a delivery order of Soiuzglavtiazhmash of May 30, 1969 and letters of the Main Procurement Board of the Ministry of the Coal Industry of the USSR of October 8, 1969, and of the Sal'vostokugol' Combine of October 16, 1969, a contract was concluded between an enterprise and the Broad Coal Pit on October 30, 1969, for the delivery in the first quarter of 1970 of a ESh-15190A track-propelled excavator.

Soiuzglavtiazhmash, by a letter of January 29, 1970, No. 62/5-51, also addressed to the Machinery Board of the Ministry of the Coal Industry of the USSR, under the allocation for the first quarter, established the end of the term in April 1970 for delivery of the excavator under the delivery order for the Broad Coal Pit.

On February 25, 1970, the supplier sent the purchaser a letter with a proposal to change the conditions of the contract in the part concerning the deadline for the supply of the excavator, and on March 4, 1970 sent a telegram with a request for confirmation of consent.

Since the Broad Coal Pit objected to the delivery deadline, the supplier, on March 18, 1970, brought an action in State Arbitration Attached to the Council of Ministers of the RSFSR to have the terms of the contract change.

By a decision of April 3, 1970, State Arbitration rejected the supplier's request for postponement of delivery deadlines, indicating in its decision that the change in the delivery deadline for the track-propelled excavator was made by Soiuzglavtiazhmash on January 29, 1970, i.e. in violation of the established procedure and time-limits provided in Par. 12 of the Statute on Deliveries of Manufactured Goods.

An appeal for reconsideration of the decision was declined by the deputy chief arbiter on the following grounds.
According to the contract of October 31, 1969, concluded on the basis of the delivery order of Soiuzglavtiazhmash, delivery of the track-propelled excavator to the Broad Coal Bit was supposed to be made in the first quarter of 1970.

In accordance with Par. 12 of the Statute on Supply of Manufactured Goods, agencies which have issued delivery orders may make changes in them in connection with redistribution of allocations and also in exceptional cases not later than 45 days before the start of the term for delivery indicated in the delivery order, simultaneously notifying the supplier, recipient, and holder of the allocation.

Siouzglavtiazhmash's letter on changing the term for delivery of the excavator was sent on January 29, 1970, i.e. after the start of the period in which the delivery was supposed to take place.

Since the question of making changes in the delivery order was made in an untimely manner in violation of Par. 12 of the Statute, and the holder of the allocation—the Ministry of the Coal Industry of the USSR objects to the extension of the term; there are no bases for changing the delivery deadline under this delivery order.

C. *Fault*

MOSCOW WOOL OUTLET WAREHOUSE "ROSTEKSTIL'TORG" vs. TROITSKAIA CLOTH FACTORY, Sovetskaia iustitsiia, 1966, No. 11, p. 31.

The Moscow Wool Outlet Warehouse "Rostekstil'torg" filed a claim with State Arbitration attached to the Council of Ministers of the RSFSR for the exaction of a sanction from the Troitskaia Cloth Factory for the violation of contractual obligations, namely the failure to make full deliveries of wool fabrics during the second quarter of 1965. The Troitskaia Cloth Factory reported that fabric of types 46118 and 10890 was not supplied to the buyer warehouse because of lack of raw material for the manufacture of the fabric and asked on this basis that the factory be freed from payment of the sanction, relying on absence of fault in the failure to make full deliveries. State Arbitration did not accept the arguments of the Troitskaia Cloth Factory and exacted a sanction from it for the following reasons:

The specifications for the contract for the supply of wool fabrics in 1965 were agreed by the supplier, the Troitskaia Cloth Factory, and the buyer, the Moscow Wool Outlet Warehouse at the inter-republican wholesale fair and according to these specifications the Troitskaia factory took upon itself the obligation to supply fabric of types 46118 and 10890. The Troitskaia factory was obliged to take all measures in order to fulfill its contractual obligations including taking care to obtain the necessary material for the making of the fabrics which were ordered. The factory did not fulfill its contractual obligations; in the second quarter of 1965, it failed to ship to the buyer the full amount of fabric of the above-mentioned types and only after the filing of a claim against it in State Arbitration for the exaction of a sanction reported that the reasons for the non-fulfillment of obligations for supply was the lack of the necessary raw material. Moreover, the factory did not present documents to State Arbitration confirming that it took exhaustive measures to obtain the necessary raw materials. Under such circumstances State Arbitration did not find any grounds for freeing the supplier from liability for violation of contractual obligations.

On the application of the Troitskaia Cloth Factory, the decision of State Arbitration was considered by way of supervision by the Deputy Chief Arbiter and was affirmed. In answer to the appeal of the Troitskaia Cloth Factory it was explained that standing alone, a reference to lack of raw material cannot serve as a basis for release from liability for failure to supply if the supplier does not show that he has taken all essential measures in order to carry out the obligations he has undertaken for supply.

KHARKOV KOOPPOSILTORG CENTER vs. CHERNIVETS CHEMICAL CONSUMER PRODUCTS FACTORY, Radians'ke pravo, 1966, No. 8, p. 95.

The Kharkov Koopposiltorg Center, in accordance with Par. 57 of the Statue of Supply of Consumer Goods, filed a claim in State Arbitration attached to the Council of Ministers of the Ukrainian SSR for the recovery of a 7500 ruble penalty from the Chernivets Chemical Consumer Products Factory for failure, in October-December 1965, to supply plastic products worth 280,000 rubles.

The Chemical Consumer Products Factory answered that the claimant had overstated the amount of the penalty since the goods were delivered directly to its warehouse. The delay in the supply was explained by the fact that the factory had only 50-55% of the polychlorvinyl chloride film needed for the fulfillment of its own plan of production. For this reason, the respondent, citing its absence of fault in failure to supply, asked to be excused for this reason from the payment of the penalty.

The State Arbiter decided that the measure of damages should be determined according to Par. 57 of the Statute on Supply of Consumer Goods. Taking into account the reduction of the production plan of the factory, the claim was allowed in the amount of 1827 rubles.

In an appeal to the Chief Arbiter, the claimant argued that although the factory's plan of production had been reduced, nevertheless the supply contract had not been changed. The Chief Arbiter found no basis for changing the decision and the award of an additional sum. Responsibility for the fulfillment of an obligation, according to Art. 209 of the Civil Code of the Ukrainian SSR may be imposed upon a party only in instance of fault, which in the present case was absent, since the failure to supply took place in connection with non-issuance of allocation permits for raw material.

ZHITOMIR MUSICAL INSTRUMENT FACTORY vs. VASIL'KIV REFRIGERATOR FACTORY, Radians'ke pravo, 1968, No. 1, p. 88.

The Zhitomir Musical Instrument Factory filed a claim with State Arbitration attached to the Council of Ministers of the Ukrainian SSR seeking to recover from the Vasil'kiv Refrigerator Factory damages caused by failure to supply in full the requisite complete sets of equipment for Zhitomir brand refrigerators during the second quarter of 1966.

Upon considering the dispute, it was found by arbitration that by the terms of the contract the duty to provide the appropriate allocation certificates for the materials and the pre-built units (tubing) necessary for the preparation of the equipment that was to be supplied was placed upon the Zhitomir Musical Instrument Factory.

The purchaser did not arrange in time the question with the planning agencies of the allocation of the necessary amount of tubing, and so the allocation permits were not issued to their factory and so were not transferred by it to the refrigerator factory.

The Ministry of Local Industry of the Ukrainian SSR to which the purchaser was subordinated, applied only at the end of June, 1966, to the State Planning Committee of the Ukrainian SSR, asking the issuance of allocation permits for tubing. The refrigerator factory repeatedly requested the purchaser to transfer allocation permits for the tubing for the preparation of the refrigeration mechanisms.

Thus, since the failure to observe the contractual obligations arose from the fault of the Zhitomir factory itself and not from the fault of the refrigerator factory, State Arbitration rejected the claim on the basis of Art. 209 [Fault as a Condition for Liability for Breach of Obligations] of the Civil Code of the Ukrainian SSR.

A request by the claimant for review of the decision was considered by way of supervision by the chief arbiter and was left without satisfaction. In approving the decision, the state arbiter in the supervisory opinion noted in particular that a claim for compensation for damages could be satisfied if it were shown that there was a direct causal connection in nonfulfillment or improper fulfillment of the contractual obligations and duties.

In seeking compensation for damanges, the purchaser was required to show that he took the necessary steps for avoiding the damages or for reducing them. Therefore the damages suffered by the factory in the payment of penalties to purchasers for failure to supply refrigerators cannot be transferred to the Vasilkiv Factory.

SEL'KHOZTEKNIKA vs. ROSTSEL'MASH, Sovetskaia iustitsiia, 1970, No. 17, inside back cover.

The Kameshkir District Combine "Sel'khoztekhnika" brought an action in State Arbitration attached to the Kuibyshev Regional Executive Committee against the Rostsel'mash Factory, for the recovery of products paid for but not received.

The decision of state arbitration placed liability for non-delivery on the shipper. In so doing, state arbitrazh proceeded from the ground that theft of the freight during shipment could not have taken place because of its heavy weight.

State Arbitration attached to the Council of Ministers of the RSFSR, checking the well-foundedness of the decision adopted, found it invalid.

As appears from the record, the Rostsel'mash Factory shipped 46 combines on open flatcars to the Kameshkir District Combine "Sel'khoztekhnika."

The freight was accepted for shipment under guard by the Minister of Transport of the USSR, which is shown by the stamp of the railway bill of lading. At the station of destination the freight arrived with a shortage of two combines. This circumstance is confirmed by a commercial attestation.

According to Art. 148 of the Charter of Railroads of the USSR, the railroad bears liability for the preservation of freight from the moment it is accepted for shipment until it is delivered to the freight recipient, if the railroad does not show that the loss, shortage, spoilage or damage to the freight occurred as the result of circumstances which it could not prevent and whose elimination did not depend upon it. The carrier must show that it was not at fault.

However, there is no evidence of the absence of fault of the carrier. The statement of the railroad that the shortage of two combines was the result of their not being loaded by the shipper, is a supposition and is contradicted by the data on the bill of lading which indicates that 46 combines were accepted for shipment. Thus, since the railroad has not shown the absence of its own fault in the shortage of freight, it must itself bear the damages caused by this shortage.

DRASNOYARSK LUMBER PROCUREMENT AND SALES BOARD vs. BISMAZHINSK LUMBER ENTERPRISE, Sovetskaia iustitsiia, 1970, No. 11, inside back cover.

State Arbitration attached to the Krasnoyarsk Territory Executive Committee on October 16, 1969, satisfied the claim of the Krasnoyarsk Lumber Procurement and Sales Board for recovery from the Bismazhinsk Lumber Enterprise in that the shortage in supply of lumber products was caused by failure of the railroad to provide cars.

This decision has been reversed by way of supervision by State Arbitration attached to the Council of Ministers of the RSFSR on the following grounds. From the tally cards of transportation plan fulfillment in the record it appears that in a number of cases the failure to supply railroad cars was explained by snowdrifts.

According to the explanation of State Arbitration attached to the Council of Ministers of the USSR of October 6, 1969, No. I-1-35, as a general rule, references by defendants to the nonallocation of means of transport within the limits of the transportation plan are not circumstances freeing from liability for the violation of obligations.

However in the present concrete case State Arbitration attached to the Krasnoyarsk Territory Executive Committee did not take into consideration that the shortage in the supply of railroad cars was caused by natural calamities. Therefore in accordance with Art. 37 of the Fundamental Principles, the shortage in supply of cars as a result of snowdrifts should be recognized as a circumstance freeing the Lumber Enterprise from liability for shortage in supply of lumber products.

BRIANSK CEMENT FACTORY vs. BRIANSK DIVISION OF THE MOSCOW RAILROAD, Sovetskaia iustitsiia, 1971, No. 8, outside back cover.

The Briansk Cement Factory brought an action in State Arbitration attached to the Briansk Regional Soviet against the Briansk Division of the Moscow Railroad for the recovery of 28, 644 rubles of fines for failure to supply transport means in July 1970 to make up shortages in shipments caused by the fault of the railroad in the previous month.

The defendant, objecting to the claim, argued that according to Art. 30 of the Charter of Railroads, the procedure for allocation of means of transport for making up shortages for shipments planned in a centralized manner must be agreed upon by the ministries.

State Arbitration found the arguments of the Briansk Division to be unfounded and adopted a decision to satisfy the claim.

The Briansk Division appealed to State Arbitration attached to the Council of Ministers of the USSR to have the decision reconsidered as violating Art. 30 of the Charter.

Since this question had been raised a number of times in the practice of the agencies of state arbitration, State Arbitration attached to the Council of Ministers of the USSR by an Instruction Letter of February 5, 1971, No. I-1-5, explained that Par. 56 of the Basic Provisions of Annual and Quarterly Planning of Transfers of Freight provides that the administration of railroad, ocean (cabotage) and river steamship lines and the administration of automotive transport (truck trusts) in case there is a failure through their fault to supply means of transport for fulfillment of the monthly plan of transport of freight, are obligated on demand of the shipper to make available means of transport to make up the undershipments during the course of the following month of the same quarter. Means of transport not supplied during the last month of a quarter must be made available in the first month of the following quarter.

In river and ocean transport the making up of under shipments is conducted within the limits of the navigation period.

The procedure for allocation of means of transport for making up undershipments is established by agreement between the transportation organization and the freight shippers. If the agreed procedure is violated, the transportation organization, for failure to supply means of transport and the freight shipper for failure to provide freight for shipment bear the responsibility provided for nonfulfillment of the plan for transport of freight.

These provisions should be followed in the settlement of disputes.

In the given case, the factory, in the agreed period sent the Administration of the Railroad a request with accounting cards attached to it and asked that freight cars be allocated to make up the shortage. The railroad made no objections and did not propose any other procedure for allocation of the freight cars for making up the shortage.

On the basis of the above, State Arbitration attached to the Council of Ministers of the USSR found the decision of State Arbitration attached to the Executive Committee of the Briansk Regional Soviet to be correct and left it in force.

PROCUREMENT OFFICE vs. RUSSIA COLLECTIVE FARM, Biulleten' Verkhovnogo Suda RSFSR, 1972, No. 4, p. 2.

The Procurement Office of the Industry Board of the Novgorod Region Soviet of Working-People's Deputies and the Russia Collective Farm concluded a procurement contract on January 28, 1970. Under the contract, the collective farm was obliged to sell 10 tons of cucumbers between August 1 and 15, 1970. Since the collective farm failed to fulfill its obligation, the Procurement Office brought an action in court to recover 120 rubles penalty and contract sanction in accordance with the procurement contract.

[A decision for the Procurement Office was reversed on the following grounds:]

In accordance with Art. 222 [Fault as a Condition of Liability for Breach of Obligations] of the Civil Code of the RSFSR and Par. 3 of the procurement contract, the collective farm is freed from liability for nonfulfillment of its obligation under the contract if it was not fulfilled as a result of natural calamity, i.e. of circumstances which could not be attributed to its fault.

Defending against the action, the collective farm relied on the ground that the cucumbers perished as the result of a natural calamity (heavy hail), which damaged the plantings in the seedbeds on August 7, 1970. However the court did not give weight to this defense, indicating in its decision that the collective farm sold 71 hundredweight of cucumbers to the food market and the district consumers' union. However in the record there is a certificate of the Borvichskii District Food Market of November 25, 1970, in which it is indicated that the Russia Collective Farm, did not supply cucumbers to the City Food Market, although under a procurement contract it was supposed to supply ten tons. The Borvichskii City Cooperative Market of the District Consumers Union in a certificate of November 25, 1970 indicated that the Russia Collective farm on August 24, 1970 had supplied it with only 244 kilograms of cucumbers. In accordance with the conditions of the contract of August

22, 1970, the collective farm sent to the Valdai Vegetable Factory a telegram in which it asked that transportation be sent for the cucumbers and only after the refusal of the vegetable factory were the cucumbers sold to the District Consumer's Union.

In affirming the decision of the People's Court, the Regional Court indicated that the collective farm was obliged to begin delivery of cucumbers on August 1, i.e. before they were damaged by hail. However no plan for supply of cucumbers by days was established by the contract, and the deadline, August 15, 1970 was not missed by the collective farm before the natural disaster.

Also unfounded is the conclusion of the court that the collective farm nevertheless did supply cucumbers to other organizations, in particular to restaurant organizations, since from the certificate of the Borovichskii Trust of Cafeterias and Restaurants of December 22, 1970, which was attached to the protest, it appears that in 1970 the Russia Collective Farm did not deliver cucumbers to their organizations.

From the certificate of the Administrative Board for Agriculture of the Borvichskii District of January 21, 1971, it appears that the plantings of cucumbers in the Russia Collective Farm were completely destroyed as a result of the hailstorm of August 7, 1970.

In these circumstances, the conclusion of the court that the responsibility for the payment of the penalties and contract sanctions for the violation of the procurement contract had to be placed upon the Russia Collective Farm appear unconvincing and require further verification taking into consideration the supplementary data presented by the defendant about the absence of fault of the collective farm in the nonfulfillment of the contractual obligation.

CASE OF THE SUPPLY AND PROCUREMENT ADMINISTRATION OF THE YAROSLAVL REGION EXECUTIVE COMMITTEE, Sovetskaia iustitsiia, 1968, No. 16, outside back cover.

By a decision of State Arbitration attached to the Yaroslavl Executive Committee, the Administration for Supply and Procurement of the Yaroslavl Region Executive Committee was freed from payment of a contract sanction for nonfulfillment of obligations for the supply in the first quarter of 1967 of 3 tons of lead crown-glass.

The decision was based upon the defendant's argument that it received the order for supply of the production only on February 16, 1967, i.e. after the expiration of the term provided for submission to the railroad of requests for receiving containers in March. Moreover the decision contained reference to the acceptance of the order by the defendant for fulfillment in the second quarter. However there was no information in the record to the effect that the supplier refused by the established procedure to fulfill the order in the first quarter or accepted it for fulfillment in the second quarter.

The claim should have been satisfied on the ground that the order was accepted for fulfillment and the supplier presented no evidence that it had taken measures for the timely and proper fulfillment of its obligations, in particular that it applied with a request to the railroad, which, in accordance with Art. 33 of the Charter of Railroads of the USSR had the right to allow the loading of freight outside the plan and above the plan (for such freight a request is submitted five days before the day of loading for shipment).

VESSANEN, TIMMERMANS, AND SEGMII vs. BALTIC SEA STEAMSHIP LINE AND USSR FOREIGN INSURANCE ADMINISTRATION, Biulleten' Verkhovnogo Suda USSR, 1970, No. 4, p. 17.

The Maritime Arbitration Commission attached to the All-Union Chamber of Commerce made a decision in the dispute of the Dutch firms of Vessalen, Timmermans, and Segmii with the Baltic Sea Steamship Line and the USSR Foreign Insurance Administration over the recovery of 44,198.19 Dutch Guilders.

Considering this decision to be incorrect, the President of the Supreme Court of the USSR brought a protest before the Judicial Division for Civil Cases of the Supreme Court of the USSR.

Having considered the case on the protest, the Judicial Division has established:

The Dutch firms shipped 7064 tons of wheat under two bills of lading of August 9 from the port of Novorossisk on the SS Mendeleev of the Baltic Sea Steamship Line to the ports of Rotterdam and Amsterdam. In unloading the vessel in the port of Amsterdam, it was established that part of the grain, loaded in the No. 2 hold of the steamship, was spoiled as a result of the fact that it was wet with fresh water. The general amount of the damage caused by the spoilage of the grain was determined by the plaintiffs to be 44,198.19 Dutch gilders. The demands of the freight recipients for compensation for the damage caused during transport of the grain were considered under the claims procedure. The claim was refused both by the Baltic Sea Steamship Company and by the USSR Foreign Insurance Administration.

In iurkollegia, acting in defense of the interests of the freight recipients—the Dutch firms, brought an action in Leningrad City Court against the Baltic Steamship Line for the recovery of damages caused by the spoilage of the grain. By agreement of the parties the action was transferred for decision by the Maritime Arbitration Commission attached to the All-Union Chamber of Commerce.

The action against the carrier for compensation for damages caused in connection with the loss of the freight—the grain accepted by the steamship line under the contract for carriage by sea, was motivated by the argument that a vessel was supplied for this trip with improper equipment and a defective waterpipe system ("Unseaworthy").

The Baltic Sea Steamship Line did not concede the claim, since it did not consider itself responsible for the failure to preserve the grain during its carriage on the SS Mendeleev. The steamship line, not contesting the fact of spoilage of the wheat, relied on the argument that the spoilage of the freight occurred under circumstances which by virtue of Art 116 of the Merchant Shipping Code of the USSR of 1929 (Pt. 1, par. "k") exclude the liability of the carrier. The steamship line would include among such circumstances the fact that the ship ran aground during its loading at the mooring in the port, listing to the left four degrees and denting the hull, which in turn caused a breakage in the flange connections of the fresh water pipes, as a result of which cause, Hold No. 2, filled with grain, was flooded, In the opinion of the steamship line, the fact that the boat ran aground during loading at the mooring in the port was a navigational error in the handling and management of the ship; the steamship line asked that it be freed from liability in the action which had been brought and that damages be assessed against the USSR Foreign Insurance Administration which was obligated to compensate under an insurance contract for damages arising as the result of mistakes in handling and management of vessels.

In the conclusion of the technical expert it is observed that the cause of the spoilage of the freight—of the grain at the port of Novorossisk was the destruction of "the solidity of the packing in the flanges of the fresh water pipes," and also the "lack of the solidity of the cutoff valve" on this pipe. A factor contributing to the flooding of Hold No. 2, according to the conclusions of the expert, was also the absence on the boat of proper organization for taking on water from the shore, the violation of the demands of the Rules for Service on Vessels of the Ocean Fleet for checking the measurement of the height of water in the holds. In the conclusion of the expert, in addition, it was observed that the spoilage of grain in Hold No. 2 occurred not only while the ship was moored in the port of Novorossisk, but also that during the voyage fresh water continued to enter Hold No. 2 through the packing of the flanges of the pipe and the cutoff valve.

Another expert, a sea captain, confirmed the correctness of the claim of the steamship line that the SS Mendelev ran aground during the loading of grain in the port of Novorossisk. However the expert did not establish a causal connection between the running aground at the mooring and the spoilage of grain in Hold No. 2.

Considering the defense offered by the steamship line against the action brought against it, on petition of the plaintiff, the USSR Foreign Insurance Administration (Ingosstrakh), which was the insurer of the freight in the contract for carriage by sea, was brought into the case as a defendant.

The Maritime Arbitration Commission entered a decision on July 3, 1969, which freed the Baltic Steamship Line entirely from liability, but satisfied in full the claims of the Dutch firms in the amount of 44,198.19 guilders, with recovery of this amount from the insurer of the freight, the Foreign Insurance Administration of the USSR.

In freeing the steamship line from liability under the claim, the Maritime Arbitration Commission relied on the provisions contained in Art. 116 of the Merchant Shipping Code of the USSR of 1929 (Pt. 1, par. "k")

In the decision of the Arbitration Commission both the fact that the SS Mendelev ran aground during loading at the mooring in the port of Novorossisk and the existence of a causal connection between this circumstances and the flooding of the grain in Hold No. 2 were taken as proved as a fact. According to the decision, the running aground of the ship at mooring in the port, although it occurred as a result of an omission of the captain (and other members of the vessel's crew), is a mistake of navigation, and therefore the Baltic Sea Steamship Line should be by virtue of the law cited above, freed from liability for the damage suffered by the owners of the freight, and the Foreign Insurance Administration of the USSR should compensate for the damage.

The Maritime Arbitration Commission did not agree with the arguments of the plaintiff that, even in the case that freight was water-damaged not by result of the unseaworthiness of the vessel, but as a result of the actions or omissions of the captain and other members of the vessel's crew, the carrier, by virtue of Art. 116 of the Merchant Shipping Code (Pt. 2, par. "k") could not be freed from liability under the claim; in the present case these actions occurred during loading, placement, and storage of the grain, and not during the voyage.

Proceeding from the ground that for the application with respect to the carrier of this legal rule it is necessary to establish that the loss or damage to the freight was in direct causal connection with the conduct of the above-mentioned loading operations (however in the present case, as is confirmed in the decision, the cause leading to the water-damage of the freight was the running aground of the boat at mooring in the port), then whether or not the occurance of this circumstance corrsponded in time with the loading operations in the vessel, the carrier, in the opinion of the Maritime Arbitration Commission, cannot bear liability to the owner of the freight for the consequences connected with it.

These considerations are placed as the basis for the decision on imposing liability in the action on USSR Ingosstrakh as the insurer of the freight carried on the SS Mendeleev since under the conditions of insurance, the insurer was obliged to compensate for damage from harm to freight, in particular including that caused by the vessel running aground.

In the protest of the President of the Supreme Court of the USSR of the decision of the Maritime Arbitration Commission it is noted that the decision was rendered on circumstances and materials in the case that had not been investigated, in connection with which the grounds on which the decision was based to free the carrier from liability in the action are found in the protest not to be convincing.

The Judicial Division for Civil Cases of the Supreme Court of the USSR, agreeing with the arguments of the protest, considers that the decision of the Maritime Arbitration Commission should be reversed and the case transferred for a new hearing for the following reasons.

Having correctly reached the conclusion that the spoilage of the grain occurred in the port of shipment during the loading of the vessel, the Maritime Arbitration Commission at the same time, without sufficient grounds, held that the shipper did not bear liability for damages caused by freight spoilage. One cannot agree with this decision, even assuming that the flooding of Hold No. 2, which was loaded with grain, occurred by reason of the ship running aground at the mooring in the port while it was being loaded and that this led to the denting of the vessel and the destruction of the integrity of its water piping system. Having agreed with the arguments of the steamship line that the running aground of the vessel during its loading at the mooring in the port is classified as a navigational error in the handling and management of the vessel, i.e. as among the circumstances provided by Art. 116, pt. 1, par. "k" of the Merchant Shipping Code of the USSR, the Maritime Arbitration Commission simultaneously came to another erroneous conclusion to the effect that the running aground of a vessel in all circumstances should be classified as among those circumstances freeing the carrier from liability for the loss or damage of freight on the ship and accepted for shipment, when the loss or damage is caused by these circumstances.

One cannot agree with these conclusions for the reason that they are made with respect to the present case in isolation from the causes which led to the running aground of the vessel, which caused the flooding of the hold loaded with grain. The Maritime Arbitration Commission did not engage in a clarification of these circumstances, but limited itself in its decision to a general statement that the running aground of the vessel at mooring in the port was connected with omissions of the captain and other members of the crew in the handling and management of the vessel, although the vessel at the time it ran aground (if this really happened) was at mooring in the port in a motionless condition.

As was already noted, the record contains the conclusions of two experts given by each of them independently, however leading to the single conclusion that the flooding of Hold No. 2 with the grain occurred as a result of defects in the water pipe system on the vessel and was not connected with the running aground of the vessel at mooring in the port.

The Maritime Arbitration Commission was not in agreement with these experts' conclusions, but did not present any substantial arguments as the basis for its position. With respect to the conclusions of one of the experts that the spoilage of grain in Hold No. 2 from the defects in the water pipe system on the vessel occurred not only in the loading port, but also later during the voyage of the vessel, the decision of the Maritime Arbitration Commission does not mention this part of the expert's conclusion. The decision also fails to give an answer to the important circumstance which is mentioned in the expert's conclusion that on the vessel during its loading a gross violation of the rules for the conduct of periodic checking of taking on fresh water from shore was committed. Moreover the expert came to this conclusion proceeding from an analysis of evidence in the record which in the hearing of the case should have been carefully studied and given an appropriate evaluation in making the decision.

Another question was not reflected in the decision of the Maritime Arbitration Commission. This was the question of the actions of the carrier to preserve the water-damaged part of the grain and to protect from spoilage the other part of the grain which had not been water-damaged after the entry of water into Hold No. 2 had been discovered at the loading port.

The clarification of all the circumstances indicated above and their proper evaluations has essential significance for the correct decision of the dispute which has arisen from the contract for carrage by sea, and also for the release of the carrier from liability for loss and damage to the freight accepted by it for carriage. It is necessary not only to establish that this was caused by one or several of the circumstances listed in Art. 116 of the USSR Merchant Shipping Code, but it is necessary in addition to show that the carrier could not prevent or eliminate the occurance of these circumstances with harmful consequences for the freight.

On the above grounds, the Judicial Division for Civil Cases of the Supreme Court of the USSR has decided to reverse the decision of the Maritime Arbitration Commission of July 3, 1969 and remand the case of the action of the Dutch firms of Vessanen, Timmermans and Segmii v. Baltic Sea Steamship Lines and the USSR Foreign Insurance Administration for the recovery as compensation for damages in the carriage of goods by sea of 44,198.19 Dutch gilders to the Maritime Arbitration Commission for a new hearing.

D. *Damages*

ADMINISTRATION OF ENTERPRISES UNDER CONSTRUCTION OF THE KAZAKHSTANNEFT' COMBINE vs. MANGYSHLAKNEFTGAZSTROI TRUST, Sovetskaia iustitsiia, 1970, No. 23, outside back cover.

During the conclusion of an annual construction contract between the Administration of Enterprises Under Construction of the Kazakhstanneft' Combine and the Mangyshlakneftgazstroi Trust, the customer proposed the inclusion in the contract of language providing for the payment of a fine if the work presented was carried out with poor quality or executed with a deviation from the designs and norms, and also for unfinished stages and structures presented.

State Arbitration attached to the Executive Committee of the Aktiubinsk Regional Council, having considered the precontract dispute which arose between the customer and the contractor, adopted a decision to include the above mentioned points in the contract.

The Mangyshlakneftgazstroi Trust appealed to State Arbitration attached to the Council of Ministers of the USSR for review of this decision. It argued that the inclusion in the contract of sanctions for nonfulfillment of obligations for the violation of which sanctions are not established by current legislation could take place only with the consent of both sides. Therefore since there were objections on the part of the contractor against the inclusion of these provisions, State Arbitration should not consider the dispute on the merits.

In the Decree of State Arbitration attached to the Council of Ministers of the USSR adopted in this case, it is indicated that Par. 67 of the Rules on Contracts for Construction provides for the possibility of inclusion in the contract of sanctions for the non fulfillment of those obligations for the violation of which sanctions are not established by current legislation. If a dispute arises over the inclusion of such sanctions in the contract or if it is a matter of their amount, then it is subject to consideration in State Arbitration by the ordinary procedure.

However in the present case the customer raises the question of inclusion in the contract of language providing for the imposition of sanctions for substandard quality in fulfillment of work and also for the submission of unfinished work, i.e. in essence for violations of the deadlines for fulfilling them. Sanctions for violating these obligations are provided by Par. 62 of the Rules on Construction Contracts. Thus, the customer's proposal amounts not to the establishment of supplementary sanctions not provided in current legislation, but to raising the amount of sanctions provided by the Rules.

In accordance with Par. 30 of the Decree of the Council of Ministers of the USSR of October 27, '67, No. 988, raising the amount of sanctions for the violation of the conditions of the contract, where the amounts are established by current legislation, may take place only with the consent of both parties. Since in the present case there was not consent of both parties to raising the amount of sanctions, the decision of State Arbitration Attached to the Executive Committee of the Aktiubinsk Regional Soviet was incorrect. On this basis the decision of State Arbitration attached to the Executive Committee of the Aktiubinsk Regional Soviet was reversed and the case was dismissed in this regard.

POLTAVA REGIONAL CENTER OF THE UKRAINIAN WHOLESALE MEAT SALES ORGANIZATION vs. KREMENCHUG MEAT COMBINE, Radians'ke pravo, 1971, No. 1, p. 107.

The Poltava Regional Center of Ukrainian Wholesale Meat Sales Organization brought an action against the Kremenchug Meat Combine for the recovery of 107,366 rubles in contract sanctions for nondelivery of meat to another union republic. Calculation of the sanction was made in accordance with Par. 28 of the Statute on Delivery of Consumer Goods, i.e. with the addition of the undelivered quantity of meat in one period to the quantity to be delivered in the following period.

Deciding this case, the regional state arbitration concurred with the plantiff's calculation and allowed recovery from the Meat Combine of a contract sanction with the calculated addition.

Exercising supervisory review over the correctness of the decision, State Arbitration attached to the Council of Ministers of the Ukrainian SSR by letter of October 6, 1970, No. P1-355 transferred the dispute for a further hearing, on the following grounds.

According to Par. 6 of Art. 37 of the Fundamentals of Civil Legislation an obligor must fulfill his obligations (supply the undelivered quantity of goods), except in cases when the planned task upon which the obligations are based, has lost its force. Since, as a rule, planned tasks last for the fiscal year, the supplier is obliged to make up the shortage by the end of the year. In the present instance, the efficacy of the planned task for the supply of meat to another republic is limited by the term of efficacy of the delivery order. Thus, the delivery orders for the shipments in dispute indicate that the term of their efficacy lapses after the end of the month for which they were issued. Therefore, after this term has passed, the delivery order—

the planned task—has lost its force. Therefore, the supplier is freed from the obligation to make up the goods which have not been supplied, and the buyer loses the right to demand such additional supply.

WESTERN SIBERIA WOOD PROCUREMENT AND SALES ADMINISTRATION vs. TOMSK CENTER OF THE MAIN COOPERATIVE SALES AGENCY, Sovetskaia iustitsiia, 1969, No. 17, inside back cover.

Western Siberia Wood Procurement and Sales Administration brought an action against the Tomsk Center of the Main Cooperative Sales Agency for the recovery of 20,500 rubles, the cost of wood not shipped and a fine for untimely presentation of copies of delivery orders for its shipment.

By decision of State Arbitration attached to the Council of Ministers of the RSFSR the demands of the plaintiff were satisfied and 20,500 and 100 rubles—fine for untimely presentation of copies of delivery orders were awarded in his favor.

The deputy chief arbiter of State Arbitration attached to the Council of Ministers of the RSFSR reversed this decision and dismissed the complaint with a reference to Par. 11 of the Decree of the Council of Ministers of the USSR of October 27, 1967, No. 988.

Paragraph 11 of this decree provides that the supplier, for untimely presentation of a copy of the order for shipment of the goods, has the right, when the time for shipment under the contract is reached, in addition to recovering the established fine for untimely presentation of the copy of the delivery order, to demand the payment of the cost of goods for which the buyer failed to give a copy of the delivery order only upon presentation of guarantees of the existence of these goods.

The shipper of wood for the Tomsk Center of the Main Cooperative Sales Agency was the Komsomolsk Wood Products Organization, which shipped wood products on the orders of the plaintiff. The plaintiff had to produce proof that the wood products organization, on the day the action was brought, had 2050 cubic meters of wood, the amount for which the defendant did not issue copies of the delivery order in the first quarter of 1968.

However, the plaintiff did not present such proofs. The plaintiff also failed to present documents showing that it had paid the amount of the cost of this wood to the Komsomolsk Wood Products Organization.

Moreover the fine in the amount of 100 rubles for untimely presentation by the defendant of copies of the delivery order should not have been exacted.

This conclusion may be reached from the Statute on Supply of Goods for Production or Technological Use, which provides that if the delivery of the goods is made not directly to the purchaser under the contract, but to other recipients not in contractual relations with the supplier, the purchaser simultaneously with the return of the signed contract to the supplier must supply it with copies of shipping orders for the recipients of the goods for the year or for the first quarter. The plaintiff prepared a counterproposal of a contract for the supply of wood products only on May

6, 1968, and, therefore, the plaintiff did not have the possiblity of making a timely presentation of a copy of the order for shipping wood in the first quarter of 1968.

SHIPPING AND TRANSPORT BOARD OF THE BELOUGOL' TRUST v. BELOVSK DIVISION OF THE WEST-SIBERIAN RAILROAD, Sovetskaia iustitsiia, 1971, No. 5, outside back cover.

The Shipping and Transport Board of the Belougol' Trust brought an action in State Arbitration attached to the Executive Committee of the Kemerovo Regional Soviet for the recovery from the Belovsk Division of the West-Siberian Railroad of a fine for nonfulfillment of a shipping plan in the third ten-day period of August 1969.

The Belovskii Division of the West Siberian Railroad brought a counterclaim for the recovery of a fine for nonfulfillment of the transportation plan for the same period in the accounting report.

State Arbitration attached to the Executive Committee of the Kemorovsk Region Soviet refused to satisfy both the basic claim and the counterclaim, setting off the excess of railroad cars supplied in one ten-day period against the failure to load enough cars in another.

By decision of the Deputy Chief Arbiter of State Arbitration attached to the Council of Ministers of the RSFSR, this decision was reversed.

The decision pointed out that, in accordance with Articles 145 and 146 of the Charter of Railroads of the USSR, a railroad and shipper are freed from liability for nonfulfillment of a shipment with a shortage in cars supplied on individual days of that ten-day period. The Charter does not provide for a setoff of an excess of railroad cars supplied (or loaded) in a given ten-day period to cover nonfulfillment of the transport plan in the following ten-day period, since the calculation of the fine is made on the results of the activity of each ten-day period.

ELISTINSK MILK FACTORY vs. FRIENDSHIP COLLECTIVE FARM, Biulleten' Verkhovnogo Suda RSFSR, 1973, No. 4, p. 13.

The Elistinsk Milk Factory brought an action against the Druzhba Collective Farm to recover 1636 rubles and 10 kopecks damages for failure to supply 190 hundredweight of milk. The amount sought was made up of profit not received by the factory, the contract sanction, and a penalty.

The Priutenskii District People's Court of the Kalmyk ASSR satisfied the claim with respect to the allowance of the contract sanction and a penalty. The remaining part of the claim was refused. Refusing to allow 1562 rubles of lost profit, the people's court indicated that according to the procurement contract, the party guilty of failure to deliver could be required to compensate for loss only in the case that as a result of the failure to deliver the enterprise was placed in a difficult position: idleness of equipment, labor, and other interruptions in work.

[This decision was reversed on the following grounds:]

Par. 4 of the Model Procurement Contract for Milk and Milk Products and Par.

41 of the Statute on the Procedure for the Conclusion and Execution of Procurement Contracts for Agricultural Products provide that independently of the payment of a sanction (of fine or penalty), the party at fault must compensate the other party for damages caused as a result of violation of the contract. Such damages may be lost profit from nonfulfillment of the supply plan.

The decision of the people's court limiting the possibility of recovery of damages to cases of idleness of equipment or labor contradicts Art. 36 [Liability for Violation of Obligations] of the Fundamental Principles of Civil Legislation.

NEVINNOMYSSKII CHEMICAL COMBINE vs. DISTRICT ENERGY BOARD OF STAVROPOL'ENERGO, Sovetskaia iustitsiia, 1970, No. 19, inside back cover.

The Nevinnommysskii Chemical Combine brought an action in State Arbitration attached to the Executive Committee of the Stavropol Regional Soviet against the District Energy Board of Stavropol'energo for the recovery of 34,757 rubles in compensation for damages caused by failure to supply electrical energy.

From the record it appears that in November 1969 there was an accident at the Nevinnomyskiii District Public Power Plant which caused a sharp voltage drop. As a result the technological system of production at the Chemical Combine was disrupted and the Combine suffered damages in the amount of 34,757 rubles.

The defendant, objecting to the claim, argued that the monetary liability of the electric power supply organization for supply of low quality electrical energy was fully exhausted by the payment of the fine provided in the Rules for the Use of Electrical Energy.

In connection with the dispute which arose in the case, a conclusion of the State Energy Supervision Agency was requested. It explained that the supply of electrical energy with characteristics making its use impossible was equivalent to the total stoppage of energy supply for the whole period of sharp deviation of the characteristics of the quality of the energy. The State Energy Supervision Agency, supporting the viewpoint of the defendant, at the same time considered that the energy supply organization bore limited liability for incompletely supplied electrical energy, within the bounds established by the Rules, of a fine in the amount of eight times the cost of the electrical energy not supplied.

A decision in the case was adopted in accordance with the conclusion of the State Energy Supervision Agency.

The Nevinnomysskii Chemical Combine appealed to State Arbitration attached to the Council of Ministers of the USSR for reconsideration of the decision which had been adopted.

The question of the limits of liability of energy supply organizations for insufficient supply of electrical energy and the supply of electrical energy of diminished quality was considered at a special session of State Arbitration attached to the Council of Ministers of the USSR. The decision of the session provided that in accordance with Art. 36 of the Fundamental Principles of Civil Legislation, in case of nonfulfillment or improper fulfillment of duties by the obligor, it was required to compensate the obligee for the damages caused thereby, in the amount not covered by the contractual sanction (for fine or penalty). For certain types of obligations limited liability for nonfulfillment or improper fulfillment of obligations may be established by the legislation of the USSR and the Union Republics. There is no legislation of the USSR or the Union Republics limiting the liability of energy supply organizations for insufficient supply of electrical energy or supply of electrical energy of diminished quality. In the Rules for Use of Electrical Energy effective from February 1, 1969, there is no language which would provide that the liability of energy-supply organizations for insufficient supply of electrical energy or supply of energy of diminished quality is limited to payment of a fine.

Therefore, on the basis of Art. 36 of the Fundamental Principles, the energy supply organizations were bound to compensate the users for damages not covered by the fine, damages sustained due to the fault of those supply organizations as the result of insufficient supply of electrical energy or the supply of electrical energy of diminished quality.

In connection with the aforesaid, the case was remanded to State Arbitration attached to the Executive Committee of the Stavropol Provincial Soviet for Supplementary consideration to adopt a decision in accordance with the recommendations of the session.

FORGING AND STAMPING FACTORY vs. AN ENTERPRISE, Sovetskaia iustitsiia, 1971, No. 15, inside back cover.

A forcing and stamping factory brought an action in State Arbitration attached to the Council of Ministers of the RSFSR against an enterprise to recover a contract sanction in the amount of 10,250 rubles for failure to supply metal under delivery order requisitions in the third quarter of 1970.

In the contract concluded between the parties for 1970, the supply periods (Sec. 5) were defined as monthly, and liability (Sec. 15) for failure to supply metal goods was provided to be quarterly.

The defendant, not denying that the metal in fact was not supplied in full, admitted the claim in the amount of 2275 rubles, but sought to reject the remaining part, relying on Sec. 15 of the contract, according to which liability for failure to supply was to be determined overall for a quarter and not monthly as the plaintiff calculated the contractual sanction.

State Arbitration satisfied the demands of the plaintiff in full on the following grounds.

Par. 59 of the Statute on Supply of Goods provides liability for late supply or failure to supply goods within the period established by the contract.

In Sec. 5 of the above-mentioned contract monthly supply periods are established. Having accepted these periods, the parties did not have the right to establish liability on totals of supply overall by quarter.

Therefore Sec. 15 of the contract, in essence limiting the liability of the parties in accordance with Par. 26 and Par. 85 of the Statute on Supply of Goods is invalid.

E. *Unplanned Contracts*

CLASSIFIED ADVERTISEMENT, Evening Moscow, advertising supplement, March 31, 1976, p. 4.
ORGANIZATION WILL TAKE A SHARE in the construction of an apartment house in Moscow or in nearby suburban Moscow with one having a plot of land and project documentation . . .

PROCURATOR OF SLOBODO-TURINSK DISTRICT ex rel. LENIN'S WAY COLLECTIVE FARM v. SLOBODO-TURINSK CONSTRUCTION AND INSTALLATION ADMINISTRATION OF THE REGIONAL COLLECTIVE FARM CONSTRUCTION ORGANIZATION, Biulleten' Verkhovnogo Suda RSFSR, 1971, No. 10, p. 5.

The Procurator of Slobodo-Turinsk District of Sverdlovsk Region brought an action in defense of the interests of Lenin's Way Collective Farm against the Slobodo-Turinsk Construction and Installation Administration of the Regional Collective Farm and the Construction and Installation Administration to have a contract declared invalid and to recover 1000 rubles.

The demands of the action are based on the fact that in accordance with an annual construction contract concluded in July 1969 between the Lenin's Way Collective Farm and the Construction and Installation Administration, the latter was obligated to construct two eight-apartment residential buildings for the collective farm.

One of these was to be ready for use in December 1969.

The Construction and Installation Administration, having finished the basic construction work by the efforts of its own employees, but not having workers for doing the stuccoing and other finishing work, on August 4, 1969, together with the collective farm concluded a construction contract with a brigade of workers headed by Pachko for doing these tasks. According to this contract, the Construction and Installation Administration would pay the brigade of workers 6000 rubles and the collective farm—1000 rubles.

Considering that this transaction with respect to the payment of 1000 rubles by the collective farm was illegal, the procurator asked that the claim be satisfied at the judicial session of the people's court.

The reprentative of the Lenin's Way Collective Farm in whose interest the present action was brought, did not support the demand of the procurator.

The representative of the Construction and Installation Administration did not recognize the claim as valid.

The Slobodo-Turinskii District People's Court dismissed the action.

The Judicial Division of the Sverdlovsk Regional Court left the decision of the people's court without change, but the presidium of the same court reversed the court decisions and remanded the case for a new hearing.

The Judicial Division for Civil Cases of the Supreme Court of the RSFSR, having considered the case on the protest of the Vice-President of the Supreme Court of the RSFSR for the reversal of the decree of the presidium of the regional court, satisfied the protest by a decision of March 16, 1971, on the following grounds.

Reversing the decision of the people's court and that of the judicial division, the presidium of the regional court relied on the ground that the Construction and Installation Administration of the Regional Collective Farm Construction Organization had not fulfilled the conditions of the annual construction contract and the requirement of Art. 368 of the Civil Code of the RSFSR, according to which the contractor is obliged to conduct all agreed work with his own forces and means, and the customer is obliged to pay the cost of the work according to the approved financial estimate account.

The violation, in the opinion of the presidium, consisted of the fact that there was an agreement between the Construction and Installation Administration and the Lenin's Way Collective Farm for the additional payment of 1000 rubles at the expense of collective farm funds above the amount paid by it to the construction administration for the construction of the building in accordance with the conditions of the construction contract. Thus, under the contract of August 4, 1969, it held that an obligation was illegally placed upon the collective farm for the payment of the above-mentioned sum to the brigade of workers which the contractor hired for carrying out its obligations to this collective farm.

These conclusions cannot be considered to be correct. In fact the relations between the contractor and the customer under a construction contract are regulated by Chapter 31, "Construction Contracts," of the Civil Code of the RSFSR (Articles 368-371).

However, neither these legal norms nor other normative acts contain indications that a collective farm does not have the right to conclude agreements with the contractor supplemental to the annual construction contract, agreements connected with the provision of manpower, materials or monetary expenditures if this speeds the finishing of construction and is economically advantageous for the collective farm.

In considering the case the people's court established that the supplementary agreement concluded by the parties on August 4, 1969, according to which the collective farm paid 1000 rubles above the estimated cost for the construction of the building according to the state appraisals was brought about for the attraction of construction specialists for the performance of finishing work, specialists that the contractor did not have.

In connection with this the construction of the building was finished early, the apartment house was put into use and the parties have no claims against one another.

The agreement for support by the collective farm of the contractor, an inter-collective-farm construction organization in the construction of the building also does not contradict the Model Charter of the Collective Farm (citation omitted), according to Par. 13 of which the disposition of the property and monetary assets of the collective farm belongs only to the collective farm itself and its agencies of administration. The decision to pay an additional 1000 rubles was adopted by the administration of the collective farm.

F. *Contracts Between State Enterprises and Private Citizens*

MODEL CONTRACT FOR THE REPAIR OF DWELLING PREMISES (SERVICE ORDER), approved by decree of the Council of Ministers of the RSFSR, Feb. 1, 1965, M. S. Makarov (editor) Spravochnik gosudarstvennogo notariata [State Notary's Handbook] (Moscow, 1972), p. 291.

City of . . . . , ..., 19. . . . .

. . . . (name of the enterprise carrying out the repairs) . . . . hereinafter called "Contractor", and citizen . . . ., residing at . . . ., hereinafter called Customer, have concluded the present contract on the following:

1. Contractor is obliged to repair the premises in Customer's apartment or in a house belonging to Customer by right of personal ownership, with Contractor's own efforts, tools, and equipment, according to the estimate attached to this contract, observing the technical conditions in effect for the repair of dwelling premises.

2. Contractor will provide materials for the repairs according to the list attached to the contract for the amount of . . . . . . rubles, ... kopecks at state retail prices.

Contractor will be responsible for poor quality material.

Contractor's material will be paid for by Customer on the conclusion of the contract in full in the amount of . . . . . rubles, ... kopecks, or not less than 50% of the cost of the material, with a final accounting after the acceptance of the completed work in the amount . . . . . rubles . . . kopecks (cross out what does not apply).

Note. The right to pay the price of the material in part with a final accounting after the acceptance of the finished work belongs to Customer, if the price of the material amounts to not less than 10 rubles. Materials provided by Contractor and the necessary equipment shall be delivered to the place of the repairs by Contractor.

3. For the repairs indicated in the present contract, Customer will supply the following materials:

_____with a value of _____rubles_____kopecks.

The value of the materials shall be determined by an agreement of the parties.

Contractor shall be responsible for incorrect use of these materials, must present Customer an accounting of their use and must return the remainder.

4. Contractor must give timely notice to Customer of: (1) unsuitability or poor

quality of material received from Customer; (2) the fact that following customer's directions threatens the suitability and strength of the work being done.

5. Contractor must begin repair of the apartment on . . . . , 19 . . . , at . . . . . . o'clock and finish it on . . . . , 19 . . . .

If it is necessary to change the time of starting or finishing work one party must inform the other party of this not later than 48 hours beforehand. An appropriate notation shall be made in both copies of the contract of any change in time.

6. In case of violation by Contractor of the time for starting or finishing work he shall pay Customer, for each day of lateness, a penalty in the amount of 0.1% of the price of the repair (including the value of Customer's materials), and if the work is not finished by the expiration of a week from the day the order was to be completed, Contractor shall pay Customer a contractual sanction in the amount of 2% of the cost of repair (including the value of Customer's materials).

If these time-limits are broken due to Customer's fault, the latter shall bear the same liability.

Customer shall pay Contractor a penalty in the amount indicated also in case of lateness in payment of obligations for materials and labor (paragraphs 2 and 10).

7. In case of compelling circumstances Customer shall have the right at anytime before the completion of the work to withdraw from the contract, paying Contractor compensation for the part of the work completed and reimbursing him for damages caused by the recision of the contract.

8. Customer must prepare the premises for the conduct of repair work: cover furniture and the floor to prevent damage, clear away objects that would interfere with the work, make room for storage of equipment and other things of the workers.

9. Contractor shall be responsible for damage or destruction of furniture, floors, electric wiring, electric appliances, bathroom fixtures, windowglass, and other property located in the premises being repaired.

10. Customer shall pay Contractor on signing the contract the cost of repair work in the amount of . . . rubles . . . . kopecks with final accounting during the two days after the acceptance of the work done (cross out whichever does not apply).

Customer has the right to pay the price of the work by giving an advance with final accounting at the end of the work if the price of the repair work amounts to not less than 10 rubles.

11. Customer must accept the finished work on the day it is completed. Claims may be made by Customer to Contractor during one month from the day of acceptance of the work. In case of disagreement between Customer and Contractor about the quality of work done, Customer has the right to demand an expert examination. Payment for the expert examination shall be made by the side against whom the decision of the expert examination is rendered.

The obligation to organize the expert examination rests upon Contractor.

If the claims are well-founded, Contractor must at its expense eliminate the shortcomings within a one-week period.

12. With respect to deviations of Contractor from the conditions of the contract worsening the quality of the work or other shortcomings in the work, Customer, whether or not he has made claims to Contractor, has the right to bring an action in court during six months, or, if the shortcomings could not be discovered by the usual mode of inspection of the work for acceptance, during one year from the day of acceptance of the work.

Signatures: Contractor
                                             Customer

A copy of this contract has been received by: Customer . . . .
19 . . .

KOZYREV vs. SPECIALIZED REPAIR AND CONSTRUCTION ADMINISTRATION, Biulleten' Verkhovnogo Suda SSSR, 1970, No. 12, p. 5.

Kozyrev brought an action in court against a specialized repair and construction administration to recover 1312 rubles in compensation for damages caused by the fault of the plaintiff.

The plaintiff motived his demands on the basis that a service contract had been concluded between him and the defendant, according to which the defendant was obligated to carry out the necessary work for bringing a gas line into his house. In carrying out the contract, the defendant did installation work in the house, and dug a trench from it to the supposed location of the main gas line. When it found that there was no gas line there, it stopped work, leaving the trench open. Water that gathered in the trench, according to the plaintiff, undermined the foundation of the house, and with the start of heavy frosts it forced and made cracks in the front and side walls of the house. The expenses for repairing the house were 1312 rubles.

In June 1969, Kozyrev died and his wife entered the case as his legal successor. She continued to press the action.

The specialized repair and construction administration objected to the claim, stating that it was without fault in the damage to the house, but that considering the financial position of Mrs. Kozyrev, it agreed voluntarily to render her aid in the repair of the house.

The case was considered a number of times by various judicial instances.

In the last consideration of the case, the Supreme Court of the Severo-Osetinsk ASSR partially satisfied the claim in the amount of 342 rubles.

In an appeal, Mrs. Kozyrev asked that the decision of the court be reversed and that her claims be fully satisfied, stating that the damage to the home was caused entirely by the fault of the defendant.

The Judicial Division for Civil Cases of the Supreme Court of the RSFSR, having considered the case on the appeals of the plaintiff and the defendant for reversal of the decision by a decision of July 23, 1970, left the decision without change and the appeals unsatisfied on the following grounds.

As appears from the record and an act of judicial-technical expert examination of April 23, 1970, the filling of the open trench with water speeded the deformation of the foundation of the house which later led to the formation of cracks in the walls.

Considering these circumstances, the court correctly placed liability under Kozyrev's action on the contractor who had taken an unconscientious attitude toward the contract work.

The conclusion of the judicial-technical expert examination on the amount of the expenses—342 rubles—which should be made in connection with the elimination of damage to the home is not confirmed by other proofs.

G. *The Economic Law Dispute*

V.V. Laptev, "LEGAL PROBLEMS OF THE ECONOMIC REFORM," Sovetskoe Gosudarstvo i Pravo, 1967, No. 4, p. 57. (Excerpts, footnotes omitted.)

The economic reform now being conducted raises a number of legal problems, and involves different branches of the law, which as a whole must be brought into accord with the new conditions of economic activity. The present article will consider not all legal aspects of the economic reform, but only certain economic-law problems connected with the realization of the reform.

The development of economic legislation is now proceeding at stormy tempos. It is characteristic that this legislation is being developed mainly by the issuance of normative acts of the government on the critical questions of the building-up of the economy.

However the issuance of numerous normative acts on economic matters will lead to very intensive increase in the volume of economic legislation. The number of legal acts on economic matters now numbers in the tens and even hundreds of thousands. Besides unwieldiness, another shortcoming of the economic legislation is the fact that different normative acts enacted at different times are poorly coordinated with one another. All this greatly complicates economic practice. Even for the experienced lawyer it is difficult at times to figure out which normative act is in force and which is not. Particular difficulties arise from this fact in the work of enterprises which do not have the possibility to undertake an exact accounting of normative acts in force.

In the circumstances which have developed it is rather difficult to put the economic legislation in order. Up till now, we have been using a method of organization of economic legislation, by which when a new decree was enacted it was usually accompanied by an assignment to work out a list of normative acts repealed and amended in connection with its enactment. However the absence of a defined core around which the acts of economic legislation could be placed leads to the situation that such lists are compiled extremely slowly. For instance, the list of normative acts repealed and amended in connection with the adoption of the Statute on the Enterprise still has not been drawn up, although a year and a half have already passed since its enactment.

The economic legislation can be put in order only by a radical change in the methods of its codification and systematization. In this respect proposals of two types have been made in the literature.

Some authors propose to conduct the organization of economic legislation by branches of the national economy and types of economic activity. It is proposed, for instance, to enact a Construction Code, a Banking Code or a Statute on Banking Operations, and other generalizing laws or codes for branches of the national economy and types of economic activity.

Other authors propose the issuance of an Economic Code of the USSR which would embrace with its norms the regulation of all branches of the national economy and types of economic activity. It should define the basic principles of socialist economic operations and at the same time the particular features of the legal regulation of economic activity in separate branches of the economy.

The second type of codification of economic legislation is, in our opinion, more preferable, for with the adoption of an Economic Code of the USSR there will be created a basis for the codification of all economic legislation and not merely of certain of its branches. If branch economic codes were issued there would arise a multiplicity of basic laws and the need for their coordination.

Of course, the full codification of economic legislation can be conducted only when the economic reform has been realized. Then the norms of economic legislation will become more stable and can be confirmed in a generalizing law—the Economic Code of the USSR. However a beginning should be made now in the work for its preparation.

The economic law orientation resulting from the economic reform appears not only in the enhancement of the role of economic legislation, but in the development of economic law as a scholarly and instructional discipline.

Certain scholars object to economic law. The essence of these objections can be formulated briefly as follows: (1) the recognition of economic law as a branch of law destroys the unity of the regulation of civil [imushchestvennykh] legal relations; (2) it violates economic accountability and the economic independence of the enterprise which are ensured by civil legislation; (3) the legal relations of parties who are equals and organizational-authoritative relations may not be joined.

Consider the first argument. Civil legal relations, whether or not economic law is recognized as an independent branch are regulated by norms of various, generally recognized branches of law—civil, collective farm, land, administrative, financial, family and labor. Thus, there is not and cannot be uniform regulation of civil legal relations by one branch of law, because the different types of these legal relations have their peculiarities which are taken account of in the norms of the different branches of law.

The second argument. Economic accountability is usually violated by superior agencies and the relations of these agencies with the enterprise are not regulated by civil legislation. Therefore the treatment of economic accountability as a purely civil law category does not strengthen but destroys the economic independence of the enterprise and leaves them without legal protection in their relations with superior agencies. On the contrary economic law, by including the regulation of these relations too in its sphere, guarantees the economic accountability of enterprises against violations which have taken place in the past just because civil law illusions were substituted for real guarantees of economic accountability.

With respect to the third argument against economic law, it is made, in our opinion without taking account of the new conditions of economic operations, which exclude the possibility of contrasting the economically—significant legal relations of "equal" enterprises and "authoritative-organizational" relations for the direction of industry. The rejection of administrative methods in the economy is leading to a situation where the relations between enterprises and superior economic agencies are no longer based merely on authority and subordination, with mutual rights and duties developed in these relations. These relations will be built more and more on bases of economic accountability and civil legal elements will appear in them. Relations between enterprises will cease to be merely civil law; the expansion of the economic rights of the enterprises by the transfer to them of certain planning functions will lead to the appearance in these relations of planning and organizational elements too.

Thus, in both horizontal and vertical economic relations there are combined at the present civil-law and planning-organizational elements, and this shows the unity in principle of these relations and the incorrectness of separating them in legal regulation. It would be wrong now to separate, for instance, the regulation of economic contract relations and of planning relations, since the economic contract is used as an instrument of planning, and the management of the economy without it is unthinkable in current circumstances.

The unity of the management of the economy and the conduct of economic activity is the basis of the economic reform. From this must proceed also the development of economic legislation regulating all the details of the single process of socialist economic operations. The economic-law orientation of the economic measures which have been taken are determinant of the further development of economic law.

S.N. Bratus', "THE CORRELATION OF ADMINISTRATIVE AND ECONOMIC METHODS IN THE REGULATION OF ECONOMIC RELATIONS," Sovetskoe Gosudarsvo i Pravo, 1966, No. 3, p. 24 (Excerpt, footnotes omitted.)

In the literature attempts are being made again and again to justify the existence in the USSR of an independent branch of Soviet law—economic law. Economic law is defined by its partisans as "the totality of legal norms defining the manner of administration and realization of economic activity and the regulation of economic relations between socialist enterprises, organizations and their structural links, with the use of the most rational scientifically-grounded methods of legal regulation."

This idea is not new and the supporting arguments are not new. They have been discussed many times in legal literature. However, since the partisans of economic law continue to insist upon the correctness of their views and proposal it is necessary once more to consider the conclusions they have drawn, taking into consideration the new situation determining the normative regulation of relations for the administration of the socialist economy.

The Fundamental Principles of Civil Legislation of the USSR and the Union Republics proceeds from the principle of the unity of the regulation of socialist property regulations independent of the nature of their participants. This unity is determined by the unity of the socialist economy, its planned character, by the interconnection of all the elements of Soviet economic circulation, the combination of the interests of society and of the individual. Socialist production develops for the purposes of satisfying the needs of society as a whole and of its members. It is subordinated to the interests of man both when consumer goods are being produced and when means of production are being produced. The latter, of course, are also goods. No one at the present time doubts the proposition of the unity of Soviet economic circulation. Therefore economic relations cannot be limited to relations arising only between socialist organizations. There exist different types of branches of the national economy serving citizens (retail trade, public services, housing, transportation, service trades, etc.)

Also wrong, both theoretically and practically is the proposal of the partisans of economic law to combine civil legal relations whose participants are socialist organizations as subjects with equal rights (on the basis of economic contracts, etc.) with relations arising from the activity of agencies for management of the economy. The partisans of economic law insist upon such a combination in proposing the issuance of an Economic Code of the USSR. As a basis for this position they advance the proposition of the existence of a single economic legal relation in which "are applied depending upon the circumstances different methods of legal regulation." However the authors are proceeding from the incorrect assumption of the possibility of combining different types of social relations (civil, based upon equality of the parties; and authoritative-organizational) as one subject of regulation. On the other hand, the proposal to limit civil legislation solely to the sphere of civil relations involving the participation of citizens is based upon the contrapositioning of this sphere of relations to civil relations arising between socialist organizations, i.e. social relations of essentially the same type are separated. But this separation of like and joining of different relations contradicts the natural principles of legal regulation of these relations. But these national principles only reflect the nature of the social relations themselves which are regulated by the rules of law. Every branch of law regulates not different types but one type of social relations.

CHAPTER XV

The Cooperatives as Supplementary Agencies

Cooperatives play a critical role in agricultural production and an increasing role in meeting many consumers' needs for housing. Still, the days of production cooperatives are numbered, for they are but a compromise with the past. The majority of communists in Lenin's time wanted to abolish cooperatives and go over to state production and state distribution, but Lenin restrained them. He anticipated a peasants' strike if they were driven too fast into land factories, and he urged preservation even of the consumers' cooperatives to meet popular demand in satisfaction of daily needs until such time as the state could fill the gap. Only the credit cooperatives looked dangerous to Lenin, and he abolished them as they had been inherited from the Empire by decree of 1918.[1] Banks were the center of the capitalist system in Lenin's analysis, and he brooked no interference with the state monopoly of credit agencies.

Stalin continued Lenin's policies, calling the cooperatives in 1926 "transmission belts" between the communist party and the masses.[2] He saw in them a school for communism, in that through association the peasants and their close cousins, the artisans and handicraftsmen of the villages, might learn to work together rather than individually. He expected that by demonstration the work in association would prove to be more productive than individual enterprise, but if the demonstration did not prove sufficiently attractive, he was prepared to use forceful persuasion. This led to the forced collectivization begun in 1929[3] and reached its climax with an incipient peasant strike so threatening that Stalin called for a reversal in a speech that came to be known as the speech on "Dizzy with Success"[4] in which he blamed his subordinates for using the pressure he had ordered and demanded that they permit the peasants to reach their own conclusion as to the desirability of association.

---

[1] December 2, 1918 [1918] I Sob. Uzak. RSFSR, No. 90, item 912
[2] J.V. Stalin, I Leninism (Eng. trans., 1934) 261 at 276
[3] Well to do peasants incurred such disfavor that they were ordered liquidated "as a class", Decree of February 2, 1930, [1930] I Sob. Zak. SSSR, No. 9, item 105.
[4] J.V. Stalin, 2 Leninism (Eng. trans. Moscow, 1933) 215.

Through less obvious but still effective persuasion in the form of special taxes placed on peasants and artisans who were not members of cooperatives as has been indicated in Chapter 11, peasants were driven into the cooperatives of various kinds, and the way was prepared for eventual absorption of the cooperatives within the state production system. The first step in this direction was taken in 1935 when the consumers' cooperatives in the various cities were abolished, and their assets, including their retail and wholesale outlets and staffs transferred to the Ministry of Internal Trade for incorporation into the state system of distribution.[5]

The progression to state absorption of the cooperatives might have been faster had the second world war not intervened. Stalin ended the war with a crisis on his hands. Production and distribution were almost nonexistent for consumers' goods. He turned again to the cooperatives, and called for their strengthening and expansion, but not to the point that they would reappear in the cities.[6] They were primarily for peasants and to help the countryside. Only in the autumn of 1952 as he wrote his last theses for the communist party did Stalin again reveal his mind. He called for development of the collective farm system of property ownership into a system of ownership by the whole people, and Khrushchev made this precise by transforming collective farms into state farms at an ever increasing rate, and even altering the basic system of payment in the collective farms to permit guaranteed money payments as a step in preparation of the peasants for transition to a wage system.

While the days of the production cooperatives are numbered, as emphasized again in late 1960[7] when artisans' cooperatives making consumers' goods were transferred to locally administered state industry, they remain a significant form of organization, especially in agriculture and in urban housing. Evidence of this has already been given in discussion of the use of the land. In this chapter the focus is on the organization of the cooperatives and the special relations that exist between members because of this form.

Cooperatives were organized in the 1920's on the pattern inherited from the cooperative movement of Europe that had extended into the Russian Empire. It is a pattern familiar to any westerner, the association of individuals who join by contributing capital in the form of shares, constitute themselves as a general meeting, adopt a set of bylaws or charter, elect an administrative body including a chairman, and an auditing commission to report directly to the general meeting so as to provide a check on the honesty and judgment of the elected administrators, and ultimately enjoy the benefits cooperation has created in the form of profits, which may be paid out to members or kept in the business, or used to provide the basis for discounts on future purchases.

---

[5]September 9, 1935, [1935] I Sob. Zak. SSSR, No. 52, item 427.
[6]November 9, 1946. Text not printed in official gazette, but in 3 Direktivy KPSS i Sovetskogo Pravitel'stva po Khoziaistvennym Voprosam (Moscow, 1957) 109.
[7]The decree has not been published, but it has been mentioned. See F. Uriupin, "Improve Control of Service Enterprises and Taxation of Handicraftsmen," Finansy SSSR, No. 10, October, 1960, pp. 14-18.

The cooperatives of the U.S.S.R. started on the familiar basis, but they soon diverged. While they were in theory to choose their own managers, their success was important not only to them but to the state which permitted them to exist for one single reason, namely to produce and distribute. If they failed in these operations, the state was interested, and it showed this interest through the introduction of candidates for managerial positions to the general meetings. As the communist party's strength in the countryside increased, an introduction was enough to assure election, and in many cases a promise of greater efficiency under the proposed candidate's expert hand had appeal. As time has passed the chairmen of collective farms have become universally the candidates of the communist party, and most frequently outsiders trained for the job. Voluntarism in the selection of management has almost passed away.

The general meeting has changed also in character, for with the amalgamation of farms, to which reference has been made in discussing the use of the land, many villages have been united in a single farm. Over a thousand families are represented, and the general meeting can have no meaning with such numbers. This has been recognized in creation in some farms of a council of deputies elected by the various villages comprising the farm.

A key feature distinguishing cooperatives in the U.S.S.R. from those of Western Europe is the limited voluntarism in what they shall do. In the west, the cooperators do what they please, but in the U.S.S.R. their production is fitted into the national economic plan. The issue has been whether the entire production should be so planned, and under Stalin that issue was being resolved in the affirmative. The collective farms were given precise orders on what to plant, and the consumers' cooperatives were fitted into the national scene by the State Planning Commission and their segment clearly defined for them through their own hierarchy headed by the Central Union of Consumers' Cooperative Societies, known as the Tsentrosoiuz.

On Stalin's death the detailed direction from headquarters was reduced as it was for industry when the regional economic councils were created in 1957 to permit exercise of initiative at lower levels.

Khrushchev's successors have made a number of important changes in policy affecting the agricultural cooperatives. Power was recentralized in the all-Union Ministry of Agriculture, and the role of the district party officials in agricultural administration was correspondingly reduced. Substantial reductions were made in farm taxes, and past farm debts were forgiven. Assurances were given that obligations to sell farm products to the state under compulsory contracts would remain stable for five years, giving farms which increased their output a guarantee of obtaining the higher free market prices. The Fundamental Principles of Land Legislation provided for a strengthening of collective farm land rights. Party leader Brezhnev promised that the collective farms would not soon be abolished and rescinded the strict limitations imposed by Khrushchev on the size of private farm plots. The farms were given a new model charter to strengthen their legal position. However events seemed to take a different turn in the summer of 1976 when the Party called for a reorganization of all Soviet farming on a large scale industrial basis.[8]

During the 1960's and 1970's the housing cooperative became an increasingly important form for the allocation and management of urban housing. It seemed to offer a middle road between the bureaucratic and economic problems of public housing and the ideological difficulties of expanding private housing.

The documents of this chapter indicate the legal structure of cooperatives and the balancing of issues between preservation of members' oportunities to influence decision making on the one hand, and the centrally directed discipline required in a planned economy on the other. This has proved and continues to be the dynamic of the cooperatives and their law.

A. *The Collective Farm and Its Members*

MODEL CHARTER OF THE COLLECTIVE FARM, Izvestia, Nov. 28, 1969, p. 1.

The collective farm system is an inalienable part of Soviet socialist society; this is the way planned by V.I. Lenin, proved by history, and the way that has answered to the peculiarities and interests of the peasantry for its gradual transition to communism.

Social ownership of the means of production, the advantages of largescale collective farming, the daily care and assistance of the party and the state has made possible the achievement of tremendous socio-economic transformations in the countryside. Thanks to the self-sacrificing labor of the collective farm peasantry, to the efforts of the working class, of all the soviet people, the collective farms have been transformed into large-scale mechanized agricultural enterprises, their social wealth has increased immeasurably, the standard of living of collective farmers has risen, the differences between town and countryside are being overcome.

The collective farm as the social form of socialist farming is fully satisfactory for the tasks of further development of productive forces in the countryside; ensures the administration of production by the collective farm masses themselves on the basis of collective farm democracy, allows the correct combination of the personal interests of the collective farms with the interests of society, of all the people. The collective farm is a school of communism for the peasantry.

Under the guidance of the Communist Party, the collective farm peasantry in close and inviolable union with the working class, participates actively in the building of communism in our country.

★ ★ ★

4. A member of the collective farm has the right:

---

[8]The Central Committee resolution was published on June 2, 1976. See Pravda and Izvestiia, pp. 1-2. Eng. trans. in Current Digest of the Soviet Press XXVII, No. 22 (June 30, 1976) p. 6.

to receive work in the social farming operation of the collective farm with guaranteed payment in accordance with the quantity and quality of labor he invests;

to participate in the administration of collective farm affairs, to elect and be elected to agencies of its administration; to introduce proposals for improvement of the activity of the collective farm, for elimination of shortcomings in the work of the administration and of officials;

to receive help from the collective farm in raising his productive qualifications and the obtaining of a specialty;

to use an auxiliary land plot for the conduct, on it, of auxiliary farming, for the construction of a dwelling house and farm buildings, and also to use collective farm pastures, social draft animals and transportation for personal needs by the procedure established in the collective farm;

to social security, every-day and cultural services and assistance of the collective farm in the construction and repair of his dwelling house and the supply of fuel.

PROCURATOR'S PROTEST AGAINST AN ILLEGAL DECISION OF THE "LENIN'S PRECEPTS" COLLECTIVE FARM. Chelovek i zakon, 1972, No. 10, p. 62.

The administration of the "Lenin's Precepts" Collective Farm of Rybin District of Iaroslavl Region decided to introduce an amendment into the collective farm charter. The amendment provided that collective farmers' children reaching the age of 16 would automatically be included in the list of members of the collective farm. However Article 3 of the Model Statute of the Collective Farm provides that citizens may be members of the collective farm if they have reached the age of 16 and have expressed the desire to participate with their labor in the social farming of the collective farm. Reception into collective farm membership is conducted by the general meeting of collective farmers on presentation by the collective farm administration and in the presence of the person who made the request.

The administration also violated Article 46 of the Model Charter, according to which the introduction of changes and additions to a previously adopted collective farm charter is in the exclusive competence of the general meeting of collective farmers.

The illegal decision was rescinded on protest of the procurator.

PROCURATOR'S PROTEST AGAINST AN ILLEGAL DECISION OF THE "ZHDANOV" COLLECTIVE FARM. Radians'ke pravo, 1968, No. 7, p. 99.

The administration of the Zhdanov Collective Farm of Mazhgir District of Zacarpathian Region adopted a decision to accept Citizen K. into membership in the collective farm on the condition that his wife would have to work on the collective farm as a milkmaid.

The district procurator entered a protest, raising the question of quashing this decision of the collective farm administration as illegal. According to Article 3 of the

Model Charter of the Collective Farm, reception into membership in the collective farm is conducted not by the administrations but by the general meeting on presentation of the administration. Moreover the indication in the decision to the effect that Citizen K. would be accepted in the collective farm only on the condition that his wife would work as a milkmaid was illegal.

The protest was satisfied and the decision of the administration was quashed. At the general meeting, Citizen K. was admitted to the collective farm without any conditions.

PROCURATOR'S PROTEST AGAINST AN ILLEGAL DECISION OF THE "UL'IANOV" COLLECTIVE FARM. Radians'ke pravo, 1968, No. 7, p. 99.

The administration of the Ul'ianov Collective Farm of Luben District of Poltava Region adopted a decision on the reduction of the size of the auxiliary plots of collective farmers T. and D. because certain members of their families did not take part in the collective farm production.

According to the decree of the Central Committee of the Ukrainian Communist Party and the Council of Ministers of the Ukrainian SSR of November 2, 1963, "On the Removal of Unwarranted Restrictions on the Individual Subsidiary Farming of Collective Farmers, Workers, and Employees," the auxiliary plot of a collective farm household may be reduced in size only by decision of the general meeting of collective farmers (or meeting of delegates) approved by the district executive committee.

Therefore the decision of the administration is illegal and was rescinded on protest of the procurator.

PROCURATOR'S PROTEST AGAINST AN ILLEGAL EXPULSION FROM A COLLECTIVE FARM. Radians'ke pravo, 1966, No. 9, p. 102.

A meeting of delegates of the Kirov Collective Farm of Veseliv County of Zaporiz'e Province adopted a decision to expel the milkmaid Isaeva from the collective farm for failure to appear for work for three days. Her husband Isaev was also expelled from the collective farm for his wife's violation of labor discipline.

The decision is a gross violation of the law. The Decree of the Central Committee of the All-Union Communist Party (Bolsheviks) and the Council of People's Commissars of the U.S.S.R. of April 19, 1938, "On Forbidding the Expulsion of Collective Farmers from Collective Farms" provides that expulsion from a collective farm may be applied as an extreme measure only after violations had already been subjected to other sanctions and these have failed to give the desired results. The Isaevs had worked conscientiously in the collective farm and had not been subjected to any sanctions. Isaeva had failed to appear for work because the collective farm childrens' nursery was not working and there was no one to watch her two small children. On protest of the procurator, the decision of the meeting was cancelled.

HUMENCHUK v. SHEVCHENKO COLLECTIVE FARM. Radians'ke pravo, 1968, No. 7, p. 95.

V. Humenchuk brought an action against the Shevchencko Collective Farm to recover 600 rubles. He stated that from November 1963 through January 1965 he worked as chief agronomist of the collective farm and for good results in crop yield and fulfillment of the agricultural production and financial plan for the collective farm he was allotted a bonus payment in the amount of 5 months salary, which constituted 600 rubles, but which was not paid to him as the result of illegal actions of the chairman of the collective farm.

Humenchuk was not a member of the collective farm, but worked as chief agronomist under the labor contract. In accordance with Paragraph 12 of the Decree of the Plenum of the Supreme Court of the U.S.S.R. of March 26, 1960, "On Judicial Practice in Collective Farm Civil Cases," the courts do not have jurisdiction over cases connected with the establishment by the collective farm of norms of production, valuation of work in labordays or money, the allocation of the amount of products and money that are distributed by labor-days for basic and bonus wages. In the present case, it was not a matter of establishment of payment of bonus wages for a collective farmer, but of a bonus payment to a person who worked under a labor contract.

Labor contracts are subject to direct judicial consideration if at the given enterprise, establishment, or organization it is not possible to organize a commission on labor disputes.

Article 5 of the Statute on the Procedure for Consideration of Labor Disputes does not provide for the organization of labor disputes commissions at collective farms. Moreover, the Temporary Statute on the Trade Union Committee of the Collective Farm likewise does not provide for consideration by this committee of labor disputes.

On this basis, labor disputes of individuals working under labor contracts on collective farms are subject to direct consideration in the court despite the fact that they have not been before the trade union committee on the collective farm.

[The case was remanded to the People's Court for a hearing on the merits.]

CASE OF DONEV, IOVCHEV, SHPAKOV, V. GREKOV AND I. GREKOV, Sotsialisticheskaia zakonnost', 1965, No. 2, p. 91.

The Odessa Provinical Court, applying Art. 206, pt. 2 of the Criminal Code of the Ukrainian S.S.R. (hooliganism) sentenced Donev to three years and six months of deprivation of freedom, Iovchev to two years and six months, Shpakov and V. Grekov to two years and I. Grekov to one year of deprivation of freedom. The Judicial Division for criminal Cases of the Supreme Court of the Ukrainian SSR altered the judgment of the regional court. The actions of the convicted Iovchev, Shpakov, V. Grekov and I. Grekov were classified under Art. 206 pt. 1 of the Criminal Code of the Ukrainian S.S.R. with a reduction in the term of punishment of Iovchev to one year of deprivation of freedom, of Shrapkov and V. Grekov to ten months each, of I. Grekov to one year of corrective tasks with a 20 percent retention of wages, of Donev to one year and six months deprivation of freedom. In the remaining part the judgment of the Odessa Regional Court was left unaltered.

Donev, Iovchev, Shpakov, V. Grekov and I. Grekov, members of the Eighth of March Collective Farm called at a meeting for special early elections of the administration of the collective farm, stating that the chairman was abusing his official position and dissipating social property. This demand was supported by other collective farmers. However the presidium of the meeting declined the proposal. Then Donev, Iovchev and the other persons convicted in the case began to shout, whistle and clap their hands. The meeting was postponed until the following day.

The Deputy Procurator General of the U.S.S.R. not finding the elements of a crime in the actions of the convicted persons protested the judgment and decision of the court on the grounds that the noise and shouts which accompanied the meeting were an expression of the indignation of the collective farmers at the improper actions of certain leaders of the collective farm and not a manifestation of hooliganism on the part of those convicted. In addition, as appears from the materials of the case, after the meeting a thorough audit was conducted at the collective farm. The audit revealed gross violations of the charter of the agricultural artel and facts of plundering of social property for which the chairman of the collective farm was removed from work and the bookkeeper was brought to criminal liability.

Agreeing with the protest of the Deputy Procurator General of the U.S.S.R., the Plenum of the Supreme Court of the Ukrainian U.S.S.R. vacated the judgment of the Odessa Provincial Court and the decision of the Judicial Division for Criminal Cases of the Supreme Court of the Ukrainian U.S.S.R. and terminated the case with respect to Donev, Iovchev, Shpakov, V. Grekov and I. Grekov because of the absence in their actions of the elements of a crime.

B. Plan and Contract on the Collective Farm

STATUTE ON THE PROCEDURE FOR THE CONCLUSION AND FULFILLMENT OF CONTRACTS FOR FUTURE DELIVERY OF AGRICULTURAL PRODUCTS Enacted by order of the State Committee on Procurement of the Council of Ministers of the U.S.S.R. of Jan. 6, 1966, No. 1. Zakonodatel'stvo o proizvodstve, zagotovkakh i zakupkakh sel'khozproduktov (Moscow, 1967), p. 117. (Excerpts.)

3. State procurement of agricultural products shall be conducted on the basis of contracts for future delivery which shall be concluded by procurement agencies and farming organizations in accordance with plans for state procurement of agricultural products transmitted to the farming organizations.

The farming organizations shall sell above-plan surpluses of agricultural produce needed by the state on a voluntary basis without the transmission to them of supplementary tasks.

Procurement of agricultural produce from farming organizations which do not have a procurement plan shall also be conducted on the basis of contracts for future delivery in the established manner. . . .

4. Nonfulfillment of obligations under contracts for future delivery is a gross violation of state discipline and shall entail liability of the guilty officials in the established manner.

The monetary liability of farming organizations and procurement agencies shall be determined by the contracts for future sale of agricultural produce and by the present Statute.

5. Superior agricultural and procurement agencies exercise control over the timely and correct conclusion of contracts for future delivery of agricultural products by farming operations and procurement agencies, and take appropriate measures for ensuring the carrying out of the contracts which have been concluded.

CASE OF MYL'NIKOV AND POPOVCHENKO, Sbornik postanovlenii Plenuma, Prezidiuma i opredelenii Sudebnoi kollegii po ugolovnym delam Verkhovnogo Suda RSFSR 1961-1963 gg. (Moscow, 1964), p. 316.

By judgment of the Chitinsk Provincial Court, Myl'nikov was convicted under Article 152-1 of the Criminal Code of the R.S.F.S.R. and Popovchenko was acquitted under the same article.

The Judicial Division for Criminal Cases of the Supreme Court of the R.S.F.S.R. considered the case on cassational appeal of the convicted person and on the cassational protest of the regional procurator for the vacation of the judgment of acquittal with respect to Popovchenko and established the following:

Myl'nikov was found guilty of issuing fictitious invoices for the receipt of wool from state and collective farms by agreement with the chairman of certain collective farms while he was working as director of a procurement office of the Olovianin district consumers' union.

Thus, under an agreement with the convicted Stepnyi he issued fictitious invoices for the receipt of 450 centners of wool and by agreement with the convicted Kalinin for 170 centners.

Myl'nikov included the fictitious invoices in his account on the fulfillment of the plan for the procurement of wool for the first half of 1962.

In all he issued fictitious documents for 1694 centners of wood, supposedly received from seven collective and state farms. In accordance with the fictitous receipts for the supposedly delivered wool Myl'nikov illegally transferred 58,600 to the account of the Il'ich collective farm.

In addition, in June 1962 he issued a fictitious delivery order for the sale of 12,900 eggs to the state farm "Zabaikal'skii," which later were formulated by fictitious documents as having been delivered to the Bokumskii workers' cooperative.

These fictitious documents were used by the procurement office in its report on fulfillment of the plan.

Popovchenko was presented with the accusation that he, working as deputy director of the procurement office of the Olovianin district consumers' union, on July 1, 1962, issued a back-dated fictitious receipt for the receipt from the state farm "Uliatuiskii" of 2826 kilograms of wool. Later, together with Myl'nikov he included this receipt in the report on the fulfillment by the procurement office of the semiannual plan for the procurement of wool.

In the judicial session Myl'nikov fully admitted his guilt and explained that he, indeed, wrote out the fictitious documents for the supposed procurement of wool and eggs in order to be one of the frontrunners in the procurement of agricultural products.

Popovchenko did not admit that he was guilty of the accusation presented to him.

The Judicial Division verified the materials of the case, considered the arguments of the cassational appeal and the cassational protest, and found the judgment with respect to Myl'nikov is well founded, but that with respect to Popovchenko should be vacated on the following grounds:

The court without sufficient grounds rendered a judgment of acquittal with respect to Popovchenko.

Both in the preliminary investigation and in the judicial session Popovchenko did not deny that he issued a back-dated receipt on July 1, 1962, but that he did not receive wool from the Uliatuiskii state farm in the amount of 2836 kilograms.

From the report of an audit conducted by a representative of the County executive committee it appears that no delivery of wool was made by the Uliatuiskii state farm at that time.

This circumstance was also confirmed in court by Myl'nikov who stated that the wool was not in the warehouse and the summary on July 1, 1962 did not correspond to reality. According to the testimony of witnesses, the workers Fillipov and Mikhenin of the Uliatuiskii state farm, no wool was delivered to the procurement office either in June or in July. It was only delivered in August 1962.

Taking into consideration the circumstance that the fictitious receipt issued by Popovchenko for the procurement of wool was included in the report on the fulfillment of the semi-annual plan, the court unjustifiably evaluated Popovchenko's actions as dereliction of duty. For these actions he must bear criminal liability in accordance with Art. 152-1 of the Criminal Code of the R.S.F.S.R. The bringing of Popovchenko to party responsibility cannot serve as a basis for the rendering of a judgment of acquittal with respect to him.

On the basis of the aforesaid, the Judicial Division for Criminal Cases of the Supreme Court of the R.S.F.S.R. left the sentence of the Provincial court with respect to Myl'nikov without change, but vacated the judgment of acquittal with respect to Popovchenko and remanded his case for new consideration in the same court with different judges.

C. *The Farm of the Future*

DECREE OF THE CENTRAL COMMITTEE OF THE COMMUNIST PARTY OF THE CPSU ON THE FURTHER DEVELOPMENT OF SPECIALIZATION AND CONCENTRATION OF AGRICULTURAL PRODUCTION ON THE BASE OF INTER-FARM COOPERATION AND AGRO-INDUSTRIAL INTEGRATION. Izvestia, June 2, 1976, p. 1.

3. The Central Committee of the CPSU notes that in spite of the positive results achieved in agriculture in recent years, its level, economic indicators and rates of growth of production of the most important products still do not satisfy our growing needs and do not correspond to the actual possibilities. So that this branch could move to the advanced frontiers opened by modern science and technology, the task of its itensification and improvement of its efficiency is moved to the forefront. One of the main ways of performing this task is specialization and concentration of agricultural production, its transfer to a modern industrial basis. Here great possibilities exist.

D. *Housing Construction Cooperatives*

PODZEMEL'NIKOVA vs. ROMASHEVSKII, Biulleten' Verkhovnogo Suda RSFSR, 1973, No. 3, p. 6.

Podzemel'nikova, in June 1968, was accepted into membership in a housing construction cooperative and by decision of its general meeting of March 11, 1969, she with her family was allotted a three-room apartment. In accordance with Paragraph 37 of the Model Charter of the Housing Construction Cooperative, the decision on the allocation of apartments in the cooperative's building was submitted to the executive committee of the local soviet for approval.

The amount of payments was determined taking into account the assignment of a three-room apartment to Podzemel'nikova.

In July 1972, the building was ready for occupancy, but the executive committee did not give Podzemel'nikova an occupancy permit for the three-room apartment. For this apartment, the occupancy permit was issued to the Romashevskiis, who, by decision of the general meeting of members of the housing construction cooperative had been allotted a two-room apartment.

Considering her right as a shareholder to have been violated, Podzemel'nikova brought an action to have the three-room apartment given to her and her family, to have the occupancy permit issued to Romashevskii held void, and to have them evicted from the apartment in dispute.

[A decision in Podzemel'nikova's favor was affirmed on the following grounds:]

In accordance with Paragraph 29 of the Model Charter of the Housing Construction Cooperative, the general meeting of the members of the cooperative has the right to allocate living quarters. Such a decision of the general meeting of the members took place on March 11, 1969. It was submitted for approval to the executive committee of the local soviet of working people's deputies, was not abrogated by anyone, no other meeting on the question of distribution of living quarters was held.

The decision of the general meeting of June 16, 1972, upon which the Romashevskii's rely in their appeal, did not decide the question on the transfer of apartments, since it "gave all functions concerning transfers of apartments to the executive committee of the district soviet."

Since the allocation of living space among members of the cooperative can only be conducted by the general meeting, it may not give that right to anyone else.

The apartment in dispute was given to Podzemel'nikova's family.

Since the occupancy permits for the living quarters in the cooperative's building were issued by the executive committee of the local soviet not in accordance with the decision of the general meeting of the members of the cooperative, the court properly found the permits void. This decision of the court is in accordance with the Model Charter of the Housing Construction Cooperative and also Paragraph 1 of the decree of the Plenum of the Supreme Soviet of the USSR of February 25, 1967, "On Certain Questions of the Application of Legislation in Judicial Consideration of Cases on Disputes between Citizens and Housing Construction Cooperatives" and Paragraph 17 of the Decree of the Plenum of the Supreme Court of the RSFSR of January 28, 1970 on the fulfillment by courts of the RSFSR of the aforementioned decree.

Taking into consideration all of the circumstances of the case, the court recognized the right to the three-room apartment to be Podzemel'nikova's and not the Romashevskiis'. The latter have the right to occupy the two-room apartment assigned to them by the established procedure.

The Romashevskiis' arguments, contained in their appeal, in respect of the fact that their family in numbers is larger than the Podzemel'nikova family, cannot serve as a basis for reversal of the decision of the court, since distribution of living quarters in a building of a housing construction cooperative is left exclusively to the general meeting of members of the housing construction cooperative.

CASE OF ZUBKOVA, Biulleten' Verkhovnogo Suda RSFSR, 1973, No. 2, p. 4.

By decision of a general meeting of the shareholders, Zubkova, who had been accepted into membership in a housing construction cooperative, was given an apartment to use. The executive committee of the district soviet of working people's deputies refused to issue her a permit for the right to occupy the apartment. Zubkova brought an action in court over the assignment of the use of the living space.

[Decisions of the lower courts against Zubkova were reversed on the following grounds:]

In dismissing proceedings in the case for want of jurisdiction, the People's Court held that Zubkova had brought an action for the assignment of an apartment whose allocation does not fall within the competence of judicial bodies. As a basis for this opinion, the court cited the explanation of the Plenum of the Supreme Court of the

RSFSR contained in Decree No. 51 of January 28, 1970.

However, this conclusion is incorrect, for the court reached it without having clarified the basis of the action. In Paragraph 4 of the Decree of the Plenum of the Supreme Court of the RSFSR, it is stated that courts do not have jurisdiction over cases of actions by members of the cooperative against the cooperative for the allocation of an apartment or summer house, since questions of distribution of quarters are decided by the general meeting of members of the cooperative. In the present case, the apartment was allocated to Zubkova by decision of the general meeting of the cooperative, but the executive committee of the district soviet of working people's deputies has not given her a permit for the right of occupancy of the apartment, without having abrogated the decision of the general meeting on accepting her into membership in the cooperative. The court did not take into account that in this case, in accordance with Paragraph 17 of the above-mentioned decree of the Plenum, the dispute is subject to jurisdiction of the court.

The Presidium of the Kursk Regional Court agreed in substance with the arguments in the protest, but dismissed it only because before the day it considered the case, the executive committee of the district soviet of working people's deputies abrogated the decision of the general meeting of shareholders to admit the plaintiff to membership in the cooperative. The decree of the presidium of the regional court is not in accordance with the law.

According to Articles 327 and 331 of the Code of Civil Procedure of the RSFSR, in considering a case by way of supervision, the court verifies the legality and basis of the decision, determination, or decree on existing and supplementarily supplied materials. However it does not have the right to establish, nor to consider proved, circumstances which were not established in the decision, determination or decree.

In violation of these rules, the Presidium of the Kursk Regional Court, in dismissing the protest, took into consideration a circumstance which occurred after the court of first instance had made its decision.

NAUMOVA vs. ZAGVOZDKINA, Biulleten' Verkhovnogo Suda RSFSR, 1971, No. 6, p. 5.

Naumova with her family occupied a two-room apartment with floorspace of 28.1 square meters in a building of the Progress Housing Construction Cooperative in Kazan. Zagvozdkina was the lessee of a three-room apartment with floorspace of 38.4 square meters in a building of the local soviet in Sokol'niki in Tula Region.

In August 1970, the parties made an exchange. However in September 1970, Naumova returned to Kazan and brought an action in court against Zagvozdkina to have the contract of exchange found void. Naumova based her claims on the argument that the exchange was conducted in violation of the law: Zagvozdkina in occupying the cooperative apartment did not contribute the cost of a share, and the plaintiff's share was not returned to her, although in joining the Progress Housing Construction Cooperative she had paid 2187 rubles.

[A decision for the plaintiff was affirmed on the following grounds:]

According to Paragraph 19(d) of the Model Charter of the Housing Construction Cooperative, a member of the cooperative has the right, with the permission of the executive committee of the local Soviet of working people's deputies, to conduct an exchange of the living quarters he occupies and other living space, including space in a building of a local soviet. However, in doing this the rules established by Paragraph 23 of the Charter must be followed: the newly admitted member of the cooperative must pay the book cost of the apartment received by contributing the corresponding share, and this share is returned to the departing member of the cooperative.

E. Other Types of Cooperatives

MAKAROVA vs. E. MAKAROVA, Biulleten' Vekhovnogo Suda SSSR, 1969, No. 1, p. 4.

Makarova and her sister E. Makarova were members of a gardening association. The association of gardeners allotted plots of land to them for their use. On one of these plots a gardening cottage was built. In connection with the fact that a dispute arose between the parties on the ownership and right of use of this cottage, Makarova brought corresponding action in the People's Court.

[The refusal of the People's Court to hear the case on the merits was reversed on the following grounds:]

The decision of the People's Court to refuse to accept the suit was motivated by the argument that the cottage built on the garden plot was the property of the association and therefore the question of the right of use of this structure was to be decided by the collective of the association.

This conclusion cannot be considered to be correct. The Model Charter of the Gardening Association does not provide for ownership by the association of gardening structures if they are built by members of the association of gardeners on plots of land allotted to them.

In accordance with Art. 17 of the Charter, a person leaving membership of the association is to be compensated by the new member of the association for the cost of the structures located on the plot.

Thus, disputes over the ownership of structures, decisions on the way they are to be used, and on eviction from them are civil law disputes and are subject to being decided in court on general bases. (Article 6 of the Civil Code of the RSFSR and Articles 3 and 25 of the Civil Procedure Code of the RSFSR).

There is no nonjudicial procedure established for the decision of these disputes.

CHIZHONOK vs. DENISENKO, Biulleten' Verkhovnogo Suda RSFSR, 1971, No. 7, p. 15.

The Chizhonoks brought an action against N. I. Denisenko to have themselves recognized as the owners of a gardening shed located on a plot of land allocated for the use of N. I. Denisenko in the gardening association of the Lengiprotrans Institute in the village of Novaia Ropsha of Lomonosov District. They claimed that the cultivation of the plot and the construction of the shed were conducted with the permission of the administration of the association and of N. I. Denisenko, but that the defendant began in 1969 to obstruct them in the use of the plot of land and the shed although the shed was entirely constructed with their labor and funds.

[A decision of the People's Court in favor of the plaintiff was overruled on review by way of supervision on the following grounds:]

In satisfying the demands of the complaint, the court followed the rules of the Civil Code which have no relation to the dispute.

Since the dispute is over a gardening shed, the court should have followed the Model Charter of the Gardening Cooperative of Workers and Employees, approved by decree of the Council of Ministers of the RSFSR of March 18, 1966.

According to Artricle 12 of the Charter, plots of land in a gardening association are allotted to workers and employees who are members of the association.

A member of the gardening association has the right to erect, on the plot allotted to him, structures which are necessary for his use of the garden.

Therefore, the right of ownership to a shed built on a plot of land belongs only to a person who is the member of the gardening association.

The plaintiffs are not and have not been members of the gardening association. Therefore their demands for recognition that they have rights of ownership to the shed erected on the plot of land are contrary to the law.

The decision of the administration of the gardening association concerning their right to use and cultivate the gardening plot allotted to the defendant is illegal and does not create a right of ownership to the shed for them.

If the plaintiffs consider that they have incurred expenses for the construction of the shed erected on the plot of land of the defendant, then they have the right to demand compensation for the expenses incurred by them.

In the present instance, as is apparent from the file of the case, Zagvozdkina, upon her admission to membership in the Progress Housing Construction Cooperative and occupancy of the cooperative apartment belonging to Naumova, did not pay in a share, and the latter did not receive her share. Accordingly, the exchange of apartments was conducted in violation of the charter. Therefore, the court, under Article 48 of the Civil Code of the RSFSR, properly entered the decision to recognize the contract of exchange as void and put the parties in their initial position. Zagvozdkina did not deny the circumstances that she did not pay her share and has refused to pay it.

The arguments of the appeal to the effect that Paragraphs 19, 22, and 28 of the Model Charter of the Housing Construction Cooperative do not exclude the possibility of occupancy of a cooperative apartment on an exchange without the payment of share contributions, if an agreement on this has been reached between the parties, are groundless, contradict the content and meaning of the above-mentioned paragraphs of the Charter, and lead to the unjust enrichment of one of the parties. Moreover, Naumova affirmed in court that she did not know of her right to receive her share in exchanging the cooperative apartment for living space located in a building of a local soviet, and in making out the departure documents was led into misapprehension by the chairman and bookkeeper of the housing construction cooperative.

NURGALEEV vs. NURGALEEVA, Biulleten' Verkhovnogo Suda RSFSR, 1971, No. 4, p. 10.

The Nurgaleevs had been married since 1963. While living together they obtained a cooperative apartment consisting of two rooms with areas of 11.6 and 19.1 square meters.

The People's Court of the Soviet District of the city of Ufa dissolved the marriage between them and divided their property including the share and the apartment, recognizing Nurgaleev as having the right to part of the share in the amount of 602 rubles and 60 kopecks and allotted the apartment with the area of 11.6 square meters to him; and to Nurgaleeva, the right to a share in the amount of 1007 rubles and 40 kopecks and the room measuring 19.1 square meters.

The decision of the court was not appealed by way of cassation.

The Presidium of the Supreme Court of the Bashkir ASSR overruled the decision of the People's Court in the part allocating the room measuring 11.6 square meters to Nurgaleev and entered a new decision to recover 602 rubles and 60 kopecks from Nurgaleeva for the use of her former husband.

The Judicial Division for Civil Cases of the Supreme Court of the RSFSR, having considered the case on the protest of the Deputy Chairman of the Supreme Court of the RSFSR asking reversal of the decree of the Presidium and the affirmance of the decision of the People's Court, satisfied the protest on the following grounds:

In reversing the decision of the People's Court, the Presidium of the Supreme Court of the Bashkir ASSR relied on the argument that in accordance with Article 25 of the Model Charter of the Housing Construction Cooperative, in case of dissolution of a marriage the share may be divided if a separate room in the apartment they occupy can be allocated to each spouse. In the present instance, as the Presidium indicated, the apartment in dispute consists of two contiguous rooms, excluding the possibility of a practical division of the apartment.

The arguments of the Presidum of the Supreme Court of the Bashkir ASSR are mistaken and may not serve as the basis for the reversal of the decision of the People's Court which satisfied Nurgaleeva's claim.

It is established in the record that the disputed cooperative apartment was obtained by the Nurgaleevs during the period they were living together and out of common funds. From this it follows that the share, as the common property of the spouses, is subject to division between them on the bases and by the procedure provided by Articles 20-22 of the Code of Marriage and the Family of the RSFSR, taking into account the limitations indicated in Article 25 of the Model Charter of the Housing Construction Cooperative, namely: in the circumstance of the dissolution of a marriage between spouses and the existence of a possibility of the allocation to each of the spouses of a separate room in the apartment occupied by them. Moreover, the division of living space in a building of a housing construction cooperative is allowed not only when the rooms are isolated from one another, but also if there are two (or more) contiguous rooms in the apartment, as is true in the present case (Subparagraph (b) of Paragraph 5 of Decree No. 51 of the Plenum of the Supreme Court of the RSFSR of January 28, 1970, "On Implementation by Courts of the RSFSR of the Decree of the Plenum of the Supreme Court of the USSR of February 25, 1967, 'On Certain Questions of Application of Legislation in Consideration by Courts of Cases of Disputes Between Citizens and Housing Construction Cooperatives.' ")

E. IA. ZHITLOVSKII vs. ZH. IA. ZHITLOVSKII, Biulleten' Verkhovnogo Suda SSSR, 1970, No. 8, p. 3.

Zhitlovskaia had been a member of the Piatiletka Dacha Building Cooperative since 1939 and had used Dacha No. 4 on Cooperative Street in the Zagorianskaia settlement in Moscow Region.

On request of Zhitlovskaia of October 16, 1965, she, by decision of the general meeting of the members of the Piatiletka Dacha Building Cooperative of April 24, 1966 was excluded from the cooperative, and her accumulated share in the amount of 5336 rubles was transferred to her son Zhitlovskii, who at the same time was accepted into the cooperative. On February 3, 1968, Zhitlovskaia died.

In September 1968, another son of the decedent, E. IA. Zhitlovskii brought an action in court for a declaration of invalidity of his mother's request that she be excluded from the cooperative and that his older brother Ah. Ia. Zhitlovskii be accepted into the cooperative. As a basis for the claims in his complaint it was indicated that Zhitlovskaia, because of extreme old age and illness, was not responsible for her actions. Moreover, Zh. Ia, Zhitlovskii did not use the dacha together with his mother, so that the share in the cooperative could not be transferred to him.

[Decisions of the lower courts in favor of the plantiff were reversed on the following grounds:]

In satisfying the claim to have Zhitlovskaia's request declared invalid, the People's Court considered that in signing the request Zhitlovskaia acted under the influence of a misapprehension, while the Judicial Division of the Regional Court considered that, in signing the request, Zhitlovskaia did not understand the significance of her actions, relying for proof on certificates of the Zagorianskaia Outpatient Clinic, Moscow Polyclinic, No. 21, and excerpts from the history of her illness made available by the Vologodskii Hospital, although only the certificate of the Moscow Polyclinic gave some bases for doubting the mental competency of Zhitlovskaia.

In these circumstances, the court should have ordered a forensic psychiatric expert inquiry. The presidium of the Moscow Regional Court was in agreement with this. However the presidium indicated that independent of whether or not Zhitlovskaia understood the significance of her actions, the decision of the general meeting of members of the Piailetka Dacha Building Cooperative of April 24, 1966, by which she was excluded from the cooperative and Zh. Ia. Zhitlovskii was accepted instead of her was illegal. The Presidium relied on the rule that in accordance with Paragraph (c) of Article 20 of the Model Charter of the Dacha Construction Cooperative a member of the cooperative has the right with the consent of the general meeting of members of the cooperative to transfer his share and right of use of the dacha to parents, spouse or children if they previously used the dacha together with the member of the cooperative. However, the Presidium of the Regional Court considered that Zh. Ia. Zhitlovskii had not used the dacha, while the plaintiff and his family had used the disputed premises, living in it in the summer together with Zhitlovskii.

This conclusion of the court does not follow from the record of the case.

On the contrary, in the record there is data providing evidence that Zh. Ia. Zhitlovskii, until his departure for the regions of the Extreme North, used the dacha from 1946 through 1958 and repaired it. While he was in the North, the defendant, by the force of the privileges established by law, preserved his right to the use of the premises. Zh. Ia. Zhitlovskii regularly rendered material aid to his mother who at the last lived with his family, where she died. In the record there are other materials providing evidence of this (the diary and letters of the decedent, testimony of a series of witnesses, etc.). This provides a basis for considering that the judicial decisions were adopted on insufficiently studied grounds, in connection with which the case needs further verification.

On the basis of the above, the Judicial Division, by a decision of December 23, 1969, reversed all decisions taken in the case and remanded the case to the Moscow Regional Court for reexamination in the first instance with the participation of the procurator.

ZHURAVLEVA vs. EKSPORTNIK COLLECTIVE OF INDIVIDUAL BUILDERS,
Biulleten' Verkhovnogo Suda RSFSR, 1971, No. 9, p. 14.

Zhuravleva brought an action in the Pervomaiskii District People's Court of Rostov-on-Don to be restored to the rights of membership in the Eksportnik Collective of Individual Builders, from which she was excluded by decision of the general meeting.

[Her action was dismissed by the lower court for want of jurisdiction, but the regional court reversed and remanded for a hearing on the merits on the following grounds:]

In refusing to accept Zhuravleva's complaint, the people's judge referred to the fact that the Eksportnik Collective of Builders was created by the "triangle" of a shop of the Rostel'mash Factory and is subordinate to it. In its legal position it differs from a housing construction cooperative. In connection with this the court recommended that she turn for decision of the dispute over the correctness of her exclusion to the "triangle" of the shop. The judicial division agreed with this reasoning.

However, according to Paragraph 14 of the Statute on Housing Construction Collectives of Individual Builders, which regulates the activity of combinations of workers and employees for the conduct of individual housing construction, civil law disputes between the participants of a housing construction collective of individual builders are decided by judicial procedure.

Zhuravleva's claim of the incorrectness of her exclusion from membership in the combine of individual builders is a civil law dispute and is connected with her right to receive an apartment in the building built by the labor of the builders.

The citation to the effect that Zhuravleva's request should be considered by the "triangle" of the shop is unpersuasive, since neither the people's judge nor the judicial division in their decisions indicated what legal acts provide for such a procedure.

ILLEGAL DECISION OF THE CHEREPOVETS CITY EXECUTIVE COMMITTEE, Sotsialisticheskaia zakonnost', 1971, No. 8, p. 7.

The Cherepovetsk City Executive Committee of Vologda Region in 1970 adopted several decisions on the assignment of plots of land to cooperatives of automobile owners, in which it prohibited the administrations of these cooperatives from accepting, without the consent of the city executive committee, new members both in place of those leaving and supplementary to the approved lists. However, according to Article 26 of the Model Charter of the Cooperative for the Construction and Exploitation of Collective Garages and Parking Areas for Automobiles of Individual Owners, the decision of the question on acceptance into or exclusion from membership in the cooperative is within the competence of the general meeting of its members.

On the protest of the procurator of the Vologodskii region, these decisions of the Cherepovetskii city executive committee were rescinded as contrary to this charter.

CHAPTER XVI

Labor Relations and Public Enterprise

Production requires people, but people will not be pushed around as planners are likely to want to do. In every modern industrial society, it has become necessary to introduce a mechanism through which the laboring man can protect himself from the remote and impersonal management evolved in large scale plants to press the primary task of production at the lowest possible cost. The U.S.S.R. has not been apart from this development. Its industrial managers are appointed by the state rather than by directors elected by stockholders, and in theory they should have wider loyalty than those who serve private owners, but in practice their careers now depend on the same performance.[1] They are promoted and given bonuses like their capitalist counterpart when they increase production and profits. They are dismissed and humiliated if they fail in this task. They differ from their counterparts in that they are fellow workers of the state with the lowliest worker in the plant they manage, but they are remote from him, physically and spiritually. They live in more attractive, spacious and isolated quarters than the bench workmen, and they do not share fully his concerns, in spite of numerous efforts to bring the two together.

Three concerns are paramount in the life of any workman in any land: security in his job, payment in just application of the formula agreed upon for his work and the dignity that comes from participation with his fellows in an organization that can stand up to management on basic issues of labor relations. All three are the subject of Soviet labor law.

Job security is provided through a set of rigid rules in the code of laws on labor on dismissal, and the courts are made available to hear disputes over those issues that require determination of the precise law among the many that is applicable or demand exercise of an element of judgment in determining whether a workman is incapable or negligent and properly subject to dismissal. A grievance procedure is provided as it is in other lands, except that in the Soviet system there is no representative of a Minister of Labor or Labor Relations Board to serve as arbiter between management and labor. The labor unions operate the grievance procedure in which management shares, but subject always to the final say of labor. What protection management needs is forthcoming from the special character of Soviet labor

---

[1] For a comparision of the Soviet and American Enterprise manager, see David Granick, The Red Executive (New York, 1960).

unions. They have been disciplined over the years so as not to oppose management by strikes or by exhibiting chronically hostile attitudes. Their relationship is one of "partnership," and this differs from the give and take of labor relations in other lands where the common good is thought to lie in the balance of equally powerful forces on both sides, with a state conciliator or arbitrator to step in if stalemate results.

Determination of payment in just application of the formulae set by law is assured again by court intervention, but only after the grievance procedure has been tried so that the foreman can explain the computation he has used and those nearest to the job can participate as courts cannot easily do in determination of what happened and in convincing a doubting worker that he has not been wronged.

Dignity has been the most difficult aspiration to meet in the framework of formal legal relationships. The problem has been created by the political philosophy underlying the Soviet state, in that as a state of the workers it is by definition administering for their benefit. Collective bargaining which is the personification of the aspiration of dignity in capitalist economies has been developed in the U.S.S.R. in special form so that the worker can see at the time of the bargaining his representative sitting at the same table with the remote and awe inspiring manager but without power to require him to concede to the workman's demands.

The role of collective bargaining is further limited by the extreme detail with which labor relations are regulated by legislation. Major new legislation in the 1970's has dealt exhaustively with duties of employers and employees, settlement of grievances, and keeping of work records.

Adversary-type collective bargaining ceased to function in the Soviet industrial complex by 1935.[2] It had no purpose once wages and hours were regulated by the planners and were compulsory for all in state industry. Then in 1947 after the war the process was restored, not as bargaining but as the preparation of collective contracts, in which management and labor union officials annually set forth their production obligations, stated in easily available form the wage and hour provisions of the law, and agree upon the precise use of the bonus fund that would become available if the plan were to be overfulfilled, as was always confidently expected. From that time the collective contract has been a much proclaimed part of the labor relationship, and a copy of the contract is placed in the hands of every workman in a plant that he may study it at leisure and appreciate its terms. Excerpts from one such contact are included in the documents of this chapter.

Until recently, Soviet labor planners have stopped short of attempting to match specific workers to specific jobs. Rather, by a combination of legal restrictions upon migration to major cities and heavy investment in industry, they have sought to ensure that no urban worker would have to look long or far for a job. Placement services were available only for persons needing special help, such as teen-agers and veterans. Assignment to jobs was practiced only for persons with a special ob-

---

[2]'Collective Bargaining in the Soviet Unions,' A Note. 62 Harvard Law Review 1191 (1949).

ligation to the state such as recent graduates of higher educational institutions. However in the late 1960's the first steps were taken toward the creation of a coordinated national labor placement service and the doctrine that such services were necessary only to deal with unemployment induced by capitalism was abandoned.

It is rare for any written document to appear in labor relations today except for the collective contract. The individual's terms of employment are defined so precisely by the law that he needs no contract. Only in unusual situations when collective farmers are induced to leave the farms for employment that may not look attractive to them have form contracts been used. An excerpt from a contract is included in this chapter. The real character of individual relations is, however, to be found in court decisions which throw light not only on the law but on the pathos of the Soviet workman's life. It is these that make up the bulk of the documents that have been reproduced, because it is here that labor relations are most clearly mirrored.

A. Basic Guarantees of Workers' Rights

CONSTITUTION OF THE U.S.S.R., December 5, 1936, as amended to January 1, 1976.

Art. 118. Citizens of the U.S.S.R. have the right to work, that is, the right to receive guaranteed employment with payment for their work in accordance with its quantity and quality.

The right to work is ensured by the socialist organization of the national economy, the steady growth of the productive forces of Soviet society, the elimination of the possiblity of economic crises, and the abolition of unemployment.

Art. 119. Citizens of the U.S.S.R. have the right to rest and leisure.

The right to rest and leisure is ensured by the establishment of a seven-hour day for industrial, office and professional workers, the reduction of the working day to six hours for a number of arduous trades and to four hours in shops where conditions of work are particularly arduous, by the institution of annual vacations with full pay for industrial, office, and professional workers, and by the provision of a wide network of sanatoria, rest homes and clubs for the accommodation of the working people.

Art. 120. Citizens of the U.S.S.R. have the right to maintenance in old age and also in case of sickness or disability.

This right is ensured by the extensive development of social insurance of industrial, office, and professional workers at state expense, free medical service for the working people, and the provision of a wide network of health resorts for the use of the working people.

Art. 121. Women in the USSR are accorded equal rights with men in all areas of economic, government, cultural, social and political activity.

The possibility of exercising these rights is ensured by women being accorded the same rights as men to work, payment for work, rest and leisure, social insurance and education, and also by state protection of the interests of mother and child, state aid to mothers of large families and single mothers, maternity leave with full pay, and the provision of a wide network of maternity homes, nurseries and kindergartens.

CODE OF LAWS ON LABOR OF THE UZBEK SSR (1971)

Art. 19 An unfounded refusal to hire is forbidden.

In accordance with the Constitution of the USSR and the Constitution of the Uzbek SSR, any direct or indirect limitation whatsoever upon right, or the establishment of direct or indirect preferences in hiring, depending on sex, race, nationality, or attitude toward religion is forbidden.

CRIMINAL CODE OF THE RSFSR, as amended through July 1, 1976.

Art. 118. Compelling a woman to engage in sexual intercourse or to satisfy sexual desire in another form by a person with respect to whom the woman is dependent financially or by her job—shall be punished by deprivation of freedom for a term of up to three years.

Art. 137. Hindrance to the legal activity of labor unions and their agencies—shall be punished by correctonal tasks for a period of up to one year, or fine of up to 100 rubles, or dismissal from a position of responsibility.

Art. 138. Illegal dismissal of a working person from a job for personal motives, failure to execute a court judgment reinstating in a job, and also any other intentional substantial violation of labor law committed by a responsible official of a state or public enterprise or office—shall be punished by correctional tasks for a term of up to one year or dismissal from the position.

Art. 139. Refusal to employ or dismissal from work of women for reasons of pregnancy, and also refusal to employ or dismissal from work of mothers who are breast feeding for these reasons shall be punished by correction tasks for a term of up to one year or dismissal from the position.

Art. 140. Violation by a responsible official of the rules for safety, industrial sanitation or other rules for the protection of labor, if this violation could cause an accident with individuals or other severe consequences—shall be punished by deprivation of freedom for a period of up to one year or correctional tasks for the same period or by fine of up to 100 rubles, or dismissal from the position.

The same violations causing bodily injury or loss of capacity to work—shall be punished by deprivation of freedom for a period of up to three years or correctional tasks for a period of up to one year.

Violations, defined in part one of this article causing death to one person or serious bodily injury to several persons—shall be punished by deprivation of freedom for a period of up to five years.

PROCURATOR'S PROTEST AGAINST DISCRIMINATION IN EMPLOYMENT,
Sotsialisticheskaia zakonnost', 1960, No. 7, P. 87.

By order of the Minister of Health of the RSFSR "On improving the selection, arrangement and preparation of scientific cadres in scientific research institutes" directors of scientific research institutes were advised to cease hiring as junior scientific assistants persons over 40 years of age.

This order was protested by the procurator of the RSFSR, as violating existing legislation, as well as the instruction approved by order of the Presidium of the Academy of Sciences of the U.S.S.R. and the Model Charter for the Scientific Research Institutes in the System of the Ministry of Health, approved by the Ministry of Health of the U.S.S.R. The law and instruction of the presidium of the Academy of Sciences of the U.S.S.R. provides no age limit for employment of persons in the position of junior scientific assistant. According to the Model Charter for Scientific Research Institutes of the System of the Ministry of Health of the U.S.S.R. (par. 24) "any person having the learned degree of candidate of science, and also those not having a learned degree but who have a completed higher education and have had enough experience and knowledge to conduct scientific research in their field of specialization may be named junior scientific assistants of the institute."

The law gives no right to the Ministry of Health of the R.S.F.S.R. to set an age limit, over which persons in accord with the requirements stated above may not be employed as junior scientific assistants. Further, establishing such limits runs counter to the rights of working people guaranteed by the Constitution of the U.S.S.R. on their employment at work.

The protest of the Procurator of the RSFSR is sutained.

PROCURATOR'S PROTEST AGAINST A LIMITATION ON HIRING, Sotsialisticheskaia zakonnost', 1965, No. 12, p. 78.

The Executive Committee of the Kopeisk City Soviet of Workers' Deputies of Cheliabinsk Region made a decision obliging managers of enterprises, organizations and institutions of the city not to hire persons other than those assigned by the City Executive Committee.

However, the decree of the Central Executive Committee and the Council of People's Commissars of the U.S.S.R. of September 13, 1931, gave state cooperative and social enterprises and organizations the right to hire workers and employees directly by agreement with persons wishing to accept jobs. For the conclusion of an agreement for hiring someone as a worker or employee no permission of the executive committee of the local Soviet is required. Thus the Kopeisk City Executive Committee's decision established an illegal limitation on hiring.

On protest of the city procurator, this decision was rescinded.

PROCURATOR'S PROTEST AGAINST A RESTRICTION ON HIRING, Sotsialisticheskaia zakonnost', 1972, No. 7, p. 85.

The Minister of Agriculture of the Kazakh SSR by an order of June 17, 1971, prohibited directors of state farms, and managers of enterprises and organizations from hiring citizens subject to a military obligation who had not registered for the draft.

The Procurator of the Kazakh SSR protested this order which limited the right of citizens to work guaranteed by the Constitution of the USSR. In the protest attention was called to the fact that neither in the Fundamental Principles of Legislation of the USSR and the Union Republics on Labor, nor in the Law on the Universal Military Obligation, is there a prohibition of the hiring of citizens subject to a military obligation if they have not been registered for the draft. According to the rules approved by the Ministry of Defense of the USSR in accordance with Article 93 of the Law on the Universal Military Obligation, the administration in the hiring procedure for engineers, technicians, workers, and employees must verify their military documents and their liability to draft registration, and if necessary propose to them that they register for the draft after they have been hired and inform the military commissariat about such persons.

The protest of the Procurator of the Republic was satisfied; the Minister has brought the order into accord with the law in force.

PROCURATOR'S PROTEST AGAINST A REQUIREMENT OF FIRE-SAFETY TRAINING FOR HIRING, Sotsialisticheskaia zakonnost', 1971, No. 8, p. 85.

The Executive Committee of the Schchuchin City Soviet of Working People's Deputies of Grodno Region by its decision obligated the managers of the district consumers' union and consumers' association to send to the fire department for instruction those persons accepted for work connected with full financial responsibility and in the absence of a certificate on the completion of a course of instruction not to accept them for work.

The procurator of the district protested this part on the following grounds. In accordance with Paragraph 3 of the Model Rules of Internal Labor Order for Workers and Employees of State, Cooperative, and Social Enterprises and Institutions, the administration of the enterprise (or institution) is obliged to demand from a person taking a job: presentation of his labor book, or if this person is taking a job for the first time presentation of a certificate from his housing administration or rural soviet about his most recent occupation; presentation of a passport in accordance with the legislation on passports. Without presentation of these documents, hiring is not allowed. In hiring for work requiring special knowledge, the administration of the enterprise (or institution) has the right to demand from the employee presentation of a diploma or other document showing completion of a higher or secondary educational institution. A demand for the presentation of other documents upon hiring is not based upon law and contradicts the decree "On Measures for Eliminating Officious Bureaucratic Distortions in the Registration of Working People at Jobs and Meeting the Consumer Needs of Citizens."

The executive committee considered the protest of the procurator and brought its decision into accord with the law in force.

PROCURATOR'S PROTEST AGAINST ILLEGAL EXTENSION OF THE WORK WEEK, Chelovek i zakon, 1973, No. 3, p. 64.

By an order for the Experimental Semibratovskii Factory of Gascleaning Apparatus, a five-day work week was established with a duration of work of 8 hours and 15 minutes a day, for the workers, engineers, technicians, and office workers of the factory.

The district procurator entered a protest against this order on the following ground. In accordance with Article 21 of the Fundamental Principles of Legislation of the USSR and the Union Republics on Labor, the normal duration of working time on enterprises, institution, and organizations cannot exceed 41 hours a week. According to the order, workers and employees of the factory worked for 41 hours and 15 minutes a week.

The protest was satisfied, and the order was brought into strict conformance with the requirements of the law.

PROCURATOR'S PROTEST OF VIOLATION OF LABOR LEGISLATION, Radians'ke pravo, 1971, No. 11, p. 110.

The procurator of Enakievo in Donets Region verified the implementation of labor legislation at the Buddetal' Factory of the Enakievzhilbud Trust and established gross violations of the laws. In violation of the law on labor protection, overtime work was often conducted at the factory without the consent of the committee of the trade union. Decisions for permission of this overtime were issued by the director of the factory after it had already taken place.

Moreover, workers and employees often worked on days off and holidays. This was also done without the written approval and permission of the factory committee of the trade union. Relying on production needs, planned tasks were fulfilled on days off, for which a significant number of workers were brought in, sometimes all the workers of the enterprise.

Without particular necessity, the director of the factory proclaimed November 7 and 8 as working days.

The management of the Enakievzhilbud Trust knew of these violations of labor legislation, but not only failed to take measures to assure that the director be held responsible and did not further violate the laws, but tried to justify the illegal actions of the management of the factory by its effort successfully to fulfill the plan.

The local procurator sent a report of the results of his inspection to the local committee of the Party. In addition, the director of the Buddetal' Factory was brought to criminal responsibility.

PROCURATOR'S PROTEST AGAINST AN ILLEGAL DEDUCTION FROM WAGES. Radians'ke Pravo, 1966, No. 2, p. 99.

By an order of the Director of Lanovets Sugar Combine of Ternopol' Province, the brigade-leader Kravchuk, the drivers Kosianchuk and Chornii were subjected to the sanction for arriving at work drunk of payment at the rate of 50% of the wage scale for one day's work.

This order depriving the workers of 50% of the regular wage for one day's work is illegal. According to Articles 22-23 of the Model Rules of Internal Labor Order for Workers and Employees of State, Cooperative, and Social Enterprises and Institutions, approved by decree of the State Committee of the Council of Ministers of the U.S.S.R. for questions of Labor and Wages with the concordance of the All-Union Central Council of Trade Unions of January 12, 1957, the administraiton has the right, for appearance at work in an intoxicated condition to apply to the guilty party one of the following sanctions: reproach (or reproval), reprimand, stern reprimand, transfer to lower paid work for a term of up to three months or transfer to a lower position for the same term; deprival of the right to a percentage bonus for seniority for a term of up to three months, discharge from work.

The procurator of Ternopol Province protested this order. The protest has been satisfied.

B. *Collective Agreements.*

CODE OF LAWS ON LABOR OF THE RSFSR, Vedomosti Vekhovnogo Soveta SSSR, 1971, No. 50, item 1007.

CHAPTER II
THE COLLECTIVE CONTRACT

Art. 7. *Conclusion of the Collective Contract*

The collective contract is concluded by the factory, plant, or local committee of the trade union in the name of the collective of workers and employees with the administration of the enterprise or organization.

The conclusion of the collective contract must be preceded by the consideration and approval of its draft at meetings (or conferences) of workers and employees.

A collective contract is to be concluded annually and enters into force from the day it is signed by the parties.

The collective contract which has been concluded shall be brought to the attention of all the workers and employees of the enterprise or organization.

Art. 10. *Settlement of Disagreements Arising During the Conclusion of a Collective Contract*

Disagreements between the administration of an enterprise or organization and the factory, works, or local committee of the trade union arising during the conclusion of a collective contract shall be decided by the superior economic and trade union agencies with the participation of the parties.

COLLECTIVE AGREEMENT OF THE ORDER OF THE RED BANNER FACTORY "SIBELEKTROTIAZHMASH" FOR 1972.

The plan for the development of the national economy of the USSR for 1971-1975 provided for by the directives of the Twenty-Fourth Congress of the CPSU is an important stage in the creation of the material and technical basis for communism, in the task of speeding the tempos of the growth of production, raising its effectiveness and the further raising of the well-being of the people.

For the achievement of these goals the most important condition is the creation in the employees of enterprises of an interest in the development and detailization of higher planned tasks, in the improvement of the use of production resources, labor force, material and financial resources, for the improvement of technology, the organization of labor according to the most advanced technology and on this technological basis the achievement of higher labor productivity and profitability of production.

For the purposes of combining and attracting all those working at the factory to the fulfillment of these most important production tasks, for the raising of the responsibility of each employee for the achievement of maximal results of work in the whole collective, and also for the strengthening of the responsibility of the economic managers and trade union organization for the improvement of the material condition of life, and cultural services for the workers of the factory, the present collective contract is concluded for the year 1972 between the director of the factory, hereinafter called the "Administration" and the workers, engineers, technicians, employees, and office workers in the person of the factory committee of the trade union hereinafter called the "factory committee."

PART I
FULFILLMENT OF THE PRODUCTION PLAN, REALIZATION OF SCIENTIFIC AND TECHNICAL PROGRESS AND OBLIGATIONS OF THE ADMINISTRATION AND COLLECTIVE OF WORKERS AND EMPLOYEES

Fulfillment of the State Plan for Output of Products, Measures for the Implementation of Economic Accountability and the Development of Socialist Competition

The administration and the factory committee of the trade union are obligated:

1. To ensure the fulfillment of the state plan on all quantitative, technical, and economic indicators and on the socialist obligations accepted for 1972:

(a) to fulfill the annual plan for sales of products by December 28, 1972, and output products above the plan in the amount of 500 thousand rubles;

(b) to achieve not less than 90% of the growth of volume of production on account of growth of productivity of labor;

(c) by conducting organizational and technical measures directed at cost reduction, to receive an above-plan profit of 100 thousand rubles;

★ ★ ★

Preparation and Raising the Qualification of Workers, Engineers, Technicians, and Employees

15. The administration is obligated to:
   (a) organize in 1972 the preparation of 460 new workers;
   (b) to raise the qualifications of 565 workers, including:
   310 at courses of production technology;
   90 at special purpose courses;
   70 at schools of advanced experience;
to teach second and mixed skills to 85 workers;
for mastering new manufactures with a leave from production and a trip to another city—10 workers;
   (c) to raise the qualifications of 295 engineers and technicians;

★ ★ ★

Improvement of Production Labor Discipline and Protection of Public Order

21. The administration is obligated strictly to obey the established duration of the working day, week, and month, and systematically to assure that the rules of internal labor order are continually posted in each shop in visible places.

22. The workers, engineers, technicians, and office employees are obligated strictly to obey the established rules of internal labor order. . .

★ ★ ★

23. The factory committee of the trade union is obligated: to improve the forms and means of educational work among the collective of the enterprise, especially among adolescents and youth;

★ ★ ★

to improve the work of the comrades' court, to enter for its consideration every instance that is allowed to occur of absence, hooliganism, drunkenness, and unworthy conduct of individual workers of the enterprise both on and off the job;

to give timely support and develop the initiative of employees in the protection of public order, strengthen the staff of the people's patrols, strictly observing in so doing the principle of voluntariness; to recognize the best members of the patrols for their active work in the protection of public order with Certificates of Honor, financial bonuses, and valuable gifts;

to pay the members of the voluntary people's patrols support in case of temporary disability occurring in connection with fulfilling a duty to protect public order in the amount of 100% of their pay.

★ ★ ★

PART II

PAY AND WORK NORMS

Formation and Distribution of Economic Incentive Funds

26. In accordance with the methodological instructions in force and on the basis of accounts for transfers from profits, the administration shall form the following

economic incentive funds: a fund for material reward, a fund for social and cultural measures and housing construction (reward funds) and a fund for the development of production.

* * *

Organization of Work, Setting Norms and Pay

* * *

33. The basis for the setting of pay for workers and jobs shall be the "Uniform Payrate-Qualification Guide for Workers of Varied Professions," 1959 edition, and the "Payrate-Qualification Guide for Jobs and Professions of Workers of the Electrotechnical Industry," 1959 with later changes and supplements.

* * *

PART III
IMPROVEMENT OF THE CONDITIONS OF WORK AND SOCIAL INSURANCE. LABOR PROTECTION.

46. The administration has the obligation, for the purposes of improving the conditions of labor of those who are working and the elimination of the causes giving rise to injuries and illness, fully to fulfill the measures for improving the state of labor protection, safety technology, and industrial sanitation provided by the agreement with the factory committee of the trade union for 1972 for an overall sum of 198 thousand rubles (appendix No. 3).

* * *

PART IV
IMPROVEMENT OF HOUSING AND LIVING CONDITIONS AND CULTURAL SERVICES FOR THOSE WORKING AND THE MEMBERS OF THEIR FAMILIES

79. For the purposes of improving the housing and living services for the collective of the factory, the administration is obligated:

(a) to formulate plans and budgets for the electrification of Buildings No. 12 and 12-a on Rimsky-Korsakov St.

(b) to prepare completely the design documentation and working drawings for the construction of a children's combine of 280 places at the Zatulinskii housing block and begin its construction;

* * *

106. The administration and the factory committee have the obligation to:

(a) ensure the continuous supervision of the collective contract by the standing commissions of the shop and factory committees together with the administration of the shops and the health division;

(b) once every six months conduct a mass verification of the fulfillment of the collective contract with the evaluation of a report by the director of the factory and the chairman of the factory committee of the trade union and conferences of workers and employees.

107. The administration has the obligation to print the present collective contract within the course of a month after its registration and to present copies to those working at the factory.

108. The term of validity of the collective contract is established as one year from the moment of its signature.

Director of the Factory A. Degtiarev
Chairman of the Factory Committee B. Lemesh

C. Individual Contract

CODE OF LAWS ON LABOR OF THE RSFSR, Vedomosti Verkhovnogo Soveta RSFSR, 1971, No. 50, item 1007.

Art. 15. *Parties to and Content of the Labor Contract*

The labor contract is an agreement between a working person and an enterprise, institution, or organization by which the working person obligates himself to perform work of a given speciality, qualification, or responsibility, in obedience to the internal labor order and the enterprise, institution, or organization obligates itself to pay the working person wages and to assure the conditions of work provided by the legislation on labor, the collective agreement, and the agreement of the parties.

Art. 17. *Term of the Labor Contract*

Labor contracts shall be concluded:

    (1) for an indefinite term;

    (2) for a fixed term of not more than three years;

    (3) for the period necessary to complete a given job;

Art. 31. *Dissolution on the Initiative of the Worker or Employee of a Labor Contract Concluded for an Indefinite Term*

Workers and employees have the right to dissolve a labor contract concluded for an indefinite term, giving the administration written notice of the dissolution two weeks in advance. At the expiration of this period, the worker or employee has the right to stop work, and the administration of the enterprise, institution, or organization is obligated to return the employee's labor book and come to an accounting with him.

Art. 33. *Dissolution of a Labor Contract on the Initiative of the Administration*

A labor contract concluded for an indefinite term and also a fixed-term labor contract before the end of its term of effectiveness may be dissolved by the administration of the enterprise, institution, or organization only in cases:

    (1) of liquidation of the enterprise, institution, or organization, or reduction of the number or staff of employees;

    (2) the discovery of inadequacy of the worker or employee for the position occupied or the work performed as a result of insufficient qualifications or condition of health preventing the continuation of the given work;

    (3) systematic nonperformance by the worker or employee without compelling reasons of the duties placed upon him by the labor contract or the rules of

internal labor order, if measures of disciplinary or social sanction were earlier applied to the worker;

(4) absence without compelling reasons (including appearance at work in an intoxicated condition);

(5) failure to appear for work during more than four months in succession as the result of temporary disability, not counting leave for pregnancy and child birth, if the legislation of the USSR has not established a longer term for preservation of a job (or office) for a specific illness. For workers and employees who have lost ability to work in connection with a job-connected injury or professional illness, the job (or office) is preserved until the restoration of the ability to work or the establishment of invalidism;

(6) the reestablishment at the job of a worker or employee who formerly had that job.

Discharges on the bases indicated in Paragraphs 1, 2, and 6 of the present article are allowed if it is impossible to transfer the employee with his consent to other work.

The discharge of a worker on the initiative of the administration during a period of temporary disability (except for discharge under Paragraph 5 of the present article) and during the period the worker is on annual leave is not allowed, except in cases of complete liquidation of the enterprise, institution, or organization.

Art. 35. *Prohibition of the Dissolution of a Labor Contract on the Initiative of the Administration without the Consent of the Factory, Plant, or Local Committee of the Trade Union*

Dissolution of the labor contract on the initiative of the administration of the enterprise, institution, or organization is not allowed without the preliminary consent of the factory, plant, or local committee of the trade union, with the exception of cases provided by the legislation of the USSR.

The administration has the right to dissolve the labor contract not later than one month after the day of receipt of the consent of the factory, plant, or local committee of the trade union, and for discharge on the grounds indicated in Paragraphs 3 and 4 of Article 33 of the present Code, within one month from the day of discovery of the offense.

Dissolution of the labor contract in violation of the first part of the present article is illegal, and the discharged worker is subject to reinstatement at his former place of work (Art. 213).

THE MODEL CONTRACT FOR COLLECTIVE FARMERS INVITED TO WORK IN THE RESTORATION OF THE MINES IN THE DON-BASIN, Annex No. 2 to the Decree of the Council of People's Commissars of the RSFSR of 10 October 1944, [1944] Sob. Post., RSFSR, No. 12, Art. 71. (Excerpt.)

Citizen . . . . , a member of Collective farm . . . . , in the village of . . . . , the County of . . . . , the Region of . . . . . . bearing Passport No. . . . . , issued by . . . . . . of the first part, and the Trust . . . . , in the person of its agent . . . . , hereafter called "Trust," of the second part, have concluded the present contract in the following terms:

Obligation of the Workman

1. Citizen . . . . obligates himself:

a.To work in the restoration of the mines of the Donets Basin of Trust . . . . as a workman from . . . . . 194— to . . . . 194—.

b. To report on . . . . 194— to the agent of the Trust at the address . . . . . , with the requisite linen, winter and summer clothing, to be sent to the place in which the work is to be performed.

c.Honestly and conscientiously to perform the work assigned to him, to protect socialist property, to take good care of any instruments put into his hands and of any tools and special clothing assigned to him, to preserve strictly labor discipline, to observe the rules of conduct for the enterprise and for the dormitory, and to carry out all orders of the administration.

Obligations of the Trust

2. The Trust obligates itself:

a.To pay the workman the sum of . . . . , as the cost of travel on the railroad (in hard class), or by water (at the tariff for third class) and by highway from his place of residence to his place of work, and also the cost of transporting the property of the workman up to fifty kilograms;

b.To give at the same time the sum of 300 rubles without obligation of repayment, of which 100 rubles shall be paid at the time the contract is concluded, and 200 rubles upon arrival at the place of work;

c.To pay during the period of travel a per diem of ten rubles a day;

d.To pay wages during the period of travel in accordance with the official tariff applying at the new place of work.

CLASSIFIED ADVERTISEMENT FROM VECHERNIAIA MOSKVA, ADVERTISING SUPPLEMENT, March 31, 1976, p. 3.

Help Wanted

Nursemaid for two twin girls (including going out to a summer home. Age 1 year and 2 months). Telephone 281-94-***. (Subway Station "Prospekt Mira").

D. Resolution of Labor Disputes

STATUTE ON THE PROCEDURE FOR THE CONSIDERATION OF LABOR DISPUTES, Vedomosti Verkhovnogo Soveta SSSR, 1974, No. 22, Item 325.

1. Labor disputes shall be considered by:

(a) Commisions on labor disputes organized at enterprises, institutions, and organizations.

(b) Factory, plant, and local committees of trade unions.

(c) District (or city) people's courts.

Labor disputes of certain categories of employees shall be decided by the superior agency in the order of subordination (Paragraph 41 of the present statute).

9. Commissions on labor disputes are the compulsory first instances for the consideration of labor disputes arising at enterprises, institutions, or organizations between workers and office workers on one side, and the administrations' on the other side, with the exception of disputes subject to consideration directly in district (or city) people's courts (Paragraphs 37 and 38) and superior agencies in the order of subordination (Paragraph 41), and also disputes on other questions set forth in Paragraph 11 of the present statute.

Art. 208. *Consideration of Labor Disputes by Factory, Plant and Local Committees of Trade Unions*

Factory, plant, and local committees of trade unions consider labor disputes on requests of workers and office workers, when the agreement of the parties was not achieved in the commission on labor disputes and on appeals of workers and office workers from the decision of this commission.

Art. 209. *Consideration of Labor Disputes in District (or City) People's Courts*

Labor disputes are considered in district (or city) people's courts:

(1) on requests of workers and office workers when they are not in agreement with the decree of the factory, plant, or local committee of the trade union, or on requests of the administration when it considers that the decision of the factory, plant, or local committee contradicts legislation in force;

(2) on requests of workers and office workers when they are not in agreement with the decision of a commission on labor disputes consisting of a trade union organizer and the director of the enterprise, institution or organization and also when at the enterprise, institution, or organization there is no factory, plant, or local committee of the trade union nor trade union organizer.

In addition, the following labor disputes are considered directly in district (or city) people's courts without resort to the commission on labor disputes and the factory, plant or local committee:

(1) on requests for reinstatement at work of workers and employees discharged on the initiative of the administration of the enterprise, institution or organization, with the exception of disputes of workers occupying a position specified in a special list (Article 220).

A labor dispute between an employee and the administration is also examined directly in the district (or city) people's court if it concerns a question of the application of labor legislation which question was previously decided with respect to this worker by the administration with the agreement of the factory, plant, or local committee of the trade union within the limits of the rights granted to them.

A. CHEKOV, "THE LABOR DISPUTE," Izvestia, May 31, 1974, p. 4.

The Presidium of the Supreme Soviet of the USSR has approved a new Statute on the Procedure for Consideration of Labor Disputes. Many of the rules of this statute differ substantially from the former ones.

More precise specification has been made of those questions which fall within the competence of commissions on labor disputes. Disputes over the legality of discharge of employees on the initiative of the administration have been excluded from their competence. These disputes will now be considered only in court. Disputes on the dissolution of the labor contract on other bases have been left in the competence of the commissions, for instance those concerning the early dissolution of a term contract for compelling reasons, disputes about the dissolution of a contract as the result of refusal of a worker or employee of a transfer to work in another place together with the enterprise and certain others.

Subject to consideration by the commissions are demands for payment for work at night, on days off, and holidays. The commissions will consider demands for payment of forced layoff if this question does not have to be decided in the consideration of a suit for reinstatement at work. The competence of the commissions includes the decision of disputes on the right to receive bonuses and their amounts, if these bonuses are provided by the system for payment for labor. These include bonuses for the achievement of the basic production indicators and also bonuses for the collection, storage, and turning in of cuttings and scraps of ferrous and nonferrous metals, for savings of fuel, electrical, and heat energy, and certain others. As a general rule demands of an employee for payment of compensation for the general annual results of the work of the enterprise are subject to consideration in the commissions. The commissions also must consider the demands of employees for the granting of an annual vacation of the established duration, payment for it, and payment of compensation for unused vacation on leaving the job.

The disputes which may not be considered in the commissions include those on such questions as the establishment of norms for processing (or norms for time), norms for service (or norms of number of personnel), and also the calculation of work seniority, when another procedure is established by legislation for the consideration of the disputes.

★ ★ ★

The new statute also provides that the factory, plant, local (or shop) committee of the trade union has the right to reverse an illegal decision of the commission not only on the appeal of the worker, but also on its own initiative or on protest of the procurator. In such an instance the committee itself considers the dispute and renders a decision on the substance of the matter.

★ ★ ★

The new statute includes a special part on the consideration of labor disputes in district (or city) people's courts. It indicates what disputes are subject to direct consideration in court, bypassing the commission and the factory, plant, or local committee.

★ ★ ★

Specially set apart are the labor disputes of managerial employees of enterprises, institutions, and organizations on questions of bonuses which are approved for payment to them by the administrators of superior agencies. These disputes are decided only by superior (in the order of subordination) agencies.

PROCURATOR'S PROTEST OF ILLEGAL DISCIPLINARY SANCTION, Sotsialisticheskaia zakonnost', 1968, No. 5, p. 85.

The Chief of the White Sea—Onega Steamship Line demoted senior mate Ponomarev to second mate and transferred him to another ship of a lower category for violation of labor discipline.

However, according to Par. 25 of the Statute on Discipline of Employees of River Transport of the USSR, "for one and the same offense, only one disciplinary penalty may be exacted. Par. 17 of the statute provides that reduction in rank and removal from the ship (with later transfer to a ship of a lower category or to shore work according to skill qualification) for a term of up to one year (subparagraphs (d) and (e)) are two independent types of administrative action. They may not be applied simultaneously for one and the same offense.

The illegal order of the Chief of the Steamship Line was protested by the procurator of the Karelian ASSR. The protest has been satisfied and the order rescinded.

OMSK BUS TRANSPORT ENTERPRISE NO. 7 vs. KOVALEV, Biulleten' Verkhovnogo Suda RSFSR 1975, No. 5, p. 2.

The Omsk Bus Transport Enterprise No. 7 concluded an agreement with Kovalev providing that he would study courses for bus drivers with a scholarship of 100 rubles a month, and after finishing the courses would work for two years. In case he quit early he would be obligated to return the cost of instruction.

In December 1973, the defendant finished the courses and during the course of half a year worked as a bus driver. On June 5, 1974, Kovalev voluntarily quit, in connection with which the Omsk Bus Transport Enterprise brought an action in court to recover 421 rubles from him.

[A decision for the defendant was affirmed on the following grounds:]

Legislation in force provides for the conclusion with persons undergoing education with leave from production of contracts obliging them to work at the given enterprise for not less than two years after the conclusion of instruction.

However in this legislation there are no norms obliging the employee to repay the expenses born in connection with the instruction in case of quitting before the expiration of the term. The provision in the contract concluded by the parties on compensation for the cost of education is illegal. Therefore the court properly dismissed the claim for recovery of 421 rubles from Kovalev.

POLIARNAIA ZVEZDA vs. SLOBODINA, Biulleten' Verkhovnogo Suda RSFSR, 1969, No. 11, p. 5.

The local committee of the editorial and printing divisions of the newspaper *Poliarnaia Zvezda* at a meeting on May 13, 1969, adopted a decision in accordance with which the administration had to give Slobodina, a typesetter in the printing division, her regular vacation for the past two years starting on June 29, 1969.

The administration, considering that the decision of the local committee contradicted the legislation in effect, brought the labor dispute for decision to the People's Court.

[On supervisory review, it was held that the case should be dismissed, on the following grounds:]

In accordance with Article 118 of the Code of Laws on Labor of the RSFSR, the time, procedure, and order for taking vacations is to be established by agreement between the administration of the enterprise (or institution) and the factory, plant, local, or shop committee of the trade union. The order for providing vacations is to be established not later than January 1 of the year in which they are to be provided.

In accordance with Article 10 of the Statute on the Procedure for considering labor disputes, disputes on the provision of regular vacations may be the subject of consideration by the commission on labor disputes, and thereafter by the court, only in the case that the administration has violated the schedule for regular vacations agreed upon with the factory, plant, or local committee, or when the right of an employee to receive a vacation at a specific time of year is provided by law. If the request of an employee to be given or have transferred a vacation is not based upon the law, the collective contract or the approved schedule of vacations, then such cases are not subject to judicial consideration, since no dispute about a legal right arises in such cases.

From the record of the case it appears that Slobodina, using her right to combine vacations during 3 years, provided by Paragraph 32 of the Instruction "On the Procedure for Presenting Privileges to Persons Working in Regions of the Extreme North and in Regions, Equated with the Extreme North Region," during the establishment of the schedule for vacations for 1969 and its approval at the session of the local committee of the trade union on January 5, 1969 did not raise the question of being given a vacation in the current year. Therefore she was not included in the schedule, of whose preparation she was timely informed.

Slobodina presented her request to be given a vacation starting on June 27, 1969 only on April 22, 1969, that is when the schedule of vacations was already agreed and approved. The administration no longer had the possibility of satisfying her request, since at the time indicated a number of editorial employees in accordance with the schedule were on vacation, and funds for giving Slobodina a vacation were not planned. Her departure could cause a delay in the publication of the Paper since in the typesetting department of the printing division only one employee would have been left who would not have been in a position to ensure the normal work of the shop.

In these circumstances, the dispute on the time of granting a vacation was not subject to judicial consideration.

RYBNOVSKII OFFICE OF THE OKHINSKII INTERDISTRICT MARKET vs. MEDVEDEVA, Biulleten' Verkhovnogo Suda RSFSR, 1971, No. 7, p. 13.

The Rybnovskii Office of the Okhinskii Interdistrict Market brought an action in court against Medvedeva to recover 216 rubles and 46 kopecks on the grounds that she, working as manager of Store No. 6, with a work-group having responsibility for the inventory, together with saleswomen Riazantseva and Kniazeva allowed the spoilage of wares in the amount of 914 rubles and 80 kopecks. Riazantseva and Kniazeva paid their shares of the damage caused, but Medvedeva has not paid in full.

[A decision in favor of the defendant was reversed on review on the following grounds:]

In dismissing the case, the people's court proceeded on the basis that in considering the criminal case on the accusation against Medvedeva of theft, the damage caused by the theft was recovered from her, which damage she has paid back in full. In addition, 1195 rubles was taken from her and transferred to the income of the state as unjust enrichment.

However, as is clear from the materials of the criminal case Medvedeva was convicted not only for theft, but also for defrauding purchasers. Therefore the court properly transferred the money taken from her to the income of the state.

As far as the damage caused as a result of the spoilage of wares is concerned, independently of the taking and payment to the income of the state of money obtained by criminal means, she as a person having responsibility for inventory is obliged to compensate for it if she does not prove that the damage was not caused through her fault. Such proofs were not presented by her, and the people's court did not receive them. In such circumstances dismissal of the claim was unjustified.

ZUBKO vs. LUNACHARSKII STATE GRAIN FARM, Biulleten' Verkhovnogo Suda RSFSR, 1969, No. 12, p. 2.

Zubko worked as a cleaning woman in the nursery at the Lunacharskii State Grain Farm. By an order of June 5, 1968 she was discharged from work for systematic violation of labor discipline. Considering her discharge improper, Zubko brought an action in court for reinstatement at work.

[A decision in her favor was affirmed on the following grounds:]

In accordance with Art. 10 of the Statutes on the Rights of the factory, plant, or local committee of the trade union, workers and office workers may not be discharged from enterprises, institutions, or organizations on the initiative of the administration without the consent of the factory, plant, or local committee of the trade union. Therefore, the director of the enterprise, institution, or organization is obliged to receive the consent of the factory, plant, or local committee for the discharge of the employee before the issuance of the order.

As is apparent from the record, the consent of the local committee for the discharge of Zubko was obtained after the issuance of the discharge order.

In accordance with Paragraph 3 of the Decree of the Presidium of the All-Union

Central Council of Trade Unions of January 8, 1965, the local committee must not consider the presentation of the administration and give consent to discharge if the administration in violation of the law has applied for the receipt of consent after the order for discharge was given.

Since the consent of the local committee to the discharge of Zubko was given after the issuance of the order for discharge, it should be considered as made in violation of the law.

The court also correctly noted that the administration in applying a disciplinary sanction, in violation of Par. 25 of the Model Rules of Internal Labor Order for Workers and Office Workers of State, Cooperative and Social Enterprises and Institutions did not receive any explanations from her.

DROZDOVA vs. EXECUTIVE BODY OF THE HOLY TRINITY CHURCH, Biulleten' Verkhovnogo Suda RSFSR, 1971, No. 1, page 15.

Drozdova brought an action in court against the executive body of the Holy Trinity Church for reinstatement at work. In the claim for relief it was stated that she had worked since 1964 under a labor contract in the church as a cleaning woman and by a decision of May 12, 1970 was discharged from this work on account of a reduction in staff improperly and without consent of the trade union committee.

[A judgment dismissing the case was reversed on the following grounds:]

The people's court and the judicial division of the city court in dismissing the case proceeded from the position that by the Decree of the Soviet Government of January 23, 1918 the church was separated from the state and that all questions connected with the conclusion and dissolution of labor contracts were to be decided by the executive bodies of religious societies. Therefore the question of the legality of the discharge of Drozdova from work could be appealed only to the superior body controlling the activity of the church.

It is impossible to agree with these conclusions. According to Article 1 of the Code of Laws on Labor of the RSFSR, the Code applies to all persons working under a labor contract.

As appears from the record, Drozdova worked as a cleaning woman under a labor contract concluded with the executive body of the Holy Trinity Church with the knowledge or consent of the group committee of the trade union of municipal service workers of the Smolninskii District of Leningrad.

No limitations on the application of labor legislation, including that connected with the resolution of labor disputes of the given category of employees is contained in the law.

On the contrary, the legislation on labor extends to persons working as employees and office workers in religious organizations.

By a decision of the central committee of workers of local industry and municipal services of August 21, 1962, a list of positions of employees to which the legislation on labor extended was approved. This list includes persons working in religious organizations only as cleaning women, watchmen, stokers, and janitors.

Discharge of them from work must be conducted with the consent of the local committee of the trade union of that primary organization where they are registered. Disputes on the reinstatement of such persons at work are decided according to the regular procedure in the commission for the consideration of labor disputes.

Therefore the court did not have grounds for dismissing the case.

KLIUEVA vs. DEPARTMENT OF EDUCATION, Biulleten' Verkhovnogo Suda RSFSR, 1975, No. 2, p. 1.

Kliueva worked as a teacher of the beginning grades in High School No. 21 of the city of Nal'chik. By an order of the Department of Education of the City of Nal'chik of February 9, 1973 she was discharged from work under Paragraph 1 of Article 33 of the Code of Laws on Labor of the RSFSR because of a reduction in staff. Considering her discharge improper, Kliueva brought an action in court for reinstatement at work.

[A decision for the Department of Education was reversed on the following grounds:]

The court correctly found that the city department of education had grounds for discharge of Kliueva because of a reduction in staff, since she was accepted for permanent work but occupied a position in addition to the regular table of staff. However, discharge on this basis is allowed only in case of impossibility of transfer of the employee with his consent to other work.

The question of whether and just what measures were taken for the transfer of the plaintiff to other work were not properly examined in the judicial session.

From the record it appears that the local committee of the trade union of the school, giving its consent to the discharge of the plaintiff asked the city education department about finding her a job. It follows from this that the approval for the discharge of the plaintiff was given before there was a clarification of the question of the possibility of the transfer of the plaintiff to other work and of her relationship to the proposed work.

The record includes a letter of the head of the city department of education about the absence of vacant places in the schools of the city. However the court did not clarify whether or not the city education department had possibilities for finding a job for the plaintiff in other institutions, or whether measures were taken for transfer to other work, in view of the fact that she was willing to transfer to work outside School No. 21, but that such work, according to her complaint, was not offered to her.

The Presidium of the Supreme Court of the Kabardino-Balkarskii ASSR, in leaving the protest unsatisfied, indicated that the duty of the administration to take measures to transfer an employee with his consent to other organizations and institutions is envisoned only for pregnant and breast-feeding women.

However, Paragraph 9 of the Decree of the Plenum of the Supreme Court of the USSR of October 19, 1971, "On the Application in Judicial Practice of the Fundamentals of Legislation of the USSR and the Union Republics on Labor" (in the

1974 version) provides that "in considering cases on the reinstatement at work of persons whose labor contract is dissolved under Paragraphs 1, 2, or 6 of Article 17 of the Fundamental Principles, the court is obligated to demand from the administration proof to the effect that the employee refused transfer to other work or that the administration did not have the possibility of transferring the employee with his consent to other work."

According to Paragraph 10 of the Decree of the Plenum of the Supreme Court of the RSFSR of December 20, 1973, "On Certain Questions of the Application of the Rules of the Code of Laws on Labor of the RSFSR to Transfers and Reassignments of Workers and Office Workers to Other Work," the courts must consider the conditions for transfer fulfilled when work has been offered in the given enterprise or organization or in other enterprises or organizations of the same population center according to the type of activity of the employee.

Since there is no data in the case to the effect that the administration took all the measures provided by law for the transfer of the plaintiff to other work, the court lacked bases for recognizing the discharge of the plaintiff as correct.

STEN'KINA vs. PENZA FORESTRY TECHNICAL SCHOOL, Biulleten' Verkhovnogo Suda RSFSR, 1974, No. 3, p. 8.

Sten'kina worked at the Penza Forestry Technical School as a teacher of the Russian language and literature.

By order of the director of the technical school of July 23, 1973, she was discharged from work for violation of the rules for administering examinations.

Considering her discharge to be incorrect, Sten'kina brought an action in court for reinstatement at work.

As a basis for her demands, the plaintiff stated that she had worked as a teacher for 25 years, including since 1970 at the technical school, that she had never been subjected to disciplinary sanctions, that she had a good attitude toward work, had not raised grades on examinations, and had repeated examinations for two graduates at the correspondence division of the technical school on the order of the former head of that division. Sten'kina also stated that she had been elected chairman of the local committee of the trade union, and according to her affirmation, she was fired because of the hostile attitude of the administration toward her. Moreover, the discharge was conducted without the preliminary consent of the local committee of the trade union.

The representative of the technical school defended against the complaint and explained that Sten'kina had grossly violated the rules for hearing the examinations of graduates and in addition was an employee of poor qualifications, and that, therefore, the administration was forced to discharge her from work.

[The decision of the regional court to reinstate her at work was affirmed on the following grounds:]

In accordance with Article 35 of the Code of Laws on Labor of the Russian Soviet Federated Socialist Republic, the dissolution of a labor contract with employees on the initiative of the administration without the consent of the factory, works, or local committee of the trade union is not allowed, and the discharged worker is entitled to reinstatement at the former job.

The fact that consent to the discahrge of Sten'kina was given by the Presidium of the Penza Regional Committee of the Trade Union of Workers of the Forest, Paper, and Wood Processing Industry, does not free the administration of the technical school from the obligation to receive consent to such a discharge from the local committee of the trade union of the technical school, since in accordance with Art. 235 of the Code of Laws on Labor, for the discharge of Chairmen and members of the factory, plant, and local committees of trade unions who are not freed from production work there is required not only the receipt of consent of the superior trade union body, but also the observance of the general procedure for discharge as a supplementary guaranty for elected trade union employees.

According to the sense of the order, Sten'kina was fired for violation of labor discipline.

Violation for these reasons, as is indicated in Paragraph 3 of Article 33 of the Code of Laws on Labor of the RSFSR may take place only in the case that measures of disciplinary or social sanction had earlier been applied to the employee.

In such circumstances the court correctly reinstated Sten'kina at work.

WEST SIBERIAN METALLURGICAL FACTORY vs. ROGOZIN, Biulleten' Verkhovnogo Suda RSFSR, 1972, No. 5, p. 3.

Rogozin worked at the West Siberian Metallurgical Factory as a duty electrician and at the same time studied by correspondence in the Kuznets Industrial Technical School. After having finished the technical school in March 1970 and having received the qualification of an electrical technician, Rogozin placed before the administration of the factory the question of providing him work in accordance with the speciality he had acquired. Since such work was not presented to him, he, in October 1970, voluntarily quit his job at the factory and began work as an electrical technician at the Novokuznets Installation and Repair Division of the Coal Energy Trust.

In November 1970, the housing and services division of the factory brought an action in court against Rogozin under Article 334 of the Civil Code of the RSFSR for his eviction from the one-room apartment received during the period of his work at the factory.

[A decision in favor of the factory was reversed on the following grounds:]

In satisfying the demands made by the plaintiff the court motivated its decision on the basis that Rogozin was working at the West Siberian Metallurgical Factory in the speciality he received after finishing the technical school, and accordingly his quitting this job was not caused by compelling circumstances.

These conclusions may not be recognized as correct.

It was stated above that Rogozin worked for the plaintiff until he finished the technical school as a duty electrician. According to the diploma which has been issued, Rogozin, after finishing the technical school was given the qualification of electrical technician. An electrical technician, as is noted in the qualification description of a technician, who has finished an industrial technical school, is prepared for work at enterprises in the positions of foreman of an electrical shop, foreman of an electrical installation shop, technician of the chief electrician's division, duty technician of a shop, etc., i.e. must be a direct organizer of the production process. The job of duty electrician is not indicated in this list; therefore there is no basis to consider that Rogozin without foundation sought to have a new job given to him or that work as a duty electrician corresponded to the specialty that he received after finishing the technical school.

The arguments of the division of the regional court to the effect that Rogozin, after he quit was offered an engineering or technical job, which he refused, are not supported by convincing proofs, and this question was not a subject of inquiry in the court of first instance.

With respect to the presidium's reference to the impossibility of the use of the defendant in the jobs of technician, foreman, etc. because of the absence of vacant jobs for middle technical personnel at the factory, and to the reference in addition to this argument to the administration's need to study the practical qualities of the defendant in more detail; these reasons cannot serve as a basis for the eviction of Rogozin. The defendant, as is apparent from the record, has worked at the factory since 1966 and the administration has had sufficient time for the study of his work characteristics.

ZHOLNEROVICH vs. BELORUSSIAN STATE INSTITUTE OF THE NATIONAL ECONOMY, Biulleten' Verkhovnogo Suda SSSR, 1971, No. 5, p. 13.

A. V. Zholnerovich, senior assistant of the Department of Economic geography of the Belorussian State Institute of the National Economy was discharged as not being attested for a renewal of her term.

[A decision to dismiss the case was reversed by the Plenum of the Supreme Court of the USSR on the following grounds:]

The supervisory courts cited as the basis for the correctness of dismissing the case, Subpar. (e) of Par. (3) of the Decree of the Plenum of the Supreme Court of the Belorussian SSR of August 26, 1970, in which it is explained that labor disputes on questions of discharge and reinstatement at work with respect to positions of senior assistants of higher educational institutions of persons found as the result of attestation to be suitable for the position occupied should be decided by the higher agency in order of subordination.

However this explanation is not based upon the law.

An edict of the Presidium of the Supreme Soviet of September 27, 1968 [citation omitted] provided that the superior agencies in order of subordination decide labor disputes on questions of discharge and reinstatement at work of employees of scientific-research, drafting, design, and technological organizations, and also of scientific-research subdivisions of higher educational institutions when employees of such institutions are found, as the result of attestation, not to be suitable for the positions occupied. Thus, the edict deals not with employees of higher educational institutions in general, but only with those who work in scientific-research subdivisions of those institutions. Senior assistants of departments of higher educational institutions are not mentioned in this edict, and, therefore, they are not included in the categories of employees whose labor disputes arise in connection with discharge, following attestation of unsuitability for the position occupied. Such disputes are decided by the superior agency in the order of subordination.

[The case was remanded for a hearing on the merits.]

EVDOKIMOV vs. LAKUTSK RIVER PORT, Biulleten' Verkhovnogo Suda R.S.F.S.R., 1967, No. 8, p. 2.

Evdokimov worked at the Iakutsk river port as a driver. By an order of September 16, 1966 he was discharged from work under Art. 47(e) of the Code of Laws on Labor of the R.S.F.S.R. on the ground that while on the job in a motor vehicle on the night of the 29th to 30th of August he was in a state of intoxication. That, as a result of this intoxication, Evdokimov ran into a pile of pulley blocks and damaged the vehicle (broke the headlights, crumpled the fender and the bumper guard in front of the radiator cover).

Previously Evdokimov had been subject to disciplinary sanctions for appearing at work in a state of intoxication.

Considering his discharge incorrect, Evdokimov brought an action in court for reinstatement at his previous job.

[A decision dismissing the action was affirmed on the following grounds:]

The Presidium of the Supreme Court of the Iakutsk A.S.S.R. in vacating the judgment of the people's court and the decision of the judicial division, argued that Evdokimov had had only one disciplinary sanction, issued under an order of March 26, 1966, and the he had committed no previous violations of labor discipline; also that no measure of social influence had been applied to him. The presidium, in addition, noted that the plaintiff had worked in the port as a driver for more than twenty years and had received no reproofs from officials of state driving inspection.

It is impossible to agree with these conclusions of the presidium. Appearing at work in an intoxicated condition is a gross violation of labor discipline. In addition, the fact must not be overlooked that Evdokimov worked as a driver and the violations he committed not only caused damage to the Port, but could have led to even more serious consequences.

The law on discharge of a worker for absenteeism does not require the existence of systematic absenteeism; a single case is enough.

According to Par. 23 of the Model Rules of Internal Labor Order, workers and employees appearing at work in a state of intoxication are considered absentees equally with those not appearing at work without compelling reasons.

The fact that Evdokimov appeared at work in a state of intoxication was established by the court.

Under these circumstances the people's court and the Judicial Division correctly denied Evdokimov's claim for reinstatement at work.

PROCURATOR'S PROTEST OF ILLEGAL ORDER OF DIRECTOR OF A STATE FARM, Chelovek i zakon, 1973, No. 6, p. 53.

The director of the Onexzhskii State Farm, by an order obligated the bookkeeper of the state farm to withhold from the pay of all workers and office workers living in the Krasnoborsk settlement, the cost of four uses of the public baths each month.

The procurator of the Pudozhskii District protested this decision as contradicting Art. 124 of the Code of Laws on Labor of the RSFSR in which it is stated that deductions from pay may be made only in instances provided by legislation of the USSR and the RSFSR. Art. 124 contains a list of the instances when withholding by decisions of the administration from the pay of workers and office workers is allowed for the repayment of their debts to the enterprise, institution, or organization where they work. But withholding for public services is not provided for.

The protest has been satisfied and the illegal order cancelled.

LIKENE vs. RAMUNE FACTORY, Biulleten' Verkhovnogo Suda SSSR, 1973, No. 5, p. 3.

Since 1964, O. I. Likene has worked as a fabric cutter for the Ramune Factory in Vilnius and her place of work has been in Fabric Sales Store No. 94 of the Vilnius City Industrial Sales Organization.

In connection with a letter from the Vilnius City Industrial Sales Organization about the impossibility after the repair of the store of equipping a location for fabric cutting in it, Likene was transferred on May 30, 1972 to work as a cutter in a shop of the same factory.

Referring to a substantial change in conditions of work in the shop and complaining against this transfer, Likene brought a suit in court for reinstatement at her former place of work.

[A decision in favor of Likene was reversed and the case was remanded for a new trial by the Plenum of the Supreme Court of the USSR on the following grounds:]

As a basis for the demands of her claim Likene indicated that when she was working as a cutter on the premises of Store No. 94, her functions included only the cutting of fabrics, while the cutters of the shop had to provide additional services for clients. Moreover, according to the plaintiff, the transfer had a significant effect on her pay, since the pay of a cutter in the shop was significantly lower than the pay for her work carried out on the premises of the store.

In adopting its decision to reinstate the plaintiff at work, the people's court did not verify the arguments of the plaintiff concerning the change in the conditions of her work in the shop in comparison with the conditions of work cutting fabric on the premises of the store. There are no data about this in the record. The representative of the Ramune Factory at the court hearing did not contradict the arguments of the plaintiff and merely referred to the elimination of the location for fabric cutting on the premises of the store.

* * *

By virtue of Art. 13 of the Fundamental Principles of Legislation of the USSR and the Union Republics on Labor, transfer to other work at the same enterprise, institution, or organization is permissible only with the consent of the worker or office worker. As is provided in Art. 35 of the Code of Laws on Labor of the Lithuanian SSR, the moving by the administration of an employee to another place of work without a change in specialty, qualification, amount of pay, benefits, privileges, or other essential conditions of labor is not considered a transfer.

The court should in connection with this have clarified if the conditions of work of the plaintiff were changed when she worked in the shop and depending upon this decide the question of whether the administration of the factory had violated labor legislation by assigning the plaintiff to work in the shop despite her objection.

[Remanded for a new trial.]

EXPERIMENTAL PRODUCTION FARM OF THE SCIENTIFIC RESEARCH INSTITUTE FOR VEGETABLE FARMING vs. ZHERDEVA, Biulleten' Verkhovnogo Suda RSFSR, 1974, No. 8, p. 3.

By order of the director of the Experimental Production Farm of the Scientific Research Institute of Vegetable Farming of November 5, 1972, Zherdeva was discharged from the position of animal technician under Par. 3 of Art. 33 of the Code of Laws on Labor of the RSFSR for reasons of systematic nonfulfillment of labor obligations. On October 3, 1973, the local committee of the labor union organization of the experimental farm ordered the recovery for the use of Zherdeva of wages for three months in connection with delay in return of her labor book.

Considering the decision to be incorrect, the administration brought the labor dispute to court for decision.

Zherdeva held to the demands she had presented previously and sought to recover her pay for the period of withholding of her labor book, i.e., from November 5, 1972 through September 14, 1973.

The representative of the defendant objected to the complaint, indicating that the defendant refused to receive the labor book.

The Moscow Regional Court, deciding the case of Zherdeva v. Experimental Production Farm, granted recovery for use of the plaintiff of 170 rubles of wages for the period from October 5 through December 21, 1972, and rejected the remaining part of the complaint.

In cassational appeals, Zherdeva sought the reversal of the decisions of the court and requested the recovery of wages through the day she received her labor book, September 14, 1973, while the Experimental Farm sought a dismissal of all claims since, in its opinion, Zherdeva had not suffered forced loss of work, but had refused to take her labor book, and had received it in September 1973 through the militia.

The Judicial Division on Criminal Cases of the Supreme Court of the RSFSR by a decision of January 16, 1974, left the decision without change on the following grounds.

In accordance with Art. 39 of the Code of Laws on Labor, the administration was obliged to return the labor book to Zherdeva on the day she was discharged. However, although the labor book had been lost, the administration of the Experimental Farm did not take the necessary measures for timely completion and tender to the plaintiff of a duplicate of the labor book.

The duplicate of the labor book was sent to Zherdeva in an insured, registered letter on December 19, 1972. On December 21, 1972, the addressee refused to accept the letter. The plaintiff explained that she knew this was done in her absence by her father.

Zherdeva did not submit to the administration a request to issue a labor book to her. Therefore it was only given to her on September 14, 1973. Despite the possession of a labor book after September 14, 1973, the plaintiff still had not begun work by the time of the hearing of the case on December 10, 1973.

The court correctly adjudged for her use wages for the period of withholding of the labor book from November 6, 1972 through December 21, 1972, since the administration during this period failed to ensure return of the labor document.

As far as the demands of Zherdeva for the recovery of wages for the time after December 21, 1972 are concerned, they are without foundation.

E. The Duty to Work

CONSTITUTION OF THE USSR, as amended through July 1, 1976.

Art. 12. Work in the USSR is a duty and a matter of honor for every able-bodied citizen, in accordance with the principle: "He who does not work, neither shall he eat."

The principle applied in the USSR is that of socialism: "From each according to his ability, to each according to his work."

SUPERVISION OF THE EXECUTION OF LAWS ON THE STRUGGLE WITH PARASITES, Sotsialisticheskaia zakonnost', 1970, No. 8, p. 85.

The Procuracy of the RSFSR has analyzed materials of supervision of the execution of legislation on the struggle with persons refusing to perform socially useful work and leading an antisocial parasitical way of life.

The analysis has shown that in connection with the application of decrees on this question [citations omitted] the councils of ministers of the autonomous republics and many executive committees of territorial and regional Soviets of working people's deputies of the Russian Federation have taken measures for the timely discovery of parasitical elements and for bringing them to socially useful work. At the same time the checkup showed that certain executive committees have not fully executed the obligations placed upon them for the organization of a struggle with persons leading an antisocial parasitical way of life. For instance, the executive committees of the Lenin and Industrial Districts of Orenburg, and the Priokskii District Executive Committee of the city of Gorky in 1971 did not consider the materials coming from the militia about parasites and did not adopt decisions concerning compelling them to take jobs. In the Mari ASSR and the Moscow region such materials were not given timely consideration.

Violations of the decree of the Council of Ministers of June 4, 1970, "On the Procedure of Job Placement on the Territory of the RSFSR of Persons Refusing to Engage in Social Useful Labor," [citation omitted] were uncovered. In a number of cities and districts of Vladimir Region, for instance, the executive committees did not designate the enterprises to which these persons should be sent, so that no supervision over their job placement and work activity was exercised.

In Irkutsk and Sverdlovsk Region in some militia offices there were violations of the terms established by law for consideration of reports of persons leading a parasitical way of life; they were not given timely notice of the necessity of getting a job, transfer of materials to the executive committees of local soviets for the decision of the question on the compulsory assignment of such persons to work was delayed. At the same time in the Chechen-Ingush ASSR and in Irkutsk and Cheliabinsk Region some employees of the police gave warnings about getting a job without legal bases to minors, invalids of the first and second group who were unable to work and women having young children.

There was not always strict control of persons sent to enterprises and construction projects by decisions of the executive committees of local soviets. In Cheliabinsk, for instance, certain parasites did not obey decisions of executive committees on getting jobs and contrary to law they were not brought to criminal liability for this; in Petropavlovsk-Kamchatsk, measures for compulsory job placement were applied to only 7.5 percent of the overall number of persons who refused to engage in socially useful labor and led an antisocial parasitical way of life who were exposed in 1971.

As a result of the intervention of the procurators the violations of legality which were exposed have been eliminated and the officials responsible for them have been brought to disciplinary responsibility.

★ ★ ★

CASE OF SHTUKATUROV, Biulleten' Verkhovnogo Suda RSFSR, 1974, No. 11, p. 13.

By a decision of the Kirov District People's Court of Leningrad, Shtukaturov was convicted under Art. 198 [Violation of Passport Rules] and Part 1 of Art. 209 [Systematic Engagement in Vagrancy or Begging] of the Criminal Code of the RSFSR. He was found guilty in that having been twice, on March 20 and 29, 1973, subjected to an administrative sanction for the violation of passport rules and warned to leave Leningrad, he did not go anywhere. He did not take measures to get a job, lived with relatives and acquaintances, also in railway stations, attics, and stairwells on chance earnings. In this manner, he systematically engaged in vagrancy for which he was detained in various districts of Leningrad.

[The conviction for violation of Art. 198 was affirmed and that for violation of Part 1 of Art. 209 was reversed on the following grounds:]

The conclusion of the court on Shtukaturov's guilt in commission of the crime provided by Article 198 of the Criminal Code of the RSFSR corresponds to the proofs gathered in the record. With regard to his conviction under Part 1 of Art. 209 of the Criminal Code of the RSFSR, the decision on this matter and all subsequent judicial decisions are subject to reversal. The case is transmitted for further investigation.

According to the sense of the law responsibility for systematically engaging in vagrancy occurs when a person over a long period of time moves from one populated area to another within the boundaries of one city, not having a permanent residence and living on non-labor income. In the decree of the Plenum of the Supreme Court of the USSR of June 29, 1973, "On Judicial Practice in Cases of Systematically Engaging in Vagrancy or Begging, Willful Refusal to Obey a Decision on Job Placement and Cessation of a Parasitical Mode of Existence and Violation of Passport Rules," it is indicated that for decision of the question of guilt and for the correct qualification of the actions of the guilty party, it is necessary to clarify data on his individual characteristics, in particular his ability to work, his sources of support and other circumstances. However, the fact that a person is unable to work is not of itself a basis for freeing him from criminal responsibility for systematically engaging in vagrancy.

As appears from Shtukaturov's explanations, after arriving in Leningrad in the early days of December 1972 he tried to obtain a residence permit for the place where his former wife lived, but she refused. In January 1973 he broke his leg and was treated as an outpatient, and in February 1973 he was in a hospital for treatment for a brain concussion, and therefore could not promptly get a job. During all this period he lived on chance earnings and on his savings. However, the question of what funds Shtukaturov lived on in this period and if he, in the condition of his health, could get a job were not investigated with sufficient thoroughness. There are no medical documents in the record confirming that Shtukaturov had a broken leg; there has been no verification of the period of time he was incapacitated in connection with this, nor what consequences resulted from this injury. Nor has it been established for how much time he suffered from the brain concussion for which he was treated in the hospital from February 20 through March 1, 1973. Nor have the circumstances been clarified under which these injuries were received, while according to the certificate of Hospital No. 17 it appears that Shtukaturov entered the hospital with this injury in a state of alcohol intoxication. Moreover his explanations to the effect that during this period he lived on money he earned have not been verified.

Considering that all these circumstances have essential significance for decision of the question of Shtukaturov's guilt and can be clarified by conducting a further investigation, the verdict must be reversed.

On the basis of the aforesaid, the Judicial Division for Criminal Cases of the Supreme Court of the RSFSR, by a decision of June 13, 1974 reversed the verdict of the People's Court and the decision of the Presidium of the City Court with respect to the conviction of Shtukaturov under Part 1 of Article 209 of the Criminal Code of the RSFSR and remanded the case for a new investigation.

EDICT OF THE PRESIDIUM OF THE SUPREME SOVIET OF THE RSFSR ON THE REPEAL OF EDICTS OF THE SUPREME SOVIET OF THE RSFSR ON THE RESPONSIBILITY OF PERSONS REFUSING SOCIALLY USEFUL LABOR AND LEADING AN ANTISOCIAL PARASITIC WAY OF LIFE, Vedomosti Verkhovnogo Soveta RSFSR, 1975, No. 33, item 699.

The Presidium of the Supreme Soviet of the RSFSR decrees:

1. The repeal of:

The Edict of the Supreme Soviet of the RSFSR of May 4, 1961, "On Strengthening the Struggle with Persons Refusing Socially Useful Labor and Leading an Antisocial Parasitic Way of Life;" [citations omitted]

The Edict of the Supreme Soviet of the RSFSR of May 6, 1963, "On the Responsibility of Persons Willfully Violating the Established System in Places of Resettlement;" [citation omitted]

2. The exclusion from the Criminal Code of the RSFSR of Art. 209-1. [Willful Refusal to Obey a Decision on Job Placement and Cessation of a Parasitic Existence.]

CHAPTER XVII

Encouragement of Inspiration

Lenin expected his revolution to prepare the way for the good life of abundance and self-disciplined order, but he emphasized that the revolution was only the first step. There had to be continuing innovation, improvement of production methods and education of citizens in conduct befitting the new society. To achieve these ends the Soviet State would have to encourage inventors, and even authors. Men of inspiration would have to prepare not only manuals explaining the new machines and techniques, but also artistic works designed to excite the public to patriotic activity by casting the new Soviet man in a hero's role.

Capitalist methods of encouragement of inventors and authors had been proven by time. Through patent law the inventor had been given a monopoly right in his invention, to exploit as he wished in producing wealth, whether by utilization in his own enterprise or by sale to another. Through copyright law the author of a book, a play, a musical composition or a work of art obtained from the state a monopoly right to reproduce and sell his production. Profit was not the sole motivation, for the personal acclaim occasioned by recognition of the inventor, or the author encouraged further creative activity, as did also the sheer enjoyment of scientific discovery and artistic triumph, but the tangible incentive was money.

For Soviet policy-makers the capitalist approach was anathema. Money was to be abandoned as an incentive as communism was achieved. This was the goal set by the communist party program of 1919. Citizens were expected to work for the good of mankind: to find their primary satisfaction not in self but in social improvement. Monopoly rights were associated in their minds with capitalism, and private monopolies were to be eliminated as fast as people learned to find inspiration in the new way. This should have meant the eventual end of patent and copyright in their conventional forms, but such a severe blow was not struck by the first acts. By decree of November 26, 1918[1] some conventional features were retained, for royalties were to be paid to authors, although in accordance with a fixed tariff measured by the objective factors of type of work and size of edition rather than skill in bargaining. Further, those productions necessary to the enhancement of the common good could be declared the property of the state by the Ministry of Education. In this way the new social emphasis and the old money incentives were paired in a working compromise.

Patents were treated in similarly traditional fashion, but with some new features designed to emphasize community welfare. Thus, by decree of June 30, 1919[2], inventions might be appropriated by the state if the Patent Committee found them useful, and the inventor would be paid a fixed fee. Other inventors were to be left to their own resources of exploitation, although being awarded a patent conferring monopoly rights of use.

With the introduction of the New Economic Policy the influence of private enterprise was again felt strongly in the economy, and two new acts[3] were adopted to bring the law of patent and copyright closer to the needs of capitalism, but the essentials of the system as they had emerged in the first two acts were retained. Property incentives were utilized, but the state was protected against the capricious author, in that it could purchase any artistic production without the author's consent and regardless of whether the work had been published, so long as it had taken concrete form. The state was continued in its right to appropriate inventions on payment of the established fees.

Not until the termination of the New Economic Policy was new thinking evi-

---

[1] [1918] I. Sob. Uzak, RSFSR, No. 86, item 900.
[2] [1919] *Ibid* No. 34. item 341.
[3] Copyright Act, May 22, 1922, [1922] I Sob. Uzak, RSFSR, No. 36, item 423.

denced. Two new acts introduced the new ideas: the copyright act of May 16, 1929, created basic principles lasting to the present time. The Act of September 12, 1924[4] relating to inventions was replaced first by an Act of March 5, 1941[5], and later by the Statute of April 24, 1959[6]. The copyright law was restated in 1961 in the Fundamental Principle of Civil Law.

For many years the patent and copyright law of the Soviet Union, like that of Tsarist Russia before it, was nationalistic, with the rights of foreigners being unclear or restricted. With the growth of international trade in the 1960's the Soviet Union adhered to the major international patent and copyright agreements and revised its patent[7] and copyright[8] laws to clarify them, modernize them and bring them into conformity with international practice.

The Soviet Union has viewed inventions made with public financing as a public good to be shared freely without payment by enterprises. This to a large extent removed research and development from the system of economic accountability and has caused many difficulties for the planning authorities. Recent developments in contracts for research and technical assistance represent a slight movement toward bringing innovation into the system of economic accountability that prevails for the legal regulation of most other types of economic activity.

To avoid creation of great private wealth, tax statutes were used in Stalin's time to siphon off large royalties received by authors and inventors, for progressively structured tax rates struck hard at large incomes. Some few unusually popular authors were placed on a no-income basis, and their bills for whatever they thought justified were paid. Some authors felt socially impelled to make large contributions to campaigns for the financing of war needs, or to revolutionary agencies working outside the U.S.S.R., or to purchase large quantities of state bonds.

Since Stalin's death the policy of reducing and ultimately eliminating income taxation has required a change in approach to the renumeration of inventors and authors. The basis of computation for invention was lowered by the 1959 statute, and the most lucrative form of realization of the works of authors, namely the moving picture, and the phonograph record were subjected to lowered tariffs. Soviet policy wishes to encourage imagination, but not to the extent of creating a segment of the population that has very large accumulations of property.

Social acclaim has not been neglected by Soviet policymakers while property incentive is continued in the laws. It has long been customary to create titles for authors as "distinguished authors" of their republics or of the U.S.S.R., and the most prominent have been awarded coveted decorations like the Order of Lenin. This approach has now been extended to the inventors and rationalizers of lesser stature by a statute creating new honors and setting the terms for their award. Here is tangible

---

[4]Act on Inventions, [1926] I Sob. Zak. SSSSR, No. 9, item 97.
[5][1941] Sob. Post. SSSR, No. 9, item 150.
[6][1959] Sob. Post. SSSR, No. 9, item 59.
[7][1973]Sob. Post. SSSR, No. 19, item 109.
[8][1973] Vedomosti Verkhovnogo Soveta SSSR, No. 50, item 525.

evidence of appeal to social recognition rather than money as an incentive.

Perhaps the ultimate incentive will be only that inner satisfaction that comes with personal recognition of a job well done, but no one is yet limiting incentives to this form of inspiration. The judicial decisions reproduced in this chapter show that property incentives still rank high in the minds of authors and inventors, even when they have been paid expressly to write or to invent and royalties will be only supplemental to their salaries. If there is to be abandonment of property incentives, it will have to wait, apparently, until money shall have ceased to circulate as a commodity and until law itself shall have withered away. Neither event is expected in the foreseeable future.

A. Rewards for Writers.

FUNDAMENTAL PRINCIPLES OF CIVIL LEGISLATION OF THE U.S.S.R. AND OF THE UNION REPUBLICS, December 8, 1961, effective May 1, 1962 [1961] Vedomosti Verkhovnog o Soveta SSSR, No. 50, item 525, as ammended Feb. 27, 1973, [1973] Vedomosti Verkhovnogo Soveta SSSR, No. 50, item 525.

PART IV. COPYRIGHT

Art. 96. Copyright extends to productions of science, literature or art regardless of the form, purpose or merits of the production and also of the means of its reproduction.

Copyright also extends to productions, whether published or not, but taking some objective form, permitting reproduction of the result of the creative activity of the author (a manuscript, sketch, picture, public utterance or performance, film, mechanical or magnetic recording, etc.)

Art. 97. Copyright to a production, first published on the territory of the USSR, or not published but existing on the territory of the USSR in any objective form, is recognized for the author and his heirs regardless of their citizenship, and also for other successors to the rights of the author.

Copyright is also recognized for citizens of the USSR, whose productions are first published or which exist in some collective form on the territory of a foreign state, as well as for the successors to their rights.

For other persons, copyright to a production first published or existing in any objective form on the territory of a foreign state is recognized in accordance with international treaties or international agreements in which the USSR participates.

For foreign successors to the rights of authors who are citizens of the USSR, copyright is recognized on the territory of the USSR if this right is transferred by the procedure established by the legislation of the USSR.

Art. 98. The author has the right:

to publication, reproduction and distribution by any means permitted by law of his production under his name, under an adopted name (or pseudonym), or without a name (anonymously).

to the inviolability of the production.

to receive royalties for the use of the production by other persons except for the situations established by law. Rates for authors' royalties are established by legislation of the USSR and of the union republics.

The procedure for transfer by an author who is a citizen of the USSR of the right to use of his work on the territory of the foreign state shall be established by legislation of the USSR.

Art. 99. The copyright of a production, created together with two or more persons (a collective production), belongs to both authors jointly, regardless of whether the production is one inseparable whole or is composed of parts, each of which has also an independent character. Each of the coauthors retains his copyright on the part of the collective production created by him, if it has an independent character.

Art. 100. A copyright is recognized as belonging to a juridical person in the circumstances and within the limits established by legislation of the U.S.S.R. and of the union republics.

The author of a production created while performing a service task in a scientific or other organization has a copyright in the production. The method by which organizations may use such a production and the circumstances of payment of royalties to the author are established by legislation of the U.S.S.R. and of the union republics.

Art. 101. Use of the production of an author (including a translation to another language) by other persons is permitted only on the basis of a contract with the author or with the successors to his rights, except in circumstances provided by law.

Model contracts for the use of a production (in publishing, in dramatic production, in moving picture scenarios and other authors' contracts) are to be approved in accordance with a procedure established by legislation of the U.S.S.R. and of the union republics.

Terms in a contract concluded with an author which worsen his situation in relatin to the status established by law or by model contracts, are without effect and are to be replaced by the terms established by law or by a model contract.

Art. 102. The translation of a work to another language for publication is allowed only with the consent of the author or of the successors to his rights.

The competent agencies of the USSR may, in a procedure established by the legislation of the USSR, allow the translation of the work to another language and the publication of this translation with the observance, in appropriate cases of the conditions of the international treaties or international agreements in which the USSR participates.

The translator shall have a copyright to the translation made by him.

Art. 103. The following are permitted without the consent of the author and without payment of authors' royalties, but with the requirement that the name of the author whose work was utilized be indicated together with the source of the original:

1. use of the published work of another to produce a new, creatively independent

production, but not including reworking of a narrative production into a dramatic play, or into a scenario, and vice versa—as well as the reworking of a dramatic play into a scenario and vice versa;
2. reproduction in scientific and critical works, textbooks and political or education publications of separately published productions of science, literature and art, and selections from these, within the limits established by legislation of the union republic;
3. information for transmission in the periodical press, in films, on the radio and through television regarding the publication of productions of literature, science and art;
4. reproduction in films, on the radio and through television of speeches and reports delivered in public and also of published productions of literature, science and art;
5. reproduction in newspapers of publicly presented speeches and reports, and also published works of literature, science, and art in the original and in translation;
6. reproduction in any form except mechanical copying by contact of works of art, located in places open to public view, except for expositions and museums;
7. copying of printed works for scientific and educational purposes without making a profit.

Art. 104. The following shall be permitted without the consent of the author but with the requirement that his name be indicated and royalties paid:
1. public presentation of published productions; but if the audience pays no admission fee, the author shall have the right to royalties only in circumstances established by legislation of the union republics;
2. recording for the purpose of public presentation or distribution of published productions on film, records, magnetic tape or other equipment, with the exception of use for the production of a moving picture, or of a radio or television program (section 4 of Art. 103 of the present Fundamental Principles);
3. use by a composer of published literary productions to compose musical productions with librettos;
4. use of works of art and also of photographs in manufactured articles; in such cases designation of the author's name is not required.

Art. 105. Copyright is effective for the life of the author and for 25 years after his death, counting from January 1 of the year following the year of death of the author.

The legislation of the union republics may establish shortened terms of effectiveness of copyright for photographic works and works of applied art. These terms may not be less than 10 years from the moment of publication of such a work by means of its reproduction.

Copyright passes by inheritance. If there is a shortened term of effectiveness for the copyright it passes to the heirs for the part of the term which has not expired at the death of the author.

The legislation of the union republics established the types of rights of authors which do not pass by inheritence.

ASTAF'EV, BORD, AND NECHAEV vs. RUNETS AND THE HIGHER SCHOOL PUBLISHING HOUSE, Sotsialisticheskaia zakonnost', 1970, No. 8, p. 86.

In April 1969, Astaf'ev, Bord, and Nechaev brought an action against Runets and the Higher School Publishing House. The action was based on the claim that in November 1966 Runets asked them to take part in the writing of a textbook for the Technical Mechanics Vocational-Technical School. The plaintiffs agreed with this proposal. Runets, on behalf of the whole group of authors was supposed to conclude a contract with the Higher School Publishing House for the publication of this book and to edit it. After they did the work and the book was brought out, it was established that Runets, without their knowledge, indicated in the preface to the book that he personally had written 70 percent of the book. In accordance with this Runets was also paid royalties in the amount of 1036 rubles. Considering that Runets illegally included himself in the list of authors of the textbook and received the royalty, the plaintiffs asked the court to exclude him from the list of authors and to recover from him for their use the excess royalty he had received in the amount of 1029 rubles.

The Judicial Division for Criminal Cases of the Supreme Court of the Belorussian SSR, by a decision of May 15, 1969 found the contract of January 6, 1967, concluded between Runets in the name of the group of authors and the Higher School Publishing House for the publication of the textbook, *Technical Mechanics* to be invalid in the part which provided that Runets was a co-author of the textbook, and it excluded him from the list of authors, since he only edited the text. In connection with this the Division decided that 951 rubles of excess royalties received by Runets should be recovered from him in favor of the plaintiffs.

After this decision was made by the court, Runets filed a complaint with the Procurator of the Belorussian SSR in which he alleged that all material included in the book, *Technical Mechanics,* was copied by the plaintiffs from other books and they were in fact not its authors. The State Committee of the Council of Ministers of the Belorussian SSR checked the text of the book and established that the plaintiffs took from other books on theoretical and technical mechanics without an indication of the source of the taking 9.3 author's quires [one author's quire is equivalent to 40,000 characters or about 20 double-spaced typed manuscript pages—translator's note.], which amounted to 60.4 percent of the length of the book.

In connection with this the Deputy Procurator of the Belorussian SSR entered a protest before the Plenum of the Supreme Court of the Belorussian SSR in which he asked the reversal of the decision of the court as made in violation of Art. 489 of the Civil Code of the Belorussian SSR (use of a work without an indicaton of the author and the source from which it was taken). The Plenum of the Supreme Court of the Belorussian SSR on December 18, 1969 left the protest unsatisfied on the ground that according to Art. 489 of the Civil Code of the Belorussian SSR the use of the published work of another to make a new work is allowed without the consent of the author; in this respect, according to the conclusion of the Plenum of the Supreme Court of the Belorussian SSR, the amount of the text taken from other works does not matter.

The Procurator General of the USSR entered a protest before the Plenum of the Supreme Court of the USSR in which he raised the question of the reversal of the judicial decisions which had taken place and of the transfer of the case for a new hearing. The protest indicated that in writing the book the authors violated Art. 489 of the Civil Code of the Belorussian SSR, that they acted in bad faith, in connection with which the publication contract concluded with them should be dissolved.

The Plenum of the Supreme Court of the USSR satisfied the protest on the following grounds.

After the decision of the case by the court of the first instance, the State Committee of the Council of Ministers of the Belorussian SSR on Publishing presented its conclusion that the plaintiffs in creating the textbook took text from other books without indicating the source of the taking. This conclusion has essential significance for the case and requires judicial evaluation. According to Article 489 of the Civil Code of the Belorussian USSR, for the creation of a new, creatively independent work, the use of the published work of another without the consent of its author is allowed without the payment of compensation for the author but with the required indication of the name of the author whose work is used and the source from which it was taken. In the present case the plaintiffs and the defendant Runets violated the requirements of this Article in not indicating the authors and the works from which they took the text.

Another circumstance also deserves attention. Article 489 of the Civil Code of the Belorussian SSR states not only that it is necessary to indicate the name of the author whose work is used and the source of the taking, but also that this taking is allowed for the purposes of creation of a new, creatively independent work. In the present case, according to the conclusion mentioned above, the text which has been taken amounts to 60.4 percent of the length of the book. (For instance the amount taken from the books: Bychkov and Mirov, *Technical Mechanics,* is 1.1 author's quires; from Shavin and Metinskii, *Technical Mechanics,* is 1.6 quires; from Sokolov and Usov, *Technical Mechanics,* 1.8 quires; from Levinson, *Theoretical Mechanics,* 1.4 quires, etc.) Therefore the question arises, whether or not the authors created a new creatively independent work.

The opinion of the Plenum of the Supreme Court of the Belorussian SSR that the plaintiffs did not commit violations of Article 489 of the Civil Code of the Belorussian SSR and that for the creation of a new work the amount of work taken in general has no significance cannot be recognized as correct.

Since in deciding the case the Supreme Court of the Belorussian SSR was not aware of the use by the plaintiffs of published works of others and the question in connection with this of whether or not they created their own work was not considered, the decision of the Judicial Division and the Decree of the Plenum of the Supreme Court of the Belorussian SSR should be reversed.

In the new consideration of the case the court should verify the materials presented by the State Committee of the Council of Ministers of the Belorussian SSR on Publishing concerning the taking by the plaintiffs of text from other books, and if necessary order an expert examination for a conclusion as to whether or not the textbook compiled by the plaintiffs can be considered as a new creatively independent work, and depending upon this, decide the case.

Agreeing with the protest of the Procurator General of the USSR, the Plenum of the Supreme Court of the USSR reversed all judicial decisions in the case and transferred it for a new hearing to the Supreme Court of the Belorussian SSR as the first instance with the participation of a procurator.

BYKHOVSKII AND DEVEL' vs. MURMANSK BOOK PUBLISHING HOUSE,
Biulleten' Verkhovnogo Suda RSFSR, 1970, No. 7, p. 5.

Bykhovskii and Debel' concluded a contract with the Murmansk Book Publishing House on February 16, 1965, in which they transferred to the publishing house the right to publish their literary work, short stories under the title "The Price of Error," 14 author's quires in length. November 1, 1965, was set as the date for presentation of the manuscript. The publishing house undertook to pay the authors at 150 rubles per author's quire and at 250 rubles for a large edition. Because of the low quality of the work presented by the plaintiffs, the publishing house declared the contract invalid, but informed the authors that it was prepared to conclude a new contracct with them, if they would present new stories. On February 16, 1966, a supplementary agreement was concluded between the authors and the publishing house, by which the contract of February 16, 1965, was reinstated subject to the fulfillment by the authors of the conditions listed in the agreement and, first and foremost, the obligatory reworking of the manuscript "The Price of Error." In addition, the authors undertook to remove from the manuscript stories which had been published earlier and also to include not less than half (by length) of materials on Murmansk themes. For its part, the enterprise undertook the obligation to send the authors observations and proposals on the improvement and finishing of the manuscript not later than March 1, 1966. The parties set a new date for submission of the manuscript—October 1, 1966.

The term for approval of the manuscript, according to the calculations of the publishing house, expired on November 5, 1966. In connection with the transfer of the manuscript on November 10, 1966 for a reading by a reviewer, the publishing house extended the term for giving written notice to the author about acceptance of the manuscript. The extension was for the whole time the manuscript was out for review. On February 1, 1967, the reviewer returned the manuscript to the publishing house. On February 3, 1967, the publisher sent to the authors a text of the book which included eight stories of the ten presented by the authors. By a telegram of

February 6, 1967, the plaintiffs complained to the publishing house about the exclusion of two stories from the book. On February 18, 1967, the publishing house communicated that it had excluded two stories from the book.

In connection with this Bykhovskii and Devel' brought an action in court against the Murmansk Book Publishing House for the recovery of royalties of 1372 rubles and 50 kopecks for the whole manuscript, since they considered that the defendant had broken the inviolabilty of the work and had missed the deadline for informing the authors of refusal to accept the manuscript.

The plaintiffs based their claims on the ground that on November 5, 1966, Chirikov, the editor of the publishing house had informed them by letter of the consent of the publishing house, in addition to the nine stories approved by the reviewer Naldeev, to include in the collection, in addition, the story "Don't Throw the Ax in the River." Thus, in the opinion of the plaintiffs, the defendant had approved ten stories with a length of 10.25 author's quires, and this was the work that the publishing house was obliged to publish.

In connection with the fact that later the publishing house published eight stories of the plaintiff's manuscript and paid them 630 rubles and 90 kopecks, the plaintiffs reduced the amount of their claim to 741 rubles and 60 kopecks.

The representative of the interests of the publisher objected to the claim, basing his objections on the ground that the contract with the authors was concluded for the publication of a collection of stories, each of which was a finished work. Therefore the plaintiffs did not have the right to demand payment of compensation for stories not suitable for publication.

The Murmansk regional court satisfied the claim in the amount of 565 rubles.

In its cassational appeal, the Murmansk Book Publisher asked that the decision of the court be reversed on the ground that the publishing house had the right to exclude from the collection presented by the authors two stories in view of their unsuitability for publication.

The Judical Division for Civil Cases of the Supreme Court of the RSFSR, having considered the case on the cassational appeal of the publishing house, left the decision of the Murmansk Regional Court without change as made in accordance with the factual circumstances and the demands of Art. 508 of the Civil Code of the RSFSR. In so holding, the Division, in its decision of February 9, 1970, indicated the following.

As is established in the record, on September 30, 1966, the plaintiffs presented to the publisher the second, revised version of the manuscript consisting of 15 stories of an overall length of 14 author's quires. On October 17, 1966, the plaintiffs sent the defendant one more story, "Don't Let Her In," with a length of two author's quires. The term for approval of the manuscript by the publishing house expired on November 5, 1966. On November 5, 1966, Chirikov, the editor of the publishing house, informed the plaintiffs by letter that the publishing house agreed with the reviewer who approved nine stories and considered it possible to include in the collection in addition the story, "Don't Throw the Ax in the River."

However the publishing house after this letter, on November 10, 1966, sent the authors' manuscript for a reading by another reviewer. He returned it to the publishing house only on February 1, 1967, i.e. after the expiration of the term for approval of the manuscript.

In these circumstances the court correctly found that the publishing house improperly excluded from the manuscript two stories, "Lew-22-17," and "Don't Throw the Ax in the River," with an overall length of 3.77 author's quires, and a royalty of 565 rubles and 50 kopecks.

The arguments of the appeal of the Murmansk Book Publisher are unconvincing, since the publisher did not refuse to publish these stories within the term provided for approval of a manuscript. Sending a manuscript for a second review does not extend the term for approval of the manuscript.

KUKLIN & SAVITSKII vs. LENINGRAD DRAMA THEATER, Biulleten' Verkhovnogo Suda RSFSR, 1971, No. 6, p. 15.

In January 1968, The Komissarzhevskaia Leningrad Drama Threater concluded a contract with Kuklin and Savitskii for the translation of the prose and verse text of a play.

The theater promised to pay compensation for the translation of the play in the amount of 800 rubles as follows: 25% on the conclusion of the contract, 50% on the acceptance of the play by the theater, and 25% after the premiere.

However the theater paid the plaintiffs only the 25% advance on the conclusion of the contract and refused to pay the 600 rubles compensation for the translation of the play.

The Kuibishev District People's Court of Leningrad satisfied the complaint.

The Judicial Division of the Leningrad City Court modified the decision of the court and reduced the amount recovered from the theater for the use of the plaintiffs to 400 rubles.

The Presidium of the same court, having considered the case on the protest of the Deputy President of the Supreme Court of the RSFSR asking that the decision of the Judicial Division be reversed and that the decision of the People's Court be left without change, satisfied the protest on the following grounds.

The Judicial Division, in modifying the decision of the People's Court and reducing the amount of the claim based its decision on the ground that according to the contract 25% of the royalty was to be paid after the premier of the play, however the play was not produced due to circumstances beyond the control of the parties, and therefore the 25% royalty was not subject to payment.

But such a conclusion contradicts the demands of Art. 512 of the Civil Code of the RSFSR, Par. 11 of the Model Production Contract, and Par. 7 of the Decree of the Plenum of the Supreme Court of December 19, 1967, "On the Practice of Consideration by Courts of Disputes Arising from Copyright."

Art. 512 of the Civil Code of the RSFSR provides that if an organization does not realize or does not begin the use of a production approved by it within the term established by contract, it is obliged on demand of the author to pay him the agreed compensation in full. The organization is freed from the obligation to pay the author the part of the compensation which he was to have received after the start of the use of the work if the organization shows that it could not use the work for reasons within the control of the author.

It was established by the court of first instance that the work of the plaintiffs on the translation of the play was accepted by the theater in April 1968 and no complaints were presented as to the quality of the translation, which was not contended by the administration of the theater. Accordingly, the theater, by virtue of Par. 9 of the Model Production Contract (par. 9 of the contract of the parties) was obliged to pay the author 50% of the compensation (400 rubles) for the accepted work.

It was also established by the People's Court that the production of the play was not accomplished by the theater within the time limits indicated in Par. 3 of the contract due to circumstance beyond the control of the authors. Therefor the theater was obliged to pay the authors for translation of the work compensation in full according to the contract, including the 25% (200 rubles) which they were to receive after the premiere of the play.

On this question, in Par. 7 of the Decree of the Plenum of the Supreme Court of the USSR of December 19, 1967, it is explained that an organization on demand of the author is obliged to pay him the agreed compensation in full, just as it must when there has been violation through its fault of the contract for the use of the work, even when a work it had approved was not presented to the public within the time provided by the contract due to circumstances not within the control of the organization.

From the record it appears that the play in the authors' translation was not produced by the theater for reasons not depending upon the authors. Therefore, they could not bear responsibility on these grounds and must receive compensation in full.

RACHMANOV, LEPING, NARKEVICH, AND LINDER vs. SOVIET ENCYCLOPEDIA PRESS, Biulleten' Verkhovnogo Suda SSSR, 1968, No. 10, p. 4.

Rachmanov, Leping, Narkevich, and Linder brought an action in court against the Soviet Encyclopedia Press for recovery of authors' royalties for the fourth edition of the *German-Russian Dictionary,* which was 87 author's quires in length. They based their demands on the ground that, according to the contract for publication concluded between them and the defendant press on September 30, 1965 they were to receive a royalty of 60% of the royalty for the first edition, however the press has refused to pay a royalty.

The Soviet Encyclopedia Press did not accept the claim and filed a counterclaim against Rachmanov and the other authors to have the contract for publication of September 30, 1965, declared invalid on the ground that it was concluded by mistake, since between the third edition of the dictionary, which appeared in September

1963, and the fourth edition of the dictionary, which appeared in July 1965 a two year term had not passed, and therefore the authors under the law had no right to receive a royalty.

The Judicial Division for Civil Cases of the Moscow City Court satisfied the autors' claims, ordering the recovery from the Soviet Encyclopedia Press of 2295 rubles for the use of Leping, 2160 rubles for Rachmanov, 2295 rubles for Linder, and 1080 rubles for Narkevich. The Judicial Division rejected the counterclaim of the Soviet Encyclopedia Press to have the contract declared invalid.

Having considered the present case by way of cassation, the Judicial Division for Civil Cases of the Supreme Court of the RSFSR in its decision of April 8, 1968, indicated the following:

From the record it appears that the first edition of the dictionary was published in 1955, for which the plaintiffs received royalties in the amount of 12948 rubles; the second was published without payment of compensation in 1956; the third edition in September 1963 with payment of compensation in the amount of 7740 rubles, and the fourth edition in July 1965.

The refusal by the press to pay royalties for the fourth edition on the grounds that a two-year period had not elapsed between the third and fourth editions cannot be considered correct.

In accordance with Art. 510 of the Civil Code of the RSFSR an organization must accomplish or begin the use of a work as provided by the contract within the term established in the same contract, a term which may not exceed two years from the day of approval by the organization of the work.

According to Par. 3 of the decree of the Council of Ministers of the RSFSR of March 20, 1962, No. 326, "On the Author's Royalty for a Work of Political, Scientific, Production-Technology, Educational, and Other Literature," each new edition of the given work is considered a republication if it is published after the expiration of the term established by contract or law after the publication of the previous edition, or within the limits of that term, but with revision or addition of new text in the form of separate chapters, parts, divisions, paragraphs, or sections.

It is established in the record that the previous edition of the dictionary, consent to which the plaintiffs had already given in 1960, was made in violation of the law without the conclusion of a publishing contract with the plaintiffs. The dictionary was sent for typesetting on October 25, 1961 and appeared in September 1963.

Since the contract for this edition of the dictionary should have been concluded with the plaintiffs not later than the beginning of the printing work for the dictionary, i.e. October 25, 1961, the two-year term which the press had for the publication of this edition expired on October 25, 1963.

The following edition of the dictionary was made after the expiration of the two-year term established by law.

The position of the press that the two-year period should run from the moment of publication of the previous edition is incorrect. According to the law the two-year period starts to run from the moment of approval of the work or equally from the moment of putting the work into production.

Thus, the defendant did not have the right to publish the latest edition of the dictionary in 1965 without concluding a publication contract with the plaintiffs, and certainly not without payment of royalties.

[Affirmed.]

SERGEEV AND LAVYGIN vs. NIZHNE-VOLZHSKAIA NEWSREEL STUDIO, Biulleten' Verkhovnogo Suda RSFSR, 1971, No. 3, p. 4.

Sergeev brought an action in court against the Nizhne-Volzhskaia Newsreel Studio for the recovery of 280 rubles, claiming that in 1969 he wrote the narrator's text and scenario plan for the film "The Crossing" and directed its production. For the production of the film the studio, instead of 560 rubles paid only 280 rubles, while it paid in full for the compilation of the narrator's text and the scenario plan.

Lavygin also brought an action in court. He sought the recovery from the film studio of 342 rubles, claiming that he, as camera operator together with director Sergeev shot the documentary film, "The Crossing" in 1969, but that instead of compensation in the amount of 400 rubles he was paid only 58 rubles.

[A decision dismissing the complaints was affirmed on the following grounds:]

From the record it appears that the film "The Crossing" was made by director Sergeev in 1968 using the materials of the earlier films "A Bridge for Gas" and "The Underground Line of Blue Fire." Only 43 meters of new material was shot for film involved. Cameraman Lavygin did the supplementary filming. This circumstance is confirmed by a certificate of the division of technical inspection, by a calculation of film involved, by a letter of December 12, 1969, from the Committee on Cinematography attached to the Council of Ministers of the USSR and its conclusion, by testimony of the witness Zhirin, and by the explanations of the plaintiff Sergeev. In this circumstance, in accordance with Par. 6 of the Temporary Statute on the Payment of Production Compensation for the production of Newsreel or Documentary Films, Film Magazines and Topical Films at Film Studios of the System of the Ministry of Culture of the USSR [citation omitted], the defendant correctly paid compensation to the director Sergeev in the proportion of 50 percent of the amount provided for films of the corresponding quality and complexity, and to the cameramen Lavygin for 43 meters of newly taken film, which corresponds to Par. 7 of the Statute.

M. vs. KAZAN UNIVERSITY PRESS, Biulleten' Verkhovnogo Suda RSFSR, 1975.

M. brought an action in court against the Kazan University Press for recovery of an author's royalty, basing his demands on the fact that the university press, in accordance with the 1973 publication plan, published his book *Economics of Management and Planning of Industrial Production,* but has refused to pay him compensation (a royalty) as an author.

The Supreme Court of the Tatar ASSR refused to satisfy the claim on the ground that the book was written by the plaintiff in fulfillment of an employment obligation for which no royalty was payable.

In his appeal, the author asked that the decision of the court be reversed on the ground that the creation of the book was not connected with his fulfillment of a plan for scientific research work and that in submitting the manuscript he reached an agreement with the director of the press on the payment of royalties.

The Judicial Division for Civil Cases of the Supreme Court of the RSFSR, which considered the case by way of cassation on February 14, 1975, affirmed the decision.

According to Art. 100 of the Fundamental Principles of Civil Legislation, authors' compensation for the publication and republication of works created in the fulfillment of employment tasks in a scientific or other organization including the planned works of employees of scientific-research institutions and higher educational institutions is paid only in the cases provided by law.

In accordance with Par. 9 of the Decree of the Plenum of the Supreme Court of the USSR of December 19, 1967, "On Practice in Court Consideration of Disputes Arising from Copyright," a work is considered planned if the individual plan for the author provides for its execution.

According to Par. (g) of Ch. XII of the Decree of the Council of Ministers of the RSFSR No. 326 of March 20, 1962, "On Royalties for Works of Political, Scientific, Production Technology, Educational and Other Literature," royalties are paid neither for dissertations prepared by the dissertation writers on a leave from production nor for planned works prepared by authors in a scientific research institution as an employment task (with the exception of standard and other textbooks for educational institutions).

From the record it appears that no publication contract as provided by Art. 505 of the Civil Code of the RSFSR was concluded between the parties and that they did not undertake any mutual obligations to one another with respect to the publication of the book and the payment of royalties to the author.

According to the plan of the Kazan Financial-Economic Institute, where M. was head of a department, work on supplementing and revising an earlier textbook, *Economics of Management and Planning of Industrial Production*, with later republication of the book was included in the individual plan of M., for the fulfillment of which in the 1971/72 academic year 400 hours was allocated. This circumstance is attested to by the individual plans of the Financial-Economic Institute which are attached to the record. The fact that this work was included in this individual plan was not disputed in substance by the plaintiff.

In this circumstance, M.'s demands for payment of royalties in addition to the salary he has received are not based upon the law, and the court correctly entered a decision to dismiss his claim.

NOVGORODOV vs. SIBERIAN DIVISION OF SCIENCE PUBLISHING HOUSE,
Biulleten' Verkhovnogo Suda SSSR, 1973, No. 8, p. 2.

In March 1971, Novgorodov brought an action in court against the Siberian Division of Science Publishing House to recover an author's royalty. As the basis for his claim he stated that in 1969 the publishing house brought out his monograph, *The October Revolution and the Civil War in Yakutia,* with a length of 25 printed quires, however no author's royalty was paid.

[The Judicial Division for Civil Cases of the Supreme Court of the RSFSR, reversed lower court decisions dismissing the claim on the following grounds:]

The People's Court dismissed Novgorodov's claim on the grounds that the monograph published by the defendant was a planned one for which no royalty was payable. In accepting the monograph for publication the editor-in-chief informed the author (the plaintiff) that the work was accepted for publication as planned (included in the plan of work of the publishing house) and would be published without payment of a royalty. The plaintiff did not present proofs that the theme of the monograph was not included in the plan of the research work of the institute where he worked at the time of completing the monograph.

In rejecting the protest, the Presidium of the Novosibirsk Regional Court based its decision on the ground that Novgorodov had defended a dissertation on "Yakutia in the Period of the Great October Socialist Revolution and the Civil War." The work of the plaintiff was planned for him, a contract was not concluded with the plaintiff, and therefore Novgorodov did not have the right to receive a royalty.

The judicial decisions which have been made in this case must be reversed on the following grounds.

The Plenum of the Supreme Court of the USSR in Par. 9 of its Decree of December 19, 1967, "On the Practice of Consideration by Courts of Disputes Arising from Copyright" indicated that according to Art. 100 of the Fundamental Principles of Civil Legislation, royalties for the publication or republication of works created in the fulfillment of an employment obligation in a research or other organization, including the planned works of employees of research and higher educational institutions are paid in the instances provided by law. A work is considered planned if its execution is envisioned in an individual plan established for the author, and also if a published work is counted with the consent of the author toward the fulfillment of the plan for his work.

There is no evidence in the record to the effect that the monograph published by the defendant was envisioned in the individual plan approved for Novgorodov or was counted with his consent in the fulfillment of the plan for his work.

The Presidium of the Regional Court, in rejecting the protest, cited new facts, in particular that the monograph was also the theme of the plaintiff's dissertation, facts which were not the subject of consideration at a court session in the presence of the parties. According to Par. 12(e) of the Decree of the Council of Ministers of the RSFSR of March 20, 1962, No. 326, "On the Author's Royalty for a Work of

Political, Scientific, Production Technology, Educational, and other Literature," a royalty is not paid for a dissertation written with a leave from production. When the monograph published by the defendant was written by the plaintiff, whether or not the text of the dissertation and the monograph coincide—these circumstances were not verified in the process of consideration of the case by the court.

As appears from the complaint and other documents in the record, Novgorodov during the course of a decade collected material on the revolutionary movement and the civil war in Yakutia. As a result of many years of work he prepared a monograph on this theme with a length of 30 author's quires. The book published by the plaintiff received many favorable reviews. It was awarded a silver medal at the Exhibition of Achievements of the National Economy for 1970.

As far as the fact is concerned that a contract was not concluded between the parties, this fact alone cannot alone serve as a basis for refusing to pay a royalty to the author.

According to the explanation of the Plenum of the Supreme Court of the USSR given in the Decree of December 19, 1967, if a work is used, the mere fact of the absence of a contract cannot serve as the basis for refusing to pay a royalty to the author. The time of release of the work (publication) should be considered as the start of the use of the work.

In the new consideration of this case, the court should more carefully verify the legality and well-foundedness of the action brought by Novgorodov.

B. Rewards for Scientists, Inventors, and Innovators

FUNDAMENTAL PRINCIPLES OF CIVIL LEGISLATION OF THE U.S.S.R. AND OF THE UNION REPUBLICS, December 8, 1961, effective May 1, 1962, [1961] Vedomosti Verkhovnogo Soveta SSSR, No. 50, item 525.

PART V.
THE RIGHT TO A DISCOVERY

Art. 107. The author of a discovery shall have the right to demand recognition of his authorship and priority in the discovery, this fact being established by a diploma which shall be issued in circumstances and in the manner provided in the Statute on Discoveries, Invention, and Rationalization proposals, approved by the Council of Ministers of the USSR.

PART VI.
AN INVENTOR'S RIGHT

Art. 110. An inventor may elect to demand either recognition only of his authorship, or recognition of his authorship and exclusive right to his invention. In the first instance an inventor's certificate shall be issued, in the second instance—a patent. Inventor's certificates and patents shall be issued under conditions and in accordance with the procedure provided by the Statue on Discoveries, Inventions and Rationalization Proposals, approved by the Council of Ministers of the USSR.

Art. 111. In those instances when an inventor's certificate is issued the right to use the invention belongs to the state, which assumes the responsibility of realizing upon the invention and accounting for the savings resulting from putting it to use.

Cooperative and social organizations may use the inventions relating to their spheres of activity on the same basis as state organizations.

An inventor to whom an inventor's certificate is issued, has the right, in the event that it is put to use, to renumeration established by a tariff related to the savings or other useful effect obtained as a result of putting the invention to use, and also the right to privileges in accordance with the Statute on Discoveries, Inventions and Rationalization Proposals.

Art. 112. A patent shall be issued for a term of fifteen years, from the day of deposit of the declaration. From that day the right of the declarer is protected. No one without the consent of the person to whom the patent belongs (the patent holder) may use the invention. The patent holder may give consent (a license) to the use of his invention or assign all rights to the patent.

An organization which prior to the declaration of the invention has independently of the inventor applied the said invention or done everything necessary to prepare for its application within the USSR shall retain the right to further use of the said invention without payment, and disputes on this matter shall be decided by a court.

In those circumstances when an invention has especially substantial importance for the state, but an agreement on concessionary use of the patent or on issuance of a license has not been reached with the patent-holder, on decision of the Council of Ministers of the USSR the patent may be purchased by the state or the organizations concerned may be given the right to use the invention, and royalties to the patent holder shall be established.

Art. 113. The author of a rationalization proposal that has been put to use shall be issued a certificate establishing his authorship. He has the right to receive the remuneration established by a tariff related to the savings or other useful effect obtained as a result of putting the proposal to use, and also the right to privileges in accordance with the Statute on Discoveries, Inventions and Rationalizing Proposals.

Art. 114. The inventors and rationalizers must cooperate actively in putting their proposals to use and in further developing them, and they shall have the right to participate in the work required to put their proposals to use, in the manner provided by the Statute on Discoveries, Inventions and Rationalization Proposals.

Art. 115. The right to receive an inventor's certificate or patent for an invention, or to a certificate for a rationalizer's proposal, and also the right to receive remuneration for inventions and rationalizers' proposals and also the exclusive right to an invention established by patent shall pass by inheritance in accordance with the procedure established by law.

Art. 116. Disputes over authorship (coauthorship) to inventions shall be decided by a court. Disputes over priority in rationalizers' proposals shall also be decided by a court, if they are not decided in the organization where the proposal has been put to use.

Disputes over the amount or manner of computation and periods of payment of remuneration for inventions and rationalizers' proposals shall be decided in accordance with the procedure provided in the Statute on Discoveries, Inventions and Rationalation Proposals, and the inventor or rationlizer who thinks the decision incorrect may take the matter to court.

CRIMINAL CODE OF THE RSFSR, effective January 1, 1961.
Art. 141. *Violation of authors' and inventors' rights.*

Issuance under one's own name of another's scientific, literary, musical or artistic production or any other appropriation of the authors' right in such a production or the illegal reproduction or distribution of such a production, as well as compulsion to accept coauthorship—shall be punished by deprivation of freedom for a term of up to one year or by fine of up to five hundred rubles.

Disclosure of an invention before announcement without the consent of the inventor, appropriation of the inventor's right to the invention, compulsion to accept coauthorship of the invention and also appropriation of the author's right to a proposal in rationalization—shall be punished by deprivation of freedom for a term of up to one year or correctional labor for the same period or by fine of up to five hundred rubles.

CASE OF IAROSHENKO, Biulletin' Verkhovnogo Suda RSFSR, 1975, No. 5, p. 5.

Iaroshenko filed an application for the establishment of his authorship of the discovery of a new physical phenomenon which was not earlier known to science. In his request he indicated that on October 19, 1973, on an application for a similar discovery a certificate was given to other persons, Tarantsov and Birfel'd, but that the priority to the discovery belongs to him, since he discovered the phenomenon even earlier, in 1954-1955.

The Moscow Regional Court refused to accept Iaroshenko's application on the ground that the dispute was not subject to the jurisdiction of the court.

In his appeal, Iaroshenko asked that the decision of the court be reversed and the case be sent for consideration on the merits on the grounds that he could not establish priorty to the discovery in any other manner.

The Judicial Division for Civil Cases of the Supreme Court of the RSFSR, having considered the case on January 10, 1975, by way of cassation, affirmed the decision of the Moscow Regional Court.

Refusing to accept the application, the Regional Court was motivated by the ground that the demands of Iaroshenko did not have the character of an action, and amounted to the qualitication of a technical proposal made earlier by him as an invention, and that, therefore, the present dispute was not within the jurisdiction of the court.

Iaroshenko has not made an application to the State Committee of the Council of Ministers of the USSR on Matters of Inventions and Discoveries, according to his statements both at the session of the Judicial Division of the Supreme Court of the RSFSR, and in court.

Iaroshenko explained in the judicial session of the second instance that he had no claims against Tarantsov and Birfel'd for use of ideas and technical documentation belonging to him, since they had been working in another agency and, therefore, could have arrived at the discovery independently.

Thus in fact Iaroshenko did not name in his application a specific defendant nor raise the question of priority to a discovery. However, disputes on novelty, priority and issuance of certificates for discoverers are not within the jurisdiction of a court.

Priority to an invention or discovery is established by the State Committee of the Council of Ministers of the USSR on matters of inventions and discoveries in accordance with the rules provided by the Statute on Discoveries, Inventions and Rationalization Proposals, approved by Decree of the Council of Ministers of the USSR No. 583 of August 21, 1973 (Pars. 144, 149).

The decision of the court to refuse to accept Iaroshenko's application was rendered in conformity with the demands of Par. 1 of Art. 129 of the Civil Procedure Code of the RSFSR.

K. vs. PETUNOV, Biulleten' Verkhovnogo Suda RSFSR, 1975, No. 11, p. 3.

K. brought an action in court against Petunov for recognition as a joint inventor of the invention "method of group soldering of output lines", an inventor's certificate for which was issued to Petunov by a decision of the State Committee of the Council of Ministers of the USSR on Matters of Inventions and Discoveries of October 30, 1974.

As a basis for his claims, the plaintiff relied on the ground that at the end of 1972, when they both were working at the Leningrad Research-Production Combine, "Red Dawn," Petunov was occupied with the development of means for the group soldering of stator output lines. In connection with a difficulty which arose, Petunov in his presence reported to sector chief Budarin that it was impossible to use the way of soldering which had been developed, soldering by submerging the output lines in a solder bath. Then he, the plaintiff, immediately proposed his method of group soldering of the output lines, by turning the stator 180°, and showed this on the table using a stator. Petunov at once checked this method in the shop and received a positive result, however he filed the application for this method of soldering only in his own name.

The defendant Petunov did not concede the claim and explained that the plaintiff did not take part in the development of the invention. K.'s proposal for rolling the stator in the solder bath was already known to him, the defendant, from Grigor'ev, technologist of the factory of automatic telephone exchanges, where this method had been in use, and did not constitute the essence of the invention.

The President of the Research-Production Combine, "Red Dawn," also objected to K.'s claim.

[A decision for the defendant was affirmed on the following grounds:]

According to Par. 4 of the Statute on Discoveries, Inventions and Rationalization Proposals, approved by decree of the Council of Ministers of the U.S.S.R. of August 21, 1973, only those persons by whose joint creative work the invention was created may be considered as coauthors of an invention.

The materials in the record establish that K. did not take a creative part in the creation of the invention in the form in which it is depicted in the specification of the invention.

From the explanations of the plaintiff, of the representative of the branch of the institute, and the testimony of the witnesses Budarin and Grigor'ev, it appears the plaintiff proposed to the defendant, who was carrying out an employment duty, to replace the generally know method of soldering output lines by submersion by another known method of placing the stator in the solder bath. However he did not make a concrete suggestion concerning the character of the placement and its technical realization. K.'s proposal in the form of advice to the inventor Petunov may not be considered to be creative participation in making the invention.

In his complaint and in the official report of January 9, 1975, made after the State Committee had adopted a decision on Petunov's application, K. gave a more detailed description of his invention, mentioning the rotation of the stator over 180° and the moving of the soldered output lines in a cycloid. However from the conclusions of the technical expert examination it is apparent that the proposal in this form does not correspond to all the characteristics of the invention.

In this situation the court properly dismissed K's action for recognition as a coinventor of the invention "means for group soldering of output lines."

KUDRIAVTSEV vs. LEMPERT ET AL., Biulleten' Verkhovnogo Suda RSFSR, 1968, No. 11, p. 10.

On May 28, 1963, The Committee on Matters of Inventions and Discoveries Attached to the Council of Ministers of the USSR issued an inventor's certificate to Lempert, Trebukhin, Safonov, Glushkov, and Beliachkov for the invention "Selfpropelled Machine for Loading Palisade Staker into Means of Transport."

In July 1967 Kudriavtsev brought an action against these persons to have himself recognized as the inventor of the invention for which an inventor's certificate was issued to them. Kudriavtsev based his action on the ground that the defendants in inventing the selfpropelled machine for loading palisade staker used the principal of operation of the working element of a staker collecting machine (for the collection and loading of staker) made by him. On November 28, 1960 he had filed an application for the machine he invented with the Committee on Matters of Inventions and Discoveries Attached to the Council of Ministers of the USSR which had wrongly refused to issue him an inventor's certificate on the ground of absence of novelty in the machine he had made.

On September 30, 1963 he filed a second application for the invention he had developed, but the Committee on Matters of Inventions and Discoveries again refused to issue an inventor's certificate citing an article published in the journal

"Peat Industry", 1963, No. 4, about the invention by the defendants of a stake-collecting machine. The Committee on Matters of Inventions adopted the decision to refuse to issue an inventor's certificate to him without taking account of his first application concerning the stake collecting machine he had invented.

The defendants did not concede, explaining that they did not know about the stake collecting machine made by Kudriavtsev and were not acquainted with the construction of this machine. The machine invented by them is the result of creative work of the whole collective and the working element of their machine is basicaly different from the construction of the working element of the machine made by Kudriavtsev.

The expert Viktorov gave the conclusion that the plaintiffs had made a machine which was basicaly different from the machine which Kudriavstev had tried to make but had not finished.

The Gorki Regional Court found the claims of Kudriavstev to be groundless and dismissed his action.

Having considered the present case by way of cassation on appeal of Kudriavtsev, the Judicial Division for civil cases of the Supreme Court of the RSFSR has indicated:

The conclusions of the plaintiff that the defendants in the development and making of the invention "Selfpropelled Machine for the Loading of Palisade Stakes on Means of Transport" took the plan and principle of operation of the working element of the machine he developed are not supported by anything and did not find support in court.

The defendants are employees of the Chistoe Peat Enterprise of Gorki Region and have never been at the Orichevskii Peat Enterprise of Kirov Region where the plaintiff worked and were not acquainted with the machine made by him in 1960.

From the copy in the record of the act of the Commission which conducted a trial of the machine proposed by Kudriavtsev, it appears that the working element of the machine was found not to be perfected. The Commission found it necessary to change the construction of the working element of the machine. As a result of the testing, the Commission came to the conclusion that the machine proposed by Kudriavtsev by its technological and construction qualities could not be recommended for use for combined work in the collection and loading of a stake nor for one of these operations.

The Committee on Matters of Inventions and Discoveries Attached to the Council of Ministers of the USSR refused to issue an inventor's certificate to Kudriavtsev on the grounds of the absence of significant elements of novelty in his proposal and also in connection with its negative conclusion on the industrial usefulness of the stake collecting machine he proposed.

The novelty of the defendants' invention was recognized by a decision of the Committee on Matters of Inventions and Discoveries with the issuance to them of an inventor's certificate.

According to Par. 45 of the Statute on Discoveries, Inventions, and Rationalization

Proposals, approved by a decree of the Council of Ministers of the USSR of April 24, 1959, disputes on the question of novelty of an invention for which an inventor's certificate has been issued are decided finally by the Committee on Matters of Inventions and Discoveries.

The decision of the Committee on this question may not be disputed in a judicial proceeding.

[Affirmed.]

BUBNOV vs. MINISTRY OF THE MEDICAL INDUSTRY OF THE USSR ET AL., Biulleten' Verkhovnogo Suda RSFSR, 1971, No. 5, p. 5.

Bubnov brought an action in court against the Ministry of the Medical Industry of the USSR, the Ministry of Health of the USSR and Akulinichev to have inventor's certificate issued to Akulinichev annulled and to recover compensation for the use of his invention.

He motivated his demands on the ground that the inventions made by Akulinichev were not distinguished by substantial novelty in comparison with his inventions for which an inventor's certificate was also given.

A member of the Moscow City Court refused to accept the complaint and explained to the plaintiff that on the question of annulling the inventor's certificate issued to Akulinichev, he should apply to the Committee on Matters of Inventions and Discoveries Attached to the Council of Ministers of the USSR. For recovery of compensation as an inventor, Bubnov could apply to the court after receiving the decision of the Ministry of the Medical Industry of the USSR if he were not in agreement with it.

[This decision was affirmed on the following grounds:]

As appears from the record, Bubnov, by bringing this action disputes the authorship of Akulinichev and the actions of those organizations which recognized Akulinichev's proposals as new and issued an inventor's certificate to him.

Since the dispute between the plaintiff and the defendant concerns the novelty of the proposals made by Akulinichev, it, according to Par. 45 of the Statute on Discoveries, Inventions, and Rationalization Proposals is not subject to the jurisdiction of the court since it is finally decided by the Committee on Matters of Inventions and Discoveries Attached to the Council of Ministers of the USSR.

The demands of the plaintiff for recovery of inventor's compensation for the use of his invention cannot be considered by the court at the present time since for this category of disputes a preliminary procedure for nonjudicial decision is established and this possibility for decision of the dispute has not been lost by the plaintiff (Par. 19 of the Statute).

Thus, the arguments of Bubnov's appeal may not be considered to be convincing, since they do not correspond to the requirements of Pars. 1 and 2 of Art. 129 of the Civil Procedure Code of the RSFSR.

SHUMILINA AND NAZAROVA vs. SARATOV TECHNICAL GLASS FACTORY, Biulleten' Verkhovnogo Suda RSFSR, 1970, No. 4, p. 7.

Shumilina and Navarova brought an action in court against the Saratov Technical Glass Factory to recover inventor's compensation.

They based their demands on the claim that the factory, in 1964, put into production an invention of theirs, but refused to pay compensation in the amount of 475 rubles of the 4300 ruble annual savings received.

The representative of the factory did not accept the claim, indicating that the plaintiffs' invention was not brought into production.

The Saratov Regional Court refused to satisfy the claim.

In a cassational appeal, Shumilina indicated that the fact of introduction of the invention by the defendant was attested by a certificate of the State Committee on Matters of Inventions and Discoveries Attached to the Council of Ministers of the USSR, while the conclusions of the expert examination were based upon a presupposition.

The Judicial Division for Civil Cases of the Supreme Court of the RSFSR, having considered the case, did not find bases for reversal of the decision rendered in accordance with Articles 521 and 526 of the Civil Code of the RSFSR which regulate questions of payment for inventions. The Judicial Division in its decision of December 23, 1969 indicated the following.

The plaintiffs are in fact the authors of the invention "Submachine Chamber for an Apparatus for Making Plate Glass," registered in the State Register of Inventions of the USSR on December 24, 1963.

However, for the satisfaction of the demands of the actions for the recovery of inventor's compensation it is necessary to establish the fact of introduction of the invention at the defendant's place of work, while the latter denies this circumstance.

The position of the defendant was complicated by the fact that the factory presented reports to the agencies of statistical information concerning the introduction of the plaintiffs' invention in the fourth quarter of 1964 with the receipt of an annual economy in the amount of 4300 rubles.

Later the factory officially denied that the invention had been introduced, stating that in 1964 only preparation for introduction of the invention had been carried out, but in fact the rationalization proposal of Engineer Noskova had been introduced with payment to her of 160 rubles compensation.

In connection with this two expert examinations were conducted in the case which established that the invention of the plaintiffs had not been introduced at the factory. The latter expertise was conducted in October 1969 in the presence of Shulina. The experts noted that both the invention of the plaintiffs and the rationalization proposal of Noskova had the purpose of improving the quality of the glass and raising the quality of production. However, there were different designs for carrying out these tasks and Noskova's proposal which did not demand significant expenditures was put into production.

This circumstance was also attested by the testimony of the factory engineers

Vanin and Omel'ianenko. Shumlina stated in court that Noskova's proposal was an independent solution of the problem, although more elementary in comparison with the plaintiffs' invention. In inspection of the equipment at the factory no signs of the introduction of the plaintiffs' invention into production were found, although the preparatory work was done for this at the factory which was the reason for the premature inclusion of the invention in the statistical report.

BEREZIUK AND PODKOVKIN vs. FACTORY, Biulleten' Verkhovnogo Suda RSFSR, 1968, No. 12, p. 6.

Bereziuk and Podkovkin brought an action in court for inventor's compensation for the use of their invention "Self-loading Barge" claiming that by order of the factory they were paid compensation only in the amount of 600 rubles. The value of their invention was incorrectly determined by the factory. In this regard they sought to have the true value of their invention established and the inventor's compensation determined accordingly.

[A decision dismissing the case was reversed by the Presidium of the Supreme Court of the RSFSR on the following grounds:]

The Volgograd Regional Court, in rendering a decision to dismiss the case relied on the ground that the right to establish the amount of compensation for an invention is given solely to the director of the enterprise, and that, therefore, this case is not subject to the jurisdiction of the court.

However, according to Par. 4 of the Decree of the Plenum of the Supreme Court of March 4, 1961, "On Judicial Practice in Invention and Rationalization Cases," disputes on amounts, procedure for calculating, and terms of payment of compensation for inventions and rationalization proposals are subject to judicial consideration if the plaintiff has observed the preliminary pretrial procedure for decision of such disputes provided in Par. 19 of the Statute on Discoveries, Inventions, and Rationalization Proposals.

If the extrajudicial procedure for the examination of a dispute is not observed, the court under Art. 221 of the Civil Procedure Code of the RSFSR must dismiss the case.

The plaintiffs dispute the correctness of the establishment of the amount of compensation of the invention according to its true value. Such a dispute is subject to judicial consideration.

In considering the claims, in which the actual value of the invention as established by the managers of the enterprise is disputed, the court in deciding this question may if necessary order an appropriate expert examination.

In doing so, it should be kept in view that the actual value of an invention whose introduction does not give savings in practice is defined by the degree of novelty of the invention, the difficulty of the technical task solved by the invention, the significance of the positive effect from the application of the invention, the amount of use and other factors.

[Remanded for consideration on the merits.]

REPIN vs. SARATOVGESSTROI Biulleten' Verkhovnogo Suda RSFSR, 1970, No. 8., p. 3.

Repin, working as head of a department of the production-technology division of Saratovgesstroi, made a rationalization proposal in August 1966. On April 5, 1967, the director of the Board for Mechanization of Construction Work (BMCW) gave him an attestation for this proposal, but no compensation was paid. In connection with this Repin brought an action in court, seeking to recover 1700 rubles from the BMCW of Saratovgesstroi.

The representative of the Board did not concede the claim, and explained that Repin's proposal was not for an improvement, since on October 20, 1969, the administration of the BMCW together with the committee of the trade union classified the proposal as an organizational measure.

Since the dispute arose over the classification of the proposal, the court entered a decision to dismiss the case for lack of jurisdiction.

Repin asked to have the decision of the court reversed and to have the case considered on the merits, on the ground that his proposal had been put in practice and recognized as a rationalization, and that, therefore, the administration of the BMCW was obliged to pay him compensation as a rationalizer.

The Judicial Division for Civil Cases of the Supreme Court of the RSFSR, having considered the case on the partial appeal of Repin, reversed the decision of the regional court, indicating in its decision of December 30, 1969, the following.

According to Par. 3 of the Decree of the Plenum of the Supreme Court of the USSR of March 4, 1961, disputes on the classification of proposals are not subject to the jurisdiction of the court.

However in this paragraph of the decree of the plenum it is stated that in instances when the proposal was introduced, but the administration of the enterprise (or institution) refuses to recognize it as rationalizing, a court which has accepted an action in a dispute about authorship (coauthorship), should stay proceedings in the case until the classification of this proposal by the superior organization. If the proposal is not found to be rationalizing, the court suspends proceedings in the case.

Repin's proposal was accepted and used, but later the administration of the BMCW of Saratovgesstroi refused to recognize it as rationalizing and did not pay rationalizer's compensation. Therefore the court did not have legal bases for dismissing proceedings in the present case.

The citation of Par. 55 of the Statute on Discoveries, Inventions and Rationalization Proposals is erroneous in the present case, since it does not decide the question which has arisen.

As is apparent from the record, by the time it was considered in the judicial decision of November 26, 1969, the decision of the Technical Council of Glavgidroenergogesstroi (the superior organization) had been made, and this decision recognized Repin's proposal as a rationalization and recommended the payment of rationalizer's compensation to the head of Saratovgesstroi.

GORBUNOV vs. RADKEVICH, KIREEV, MAKAROV AND THE NEZHDANNAIA MINE, Biulleten' Verkhovnogo Suda RSFSR, 1972, No. 5, p. 4.

In June 1967, Gorbunov brought an action in court against Radkevich, Kireev, Makarov and the Nezhdannaia Mine for the recognition of his priority to a rationalization proposal. Gorbunov based his demand on the ground that he, working at the Nezhdannaia Mine, on March 28, 1956 made a proposal about a means for automation of the control of branched conveyor lines. This proposal was accepted by the administration of the Nezhdannaia Mine and was implemented. In 1960 he published his proposal in a scientific and technical bulletin in an article "Automation of Control of Branched Conveyor Lines at the Nezhdannaia Mine." On September 7, 1968, Radkevich, Kireev, and Makarov made a proposal at the Nezhdannaia mine. Their proposal, which was called "Plan for Automation of Branched Conveyer Lines," was recognized as rationalizing and the authors were paid compensation. Gorbunov considered that their proposal was identical to the proposal that he had made earlier at that mine.

An action was brought in court in connection with the fact that the administration of the Nezhdannaia Mine had refused to recognize Gorbunov as having priority.

The representative of the Shakhtantratsit Trust and Makarov contested the claim on the ground that Gorbunov's proposal was not recognized as rationalizing.

[Lower court decisions rejecting Gorbunov's claim were reversed on the following grounds.]

According to Par. 56 of the Statute on Discoveries, Inventions and Rationalization Proposals [citation omitted] of 1959, if one and the same rationalization proposal are made at one and the same enterprise at different times by different persons, priority is recognized as belonging to that person who made the proposal first. This rule is also applied in the case if the first proposal made was refused, but the actions of the manager of the enterprise refusing to implement the proposal were not appealed in time by the maker of the proposal.

Accordingly, for judicial consideration of a dispute on the priority for a rationalization proposal (as distinguished from a dispute over authorship) it is not obligatory that the proposal made earlier by the plaintiff have been recognized as rationalizing by the established procedure.

A necessary prerequisite for the consideration of a dispute over priority is the recognition of the proposal made later as rationalizing. Therefore, the refusal of the managers of the mine and trust to classify Gorbunov's proposal as rationalizing may not serve as the basis for dismissing proceedings in the case on the dispute on priority. In the judicial consideration of the case, both proposals must be compared, and if they are identical, the proposal made earlier must be considered to be rationalizing and priority must be recognized as belonging to the person who made this proposal.

In the present case Gorbunov claimed that the proposal made by him in 1956 was identical to the proposal of Radkevich, Kireev, and Makarov which was recognized by the established procedure as rationalizing. Therefore, he asked the court to establish the identity of his proposal with the defendants' proposal and on this basis to recognize his priority. The claim made by Gorbunov is a dispute on priority, and this dispute by virtue of Art. 56 of the Statute is subject to the jurisdiction of the court.

Since the plaintiff has used different names for his proposal, it is necessary to have him clarify exactly what proposal of his he considers identical to the rationalization proposal of the defendants, when he made it, and to demand from the Nezhdannaia Mine Gorbunov's statement in which he formulated his proposal and the documents attached to it. There also should be demanded the attestation for the rationalization proposal made by the defendant, the statement and other materials on the basis of which this attestation was issued.

COPYRIGHT PROTECTION BOARD OF THE USSR ARTISTS' UNION v. MINISTRY OF LIGHT INDUSTRY OF THE USSR AND KOMSOMOL'SKAIA PRAVDA, Biulleten' Verkhovnogo Suda RSFSR, 1970, No. 11, p. 2.

In June, 1966, the Ministry of Light Industry of the USSR and the editorial board of the newspaper *Komsomol'skaia Pravda* announced an all-union contest for the best models of toys and of amateur creations of children and adolescents. Among other persons the artist L. N. Smorgon presented in the contest seven models of dolls under different names, from which the contest jury selected four with the names "Cleopatra," "Irishka," "Murik," and "Pelenashka," joined them into one group and awarded it a second prize in the amount of 350 rubles.

The Copyright Protection Board of the USSR Artists' Union brought a suit in defense of the interests of the artist L. N. Smorgon against the organizers of the contest to recover for the use of the artist three second prizes announced for the contest. The Board based its demand on the ground that under the conditions of the contest, the jury did not have the right to join into a single group examples of toys submitted under different names and to award a single prize to them. Since the jury had found all four types of dolls worthy of a second prize, then according to the conditions of the contest a prize should be awarded and paid for each of these types.

L. N. Smorgon supported the action on the same grounds.

The Ministry of Light Industry of the USSR contested the satisfaction of the claim on the ground that the jury had the right to award one prize to several items submitted under different names if they had a single artistic touch and an identical pedagogical value. The four types of dolls selected in the judging were executed in a single style and bore one characteristic artistic touch. Therefore, the contest jury properly joined them in a single group and awarded them one second prize.

After the tallying of the results of the voting, the envelopes with the names were opened and it turned out that the author of all four works was L.N. Smorgon.

[Lower court decisions against the artist were reversed on the following grounds:]

According to Articles 439 and 440 of the Civil Code of the RSFSR the announcement of a contest obliges the organizer to pay the promised compensation to the person whose work is recognized as worthy of an award in accordance with the conditions of the contest. By force of the same law, the announcement of the contest must contain a statement of the task, the term for its performance and the other conditions including the procedure and terms for the comparative evaluation of the works.

The conditions of the contest are obligatory both for the contestants and for the organizer and jury. A change in the conditions of a contest is allowed only during the first half of the term established for the presentation of works. A change in the conditions of the contest must be communicated in the same manner as the contest was announced.

From the "Conditions for the Conduct of the All-Union Contest for the Best Models of Toys and of Amateur Technical Creations of Children and Adolescents" attached to the record it follows that models of toys and of amateur technical creations of children and adolescents should be entered in the contest and that the best of them were to be awarded prizes. Therefore, according to the conditions of the contest, the competing work was to be a single model of a toy, in the present case a doll, and not a series of models. Each model of a toy was to be submitted under a specific name and the name of the author was to remain unknown to the jury until the completion of the evaluation of the works presented and the award of prizes.

The conditions of the contest did not provide that several different models of dolls, presented under different names, could be combined into a single group and be awarded one prize.

The arguments of the Ministry of Light Industry that under the conditions of the contest the jury had the right to award to one or several models, submitted under one or several names, but having a single artistic touch and identical pedogogical value a single prize, does not correspond to the character of the contest.

The artist Smorgon presented every model of toy as an independant work. In the consideration of the case no evidence was presented that these models taken separately or several of them did not satisfy the demands for independent competing work.

In leaving unsatisfied the protest of the Deputy President of the Supreme Court of the RSFSR, the Presidium of the Moscow City Court relied on the ground that the conditions of the contest did not forbid the joining of several models of dolls into a single group and that, therefore, such a joining and the award of one premium for a group was possible. However this conclusion of the Presidium, as was mentioned above, contradicts the character of the conditions of the contest.

At the same time, the substantiation should be verified for the conclusion of the Copyright Protection Board that the four models of dolls of the artist Smorgon were recognized by the jury as worthy of a second prize. It is necessary, in particular, to clarify how many votes of members of the jury had to be received by a submitted work for it to be awarded second prize and which models of dolls of the artist Smorgon received the necessary number of votes.

THE SOVIET LEGAL SYSTEM

Contemporary Documentation and Historical Commentary

PART III

PRIVATE LEGAL RIGHTS AND OBLIGATIONS OF SOVIET CITIZENS

FOREWORD

Relations between individuals in which the state plays no direct role have been called "private" ever since the emergence of Roman law. In modern Romanist systems their regulation is classified as private because the state has only a limited concern and responsibility in these relations. A forum for resolving disputes between citizens and a set of procedural rules to be observed in their resolution are provided by the public authorities, but the parties themselves are left free to decide whether to have recourse to the courts or to alternative remedies. While the common law traditionally recognized no such dualism, conceiving of the legal order in monistic terms, contemporary common lawyers have no difficulty in understanding the dualistic treatment of law, and in fact even in the common law a distinction is drawn between the public and private sectors.

The practice of separating a large body of law and denominating it "private law" and distinguishing it from "public law" affords adequate reason to establish as a separate part of this study of the Soviet legal system the Soviet legislation and practices of Soviet courts in what has traditionally been the private sector of other legal orders. Scholars from the common and Romanist legal systems can expect to find the law relating to personal contracts, actions for injury to the person and to property, disputes over ownership, inheritance, and domestic relations.

Most Soviet jurists regard a separation of law into public and private law as unrealistic in this sense. They regard as basic to all legal systems the pursuit of state aims, distinguishing the Soviet legal system on the basis of the degree to which the state has an interest in what transpires in every field of social endeavor, and in its express admission that such a public or social interest exists. Lenin reinforced such thinking when he declared that all law is "public,"[1] and Soviet jurists have reiterated his words ever since. There are other ways, however, in which Soviet law distinguishes between "public" and "private" law, notably in debating the respective bounds of civil law and economic law and in distinguishing private international law from public international law.

[1] V. I. Lenin, 29 *Sochineniia* (3d ed., 1928–1937), 419.

For anyone seeking to understand those features of Soviet law that, in the Soviet view, justify a claim to distinctiveness for the Soviet system, the traditionally private sector merits special examination. It is in this domain that the maximum correlation exists between Soviet code provisions and the models in Romanist systems after which many of these provisions were patterned, although traces of the Romanist models are less evident in the codes of the 1960-70s than in the codes of the 1920s. Yet, in this sphere of the Soviet legal system as much as in the less traditional areas encompassed in Parts I and II of this study, Soviet jurists find metamorphosis. Part III presents materials contributing to an assessment of this claim.

CHAPTER XVIII

Personal Property Rights and Their Scope

"Private property," wrote Lenin, "is robbery, and a state based on private property is a state of robbers who fight to share in the spoils."[1]

Consistent with this observation and with the guiding principles laid down by Marx and Engels, a primary goal of the Bolsheviks after coming to power was the elimination of private ownership of the instruments and means of production. The basic theory was: abolition of private ownership of the instruments and means of production would prevent capital assets and income from accruing to individuals and being used to exploit the labor of others. The individual's right of ownership would be limited to articles intended for personal use or consumption and acquired by earnings from their own labor. The practical application of this formula proved to be more complex when it came time for the Soviet legislators and judges to translate this objective into reality.

The nationalization of land, while it vested title to all land in the state, gave rise to the development of a whole new series of property relationships based on use rather than ownership (See Part II, Chapter 11). And even though the land under his house had passed to the state, the house owner retained the title to his home.[2]

With the nationalization of the banks and the cessation of trading in securities (including the prohibition against payment of dividends and interest), private property rights in intangibles were eliminated, except for those of small depositors in their bank accounts.[3] The private ownership of industry was liquidated more gradually. Large enterprises were nationalized in 1918,[4] whereas the smaller enterprises continued to function in private hands until 1920, when all enterprises employing more than five persons using mechanical tools or ten persons not using mechanical tools were nationalized.[5]

---

[1] V.I. Lenin, 31 Sochineniia [Collected Works] (3d ed., 1928–1937) 300.
[2] February 19, 1918, [1918] Sob. Uzak., RSFSR, No. 25, item 346; August 20, 1918. [1918] Sob. Uzak., RSFSR. No. 62, item 674.
[3] December 14, 1917, [1917] Sob. Uzak., RSFSR, No. 10, item 150.
[4] July 28, 1918, [1918] Sob. Uzak., RSFSR, No. 47, item 559.
[5] November 20, 1920, [1920] Sob. Uzak., RSFSR, No. 93, item 519.

The advent of the New Economic Policy, which, in Lenin's own words, was to permit rivalry temporarily between socialism and capitalism, brought to a halt the implementation of Marxist property theory. The great bulk of the means of production and of transport remained, however, even during the NEP, in the hands of the state.

The RSFSR Civil Code, which became effective on January 1, 1923,[6] represented an early attempt at codification and was drafted to meet the exigencies of the NEP with its qualified recognition of private enterprise. For this reason Article 54, in defining the objects capable of being owned by individuals, included small private enterprises and instruments of production as well as articles for individual use and income from labor. The Code defined these and other objects as being capable of being the subjects of "private"(*chastnaia*) property, rather than "personal" (*lichnaia*) property, the term later adopted in the 1936 USSR Constitution and in the 1961 Fundamental Principles of Civil Legislation of the USSR and Union Republics.[7]

Although the provisions relating to the ownership and conduct of private enterprises lost importance with the introduction of national economic planning in 1928, the remaining provisions relating to the ownership and use of houses and personal belongings retained their importance. Post-NEP recognition was given these provisions in Article 10 of the 1936 USSR Constitution, which guaranteed the protection of "personal" property rights in income and savings from labor, in dwelling houses, household articles and items for personal use, as well as the right of inheritance. The 1961 Fundamental Principles and the union republic civil codes promulgated on the basis thereof have followed closely the constitutional provisions.

The right of a property owner to possession, use, and alienation of his property was reaffirmed in Article 27 of the 1961 Fundamental Principles. These rights are expressly subject to whatever limitations are fixed by law. Some materials in this chapter will demonstrate that the problems of defining personal ownership and the permissible limits of use and alienation have both created conundrums for Soviet jurists and also evolved as the material requisites of life have become more abundant.

The great bulk of the litigation in Soviet courts involving personal rights of ownership relates to the ownership and use of houses. Material relating to land use for the construction of private dwellings has been included in Part II, Chapter 10. The selections in this chapter are intended to illustrate the multiplicity of problems faced in settling disputes between citizens involving the rights of ownership and use in a private dwelling, a collective farm household, and sundry items of personal use.

---

[6]November 11, 1922, [1922] Sob. Uzak., RSFSR, No. 71, item 904.
[7]December 8, 1961, [1961] Vedomosti Verkhovnogo Soveta, SSSR, No. 50 (1085), item 525.

A. Socialist theory of the nature of personal ownership

M. I. Braginskii, "Right of Personal Ownership," In O. S. Ioffe (ed.), OSNOVY SOVETSKOGO PRAVA, [The Fundamentals of Soviet Law] (Minsk, 1970), 140–141.

The essence of the right of personal ownership. In a socialist society there exists not only social, but also individual ownership, which takes the form of *personal ownership*. Personal ownership has a number of criteria. First, it is created by personal labor, excluding the exploitation of man by man. Karl Marx and F. Engels indicated: "Communism does not take away the possibility of appropriating social products; it takes away only the possibility of enslaving another's labor by means of such appropriation." Second, labor and social production are the basic source of personal ownership. Personal ownership may be created by such labor in its subsidiary husbandry. However, subsidiary husbandry also is linked with the participation of the person in social production, inasmuch as it is realized on land plots granted to collective farmers, workers and employees of enterprises, and organizations as such. This makes it possible in all instances to regard personal ownership as derived from socialist ownership. Third, the special purpose of personal ownership consists of satisfying the personal requirements of citizens, which also determines the circle of its possible objects. As Karl Marx pointed out, under socialism "nothing may pass to the ownership of individual persons except individual articles of consumption".

In conditions of the construction of communism, the party and government devote great attention to the development of personal ownership as one of the most important prerequisites of constantly raising the material welfare of the people. . . . Unfounded restrictions which existed in regard to personal subsidiary husbandry of workers, employees, and collective farmers have been abolished.

ANSWERS TO QUESTIONS, Kommunist, 1965, no. 1, p. 117.
To Comrade Z. Saiapov (from Shtanda, Bashkir ASSR)

Esteemed Comrade Saiapov! Having touched upon a series of problems concerning our social development in your letter, you expressed the opinion that personal ownership negatively influences the building of communism. It represents to you an almost fundamental obstacle to our movement. "All the bad habits people have," it says in the letter, "are so-called survivals not only from capitalism, but above all, from personal ownership." The sense of your suggestion can be reduced to the following: for the successful advancement of communism it is necessary to begin with the "curtailment" of personal ownership or even, as you write, the "rejection" of it from our life. And numerous survivals must vanish together with it. Thus the question of the abolition of personal ownership under socialism arises . . .

In history there is not and can not be a society composed of no form of property. Of course, if there were a man who labored and lived in utter solitude without any social links, then it would be senseless to speak of ownership or of "mine", "yours", or "ours", inasmuch as no one except him would profit from the fruits of his labor. But in the process of the production and the utilization of goods, people are always situated in definite relations with each other, including relations of personal ownership. In every society people assume the ownership of goods for individual consumption (for example, clothes, shoes) which are at their disposal for the satisfaction of personal needs. A person in a communist society could not do without the items included under personal ownership.

It is impossible for personal ownership to be unchanging during the various stages of social development: its character changes with the alteration of the character of ownership within the means of production. Thus, to whom the land, machines, industrial buildings, raw materials, and the like belong depends specifically on the status of people in society who assume possession and disposition of the share and form of consumer goods.

Socialism radically changes the economic content of personal ownership. Derived from the means of production of socialist social ownership, it expresses the attitude of free men to the exploitation of people. Under the conditions of socialism, labor becomes a singular, historical material blessing working for the personal ownership of the members of the society. "He who does not work, neither shall he eat" is the principle of a society which has done away with exploitative and parasitic classes.

One of the essential features of personal ownership under socialism is its continuous link with the distribution of labor. The material-technical base of society can no longer provide an abundance of material blessings. Furthermore, labor under socialism still has not become the first vital requirement of men because the significant distinctions between easy and difficult, skilled and unskilled, and mental and physical still remain. The most important stimulus in the development of economies appears to be the personal material incentive, working toward the results of production, and granting to the toiling people the basic mass of goods necessary for compliance with the expenditure of their labor. How is this manifested in personal ownership? Insofar as the unequal contributions of labor by various people in the national economy are concerned, those people have been paid diversely by society, and there arose the well-known distinctions among the material conditions and amount of the personal ownership of people. And this distinction has been impossible to eliminate at once since it arises from the objective necessity of the distribution of consumer goods in return for labor, and by necessity, it strengthens personal material incentive.

The extent of development of socialist production influences the essential form of the character of personal ownership. Socialism can not at once provide to everyone dwellings from the social fund, rest homes, or a universal public food supply. Therefore, not only such goods for individual comsumption as clothes or shoes, not only income and savings from labor from which some means of transport (cars, motorcycles) can be purchased, but also dwelling houses and subsidiary husbandry are in personal ownership under socialism.

You ask what will happen to personal ownership under communism. The single, social communist ownership, the means of production, presupposes the enormous rise of the role of the social fund in the organization of personal consumption from personal ownership. It is necessary to keep in mind that the rapid development of collective structures for the satisfaction of needs renders and will render to all an accelerated influence on the role of personal ownership in contemporary conditions and in the higher stages of communism. For example, when our society will be able to provide to all people comfortable apartments and to organize a network of public rest homes, the existence of dachas and houses will become senseless and irrational ownership. The development of social food resources, and the improvement of everyday repairs and other services will entail a sharper reduction of housekeeping. Further development will include instituting a network of public education for children and medical services. All these diverse social structures for the satisfaction of needs are characterized as the communist road to the increase of social welfare. Their instillation promotes man's formation of the collective tradition, surmounting the survivals of bourgeois individualism and egoism.

Communism, by comparison to socialism, imparts a new trait to remaining personal ownership. Thus, as under socialism, every man will receive consumer goods for his needs, but the principle of personal ownership in accordance with the expenditure of labor will be eliminated. It follows that material inequality in personal ownership, which was still preserved under socialism, will not be reflected under communism. Or to take, for example, such an element of personal ownership as a money economy: the need for them fades away with the disappearance of commodity-monetary relations. And the need to create a reserve of goods for personal consumption equally disappears.

V. Radaev, candidate of economic sciences.

B. *Nature and Scope of Personal Property Rights*

CONSTITUTION OF THE U.S.S.R., December 5, 1936
Art. 10. The right of personal ownership of citizens in the income and savings from their labor, in a dwelling house and subsidiary husbandries, in household articles, and in articles of personal use and convenience, as well as the right to inherit the personal ownership of citizens, shall be protected by the law.
CIVIL CODE, R.S.F.S.R. (1964)
Article 92. *Rights of an Owner*

An owner shall have the right to possess, use, and dispose of property within the limits established by law.
Article 105. *Objects of the Right of Personal Ownership*

Citizens may have in personal ownership property intended for the satisfaction of their material and cultural requirements.

Each citizen may have in personal ownership labor income and savings, a dwelling house (or part thereof) and subsidiary household economy, household articles, and articles of personal use and convenience.

Property in the personal ownership of citizens may not be used to derive nonlabor income.

Article 106. *Right of Personal Ownership in a Dwelling House*

A citizen may have one dwelling house (or part of one house) in personal ownership.

Spouses living together and their minor children may have only one dwelling house (or part of one house) belonging by right of personal ownership to one of them or in their common ownership.

The right of ownership of one or several citizens from those specified in paragraph two of the present Article shall not deprive the rest of these citizens of the right of ownership in another part (or parts) of this house. However, in a multiple-apartment house of a housing construction collective of individual builders, spouses living together and their minor children may have only one apartment.

The maximum size of a dwelling house or part (parts) thereof belonging to a citizen by right of personal ownership should not exceed sixty square meters of living space.

However, the executive committee of a district or city Soviet of Working People's Deputies may authorize a citizen who has a large family or who has a right to additional living space to build, acquire, or retain in ownership a house (or part of a house) of larger size. In this event, the living space of the house (or part of the house) should not exceed the size determined for the particular family according to norms for lessees in houses in local Soviets of Working People's Deputies, taking into account the right to additional living space (Article 316).

Article 151. *Recovery of Property by an Owner from Another's Illegal Possession*

An owner shall have the right to recover his property from another's illegal possession.

Article 152. *Recovery of Property from a Good-faith Acquirer*

If property is acquired for value from a person who did not have the right to alienate it, of which the acquirer did not know and should not have known (good-faith acquirer), then the owner shall have the right to recover this property from the acquirer only when the property has been lost by the owner or person to whom the property was transferred in possession by the owner, or has been stolen from one or the other, or otherwise left their possession against their will.

The recovery of property on the grounds specified in paragraph one of the present Article shall not be permitted if the property was sold in the procedure established for the execution of judicial decisions.

If the property was acquired gratuitously from a person who did not have the right to alienate it, the owner shall have the right to recover the property in all instances.

Article 156. *Protection of Rights of an Owner from Infringements Not Connected with Deprivation of Possession*

An owner may demand the elimination of any violations of his rights, even though such infringements were not linked with deprivation of possession.

Article 157. *Protection of the Rights of a Possessor Who is Not an Owner*
The rights provided by Articles 151-156 of the present Code also shall belong to a person even though not an owner who possesses property by virtue of law or contract.

SHCHERBAKOVA AND LARINA vs. MASHKOV et al, Biuileten' Verkhovnogo Suda RSFSR, 1973, no. 10, pp. 13–14.

House No. 12 on G. Uspenskii Street in the city of Tula belongs by right of share ownership to Mashkov, Romashchenko, Nikitina, and the Larins.

Shcherbakova bought part of the house from Mashkov, and the Larins, from Romashchenko.

Shcherbakova and the Larins brought suit in court against Mashkov, Romashchenko, and Nikitina to determine the procedure for using the land plot in accordance with the shares of the house belonging to them, citing the fact that the respondents B. Mashkov and Romaschenko are impeding them in the use of the land plot.

[After lower courts refused to hear the suit, the regional court returned the case for new consideration]. In refusing to satisfy the plaintiffs' claims, the court referred to the fact that since 1943 only the respondents actually used the land plot and had fruit trees thereon, and, in buying part of the house in 1968, the plaintiffs did not acquire the right to use the land plot inasmuch as at that time a procedure for using the plot had formed among the respondents, and the plaintiffs presented no evidence that the purchase of the share of the house was with the right to use the land plot. The court pointed out that Shcherbakov acquired part of the house from A. Mashkov, who was a I group invalid and who because of his state of health could not use the plot corresponding to his ideal share in the house, which was in the use of his brother B. Mashkov.

However, in accordance with Article 134 of the RSFSR Land Code, the procedure for the use of a common land plot shall be determined by taking into account the share of the structure belonging to citizens. The court resolving the dispute should have had this in view.

The reference in the decision to the fact that when drawing up the purchase-sale contract for the share of the house between the parties there was no agreement concerning the right to use the land plot is not evidence of the voluntary waiver by the plaintiffs of their rights. It is clear from the materials of the case that after the purchase of the share of the house, they used the land plot until the end of 1971, the respondents not obstructing them. Moreover, the agreement itself between the parties, according to which the plaintiffs would be deprived of the right to use the land plot, could not be deemed legal inasmuch as it contravenes Article 134 of the RSFSR Land Code.

The fact that A. Mashkov by reason of his health could not use the land plot, having re-ceded his right of use to his brother, could not deprive new owners of his share of the house of the right to use the plot. According to Article 87 of the

RSFSR Land Code, in the event of the transfer of a right of ownership to the structure (or part thereof), the right of use of the land plot or part thereof also is transferred.

The people's court, having mistakenly interpreted the instruction in Article 134 of the RSFSR Land Code on taking account of the procedure for use of the land plot which actually has formed, came to the incorrect conclusion concerning the possibility of wholly depriving the plaintiffs of the right to use the land plot.

In so doing, the court recognized that the change of procedure for a use already formed materially violated the interests of the respondents but did not take into account the fact that the preservation of this procedure leads to a greater violation of the plaintiff's interests.

KOLESNIKOV vs. UNUKOVA, Biulleten' Verkhovnogo Suda RSFSR, 1969, no. 11, pp. 8–9.

Kolesnikov possesses by right of personal ownership in the city of Krasnodar the western portion of the wing of house No. 348 on Golovatyi Street.

One meter from this wing is situated part of house No. 346, belonging to Unukova.

Kolesnikov brought suit against Unukova to eliminate obstacles to the use of the house, since she had rebuilt without authorization the part of the house belonging to her, increasing its size and blocking the kitchen window of his wing. As a result, use of the kitchen became impossible.

[After several appeals, the Krasnodar Territorial Court ordered Unukova to free the western wall of the house and the window from unauthorized structures at her own expense within a designated period; if she failed to do so, Kolesnikov was authorized to do so at his expense and recover these through the court. Unukova appealed to the Judicial Division for Civil Cases of the RSFSR Supreme Court, alleging that the structural modifications had been made in 1960 with Kolesnikov's consent because water from the roof of his house had been damaging her walls and also because her family badly needed additional living space. The Judicial Division ruled on June 5, 1969]:

The materials of the case indisputably establish that the rebuilding of Unukova's house was done without authorization, since the Executive Committee of the First of May District Soviet of Working People's Deputies by decision of September 29, 1965, refused to formalize the technical documentation for a housing extension. By a decision of May 19, 1966, the same Executive Committee submitted to the First of May District Procurator the question of bringing Unukova to criminal responsibility for unauthorized construction. Therefore, irrespective of what year in which the premises were re-equipped, even with the consent of Kolesnikov, it was contrary to law.

The materials of the case also established that the premises adjacent to Unukov's house are used by Kolesnikov as a kitchen. However, in the absence of a window, Kolesnikov is not allowed to use gas. Therefore, the demand of Kolesnikov to eliminate the obstacles created by Unukova in the use of his kitchen were justifiably deemed by the court as deserving attention.

At the judicial session, Kolesnikov modified his initial demand to restore in full the previously existing gap between the house and requested the court to oblige Unukova only to free the kitchen window looking out on Unukova's yard. The territorial court in this connection correctly obliged Unukova, in accordance with Article 156 of the RSFSR Civil Code, partially to remove the extension built by her so as to free the kitchen window of the plaintiff Kolesnikov and thereby restore his right to use of the kitchen in the house belonging to him.

On the basis of the foregoing, the Judicial Division left the decision of the Krasnodar Territorial Court without change, and the appeal of Unukova without satisfaction.

CONSTITUTION OF THE U.S.S.R., December 5, 1936
Art. 7. . . . Each collective farm household shall, in addition to its basic income from the social collective farm economy, have for personal use a small household plot and in personal ownership a subsidiary husbandry on the household plot, a dwelling house, livestock, poultry, and minor agricultural implements, in accordance with the charter of the agricultural artel.

CIVIL CODE, R.S.F.S.R. (1964)
Article 126. *Ownership of a Collective Farm Household*
The property of a collective farm household shall belong to its members by right of joint ownership (Article 116).

A collective farm household may have in ownership the subsidiary husbandry on its household plot, a dwelling house, livestock, poultry, and minor agricultural implements, in accordance with the charter of the collective farm.

In addition, there belongs to a collective farm household the labor income transferred to its ownership by members of the household from participation in the general economy of the collective farm or other property transferred by them to the ownership of the household, as well as household articles and articles of personal consumption acquired with common funds.

Article 127. *Possession, Use and Disposition of Property of a Collective Farm Household*
Possession, use, and disposition of the property of a collective farm household shall be carried out with the consent of all its members.

A dispute over the possession, use, or disposition of household property shall be decided by a court in a suit by any member of a household who has attained sixteen years of age.

Members of a household from fifteen to sixteen years of age shall bring such suits with the consent of their parents, adoptive parents, or guardians, and suits in the interests of household members who have not attained fifteen years of age shall be brought by their parents, adoptive parents, or guardians.

Article 129. *Determination of Shares in Household Property*

The share of a member of a collective farm household in the household property shall be determined upon his departure from the household without forming a new household (separation), upon partition of the household, and also in the event of an exaction in regard to his personal obligations.

The size of the share of a household member shall be established proceeding from the equality of shares of all household members, including those who have not attained majority and disabled persons.

The share of an able-bodied member of a household in the household property may be reduced by virtue of the brevity of his stay in the household or the insignificance of participation by his labor or funds in the economy of the household.

Article 130. *Separation from a Collective Farm Household*

In the event of the departure of one or several collective farm household members, a separation of shares shall be made in kind so as not to deprive the household of buildings, livestock, or agricultural implements necessary to carry on subsidiary husbandry.

If it is impossible to separate the share of property due to a household member in kind, its value shall be paid in money.

The right to demand a separation of property upon the departure from the household shall appertain to household members who have attained sixteen years of age. Household members from fifteen to sixteen years of age may demand a separation with the consent of their parents, adoptive parents, or guardians. In the interests of household members who have not attained fifteen years of age, their parents, adoptive parents, or guardians may demand a separation.

Article 131. *Partition of a Collective Farm Household*

In the event of a partition of a collective farm household, its property shall be divided among the newly formed households in accordance with the share of their members and taking into account the economic needs of each household.

The right to demand a partition of the collective farm household shall appertain to members of a household who are of legal age and who are members of the particular household.

Article 132. *Loss of the Right to a Share in Collective Farm Household Property*

An able-bodied collective farm household member shall lose the right to a share in the household property unless he participates for three years in succession with his labor and funds in the common economy of the household. This rule shall not apply if the member has not participated in the common economy as a consequence of being called to active military service, study at an educational institution, or illness.

Article 133. *Partition of Collective Farm Household Property after its Termination*

Partition of property belonging to a collective farm household and retained after termination of the collective farm household shall be according to the rules of Articles 129 and 132 of the present Code.

Article 134. *Ownership of an Individual Peasant Household*

Working livestock (with the consent of the autonomous republic Council of Ministers or the executive committee of the territory, or region soviet of working people's deputies) and agricultural implements needed to work the land allocated to the use of the household without the use of another's labor may be in the ownership of an individual peasant household in addition to the property specified in Article 126 of the present Code.

The property specified in paragraph one of the present Article may not be in the personal ownership of individual members of an individual peasant household.

The property of an individual peasant household specified in the present Article shall belong to its members by right of joint ownership (Article 116).

Articles 127–133 of the present Code shall be applied respectively to the right of joint ownership of an individual peasant household.

MODEL COLLECTIVE FARM CHARTER, November 28, 1969

42. The family of a collective farmer (or collective farm household) may have in ownership a dwelling house, farm buildings, productive livestock, poultry, bees, and minor agricultural implements for work on the personal plot.

A personal plot of land shall be granted for use to the family of a collective farmer (or collective farm household) for a kitchen-garden, garden, and other needs, up to one-half hectare in size, including the land occupied by buildings, and on irrigated lands, up to one-fifth hectare.

. . . The personal plot shall be granted to the family of a collective farmer (or collective farm household) by decision of the general meeting of collective farm members, and its size shall be established taking into account the number of family members of the collective farmer (or collective farm household) and their labor participation in the common economy of the collective farm. . . .

The personal plot may not be transferred to the use of other persons or worked with the use of hired labor.

The collective farm board shall be obliged systematically to control the observance of the established sizes of personal plots. In the event of the arbitrary increase of the sizes of personal plots, the surpluses above the established norms shall be confiscated by the board, transferring the crop harvested therefrom to the collective farm without reimbursing expenditures made from the period of illegal use.

43. The family of a collective farmer (or collective farm household) may have one cow with issue up to one year and one head of younger horned livestock up to two years of age, one sow with issue up to three months of age, or two pigs being fattened, up to 10 sheep and goats together, bee hives, poultry, and rabbits.

An increase of the norms for keeping livestock in the personal ownership of the collective farmer's family (or collective farm household) and the substitution of one species of livestock by others in individual areas, taking into account the national peculiarities and local conditions, shall be permitted by decision of the union republic Council of Ministers. . . .

FINOGENOV vs. FINOGENOVA, Biulleten' Verkhovnogo Suda RSFSR, 1972, no. 4, p.4

The Finogenovs had been married since 1944 and resided in the house of the defendant's parents. In 1947 they built a house in the village of Kishkino, Domodedovskii District, Moscow Region, on a land parcel allotted to them by the collective farm and began to keep an independent house of the collective farm household type. In connection with the reorganization of the farm and the creation of a state farm, the said house was relegated to the type for workers situate in a rural locality. Until 1968 the Finogenovs lived together, repaired the house from common funds, and built several extensions, but in 1969 formalized a divorce.

Finogenov brought suit against Finogenova for recognition of his right of ownership in half the house and for a division of it and the fruit plantings. He referred to the fact that the house and extension thereto were erected during their life together from common funds. The premises he needed to use during the summer time as a second group invalid of the Fatherland War.

Finogenova acknowledged the suit in part. She did not object to paying the plaintiff monetary compensation for the extension to the house and the shed. According to her submission, the principal house and the household were erected from her parents' funds with the labor participation of relatives, and the plaintiff rendered no assistance in the construction. She referred to the fact that Finogenov took an insignificant part in keeping the house since he lived for individual periods of time at his sister's. In 1965 he obtained a room in a comfortable house in the city of Dolgoprudnyi and was supplied with living quarters.

Moreover, the defendant pointed out in the judicial session that in 1968 she transferred 300 rubles to the plaintiff for the share of the house due to him.

[The lower court found for the plaintiff, which was affirmed by the Judicial Division for Civil Cases of the RSFSR Supreme Court, declaring:] According to Article 129 of the RSFSR Civil Code, in the event of separation from a collective farm household the size of the share in property of the household member shall be established, proceeding from the equality of shares of all household members, including those who have not attained majority and disabled persons.

These same rules shall be applied in the partition of property belonging to the collective farm household and retained after its termination (Article 133, RSFSR Civil Code).

The house in dispute was erected in 1947, when the parties were married, lived together, and kept a common house of the collective farm household type. According to the information of the rural Soviet, the head of this house was the plaintiff, Finogenov. Therefore the court correctly recognized his right of ownership in half of the said property retained after the termination of the collective farm household. . . .

It is clear from the materials of the case that Finogenov contributed his assets to the construction of the principal house and other structures since he worked at that time on the collective farm and at other organizations and received a pension as an invalid of the Fatherland War.

The division of the house and household structures in kind, made by the court, also is correct in accordance with the opinion of an expert to the effect that such a division is possible and that material expenditures were not required for isolation of the premises. In this event, the court did not have the right to award monetary compensation to the plaintiff without his consent.

The reference in the appeal to the fact that Finogenov was provided with living space in a house of the local Soviet and did not require living quarters is unconvincing inasmuch as he could not be deprived of the right of ownership in part of the house only because he has living premises in another populated settlement. Being a second group invalid of the Fatherland War, Finogenov intended to use the part of the house allotted to him in the summer time as a dacha.

IN RE L. LIAKHOVA, Biulleten' Verkhovnogo Suda RSFSR, 1973, no. 10, pp. 14–15.

After entering into marriage with V. Liakhov, L. Liakhova became a member of a collective farm household, the head of which was K. Liakhova.

In connection with the termination of family relations in September 1971, L. Liakhova brought suit for a separation of half the value of the collective farm household property for herself and a child, indicating in so doing that she had participated in the improvement of the husbandry with the repair and reconstruction of the house, the erection of new structures, and the acquisition of belongings.

In a supplementary petition the plaintiff changed her claim: she asked that a division of the household property be made and her right to part of the house and structures be recognized in order to form a new husbandry. . . .

[The lower courts found for the plaintiff, awarding her 17/46 of the house and various articles; their decision was protested by the deputy chairman of the RSFSR Supreme Court to the Presidium of the Rostov Regional Court, which returned the case for a new hearing on the following grounds:]

According to Article 131 of the RSFSR Civil Code, the right to demand a partition of a collective farm household belongs to household members who have attained majority and who are members of the particular collective farm.

Only K. Liakhova is a member of the collective farm to whom a land parcel was allotted for the persons residing in the house in dispute. L. and V. Liakhov worked in various organizations in the city. This fact was adequately confirmed and was not disputed by the parties.

In deciding the question of the partition of the household and thereby the creation of a new collective farm household, the court did not verify whether the integrity of the house in dispute would be preserved and did not take into account that this requires the granting of a personal land plot to the newly formed household.

Moreover, the use of land within the farm allotted by the collective farm in virtue of Article 51 of the RSFSR Land Code is to be carried out on the basis of the collective farm charter, and according to Article 42 of the Model Collective Farm

Charter the personal land plot is to be granted by decision of the general meeting of collective farm members for the use of the family of the collective farmer.

The plaintiff in practice is deprived of the possibility of forming a new husbandry, which is confirmed by a letter in the file of the case signed by the collective farm chairman, from which it seems that the collective farm board objects to the partition of the land plot granted to the family of collective farmer K. Liakhova since this could lead to the breaking up and liquidation of the collective farm household.

In the said circumstances the consent of the executive committee of the rural Soviet of Working People's Deputies for the partition of the house could not be significant, . . . since the particular dispute arose in connection with the partition of the collective farm household and not of common ownership. . . .

C. *Restrictions on rights of personal ownership*

1. Restrictions Relating to Nature of Property

CIVIL CODE, R.S.F.S.R. (1964)
Article 137. *Articles which may be acquired only by special authorization.*
A list of articles which by virtue of their significance for the national economy, considerations of state security, or other reasons, may be acquired only by special authorization (weapons, aircraft, highly toxic poisons, etc.), and also the procedure for issuing such authorizations, shall be determined by legislation of the USSR and decrees of the RSFSR Council of Ministers.

Gold, silver, platinum, and metals of the platinum group in coin, ingot, and raw form, foreign currency, and payment documents in foreign currency (bills of exchange, checks, remittances, etc.), and also foreign securities (stocks, bonds, coupons, etc.) may be acquired only in the procedure and within the limits established by USSR legislation.

2. Restrictions As to Quantity

CIVIL CODE, R.S.F.S.R. (1964)
Article 106. *Right of Personal Ownership in a Dwelling House*
One dwelling house (or part of one house) may be in the personal ownership of a citizen.

Spouses living together and their minor children may have only one dwelling house (or part of one house) belonging by right of personal ownership to one of them or in their common ownership.

The right of ownership of one or several citizens of those specified in paragraph 2 of the present Article shall not deprive the rest of these citizens of the right to have in ownership another part (or parts) of the same house. However, spouses living together and their minor children may have only one apartment in a multiple-apartment house of a housing construction collective of individual builders.

The maximum size of a dwelling house or part(or parts) thereof belonging to a citizen by right of personal ownership should not exceed 60 square meters of living space.

However, the executive committee of a district or city Soviet of Working People's Deputies may authorize a citizen having a large family or the right to additional living space to build, acquire, or retain in ownership a house (or part of a house) of larger size. In such event the living space of a house (or part of a house) should not exceed the size determined for the said family pursuant to the norms for lessees in houses of the local Soviets of Working People's Deputies, taking into account the right to additional living space (Article 316).

Article 107. *Termination of the Right of Personal Ownership in More Than One Dwelling House.*

If it happens that more than the one house permitted by law is in the personal ownership of a citizen or of spouses living together and their minor children, the owner shall have the right, at his election, to retain any of the houses in his ownership. The other house (or houses) should be sold, given, or alienated by other means within one year by the owner.

The period of one year for the voluntary alienation by the owner of a house (or houses) shall be calculated from the day upon which the right of ownership in the second house (or houses) arises.

If the owner fails to alienate the house in some manner within the one-year period, this house shall, by decision of the executive committee of the district or city Soviet of Working People's Deputies, be subject to compulsory sale in the procedure established by the RSFSR Code of Civil Procedure for the execution of judicial decisions. Amounts obtained from the sale shall, after compensating the expenses connected with carrying out the compulsory sale, be transferred to the former owner of the house.

In instances when the sale of the house in a compulsory procedure fails to take place for the lack of buyers, the house, by decision of the executive committee of the district or city Soviet of Working People's Deputies, shall be transferred to the ownership of the state without compensation.

The rules of the present Article shall be applied respectively in instances when it happens, on the grounds permitted by law, that there are in the personal ownership of a citizen or spouses living together and their minor children:

(1) in addition to one house, part (or parts) of another;

(2) parts of different houses;

(3) part (or parts) of one house exceeding the dimensions specified in Article 106 of the present Code;

(4) more than one apartment in a multiple-apartment house of a housing construction collective of individual builders.

Article 108. *Consequence of the Acquisition of the Right if Personal Ownership in a Dwelling House when one Has an Apartment in a House of a Housing Construction Cooperative.*

If a citizen or spouses living together and their minor children happen to have a dwelling house (or part of a house) in personal ownership on the grounds permitted by law and simultaneously an apartment in a house of a housing construction cooperative, the owner of the house (or part of a house) shall have the right, at his election, to retain the house (or part of a house) or apartment in the house of the housing construction cooperative. In the latter instance, the owner should alienate his house (or part of a house) within one year from the day the right of ownership in the house (or part of a house) arises or from occupying the apartment of the housing construction cooperative. The failure to fulfill this requirement shall incur the consequences provided for by paragraphs 3 and 4 of Article 107 of the present Code.

Article 112. *Maximum Quantity of Livestock Which a Citizen May Have in Personal Ownership.*

The maximum quantity of livestock which may be in the personal ownership of a citizen shall be established by RSFSR legislation.

LAW ON THE PROTECTION AND USE OF MONUMENTS OF HISTORY AND CULTURE, U.S.S.R., October 29, 1976. [1976] Vedomosti Verkhovnogo Soveta SSSR, no 44, item 628.

Article 4. *Ownership of Monuments of History and Culture.*

Monuments of history and culture shall be the ownership of the state, as well as of collective farms, other cooperative organizations, their combines, social organizations, and in the personal ownership of citizens.

The sale, gift, or other alienation of monuments of history and culture shall be permitted with the obligatory preliminary notification of state agencies for the protection of monuments. In the event of the sale of monuments, the state shall have a priority right of purchase.

Article 12. *State Registration of Monuments of History and Culture in the Personal Ownership of Citizens.*

Articles of antiquity, works of decorative and applied art, structures, manuscripts, collections, rare printed publications, and other articles and documents in the personal ownership of citizens and of significant historical, scientific, artistic, or other cultural value shall be deemed monuments of history and culture and shall be subject to state registration for the purpose of fully making known the monuments and rendering assistance in ensuring their preservation.

Citizens in whose personal ownership there are monuments of history and culture shall be obliged to observe the rules for the protection, use, registration, and restoration of monuments.

Article 27. *Collecting of Monuments of History and Culture.*

The collecting of antique documentary monuments, ancient paintings, and ancient applied art by organizations or citizens shall be permitted if there are special permits issued and registered in the established procedure.

Article 28. *Prohibition of Exporting Monuments of History and Culture Beyond the Limits of the USSR.*

The export of monuments of history and culture beyond the limits of the USSR shall be prohibited.

An exception from this rule shall be permitted only with the special permit in each individual instance issued in the procedure defined by USSR legislation.

R. Abdullin, THE CONCERNS OF A COLLECTOR, Izvestia, August 29, 1976, p. 2.

I have attentively familiarized myself with the draft USSR Law "On the Protection and Use of Monuments of History and Culture". This is one more evidence of the fact that in recent years the educational role of monuments of history and culture in the life of the Soviet people has revived significantly and grown visibly in significance.

In this sense it is no accident that collectors are mentioned in the draft. Tens of thousands of people in our country engage in an intriguing, useful, and important cause—the collecting of various articles of antiquity and rare forms (the writer also is guilty). Not long ago I read in *Nedelia* that a brick collector, L. Antropov, can establish from the marks on their face the year in which practically any building was constructed. Is this not important for science? Is it not needed in practice? The painstaking, difficult work of a collector deserves, it seems to me, not only respect but also every encouragement. Yet all, irrespective of the significance of their collections, are in the position of ordinary owners of various articles. Only philatelists are more or less enveloped with public attention: there are catalogs, stores, clubs. Basically, collectors are, pardon me, homeless waifs linked only by accident, with nowhere to assemble and nowhere to exhibit. But even worse: sometimes the actions of a collector are readily interpreted as criminal.

According to the new law, all ". . . collections and other articles and documents in the personal ownership of citizens, if they have historical, scientific, artistic, or other cultural value, shall be deemed monuments of history and culture in the procedure established by USSR and union republic legislation" and shall be subject to state registration (Articles 8, 11 of the draft). To them will be extended in the established procedure the expenditure of state and social funds connected with the protection, repair, and restoration of monuments (Article 13 of the draft). No less important: if a private individual wishes to sell his collection, the state guarantees a priority right to acquire it with reimbursement of all expenditures made by him in the course of accumulating and keeping the collection. At the same time, citizens in whose personal ownership there are registered collections will be obliged to observe all established rules for the protection and use of the monuments.

Moreover, with the adoption of this law the dispersed and unknown private collections, creations of human hands, will become accessible for cultural and educational work, for science, enlightenment, patriotic, and esthetic nurturing of the working people. But it is necessary to formulate precisely in the draft law: *what is understood by collection, collecting, and what are the rights and duties of collectors and their voluntary societies.*

FEEDING BREAD TO ANIMALS, Sotsialisticheskaia zakonnost', 1972, no. 11, pp. 86–87.

The procurators of the Barysh and Tsil'ninsk Districts of the Ul'ianov Region organized a verification of the execution of prevailing legislation on responsibility for the buying-up in state or cooperative stores of baked bread, flour, groats, and other bread products and feeding them to cattle and poultry.

It was established that in a number of trade organizations proper control was not effectuated over the proper consumption of state grain resources and norms for the sale of bread and bread products to a single person were not observed. As a result, some citizens, taking advantage of lower prices for bread and higher procurement prices for meat, bought up baked bread in stores in order to feed it to cattle and poultry. Thus, I., having pigs, cocks, and ducks in his personal husbandry, fed them daily about 8 to 10 kilograms of bread bought up in stores; G. daily bought up and fed to a cow and horse up to 5 kilograms of baked bread. The guilty persons were convicted under Article 154-1 of the RSFSR Criminal Code. There also were instances when trade workers sold baked bread to some collective farms to feed their cattle. At the instruction of the chairman of the B.-Magatinskii rural consumers' society of the Tsil'ninsk District, Buteikin, for example, sold more than 35,000 tons of bread to collective farms for feeding to cattle. For these illegal activities, also involving an interruption in the proper supply of the population with bread, Buteikin was convicted.

Some bread plants of the city of Ul'ianovsk violated the technology for baking bread and sometimes delivered to the trade network poor-quality bread. The procuracy has initiated a criminal case in regard to these facts.

The regional procurator has informed the regional committee of the Communist Party of the Soviet Union about violations uncovered. A number of officials of trade organizations and collective farms have been brought to strict party responsibility.

IN RE EFIMOVA, Biulleten' Verkhovnogo Suda RSFSR, 1969, no. 4, p. 4.

The notary of the Magnitogorsk Notarial Office refused to certify Efimova's purchase-sale contract for one-half of a house on the grounds that from the moment of sale of her first dwelling house three years had not passed.

Considering the refusal of the notary to be improper, Efimova brought an appeal to a people's court in which she requested that the notarial office be obliged to certify the purchase-sale contract for the part of the house. The petitioner referred to the fact that she intended to change her place of residence and the building would be left without supervision and would lose its initial value.

[The city people's court ruled in favor of Efimova, which was upheld on appeal by the Regional Court. The Judicial Division for Civil Cases of the RSFSR Supreme Court considered the case together with others and ruled that Efimova's appeal must be rejected]:

According to Article 238 of the RSFSR Civil Code a dwelling house (or part thereof) in the personal ownership of a citizen or of spouses living together and their minor children may be the subject of purchase-sale, observing the rules of Article 106 of the present Code and also on condition that the owner had not sold more than one house (or part of one house) within three years, except for instances of sale provided for by Article 107 of the Civil Code.

It is clear from the file of the case that Efimova sold on April 18, 1966, a dwelling house on Parkhomenko Street in the city of Magnitogorsk and bought one-half of a dwelling house on the Ninth of January Street.

Inasmuch as Efimova had intended to sell this part of the house before the expiry of three years from the moment of sale of the first house, the conclusion of this transaction cannot be deemed legal. In the present instance, the purchase-sale transaction for part of the house could exist only on condition that Efimova found herself with more than one house on the grounds permitted by law. However, in the present case such facts have not been established.

In obliging the notarial office to certify the purchase-sale contract, the people's court referred to the fact that Efimova could not, by reason of health, fulfill the work connected with maintenance of the house and was obliged to lodge with relatives also living in the city of Magnitogorsk.

However, these arguments are not provided by law as grounds for certifying in the present instance the purchase-sale contract for the house.

3. Restrictions As To Use

CIVIL CODE, R.S.F.S.R. (1964)
Article 111. *Confiscation of property used to derive nonlabor income.*

If a dwelling house, dacha (or part of a house, dacha) or other property in the ownership of a citizen is used systematically by the owner to derive nonlabor income, this house, dacha (or part of a house, dacha) or other property shall be subject to confiscation without compensation in a judicial proceeding in a suit brought by the executive committee of the local Soviet of Working People's Deputies. The house (or dacha) or part of a house (or dacha) confiscated by decision of a court shall be added to the fund of the local Soviet of Working People's Deputies.

The rule of paragraph one of the present Article shall not apply in instances of the leasing of dwelling houses, dachas, and premises therein if the conditions provided for by Article 304 of the present Code are observed.

The rules established by paragraph three of Article 109 of the present Code shall apply in the event of the confiscation without compensation of a dwelling house (or dacha) or part of a house (or dacha) from the owner by decision of a court and its being added to the fund of the local Soviet of Working People's Deputies.

CRIMINAL CODE, R.S.F.S.R. (1960)
Article 154. *Speculation.*

Speculation, that is, the buying up and selling of goods or other articles for the purpose of gain, shall be punishable by deprivation of freedom for a term of up to two to seven years with confiscation of property.

Petty speculation, committed repeatedly, shall be punishable by correctional tasks for a period of up to one year, or by a fine of up to two thousand rubles, with confiscation of the objects of speculation.

IN RE KUDAINETOV, Biulleten' Verkhovnogo Suda RSFSR, 1967, no 2, p. 14.

The senior notariat of the Maikop state notarial office of the Adygei Autonomous Region by a decree of June 8, 1967, refused to certify for Kudainetov a contract granting a land plot for use in perpetuity for the construction of an individual dwelling house in the city of Maikop on the grounds that the said contract was contrary to a normative act, in particular, the decree of the RSFSR Council of Ministers of September 3, 1963.

Considering the refusal to be incorrect, Kudainetov appealed to the Maikop City People's Court, requesting that the notarial office be obliged to certify the contract, citing in this connection an extreme need for living space.

[The Maikop City Court ordered the notarial office to certify the contract but was reversed by the Presidium of the Adygei Regional Court on the following grounds]:

According to the decree of the RSFSR Council of Ministers of September 3, 1963, No. 1102 "On the Course of Fulfillment of the Plan for Cooperative Housing Construction in the RSFSR in 1963", the allotment of land plots for individual housing construction in regions, territories, and republics (autonomous republics), centers, and industrial cities with a population exceeding 100,000 persons, as well as in all resort cities, was prohibited as from January 1, 1964.

From the materials of the file of the case it is clear that Kudainetov was granted a land plot of 473 square meters in the city of Maikop, which is a regional center with a population exceeding 100,000 persons.

Inasmuch as the decision on granting Kudainetov a land plot for the construction of a dwelling house was rendered after January 1, 1964, the people's court did not have the right to oblige the notarial office to certify this contract.

ISMAILOVA vs. AKHABOV AND AKHABOVA, Biulleten' Verkhovnogo Suda SSSR, 1971, no. 4, pp. 27–28.

In 1968 Sh. G. Ismailova received from her mother by contract of gift 1/6 of a house. In accordance with this share Ismailova thereupon was allocated two rooms in this house.

In September 1969 Ismailova brought suit for eviction against A. D. Akhadov and his sister M. D. Akhadova, who resided in these rooms. In justification of the suit Ismailov referred to the fact that she needed living space.

[The people's court in Baku twice ruled for the plaintiff and was twice reversed by the Judicial Division for Civil Cases of the Azerbaidzhan SSR. Hearing the case on protest, the Judicial Division for Civil Cases of the USSR Supreme Court found the protest justified and returned the case for new consideration on the following grounds]:

Ismailova received in ownership part of the house, and the Akhadovs did not contest this right. From the moment of moving in, the Akhadovs paid apartment rent. This duty was provided for in the "apartment lease" of April 5, 1955, joined to the file of the case. Referring to this lease, the Judicial Division for Civil Cases of the republic Supreme Court came to the conclusion that the rooms in dispute had been purchased by the father of the defendants. But the lease speaks of leasing the premises, and not of a sale to the Akhadovs.

Thus, the argument of the republic Supreme Court that the defendants use the rooms in dispute as they were acquired by their father does not follow from the materials of the case.

The argument of the court that the plaintiff did not need the living space in dispute for personal use also is not based on the materials of the file of the case. When considering the case it was established that since 1932 Ismailova lived with her family as a lessee in two rooms of a house belonging to citizen Khanputaeva. One room, 17 square meters, is unfinished; the second room, 10 square meters, has no natural light. Together with the plaintiff in this space live her two daughters, son-in-law, and grandchild. In the opinion of the housing office of the housing administration, Khanputaeva's house is dangerous, and the premises occupied by the plaintiff are unsuitable for further residence therein.

As regards the reference in the judicial decision that the plaintiff may be provided with housing in the house of her mother, Nurieva, the court did not take into account that the plaintiff, her daughters, son-in-law, and grandchild are not members of Nurieva's family, do not reside jointly with her, and have no right to living space in her house. Moreover, as is evident from the materials of the case, there is no free living space in Nurieva's house: part of the living premises are occupied by apartment lessees. The need of the plaintiff for housing can not serve as the basis for their eviction, inasmuch as she is not a member of the mother's family and herself has the right of personal ownership in another living space.

According to Article 58(2) of the Fundamental Principles of Civil Legislation, a lessee may be evicted from a house belonging to a citizen by right of personal ownership if the premises occupied by him are needed for the personal use of the owner of the house and members of his family.

CONFISCATION FOR EXCESSIVE RENT, Sotsialisticheskaia zakonnost', 1971, no. 7, p. 90.

By decision of the people's court in the city of Evpatoriia, left without change by ruling of the Judicial Division for Civil Cases of the Crimean Regional Court, a 3/20 share of a house was confiscated from Palkin for the fund of the Evpatoriia municipal housing section.

The Deputy Procurator General of the USSR brought a protest by way of supervision in this case on the following grounds:

Palkin, an owner of a house, had leased since 1958 for more than four years to a bookstore his part of a house for a rental of 25 rubles per month. The Procurator of the city of Evpatoriia brought suit against Palkin to confiscate his part of the house in connection with the fact that he was deriving nonlabor income. The court satisfied the suit. However, the law does not prohibit the owners of houses to lease premises belonging to them to citizens or organizations, but there is a limitation on the payment exacted (Article 57, Fundamental Principles of Civil Legislation of the USSR and Union Republics). According to Article 36 of the previously prevailing decree of the USSR Central Executive Committee and Council of People's Commissars of October 17, 1937, house owners were permitted to recover surcharges on the rates of apartment rent established by law in an amount not exceeding 20 per cent.

It is provided by the prevailing rules that rental payment should comprise on average not more than 4 rubles and not less than 2 rubles annually for one square meter. Palkin had the right to lease premises to the bookstore, but the court did not disclose the size of premises which he leased nor the amounts of rents which he had the right to recover. Only after uncovering these material facts could the court, according to Article 25 of the Fundamental Principles of Civil Legislation of the USSR and Union Republics, decide the question of confiscating the part of the house in dispute or recover for state revenues the amounts received by the defendant in excess of the rates of rent established by law.

D. *Loss of rights of personal ownership.*

CIVIL CODE, R.S.F.S.R. (1964)
Article 141. *Neglectful Maintenance of a House*

If a citizen neglectfully treats a house belonging to him, allowing its delapidation, the executive committee of the local Soviet of Working People's Deputies may designate a reasonable period for the owner to repair the house. If the citizen without justifiable reasons does not carry out the necessary repair, the court may, upon the suit brought by the executive committee of the district or city Soviet of Working People's Deputies, confiscate without compensation the neglectfully maintained house and transfer it to the fund of the local Soviet of Working People's Deputies.

Article 142. *Neglectful Maintenace of Cultural Valuables.*

If a citizen neglectfully treats property belonging to him which has significant historical, artistic, or other value for society, the state organizations whose task is the protection of such property shall give the owner a warning about terminating his neglectful treatment of the property. If the owner does not fulfill this requirement, upon the suit of the appropriate organization a court may confiscate this property, which shall be transferred to state ownership. The citizen shall be compensated for the value of the confiscated property in an amount established by agreement, and in the event of a dispute, by the court.

In the event of urgent need, a suit for the confiscation of the said property may be brought without a preliminary warning.

Article 143. *Abandoned Property.*

Property which has no owner or whose owner is unknown (abandoned property) shall pass to the ownership of the state by decision of a court rendered upon the petition of a financial agency. The petition shall be submitted upon the expiry of one year from the day the property is accepted for registration.

Abandoned property belonging to a collective farm household shall pass to the ownership of the collective farm on whose territory the property is situated by decision of a court rendered upon the petition of the collective farm. The petition shall be submitted upon the expiry of one year from the day this property is accepted for registration by the executive committee of the rural Soviet of Working People's Deputies.

The procedure for the discovery and registration of abandoned property shall be determined by the RSFSR Ministry of Finances.

Article 149. *Requisition and Confiscation.*

The confiscation by the state of property from an owner for state or social interests with the payment to him of the value of the property (requisition), as well as the confiscation without compensation by the state of property as sanction for a violation of law (confiscation) shall be permitted only in the instances and in the procedure established by legislation of the USSR and RSFSR.

Article 150. *Confiscation of Precious Metals and Diamonds.*

The value of confiscated valuables shall be paid to owners of precious metals, (gold, platinum, silver) in ingots, concentrates, or raw ore, semi-finished goods, and articles intended for manufacturing or laboratory purposes, as well as diamonds, confiscated by decrees of investigative or judicial agencies in the event these owners are convicted without confiscation of property, or a verdict of acquittal is rendered, or the case is terminated, and the valuables themselves shall be given over to the state fund of the USSR.

EDICT OF THE PRESIDIUM OF THE RSFSR SUPREME SOVIET, September 25, 1969, "On the Confiscation of Firearms from Persons Who Have Committed Anti-Social Offenses", [1969] Vedomosti Verkhovnogo Soveta RSFSR no. 40, item 1231.

With a view to the further intensification of the struggle against violations of the procedure for keeping and using firearms, the Presidium of the RSFSR Supreme Soviet decrees:

1. To establish that hunting weapons and other firearms and ammunition for them belonging to persons who systematically violate public order, abuse alcoholic beverages, or suffer from psychiatric illnesses, may be confiscated from them in an administrative procedure by decisions of rural or settlement Soviets of Working People's Deputies, their executive committees, or decrees of administrative commissions attached to the executive committees of district, city, rural, or settlement

Soviets of Working People's Deputies.

The confiscated battle and small caliber arms, including rifled hunting weapons and ammunition for them, shall be handed over to agencies of internal affairs, and smooth-bore hunting weapons shall be appraised and transferred to trade organizations for sale on a commission basis in the established procedure. Monies received from the realization of the weapons shall be given to the owner of the weapon.

2. To grant to police agencies the right to seize the weapons and ammunition enumerated in Article 1 of the present Edict and to keep them until consideration of the material by the rural or settlement Soviet of Working People's Deputies, their executive committees, or by the administrative commission attached to the executive committee of a district, city, rural, or settlement Soviet of Working People's Deputies.

The weapons and ammunition in these instances shall be confiscated according to a reasoned decree of the head of the district or city agency of internal affairs or his deputy.

PROCURATOR'S PROTEST, Chelovek i zakon, 1973, no. 5, p. 98

The Administrative Commission attached to the executive committee of the Slavgorod District Soviet of Working People's Deputies (Mogilev Region) adopted a decree concerning the confiscation from citizen A. of a hunting weapon without compensation of the value on the grounds that he had no right to keep it.

The procurator of the Slavgorod District brought a protest against this decree, since in accordance with the decree of the Belorussian Council of Ministers of March 3, 1959, No. 130 "On Regulating the Registration and Trade of Hunting Weapons" (*SZ BSSR,* 1959, no. 3, item 85), it shall be confiscated from a person who maliciously avoids registration of smooth-bore weapons by police agencies and shall be realized through commission stores, and the monies received, less the commission fee, shall be handed over to the owner of the weapon. It seems the administrative commission adopted a decree in regard to a question whose consideration is relegated to the competence of police agencies, and moreover allowed the violation of the rights of a citizen to compensation for the value of the weapon confiscated from him.

The protest was satisfied, and the illegal decree repealed.

IN RE UL'IANOV, Biulleten' Verkhovnogo Suda RSFSR, 1968, no. 9, pp. 11–12.

By judgment of the Kuibyshev District People's Court of Moscow, Ul'ianov was sentenced on December 18, 1962, to four years deprivation of freedom under Article 92(2) of the Criminal Code.

Compensation of 1090 rubles was exacted from him for damage caused.

Ul'ianov was deemed guilty in that he, while working as the production head of a railway restaurant car and by arrangement with other persons convicted in this case, systematically stole products which were sold through the restaurant car and the monies withdrawn and appropriated.

On December 13, 1961, during a search at Ul'ianov's, the agencies of investigation confiscated two cameras, "Kiev", and "Zorkii-3".

The court did not resolve the question of these cameras in the decree of judgment.

Subsequently, the people's court, as indicated above, by a ruling of March 27, 1963, converted these cameras to the income of the state (as acquired by criminal means).

[The Judicial Division for Criminal Cases of the RSFSR Supreme Court upheld the protest of the Deputy USSR Procurator General as follows]:

In accordance with Article 86(4) of the RSFSR Code of Criminal Procedure, money and other valuables acquired by criminal means shall be subject to conversion to the income of the state by the judgment of a court.

As is obvious from the materials of the case, the said cameras were not converted to the income of the state by the judgment of the court.

Thus, the court ruling, rendered in violation of Article 86(4) of the RSFSR Code of Criminal Procedure, is subject to repeal. It should be noted that it was not indicated in the people's court ruling that the cameras were acquired with assets procured by criminal means.

IN RE ITSKHAKOVICH, Biulleten' Verkhovnogo Suda RSFSR, 1973, no. 2, p. 3.

By decision of the executive committee of the Makhachkalin City Soviet of Working People's Deputies, Itskhakovich was authorized to carry on capital restoration repair of a house within the former dimensions, raising the plinthe part of the wall to 1.6 meters and building a semi-basement in connection with the proximity of underground waters. To perform the work she concluded a contract with the construction-assembly administration (SMU) and paid the cost of the work. After confirmation of the plan by the chief architect of the city of Makhachkalin, the SMU commenced work.

Having discovered that the SMU was erecting the house with deviations from the dimensions specified in the decision of the executive committee, the municipal housing administration proposed that Itskhakovich remove the second floor within a month and bring the first into conformity with the dimensions of the previously existing house. The administration warned her in this connection that the failure to fulfill this demand would lead to the question being raised of the confiscation of the house and its transfer to the fund of the City Soviet.

Inasmuch as the defendant did not make the necessary corrections within the established period in the construction, the municipal housing administration brought suit in court to confiscate from Itskhakovich the inadequately constructed house and to transfer it without compensation to the fund of the local Soviet.

[The city people's court found for the city Soviet, which decision was confirmed by the Dagestan ASSR Supreme Court and the Presidium thereof. The Judicial Division for Civil Cases of the RSFSR Supreme Court heard the case upon the protest of the Deputy USSR Procurator General that the facts of the case had been inadequately investigated and reversed the previous decisions on the following grounds]:

From the materials of the case it is clear that the construction of Itskhakovich's house was carried out by the SMU in accordance with the plan and estimate confirmed by the city architect. However, the plan did not correspond to the decision of the executive committee of June 13, 1969. The court did not elucidate how this discrepancy could have arisen nor by whose fault it occurred.

The court should investigate more carefully the question of what the defendant was authorized to erect by the decision of the executive committee and by the plan; what was in fact erected; and how material were the deviations which it allowed.

From the explanations in the judicial session of the chairman of the municipal housing section of the city executive committee it seems that the chief architect is at fault in that, when confirming the plan, he did not take into account the decision of the executive committee of the city Soviet.

It is clear from the materials of the case that the procurator of the Dagestan ASSR raised the question of the responsibility of the deputy chief city architect for confirming the illegal plan for the construction of Itskhakovich's house, and also of the chief architect for the absence of architectural supervision over observance of the construction rules.

Therefore, the court should elucidate whether Itskhakovich is at fault in that in constructing the house deviations from the decision of the executive committee were allowed with the proviso that these deviations were authorized by the city architect.

It is clear from the materials of the case that Itskhakovich, after receiving the warning about removing within a month the second floor and bringing the construction into conformity with the decision of the executive committee, took measures to fulfill this warning; however, she was not in a position to fulfill it with her own efforts, and the SMU, having done the work, refused to do so.

Therefore, in a new consideration of the case, the court should carefully investigate the question of whether Itskhakovich is at fault in the failure to fulfill the instruction of the executive committee to bring the construction of the house into proper form.

The uncompensated confiscation of a house on the basis of Article 109 of the RSFSR Civil Code is possible only if guilty conduct of a citizen who has permitted unauthorized construction is established.

IL'CHENKO vs. KHIZHINETS RURAL SOVIET OF WORKING PEOPLE'S DEPUTIES, Biulleten' Verkhovnogo Suda SSSR, 1971, no. 2, pp. 18-20.

Until March 1944 I. I. Il'chenko lived with his family in the settlement of Khizhinets in a house belonging to him by right of personal ownership.

At the beginning of 1945, Il'chenko went to the city of Nemirov, Vinnits Region, where he also had a dwelling house by right of personal ownership comprising a room and a kitchen. The house which he left in the settlement of Khizhinets was leased until 1947 by Il'chenko's wife, and in 1948 was transferred by the rural Soviet to the use, without compensation, of citizen Sennikov.

By judgment of a military tribunal of September 8, 1951, Il'chenko was sentenced to a lengthy term of deprivation of freedom with confiscation of property. In April 1955 the said judgment was modified, the term of punishment reduced to five years deprivation of freedom, with the release of Il'chenko from further serving the punishment pursuant to an amnesty.

In executing the judgment the part of the house (one room) in the city of Nemirov was confiscated; the house in the settlement of Khizhinets was not included in the inventory of property and was not confiscated.

By a ruling of the Military Division of the USSR Supreme Court of March 3, 1960, the judgment in respect of Il'chenko was vacated and the proceeding terminated for lack of the constituent elements of a crime.

In August 1955 Il'chenko brought suit in court for recognition of the right of ownership and the return of the house belonging to him in the settlement of Khizhinets. This claim was twice considered by the Vinnits District People's Court and deemed well-founded; however, subsequently both judicial decisions were vacated and the case accepted by the Vinnits Regional Court.

Having considered the case on June 5, 1957, the Vinnits Regional Court left Il'chenko's suit without satisfaction, referring to the fact that the house which belonged to him was deemed abandoned and in December 1953 was transferred to the Khizhinets Rural Soviet of Working People's Deputies.

Moreover, the court pointed out that by virtue of Article 60 of the Ukrainian SSR Civil Code (1922 version), an owner had the right to demand property belonging to him from a good-faith acquirer only if such property was lost by him or stolen from him.

The Judicial Division for Civil Cases of the Ukrainian SSR Supreme Court on July 8, 1957, left the decision of the regional court without change, recognizing that the house was abandoned and therefore lawfully accepted into the balance of the rural Soviet.

On these same grounds the Plenum of the Ukrainian SSR Supreme Court on March 10, 1961, left without satisfaction the protest of the deputy chairman of the republic Supreme Court to repeal the judicial decisions in regard to the case and send the case for new consideration.

Finding this decree incorrect, the chairman of the USSR Supreme Court brought a protest to the Plenum of the USSR Supreme Court in which the question was raised of sending the case for new consideration.

Having considered the materials of the case, the Plenum of the USSR Supreme Court satisfied the protest on the following grounds:

When resolving the said dispute, the court permitted material violations of the norms of material law which established the conditions and procedure for recognizing structures belonging to citizens by right of personal ownership as abandoned, and also did not investigate a number of facts having essential significance for taking a legal and well-founded decision.

Both the Vinnits Regional Court and the Supreme Court of the Ukrainian SSR proceeded from the fact that inasmuch as Il'chenko and members of his family did not live in the house, acceptance of the house into the balance of the rural Soviet was done lawfully. However, not one of the judicial decrees indicated on the basis of what normative acts establishing the procedure for the transfer to the state of abandoned houses this conclusion was drawn.

According to Article 68 of the Ukrainian SSR Civil Code, which prevailed until 1964, property was deemed abandoned if it did not have owners or the owner was unknown.

It also was established by the Statute on the Procedure for the Registration and Use of Nationalized, Confiscated, Escheated, and Abandoned Property, confirmed by decree of the USSR Council of People's Commissars on April 17, 1943, no. 404, and the Instruction of the USSR People's Commissariat of Finances of May 31, 1943, No. 311, adopted on the basis of this Statute, that abandoned property embraces, for example, the property of persons deemed deceased in the established procedure if there are no legal heirs, and others.

Moreover, it is established in the file of the case that, in accepting the house for its balance, the rural Soviet had available data that Il'chenko was the house owner, who was serving punishment in places of deprivation of freedom in connection with a sentence in a case considered at a circuit session of the court in the settlement of Khizhinets. There also was information that Il'chenko's family lived in the city of Nemirova.

In addition, in accordance with the decree of the Ukrainian SSR Council of Ministers of August 4, 1950, No. 2398, the right to sell abandoned dwelling houses situated in a rural locality was granted to the executive committees of regional and district Soviets, whereas the house belonging to Il'chenko was sold by decision of the executive committee of a rural Soviet.

Under these circumstances, the conclusion of the court concerning the lawfulness of the confiscation of the house in dispute can not be deemed well-founded in law, and in connection therewith the case is subject to being remanded for new consideration.

FROM THE PRACTICE OF PROCURATORIAL SUPERVISION, Sotsialisticheskaia zakonnost', 1971, no 12, p. 71.

The executive committee of the Leningrad City Soviet of Working People's Deputies adopted a decision which prohibited transport enterprises from conveying imported furniture, refrigerators, and motorcycles acquired by citizens in stores, from Leningrad.

The procurator of Leningrad protested this decision as it contravened the Railway Statute of the USSR and the Automotive Transport Statute of the RSFSR in which there were no provisions for restricting the rights of citizens in the use of railway or automotive transport services for the carriage of baggage belonging to them. Only the carriage as baggage of highly inflammable and other dangerous cargoes, a list of which was established by the rules, was prohibited by the statutes.

Taking advantage of the introduction of an illegal restriction on the carriage of furniture from Leningrad, certain smart operators set out on the path of bribery and other abuses. Thus, a worker of the transport agency, A. Grigor'eva, acting as a middle-man in transferring bribes for the acquisition of new furniture in store No. 14 of the Leningrad Furniture Mart, for compensation of 100 rubles aided P. Mkhitarian in despatching an imported suite which he purchased in this store as though it had been acquired in a commission store. For this purpose, Grigor'eva made contact with the bookkeeper of a commission store, where fictitious documents "for the acquisition" of furniture were drawn up. The driver of a cargo taxi of automotive enterprise No. 104, A. Mitroshkin, for 125 rubles received from S. Abelian, without authorization or proper formalization, carried a container from the Leningrad-Freight-Finland Station and delivered the furniture acquired by Abelian to Narva Station, where it was detained by police workers. A crane machinist of a locomotive depot, V. Mochenkov, systematically forged authorization signatures for the receipt of containers and the despatch therein of household articles by railway. It was established by investigation that the middle-men received for each despatched new imported suite about 400 or more rubles, which was then divided among other participants. The persons established as guilty of giving and receiving bribes and their accomplices were brought to criminal responsibility.

The protest of the procurator was considered by the executive committee of the Leningrad City Soviet and the illegal decision concerning the prohibition of the carriage of imported furniture, refrigerators, and motorcycles from Leningrad was repealed.

CHAPTER XIX

Inheritance and Socialism

One of the early reforms of the Bolsheviks after coming to power was to curtail sharply the right of inheritance, an institution regarded by classical Marxism as owing its raison d'être to the desire to perpetuate the ownership and control of the instruments and means of production in the hands of a capitalist oligarchy. The Communist Manifesto had made the abolition of inheritance a cornerstone of the socialist program, and like other early Soviet enactments, the decree of April 27,

1918,[1] which curtailed succession by will as well as by operation of law, was symptomatic of the early phase of Soviet power during which the Bolsheviks sought to translate revolutionary theory into direct government action.

This early decree on inheritance provided that all property owned by individuals at the time of their death escheated to the state except for families of a deceased working male which might otherwise be left without any means of support. Thus, the 1918 decree stipulated that estates not exceeding 10,000 rubles in value and consisting of a house, household furnishing, or a workman's means of production could pass to relatives living with and dependent on the decedent. A similar provision was made for peasant households, though without any limitation as to the value of the estate. Estates valued in excess of 10,000 rubles passed to the local Soviet, which had the duty of providing for needy relatives limited to a surviving spouse, descendants or ascendants, and siblings, whether of full or half-blood.

Mention has already been made (see introduction to Chap. 17) of the fact that the 1922 RSFSR Civil Code, drafted to meet the exigencies of Lenin's New Economic Policy, reflected the temporary compromise with capitalism which marked the period preceding the introduction of the first five-year plan in 1927.

The adoption of the 1922 Civil Code signaled a return to traditional notions of inheritance, but the law continued to limit both the size of estates capable of descent and the circle of heirs capable of sharing in it. Thus the maximum amount includable in an estate for purposes of distribution to heirs was fixed at 10,000 rubles.[2] The circle of heirs eligible to share in the estate was limited to the spouse of the deceased, his descendants, and relatives or strangers incapable of working who had been dependent on the deceased for at least one year prior to the date of his death.[3]

Property was permitted to pass by will, but only to beneficiaries chosen from among the statutory circle of heirs eligible to participate as intestate takers. Property was distributable to the heirs per capita, with no right of representation. Simultaneously with the introduction of the Civil Code, a separate law introduced a progressive inheritance tax, the maximum rate being 50 per cent.[4]

The limitation concerning the maximum value of an estate capable of descent was abolished in 1926,[5] but this measure was accompanied by the adoption of a progressive estate tax, with rates as high as 90 per cent for estates whose value exceeded 500,000 rubles.[6] The impact of the tax and the limitation on the circle of heirs was softened two years later when the law was amended to provide that government securities on deposit in banks were not includable in the estate and thus not subject

---

[1]April 27, 1918, [1918] 1 Sob. Uzak., RSFSR, No. 34, item 456.
[2]Art. 416.
[3]Art. 418.
[4]November 11, 1922, [1922] 1Sob. Uzak., RSFSR, No. 71, item 905.
[5]January 29, 1926, [1926] 1 Sob. Jak., USSR, No. 6, item 37.
[6][1926] I Sob. Uzak., RSFSR, No. 12, item 88; *Ibid.* No. 53, item 355; [1928] Sob. Uzak., RSFSR, No. 54, item 41.

to the normal rules of succession.[7] This exemption was extended in 1935 to include cash deposits. The progressive tax as such was abolished in 1942[8] and replaced by a schedule of notarial fees applicable to the issuance of a certificate of inheritance to an heir.[9] The schedule provided for flat fees ranging from 10 rubles for inheritances of less than 300 rubles to 100 rubles on inheritances exceeding 3,000 rubles but not exceeding 5,000 rubles. Fees on inheritances exceeding 5,000 rubles were collected at a rate of 5 per cent for amounts not exceeding 10,000 rubles and at a maximum rate of 10 per cent for those in excess of that sum.

The comprehensive reform of inheritance law in 1945[10] brought additional changes tending to liberalize the law of succession, that is, to broaden the circle of persons eligible to take upon the intestacy of the decedent and those eligible to take under a will. Thus, the circle of intestate takers was expanded to include parents of the deceased incapable of working and brothers and sisters, who, however, were eligible to take only if there were no spouse, no children, and no descendants or parents eligible to take. The 1945 amendment also provided that in the absence of surviving heirs by operation of law, property could be bequeathed to anyone, including someone not included in the statutory circle of intestate takers. In addition, the 1945 decree replaced per capita distribution with distribution per stripes. Escheat to the state resulted from the total absence of heirs or from their failure to accept their inheritance within the statutory period—three months for heirs present at the place of opening of the estate, and six months for absent heirs. Since the law required no mandatory notification of heirs, the possibility of so-called "laughing heirs" making claims was virtually excluded.

The 1961 Fundamental Principles of Civil Legislation of the USSR and Union Republics, by eliminating any restriction on persons to whom property may be willed, evidenced a continued trend toward traditional civil law notions of inheritance. Naturally, Soviet jurists have not viewed the history of the Soviet law of inheritance in this light, but have argued rather that the institution of inheritance is intimately related to property, the curtailment of inheritance in 1918 was intended as a provisional measure until all vestiges of private property had been eliminated and individual ownership of property placed on a new basis commensurate with socialist notions of the extent and nature of personal ownership.

Whatever the theoretical explanations, the adoption of the 1961 Fundamental Principles and the union republic civil codes constitute a new phase in the development of the Soviet inheritance law in which an individual owner's right to dispose of his property after death will be limited only by socialist definitions of the scope of property capable of individual ownership and the notion, almost universally recog-

---

[7]Charter of State Toilers' Savings Banks of the USSR, Approved by Council of Ministers of USSR, November 20, 1948, [1948] Sob. Post., SSSR, No. 7, item 89, sec. 19.
[8]Law of January 9, 1943, 2 Sbornik Zak. SSSR, 1938–1944 (1945), p. 187.
[9]Deceree of April 10, 1942, 2 Sbornik Zak. SSSR, 1938–1944 (1945), p. 184.
[10]Decree of March 14, 1945, 3 Sbornik Zak., SSSR. 1945–1946 (1947), p. 163.

nized, of protection of the rights of close relatives dependent on the decedent and incapable of providing for themselves.

The increasing affluence of Soviet society could present the problem of the fromation of an increasingly large group of persons who have acquired substantial wealth through inheritance. It is possible that this may be avoided by a greater reliance on distribution of property in accordance with status or need, with ownership retained by the state. Alternatively, as the general standard of living improves, such concentrations of personal ownership may be less objectionable and regulated to the extent necessary through estate taxation.

A. Fundamental principles of inheritance under socialism

U.S.S.R. CONSTITUTION, December 5, 1936

Article 10. The right of personal ownership of citizens. . . , as well as the right of citizens to inherit personal ownership, shall be protected by law.

FUNDAMENTION PRINCIPLES OF CIVIL LEGISLATION OF THE USSR AND UNION REPUBLICS, December 8, 1961; effective May 1, 1962. [1961] Vedomosti Verkhovnogo Soveta SSSR, no. 50, item 525.

Article 117. *The Bases of Inheritance*

Inheritance shall be effectuated by operation of law and by will.

Inheritance by operation of law shall take place when and insofar as it has not been altered by will.

If there are no heirs either by operation of law or by will, or if none of the heirs has accepted the inheritance, or if all heirs have been disinherited by the testators, the property of the deceased shall pass to the state by right of succession.

Article 118. *Inheritance by Operation of Law*

In the event of inheritance by operation of law, the heirs of the first class, in equal shares, shall be the children (including adopted children), the spouse, and the parents (or adoptive parents) of the deceased. A child of the deceased born after his death also shall be an heir of the first class.

The grandchildren and great-grandchildren of the deceased shall be heirs by operation of law if at the time of the opening of the inheritance none of their parents are living who would be an heir. They shall inherit in equal share that which their deceased parent would have received in the event of an inheritance by operation of law.

The legistlation of the union republics may designate additional groups of heirs by operation of law. Heirs of this additional class shall inherit by operation of law only if there are no heirs belonging to the preceding class or in the event of their failure to accept the inheritance.

Among the heirs by operation of law shall be disabled persons who were dependent on the deceased for not less than one year before his death. If there are other heirs, they shall inherit equally with heirs of the class entitled to inherit.

Articles of ordinary household furnishing or use shall pass to heirs by operation of law who live together with the decedent irrespective of their class or their share of the inheritance. The terms of the inheritance of such property shall be determined by union republic legislation.

Article 119. *Inheritance by Will*

Every citizen may leave all of his property or part thereof by will (including articles of ordinary household furnishings or use) to one or several persons, either within or not within the circle of heirs by operation of law, as well as to the state or to individual state, cooperative, or social organizations.

Minors or disabled children of the decedent (including adopted children), as well as the spouse, the parents (or adoptive parents), and the dependents of the deceased who are unable to work, shall inherit, irrespective of the content of the will, not less than two-thirds of the share which would have been due each of them in the event of inheritance by operation of law (statutory share). In determining the amount of the statutory share, the value of the estate property consisting of articles of ordinary household furnishing or use also shall be taken into account.

The procedure for the disposition, in the event of death, of deposits in state savings banks or in the State Bank of the USSR according to the special instructions of the depositors shall be determined by the statutes of the said financial institutions issued in accordance with the established procedure.

Article 120. *Liability of Heir for Debts of Decedent*

An heir who has accepted an inheritance shall be liable for debts of the decedent within the limits of the actual value of the estate property which has passed to him. The state shall be liable on the same bases for property which has passed in the procedure of Articles 117 and 119 of the present Fundamental Principles.

Article 121. *Place of Opening an Inheritance*

The place of opening an inheritance shall be deemed the last permanent place of residence of the decedent, and if it is unknown, the place where the property or the principal part thereof is located.

Article 127. *Law Applicable to Inheritance.*

Relations relating to inheritance shall be determined by the law of the country where the decedent had his last permanent place of residence.

The capacity of a person to draw up and revoke a will, as well as the form of the will and act of revocation, shall be determined by the law of the country where the testator had a permanent place of residence at the moment the act was drawn up. However, the will or its revocation may not be deemed invalid as a consequence of the failure to observe the form if the latter satisfies the requirements of the law of the place of drawing up the act or the requirements of Soviet law.

The inheritance of structures situated in the USSR shall be determined in all instances by Soviet law. The capacity of a person to draw up or revoke a will, as well as the form of the latter if a structure situated in the USSR is bequeathed, shall be determined by the same law.

A. N. Makarova, "Inheritance Law" in O. A. Krasavchikov (ed.), SOVETSKOE GRAZHDANSKOE PRAVO [Soviet Civil Law] (Moscow, 1969), Vol 2, 493–494.

1. Significance of Inheritance Law. The institution of inheritance law is inextricably linked with the law of ownership. In sharply criticizing the narodnik Mikhailovskii, who preached that only family relations give birth to inheritance law, V. I. Lenin wrote: ". . . the institution of inheritance presupposes private ownership, and the latter arises only with the emergence of exchange."

In an exploitative state the law of inheritance reflects and consolidates the interests of the dominant class. Thus, in bourgeois society inheritance law furthers the strengthening of capitalist productive relations and capitalist private ownership. ". . . it leaves," as K. Marx pointed out, "for the heir the right which the deceased possessed *during life,* namely, the *right* with the aid of ownership to *appropriate the products of another's labor.*"

The classics of Marxism-Leninism sharply opposed utopian and reformist views on the essence of the law of inheritance. Ideologues of these views (Saint-Simon, Bakunin, and their followers) saw in the law of inheritance the principal reason for the existence of private ownership, economic inequality, and class organization of society. In this connection they imagined it possible to transform society by abolishing the right of inheritance. In criticizing the profound mistakenness of these views, K. Marx pointed out that ". . . the laws on inheritance are not the *cause,* but the *consequence,* the *juridical conclusion* of the *existing economic organization of society,* which is based on private ownership of the means of production . . ." Therefore, a social revolution is necessary. *"Disapearance of the right of inheritance* will be the natural result of such a social restructuring which abolishes private ownership of the means of production; but *abolition of the right of inheritance* can never become the starting-point of such a social transformation."

The classics of Marxism-Leninism considered abolition of the right of inheritance of private ownership to be a necessary measure which would be effectuated in a complex with others after the victory of the proletarian revolution.

Under socialism the institution of inheritance law is closely linked with the right of personal ownership of citizens. The right of inheritance of personal ownership is among the constitutional rights. According to Article 10 of the USSR Constitution, "the right to inherit personal ownership of citizens shall be protected by law". The institution of inheritance law allows each Soviet citizen freely to dispose, within the limits established by law, of his property in the event of death. In the absence of any dispositions of the testator, the law deems persons close to the deceased to inherit by virtue of relationship, marriage, or dependence. Thus, inheritance law to a certain extent furthers the strengthening of marital and family relations of citizens and protects the interests of minor children and heirs who were disabled.

B. S. Antimonov and K. A. Grave, SOVETSKOE NASLEDSTVENNOE PRAVO [Soviet Inheritance Law] (Moscow, 1955), 7.

In the text of the first draft of the USSR Constitution this link [the link between the institution of inheritance, the institution of property, and the Soviet economic and socio-political structure] did not as yet find any reflection. Article 10 of the draft spoke not of the right of personal ownership of citizens, but simply of their personal property. About the right to inherit personal ownership there was absolutely no mention.

The Drafting Commission of the Extraordinary VII Congress of Soviets proposed the adoption of a new redaction of Article 10 of the draft USSR Constitution, which later came into the text of our basic law. At present, Article 10 of the USSR Constitution contains the term "right of personal ownership". . . , and the words, "as well as the right to inherit", complete this article, expressing the indissoluble link between the right of inheritance and the right of personal ownership.

The USSR Constitution views the institution of inheritance as a part of the broader question of the right of personal ownership of citizens.

IN RE S. P. TSYMBALIUK, Biulleten' Verkhovnogo Suda SSSR, 1969, no. 3, p. 39.

Tsymbaliuk was convicted by the Military Tribunal of the Privolzhskii Military District of the murder of his father because of a family quarrel.

The Military Tribunal, having considered a civil suit for 406 rubles brought against Tsymbaliuk by A. O. Tsesarskaia, satisfied it.

Simultaneously with the judgment, the court rendered a ruling wherein the court decreed that the civil suit be compensated from monetary savings of the murdered P. P. Tsymbaliuk, deposited in a savings bank.

Having considered the record of the case upon the protest of the chairman of the Military Division of the USSR Supreme Court, the Military Division finds that the said ruling is illegal and subject to repeal since according to Article 531 of the RSFSR Civil Code Tsymbaliuk has no right to inherit the property of his parents, including monetary deposits.

In connection therewith the ruling of the military tribunal can not be executed. Insofar as the judgment in the case of S. P. Tsymbaliuk has entered into legal force, it is subject to execution as regards the civil suit in accordance with the procedure established by Articles 340 and 368 of the RSFSR Code of Civil Procedure.

N.A. FILIMONOVA vs. DACHA CONSTRUCTION COOPERATIVE, Biulleten' Verkhovnogo Suda RSFSR, 1973, no. 6, p. 4.

K. A. Filimonova was a member of the Dacha Construction Cooperative attached to the Leningrad Admiralty Plant and used the dacha of the dacha construction cooperative located at the Orekhovo Station, Sosnovskii District, Leningrad Region. In August 1971 Filimonova died and in her place, by decision of the general meeting of members of the Dacha Construction Cooperative, Ksenofontova, with whom Filimonova had been friends for many years, had built the dacha together, had worked the land plot, and had used the dacha building, was admitted to membership in the cooperative.

N. A. Filimonova, the sister of the deceased, brought a claim in court to oblige the Dacha Construction Cooperative to admit her to membership in the cooperative and to grant her the sister's dacha and land plot, referring to the fact that she is the heir of K. A. Filimonova, used the dacha, and therefore has a preferential right to join the cooperative.

The Leningrad City Court rejected the suit.

The Judicial Division for Civil Cases of the RSFSR Supreme Court, having considered the file of the case by way of cassation, left the decision by a ruling of January 26, 1973, without change on the following grounds:

In accordance with section 23 of the Model Charter of a Dacha Construction Cooperative and the Charter of the Dacha Construction Cooperative attached to the Admiralty Plant, a preferential right to join the cooperative is accorded only to members of the family and to heirs of the deceased who have used the dacha premises jointly with them.

Heirs who have not used the dacha premises during the life of the decedent do not possess such a right and may claim payment by the cooperative of the value of the share or portion which they have inherited.

It was established in the case that N. A. Filimonova was not a member of the deceased Filimonova's family, and she did not contest this fact.

Her arguments that in the period 1966–1971 she and members of her family used the dacha premises granted to the deceased were disproved by evidence in the case during the course of the judicial examination.

The neighbors of the deceased K. A. Filimonova at the dacha settlement, witnesses Kondratovich, Bogov, Potemkin, and others, testified in court that the dacha was erected with the labor and assets of Ksenofontova and K. A. Filimonova, and that the plaintiff and members of her family did not take part either in erecting the dacha nor in exploiting the land plot.

The same fact was confirmed also in the statement of the plaintiff's husband, Ukhanov, of July 25, 1967, who was an initial member of the Dacha Construction Cooperative, wherein it is indicated that, inasmuch as the house and plot were fully exploited by K. A. Filimonova, and he, Ukhanov, took practically no part in these works, he requested the plot be transferred to K. A. Filimonova.

The plaintiff herself did not deny in court that she resides permanently in Leningrad, she took and takes her holidays in the Crimea or the Caucasus, and never lived at Orekhovo (at the dacha) in the summer nor was at the dacha in 1970–71. According to information of the Leningrad Admiralty Combine, the plaintiff's husband, Ukhanov, in the summer seasons beginning from May 1966 up to October 1, 1971, performed the duties of the head of the plant leisure base in the Manol settlement, Vyborg District, and consequently also did not use the dacha premises of the deceased.

The fact that during K. A. Filimonova's life the plaintiff and her adult son sometimes visited the now deceased decedent, to which some witnesses testified, and to which the plaintiff referred, cannot serve as a ground for satisfying the claims petitioned for, inasmuch as these visits were of an occasional nature. They may not be regarded as evidence of the joint use of the dacha with K. A. Filimonova which gives a preferential right to the plaintiff for future use of this premise.

In accordance with Article 532 of the RSFSR Civil Code and section 23 of the Charter of the Dacha Construction Cooperative, the plaintiff shall have the right in such event to demand from the respondent only payment of the value of the inherited share, to which the latter did not object.

INHERITANCE OF INSURANCE ON SIMULTANEOUS DEATH OF THE INSURED AND THE BENEFICIARY, Sovetskaia iustitsiia, 1970, no. 18, p. 32.

V. E. Shadrina concluded an insurance contract with agencies of Gosstrakh. She designated her daughter as the beneficiary of the insured sum. On September 10, 1969, they perished simultaneously.

In connection therewith the sister of the insured, Semenova, petitioned the Noril'sk notarial office to issue her a certificate of the right to inheritance in deposits, the insured sum, and other property.

In considering this question, the question arose as to whether the notary could issue a certificate of the right to ineritance by operation of law to the sister of the decedent if another person who had died on the same day as the insured decedent had been designated the beneficiary of the insured sum.

The notarial section of the RSFSR Supreme Court explained that according to section 25 of the Rules for Joint Life Insurance confirmed by the USSR Ministry of Finances, the insured sum shall be paid to heirs of the insured in the event of the simultaneous death of the insured and the person designated to receive the insured sum unless otherwise provided in the insurance contract. In the insurance policy submitted for review, there is no provision on this question. Consequently, the insured sum shall be subject to payment to the heir of the insured person on the basis of the certificate on the right to inheritance by operation of law issued by the notarial office.

B. *Inheritance by will*

CIVIL CODE, RSFSR (1964)
Article 534. *Right of a Citizen to Bequeath his Property at his Discretion.*

Every citizen may leave by will all his property or a part thereof (including ordinary household furnishing and articles) to one or several persons who are within or are not within the circle of heirs by operation of law, as well as to the state or to individual state, cooperative, and social organizations.

A testator may in the will disinherit one, several, or all heirs by operation of law.
Article 535. *Right to Statutory Share in an Estate*

Minors or disabled children of the decedent (including adopted children), as well as a disabled spouse, parents (or adoptive parents) and dependents of the deceased, shall inherit, irrespective of the content of the will, not less than a two-thirds share which would be due each of them in the event of inheritance by operation of law (statutory share). In determining the amount of a statutory share, the value of the inherited property consisting of ordinary household furnishing and articles also shall be taken into account.

Article 536. *Designation of an Alternate Heir*

A testator shall have the right to specify in a will another heir in the event the heir he designated dies before the opening of the estate or does not accept it.

Article 537. *Inheritance of the Part of the Property Not Bequeathed*

The part of the property not bequeathed shall be divided among the heirs by operation of law who are deemed to inherit in accordance with the procedure of Articles 532 and 533 of the present Code.

Among such heirs are those heirs by operation of law to whom another part of the property was left by will insofar as is not provided otherwise in the will.

Article 538. *Testamentary Charge*

A testator shall have the right to impose on an heir by will the execution of any obligation (or testamentary charge) to the benefit of one or several persons (beneficiaries of a testamentary charge) who shall acquire the right to demand its execution. Persons both within and not within the circle of heirs by operation of law may be beneficiaries of a testamentary charge.

A testator shall have the right to entrust to an heir to whom a dwelling house passes the obligation to grant to another person the use of his house for life or a certain part thereof. In the event of the subsequent transfer of the right of ownership in a house or part thereof, the right of use for life shall retain force.

An heir who is entrusted by a testator with the execution of a testamentary charge should execute it only within the limits of the actual value of the inherited property which passed to him, deducting that portion of the decedent's debts falling on him.

If an heir by will who is entrusted with the execution of a testamentary charge has the right to a statutory share in an estate, he shall execute the testamentary charge only within the limits of the value of the inherited property which passed to him that exceeds the amount of his statutory share.

In the event of the death of the person, before the opening of the estate who has been entrusted with the execution of a testamentary charge, or in the event of his failure to accept the inheritance, the duty to execute the testamentary charge shall pass to the other heirs who have received his share.

Article 539. *Entrusting to an Heir the Performance of Actions for Generally Useful Purposes*

A testator may impose on an heir the execution of any actions directed to the implementation of any generally useful purpose. If such actions are of a financial nature, the rules of Article 538 of the present Code shall apply respectively.

Article 540. *Notarial Form of a Will*

A will should be drawn up in writing, indicating the place and time of its compilation, and be personally signed by the testator and notarially certified.

Article 541. *Wills Equivalent to Notarially Certified Wills*

There shall be equivalent to notarially certified wills:

(1) wills of citizens being treated in hospitals, other in-patient medical institutions, sanatoriums or residing in homes for the aged and disabled, which are certified by the chief doctors, their medical deputies, or duty doctors of these hospitals, medical institutions, sanatoriums, as well as directors and chief doctors of the said homes for the aged and disabled;

(2) wills of citizens on sea-going vessels of internal navigation sailing under the flag of the USSR which are certified by the masters of these vessels;

(3) wills of citizens in prospecting, arctic, and other similar expeditions which are certified by the heads of these expeditions;

(4) wills of military servicemen and other persons being treated in military hospitals, sanatoriums, and other military medical institutions which are certified by their heads, their medical deputies, the senior and duty doctors of these military hospitals, sanatoriums, and other military medical institutions;

(5) wills of military servicemen, and at points where military units, formations, institutions, and military training institutions are situated where there are no state notarial offices or other agencies performing notarial activities, also the wills of workers and employees, members of their families, and family members of military servicemen, which are certified by the commanders (or heads) of these units, formations, institutions, and educational institutions;

(6) wills of persons in places of deprivation of freedom which are certified by the heads of the places of deprivation of freedom.

Article 542. *Signing of a Will by Another Person*

If a testator, by virtue of physical defects, illness, or other reasons, can not personally sign a will, it may be signed at his request in the presence of a notary or other official (Article 541) by another citizen, indicating the reasons by virtue of which the testator could not sign the will personally.

NOTARIAL PRACTICE, Sovetskaia iustitsiia, 1969, no. 2, p. 29.

A citizen requested a notarial office to certify in his name a will wherein a dwelling house belonging to him should pass to his son. In addition, the testator indicated in this will that his son shall not have the right after the father's death to sell the house which passed to him by right of inheritance without the consent of the other children of the decedent.

The notary refused to certify the will.

The notarial section of the RSFSR Supreme Court explained that the will is itself a free and strictly personal disposition by a citizen of his property in the event of death made in the form established by law. However, the freedom of testamentary dispositions is not unlimited.

The testator may not limit the heir in the right to dispose of inherited property which passed to him as a consequence of the right of inheritance.

From the moment inherited property passes to an heir, he becomes the owner of this property and may dispose of it (sell, give, bequeath, etc.) at his discretion in accordance with Article 92 of the RSFSR Civil Code.

Consequently, the notarial office may not certify a will which contains an instruction limiting the right of an heir to use, dispose, and possess property which passes to him in ownership by right of inheritance.

CERTIFICATION OF A FOREIGNER'S WILL, Sovetskaia iustitsiia, 1971, no. 5, p. 62.

The question arises in the practice of state notarial offices whether a notarial office has the right to certify a will in the name of a citizen of a foreign state.

A foreigner in the Soviet Union may draw up a will, as well as change or revoke a will which he has drawn up, and the notarial office shall certify it.

Article 127 of the Fundamental Principles of Civil Legislation establishes that the capacity of a person to draw up and revoke a will, as well as the form of the will and act revoking it shall be determined according to the law of that country where the testator had a permanent residence at the moment of drawing up the act. However, a will or its revocation may not be deemed invalid as a consequence of the failure to observe the form if it satisfies the requirements of the law of the place where the act is drawn up or the requirements of Soviet law. If a dwelling house in the USSR is bequeathed, the form of the will shall be determined according to Soviet legislation, pursuant to which the will should be drawn up in writing, signed by the testator, and this signature must be notarially certified.

It is provided in treaties on legal assistance concluded by the USSR with other socialist countries that the form of the will of citizens shall be determined according to the law of the country of their citizenship, Moreover, the treaties establish the competence of the will if the legislation of that state on whose territory the will was drawn up is observed.

G. N. BABLIDZE vs. V. E. BABLIDZE, Biulleten' Verkhovnogo Suda SSSR, 1969, no. 5, pp. 37-37.

G. N. Bablidze brought suit in a people's court against V. E. Bablidze for recognition of the right of ownership in half of a house and for recognition of a will as void wherein the entire house had been bequeathed to the defendant by his now deceased father, E. G. Bablidze.

G. N. Bablidze's claim was based on the fact that until 1942 she was de facto married to the father of the defendant, E. G. Bablidze, and in 1942 registered the marriage with him. She took part in constructing the house together with him. The house then consisted of a single room, 29.89 meters square in area. During the period of their life together, the spouses built, with the appropriate permits, two more rooms of 15 and 16 square meters. Despite this, the deceased spouse left the entire house in 1967 by will to the son of his first marriage, the defendant V. E. Bablidze, which deprived her, the plaintiff, of the possibility of receiving the statutory share of the estate according to law.

[The people's court decided in favor of the plaintiff and deemed the will void; on cassational review, the Presidium of the Georgian Supreme Court awarded the plaintiff 2/3 of the house, considering her entitled to a full statutory share as a spouse unable to work. This decree was protested by the deputy chairman of the USSR Supreme Court to the Plenum of the Georgian Supreme Court on the following grounds]:

It is acknowledged in the protest that the presidium of the Georgian Supreme Court correctly pointed out the erroneous conclusions of the people's court and the cassational instance, that the court supposedly had the right to increase the statutory share of the estate, that is, to fix it in a larger amount than is provided for in law (more than two thirds of the share due to each heir in the event of inheritance by operation of law).

In accordance with the Fundamental Principles of Civil Legislation of the USSR and Union Republics, it was affirmed in the protest that minors or disabled children of the decedent (including adopted children) and dependents of the deceased shall inherit irrespective of the content of the will not less than two-thirds of the share which would be due each of them in the event of inheritance by operation of law (statutory share).

This means, it was pointed out in the protest, that if the decedent did not mention minors or disabled heirs in the will or fixed for them less than two-thirds of the share which would be due each of them by operation of law (statutory share), the court in considering a dispute regarding the inheritance property left shall ascertain the right of each of the said heirs to a statutory share of the property in the amount of two-thirds of the share which would be due each of them in the event of inheritance by operation of law.

It also is necessary to have the following in mind. The people's court established that part of the house was built during the life of the plaintiff together with the decedent. The property acquired by the spouses by their joint labor during the marriage shall, according to Article 17 of the Code of Laws on Marriage, Family, and Guardianship of the Georgian SSR, be considered as belonging to both spouses in equal shares. In connection therewith, in the present instance the estate property is not the entire house, but only part of it.

Proceeding from the aforesaid, the people's court had grounds to satisfy the suit of G. N. Bablidze and correctly recognized her right of ownership in half of the house which she actually enjoys at the present time.

[The Plenum of the Georgian Supreme Court concurred with the protest, reversed the decree of the Presidium of the Georgian Supreme Court, and restored the decisions of the people's court and the cassational ruling].

C. Inheritance by operation of law

CIVIL CODE, RSFSR (1964)
Article 532. *Heirs by Operation of Law*

In the event of inheritance by operation of law, the heirs in equal shares shall be:

of the first class: the children (including adopted children), the spouse, and the parents (or adoptive parents) of the deceased, as well as the child of the deceased born after his death;

of the second class: the brothers and sisters of the deceased, his grandfather and grandmother both on the father's and the mother's side.

Heirs of the second class shall be deemed to inherit by operation of law only in the absence of heirs of the first class or their failure to accept the inheritance, and also in the event all heirs of the first class have been deprived by the testator of the right to inherit.

Among the heirs by operation of law shall be disabled persons who are dependent on the deceased at least one year before his death. If there are other heirs, they shall inherit equally with the heirs of that class which is deemed to inherit.

Grandchildren and great-grandchildren of the decedent shall be heirs by operation of law if at the time the estate is opened none of their parents who would be an heir is alive; they shall inherit in equal parts that share which would have been due their deceased parent in the event of inheritance by operation of law.

Adopted children and their descendants shall not inherit after the death of the parents of the adopted person, his other blood relatives in a direct line, as well as his blood brothers and sisters.

The parents of an adopted person and his other blood relatives in direct line, as well as his blood brothers and sisters, shall not inherit after the death of the adopted person and his descendants.

Article 533. *Inheritance of Articles of Ordinary Household Furnishings and Use.*

Articles of ordinary household furnishings and use shall pass to heirs by operation of law who live together with the decedent before his death for at least one year, irrespective of their class or their share of the inheritance.

IN RE MALOVA, Biulleten' Verkhovnogo Suda RSFSR, 1968, no. 6, p. 10.

Malova petitioned a court to establish the fact that her son, Anatolii Malov, born in 1954, was a dependent of Krupskii, who died on January 19, 1967. She referred in this connection to the fact that the son was born from her life together with Krupskii. Anatolii Malov was a dependent of Krupskii, whose earnings significantly exceeded the mother's earnings. Establishment of this fact was necessary for her son to receive the estate left after Krupskii's death.

Inasmuch as other heirs to Krupskii's property were not found, the Kalinin District Finance Section of Moscow was enlisted to participate in the case as an interested person.

[The Judicial Division of the Moscow City Court concluded that the child was a dependent, which decision was left unchanged by the Judicial Division for Civil Cases of the RSFSR Supreme Court on appeal by the Kalinin Finance Section]:

In its ruling of January 25, 1968, the Division pointed out the following.

It was established by the materials of the case that in 1959 Malova had settled with the son in the living quarters of Krupskii as a member of his family. Krupskii's earnings were the basic source of funds for the existence of Anatolii Malov. Krupskii acquired things for the child and organized his vacation during the holidays. He considered Anatolii Malov to be his son and manifested care for him as a father.

The said facts have been confirmed by witness testimony of Krupskii's relatives, his close friends, associates at work, and apartment neighbors.

Letters annexed to the file of the case and certificates of children's and medical institutions also testify to Anatolii Malov living at Krupskii's as a member of the family.

Taking into account the aforesaid, the court correctly established the fact that Anatolii Malov was a dependent of the deceased Krupskii.

The reference in the appeal of the district finance section to the fact that Malova received for her son an allowance as an unmarried mother and that she herself worked, receiving a wage sufficient to support the child, and that therefore the child could not be deemed a dependent of the deceased, can not serve as grounds to vacate the decision of the court.

In point 4 of the decree of the Plenum of the USSR Supreme Court of February 25, 1966, "On Judicial Practice in Cases Concerning the Establishment of Facts Having Legal Significance", it is indicated that the existence of earnings, receipt of pensions, stipends, and so forth can not be a grounds for refusing to establish the fact of the dependence of a person if the funds granted by the deceased were the basic and permanent source of existence for this person.

NOTARIAL PRACTICE, Sovetskaia iustitsiia, 1974, no. 5, p. 60.

After the death of N., his daughter was adopted by G. The daughter of the deceased requested the notarial office to issue a certificate of the right to inheritance left after the death of her natural father. The notary raised the question of whether he has the right to issue her a certificate of the right to inheritance left after the death of the father, having in view that according to Article 532 of the RSFSR Civil Code adopted persons and their descendants shall not inherit after the death of the parents of an adopted person, his other blood relatives in direct line, as well as his blood brothers and sisters.

The notarial section of the RSFSR Ministry of Justice explained that inasmuch as the death of the decedent had taken place earlier than the adoption, the daughter consequently had not lost her right to the estate left after the father's death.

Citizen K. during his father's life was adopted by a step-father in 1939. The step-father was mobilized in 1941 at the front of the Great Fatherland War and at the end of the war did not return to the family nor thereafter bring up the step-son which he had adopted.

Having become disabled, the step-father brought suit in 1969 to recover maintenance from the stepson.

Taking into account that the step-father had avoided maintaining the stepson which he had adopted, the people's court rejected the suit.

Citizen K. searched for and found his natural father. In April 1970 the father of citizen K. died. In connection therewith, K. requested the notarial office to issue him a certificate of the right to inheritance left after his father's death. The State Notarial Office, being guided by Article 532 of the RSFSR Civil Code, refused to issue the certificate of the right to inheritance.

To the appeal submitted by citizen K., the notariat section of the RSFSR Ministry of Justice explained that he cannot be deemed an heir inasmuch as during his father's life he was adopted by another person and the father's will left nothing to his benefit. The fact that the court rejected his step-father's suit for maintenance has significance in the present case since the court rejected the suit because the step-father, having adopted a stepchild, avoided supporting him. (article 78, RSFSR Code on Marriage and the Family).

SUSHKO vs. THE VINOKUROVS, Biulleten' Verkhovnogo Suda RSFSR, 1969, no. 2 p. 8

Sushko petitioned the court to recognize de facto marital relations with Voinova and the right to an inheritance of a savings account in the amount of 816 rubles, referring to the fact that he had entered into de facto marital relations with Voinova in 1943 and lived with her as a single family until the day of her death, which occurred December 4, 1965. The savings account in the amount of 816 rubles in Voinova's name at the savings bank constitutes the property acquired by them during their life together. In connection with the fact that the marriage between them had not been registered, his right to inherit the account had not been recognized.

The sister and brothers of the deceased Voinova, the Vinokurovs, brought a counter-suit against Sushko to recognize them as heirs. They referred to the fact that they are the sole heirs of their sister's property, and Sushko did not permanently live with Voinova nor keep a common household, co-habited with other women, taunted the sister, and had no intention to form a lasting family with her.

By decision of the Judicial Division of the Bashkir ASSR Supreme Court it was recognized that Sushko and Voinova had de facto marital relations from 1943-December 4, 1965. Sushko, moreover, was recognized as the heir of the account. The Judicial Division rejected the Vinokurovs' suit to recognize them as the heirs.

[In a cassational appeal the Vinokurovs sought reversal of the decision on the grounds that Sushko did not take part in the accumulation of Voinova's property and, systematically abused alcoholic beverages. On June 11, 1968, the Judicial Division for Civil Cases of the RSFSR Supreme Court rejected the appeal on the following grounds]:

In point 6 of the decree of the Plenum of the USSR Supreme Court of February 25, 1966, "On Judicial Practice in Cases Concerning the Establishment of Facts Having Legal Significance", it was indicated that by virtue of Article 247, point 4 of the RSFSR Code of Civil Procedure the establishment of the fact of the existence of de facto marital relations may occur if such relations arose prior to the promulgation of the Edict of the Presidium of the USSR Supreme Soviet of July 8, 1944, and continued until the death of one of the spouses.

The Judicial Division established that Sushko and Voinova had entered into de facto marital relations in 1943 and lived as a single family until the latter's death, that is, until December 4, 1965.

This fact, which is of decisive significance for the present case, is confirmed by the documents submitted by Sushko and by the testimony of witnesses Shumakov, Dolgovaia, and Zinov'ev.

Sushko, as Voinova's spouse, is the heir of the first class of property remaining after her in accordance with Article 532 of the Civil Code.

Therefore, the judicial division of the Bashkir ASSR Supreme Court correctly recognized Sushko's right to inherit the account in the amount of 816 rubles kept in the savings bank in Voinova's name.

The counter-suit of the Vinokurovs to recognize their right to inherit the property of Voinova is unfounded. The decision in this respect corresponds to the requirements of Article 532 of the Civil Code, according to which the brothers and sisters are heirs of the second class. Heirs of the second class are deemed to inherit by operation of law only in the absence of heirs of the first class (spouse, children, parents) or if they fail to accept the inheritance, as well as when all heirs of the first class are deprived by the testator of the right of inheritance.

Inasmuch as in the present Sushko is the heir of the first class, the Vinokurov brothers and sister as heirs of the second class may not be deemed to inherit the property of the deceased.

The Vinokurovs' arguments that Sushko did not live with Voinova permanently and did not take part in acquiring the property are confirmed by nothing in the file of the case. During life together with Sushko, Voinova was dependent on him and worked only for three years as a cleaner in a house administration.

D. *Inheritance in the collective farm household*

CIVIL CODE, RSFSR (1964)
Article 560. *Inheritance in the Collective Farm Household*

In the event of the death of a member of a collective farm (or single peasant) household, inheritance in the property of the household shall not arise.

If after the death of a member of a collective farm (or single peasant) household there remain no other members of the household, the rules of the present section shall apply to the property of the household.

NOTARIAL PRACTICE, Sovetskaia iustitsiia, 1968, no. 16, p. 69.

In the practice of the 1st Astrakhan State Notarial Office the question arose of whether an automobile or motorcycle left after the death of a member of a collective farm household passes into the ownership of a collective farm household if it was acquired from the common assets of the household members.

The notariat section of the RSFSR Supreme Court explained that agencies of the State Motor Vehicle Inspectorate have the right to re-register an automobile or motorcycle acquired from the common assets of members of the household left after the death of a member of the collective farm household and belonging to him by right of common ownership, to another member of this household. Such re-registration is permissible with the consent of all the other members of the household.

For this purpose the following documents should be submitted to agencies of the State Motor Vehicle Inspectorate: (a) a certificate of the executive committee of the rural soviet of working people's deputies that the household is a collective farm household and the membership of the household; (b) a declaration from all household members of consent to re-registration of the automobile or motorcycle and that it is in the common ownership of a collective farm household.

DUREEVA vs. PETRIIAKINA, Biulleten' Verkhovnogo Suda RSFSR, 1976, no. 2, pp. 8–9.

On May 19, 1971, the notary of the Dmitriev State Notarial Office issued Petriiakina a certificate of the right to inheritance by will of one-half a house in rural village of the Khonutovskii District, Kursk Region and which belonged to Dureev, who died November 13, 1970.

Dureeva brought suit against Petriiakina to recognize as void the will certified by the Dmitriev State Notarial Office and the certificate of the right to inheritance by will.

The suit of Dureeva was motivated by the fact that the farm (or house) appertains to a collective farm household of which she is a member. After the death of her husband, Dureeva did not open the inheritance, and she is the owner of all the property as a member of the collective farm household.

Petriiakina did not acknowledge the suit and explained that the farm of her brother, Dureev, appertained to the category of a farm of workers and employees, and therefore he had the right to bequeath his property. Moreover, Petriiakina requested her right of ownership in one-half the house be recognized. In justification of her counter-suits Petriiakina referred to the fact that she took part in the construction of the house with her personal labor and assets, on the occasion of which a dispute arose. She transferred 900 rubles of her personal savings to her brother Dureev for building the house, painted and whitewashed the house, and had an arrangement with her brother to build the house for her residence. To this end, a second brother also helped build the house.

The Kursk Regional Court satisfied the basic suit and rejected the countersuit.

The Judicial Division for Civil Cases of the RSFSR Supreme Court, having considered the case by way of cassation, left the decision without change by a ruling of May 13, 1974, on the following grounds.

According to Article 126 of the RSFSR Civil Code, the property of the collective farm household belongs to its members by right of joint ownership.

From the certificates of the "Victory" collective farm and the Lenin collective farm (later unified into a single collective farm), and also from the farm books of the Romanov Rural Soviet of Working People's Deputies appended to the file of the case it is clear that the Dureev farm appertains to the collective farm household type. The household members were: Dureev and his first wife, a collective farmer who died July 28, 1969.

Dureeva began to live together with Dureev from September 1969, moved in with him as a member of the family, and then registered a marriage with him.

From September 1969 she worked in the Lenin Collective Farm, taking part in keeping the collective farm household. The protocol of the general meeting of the collective farmers of the Lenin Collective Farm of February 22, 1974, also testifies to this.

In accordance with Article 560 of the RSFSR Civil Code, in the event of the death of a member of a collective farm household, inheritance in the property of the household does not arise. As is obvious from the file of the case, Dureeva is a member of the collective farm household and all property of the collective farm household belongs to her by virtue of the law.

With such data the court justifiably recognized as void the will of August 6, 1970, and the certificate on inheritance of May 19, 1971, issued by the Dmitriev State Notarial Office to Petriiakina recognizing her as the heir to one-half the house.

The arguments of Petriiakina's appeal that after the death of the first wife of Dureev, the collective farm can not be deemed correct since the legal regime of the farm did not change. This is confirmed by the fact that Dureev in the period from July 28-September 1969 enjoyed the exemptions and privileges established for the collective farm household.

The counter-suit of Petriiakina to recognize the right of ownership in one-half the house was correctly deemed by the court unjustified.

In itself the participation of a non-member of a collective farm household in the construction of a house with personal labor or assets erected by the collective farm household does not create for this person the right of ownership in a share in the property of the collective farm household.

Moreover, from the farm book of the Romanov Rural Soviet of Working People's Deputies it is clear that the house was built in 1963 (in place of the old house) and from that time Dureev lived in the house with his first wife and after her death with Dureeva.

Petriiakina never lived in the house. During the brother's life there were no claims submitted for her right of ownership in one-half the house.

The house was built for the residence of one family therein, with one entrance, and it consists of two living rooms.

Witnesses Burenkov, Kovalev, and Reviakin confirmed in court that the house was erected by Dureev personally for his family with the participation of Petriiakina, and there was no arrangement between the brother and sister to create common ownership in the dwelling house.

Evidence which confirmed that Petriiakina transferred 900 rubles to Dureev for construction of the house was lacking.

The chairman of the rural soviet of working people's deputies, Burenkov, explained in court that neither Petriiakina nor Dureev applied to the rural soviet for permission concerning the joint construction of a house.

E. *Probate and estate administration*

CIVIL CODE, RSFSR (1964)
Article 528. *Time of Opening an Estate*

The date of death of the decedent shall be deemed the time of opening an estate, and in the event of declaring him to be dead, the date specified in Article 21, paragraph 3, of the present Code.

Article 529. *Place of Opening an Estate*

The last permanent place of residence of the decedent (Article 17) shall be deemed the place of opening an estate, and if this is unknown, the place where his property is located or the basic part thereof.

Article 544. *Execution of a Will.*

The execution of a will shall be entrusted to the heirs designated in the will.

The testator may charge to execute a will a person specified in the will who is not an heir (executor). In this event the consent of the executor is required, expressed in his signature on the will itself or in a declaration attached to the will.

Article 545. *Powers of an Executor*

The executor shall have the right to perform all actions necessary for execution of the will.

The executor shall not receive compensation for his actions relating to execution of the will, but shall have the right to compensation from the estate for necessary expenses incurred in the protection of estate property and the management of this property.

Upon executing the will, the executor shall be obliged to submit a report to the heirs at their request.

Article 546. *Acceptance of an Inheritance*

In order to acquire an inheritance, the heir should accept it. An acceptance of an inheritance on condition or with reservation shall not be permitted.

An heir shall be deemed to have accepted an inheritance when he comes into actual possession of the estate property or when he has submitted to a notariral agency at the place of opening an estate a declaration accepting the inheritance.

The actions specified in the present article should be performed within six months from the date of opening the estate.

Persons for whom a right of inheritance arises only in the event of the failure of other heirs to accept an inheritance may declare their consent to accept the inheritance within the remainder of the period for accepting the inheritance, and if this period is less than three months, it shall be extended to three months.

The accepted inheritance shall be deemed to belong to an heir from the time of opening estate.

Article 547. *Extension of the period for Accepting an Inheritance*

The period for accepting an inheritance established by Article 546 of the present Code may be extended by a court if it recognizes the reasons for passage of the period to be justifiable. An inheritance may be accepted after expiry of the said period and without recourse to a court on condition that all the remaining heirs who have accepted the inheritance consent.

In such instances an heir who has allowed the period for accepting an inheritance to pass shall receive only that property due him as has been retained in kind by the other heirs or been transferred to the state, as well as monies obtained from realization of the other part of the property due him.

Article 548. *Transfer of the Right to Accept an Inheritance*

If an heir deemed to inherit by operation of law or by will dies after the opening of an estate without having succeeded in accepting it within the established period (Article 546), the right to accept the share of the estate due him shall pass to his heirs.

This right of the deceased heir may be exercised by his heirs on the general provisions during the remaining part of the period to accept the inheritance. If the remaining part of the period is less than three months, it shall be extended to three months.

Article 549. *Rights of an Heir Who Has Entered into Possession or Administration of Inherited Property Before the Appearance of Other Heirs.*

An heir who has entered into possesion or administration of inherited property without expecting the appearance of other heirs shall not have the right to dispose of the inherited property (sell, pledge, etc.) before expiry of six months from the date of opening the estate or until receiving a certificate of the right to inheritance.

Before expiry of the said period or receipt of the certificate of the right to inheritance, an heir shall have the right to make expenditures from the estate only for:

(1) covering expenditures for the care of the decedent during his illness, as well as for his funeral;

(2) supporting citizens dependent on the decedent;

(3) satisfying claims for wages and claims equivalent thereto;

(4) protecting the estate property and its management.

Article 550. *Refusal of an Inheritance*

An heir by operation of law or by will shall have the right to refuse an inheritance within six months from the date of the opening of the estate. He may indicate that the inheritance is refused to the benefit of other persons from among the heirs by operation of law (Article 532) or by will (Article 534), to the benefit of the state, or of an individual state, cooperative, or social organization.

Refusal of an inheritance without indicating to whose benefit the heir is refusing the inheritance shall entail the same consequences as the failure to accept an inheritance.

Refusal of an inheritance shall not be permitted if an heir submitted to a notarial office at the place of opening the estate a declaration accepting the inheritance or concerning the issuance to him of a certificate of the right to inheritance.

Refusal of an inheritance shall be performed by the heir submitting a declaration to the notarial office at the place of opening the estate.

Article 554. *Procedure for Submitting Claims by Creditors*

Creditors of the decedent shall have the right within six months from the date of opening the estate to submit their claims to heirs who have accepted the inheritance or to the executor, or to the notarial office at the place of opening the estate, or to bring suit against the estate property in court.

Claims shall be submitted irrespective of whether the period of the respective demands has come due.

The failure to observe these rules shall entail the loss by the creditors of the rights to a claim belonging to them.

NOTARIAL PRACTICE, Sovetskia iustitsiia, 1969, no. 5, cover.

Sometimes citizens request notarial offices to certify the genuineness of signatures on their declarations concerning the issuance of a certificate of the right to inheritnace. It is necessary to send such a declaration to a notarial office at the place of the opening of an inheritance, although they have sent (within six months from the day of opening the estate) to the said notarial office a declaration accepting the inheritance, but the authenticity of the signature of his declaration is not certified. Individual notaries refuse to perform this act, referring to the passage of the period established for accepting the inheritance.

The notariat section of the RSFSR Supreme Court explained that when at the notarial office at the place of the opening of an estate a declaration is received from an heir accepting the inheritance within the six-month period from the day the estate is opened, irrespective of whether the authenticity of the heir's signature on this declaration is certified or not, he should be considered as having accepted the inheritance. However, to receive a certificate of the right to inheritance he is obliged to appear either personally at the notarial office at the place of opening the estate or to receive it through his representative, or to send another declaration. The signature of the heir on this declaration should be certified by the notarial agency or organization in which the heir works or studies or the house administration or administration of a medical institution in which he is situated for treatment, irrespective of the expiry of the six-month period from the day the estate is openend.

The refusal of a notary to certify the genuineness of a signature of an heir on the said declaration for reasons of the passage by the heir of the period established by law to accept an inheritance is not based on law (Article 59, Statute on the State Notariat of the RSFSR). The question of the possibility of issuing a certificate on the right to inheritance relating to this declaration shall be decided by the notary issuing the certificate.

STATE BANK vs. GRETSKAIA, Biulleten' Verkhovnogo Suda SSSR, 1973, no. 4, pp. 10–11.

On April 17, 1968, N. K. Gretskii obtained at the Shklovskii branch of the State Bank an interest-free loan for the construction of a house in the amount of 1000 rubles, to be paid off over 10 years commencing from April 1971 at the rate of 25 rubles quarterly. On November 7, 1969, Gretskii died. In October 1971 the Shklovskii branch of the State Bank brought suit in court against Gretskii's spouse, V. N. Gretskaia, to recover the indebtedness on the loan inasmuch as after the death of her husband she became the owner of the house built from the loan received.

The Shkolvskii District People's Court, Mogilev Region, rejected the State Bank's suit on November 11, 1971, justifying its decision by the fact that the plaintiff let pass the six month period established by the Belorussian Civil Code for the submission of claims to heirs of the deceased Gretskii for debts of the decedent.

[The Judicial Division for Civil Cases of the Mogilev Region and the Judicial Division for Civil Cases of the Belorussian Supreme Court and the Plenum of that Court affirmed this decision. The USSR Procurator General brought a protest to the Plenum of the USSR Supreme Court, which satisfied the protest on the following grounds]:

In violation of Article 16 of the Fundamental Principles of Civil Procedure of the USSR and Union Republics the people's court did not elucidate whether Gretskii had built the house and whether the house has passed by right of inheritance to the defendant. The elucidation of this question has important significance for the correct resolution of the dispute.

According to point 12 of the Instruction of the USSR State Bank on long term credits for the rural population for individual house construction, confirmed October 1, 1966, the issuance of loans shall be on condition that a land plot is allotted to the builder for the construction of the house. As is indicated in point 10 of the said Instruction, notification of the bank about a loan issued to a builder for the construction of a house appropriately registered by a notarial office shall have the force of a mortgage of the property.

In the event of the failure to perform the obligation to pay off the loan secured by a mortgage on the constructed house, the bank as holder of the mortgage may, in accordance with Article 169 of the Belorussian Civil Code, receive satisfaction from the value of the mortgaged property.

It follows from the provisions of Article 178 of the Belorussian Civil Code that the right of the mortgage does not terminate with the death of the mortgagee. Consequently, in the event of the transfer of a right of ownership in the mortgaged property to another person, which is possible also with an inheritance, the right of the mortgage retains force. Thus, the right of possession, use, and disposition of inherited property under mortgage is restricted for the heir. The right to receive satisfaction from the value of the mortgaged property provided by law belongs to the mortgagor in this event. Taking this into account, it should be acknowledged that Article 549 of the Belorussian Civil Code referred to by the judicial instances which considered the present case in its decisions in justification of rejecting the suit, does not apply to the present legal relations.

Moreover, the court did not take into consideration the fact that in view of the joint construction of the house with the deceased Gretskii with a loan obtained from the bank, the defendant according to Article 24 of the Code on Marriage and Family of the Belorussian SSR should be liable for the obligation of her spouse from property in their common joint ownership.

TUMANOVA vs. TUMANOVA, Biulleten' Verkhovnogo Suda RSFSR, 1969, no. 1, p. 5

Tumanov died on November 18, 1966. After his death property and a savings account remained. The daughter of the deceased V. Tumanova (of her first marriage) brought suit in court against G. Tumanova (wife of the deceased) for a division of the estate property. Inasmuch as her sister Antipova refused her share in the estate to her benefit, V. Tumanova requested that her right be recognized in part of the savings account and in .34 share of the house and that a room 15,8 square meters be allotted to her in kind, as well as part of the hall.

Antipova brought suit against G. Tumanova for a division of the estate property and against V. Tumanova to recognize as void the refusal of the inheritance.

After consideration of the case in various judicial instances, it was accepted by the Supreme Court of the Severo-Osetian ASSR. By a decision of July 24, 1968, the court exacted from G. Tumanova to the benefit of V. Tumanova and Antipova 552 rubles each as a form of compensation for the share in the house and also divided between them the bank account, each being allotted 149 rubles.

In a cassational appeal V. Tumanova requested the court decision be vacated, referring to the fact that the court without sufficient grounds recognized the refusal of the inheritance by Antipova as void, as well as rejected without justification her allocation in kind of .34 share of the house. Her family needed housing space.

G. Tumanova in her cassational appeal considered the conclusion of the court incorrect that her portion of the estate comprised one-half of the house. The court did not take into account that the greater part of the funds for the purchase of the house had belonged to her before the marriage. In the opinion of G. Tumanova, the share of the heirs should comprise .09 of the house, the value of which she agreed to pay them.

Having verified the materials of the case, the Judicial Division for Civil Cases of the RSFSR Supreme Court left the decision of the Supreme Court of the Severo-Osetian ASSR, and the appeals of V. Tumanova and G. Tumanova without satisfaction.

In its ruling of September 12, 1968, the Division pointed out the following:

According to Article 550 of the RSFSR Civil Code, an heir by operation of law or by will has the right to refuse an inheritance within six months from the date of opening the estate. He may indicate that the inheritance is refused to the benefit of other persons from among the heirs by operation of law (Article 532) or by will (Article 534), to the benefit of the state, or to an individual state, cooperative, or social organization.

From the materials of the file of the case it is clear that extremely hostile relations were formed between the sisters in connection with the division of the estate property. V. Tumanova, wishing to receive a large share of the estate property, demanded that Antipova refuse her share of the estate, threatening to divulge her family secret.

Antipova, under the influence of the threat, filed a declaration at the notarial office refusing the estate.

Inasmuch as the refusal of inheritance took place under the influence of a threat, the court correctly deemed it void.

G. Tumanova's assertion that .45 share of the house should belong to her does not follow from the materials of the case. The house was acquired by G. Tumanova and the deceased Tumanov in 1956 in the period of their life together. The fact that the purchase of the house was defrayed by funds from the sale of a house on Gabidov Street could not serve as evidence that any part of it belonged to G. Tumanova alone since the house on Gabidov Street was acquired in 1941, *i.e.*, also in the period of the spouses' marriage.

Inasmuch as the court recognized for V. Tumanova the right to a 1/6 share of the property and allotted her a corresponding share of the house in kind, the court did not find it possible to award her monetary compensation in accordance with Article 121 of the Civil Code.

F. Inheritance of copyright

CIVIL CODE, R.S.F.S.R. (1964)
Article 496. *Period of Validity of Copyright*

A copyright shall be valid throughout the entire life of the author and for twenty-five years after his death, commencing from January 1st of the year following the year of the author's death.

A copyright shall pass by inheritance. The copyright in a name and the right to the integrity of a work shall not pass by inheritance.

After an author's death, the protection of his name and the integrity of a work shall be effectuated in accordance with the provisions of Articles 480 and 481 of the present Code.

U.S.S.R. DECREE "ON RATES OF STATE DUTY" (1942), *SP SSSR,* 1973, no. 4, item 15.

On February 8, 1973, the USSR Council of Ministers decreed to amend Section I, point 3(r) of the decree of the USSR Council of People's Commissars of August 29, 1942, No. 598 "On Rates of State Duty" by adding a paragraph as follows: "The monetary appraisal of a copyright and the amounts of author's royalties which pass to the heirs of an author shall not be included when computing the state duty in the total appraisal of the estate property."

CHAPTER XX

Private Contracts

The eminent French civil lawyer, Planiol, once wrote: "It is constantly repeated that obligations form an immutable part of the law; it seems that their principal rules are universal and eternal truths like those of geometry and arithmetic. This is but an illusion. While it may be that this area is less subject than others to the vicissitudes of political revolutions, it does not escape them altogether, even though the transformations are slower."[1]

The 1922 RSFSR Civil Code drew heavily upon continental patterns of the law of contract, adapting these to the exigencies of the New Economic Policy and to the principles of revolutionary Marxist theory. Germanic influence was particularly marked, for many of the early Soviet civilists trained before the Revolution had been steeped in the writings of German jurists and the German civil code, then the most modern of the European models. Also influential on Soviet thinking was a draft Russian civil code prepared in the twilight days of the Empire. A prominent architect of the 1922 RSFSR Civil Code, A. G. Goikhbarg, had played an important part in preparing the Imperial draft.

The principles governing the Soviet law of obligations, including especially contract, have increasingly been adapted to national economic planning and to the special functions contract has in relations among socialist organizations, giving rise to the conviction among many Soviet jurists that a code of economic law should be created especially for obligations of this type. The role of private contracts has correspondingly diminished between citizens, the principal area of application now being agreements between individuals and socialist organizations, *e.g.*, for the purchase of goods, the rental or sale of housing, and the like.

[1]Planiol, Traite du Droit Civil, Vol. II, 8th Ed., p. 56.

With the advent of a communist society in which goods are plentiful for all, some Marxist jurists have speculated that private agreements will no longer require means of enforcement.[2] In the interim some jurists have predicted that the role of private contracts will grow as the supplies of consumer goods expand. But even this growth is dwarfed by the greater reliance under the post-1965 economic reforms upon economic contracts to regulate relations among socialist organizations.

The materials in this chapter illustrate some of the ways in which Marxian socialism has altered traditional principles of contract. We already have noted the dwindling number of contracts, in relative terms, concerned with private matters. Common lawyers will note that in deciding whether a contract exists between parties, the emphasis is upon agreement, and not promise. Nor is consideration a requirement; rather, the purpose of the agreement must be indicated. Soviet contract law also gives priority to specific performance and accordingly is not partial to the concept of liquidated damages. On the other hand, there is a great insistence upon the observance of the forms of contract law. Written agreements or notarized written agreements are mandatory in many instances, depending on the value of the contract or its purpose. Some of these principles have counterparts in modern European codes; others find their raison d'être in the mores or practices of a socialist society.

A. Concept and purpose of contracts under socialism

O. S. Ioffe, OBIAZATEL'STVENNOE PRAVO [The Law of Obligations] (Moscow, 1975), pp. 10–11.

The basic purpose of obligations in a capitalist society is determined by the fact that they are a legal means of realizing the surplus value produced by workers and appropriated by capitalists, as well as a legal mode for extracting elements from circulation which are necessary for the repetition of production cycles, each of which serves as a source of new profits. The bourgeois law of obligations is subordinated to the purposes of capitalist exploitation to the same extent as the law of ownership and as all institutes and branches of bourgeois legislation in general. Therefore, bourgeois jurisprudence always aspires in its theoretical constructions to present the obligations of capitalist society in an impersonal class form, as though this did not contravene reality. At various stages in the development of capitalism, the said aspirations are manifested in various forms. . . .

In the system of norms of modern bourgeois legislation, the norms of the law of obligations are one of the strongest means for consolidating the positions of capitalist monopolies. As even some official politicians of capitalist countries recognize, the basic purpose of contract in bourgeois society is to serve as a means of surbordinating the market, seizing spheres of influence, and displacing competitive producers.

[2]R.O. Khalfina, Znachenie i Sushchnost Dogovora v Sovetskom Sotsialisticheskom Prave [The Significance and Substance of Contracts in Soviet Socialist Civil Law], (Moscow, 1954) 47.

The very structure of contractual ties applied in capitalist countries is used for this purpose . . . These and other analogous phenomena oblige modern bourgeois civilistics to reject the treatment of the contract as a freely individual act based on the autonomy of parties. Some say that the individualist understanding of a contract harmonious with the economic conditions of the early nineteenth century is contrary to the new organization of society, and this, in their view, constitutes one aspect of the socialization of the civil law . . . Others, without excluding the use within certain limits of the ordinary type of contracts, note that now, when the high level of production attained can not be satisfied by the activity of individual persons but requires the efforts of many people and even of all of society, state contracts are beginning to occupy the key positions . . . Others either reject completely the volitional nature of contract or restrict it within such limits that there is essentially no place left for free will . . . It is evident however that neither the frank acknowledgements to which bourgeois civilists sometimes resort nor their aspiration to misconstrue the essence of capitalist obligations in any way changes the class orientation of the norms of the bourgeois law of obligations, which are in the service of monopoly capital and used for the purpose of securing and protecting their predatory interests.

A. Iu. Kabalkin, "General Provisions on Contracts," in V. A. Riasentsev (ed.), SOVETSKOE GRAZHDANSKOE PRAVO [SOVIET CIVIL LAW] (2d ed., MOSCOW, 1975), p. 441

The property and contractual relations in the sphere of services, having the object of satisfying the constantly growing economic and cultural demands of Soviet citizens by organizations, are several (for example, retail sale contracts, lease of housing, rentals, orders). Author's contracts of citizens with cultural-enlightenment and entertainment organizations (publishing, staging, and others) are widely used. The fulfillment by organizations of obligations assumed under such contracts is of primary significance for ensuring not only the financial but also the personal non-financial rights of citizens.

The contract form is used by citizens when disposing of things belonging to them by right of personal ownership. Inasmuch as the populace basically satisfies its material and spiritual requirements by concluding contracts with specialized organizations, the total number of contracts between citizens is comparatively modest.

"ON THE DRAFT USSR LAW 'ON THE OFFICE OF STATE NOTARY.' SPEECH OF THE U.S.S.R. MINISTER OF JUSTICE, DEPUTY V. M. TEREBILOV", Izvestia, July 20, 1973, p. 5, col. 1.

What kind of questions does the Office of State Notary decide? For example, the notaries annually certify about 300,000 contracts concerning purchase-sale and gifts of dwelling houses, without which the contract would be void; they issue more than 300,000 certificates on the right of inheritance, without which one can not receive an inheritance.

B. Basic Formalities Relating to Conclusion of Contracts

CIVIL CODE, RSFSR (1964)
Article 41. *Concept and Types of Legal Transactions*

Actions of citizens and organizations aimed at the establishment, modification, or termination of civil rights or duties shall be deemed legal transactions.

Legal transactions may be unilateral and bilateral or multilateral (contracts).

Article 42. *Form of Legal Transactions*

Legal transactions shall be performed orally or in writing (ordinary and notarized).

A legal transaction for which a definite form has not been established by law shall be considered performed also if from the conduct of a person his will to perform the legal transaction is manifest.

Silence shall be deemed an expression of the will to perform a legal transaction in instances provided by legislation of the USSR or RSFSR.

Article 43. *Oral Legal Transactions*

Legal transactions executed at the time of their performance may be agreed orally unless USSR or RSFSR legislation has established otherwise.

Article 44. *Legal Transactions in Writing*

The following must be performed in writing:

(1) legal transactions of state, cooperative, and social organizations between themselves and with citizens, except for legal transactions specified in Article 43 of the present Code and individual types of legal transactions for which legislation of the USSR or RSFSR provides otherwise;

(2) legal transactions of citizens between themselves for an amount exceeding 100 rubles, except for legal transactions specified in Article 43 of the present Code and other legal transactions specified in USSR or RSFSR legislation;

(3) other legal transactions of citizens between themselves with respect to which the law requires observance of the written form.

Legal transactions in writing should be signed by the persons who have performed them.

If a citizen as a result of physical inability, illness, or any other reasons can not personally sign, then upon his commission another citizen may sign. The legal organization in which the citizen performing the legal transaction works or studies or the house administration in which he lives, or the administration of the in-patient medical institution in which he is receiving care, or a notarial agency, must certify such other signature, indicating the reasons by virtue of which the person performing the legal transaction could not personally sign it.

Article 45. *Consequences of the Failure to Observe the Form of Legal Transactions*

The failure to observe the form required by law shall entail the invalidity of the legal transaction only in the event such a consequence is expressly specified in law.

The failure to observe the form of foreign trade transactions and the procedure for their signature (Article 565) shall entail the invalidity of the legal transaction.

Article 47. *Requirement of the Notarial Form and Consequences of the Failure to Observe it*

Notarial certification of a legal transaction is obligatory only in instances specified in law. The failure to observe the notarial form in these instances shall entail the invalidity of the legal transaction with the consequences provided for by Article 48, paragraph 2, of the present Code.

If one of the parties has fully or partially executed the legal transaction requiring notarial certification, and the other party avoids notarial formalization of the legal transaction, the court shall have the right at the demand of the party which has executed the legal transaction to recognize the legal transaction as valid on condition that the legal transaction does not contain anything contrary to law. In such event, the subsequent notarial formalization of the legal transaction shall not be required.

Article 158. *Concept of an Obligation and the Bases of its Origin.*

By virtue of an obligation, one person (the obligor) shall be obliged to perform for the benefit of another person (the obligee) a certain action such as to transfer property, fulfill work, pay money, and so forth, or to refrain from a certain action, and the obligee shall have the right to demand the execution of the duty from the obligor.

Obligations shall arise from a contract or other bases specified in Article 4 of the present Code.

Article 160. *Conclusion of a Contract.*

A contract shall be considered concluded when an agreement regarding all its essential points is achieved in the appropriate form required.

Those points of the contract are essential which are so deemed by law or are necessary for contracts of the particular type, as well as all those points relative to which agreement must be achieved at the request of one of the parties.

A contract may be concluded by means of accepting an order for execution and between socialist organizations in the instances provided by law by accepting for execution an order or procurement permit.

KUZNETSOVA vs. THE KOPYLOVS, Biulleten' Verkhovnogo Suda RSFSR, 1968, no. 6, p. 9

Kuznetsova brought suit in court to recover 150 rubles from Kopylova and Kopylov. In justification of the suit she pointed out that in April 1967 she transferred 200 rubles to the defendants by a loan contract with the obligation to repay the amount of the debt within a month. However, the defendants repaid only 50 rubles and are avoiding repayment of the balance.

The defendants opposed the suit, referring to the fact that they borrowed not 200, but 180 rubles, from Kuznetsova and repaid this amount in full.

[The Judicial Division of the Tula Regional Court satisfied the suit; in a cassational appeal the Kopylovs reaffirmed their position, but the lower court decision was upheld by the Judicial Division for Civil Cases of the RSFSR Supreme Court on the following grounds]:

According to Article 269 of the RSFSR Civil Code, a loan contract for an amount exceeding 50 rubles must be in writing.

In conformity with Article 271 of the Civil Code, a borrower shall have the right to contest a loan contract on the ground of "money not received," proving that money or articles in reality were not received by him from the lender or were received in lesser quantity than specified in the contract.

In those instances when the loan contract should be in writing (Article 269) it shall not be permitted to contest it on the ground of "money not received" by witness testimony except for instances of criminally punishable acts.

Kuznetsova submitted two receipts in confirmation of the fact that the defendants received 200 rubles from her in the form of a loan.

The Kopylovs submitted no documents regarding the receipt of a lesser amount of money than specified in the receipts.

The fact of the repayment to the plaintiff of the entire amount of money is confirmed by nothing in the file of the case, as the defendants assert.

In such circumstances the decision of the court should be deemed correct.

"NOTARIAL PRACTICE," Sovetskia iustitsiia, 1970, no. 14, p. cover

Citizens G. and Ch. requested the Gvardeiskii State Notarial Office to certify a contract for the lease of housing. According to the contract, citizen G. leases housing space 49.2 square meters in size for three years in a house belonging to him by right of personal ownership.

The question arose for the state notary as to which normative act should guide him in certifying such a contract and how to determine the amount necessary for computing the state duty.

The notariat section of the RSFSR Supreme Court explained that in certifying a contract for the lease of housing belonging by right of personal ownership, a notarial office is obliged to be guided by the decree of the RSFSR Council of Ministers of August 9, 1963, No. 983, "On the Maximum Rates of Payment for Housing and Dacha Premises Leased in Houses and Dachas Belonging to Citizens by Right of Personal Ownership" (SP RSFSR, 1963, no. 15, item 102).

When determining the amount for computing the state duty, one should have in view that the payment for use of living premises leased to individuals in houses belonging to citizens by right of personal ownership shall be determined by agreement of the parties, but may not exceed the maximum rate: 16 kopecks for 1 square meter of living space per month. Proceeding therefrom, the amount of payment under the contract being taken as an example will constitute 283 rubles, 40 kopecks. For certifying this contract a state duty in the amount of 11 rubles should be levied (e.g., 3% of 283 rubles, 40 kopecks or 8 rubles, 50 kopecks for certification of the contract and 2 rubles, 50 kopecks for technical services).

BEZRODNYI vs. NORTH KURILES FISHERY KOMBINAT, Biulleten' Verkhovnogo Suda RSFSR, 1970, no. 3, p. 9.

Bezrodnyi brought suit in court against the North Kuriles Fishery Kombinat to recover 1032 rubles for house no. 35 on Osvobozhdenie Street in the city of Severo-Kuril'sk belonging to him by right of personal ownership which was transferred to the fishery kombinat, inasmuch as the fishery kombinat had not fulfilled its obligation to pay the money.

[Bezrodnyi's suit was satisfied by the district people's court and affirmed by the Judicial Division for Civil Cases of the Sakhalin Regional Court. The Presidium of the latter court, considering the case upon the protest of the deputy chairman of the RSFSR Supreme Court, returned the case for new consideration on the following grounds]:

The people's court, in satisfying the suit, and the judicial division, in leaving the decision of the people's court without change, proceeded from the fact that a purchase-sale contract for the house was concluded.

However, this conclusion is not based on the materials of the file of the case.

In accordance with Article 239 of the RSFSR Civil Code, a purchase-sale contract for a dwelling house should be notarially certified, the failure to observe the rules of this article entailing the invalidity of the contract. A notarially certified purchase-sale contract for the house is lacking in the file of the case.

At the same time it is clear from the materials of the case that although the fishery combinat had the intention to buy the house, a purchase-sale contract for the house did not exist since the superior organization had not given authorization for the fishery combinat to conclude such a legal transaction, and on July 10, 1965, a lease contract was concluded between the parties. This fact also is confirmed by a letter of the fishery combinat to Bezrodnyi of April 10, 1968, that the rental payment in the amount of 136 rubles, 22 kopecks, is being transmitted to him for use of the house.

In the new consideration of the case it is necessary for the court to take into account the foregoing and to decide the dispute in accordance with the facts of the case and the requirements of the law.

C. *Invalidity, illegality, and their consequences*

CIVIL CODE, RSFSR (1964)

Article 46. *Consequences of the Failure to Observe the Simple Written Form*

The failure to observe the simple written form required by law (Article 44) shall deprive the parties of the right in the event of a dispute to refer in confirmation of the legal transaction to witness testimony, and in instances expressly indicated in law, shall entail the invalidity of the legal transaction with the consequences provided by Article 48, paragraph 2, of the present Code.

Article 48. *Invalidity of Legal Transactions Not Conforming to the Requirements of Law*

A legal transaction not conforming to the requirements of law shall be void.

In an invalid legal transaction each party shall be obliged to restore to the other party everything received in respect of the legal transaction, and if it is impossible to restore that which was received in kind, to reimburse its value in money unless other consequences of invalidity of the legal transaction are provided for in law.

Article 49. *Invalidity of a Legal Transaction Performed for Purpose Contrary to the Interests of the State and Society*

If a legal transaction is performed for a purpose knowingly contrary to the interests of the socialist state and society, if both parties have such an intent—in the event the legal transaction is executed by both parties—everything received by them in respect of the transaction shall be recovered for the income of the state, and in the event the legal transaction is executed by one party, from the other party shall be recovered for the income of the state everything received by it and everything due from it for the first party in compensation of that received; if only one party has such intent, everything received by it in respect of the legal transaction should be returned to the other party, and that received by the latter or due it in compensation for that executed shall be recovered for the income of the state.

Article 50. *Invalidity of a Legal Transaction of a Juridical Person Contrary to its Purposes*

A legal transaction performed by a juridical person in contravention of the purposes specified in its charter, in statutes concerning it, or in the general statute concerning organizations of the said type, shall be void.

The rules provided for by Articles 48 and 49 of the present Code shall apply respectively to such legal transactions.

Article 51. *Invalidity of a Legal Transaction Performed by Minors Who Have Not Attained Fifteen Years.*

A legal transaction performed by a minor who has not attained fifteen years of age shall be void, except for legal transactions provided for by Article 14, paragraphs two and three, of the present Code.

Each party shall be obliged with respect to this transaction to restore to the other party everything received in respect of the legal transaction, and if it is impossible to restore that received in kind, to reimburse its value in money.

The party having legal capacity shall be obliged, in addition, to reimburse to the other party all expenses, loss, or damage of its property incurred if the party having legal capacity knew or should have known about the other party's lack of legal capacity.

Article 52. *Invalidity of a Legal Transaction Performed by a Citizen Deemed to Lack Legal Capacity*

A legal transaction performed by a citizen deemed to lack legal capacity as a consequence of mental illness or feeble-mindedness shall be void. The rules provided for by Article 51 of the present Code shall apply to such legal transactions.

Article 53. *Invalidity of a Sham or Feigned Legal Transaction*

A legal transaction performed only for form, with no intention to create legal consequences, shall be void.

If a legal transaction was performed for the purpose of concealing another legal transaction, the rules relative to that legal transaction which the parties actually had in mind shall be applied.

Article 54. *Invalidity of a Legal Transaction Performed by Minors from Fifteen to Eighteen Years of Age*

A legal transaction performed by a minor from fifteen to eighteen years of age without the consent of his parents, adoptive parents, or guardians, shall be deemed void by a court upon the suit of the parents, adoptive parents, or guardians.

If such a legal transaction is deemed void the rules provided by Article 51 of the present Code shall be applied.

The rules of the present Article shall not extend to a legal transaction of minors from fifteen to eighteen years of age which was concluded in accordance with Article 13, paragraphs two and four, of the present Code.

Article 55. *Invalidity of a Legal Transaction Performed by a Citizen Who Abuses Alcoholic Beverages or Narcotics*

A legal transaction relating to the disposition of property performed without the consent of the guardian of a citizen whose legal capacity is restricted as a consequence of the abuse of alcoholic beverages or narcotics shall be deemed void by a court upon the suit of the guardian.

If such a legal transaction is deemed void, the rules provided for by Article 51 of the present Code shall apply.

The rules of the present Article shall not extend to legal transactions concluded in accordance with Article 16, paragraph two, of the present Code.

Article 56. *Invalidity of a Legal Transaction Performed by a Citizen Incapable of Understanding the Significance of his Actions*

A legal transaction performed by a citizen, although having legal capacity but at the moment of its performance in such a state that he could not understand the significance of his actions or direct them, shall be deemed void by a court upon the suit of this citizen.

If such a legal transaction is deemed void, each party shall be obliged to restore to the other party everything received in respect of the legal transaction, and if it is impossible to restore that received in kind, to reimburse its value in money.

To the party which at the moment of performing the legal transaction could not understand the significance of his actions or guide them, the other party in addition should reimburse the expenses, loss, or harm of its property if it knew or should have known about this state of the citizen who concluded the legal transaction with it.

Article 57. *Invalidity of a Legal Transaction Performed Under the Influence of Mistake*

A legal transaction performed under the influence of a mistake which is of material significance shall be deemed void upon the suit of the party which acted under the influence of the mistake.

If such a legal transaction is deemed void, each party shall be obliged to restore to the other party everything received in respect of the legal transaction, and if it is impossible to restore that received in kind, to reimburse its value in money.

The party upon whose suit the legal transaction is deemed void shall have the right to demand of the other party the reimbursement of expenses, loss, or damage of its property if it is proved that the mistake arose at the fault of the other party. If this is not proved, the party upon whose suit the legal transaction is deemed void shall be obliged to reimburse to the other party the expenses, loss, or damage of its property.

Article 58. *Invalidity of a Legal Transaction Performed Under the Influence of Fraud, Duress, Threats, Ill-Intentioned Agreement of the Representatives of One Party with the Other Party, or the Coincidence of Grave Circumstances*

A legal transaction performed under the influence of fraud, duress, threats, ill-intentioned agreement of a representative of one party with the other party, as well as a legal transaction which a citizen was obliged to perform as a consequence of the coincidence of grave circumstances on conditions extremely disadvantageous for him, shall be deemed void upon the suit of the victim or upon the suit of a state, cooperative, or social organization.

If a legal transaction is deemed void upon one of the said grounds, then to the victim shall be returned by the other party everything received by it in respect of the legal transaction, and if it is impossible to return that received in kind, to reimburse its value in money. The property received in respect of the legal transaction by the victim from the other party, as well as that due it in compensation for that transferred to the other party, shall be converted to the income of the state. If it is impossible to transfer the property to the income of the state in kind, its value shall be exacted in money.

In addition, the victim shall be compensated by the other party for expenses, loss, or damage of its property incurred.

PROCURATORIAL SUIT TO VOID GIFT CONTRACT, Sotsialisticheskaia zakonnost', 1970, no. 11, pp. 89–90

A house on Revolution Street in the city of Kalinin belonged by right of personal ownership to L. Nekrasova. In 1964 she applied for membership in a housing construction cooperative, which was rejected in view of the fact that she was provided with housing premises. In 1965 she again sought membership in the housing construction cooperative and proposed at the same time to transfer her house free of charge to the executive committee of the local Soviet. By decision of the Kalinin

City Executive Committee of November 25, 1965, it was decreed by way of exception to admit L. Nekrasova to membership in the housing contruction cooperative, and on October 15, 1968, Nekrasova was permitted by the executive committee of the City Soviet to sell the house for demolition in view of its dilapidated condition and because the general plan presupposes the reconstruction of Revolution Street. On June 11, 1969, Nekrasova gave the house belonging to her to her sister, K. Nekrasova. In November 1969 the procurator of the Proletarskii District of the city of Kalinin brought suit in court to recognize the gift contract as void, referring to the fact that K. Nekrasova, having received the house as a gift, is attempting to sell it not for demolition. Having considered the case, the Proletarskii District People's Court in the city of Kalinin satisfied the suit of the procurator and dissolved the contract of gift. The court referred to the fact that the defendant made a gift of the house, whereas she was authorized to sell the house for demolition taking into account the fact it was dilapidated. The decision of the court was left without change by a ruling of the Judicial Division for Civil Cases of the Kalinin Regional Court.

Having considered the protest of the Deputy USSR Procurator General which raised the question of vacating the said judicial decrees, the presidium of the Kalinan Regional Court has satisfied it on the following grounds.

By virtue of Article 92 of the RSFSR Civil Code there belongs to an owner the right of possession, use, and disposition of property within the limits established by law. A limitation of a gift of property on the grounds of its dilapidation is not provided for by law. In accordance with Article 108 of the RSFSR Civil Code, if a citizen has, on the grounds permitted by law, a dwelling house (or part of a house) by right of personal ownership and at the same time an apartment in a housing construction cooperative house then the owner of the house (or part of the house) shall have the right at his selection to retain the house (or part of the house) for himself or the apartment in the housing construction cooperative house. In the latter case, the owner should alienate his house within one year from the day on which the right of ownership in the house arose or of moving in to the apartment of the housing construction cooperative. In this event the other house should be sold by the owner, given, or alienated by other means (Article 107, RSFSR Civil Code). Thus, the gift contract concluded by the defendant is legal, and the court had no grounds to dissolve it.

Taking into account that the facts of the case established by the court of first instance are complete and correct but that an error was made in applying the norms of substantive law, the presidium of the regional court has vacated the decision of the Proletarskii District People's Court in the city of Kalinin and the ruling of the Judicial Division for Civil Case of the Kalinin Regional Court and rejected the suit of the procurator for dissolution of the gift contract for the house.

KHOKHLOV AND MERKULOV vs. IANKIN, Biulleten' Verkhovnogo Suda RSFSR, 1970, no. 10, pp. 1–2

In 1967 the Construction-Assembly Administration (SMU) of the Orlov Regional

Consumers Union had to build a vegetable store for the Khotynets Drying Plant. On June 2, 1967, the SMU and Iankin concluded a contract whereby Iankin had to fulfill part of the work in constructing the vegetable store before July 20, 1967, and the SMU was obliged to pay him 4500 rubles.

To take part in the fulfillment of the construction work provided for by the contract, Iankin at his discretion enlisted certain citizens, including Khokhlov and Merkulov.

Khokhlov brought suit to recover 1121 rubles from Iankin, and Merkulov, 30 rubles, referring to the fact that the defendant had not settled accounts with them for work in the construction of the vegetable store.

Iankin opposed satisfaction of Khokhlov's suit, asserting that he had paid him in full according to their oral arrangement. The defendant acknowledged Merkulov's suit in the amount of 20 rubles.

The SMU of the Orlov Regional Consumers Union was joined as a co-defendant in the case, the chairman of which believed their enterprises had no obligations to Khokhlov and Merkulov.

The Orlov Regional Court, having accepted the case for hearing as a court of first instance, established that the head of the SMU of the Orlov Consumers Union had, when concluding the contract with Iankin, illegally fixed the amount of payment for the fulfillment of work in building the vegetable store too high, and Iankin was overpaid 1124 rubles in this connection. The court deemed the contract of June 2, 1967, to be void in the part fixing the amount of payment too high in the amount of 1124 rubles, as being contrary in this respect to the interests of the socialist state and society, and on the basis of Article 49 of the RSFSR Civil Code recovered for the income of the state from Iankin and from the SMU of the Orlov Regional Consumers Union 1124 rubles each. In addition from Iankin was recovered 35 rubles, 80 kopecks for the benefit of Khokhlov and 30 rubles for the benefit of Merkulov.

The Judicial Division for Civil Cases of the RSFSR Supreme Court left the decision of the court without change by a ruling of April 18, 1968.

The Deputy USSR Procurator General brought a protest to the Presidium of the USSR Supreme Court to vacate the decision of the regional court and the ruling of the Judicial Division of the RSFSR Supreme Court as to the part recovering for the state from the SMU of the Orlov Regional Consumers Union 1124 rubles and to reduce the recovery for the state from Iankin to 900 rubles.

The protest was based on the fact that, by virtue of Article 49 of the RSFSR Civil Code, everything received by the parties in respect of the legal transaction is to be recovered for the state. In the present instance 1124 rubles were received by Iankin in regard to an illegal transaction. The SMU did not receive this amount and, therefore, there are no grounds to recover this from them. When determining the amount of the sum subject to recovery from Iankin, one should take into account that income tax was withheld from the 3150 rubles.

By a decree of April 1, 1970, the Presidium of the RSFSR Supreme Court satisfied the protest in part on the following grounds.

According to Article 49 of the RSFSR Civil Code, if a legal transaction is performed for a purpose knowingly contrary to the interest of the socialist state and society, if both parties have such an intent—in the event the legal transaction has been executed by both parties—everything received by them in respect of the transaction shall be recovered for the state, and in the event the legal transaction has been executed by one party, there shall be recovered for the state from the other party everything received by it and everything due to it from the first party, in compensation for its performance.

It was established by the regional court that for the entire amount of work provided for by the contract between the SMU and Iankin, wages could be computed in an amount of 2026 rubles. Therefore, the court correctly deemed the legal transaction void on the basis of Article 49 of the RSFSR Civil Code as to the part exceeding the amount of compensation provided by the contract above the amount of wages according to the estimate.

However, not only is the over-payment to Iankin of 1124 rubles illegal under Article 49 of the RSFSR Civil Code, but also the agreement relating to the entire amount for which compensation under the contract exceeds the amount of wages according to the estimate, e.g., 2475 rubles (4500-2026).

The monies received by Iankin as compensation under the contract should be recovered from him for the state.

It was correctly pointed out in the protest that the court mistakenly recovered from the SMU the same sum as from Iankin for the state. In this respect the decision by the court is not supported by anything.

At the same time there are no grounds to exempt the SMU from the responsibility provided for by Article 49 of the RSFSR Criminal Code. The SMU was a party to a contract under which it had not paid over fully that due from it to the other party. In this event it is necessary to recover from the SMU for the state that which was due from it to Iankin but was not paid, that is, 1350 rubles (4500-3150). Thus, the decision of the court in this respect should be changed.

The question was correctly raised in the protest about reducing the amount recovered from Iankin by 141 rubles, 12 kopecks, withheld from him as tax.

On the basis of the foregoing, the Presidium of the RSFSR Supreme Court changed the decision of the Orlov Regional Court and the ruling of the Judicial Division for Civil Cases of the RSFSR Supreme Court, increasing the amount recovered for the income of the state to 1350 rubles from the SMU of the Orlov Regional Consumers Union and reduced the amount recovered for the income of the state from Iankin to 982 rubles, 88 kopecks, and left the remaining part without change.

TILIB vs. VIKUL, Biulleten' Verkhovnogo Suda SSSR, 1970, no. 3, pp. 32–34.

On January 17, 1968, E. T. Tilib notarially formalized a contract for the sale to M. E. Vikul of one-half of a dwelling house belonging to her by right of personal ownership and situated in the city of Iurmal. The contract was registered in the municipal housing section of the Iurmal city executive committee.

In February 1969 Tilib brought suit in court to declare the purchase-sale contract void, referring to the fact that this legal transaction was of a fictitious character; in fact she did not sell part of the house and did not receive the money from Vikul.

The Iurmal People's Court rejected the suit on April 14, 1969. The Judicial Division for Civil Cases of the Latvian Supreme Court vacated the decision of the people's court on July 9, 1969, for the failure to investigate the facts of the case, and the Supreme Court of the republic accepted the case for consideration at first instance.

Having considered the file of the case, the Judicial Division for Civil Cases of the Latvian Supreme Court on September 29, 1969, rendered a decision declaring void the purchase-sale contract. The decision reasoned that a fictitious contract was concluded between the parties with no intention to give rise to legal consequences; the legal transaction was performed for the purpose of creating the appearance that the house belonged to two co-owners, and this was necessary so that the former spouse of the plaintiff could not claim further residence in her home. Subsequently, a suit was brought by the plaintiff and defendant to evict the former husband of the plaintiff from the house belonging to her.

The Deputy USSR Procurator General brought a protest against the decision of the Judicial Division and the ruling previously rendered and requested that the decision of the Iurmal People's Court on April 14, 1969, refusing to satisfy the suit of E. T. Tilib be left in force.

It is pointed out in the protest that the conclusion of the Judicial Division concerning the fictitiousness of the purchase-sale contract does not correspond to the materials of the case. The contract was signed by the parties and notarially certified; the defendant entered into possession of half of the house acquired by her. The reference to witness testimony in confirmation of the fictitiousness of the purchase-sale contract is unfounded. Contesting a contract by witness testimony is not based on the requirements of law inasmuch as by virtue of Article 17 of the Fundamental Principles of Civil Procedure of the USSR and Union Republics and Article 53 of the Latvian Code of Civil Procedure, the facts of the case which by law should be confirmed by specific means of evidence may not be confirmed by any other means of evidence.

In discussing the arguments set forth in the protest, the Judicial Division found no grounds for satisfying it.

The signature by the parties of a purchase-sale contract for a dwelling house, notarial certification of the contract, and the entry of the buyer into possession of the property acquired can not prevent annulment of the contract if the court comes to the conclusion that the facts which entail deeming the legal transaction void at law are conclusive.

As noted above, having investigated the materials of the case and properly assessed the evidence in its totality gathered in the file of the case, the Judicial Division for Civil Cases of the Latvian Supreme Court established that in entering into the said legal transaction, the parties in fact had not pursued the purpose of selling a part of the house and the contract formalized by them was fictitious. This conclusion does not contravene the materials of the case nor the requirements of law.

It is clear from the case that after the parties concluded the purchase-sale contract, the entire house, as previously, remained in the possession and use of the plaintiff. She, as formerly, continued to pay the taxes and insurance premiums due from her for the entire house, and not for part of it, and continued to repair as well that part of the house which supposedly was sold to the defendant. Those tenants living in the disputed part of the house paid the plaintiff the apartment rent for 1968, and not the defendant. The witnesses questioned in the judicial proceeding, Polonskia, Ozolniek, Vodnietse, and others explained that after formalization of the contract the husband of the defendant, Ia. Vypulis, repeatedly declared that only the plaintiff was the owner of the house. There also is no convincing evidence in the file of the case which would testify that the defedant had transferred money to the plaintiff under the contract.

The fact that the defendant and her husband, who lived in the city of Riga, in December 1968, that is, almost a year after the purchase-sale contract was formalized, brought to the plaintiff's house, in her absence and against her wish, a number of things can not be deemed, taking into account the above, as the actual entry of the defendant into possession of the disputed part of the house.

The considerations set forth in the protest concerning the inadmissibility of witness testimony confirming the fictitiousness of the purchase-sale contract for the dwelling house also are unconvincing.

According to Article 248 of the Latvian Civil Code, the purchase-sale contract for a dwelling house should be notarially certified, even though one of the parties is a citizen, and registered at the executive committee of the local Soviet of Working People's Deputies. The failure to observe this rule entails the invalidity of a purchase-sale contract for a dwelling house.

It follows from this that a notarially certified contract registered at the executive committee of the local Soviet should be submitted in confirmation of the fact of the conclusion in proper form of a purchase-sale contract for a dwelling house.

At the same time, the law contains no prohibition against confirming with witness testimony, just as with other forms of evidence provided for by Article 17 of the Fundamental Principles of Civil Procedure, the fictitiousness of a contract (in particular when the legal transaction is performed only for appearances, with no intention to create legal consequences) if the interested person brings suit in court to recognize the contract as void on this ground. This also appertains completely to the possibility of confirming on the basis of witness testimony the facts affecting execution of a contract. The principle contained in Article 17 of the Fundamental Principles of Civil Procedure of the USSR and Union Republics that individual facts may be established by a court with the aid of strictly defined forms of evidence extends only to instances expressly provided for by law (Articles 46, 287, of the Latvian Civil Code).

BOLSHAKOVA vs. MIKHEEV, Biulleten' Verkhovnogo Suda RSFSR, 1971, no. 1, p. 2.

Bolshakova brought suit in court against Mikheev to recognize as void a contract for the exchange of living space by which she moved from a room 28.17 meters square in Moscow to a two-room apartment of the defendant, 31.6 meters square in the city of Kuibyshev. She based her claim on the fact that the exchange contract was concluded by her under the influence of a material mistake. The apartment of the defendant was not on the second floor, as he indicated in his exchange statement, but on the third, was damp, and was dirty. By reason of age and state of health she could not use this apartment on the third floor of the house without a lift.

The Moscow City Court rejected Bolshakova's suit.

Having considered the file of the case by way of cassation upon the appeal of Bolshakova, the Judicial Division for Civil Cases of the RSFSR Supreme Court by a ruling of February 12, 1970, left the decision of the city court without change and the appeal without satisfaction, indicating the following.

It seems from the materials of the case that the housing space was exchanged by the parties voluntarily in accordance with the Instruction "On the Procedure for the Exchange of Housing Premises" No. 12, confirmed by the Minister of Municipal Housing of the RSFSR on January 9, 1967.

According to point 11 of the said Instruction, the exchange of housing premises is considered to be performed from the moment the exchanging parties receive exchange orders. On March 4, 1969, the parties received exchange orders and the exchange contract was executed.

Bolshakova's arguments that the exchange contract was performed by her under the influence of a material mistake both with respect to the subject of the contract and the reasons for the exchange are unfounded.

In accordance with Article 57 of the RSFSR Civil Code, a legal transaction performed under the influence of a mistake which is of material significance shall be deemed void upon the suit of the party which acted under the influence of the mistake.

A representation concerning some facts essential for the particular legal transaction or the ignorance thereof are considered a mistake which is of material significance not corresponding to reality.

Such facts have not been established in the case. Mikheev performed no bad-faith actions in formalizing the exchange.

The information specified by him in the statement concerning the exchange of the apartment, in particular that the apartment is located on the second floor and that there is no lift in the house, correspond to reality.

Bolshakova had been informed in detail about the condition of Mikheev's apartment by her nieces, Grishaeva and Krivorotova.

Arriving in Kuibyshev on March 10, 1969, she moved into the apartment at once, registered her niece Grishaeva with her, and submitted no claims within two months.

From letters of the executive committee of the Lenin District of the Kuibyshev Soviet of Working People's Deputies attached to the file of the case, the opinions of construction organizations, as well as of the chief sanitary doctor of Kuibyshev, and copies of the house floor plan it appears that the apartment is located in a house with all conveniences in the center of the city. It is on the second floor, well constructed, dry, in good technical and sanitary condition, the height of the premises is 3 square meters, and a window looks to the south. In the apartment are a kitchen of 10 square meters, separate toilet and bath, built-in shelves in the corridor, mezzanine, balcony, and telephone.

The reference of Bolshakova to a medical certificate of June 16, 1969, recommending that she live not higher than the first floor or in a house with a lift can not be taken into account. At the moment of performing the exchange the state of her health was the same and she considered it possible to live on the second floor without a lift. She can exchange for an apartment located on the first floor of a house. According to Grishaeva, there is such a variant of exchange.

D. Remedies for breach of contract

CIVIL CODE, RSFSR (1964)
Article 186. *General Provisions*

The performance of obligations may be secured according to law or a contract by a forfeiture (fine, penalty), a pledge, or a surety.

In addition, obligations between citizens or with their participation may be secured by a deposit, and obligations between socialist organizations, by a guarantee.

Article 187. *Forfeiture*

A sum of money determined by law or by contract which an obligor is obliged to pay to an obligee in the event of the failure to execute, or of the improper execution of an obligation, in particular in the event of delay of execution, shall be deemed a forfeiture (fine, penalty).

Only a valid claim may be secured by a forfeiture (fine, penalty).

An obligee shall not have the right to demand the payment of a forfeiture (fine, penalty) unless the obligor is liable for the failure to execute or for the improper execution of the obligation (Article 222).

Article 189. *Forfeiture and Losses*

If a forfeiture (fine, penalty) has been established for the failure to execute or for the improper execution of an obligation, the losses shall be compensated in that part not covered by the forfeiture (fine, penalty).

Instances may be provided for by law or contract when only the exaction of a forfeiture (fine, penalty) is permitted, but not for losses; when losses may be exacted in the full amount above the forfeiture (fine, penalty); when at the choice of the obligee either a forfeiture (fine, penalty) or losses may be exacted.

Article 191. *Duty of Obligor Who Has Paid a Forfeiture Specifically to Perform an Obligation*

The payment of a forfeiture (fine, penalty) established in the event of delay or other improper execution of an obligation shall not release the obligor from specific performance of the obligation except for instances when a planning task on which the obligation between socialist organizations is based has lost force.

Article 218. *Consequences of the Failure to Execute an Obligation to Fulfill Particular Work*

In the event of the failure of an obligor to execute an obligation to fulfill particular work, the obligee shall have the right to fulfill this work at the obligor's expense unless the contrary follows from the law or contract, or he may demand compensation for losses.

Article 219. *Duty of an Obligor to Compensate Losses*

In the event of the failure to execute or of the improper execution of an obligation by an obligor, he shall be obliged to compensate the obligee for losses caused thereby.

"Losses" includes expenses incurred by an obligee, the loss of or damage to his property, as well as revenues not received by an obligee which he would have received if the obligation had been executed by an obligor.

Compensation of losses in instances when a forfeiture (fine, penalty) is established for the failure to execute or for the improper execution of an obligation shall be determined by the rules of Article 189 of the present Code.

Article 220 *Limitation of Liability Regarding Obligations*

Limited liability for the failure to execute or for the improper execution of obligations may be established for individual types of obligations by legislation of the USSR and RSFSR.

An agreement between socialist organizations to limit their liability shall not be permitted if the amount of liability for a particular type of obligation is determined precisely by law.

Article 221. *Duty of an Obligor Who has Compensated Losses Specifically to Perform an Obligation*

Compensation of losses caused by the improper execution of an obligation shall not release the obligor from specifically executing the obligation except for instances when the planning task on which the obligation between socialist organizations is founded has lost force.

Article 222. *Fault as a Condition of Liability for Breach of Obligations*

A person who has not executed an obligation or has executed it improperly shall be financially liable only in the presence of fault (intent or negligence) except for instances provided for by law or contract. The absence of fault shall be proved by the person who has breached the obligation.

BRUN'KO vs. UNIVERMAG, Biulleten' Verkhovnogo Suda RSFSR, 1970, no. 5, p. 12.

On August 15, 1966, Brun'ko purchased a "Rubin-106" television set at a cost of 426 rubles from the Department Store in the city of Sverdlovsk.

In December 1968 she brought suit in court against the Department Store and Teleatelier No. 1 (now the production sector attached to the Sverdlovsk Directorate for Television Network Reception) to recover the cost of the television set. She justified her suit by the fact that the television set was defective and was brought in for repair to Teleatelier No. 1, where they broke it. For more than two years she was deprived of the possibility of using the television set.

The Judicial Division for Civil Cases of the Sverdlovsk Regional Court satisfied Brun'ko's suit and exacted 426 rubles from the Department Store, obliging Brun'ko to hand over the television set she had purchased to the Department Store.

The Judicial Division for Civil Cases of the RSFSR Supreme Court, having considered the case on cassational appeal of the Department Store, left the decision of the regional court without change and the cassational appeal without satisfaction, specifying in a ruling of December 20, 1969, the following:

According to Article 248 of the RSFSR Civil Code, a buyer may within the guarantee period submit a claim to the seller in regard to defects of the article sold which prevent its normal use. The seller shall be obliged to ensure the elimination of the defects in the article free of charge or to take it back and return to the purchaser the amount paid for it unless it is proved that the defects arose as a consequence of the purchaser's violation of the rules for the use of the article or for storing it.

It was established by the court that Brun'ko, after installing the television set in September 1966, immediately filed a claim with the Department Store in respect of the unclear picture and hands on the screen. At the suggestion of the Department Store she went to the teleatelier for the purpose of eliminating the defects in the television set. Workers of the teleatelier repeatedly came to Brun'ko's apartment and attempted to find the reason for the defects in the television set. Only in July 1967 the master of the teleatelier suggested the television set be brought to the teleatelier for repair and replacement of the picture tube. Before then, when attempting to replace the picture tube in Brun'ko's apartment, the atelier workers had broken the front of the television set. Only in August 1967 was the picture tube replaced and a new front for the television set mounted. However, after this the television set did not work normally for a long time.

According to the Rules for the Exchange of Manufactured Goods Purchased in Retail Trade Network, of September 13, 1965 (with subsequent additions), television sets, radio combinations, and others, if manufacturing defects are discovered in them, shall be exchanged within the guarantee period when the manufacturing enterprise or shop (atelier) performing the guarantee servicing cannot within ten days after the application of the purchaser eliminate the manufacturing defects because of the complexity of the repair or the absence of necessary spare parts.

In the present case the teleatelier eliminated the defects of the telvision set only after a year. Moreover, the teleatelier workers in attempting to replace the picture tube of the television set on a house call broke the front of the television set, as a consequence of which the latter lost its previous marketable form.

BOCHARNIKOVA vs. THE SYROEDINS, Biulleten' Verkhovnogo Suda RSFSR, 1970, no. 11, pp. 7-8

By a contract of gift Bocharnikova transferred to the spouses Syroedins a house belonging to her by right of personal ownership at No. 13, V. Cherepanov Street in the city of N. Tagil, and the Syroedins assumed the obligation to support Bocharnikova for life, formalizing this in a signed paper.

After several years passed, Bocharnikova brought suit in court against the Syroedins to recognize the contract of gift for the house as void, referring to the fact that she had become gravely ill. The Syroedins took poor care of her, and she was obliged to leave the house and go to the Mikhailov family.

The case was considered repeatedly by various judicial instances, after which it was accepted by the Sverdlovsk Regional Court.

By a decision of December 10, 1969, the Sverdlovsk Regional Court satisfied Bocharnikova's suit.

Having considered the case by way of cassational appeal of the defendants, the Judicial Division for Civil Cases of the RSFSR Supreme Court by a ruling of February 10, 1970, left the decision of the regional court without change and the cassational appeal without satisfaction on the following grounds.

The decision of the regional court is rendered in accordance with the actual facts of the case and the requirements of law.

From the materials of the case it is clear that in fact a purchase-sale contract for a dwelling house was concluded between the parties with the condition that the seller be supported for life, that is, the parties entered into legal relations regulated by Article 253 of the RSFSR Civil Code.

In accordance with Article 254 of the RSFSR Civil Code, a purchase-sale contract for a dwelling house with a condition that the seller be supported for life may be dissolved at the request of the seller if the purchaser does not perform the duties assumed under this contract.

The Syroedins are not fulfilling the obligations assumed to support the plaintiff. The regional court came to this conclusion on the basis of information in the file of the case and verified in the judicial session.

In November 1965 Bocharnikova was gravely ill. The Syroedins devoted little attention to her throughout the period of her illness and afterward when she was paralyzed.

At this time the defendants with the plaintiff's consent sold a cow belonging to her. The monies from its sale Bocharnikova received, but the Syroedins placed it in a savings bank in their own name, and when the plaintiff improved and began to demand the deposit be placed in her name, the Syroedins refused and transferred part of the money only after the intervention of the procurator. From this moment extremely hostile relations existed between them.

The residence of the parties together in a single house became impossible. Consequently the plaintiff requested Pologova to take her in to her apartment.

Since Pologova refused Bocharnikova's request, she moved to live in May 1967 with the Mikhailovs, where she now lives.

The reference in the Syroedins' appeal to the fact that they fulfilled the obligations assumed to support Bocharnikova but that she herself preferred not to live with them and went to the Mikhailovs is unfounded and cannot serve as grounds for vacating the court decision and rejecting Bocharnikova's suit.

The defendants did not deny in the judicial session the fact that they had not objected when Bocharnikova left them and that during the time she lived at the Mikhailovs they had not once been there nor been interested in how she lived, what she required, nor rendered any assistance to her.

Therefore the regional court justifiably pointed out in the decision that during Bocharnikova's residence at the Mikhailovs (people who were strangers to her) the Syroedins took no measures toward a reconciliation. They did not meet with her. For about three years the defendants supplied no support for the plaintiff and thereby did not fulfill the obligations assumed. The arguments of the Syroedins in the appeal that Bocharnikova did not wish to live together with them and receive support from them are unfounded.

IVANOVO MUNICIPAL HOUSING SECTION vs. MALYSHEV, Biulleten' Verkhovnogo Suda RSFSR, 1968, no. 12, pp. 7–8.

The Municipal Housing Section of the Lenin District Soviet of Working People's Deputies in the city of Ivanovo concluded a contract in 1959 with Malyshev granting him use in perpetuity of a land plot for the construction of an individual dwelling house by right of personal ownership.

According to this contract, Malyshev was obliged to complete the building of the house within three years, *i.e.*, by July 24, 1962. However, he did not fulfill his obligation within the established period.

By a decision of the executive committee of the Lenin District Soviet of November 16, 1964, the period for building the house was extended for Malyshev to November 1, 1965. But Malyshev did not build the house within this period.

In connection with the violation by Malyshev of the periods for completing the construction of the house, the Lenin District Municipal Housing Section brought suit in court to recover 230 rubles forfeiture from Malyshev, at two rubles, 50 kopecks for each day of delay.

The Lenin District People's Court recovered a forfeiture in the amount of 100 rubles from Malyshev.

In August 1966 the Lenin District Municipal Housing Section brought suit in court for a second time to recover a forfeiture of 490 rubles from Malyshev for violation of the construction period.

The Lenin District People's Court recovered 450 rubles from Malyshev.

The Judicial Division for Civil Cases of the Ivanovo Regional Court left the decision of the people's court without change.

The Presidium of the same court rejected the protest of the Ivanovo Regional Procurator to change the decision of the people's court and the ruling of the regional court and reduced the amount awarded against Malyshev to 250 rubles.

Having considered the present case by way of supervision upon the protest of the deputy Procurator of the RSFSR, the Judicial Division of the RSFSR Supreme Court, agreeing with the arguments of the protest, indicated the following in its ruling of March 11, 1968:

According to Article 190 of the RSFSR Civil Code, the court shall have the right to reduce the amount of a forfeiture subject to payment taking into account the extent of the fulfillment of the obligation by the obligor, as well as his financial position.

In his explanations to the court Malyshev asserted that he could not fulfill his obligation within the period because of the financial difficulties. The court unjustifiably did not take into account these arguments of the defendant nor consider them when rendering the decision to satisfy the suit.

It is clear from the file of the case that the average monthly earnings of Malyshev constitute 111 rubles. From this amount is withheld by decision of a people's court 33% alimony and 17% for the revenues of the state.

The reference in the ruling of the Judicial Division of the Regional Court and the decree of the Presidium of the same court that Malyshev deliberately delayed construction of the house for the purpose of keeping a room in a municipal apartment for his son who has not attained majority does not follow from the materials of the case. The people's court did not investigate this question.

It is clear from the investigative document concerning the daily living conditions of Malyshev that his financial position is extremely difficult.

At present 208 rubles, 60 kopecks, has been withheld from Malyshev and transferred to the income of the state in cancellation of the forfeiture exacted.

Taking into account all these circumstances, the Judicial Division for Civil Cases of the RSFSR Supreme Court has changed the decision of the people's court, the ruling of the judicial division, and the decree of the presidium of the Ivanovo regional court, reducing the amount of the forfeiture recovered from Malyshev from 450 rubles to 250 rubles.

CHAPTER XXI

Torts and Social Insurance

Actions by irate peasants for injury caused to their crops by straying cattle were among the first tort actions brought in Soviet courts after the revolution. The courts raised no question of the role that tort law would play in the new society.[1] They proceeded to look for causation and fault in the conventional manner, even though at the time they were functioning under an early Soviet decree authorizing courts to reject principles of Imperial Russian law if these appeared to be contrary to the revolutionary consciousness of the judges.[2] Since then, the law of tort has had a place in the Soviet legal system, although there have been occasions when official doubt as to its permanent value has been expressed.

In the 1920s Soviet jurists had their heart set on the evolution of a social insurance law to meet the needs of accident victims; with the eventual withering away of the state, the protection of private interests in property was expected to become unnecessary. The first social insurance law was enacted in 1918,[3] while hopes were still bright that the law of the market place would soon disappear. Even when it became evident that the achievement of full communism would transpire in the indefinite future, social insurance continued to play a part in relation to tort law, for not only was it continued after the enactment of the 1922 RSFSR Civil Code, but its coverage was widened and the amount of benefits increased.[4]

Protection for accident victims is presently afforded outside the civil codes, not only through social insurance, but through public health legislation. Medical care is

---

[1] Bazhenkov v. Vshivskii Village Community, and Kormakov v. Vshivskii Village Community, reported in Kurskii, Comments on the people's court, Prol. rev. i pravo, No. 2 (August 15, 1918) pp. 17–18.

[2] Decree No. 1 on the courts, November 24, 1917, [1917–1918], I Sob. Uzak. RSFSR, No. 4, item 50.

[3] Decree of October 31, 1918, [1918] I Sob. Uzak. RSFSR, No. 89, item 906.

[4] Following federation of the republics, a law of February 6, 1925, coordinated the various republic laws. [1925] I Sob. Zak. SSSR, No. 8, item 74. A new basic federal statute was enacted on February 13, 1930. [1930] *ibid.* No. 11, item 132 and No. 51, item 528. After frequent amendment, this was replaced by a regulation approved by the Council of Labor Unions, January 23, 1955, on temporary disability, and a law on state pensions of July 14, 1956. Both are printed in Sbornik Zak. i Aktov o Trude [Collection of Legislative Acts on Labor]. (Moscow, 3d ed., 1960) 540–630.

provided without charge, or with minimal charges for collateral medical expenses, to all. The social insurance system is somewhat more restrictive, covering those who are workers and employees and certain other analogous categories. Most self-employed persons, housewives, and children are excluded. Members of cooperatives, including the collective farms, were brought within social insurance during the 1960s. Individuals not covered by social insurance can recover for personal injuries only under the general provisions of tort law. The law of tort accordingly has retained considerable value as the means by which the financial needs of a still significant portion of the population are met after an accident, although for the majority of the population, it is only a secondary line of protection against potential impoverishment.

In spite of limited coverage, social insurance provides protection not only against financial loss resulting from employment-connected injuries, but also against loss resulting from any injury or illness, even if unconnected with employment. Elements of accident such as compensation for pain and suffering, or for loss of future earnings, are not recoverable in Soviet law under social insurance nor the law of tort. Many personal injury cases that traditionally congest courts in other lands would be divided between the social insurance agencies and the courts in the Soviet Union. Cases involving injury without a social insurance dimension are rarely encountered in published Soviet judicial decisions.

Until revised by the Fundamental Principles of Civil Legislation in 1961, and the union republic civil codes enacted pursuant thereto, Soviet statutory tort law retained many distinctive marks of its origin, including the lacunae, in the early years when the draftsmen assumed its function would be to protect the worker under conditions of the New Economic Policy. To an unusual extent in Soviet civil law, the law of tort was to be found in the civil codes, in ancillary legislation, and in decrees and guiding explanations of the highest courts. Even today, in respect of certain kinds of tort liability, recourse must be had to the codes together with other legislation and to court decisions and decrees.

The basic tort provision in the 1922 RSFSR Civil Code, Article 403, contained no requirement of fault as a prerequisite to tort liability. The draftsmen explained that their intention was to make fault unnecessary.[5] As late as 1929, a court required a husband to pay damages to his common-law wife for injury resulting from an abortion he had not performed on the ground that the child had been fathered by him.[6] This tenuous causal relation sufficed for the court, which was following the pattern of the expansive interpretation of the code established in early years to favor weaker parties, regardless of fault or relevant causation.

Article 406 authorized a court to require a defendant to pay damages to an injured party, even though no actionable wrong had been committed, if the defendant's fi-

---

[5]For a survey of the law of the 1920s, see A.B. Holman and M. Spinner. Basis of Liability for Tortious Injury in Soviet law, 22 Ia. L. Rev. 1–38 (1936).
[6]Case No. 339. Sud. Prak. RSFSR, No. 8 (May 7), 1929, p. 5.

nancial means were relatively superior to those of the injured party. With the passage of time and the disappearance of the conditions created by the New Economic Policy, the "soak the rich" policy disappeared. As early as 1947, the authors of a textbook on civil law declared that Article 406 no longer had validity, except in very unusual cases, because "the absence in the USSR of any possibility of exploiting the work of others, and the guarantee to all Soviet citizens of the right to work gives no possibility for the development of sharp differences between the property status of working people."[7]

With the expansion of the social insurance system and the fading away of the NEP, the law of tort moved into a new phase. Its function became, in addition to the recoupment of a victim's expenses and loss of earnings, deterrence and education, in the expectation that future negligence would be averted. This reorientation suggested to Soviet jurists that there was reason to compare the law of torts with criminal law, since both were related to the prevention of socially undesirable acts.[8] To assure the effectiveness of a policy of deterrence through tort law, while at the same time retaining social insurance coverage for financial losses due to unlawful injury, the two concepts had to be interwoven.

Soviet draftsmen found an appropriate model in Western Europe, where the social insurance agency that pays benefits may sue the tortfeasor for the recoupment of its payments by way of subrogation to the rights of the victim.[9] The employer was treated in traditional fashion and given protection, but only to the extent that he had not been guilty of a "criminal act or omission". Whatever restrictive meaning this formula may have had in the early years, subsequent court practice eroded it to such an extent that by 1950 an author was able to write that "criminal negligence" was present whenever there had been failure to protect workers or to adopt proper safety rules.[10] In short, the protection obtained through purchase of insurance became less important. The courts seem to have favored absolute liability, at least for employment injuries, and this would seem to lessen the deterrent effect of tort law.

The deterrent function of tort law has been evident in the fixing of social insurance benefits, after a period of "temporary disability" when benefits amounting to full wages are paid, at less than full wages. This feature obliged victims permanently disabled to bring suits to recover the difference between their insurance benefits and their former wages, or such part of their former wages as medical examiners believed them incapable of earning in their disabled condition. If the defendant were their employer, the code as already noted allowed recovery only if the employer's act or omission could be categorized as "criminal". If the tortfeasor were not the employer, the victim was required to prove only ordinary negligence,

[7]M. V. Zimeleva, V.I. Serebrovskii, Z.I. Skundin, Grazhdanskoe Pravo [Civil Law.] (Moscow, 1947) 347.
[8]2 Grazhdanskoe Pravo [Civil Law] (Moscow, 1938) 389.
[9]Civil Code, RSFSR, 1922, Art. 413.
[10]See Matveeev, Cases concerned with compensation for injury. Sots. Zak., 1950. No. 2, p. 32. Compare Dobrovolskii, What's New in Judicial Practice in Tort Cases, Sots. Zak., 1960, No. 8, p. 54.

whether he were insured or not, and the insurance agency would recover any benefits it may have been required to pay the victim under the insurance system without proof of criminal negligence.[11]

Since punitive elements have, at least in theory, been present since the NEP, the courts have examined the primary elements of causation and fault without which the therapeutic consequences of punitive action would not follow. Because the burden of proof is on the person causing the injury to show absence of fault, the nature of this examination has differed from that in Western courts.

To the general rule that liability is based on fault there has been one exception, commonly found in Western legal systems, whether they be of Romanist or common law origin, namely the exception for extra-hazardous activity. Such an exception is justified in societies where social insurance is not developed because it provides a form of compulsory private insurance on the part of industries where injury is so common as to constitute a cost of production or of conducting the activity. In Soviet society, where most enterprises are economically accountable for their operations, strict liability for extra-hazardous activity assists in assigning the costs for that activity to the responsible enterprises and institutions. This is especially evident in the rather unusual stipulation in Soviet law that the operation of automobiles is included among the extra hazardous types of acitvity.[12] Although the numbers of privately-owned vehicles are growing substantially, most vehicles are owned by state institutions and enterprises, who are better able to absorb the cost of accidents. The increasing number of privately-owned vehicles has been accompanied by another phenomenon: the underwriting by the State Insurance Agency (Gosstrakh) of insurance policies for property and life insurance.

Since 1961, victims of employment-related injuries are required to seek administrative remedies before bringing a suit in court. This modified form of workmen's compensation may well reduce the number of tort cases in the Soviet courts.

Not all Soviet state agencies have been subjected to tort actions. The 1922 RSFSR Civil Code took an ambiguous position, exempting state institutions from liability unless contrary provision was established by law.[13] This rule appeared to create the exemption from liability of Romanist systems for state agencies engaged in the governing process. Statutes implemening the 1922 code brought many government agencies within the law of torts. They covered the Ministry of Railways, the Ministry of Communications, the Ministry of Defense, and state harbor pilots almost at once.[14] Judicial decisions in cases decided after these early statutes declared that the exemption was one to be strictly applied, and in 1926 the Supreme Court of the RSFSR issued a directive that Article 407 was not to be applied to

---

[11]Civil Code, RSFSR, 1922, Art. 414.
[12]Civil Code, RSFSR, 1922, Art. 404.
[13]Civil Code, RSFSR, Art. 407.
[14]Decrees of July 12, 1922, [1922] I Sob. Uzak, RSFSR, No. 38, item 445; July 17, 1923, [1923] ibid., No. 83, item 812; September 18, 1923, [1923] ibid. No. 100, item 999 and October 17, 1921, [1921] ibid. No. 70, item 564, sec. 17.

give immunity to a governmental agency when the function performed and causing damage was an economic one.[15] The 1961 Fundamental Principles and union republic civil codes go further and make an agency liable unless exempted from liability by statute.

Other Romanist principles characterize Soviet tort law, such as the rule of comparative negligence, and the rule that damages be paid in monthly installments rather than in a capitalized form of a lump sum. This latter requirement has a socialist ring, for, under Soviet conditions, lump sums could not be invested to provide income sufficient to meet continuing needs. On the other hand, if an enterprise owing monthly installments to various individuals for injury claims should be liquidated, its obligations in this respect are capitalized and paid to the state social insurance agency, which then assumes the responsibility for paying out the monthly installments. Yet, it should be noted the installment concept was not an invention of Soviet draftsmen, but is to be found in other Romanist-inspired systems such as that of Mexico.

Finally, a word needs to be said about the duty to rescue, for the USSR Constitution of 1936 requires citizens to observe the "rules of socialist community life" and to "safeguard and strengthen social, socialist ownership."[16] Soviet jurists have asked themselves whether this created a duty to rescue and liability in tort for those who fail to perform their duty. No doubt was expressed on this score in a 1938 textbook, and a hypothetical case was given in which damages would be recoverable.[17] Today it is felt that Soviet Man has a duty to rescue, and the union republic civil codes allow recovery for injury received while rescuing socialist property; this principle has even been extended to the rescue of human life.

A. General principles of tort liability

CIVIL CODE, RSFSR (1964)
Article 444. *General Bases of Liability for Causing Harm*

Harm caused to the person or property of a citizen, as well as harm caused to organizations, shall be subject to compensation in full by the person who has caused the harm.

One who has caused harm shall be relieved from compensating it if he proves that the harm was caused not by his fault.

Harm caused by lawful actions shall be subject to compensation only in the instances provided for by law.

Article 448. *Harm Caused in Necessary Defense*

Harm caused in necessary defense, if it does not exceed its limits, shall not be subject to compensation.

---

[15]See E.A. Fleishits, Obiazatel'stva iz Prichineniia Vreda i iz Neosnovatel'nogo Obogashcheniia [Obligations from Causing Inusry and from Unjust Enrichment]. (Moscow, 1951) p. 113.
[16]U.S.S.R. Constitution, 1936, Arts. 130,131.

Article 449. *Liability for Harm Caused in Extreme Necessity*

Harm caused in extreme necessity should be compensated by the person who has caused it.

Taking into account the circumstances under which such harm was caused, the court may impose the duty to compensate it on a third person in whose interests the person causing the harm acted or relieve in full or in part the third person and the person who caused the harm from compensating the harm.

Article 452. *Liability for Harm Caused by a Citizen Deemed to Lack Legal Capacity*

For harm caused by a citizen deemed to lack legal capacity (Article 15), his guardian or the organization obliged to keep supervision over him shall be liable unless they prove that the harm arose not by their fault.

Article 453. *Liability for Harm Caused by a Citizen Not Capable of Understanding the Significance of His Actions*

A citizen having legal capacity who has caused harm in a state when he could not understand the significance of his actions nor direct them shall not be liable for the harm he has caused. However, he shall not be relieved from liability if he brought himself into such a state by the abuse of alcohol or narcotics or by other means.

Article 455. *Liability for Harm Jointly Caused by Several Persons*

Persons who jointly cause harm shall bear joint liability to the victim.

Article 457. *Amount, Character, and Extent of Compensation for Harm*

In awarding compensation for harm, a court, arbitrazh, or conciliation court shall in accordance with the facts of the case oblige the person liable for the harm to compensate it in kind (give over a thing of the same kind and quality, rectify the thing damaged, etc.) or to compensate in full the losses caused (Article 219).

Article 458. *Taking Account of the Fault of the Victim and Financial Status of the Person Who caused the Harm*

If the gross negligence of the victim himself facilitated the origin or the aggravation of the harm, then depending on the extent of the victim's fault (and if the person who caused the harm is at fault, also depending upon the extent of his fault), the amount of compensation unless otherwise provided for by a law of the USSR, should be reduced or compensation of the harm should be denied.

A court may reduce the amount of compensation for harm caused by a citizen, depending on his financial status.

O. A. Krasavchikov, "Concept of the Obligation to Compensate Harm," in SOVETSKOE GRAZHDANSKOE PRAVO (Moscow, 1969), pp. 363-365.

The legal institute of compensation for harm caused is a well-known complex of norms of Soviet civil law defining the group of subjects having rights and duties and the bases and procedure for compensation of harm caused by one person to another . . . The legal institute being considered has certain specific features . . . The majority of institutes of the law of obligations contains two kinds of Norms:

imperative norms and dispositive norms. The latter allow parties of civil legal relations to determine the bounds of their conduct otherwise than is written in the dispositive norm. In contrast to these legal institutes, the institute of compensation for harm unlawfully caused consists exclusively of imperative norms whose effect may not be modified by agreement of the parties. . . .
Concept of the Obligation for Compensation of Harm. . . .
1. By their economic essence, obligations for compensation of harm caused are a legal form of relations for the redistribution of financial benefits (chiefly sums of money). The one who causes harm compensates the harm caused by his actions without equivalence; there is no counter submission from the victim nor is any presupposed.
2. From the viewpoint of legal nature, the obligations being considered are a legal form of realizing civil law liability, to which the one who causes harm is brought in accordance with the provisions of the law.
3. The basic function of obligations arising from the unlawful causing of harm also is a specific one. The essence of this function is that the particular obligations aim to restore the financial position of the victim to what it was before the harm was caused. One should bear in mind that the restorative function, being a basic one, is combined with the educational influence on the violator.
4. A peculiarity of measures of civil law liability realized through obligations from the causing of harm is that they do not exert direct influence on the individual violator. If harm is caused, the person causing the harm undergoes a pinching of his financial interests. This pinching is reflected in that the person causing harm is compelled to compensate all financial losses incurred by the victim, proceeding from the principle of full compensation for harm.
5. The grounds for the obligations being considered to arise also are distinctive; they arise when conditions exist which are provided for by law, and in any event only when harm is caused by unlawful actions. Compensation for harm caused lawfully goes beyond, in essence, the limits of the present legal institute. Its rules also do not extend to instances of compensation for harm caused as a consequence of the failure to perform obligations assumed by the parties under a contract or other analogous legal bases. Liability in such instances is contractual.
6. Compensation of harm, depending on the character of the harm caused, and the possibility for compensating it in a particular form for a number of other essential obligations may be reflected in compensation for harm in kind . . . or by full compensation for losses caused.

FRUNZE CITY PROCURATOR vs. IABLONSKII, Biulleten' Verkhovnogo Suda SSSR, 1975, no. 3, pp. 20–21.

Alexander Iablonskii, aged 14, left home in December 1968. In the evening he climbed into the attic of the main building of the Polytechnic Institute, where in a wooden structure with a heater he spent the nights of December 10 and 11th. On the night of December 12th he made a camp fire in a small metal box on the spot to warm himself and fell asleep. Beneath the hot box the wooden floor burned. Iablonskii, seeing the flame, became frightened, gathered his belongings, and fled, not telling anyone what had happened. As a result of the fire, the wooden structure of the attic burned and the roof above the documents room of the Institute collapsed. Besides the damage to the Institute building, the chairs, tables, decorative panels, and other property in the documents room were damaged.

Because of his age, Alexander Iablonskii could not bear criminal responsibility under Article 91 of the Kirgiz Criminal Code, and the criminal case with respect to him was terminated.

The Frunze City Procurator brought suit against I. B. Iablonskii to recover 28, 319 rubles in compensation for damage caused by the fire which originated through the fault of his minor son, Alexander.

[The Frunze People's Court satisfied the suit in full, and its decision was left without change by the Judicial Division for Civil Cases of the Kirgiz Supreme Court. The Presidium of the Kirgiz Supreme Court rejected a protest to reduce the amount of recovery, but a further protest to the Plenum of the Kirgiz Supreme Court in this connection was satisfied on the following grounds].

In imposing financial liability on B. I. Iablonskii for the damage caused in full, the court did not take into account the fact that in accordance with Article 468 of the Kirgiz Civil Code, when determining the amount subject to compensation, the degree of fault of the victim in the origin of the harm and the financial status of the person who caused the harm must be taken into account.

The materials of the case indicate that the administration of the Polytechnic Institute did not exercise proper protection of the building, the attic of which was repeatedly frequented by youths. The attic was enclosed with wooden blocks. Alexander Iablonskii, as he confirms, found kerosene there with the aid of which he lit the fire. The court did not appraise these facts sufficiently.

Nor did the court take into account the financial status of the defendant, who with earnings of 115 rubles per month had dependent on him, besides a son, an ill daughter.

As is clear from the receipt issued July 20, 1974, by the bookkeeper of the plant at which Iablonskii works, for the period May 1, 1969 to June 1, 1974, a thousand rubles were withheld from his wages.

Iablonskii and his wife, who is a pensioner, were participants in the Great Fatherland War.

Taking account of the circumstances of the causing of harm and the financial status of the defendant, the Plenum of the Kirgiz Supreme Court has vacated the decision of the Lenin District People's Court in Frunze and the ruling of the Judicial Division for Civil Cases of the Kirgiz Supreme Court has been changed, the amount subject to recovery from I. B. Iablonskii being reduced to 1500 rubles.

MEZHOVA vs. STAROVOITOV, Biulleten' Verkhovnogo Suda RSFSR, 1969, no. 6, p. 2

Mezhova brought suit in court against Starovoitov for compensation of harm caused to health, referring to the fact that on August 22, 1965, the defendant, stimulated by hooligan motives, caused her grave bodily injuries with a shot from a gun. In connection with the injury received, she lost 80% of her professional capacity to work and 60% of her general capacity. The fault of Starovoitov in causing her grave bodily injuries was established by a judgment of the Khakass Regional Court of December 22, 1965.

[The people's court satisfied the suit, but was reversed by the Presidium of the Khakass Regional Court. The Judicial Division for Civil Cases of the RSFSR Supreme Court, hearing the case upon the protest of the chairman of the RSFSR Supreme Court, reinstated the decision of the people's court.]

In vacating the decision of the people's court and rejecting Mezhova's suit, the presidium of the regional court referred to the fact that the plaintiff was not working at the moment she suffered the injury, was an elderly person, received a pension, and there had been no real loss of earnings.

One can not concur with these arguments of the court.

A decree of the USSR Council of Ministers of February 26, 1964, "On Increasing the Financial Interest of Pensioners in Production Work" recommended that the managers of enterprises, institutions, and organizations hire, in the event of production need, able-bodied pensioners who receive an old-age pension.

It was established in the case that Mezhova actually was a pensioner and received a pension. However, she constantly worked. From the receipts in the file of the case it is clear that the plaintiff worked in a technical school. As a consequence of the criminal actions committed by the defendant, she now can not work since the radial nerve of her left shoulder is injured.

According to the opinion of the VTFK of November 2, 1965, the plaintiff lost 80% of her professional capacity to work in connection with the injury received.

In this situation, in accordance with Article 459 of the RSFSR Civil Code, the people's court recognized with good reason that Mezhova has the right to compensation for the loss under the general provisions provided for by law and obliged Starovoitov to pay her 16 rubles monthly until the time she is recertified.

The presidium of the regional court had no basis to vacate the said decision of the people's court and to reject the plaintiff's claim.

VINTER vs. SHCHEKIN AND OLOKHOV, Biulleten' Verkhovnogo Suda RSFSR, 1974, no. 3, pp. 7–8.

Shchekin and Olokhov were convicted under Article 146, paragraph 2(a)-(c), Article 15, and Article 102(a) and (e) of the RSFSR Criminal Code with the recovery from them of 800 rubles jointly for the benefit of Vinter in compensation of financial loss by a judgement of the Cheliabinsk Regional Court of May 25, 1972.

They were deemed guilty of possessing as a result of an assault at the apartment of Vinter various articles valued at 800 rubles and of the attempted murder of the eleven-year old son of Vinter, Evgenii, from mercenary motives and with a view to concealing the crime committed, as a result whereof he was caused grave bodily injuries dangerous to life.

The Judicial Division for Criminal Cases of the RSFSR Supreme Court left the judgment without change.

The deputy chairman of the RSFSR Supreme Court brought a protest to the Presidium of the RSFSR Supreme Court which raised the question of vacating the judgment in respect of the civil suit and sending this part of the case for new consideration in a civil proceeding.

In concurring with the protest, the Presidium of the RSFSR Supreme Court indicated the following in a decree of September 19, 1973:

The guilt of Olokhov and Shchekin in committing the crime has been proved, they were justifiably convicted, their actions were classified properly; however, the question of the civil suit was decided by the court incorrectly, and in this respect the judgment and cassational ruling are subject to being vacated.

When deciding the question of civil suit, the court failed to take into account that the victim Vinter had taken out with the State Insurance inspectorate for the Traktorzavod District in the City of Cheliabinsk on July 14, 1971 a voluntary household property insurance policy, covering, among other events, the theft of property.

In execution of the terms of this policy the State Insurance inspectorate paid her insurance compensation in the amount of 690 rubles, 60 kopecks, after the commission by Olokhov and Shchekin of the assault at Vinter's apartment on April 18, 1972.

At the same time, 800 rubles was recovered from the convicted persons for the benefit of Vinter in compensation of the value of the stolen articles.

Thus, for the stolen property Vinter received compensation from the State insurance agencies, and in addition the full value of this was recovered by the court from the convicted persons for her benefit.

In accordance with point 28 of the Rules for Voluntary Household Property Insurance confirmed by Order of the Minister of Finances of the USSR, No. 272, of November 12, 1968, which were in force when the case was considered by the court, the right to claim compensation, which the insured has against the person liable for the loss caused, passes within the limits of this amount to the State Insurance agencies which paid this amount.

An analogous provision is found also in point 28 of the new Rules for Voluntary Household Property Insurance confirmed by the USSR Ministry of Finances on August 7, 1972.

On the basis of this provision the State Insurance inspectorate for the Traktorzavod District in the city of Cheliabinsk brought suit in court against the convincted Olokhov and Shchekin to recover the amount of 690 rubles, 60 kopecks, paid by the State Insurance Agency.

The loss already has been recovered from the convicted persons by judgment of the court in full to the benefit of Vinter.

Moreover, the latter in the present instance have the right to claim recovery from the convicted persons not the full value of the property stolen by them (800 rubles) but only the difference between this value and the amount which she received from State Insurance agencies.

MORGUNOV vs. DMITRIEVA, Biulleten' Verkhovnogo Suda RSFSR, 1971, no. 12, pp. 9–10.

On May 25, 1969, 17-year old Dmitrieva together with friends and a three-year old nephew walked near children playing in the street. 11-year old Kostia Shevelev threw a stick to Dmitrieva's nephew, who caught it and threw it to Shevelev. The stick struck a tree and, bouncing off, poked the eye of nine-year old Natasha Morgunova. A partial dulling of the crystalline lens of the left eye was established by the bureau of forensic medical expertise.

The father of the victim, Morgunov, brought suit against Dmitrieva to recover 1042 rubles in compensation of expenses for a high-caloric diet during the girl's stay in hospital for 21 days in the amount of 126 rubles at 6 rubles per day, expenses for taxi fares to the hospital on the day the injury was received in the amount of 5 rubles, the cost of glasses and medicine, ten rubles. In addition, in the opinion of forensic medical experts the daughter requires a supplemental diet whose cost, according to the plaintiff's figures, is one ruble per day, and for the time which has passed since the injury was received until the day of recertification on December 3, 1970, expenses for supplemental diet amount to 901 rubles.

[The people's court satisfied the suit in part, recovering 450 rubles to the plaintiff's benefit; the decision was not appealed by way of cassation. The Presidium of the Moscow Regional Court, hearing the case upon the protest of the chairman of that court, returned it for new consideration]

In rendering the decision partially to satisfy the suit, the people's court proceeded from the fact that Morgunov's claim in the amount of 1042 rubles was well-founded and the degree of fault of the person who caused the harm was insignificant. The court also took into account the financial status of the defendant.

However, the amount of the claim was in no way confirmed, and it remains unknown why the court came to the conclusion that the account submitted by the plaintiff was correct.

Information is lacking in the file of the case confirming the expenses for the acquisition of medicines, glasses, and taxi fares.

The basic amount of the suit constitutes the expenses for the high-caloric and supplemental diet.

In the opinion of the forensic medical expertise bureau the victim needs a supplemental diet whose cost, according to the institute's data, is 51.5 kopecks per day. The plaintiff considered that he must be compensated for expenses for the supplemental diet at one ruble per day.

There is no medical expert opinion concerning the victim's need for a high-caloric diet.

According to point 16 of the decree of the Plenum of the USSR Supreme Court of October 23, 1963, "On Judicial Practice Regarding Suits for Compensation of Harm", the court may impose on the person who has caused harm the duty to compensate the victim for expenses actually incurred for a supplemental diet, prosthetics, sanatorium and resort treatment, and other expenses if the victim in the opinion of medical expertise requires the said assistance and does not receive it through the respective organizations free of charge.

When deciding the given dispute, the law was applied incorrectly by the court. In satisfying the claim partially, the court, in addition to the financial status of the defendant, took into account also the insignificant degree of fault of the person who caused the harm. According to point 16 of the decree of the Plenum of the USSR Supreme Court of October 23, 1963, when determining the amount of supplemental expenses, the rules allowing a reduction of the amount of compensation depending on the degree of the fault of the victim shall not apply.

IN RE GRACHEV, Biulleten' Verkhovnogo Suda RSFSR, 1972, no. 6, p. 10

On January 13, 1970, a driver of the second motor bus pool of Moscow, Khokhlov, driving a motor bus on route 593, crashed into a Pobeda motor vehicle belonging to Grachev. By a judgment of the Liuberets City People's Court of April 7, 1970, he was convicted under Article 211, paragraph 1, of the RSFSR Criminal Code to one year of correctional tasks. By this same judgment 748 rubles was recovered from the second motor bus pool for the benefit of Grachev, including 694 rubles in compensation for the restorative repair of the motor vehicle.

The Presidium of the Moscow Regional Court vacated the judgment in respect of the civil suit and sent the case in this part for new consideration as a civil proceeding.

After repeated consideration, it was accepted by the regional court for jurisdiction as first instance.

Grachev requested that 2425 rubles be recovered from the motor bus pool in compensation for expenses relating to the assemblage of a new motor vehicle.

The chairman of the motor vehicle pool acknowledged the suit in the amount of 731 rubles, taking into account the money paid in execution of the judgment.

Having participated in the case as a third person, Khokhlov did not acknowledge the suit.

The Moscow Regional Court satisfied the suit in the amount of 2459 rubles, 16 kopecks, deducting the amount of 694 rubles previously paid to the plaintiff. At the same time, the court obliged Grachev to transfer the Pobeda motor vehicle to the defendant in the condition in which it was after the accident.

The second motor bus pool appealed the decision and requested that it be vacated. In a cassational appeal it was indicated that the determination of the amount of compensation for harm was incorrect.

The Judicial Division for Civil Cases of the RSFSR Supreme Court, having considered the case by way of cassation, left the decision of the regional court without change by a ruling of January 21, 1972, on the following grounds.

The fact harm was caused to Grachev's motor vehicle as a result of a collision with a motor bus belonging to the defendant is not disputed by the latter. In such circumstances the motor bus pool as the owner of a source of increased danger is obliged by virtue of Article 454 of the Civil Code to compensate the harm caused to the property of the plaintiff.

The court appointed a technical expert to determine the amount of compensation for harm, commissioning the bureau of goods expertise of the trade administration of the Moscow Regional Executive Committee to do it.

It was correctly indicated in the cassational appeal that the expert submitted three different opinions regarding the amount of the real value of the motor vehicle before the accident.

Thus, the true value of the Pobeda motor vehicle was fixed at 1320 rubles, 2459 rubles, and 2028 rubles.

However, the different appraisal of the motor vehicle's value is explained not as a mistake of the expert but by the following circumstances.

In establishing the real value of the motor vehicle before the accident, the expert in this first instance proceeded from the fact that the motor vehicle was acquired in 1956 for 3000 rubles. In the second instance the expert took into account that the prices of the Pobeda motor vehicles were increased in 1963 to 3900 rubles and, moreover, the plaintiff in 1968 replaced the motor. In the third instance the expert proceeded from the price of the motor vehicle at 3000 rubles but took into account the replacement of the motor in 1968. In all three opinions the expert took into account that the motor vehicle had 140,000 kilometers mileage, in connection wherewith a scale was applied for depreciation, including a separate computation for the depreciation of a new motor in the second and third opinions.

The court recognized that the true value of the motor vehicle was 2459 rubles, 16 kopecks. Thus the decision corresponds to Article 457 of the Civil Code defining the amount, character, and extent of compensation for harm.

To compensate the harm in kind, that is, to give Grachev a Pobeda motor vehicle, is not possible for the defendant, since this model was long ago removed from production. One can not repair it, since the body cannot be restored and there are no spare parts. In such circumstances, the court correctly based its computation on the real harm, in the amount of 2459 rubles, 16 kopecks.

The period in which the motor vehicle was used and the fact the motor was replaced are confirmed by documentation, and the conclusions of the expert are in no way discredited.

Inasmuch as the full value of the motor vehicle has been recovered for the benefit of the plaintiff, it was correctly pointed out in the court's decision that he is obliged to transfer the motor vehicle to the defendant in the same condition in which it was after the accident.

It was established in the judicial session that parts from Grachev's damaged motor vehicle were not used in assembling the new motor vehicle. This fact, in particular, the expert confirmed.

The reference in the appeal to the fact that the court actually recovered compensation of expenses for the plaintiff in the assembly of a new motor vehicle are not well-founded and are refuted by the evidence set forth.

RULES OF VOLUNTARY INSURANCE FOR MEANS OF TRANSPORT BELONGING TO CITIZENS, Confirmed by Order of the USSR Ministry of Finances, August 7, 1972, No. 146

I. General Provisions

1. Contracts of voluntary insurance for means of transport shall be concluded by Gosstrakh with citizens of the USSR, as well as with foreigners and stateless persons permanently residing in the USSR.

2. The following means of transport subject to registration in the established procedure may be insured by a contract:
   (a) automobiles;
   (b) motorcycles, motor-scooters, motorized wheel-chairs, mopeds;
   (c) motor, sail, and row boats (except pneumatic), cutters, and other vessels.

3. Means of transport shall be insured in the event of loss or damage as a result of accident, fire, explosion, flood, snow-storms, hurricane, torrential rain, hail, land-slip, landslide, flood from thawing, settlement, strike by lightning, earthquake, and also in the event of the theft of a means of transport and its loss or damage connected with a theft or highjacking or an attempted theft (or high-jacking).

Note· An accident shall be deemed a collision with another means of transport, with moving or non-moving objects, the falling of means of transport, or any object thereon, dumping, short-circuiting of current.

The aforesaid events hereinafter are insured events.

4. There shall not appertain to insured events:
   damage (or loss) of rubber tires unless other damage (or loss) of the means of transport also occurred;
   the theft of individual parts and appurtenances of means of transport unless the means of transport itself was stolen (or high-jacked), except for the theft of an outboard motor.

5. Means of transport shall be considered insured only on USSR territory.

6. Insurance contracts shall be concluded for a period of from 2 to 11 months inclusive or for one year.

B. Strict liability arising out of extra-hazardous activities

AIR CODE OF THE USSR (effective January 1, 1962). Confirmed by Edict of December 26, 1961 [1961] Vedomosti Verkhovnogo Soveta SSSR, No. 52, item 538.

Article 101. The carrier shall bear financial liability established by legislation of the USSR and union republics for the death, mutilation, or other injury to health caused to a passenger during the take-off, flight, or landing of an aircraft, as well as during the boarding or disembarking of a passenger unless it proves that the harm occurred as a consequence of the intention of the victim himself.

In the event of death, mutilation, or other injury to health caused to a passenger as a result of insuperable force, the carrier shall bear the established liability unless it proves that the harm originated or was aggravated by the intention or gross negligence of the victim himself. In other instances when the carrier proves that the gross negligence of the victim himself facilitated the origin or aggravation of the harm, the extent of compensation for harm in accordance with the general norms of civil legislation should be reduced, or compensation for harm should be denied.

CIVIL CODE, RSFSR (1964)
Article 454. *Liability for Harm Caused by a Source of Increased Danger*

Organizations and citizens whose activity is connected with an increased danger for surrounding persons (transport organizations, industrial enterprises, construction sites, owners of automobiles, etc.) shall be obliged to compensate harm caused by a source of increased danger unless they prove that the harm arose as a consequence of insuperable force or the intention of the victim.

NESTEROV vs. KONDRAT'EV, Biulleten' Verkhovnogo Suda RSFSR, 1968, no. 10, p. 2

On August 22, 1966, on the Moscow-Simferopol' motorway a collision occurred between a Pobeda car belonging to Kondrat'ev and a motorcycle Iava which belonged to Nesterov.

As a result of the collision, Nesterov received grave bodily injuries, and his motorcycle was destroyed.

Referring to the fact that the damage occurred through the fault of Kondrat'ev, who flagrantly violated the traffic rules, Nesterov brought suit for compensation of the damage caused him in connection with his failure to receive wages in the amount of 548 rubles through illness (from August 22-October 16, 1966), repair of the motorcycle in the amount of 249 rubles, soiling of clothing in the amount of 70 rubles, expenses for transport of the motorcycle from the city of Kursk to Leningrad in the amount of 30 rubles, and other expenses.

Kondrat'ev, not acknowledging the suit and considering Nesterov to be at fault in the accident, brought a counter-suit to recover from Nesterov the cost of the repair of the car in the amount of 134 rubles and expenses connected with his travel to Leningrad in the amount of 207 rubles.

The Leningrad City Court satisfied Nesterov's suit in the amount of 680 rubles, taking into account the financial status of Kondrat'ev. The counter-suit of the defendant was rejected by the court.

Having considered the present case by way of cassation, the Judicial Division for Civil Cases of the RSFSR Supreme Court indicated the following in its ruling of July 14, 1968:

The court established that Kondrat'ev, following a car and intending to make a left turn from the highway where there was no crossing, in violation of points 27, 41–43 of the Traffic Rules for Streets of Cities, Populated Points, and Roads of the USSR, without being convinced it was safe, turned left and thereby obstructed the motorcycle coming from behind driven by Nesterov, which was the cause of the accident.

The said facts are confirmed by the explanations of the victim and other evidence: the conclusions of the forensic highway-transport expert examination, the materials of the criminal case initiated against Kondrat'ev (later the case was terminated), the sketch of the road accident and the protocol of the occurrence of the highway-transport accident, and the testimony of witness Chernyshov.

The evidence testifies to the fact that Kondrat'ev was negligent and as the owner of a source of increased danger (a motor vehicle) is obliged, by virtue of Articles 454 and 459 of the RSFSR Code, to compensate the harm to the victim.

Taking into account that the defendant supports his two dependent children and mother, the court justifiably rendered a ruling to satisfy the claims of Nesterov not in the full amount, but in the amount of 680 rubles.

On the above grounds, the Judicial Division for Civil Cases of the RSFSR Supreme Court left the decision of the judicial division of the city court without change.

IGONINA vs. GLAZUNOV, Biulleten' Verkhovnogo Suda RSFSR, 1970, no. 1, p. 10

While driving a Moskvich-407 automobile, Glazunov struck Igonin, who died from injuries received. The spouse of the deceased Igonin brought suit in court against the owner organization of the source of increased danger and Glazunov, who was sentenced under Article 211, paragraph 2, of the RSFSR Criminal Code to six years deprivation of freedom, for compensation of damage in connection with the loss of a breadwinner.

Two small children were dependent on the deceased breadwinner.

The Kamenskii District People's Court of the Sverdlov Region satisfied Igonina's suit and recovered to her benefit from the owner organization of the source of increased danger a single payment of 118 rubles and 23 rubles for each child monthly.

By a ruling of the Sverdlov Regional Court upon the cassational protest of the

Procurator of the Kamenskii District, the decision of the people's court was vacated and the case accepted by the regional court at first instance.

Igonina supported her suit in the judicial session. The representative of the owner organization of the source of increased danger did not recognize the suit, asserting that driver Glazunov, taking advantage of the absence of a guard at the garage, took the vehicle from the garage at midnight and at 4:00 a.m. on August 28, 1968, struck Igonin. Inasmuch as the source of increased danger had left the possession of its owner as a result of the unlawful actions of Glazunov, liability for compensation of harm to the plaintiff should be imposed on the latter.

The Sverdlovsk Regional Court recovered monthly from Glazunov 17 rubles for each child of the deceased, and a single payment of 242 rubles for the benefit of the plaintiff. The suit against the owner organization of the source of increased danger was rejected by decision of the court.

In a cassational appeal Glazunov requested the decision of the court be vacated since he took the motor vehicle from the garage not arbitrarily but by arrangement with the administration, which permitted him to take the car from the garage at any time in his discretion. The travel sheet was written out to him for a week or a month and when finishing work neither the travel sheet nor the key from the garage were taken from him.

The Judicial Division for Civil Cases of the RSFSR Supreme Court vacated the decision of the regional court and sent the file of the case for new consideration.

In this connection the Division indicated the following in its ruling of July 25, 1969:

According to Article 454 of the RSFSR Civil Code, organizations and citizens whose activity is connected with increased danger for surrounding persons (transport organizations, industrial enterprises, construction sites, owners of motor vehicles, etc.) shall be obliged to compensate harm caused by the source of increased danger if it does not prove that the harm arose as a consequence of insuperable force or the intention of the victim.

As is indicated in point 5 of the decree of the Plenum of the USSR Supreme Court of October 23, 1963, "On Judicial Practice Regarding Suits Concerning Compensation of Harm", the owner of a source of increased danger shall not be liable for harm caused by the action of this source if it is proved that the latter left the possession of the owner not by his fault but as the result of unlawful actions of third persons.

As is clear from the materials of the case, the garage in which the motor vehicle was located was not guarded, the driver Glazunov had the key from the garage, and he had access to the vehicle at any time. Consequently, Glazunov's trip in the car about the city early on the morning of August 28, 1968, when he struck Igonin became possible from the owner's failure to ensure proper protection of the vehicle in the garage during non-working hours.

Glazunov's assertion in the cassational appeal that the travel sheet was issued to him for a week or a month and that, when finishing work neither the travel sheet nor the garage key nor the ignition key for the vehicle were taken from him nor handed in for keeping to an appropriate official, were not verified by the court in the judicial session. These facts have material significance for the correct resolution of the case.

DROZDOV vs. GORKY RAILWAY ADMINISTRATION, Biulleten' Verkhovnogo Suda RSFSR, 1972, no. 6, p. 6

Drozdov brought suit against the Gorky Railway Administration for compensation of harm causing mutilation, basing his claim on the fact that on April 3, 1970, he was knocked down by an electric train while crossing the permanent way, as a result of which he lost both feet, was deemed a second group invalid, and had loss of earnings. The Moscow Railway Administration and the Moscow-Kursk Division of the Moscow Railway were joined as co-defendants during the trial.

The Vladimir Regional Court granted the plaintiff compensation for harm from the Moscow Railway Administration.

The Judicial Division for Civil Cases of the RSFSR Supreme Court, having considered the case by way of cassation, vacated the decision by a ruling of February 17, 1972, and sent the case for new consideration on the following grounds.

In accordance with Article 454 of the RSFSR Civil Code organizations and citizens whose activity is connected with an increased danger for surrounding persons (transport organizations, industrial enterprises, construction sites, owners of motor vehicles, etc.) shall be obliged to compensate for harm caused by a source of increased danger, unless it is proved that the harm arose as a consequence of insuperable force or the intention of the victim.

The court, in releasing the Gorky Railway Administration from liability for the harm caused, referred to the fact that the harm was caused to the plaintiff as a result of the action of a source of increased danger: electric locomotive No. 2355 belonging to the Orekhovo-Zuev Depot of the Moscow-Kursk Division of the Moscow Railway. The fact that the plaintiff's accident occurred on the railway lines of the Gorky Railway Administration can not serve [in the trial court's view] as a basis for imposing liability for harm on this railway administration, inasmuch as the railway line, as well as the platform, are not a source of increased danger. The court cannot concur with this argument.

The Plenum of the USSR Supreme Court in point 5 of decree No. 16 of October 23, 1963, "On Judicial Practice Regarding Suits for Compensation of Harm" explained that by "owner of a source of increased danger" should be understood an organization or citizen using the source of increased danger either by virtue of its belonging to him by right of ownership or right of operative management, or also on other grounds (for example, by contract of lease, hire, or by arrangement), as well as by virtue of regulations of competent agencies concerning the transfer to organizations of the temporary use of a source of increased danger.

From the copy of a letter of the legal section of the USSR Ministry of Railways, No. TsIu-25 of April 7, 1971, attached to the cassational appeal, it seems that in railway transport the owner of a source of increased danger applicable to rolling stock is that railway which is using the source of increased danger at the time of the accident, and on the basis of departmental rules the respective agencies of this railway are obliged to conduct the official investigation of accidents. Inasmuch as electric locomotive No. 2355 at the moment of the accident with the plaintiff was in the operative management of the Gorky Railway Administration and being used by it, it is of no significance that the owner of the electric locomotive is the Orekhovo-Zuev Depot of the Moscow-Kursk Division of the Moscow Railway. There are no grounds also for imposing liability for the harm caused to the plaintiff on the Moscow Railway Administration.

VORONOVA vs. KALININ FREIGHT TRANSPORT ENTERPRISE, Biulleten' Verkhovnogo Suda RSFSR, 1971, no. 2, p. 4

On February 23, 1970, Voronov was knocked down by a motor vehicle belonging to the Kalinin Freight Transport Enterprise No. 5 and died from injuries received.

Voronova brought suit against the transport enterprise for compensation of harm causing the death of a breadwinner.

The Kalinin Regional Court satisfied the suit in part.

The Judicial Division for Civil Cases of the RSFSR Supreme Court, having considered the case by way of cassational appeal instituted by Voronova to change the decision of the regional court, left it without change and the appeal without satisfaction, indicating the following in its ruling of August 27, 1970:

According to Article 454 of the RSFSR Civil Code, organizations and citizens whose activity is linked with increased danger for surrounding persons (transport organizations, industrial enterprises, construction sites, owners of motor vehicles, etc.) shall be obliged to compensate harm caused by a source of increased danger if it does not prove that it arose as a consequence of insuperable force or the intention of the victim.

Voronov perished as a result of the actions of a source of increased danger, the owner of which, enterprise No. 5, is obliged to compensate the harm.

However, in accordance with Article 458 of the RSFSR Civil Code, if the gross negligence of the victim himself facilitated the origin of or the aggravation of the harm, then depending upon the extent of fault of the victim (and if the person who caused the harm is at fault, also depending upon the extent of his fault), the amount of compensation should be reduced or compensation of the harm should be refused.

It is clear from the decree terminating the criminal case that the actions of driver Maznenkov lacked the constituent elements of a crime. It was noted in the decree that Voronov, in a state of intoxication, ran into the road and the driver, seeing him only four meters from the motor vehicle, braked but could not avert the crash since the full stopping distance was 42.5 meters.

Witnesses Pinigii and Mikhailov confirmed that Voronov ran into the road in direct proximity to the motor vehicle.

Given such data, the court correctly came to the conclusion that Voronov was grossly negligent and, having determined the extent of his fault, satisfied the suit in part.

BASHLYKOV vs. GUSEV TIMBER INDUSTRY ENTERPRISE, Biulleten' Verkhovnogo Suda RSFSR, 1969, no. 8, p. 2

Mel'gunov was riding on a Voshkhod motorcycle with a passenger along the Vladimir-Gus'-Khrustal'nyi Highway. He was driving on the left hand side of the lane. Coming toward him was a freight truck ZIL-150 of the Gusev Timber Industry Enterprise driven by chauffeur Alferov. Wishing to avoid a collision with the motorcycle, Alferov drove the vehicle into a ditch and ran over Bashlykov, sitting on the edge of the road, whom he did not see. As a result, Bashlykov was caused grave bodily injuries, in connection with which he was deemed a group II invalid.

Inasmuch as the pension assigned to Bashlykov does not compensate him for earnings lost as a consequence of mutilation, he brought suit in court against the Gusev Timber Industry Enterprise and the owner of the motorcycle for compensation of harm caused by the injury to health.

The Judicial Division of the Vladimir Regional Court satisfied the suit of Bashlykov to recover compensation for harm from the Gusev Timber Industry Enterprise.

In a cassational appeal the Gusev Timber Industry Enterprise requested that the decision of the court be vacated, since Mel'gunov created the accident situation on the road. He was convicted for this in a criminal proceeding, and, therefore, should compensate the material loss suffered.

Having considered the case, the Judicial Division for Civil Cases of the RSFSR Supreme Court left the decision of the Vladimir Regional Court without change and the cassational appeal without satisfaction, citing the following in its ruling of March 10, 1969.

As established in the case, harm was caused to Bashlykov as a result of a motor vehicle belonging to the Gusev Timber Industry Enterprise running him over.

According to Article 454 of the Civil Code, an organization or citizen whose activity is connected with an increased danger for surrounding persons (transport organizations, industrial enterprises, construction sites, owners of automobiles, etc.) shall be obliged to compensate the harm caused by a source of increased danger if it does not prove that the harm arose as a consequence of insuperable force or the intention of the victim.

The owner of a source of increased danger may be relieved of liability for harm also in the event the harm was caused as a result of the creation of the accident situation by a third person.

Taking this into accont, the court correctly imposed financial liability for harm caused to Bashlykov on the Gusev Timber Industry Enterprise.

NIKOLAEV vs. RUZAEVSKII DIVISION OF THE KUIBYSHEV RAILWAY,
Biulleten' Verkhovnogo Suda RSFSR, 1970, no. 6, pp. 1–2

Nikolaev brought suit against the Ruzaevskii Division of the Kuibyshev Railway for compensation of loss caused by mutilation. In justification of his claims Nikolaev pointed out that on November 27, 1965, he was riding as a passenger in the city of Orenburg. At Sura Station of the Kuibyshev Railway he left the car during the train stop, and when getting back on the car of the already moving train he slipped and fell under the wheels, as a result of which he received injuries. After treatment he at first was deemed a first group invalid, and subsequently a second group with loss of 100% general and professional capacity to work. A pension has been assigned to him at present and is paid in the amount of 51 rubles, 26 kopecks per month. His average earnings before the accident amounted to 166 rubles per month.

[The Pskov City Court satisfied the suit and awarded Nikolaev 54 rubles, 74 kopecks monthly. Both the Judicial Division of the Pskov Regional Court and its Presidium left the procurator's protest against the decision without satisfaction. The Judicial Division for Civil Cases of the RSFSR Supreme Court accepted the procuratorial protest and vacated all previous decisions and decrees, sending the case for new consideration. In its ruling of November 20, 1969, the Court indicated:]

In accordance with Article 458 of the RSFSR Civil Code, if the gross negligence of the victim himself facilitated the origin or the aggravation of the harm, then depending on the extent of the victim's fault the amount of compensation should be reduced or compensation of the harm should be refused.

The people's court, in deciding the dispute, did not discuss the question of the presence or absence of gross negligence in the actions of the victim himself. The Judicial Division and the presidium of the regional court did not see gross negligence in Nikolaev's actions. It is clear from the materials of the case that Nikolaev, in riding on the railway train and leaving the car during the stop at Sura Station, endeavored to get back on the car of a train already moving but slipped and fell under the wheels. His endeavor to board a moving train cannot be anything other than gross negligence. Therefore, the reference of the judicial division and presidium of the regional court to the fact that there was no gross negligence in Nikolaev's actions but was simply imprudence does not correspond to the data in the file of the case concerning the occurrence of the accident.

In the new consideration of the suit the court shall take proper account of the foregoing and investigate more carefully the materials of the case. Depending on the information established in the case, the court should discuss the question of the extent of Nikolaev's fault in causing the accident, and the application of mixed liability.

Moreover, the court should have in view that the opinion of a forensic medical expert is absent in the file of the case concerning the extent to which Nikolaev has lost general and professional capacity to work.

The VTEK establishes loss of capacity to work only for workers and employees who have been maimed or otherwise injured in health in connection with the Rules confirmed by decree of the State Committee of the USSR Council of Ministers for Labor and Wages and the Presidium of the All-Union Central Council of Trade Unions of December 22, 1961.

SEREBRIANNIKOV vs. KRASNOE STATE FARM, Biulleten' Verkhovnogo Suda RSFSR, 1969, no. 10, p. 2

On July 21, 1967, house no. 15 on Sovetskii Street in the village of Novosel'e, Strugokrasnenskii District, Pskov Region, the household property, and livestock belonging to Serebriannikov burned. Considering that the Krasnoe State Farm, Strugokrasnenskii District, was at fault in the origin of the fire, Serebriannikov brought suit to recover 5323 rubles in compensation of the damage caused by the fire.

Serebriannikov's suit was justified by the fact that the Krasnoe State Farm, being the owner of low-voltage and high-voltage electric transmission lines, maintained them in an improper state. As a result of violations of the requirements of clearance space where the lines cross, there occurred a locking of the high-tension lines (10,000 volts) with the low voltage lines (220 volts), which resulted in increasing the current in the low-voltage lines; the electric wiring in the house catching fire, and a fire. In support of these conclusions, the plaintiff pointed to the fact that as a result of the improper maintenance of the low-voltage lines there were fires in a number of other houses of the settlement.

The case was considered by various judicial instances.

In a subsequent consideration of the case by the Pskov Regional Court plaintiff Serebriannikov reduced his claim to 5622 rubles, taking into account the extent of depreciation in value of the destroyed items as the result of wear.

The representative of the Krasnoe State Farm objected to the suit, referring to the fact that the fire in the plaintiff's house originated in switched on electric wires left without supervision and not from the poor state of the electric lines. The Pskov Regional Court rejected the suit.

The Judicial Division for Civil Cases of the RSFSR Supreme Court by a ruling of May 22, 1969, left the decision of the regional court without change and Serebriannikov's appeal without satisfaction on the following grounds.

According to Article 454 of the RSFSR Civil Code . . .

However, the said rule does not relieve the plaintiff from the duty to prove that harm was caused to him by that person whom he has sued.

Witnesses interrogated by the court, who by the nature of their work had a relationship to the use of the electric lines of the state farm or who lived near them, testified that they were not eyewitnesses of the locking of the high- and low-voltage lines. There were no instances of the burning of overhead cables of electric transmission lines, and these cables have no traces of locking at the place where the two lines cross.

Forensic electrical and fire experts established that the fire in Serebriannikov's house could not occur from a locking of high- and low-voltage lines since there was no locking. This conclusion of the experts was confirmed in court. The specific cause of the fire the experts did not succeed in establishing because of the time since the fire itself and because of the superficial initial investigation of the causes of its origin.

Inasmuch as it was not proved by the plaintiff that the house burned because of the poor state of the low-voltage electric transmission line, the court correctly rejected the suit.

Certain violations allowed by the Krasnoe State Farm in the installation and use of electric transmission lines in the village of Novosel'e, as the court established, were not the cause of the fire. Other fires in the village since July 21, 1967, arose for reasons not connected with the use by the state farm of the electric transmission lines.

KISELEVA vs. TYDINSKII MOTOR TRANSPORT DEPOT, Biulleten' Verkhovnogo Suda RSFSR, 1969, no. 5, pp. 4–5

Kiseleva brought suit against the Tyndinskii Motor Transport Depot "Aiamtrans" for compensation of damage caused by the loss of a breadwinner. In justification of the suit she referred to the fact that her husband Kiselev perished in an automobile accident while on an official business trip to Iakutsk, on June 30, 1967. Two minor children were dependent on Kiselev, for the support of which a pension is assigned at present in the amount of 53 rubles. Believing that the death of the husband occured through the fault of the administration of the depot, Kiselev requested that compensation for the harm caused be recovered from the depot.

[The people's court found for the plaintiff, recovering a single payment of 244 rubles and monthly payments of 60 rubles to support the two children. On cassational appeal, the Judicial Division for Civil Cases of the Amur Regional Court modified the period for exaction of the compensation, fixed by the lower court at 60 rubles monthly from January 1, 1968, until the children were sixteen years old or, if studying, until 18 years old. Reviewing the case upon the protest of the RSFSR Deputy Procurator, the Judicial Division for Civil Cases of the RSFSR Supreme Court vacated all previous decisions and rulings and returned the case for new consideration]:

In accordance with Article 460 of the RSFSR Civil Code . . .

In satisfying the suit of Kiseleva, the people's court referred to the fact that the accident with her husband occurred both through the fault of the defendant and the fault of the victim himself; therefore the principle of joint liability applied.

However, the conclusion of the court regarding joint fault does not follow from the materials of the case. Kiselev worked as a chauffeur for the Tyndinksii Motor Transport Depot "Aiamtrans". On June 30, 1967, being on a business trip in Iakutsk and driving an automobile in a state of intoxication, he exceeded the speed limit, did not manage the wheel, drove into the ditch, where the automobile overturned. In the accident which occurred, Kiselev perished and also a passenger, Popov, riding in the car.

Thus, the cause of Kiselev's death was the flagrant violation by him of the Traffic Rules on Streets of Cities, Populated Points, and Roads of the USSR.

There is no fault of the administration of the motor transport depot in the present accident. The reference of the court in the protocol of the highway-transport accident, in which the indirect persons at fault in the accident supposedly are officials of the motor transport depot for not taking measures to strengthen labor discipline of transport drivers, cannot serve as grounds for imposing the duty to compensate harm on the Tyndinskii Motor Transport Depot "Aiamtrans". Chauffeurs are categorically prohibited from using alcoholic beverages when driving an automobile. Knowing this, Kiselev, while on a business trip, deliberately flouting the established rules, sat at the wheel in a state of intoxication and had an accident. The motor transport depot, naturally, cannot be obliged to compensate the harm which ensued in connection with the given accident while Kiselev was in a state of intoxication on a business trip. Facts are not established in the materials of the case which would testify to shortcomings of the administration of the motor transport depot in work with cadres.

C. Employment-related injuries

CIVIL CODE, RSFSR (1964)
Article 445. *Liability of an Organization for Harm Caused by the Fault of its Workers*

An organization shall be obliged to compensate harm caused by the fault of its workers during the performance by them of their labor (or official) duties.

Article 460. *Liability for Injury to Health and for Death of a Citizen for Whom the Person Who Has Caused the Harm is Obliged to Pay Insurance Premiums*

If a worker in connection with the performance by him of his labor (or official) duties is caused mutilation or other injury to health by the fault of the organization or citizen obliged to pay premiums for state social insurance for him, this organization or citizen should compensate the victim for the harm in that part exceeding the amount of benefit received by him or assigned to him after the injury to his health and the pension actually received by him. Exceptions from this rule may be established by USSR legislation.

In the event of the death of the victim, the right to compensation for harm shall appertain to persons unable to work who were dependent on the deceased or had on the day of his death the right to receive support from him, as well as a child of the deceased born after his death. The harm shall be compensated to the said persons to the extent of the share of the earnings of the victim which they received or had the right to receive for their support during his life.

Harm shall be compensated to:

minors—until attaining sixteen years of age, and students, to eighteen years;

women more than fifty-five years old and men more than sixty years old—for life;

invalids—for the period of disability;

spouse or parent of the deceased irrespective of age and capacity to work, who are not working and who are engaged in caring for children, grandchildren, brothers, or sisters of the deceased who have not attained eight years of age—until the attainment by them of eight years of age.

Article 461. *Liability for Injury to Health and Death of a Citizen for Whom the Person Who Has Caused the Harm is not Obliged to Pay Insurance Premiums*

If mutilation or other injury to health is caused to a citizen who is subject to state social insurance by an organization or citizen not obliged to pay for the victim's premiums under state social insurance, this organization or citizen should compensate the victim for the harm according to the rules of Articles 444, 445, and 454 of the present Code in that part exceeding the amount of benefits received by him or the pension assigned to him after the injury to his health and in fact received by him.

In the event of the death of the victim, the right of compensation for harm shall appertain to the citizens specified in the second paragraph of Article 460 of the present Code within the amounts established by this paragraph and for the periods provided for by paragraph three of the same Article.

LABOR CODE, RSFSR (1972)

Article 159. *Financial Liability of Enterprises, Institutions, Organizations for Damage Caused to Workers and Employees by Injury to their Health*

Enterprises, institutions, and organizations shall bear financial liability in accordance with USSR and RSFSR legislation for damage caused to workers and employees by mutilation or other injury to health connected with the performance by them of their labor duties.

Article 236. *Extension of Social Insurance to All Workers and Employees*

All workers and employees shall be subject to compulsory state social insurance.

Article 237. *Social Insurance Funds*

State social insurance of workers and employees shall be effectuated at the expense of the state.

Premiums for social insurance shall be paid by enterprises, institutions, and organizations without any deductions from the earnings of workers and employees. The failure of an enterprise, institution, or organization to pay insurance premiums shall not deprive workers and employees of the right to security under state social insurance.

Article 243. *Pensions for Disability and in the Event of the Death of a Breadwinner.*

Pensions for disability and in the event of the death of breadwinner shall be assigned when the disability of a worker or the death of a breadwinner occurred as a consequence of labor mutilation, professional illness, general illness or mutilation not connected with work.

"ARBITRATION PRACTICE," Sovetskaia iustitsiia, 1975, no. 8, p. cover

The Iaroslavl' Regional Social Security Section brought suit against the Novoiaroslavl' Station in State Arbitrazh attached to the Executive Committee of the Iaroslavl' Regional Soviet of Working People's Deputies for the recovery of 643 rubles, 86 kopecks by way of a recourse claim, the amount of a pension paid for the loss of a breadwinner. The defendant considered that its liability to the social security agencies should be fixed at 30% of the amount of the suit, since the joint fault established by the court was the victim (70%) and the station (30%). The social security section insisted on compensation for the full amount, supposing that the station is obliged by way of a recourse suit to compensate the entire amount of the pension irrespective of whose fault the accident occurred.

By a decision of State Arbitrazh the suit was satisfied in the amount of 433 rubles, 91 kopecks. The remaining portion of the suit was rejected because the period of limitations has passed; *i.e.*, state arbitrazh proceeding from the fact that the amount in dispute is subject to compensation in full irrespective of the fact that the joint fault of the victim and the station was established.

State Arbitrazh RSFSR verified the correctness of the decision adopted by way of supervision at the application of the station. The verification showed that by the decision of the Krasnoperekopskii District People's Court in the city of Iaroslavl' the joint fault (the victim, 70%; the station, 30%) was established in the occurrence of the accident. Article 94 of the Fundamental Principles of Civil Legislation establishes that an organization liable for harm caused shall be obliged by a recourse claim of a state social insurance agency or social security agency to compensate the amount of the benefits or pensions which are paid by them. In instances when the amount of compensation for harm is reduced, the amount of compensation under the recourse claim also is to be reduced repectively. Consequently, the suit of the social security section was subject to satisfaction within the limits of the period of limitations in the amount of 30% of the claim, *e.g.*, 130 rubles, 17 kopecks.

By decree of the Deputy Chief Arbitrator of State Arbitrazh RSFSR, the decision in the case was modified. The suit was satisfied in the amount of 130 rubles, 17 kopecks, and the remaining part of the suit rejected.

NEPOMNIASHCHII vs. CORRECTIONAL LABOR CAMP, Biulleten' Verkhovnogo Suda RSFSR, 1973, no 8, pp. 3–4

By a judgment of the Petropavlovsk City People's Court of August 13, 1966, Nepomniashchii was sentenced under Article 206, paragraph 2, of the RSFSR Criminal Code to deprivation of freedom. In serving the sentence, he worked from September 26, 1970, in a shop. On October 13, 1970, at night, Nepomniashchii fell into an open cell not having a guard and received an injury to his left hand. In connection with the injury he was treated in a hospital from October 14, 1970 to

January 25, 1971, and until November 4, 1971, there was established for him a second, and then a third; group disability.

On April 10, 1972, Nepomniashchii was released from the place of confinement according to an act of pardon and brought suit for compensation of harm. It was acknowledged by the opinion of a technical expert that the plaintiff's accident occurred through the fault of the enterprise. In the opinion of the medical-labor expert commission the plaintiff lost 20% of ordinary and 40% of professional capacity to work.

The Kamchatka Regional Court satisfied Nepomniashchii's suit partially, recovering to his benefit a single payment, 234 rubles, and from January 1 to May 23, 1973, 32 rubles, 63 kopecks monthly for loss of earnings.

In a cassational appeal Nepomniashchii requested that the decision of the court be modified, referring to the fact that the compensation for harm was subject to recovery from the date the harm was caused and not from the moment of release from the place of deprivation of freedom, as the court decided. Moreover, the plaintiff believed the court had incorrectly determined the average earnings and consequently the amount of payments recovered.

The Judicial Division for Civil Cases of the RSFSR Supreme Court by a ruling of February 7, 1973, left the decision without change on the following grounds.

According to Article 42 of the RSFSR Correctional Labor Code, persons who have lost the capacity to work while serving a sentence shall, after release, have the right to a pension and to compensation for harm.

Nepomniashchii was released from a place of deprivation of freedom on April 10, 1972, His accident occurred while serving a sentence. Therefore, the court justifiably came to the conclusion to recover for the benefit of the plaintiff compensation for harm caused from April 10, 1972.

The arguments of the plaintiff in the appeal concerning recovery for his benefit of payments from the date the harm was caused are not based on law.

In accordance with the requirements of point 12 of the Rules for Compensation by Enterprises, Institutions, and Organizations of Damage Caused to Workers and Employees by Mutilation or Other Injury to Health Connected with Their Work, the average monthly earnings for determining the extent of compensation for damage shall be taken from the twelve calendar months preceding the mutilation, excluding months during which the worker worked an incomplete number of days.

Taking into consideration the document in the file of the case, the court took note of the earnings of the plaintiff for 12 complete calendar months preceding the accident, which came to 978 rubles, 86 kopecks, making an average monthly earnings of 81 rubles, 57 kopecks.

The plaintiff having lost 40% of professional capacity to work, the damage subject to recovery to the benefit of the plaintiff was determined to the extent of 32 rubles, 63 kopecks monthly from April 10, 1972.

UGREVATYI vs. NARVA AUTOBUS-TAXI MOTOR POOL, Biulleten' Verkhovnogo Suda SSSR, 1973, no. 5, pp. 27–29

P. M. Ugrevatyi worked as a chauffeur of an autobus at the Narva Autobus-Taxi Motor Pool (ATP) and served the inter-city route No. 4, Narva-Ivangorod.

On March 30, 1968, while driving in Ivangorod on Pastorov Street, the autobus struck a large hummock and the wheel broke loose from the hands of the chauffeur Ugrevatyi; and when he began to straighten it out, he received a blow from the spoke of the steering wheel on the palm of his left hand. This injury led to a paralysis of the shoulder joint with a sharp limitation of mobility. As a result of the injury received, Ugrevatyi was deemed a third group invalid from January 31, 1969, to May 20, 1970, with a loss of professional capacity of work of 50%, and he was assigned a pension of 30 rubles, 13 kopecks, per month. Later the payment of the pension was terminated, since the disability group had not been determined for Ugrevatyi; however, in the opinion of the VTEK he had lost 20% of professional capacity to work.

Ugrevatyi was transferred to light work, his earnings were reduced, and he claimed compensation for harm against the administration of the Narva ATP. Inasmuch as this was denied him, he turned to the local trade union, which obliged the administration to compensate the harm caused.

At the petition of the Autobus-Taxi Motor Pool, this question was brought to a people's court for consideration.

The case was considered repeatedly in the courts.

The Narva City People's Court on August 17, 1971, obliged the defendant to compensate Ugrevatyi for the harm, to pay him a single payment of 932 rubles, 54 kopecks, and from May 1971 to January 1972 to pay 32 rubles, 15 kopecks per month, having granted the right for payment of amounts exceeding 160 rubles, 15 kopecks per month (the average monthly earnings of the victim before the injury).

The Judicial Division for Civil Cases of the Estonian Supreme Court on September 14, 1971, vacated this decision, having accepted the case for hearing.

Having considered the case on October 14, 1971, the Judicial Division for Civil Cases of the Estonian Supreme Court rejected the suit, reasoning that the autobus was sent on its route in a proper state and that the pool administration should not bear liability for the state of the road.

The Deputy Chairman of the USSR Supreme Court brought a protest to the Judicial Division for Civil Cases of the USSR Supreme Court to vacate the cassational ruling of the Judicial Division for Civil Cases of the Estonian Supreme Court of September 14, 1971, the decision of this division of October 14, 1971, and to leave in force the decision of the Narva City People's Court of August 17, 1971, which had satisfied Ugrevatyi's suit.

Having considered the materials of the case, the Judicial Division for Civil Cases of the USSR Supreme Court has satisfied the protest.

It is clear from the materials of the case that route No. 4, which the autobus driven by the plaintiff followed, had segments of road dangerous for travel, and this was known to the ATP administration.

In the file of the case is a document drawn up on February 8, 1968 (less than two months before the accident) by a competent commission with the participation of the chairman of the Narva ATP, a traffic safety engineer. It is said in the document that the thoroughfare of Pastorov Street was ice-covered with deep pot-holes, as a result of which transport was being smashed to pieces. This gives rise to a threat of collision with on-coming transport and could lead to human casualties. The commission came to the conclusion that the route should be closed until this part of the thoroughfare was put in a proper state.

Thus, the administration of the autobus-taxi motor pool knew that the bus route on Pastorov Street was dangerous and should be changed until the street was put in a state suitable for travel. This also is confirmed by testimony of the representative of the defendant in the judicial session that the administration raised the question with the executive committee to curtail traffic on the dangerous part of the road. Route No. 4 was curtailed only for a brief time, and despite the fact that the road was not repaired, the pool administration began anew to send autobuses on the former route, subjecting the drivers of the autobuses and the passengers to danger.

Chauffeurs Gorvunov and Kezonen, who had worked on route No. 4, testified in the judicial session on July 29, 1971, that the road on the Ivangorod side was in a poor state also in the month of March—pot-holes and pockets, and local buses did not travel on dangerous parts of the road. Autobuses of the Narva ATP frequently broke down on route No. 4, and the chauffeurs declared to the administration that it was necessary to shut down route No. 4 and not travel on Pastorov Street, but only after Ugrevatyi's accident occurred was the route changed.

Witness Bleshchenko, a people's controller of the Narva ATP, testified that the road to Ivangorod was in a neglected state, required repair, and he, with a safety engineer, repeatedly drew up documents with the participation of the State Motor Vehicle Inspectorate regarding the need to take measures for the repair of the road to avoid accidents.

It follows from this that in sending autobus driver Ugrevatyi on a route where parts of the road were in a poor state the administration of the Narva ATP placed the victim in dangerous labor conditions.

All the above facts were acknowledged as established by the judicial division for civil cases of the Estonian Supreme Court and the people's court.

In justification of its decision, the judicial division of the Estonian Supreme Court pointed out that putting the road in order is not a duty of the ATP. However, the judicial division did not take account that the administration of any enterprise in accordance with Article 57 of the Fundamental Principles of the USSR and Union Republics on Labor is obliged to ensure safe labor conditions for its workers.

The Judicial Division for Civil Cases of the USSR Supreme Court under these circumstances came to the conclusion that the decision of the Narva City People's

Court of August 17, 1971, to satisfy Ugrevatyi's suit was rendered in accordance with the materials of the case and Article 464 of the Estonian Civil Code.

RULES FOR COMPENSATION BY ENTERPRISES, INSTITUTIONS, AND ORGANIZATIONS OF DAMAGE CAUSED TO WORKERS AND EMPLOYEES BY MUTILATION OR OTHER INJURY TO HEALTH CONNECTED WITH THEIR WORK, Confirmed by Decree of the State Committee of the USSR Council of Ministers for Labor and Wages and the Presidium of the All-Union Central Council of Trade Unions, December 22, 1961. Biulleten' Gosudarstvennogo Komiteta Soveta Ministrov SSSR po voprosam truda i zarabotnoi platy, 1962, no. 1; 1963, no. 10

I. General Provisions

1. Enterprises, institutions, and organizations shall bear financial liability for damage caused to workers and employees by mutilation or other injury to health connected with their work and which occurred:
    (a) on the territory of the enterprise, institution, and organization;
    (b) outside the territory of the enterprise, institution, and organization during the fulfillment by them of their labor duties, as well as during travel to the place of work and from work on transport of the enterprise, institution, and organization.

Such liability shall ensue if the mutilation or other injury to health of the worker or employee occurred by the fault of the enterprise, institution, or organization.

2. The fault of an enterprise, institution, and organization in causing mutilation or other injury to health to the worker or employee connected with his work shall be established taking into account the specific facts and available evidence regarding each instance. Such evidence, in particular, shall include:
    (a) a document concerning the accident connected with production;
    (b) an accusatory judgment of a court;
    (c) a decree of investigative agencies or a court terminating a criminal case because of its insignificance or in connection with an act of amnesty;
    (d) a decree imposing an administrative exaction (or fine) by agencies (or officials) exercising control and supervision over the state of labor protection, or the opinion of such agencies (or officials) concerning the causes of the mutilation or other injury to health;
    (e) an order imposing a disciplinary sanction on specific persons at fault in the particular mutilation or other injury to health;
    (f) a decree of a factory, plant, or local trade union committee concerning compensation of expenses by the enterprise, institution, or organization to the state social insurance budget for payment to a worker or employee of a benefit for temporary incapacity to work in connection with labor mutilation or professional illness.

3. Compensation of damage shall consist of the payment to the victim of a sum of money to the extent of the earnings of which he was deprived as a consequence of the loss of capacity to work from the given mutilation or other injury to health.

In instances when the victim in connection with the mutilation or other injury to health is temporarily transferred to lower-paid work, the difference between the former earnings and the new earnings for the lower-paid work shall be paid to him until the moment the capacity to work is restored or disability is established.

4. In addition to compensation for lost earnings, an enterprise, institution, or organization shall compensate the victim also for expenses for his care, for a supplemental diet, prosthetics and sanatorium or resort treatment (including travel fares), and other expenses if it is deemed necessary by the medical-labor expert commission in such types of assistance in connection with the particular injury to health and is not received free of charge from the respective enterprise, institution, or organization.

An opinion on the need for care is not required for victims deemed by a medical labor expert commission to be group I invalids.

5. In those instances when the mutilation or other injury to health of a worker was a result not only of the failure of the administration of the enterprise, institution, or organization to ensure safe labor conditions, but also the gross negligence of the worker himself (for example, flagrant violation by a worker of safety with which he is familiar), joint liability shall be applied.

Under joint liability the extent of compensation shall be determined by taking into account the specific facts of the case, depending on the degree of fault of the administration and the victim. The degree of fault of the victim (in percentages) shall be established by the administration, taking into account the opinions of the labor protection commission of the factory, plant, and local trade union committee.

D. *Liability for Injury to Rescuers*

CIVIL CODE, RSFSR (1964)
Article 472. *Compensation of Harm Sustained When Saving Socialist Property*

Harm sustained by a citizen when saving socialist property from a danger threatening it should be compensated by that organization whose property was saved by the victim.

The rules of Article 444, paragraph one, Articles 455, 457, 459, 460, paragraphs two and three, 461, 462, and 464-471 of the present Code shall apply respectively to compensation of such harm.

P. Stavisskii, "MUZHESTVO I ZAKON," [Courage and the Law], Izvestia, March 30, 1971, p. 3

The reader may possibly recall the question raised [in a previous issue] about the need to compensate a citizen (and if he perished, his family) for financial loss sustained by him when saving the life and health of another person. Civil legislation does not evade this issue in silence, but in legal practice a mass of difficulties arise which require resolution: when is it appropriate to compensate such loss? Without entering into a polemic of a theoretical character, I shall tell you how this was resolved by a court in one specific instance.

Filipp Aleksandrovich Poltavskii worked at the port in the city of Reni in the routine unloading of a ship. Returning from work, he heard a child's cry. At the corner of Ovrazhnaia and Zelenaia Streets a torn electric cable dangled from the pole to the ground. At night there had been a strong rain (and even now it drizzled). In a puddle stood a five-year old girl in swimming trunks and around her bare feet, like a snake, the electric cable. It was decided instantaneously. Poltavskii jumped from his bicycle and threw the child clear. Threw her from death . . .

Everything happened so quickly that a man passing nearby did not even see what was the matter. He only noted how Poltavskii threw the child aside and how next they both fell. Both were unconscious. People came running, found a dry stick, and threw the cable aside. Then the ambulance arrived.

Vitia Kukobnikov quickly regained consciousness in the hospital; only the burns from the cable remained on her legs below the knees. Filipp Poltavskii was given artificial respiration for a long time; no one wanted to believe he had passed away.

The entire port buried Poltavskii. Here, in Reni, he was born and grew up, here he studied. From here he went into the army and from there, following the example of his father, an old port hand, returned after army service, became a crane operator 1st class, headed the crew of a large port crane. He was an excellent worker, a good and loving father.

Elena Efimovna Poltavskaia was left alone with three children. She wrote a letter to the management of the Izmail Electric Grid District requesting compensation for the children for the lost earnings of a breadwinner. A refusal followed. In the name of the minor children, she brought suit in court against the electric grid district.

The Division for Civil Cases of the Odessa Regional Court is on circuit in Reni. The defendant does not acknowledge the suit: Poltavskii apparently violated flagrantly the safety rules; he knew that "one should never have direct contact with a bare cable of phased voltage . . . and took the cable with his bare hands". So, Poltavskii was supposed to come running with rubber gloves! . . .

Meanwhile, the court hears eyewitnesses of the accident and the mother of the rescued Vitia. Then the chief technical inspector of the Odessa Trade Union Council gives an opinion. He calls the attention of the judges to the flagrant violations of the rules for maintaining the electric lines: there was not, in particular, secondary grounding; the branches of trees growing along the line had not been trimmed in good time, etc. All this led to the breaking of the cable, created a threat for the life of people. The social representative who spoke at the judicial session transmitted to the court a protocol of a general meeting of the port workers. The collective requested that the suit of Poltavskii's family be satisfied, stressing the courage and selflessness he manifested in fulfilling his civic duty.

The court adjourned for a meeting. And we ponder: what decision most fully responds to the principles of Soviet justice?

It is not easy to render a decision regarding this case. It only seems simple and clear. It encompasses several legal problems. Not perfunctorily did the Judicial Division for Civil Cases of the Moscow Regional Court reject the suit of Valentin Suroviatkin . . . Suroviatkin, who while saving a drowning person, himself suffered and became an invalid. The Moscow Regional Court did not consider it possible to impose the duty of compensating the loss on the state farm which had not secured the safety of bathers in a pond belonging to it, and the basic reason for rejecting the suit was that compensation for harm sustained when saving the life of a person was not provided for by law. Such a norm there is not, and the true way out of the situation would be to adopt an appropriate norm. But what to do now?

First of all, in deciding the suit of Poltavskii's widow the court had to decide: could it, without violation of prevailing legislation, in the absence of a norm expressly regulating the relations which had come into being, compensate the harm sustained when saving a person? It seems to us there is such a possibility. Our conclusion is based first on the general moral and social criteria of Soviet laws. In throwing oneself to the aid of a person who has fallen into misfortune, a citizen fulfills his duty. Poltavskii performed an heroic deed in exceptional circumstances. Being an electrician, he could not but understand that rubber gloves, a dry object, or at least a dry coat are necessary. But there were none of these. His shirt, and this was wet from the rain. To run for a stick or a board? One careless move of the child, and he is dead. And Poltavskii made the decision, knowing the degree of risk. He rescued another's child, and three of his own remain orphans. Proceeding from the fact that Poltavskii's actions in rescuing a person correspond to the principles of Soviet legislation, and leaving those who suffered without compensation for loss sustained is contrary to these principles, the question may be resolved on the basis of prevailing legislation.

Article 4 of the Ukrainian SSR Civil Code provides that "civil rights and duties arise on the grounds provided by legislation of the USSR and Ukrainian SSR, as well as from actions of citizens and organizations which, although not provided by law, but by virtue of general principles and the meaning of civil legislation give rise to civil rights and duties."

On the basis of this article the court could, applying the general principles of the legislation, use the so-called analogy of law. The way out is temporary, until the adoption of a norm regulating this circumstance, but there is one! (Incidentally, the obligations for compensating loss sustained while saving socialist property were initially recognized by judicial practice and only later received legislative regulation). And the Judicial Division of the Odessa Regional Court came to its decision in the Poltavskii case by precisely this route.

"F. A. Poltavskii perished while saving the life of a child. Article 467 of the Ukrainian SSR Civil Code provides for compensation of harm sustained while saving property. The Judicial Division considers that the more so should be compensated loss sustained by a citizen while saving a life of a person. The absence in the Civil Code of the Ukrainian SSR of an article regulating compensation of harm cannot serve as a basis for rejecting the suit. Rejection of the suit on these grounds in the opinion of the Judicial Division would be contrary to both the general norms of civil law and the principles of communist morality." After the decision in principle of the question of the necessity of compensating loss, another very complex problem faced the court. On whom should be imposed the duty to compensate the loss?

". . . the Judicial Division takes into account that the Izmail Electric Grid District did not exercise proper control over the use of the electric wires. The untimely trimming of branches of trees growing near the electric lines led to the breaking of the cable, and this created the situation constituting a threat to the life of citizens. Moreover, the cause of the accident was the absence of secondary grounding at the end of the line. The defendant's arguments that the victim himself was flagrantly negligent can not be taken into account since, having seen the real threat to a child's life, F. A. Poltavskii had neither the time nor the opportunity to take measures for personal safety."

The importance of this decision, in our view, is not settled by the particular event. In essence, a *legal precedent has been created,* because the court for the first time expressly favored compensation for harm sustained when saving the life of a person and applied clearly the analogy of law (in criminal legislation analogy is inadmissible, however it is applied in civil law) in connection with the absence of a special norm. And, finally, the court favored the view that the duty to compensate harm in the instances considered should be imposed on those at fault in creating the threat to the life of people.

CHAPTER XXII

Marriage and Divorce

The church, the mosque, and the synagogue dominated family life in pre-revolutionary Russia. Under Tsarist law the ecclesiastical law of the various denominations within the Empire governed marriage, divorce, and family responsibilities. Registration of births, marriages, and deaths was in the hands of the parishes. For the great majority of the Tsar's subjects this meant that the governing law was that of the Russian Orthodox Church, which permitted dissolution of a marriage on only the most limited grounds.[1]

---

[1] Harold J. Berman, Soviet Family Law in the Light of Russian History and Marxian Theory, 56 Yale L.J. 26 (1946).

For the Bolsheviks, with their Marxist antipathy toward religion as the opiate of the people, the influence of the ecclesiastical authorities over the family was unacceptable. Moreover, the family represented the major institution through which the traditions of the past were transmitted to future generations. If the new regime was to root out the mores and inequities of bourgeois civilization, it could not content itself with laws affecting merely the superficialities of everyday life. It would be necessary to destroy obsolete bourgeois notions of the family and the home.

The early postrevolutionary literature is replete with comments of persons who added to these political and social arguments the espousal of free love,[2] calling it the essence of communist living, with all as free as the tribal communities of the past, in which matriarchies developed because no clear line of descent from a given male could be readily determined.

Early Soviet family legislation thus aimed to redress fundamental inequities in the pre-existing social order by transforming the status of women to one of equality in the marital relationship and in political life, removing the constraints imposed by religion, relying upon childbirth as the principal family bond, and furthering economic equality through equal wages and employment opportunities.

Within one month after the revolution, the Soviet Government removed divorce from the domain of the ecclesiastical authorities by placing sole authority over dissolution of marriage in the courts.[3] No grounds had to be specified; divorce was to be had for the asking by either or both parties. The authorities evidenced a desire, however, to remain less radical than the proponents of free love, for they placed jurisdiction in the courts rather than in administrative agencies. Years later it was acknowledged that the courts were chosen because it was felt the inherited respect for courts would restrain the thoughtless from seeking a divorce more than would recourse to a less formal institution such as an administrative agency.

A concomitant decree on marriage provided that only civil marriages concluded before secular authorities would be recognized.[4] Marriages could still be celebrated by religious authorities but would have no legal effect.

In 1918 these two decrees were combined with others into a unified family code[5] which remained in effect until 1926, when various new union republic family codes liberalized the law still further.[6] Under these 1926 codes not even registration was required for either marriage or divorce. Registration was encouraged, however, to facilitate the preparation of statistics and simplification of inheritance proceedings; a *de facto* marriage could be registered retroactively to the date when cohabitation commenced. Subsequent judicial decisions permitted women with no formal marriage ties to inherit property from men with whom they had maintained the *de facto*

---

[2] Aleksandra Kollontai, Communism and the Family (1920). Translated in R. Schlesinger, Changing Attitudes in Soviet Russia: The Family (London, 1949).
[3] Decree of December 19, 1917, [1917] I Sob. Uzak. RSFSR, No. 10, item 152.
[4] Decree of December 18, 1917, [1917] I Sob. Uzak. RSFSR, No. 11, item 160.
[5] [1918] *idem,* Nos. 76–77, item 818.
[6] [1926] *idem,* No. 82, item 612.

relationship of husband and wife. This practice went so far as to permit inheritance by two women with whom a man had maintained simultaneous continuing relationships, seemingly circumventing criminal sanctions against bigamy.

In 1944, toward the end of the war, there was a significant reversal of divorce policy. In that year an all-union statute, superseding the relevant articles of the union republic family codes, prohibited a court of first instance from granting a divorce and required it to attempt to reconcile the parties, if possible, with the help of a full hearing, including testimony of witnesses.[7] Only if reconciliation was shown to be impossible could the parties proceed to the next highest court, where there would be a rehearing and a new determination. No grounds for divorce were specified in the statute. Courts therefore were free creatively to fill the gaps. This they did, taking a strict line and permitting divorce only if there appeared to be no possibility of reconciliation because of the separation of the spouses and the creation by one or both of them of new unregistered but enduring liaisons manifested in part by the birth of children.

The 1944 legislation restored the requirement that marriages be registered, which had been dropped in 1926, and provided that an unregistered marriage contracted before the date of the enactment was to have no legal effect.

As time passed there was a growing demand that divorce laws be liberalized once again. It was evident from judicial practice that divorces were for many years difficult to obtain unless there had been children of new unions. At that point legitimation of the new children was possible only if the earlier marriage was dissolved and the subsequent one permitted to be registered. In the 1950s, however, there was a change in the direction of greater willingness on the part of courts to grant divorce petitions, and the possibility of relaxing divorce requirements was discussed extensively. In 1965 the people's courts had power to grant divorces if efforts at reconciliation failed. No longer was the two-tiered procedure necessary. In addition, the people's courts were granted jurisdiction, indeed the duty, to determine all questions relating to the division of community property, alimony, and custody of children.

On October 1, 1968, the long-awaited Fundamental Principles of Legislation of the USSR and Union Republics on Marriage and the Family entered into effect. This enactment and the union republic family codes enacted pursuant thereto made two major changes in marriage and divorce which had been debated for years. A one-month waiting period after an application for registration of a marriage has been filed before the marriage can take place was introduced, and the marriage should be performed in a ceremony rather than by means of a simple registration, as previously. Some commentators believed this waiting period should be increased to as much as six months, but while the Fundamental Principles allow reduction of the period by union republic legislation, nothing is said regarding the power to increase the period; some union republic codes do allow this under certain conditions.

The major change concerning divorce was that spouses who have no minor chil-

---

[7]Decree of July 8, 1944, [1944] Ved. Verkh. Sov. SSSR, No. 37.

dren might dissolve their marriage by mutual consent through simple registration. On the basis of such registration, the divorcing spouses become entitled to a court decree dissolving their marriage three months from the date of application. Divorce by similar administrative action also is permitted in cases where one of the spouses has disappeared and been declared absent under the appropriate procedure, where one of the spouses has become incompetent, or has been sentenced to deprivation of freedom for three years or more. This provision may perhaps encourage trial marriages in which the rearing of a family is delayed until such time as the spouses feel sure that the marriage is a lasting one. Fees payable when a divorce is granted remain significant, and though not a barrier to dissolution of marriage, they too may serve as a deterrent to hasty action.

The duty of family members to maintain one another and, in the event of divorce, to pay alimony has been strengthened in the 1968 Fundamental Principles and union republic family codes. Evasion of alimony was made far more difficult with the requirement that an appropriate entry be made in an offender's passport and that officials may be penalized for failure to withhold alimony as required. Maintenance orders may be obtained by either spouse, if required, and may continue in force even after a divorce. Parents, children, and other relatives also may secure a maintenance order, and maintenance considerations may influence the division of marital property by a court.

A. Fundamental concepts of family, marriage, and divorce

CONSTITUTION OF THE USSR, December 5, 1936

Art. 14. The competence of the Union of Soviet Socialist Republics as represented by its highest agencies of state power and agencies of state administration shall embrace:

(w) the establishment of fundamental principles of legislation on marriage and the family;

Art. 122. In the USSR women shall be granted equal rights with men in all domains of economic, state, cultural, and socio-political life.

The possibility of exercising these rights of women shall be guaranteed by providing women with an equal right with men to labor, payment for labor, rest and leisure, social insurance, and education, by state protection of the interests of mother and child, by state aid to mothers with many children and to unmarried mothers, by providing holidays for women during pregnancy while retaining maintenance, and by an extensive network of maternity homes, day nurseries, and kindergartens.

CODE ON MARRIAGE AND THE FAMILY, RSFSR (1969)

Concern for the Soviet family, in which the social and personal interests of citizens are harmoniously combined, is one of the most important tasks of the Soviet state.

The most favorable conditions for the strengthening and flourishing of the family have been created in the Soviet Union, of which the Russian Soviet Federated Socialist Republic is a member on the basis of voluntary union and equality with the other union republics. The material well-being of citizens is growing steadily, and the housing and cultural conditions of life for the family are improving. Socialist society devotes great attention to the protection and encouragement of motherhood and to ensuring a happy childhood.

A communist upbringing for the growing generation and the development of its physical and spiritual forces are the most important duty of the family. The state and society help in every possible way the family in the upbringing of children, and the network of kindergartens, day nurseries, boarding schools, and other children's institutions is expanding.

The necessary social and domestic conditions are provided to Soviet woman in order to combine a happy motherhood with an ever more active and creative participation in production and socio-political life.

Soviet legislation on marriage and the family is called upon actively to promote the final cleansing of family relations from material calculations, to eliminate the remnants of the unequal status of women in daily life, and to create a communist family in which the deepest personal feelings of people find their complete satisfaction.

Section I. General Provisions

Article 1. *The Tasks of the RSFSR Code on Marriage and the Family*

The tasks of the Code on Marriage and the Family of the Russian Soviet Federated Soviet Republic shall be:

the further strengthening of the Soviet family based on principles of communist morality;

the structuring of family relations on a voluntary marital union of a woman and a man on feelings of mutual love free from material calculations and of friendship and respect for all family members;

the bringing up of children of the family in an organic union with social nurturing in a spirit of devotion to the Motherland, of a communist attitude toward labor, and of training children actively to participate in the construction of a communist society;

all possible protection of the interests of the mother and children and ensuring a happy childhood to each child;

the final elimination of harmful survivals and customs of the past in family relations;

nurturing a feeling of responsibility toward the family.

Article 2. *Relations Regulated by the RSFSR Code on Marriage and the Family*

The present Code shall, in accordance with the Fundamental Principles of Legislation of the USSR and Union Republics on Marriage and the Family, establish the procedure and conditions of entry into marriage between spouses, between parents and children, between other family members, relations arising in connection with adoption, guardianship, and curatorship, the adoption of children for upbringing, the procedure and conditions for the termination of marriage, and the procedure for the registration of acts of civil status.

Article 3. *Equality of Women and Men in Family Relations*

The woman and man shall have equal personal and property rights in family relations.

Equality of rights in the family shall be based on the equal rights of a woman with a man consolidated by the USSR Constitution and RSFSR Constitution in all domains of state, socio-political, economic, and cultural life of the country.

Article 4. *Equality of Citizens in Family Relations Irrespective of Their Nationality, Race, or Attitude Toward Religion*

All citizens, irrespective of nationality, race, and attitude toward religion, shall have equal rights in family relations.

Any direct or indirect limitation of rights or the establishment of express or indirect privileges when entering into a marriage or family relations dependent on national or racial affiliation or attitude toward religion shall not be permitted.

Article 5. *Protection and Encouragement of Motherhood*

Motherhood in the RSFSR, just as in the entire Soviet Union, shall be honored and respected by all the people and shall be protected and encouraged by the state.

The protection of the interests of mother and child shall be ensured by the organization of a broad network of maternity homes, children's day nurseries and kindergartens, boarding schools, and other children's institutions, by granting to a woman leave for pregnancy and birth while retaining maintenance, by establishing privileges for pregnant women and mothers, protection of labor in production, the payment of state benefits to mothers of one child or many children, as well as other state and social assistance to the family.

Article 6. *Legal Regulation of Marriage and Family Relations by the State*

Legal regulation of marriage and family relations in the RSFSR shall be exercised only by the state.

A marriage concluded only in state agencies for the registry of acts of civil status shall be recognized. A religious marriage rite, just as other religious rites, shall have no legal significance.

This rule shall not appertain to religious rites performed before the formation or restoration of Soviet agencies of acts of civil status or to documents concerning birth, the conclusion of a marriage, dissolution of a marriage, and death obtained therein.

Article 7. *Legislation Concerning Marriage and the Family*

Legislation concerning marriage and the family shall consist of the Fundamental Principles of USSR and Union Republic Legislation on Marriage and the Family and other legislative acts of the USSR, the present Code, and other legislative acts of the RSFSR promulgated in accordance with them.

The present Code and other RSFSR legislation on marriage and the family shall, in accordance with the Fundamental Principles, decide questions relegated to the jurisdiction of the union republics by the Fundamental Principles, and questions of marriage and family relations not expressly provided for by the Fundamental Principles.

Article 8. *Application in the RSFSR of Legislation on Marriage and the Family*

The conclusion of a marriage in the RSFSR, relations between spouses, between parents and children, adoption, the establishment of paternity, the recovery of alimony, guardianship and curatorship, dissolution of marriage, and registration of acts of civil status shall be regulated by RSFSR legislation.

The validity of a marriage, adoption, establishment of guardianship and curatorship, and the validity of acts of civil status shall be determined by legislation of the union republic on whose territory the marriage was concluded, the adoption performed, the guardianship or curatorship established, or the act of civil status registered.

V. A. Riasentsev, SEMEINOE PRAVO [Family Law] (Moscow, 1971), 5–8, 43–46

1. Basic Tenets of Marxist-Leninist Doctrine on Marriage and the Family.

1. Marxist-Leninist doctrine on marriage and the family serves as the ideological basis of Soviet family law. The material life of society takes shape from the jointly existing aspects of social activity having varying significance: 1) production of the means of existence (food, clothing, housing, instruments of production); 2) producing another life through birth as a process of continuing the human species. The production of material benefits and means of existence are of primary, decisive significance in the life of society. The family is the social form of continuing the human species and population growth.

2. Marriage and family have undergone a number of forms in their historical development. The transition from one form to another was caused by basic changes in the mode of production. With the emergence of private ownership, of classes, and of the state, the so-called monogamous family arose. In contrast to preceding forms of family, its basis was private ownership.

In exploitative formations a characteristic feature of the family is the arbitrary, oppressed position of women. The domination of the husband is the simple consequence of his economic domination. Monogamy is observed strictly only for women. Men retain the freedom to change spouses.

However, the monogamous family has distinctive features in each of the antagonistic formations: slave-owning, feudal, and capitalist. Within the limits of a particular formation, the laboring family differs substantially from the family of the ruling class.

Bourgeois legislation strengthens the dominant position of the man in the family, his priority in personal and property relations of spouses, in questions of bringing up children, exercising guardianship over them, and so forth.

3. Within the depths of capitalist society, amongst the proletariat, is born a model

family of a new type: the socialist family. It was said even in the Communist Manifesto: "The proletariat have no property; its attitude toward the wife and children has nothing in common with bourgeois family relations." Marriages amongst the oppressed class more often are concluded freely, on the basis of love. Marital disloyalty plays an insignificant role here. Equating the man and woman in the proletarian milieu furthered the involvement of the woman and siblings of both sexes in large-scale industry, as a result of which the woman acquired a certain economic independence. However, the participation of the woman in capitalist production, where she was subjected to cruel exploitation, led to her frequently being deprived of the opportunity to have a family and to fulfill her maternal duties. At the same time, the grave conditions of life of the proletariat in capitalist society and the constant threat of unemployment and destitution give rise to an artificial restriction of child-birth, which is extremely unfavorable for the proletarian family.

4. The Soviet family as a family of a new type originates and develops on a completely different socio-economic basis from that of the bourgeois family. The essence of the bourgeois family is conditioned by private ownership, and the social nature of the Soviet family is determined ultimately by the socialist system of the economy and socialist ownership of the instruments of production. The Soviet family, together with the natural function of reproduction of human life, also has other functions: communist upbringing of children, mutual assistance of its members, and provision of the necessities of household consumption.

The Soviet family, being a link of socialist society, occupies a special place in the system of socialist societal relations.

The material aspect of the family comprises the natural biological and household consumption relations (maintaining the household, satisfying the daily requirements of family members); household consumption relations are conditioned by the character of production and distribution in socialist society. The legal, moral, and psychological relations shape the spiritual, ideological aspect of the family.

The natural biological life of the family, which determines population growth (interacting with other factors), is inextricably linked with the productive forces of society; the household consumption relations in which the family enters are chiefly the consumer cell of society, entering into the basis and not the material superstructure of society. The said nature of the family allows one to regulate within certain limits the intra-family relations, to influence the conduct of family members with the aid of legal norms. The large role of law in ensuring the development of the family under socialism is explained by this.

5. Marriage in the USSR differs fundamentally from bourgeois marriage, which is based on private ownership and financial accounts.

V.I. Lenin contrasted the proletarian civil marriage with love to the merchant, intelligentsia, peasant marriage in bourgeois society, which is frequently concluded without love, and thus is vulgar and sullied.

Marriage in the USSR is concluded, as a rule, on the basis of love for the normal spiritual and physical community and development of both spouses with a view to the birth and upbringing of children. The Soviet family is characterized by the complete equality of spouses. The liberation of women in the USSR from the authority of the father, and husband, and the attainment by her of factual equality was the result of the involvement of women in social production and their mass training in various specialities. The collective farm stratum has formed family relations within the collective farm milieu.

With the building of socialism it has become possible for the expenditure of enormous and ever growing resources for the protection of motherhood and childhood, the encouragement of childbirth, rendering aid to mothers with many children.

One of the most important tasks of socialist society is to ensure the communist upbringing of children and the normal prosperous life of the spouses themselves, without which one cannot achieve a harmonious development of the individual. Therefore, socialist society is interested in strengthening the family in every possible way. A thoughtless attitude toward marriage and children is alien to socialist ideology.

V. I. Lenin emphasized the important social character of marriage and family relations, their inextricable link with the interests of a new socialist system, and called for the entire cause of bringing up, educating, and teaching youth to be subordinated to nurturing them in communist morality. . . .

1. Concept of the Family in the Sociological and Legal Sense

1. There exist a general (sociological) and special (legal) concept of the family. The sociological understanding of the family is a *union* of persons based on marriage or kinship (or only kinship), the acceptance of children for upbringing, being characterized by a community of life, interests, and mutual concern.

In the family union are manifested moral, psychological, physiological, and household consumption links between a small group of persons which give birth to a community of their life and interests. The family union is a specific and complex social relation which includes a unique unity of various links not encountered among other social phenomena.

The family represents a social, socially organized combination of people. Its beginning is usually based on a marriage; therefore, childless marriages create a family also. Thereafter, with the birth of children, the family grows. The family where there are children together with the spouses is typical.

Parents and children form the most integrated family entity. Very close and tight family relations exist between them.

The said persons constitute the nucleus of the Soviet family. But, in addition, a family may comprise other persons, including relatives: parents and sometimes the brother or sister of the husband or wife.

From the standpoint of its social content, the family usually represents three interlocked groups of social phenomena: marriage as its basis, conjugal relations as a result of the marriage, relations between parents and children as a result of conjugal relations. Besides these most typical relations, there also are family relations between a widowed mother with her children, other relatives, and in a number of instances also between non-relatives (adoptive and adopted persons, educators, and pupils).

The temporary absence of a member of such a family does not violate the community (being drafted into the army, leaving for training, working under a contract, etc.). But in consequence of certain circumstances the said union may be terminated. This means that the particular family ceases to exist. Thus, if the spouses have in fact broken relations with each other or even created a new family with other persons, then the previous family has disintegrated. In certain instances, despite the kinship link between parent and child, a family does not arise in this sense. Thus, if a citizen even before the birth of his child has left its mother and, despite his being deemed the father of this child by a court, he avoids payment of alimony and other concerns for the child, one can not maintain that there exists a family composed of these persons; there is a family only of a mother and child.

2. In the *legal* sense, the family is a juridical link. The legal character of family relations is imparted by their being regulated by norms of law to the extent and within the limits in which the state may with the aid of binding rules influence the conduct of family members and further its development in a direction desirable for a socialist society.

A registered marriage and close kinship as legal facts are the most important legal bases for the origin of family law links. The latter may arise also apart from a registered marriage. The mother of children who is not in a registered marriage with their father forms, together with the children, a family whose legal basis is merely kinship. Family law relations may also arise in the absence of marriage and kinship; as a result of adoption of a child by an unmarried woman or unmarried man. Family law relations also may arise when children are accepted by single people for permanent upbringing as dependents, without adoption.

On the basis of the aforesaid, the Soviet family in the legal sense can be defined as the group of persons linked by rights and duties arising from marriage, kinship, adoption, or other form of accepting children for upbringing and deemed to promote the strengthening and development of family relations on the principles of communist morality.

The family as a legal link usually is preserved in the event of the actual disintegration of the family in the first meaning. Thus, in the event of the termination of a family whose spouses have actually broken relations with each other, in the legal sense of the family legal relations still exist between them since they have not dissolved the marriage with all the legal consequences arising therefrom (the right to demand financial aid, the division of jointly acquired property, the right of inheritance, the right to a pension after the death of a spouse).

Although in fact there is no family of a child with a father in the said example, the family is preserved in the juridical sense as a legal link based on kinship: the child has a right to receive upbringing, alimony, the father's surname, etc.

When Karl Marx said that divorce is the establishment of the fact that a particular marriage is a dead marriage, marriage as an actual family relationship between spouses is called the "dead marriage" and not the legal relationship between them preserved up until a divorce.

One must distinguish actual family relations and family legal relations; it is a mistake to believe that family legal relations always testify to the existence of a family.

A mother who transfers a child for upbringing to a children's institution and does not remember him for years does not form a family with him in the said sociological sense, although the family law link with the child exists. The father of a child who has never been concerned with his upbringing and has rendered him no financial support does not in fact form a family with him and his mother, even though family law relations have arisen.

Therefore, family law relations may exist not only within one family but also between individual members of various families. Thus, grown-up children form their own family, but they have duties with respect to their minor brothers and sisters who reside in other families. A husband and father in one family has family law relations with his children of a first marriage being brought up by their mother and forming a separate family.

But family relations are not always legal relations. Thus, there is the *de facto* family, for example, the cohabitation of a man and woman who are not married, who keep a common household, and not giving rise to family law relations since the *de facto* marriage not formalized in the established procedure is not regulated by norms of family law and family rights and duties do not arise for such persons.

Consequently, persons within a single family are, in the overwhelming majority of instances, linked by rights and duties, but those who have family rights and duties do not always form a single family. It presupposes the existence of a community of life and interests, which are lacking in the said instances.

E. M. Vorozheikin, PRAVOVYE OSNOVY BRAKA I SEM'I [Legal Bases of Marriage and the Family] (Moscow, 1969), 5–12

1. Functions of the Family and Legal Regulation of Family Relations

Which are the social functions of the family? As the first of these, Marx and Engels pointed to the reproduction of new life or the continuation of the species. The birth of a child in a family always is a happy event for the parents and their close relatives. But birth also is a biological act. The majority of living organisms do not have the facility to direct it. Man possesses the gift consciously to direct the biological phenomenon, the capacity to subordinate it to his will. By virtue of this, birth has ceased to be a category solely biological. It is becoming a social category. But the main point is that birth as a biological category forms the social category when one speaks of the aggregate of births . . .

In our country all conditions are present for a significant population increase: territorial, natural, economic, and political. The social system of socialism promotes best of all the all-round flourishing of the human personality.

How is the task of reproduction resolved in the Soviet family?

From 1926 to the present in our country the annual average birth-rate has declined. In 1926 there were 44 births per 1000 persons, and in 1955–59 census, 25. Loss of the number of souls in a single family goes on. According to the 1959 census, the average family was 3.7 souls. Consequently, for one married couple, 1.7 children. Now this figure has become still lower. The view that two children per family would fully resolve the task of maintaining the population at the same level is incorrect. Economists and demographers believe that to support the existing population even in conditions of a low death-rate, there must be not two children, but 2.7 or 270 children per 100 married couples. Otherwise, the population will systematically decline . . .

Legislative measures also may materially influence the regulation of the birth-rate in the family in the necessary direction. They are used by the state. For example, the establishment of a tax on single persons and small families had the purpose of stimulating the birth-rate in the postwar period. The honorary titles and governmental awards introduced by law for mothers with many children also had the task of partially resolving the problem. The significant improvement of regulating family relations in the Fundamental Principles also will give results. This especially appertains to such institutes of family law as the possibility of establishing paternity by the joint consent of the spouses or through a court, subsequently recovering assets for maintenance of the child and others . . .

Here one must take into account as well the fact that disputes arising out of family marital relations comprise a significant number of cases in courts of the total number of civil law disputes. In 1967 they amounted to more than half of the civil cases brought to court. Among them: 30.6% for the dissolution of marriage; 22.8% for recovery of alimony for children; 2.5% for the recovery of financial support for other relatives. In addition, legal facts arising out of family relations (dependence, kinship relations, and others) were established in a judicial proceeding.

B. Marriage

CODE ON MARRIAGE AND THE FAMILY, RSFSR (1969)

Article 13. *Conclusion of a Marriage*

A marriage shall be concluded in state agencies for the registry of acts of civil status.

The registration of a marriage shall be established both in the interests of the state and society and also with a view to protection of the personal and property rights and interests of spouses and children.

Article 14. *Procedure for Conclusion of a Marriage*

The conclusion of a marriage shall take place upon the expiry of a month after those wishing to marry file an application at the state agency for the registry of acts of civil status.

If there exist justifiable reasons, the month period may be reduced or increased, but not more than three months, by the head of the section (or bureau) of the registry for acts of civil status of the executive committee of a rural (or city) soviet of working people's deputies, and in a rural locality or settlement, by the chairman of the executive committee of a rural (or settlement) soviet of working people's deputies.

Article 15. *Conditions for Conclusion of a Marriage.*

The mutual consent of the persons entering into a marriage and the attainment by them of marriageable age are necessary for the conclusion of a marriage.

Marriageable age shall be established as eighteen years.

The executive committees of district (or city) soviets of working people's deputies may, in individual exceptional instances, reduce the marriageable age, but by not more than two years.

Article 16. *Obstacles to the Conclusion of a Marriage.*

The conclusion of a marriage shall not be allowed:

between persons one of whom already is married;

between relatives in direct line of ascendance or descendence, between full or half brothers or sisters, and also between adoptive and adopted persons; between persons one of whom is deemed by a court to lack capacity as a consequence of mental illness or feeble-mindedness.

Article 17. *Origin of Rights and Duties of Spouses*

The rights and duties of spouses arise only from a marriage concluded in state agencies for the registry of acts of civil status.

Article 20. *Common Joint Ownership of Spouses*

The property acquired by spouses during marriage shall be their common joint ownership. Spouses shall have equal rights to possession, use, and disposition of such property.

Spouses shall enjoy equal rights to property also in the event that one of them was occupied with keeping the household, caring for children, or for other justifiable reasons had no independent earnings.

Article 21. *Determination of the Share in Common Joint Ownership of Spouses When Dividing Property*

In the event of a division of property in the common joint ownership of spouses, their shares shall be deemed equal. In individual instances a court may depart from this rule, taking into account the interests of minor children or the interests of one of the spouses deserving attention. The share of one spouse, in particular, may be increased if the other spouse avoided socially useful labor or spent common property to the detriment of the family interests.

In the event of a division of property in the common joint ownership of spouses, the court shall determine which articles are subject to being transferred to each of them. In instances when articles whose value exceeds the share due are transferred to one spouse, the other spouse may be awarded appropriate monetary compensation.

A three-year period of limitation shall be established for claims concerning the division of property.

Article 22. *Personal Ownership of Each Spouse*

Property belonging to spouses before marriage, and also received by them during marriage as a gift or by way of inheritance, shall be the ownership of each of them.

Articles of individual use (clothes, shoes, etc.), except for jewelry and other luxury articles, although acquired during the marriage at the expense of common assets of the spouses, shall be deemed the personal ownership of that spouse who used them.

The property of each spouse may be deemed their common joint ownership if it will be established that during the marriage investments were made which significantly increased the value of this property (capital repair, construction, refurnishing, etc.).

CRIMINAL CODE, RSFSR (1960)

Article 232. *Payment and Acceptance of Bride Price*

The acceptance of a bride price by the parents, kinfolk, or relatives by marriage of a bride in the form of money, cattle, or other property shall be punished by deprivation of freedom for a term not exceeding one year, the bride price being confiscated, or by correctional tasks for the same term, the bride price being confiscated.

The payment of a bride price by a groom, his parents, kinfolk, or his relatives by marriage shall be punished by deprivation of freedom for a term not exceeding one year or by social censure.

Article 233. *Compelling a Woman to Enter into Marriage or Obstruction of Entry into Marriage*

Compelling a woman to enter into marriage or to continue marital cohabitation, or the obstructing of a woman from entering into marriage, or the abducting of her for entry into marriage shall be punished by deprivation of freedom for a term not exceeding two years.

Article 234. *Concluding a Marital Agreement with Person who has not Attained Marriageable Age*.

The concluding of a marital agreement with a person, in accordance with local customs, who has not attained marriageable age shall be punished by deprivation of freedom for a term not exceeding two years or by correctional tasks for a term not exceeding one year.

The commission in this connection of rape or the entering into sexual intercourse with a person who has not attained puberty shall entail responsibility in accordance with appropriate articles of the present Code.

Article 235. *Bigamy or Polygamy*

Bigamy or polygamy, that is, the cohabitation in a common household with two or more women, shall be punished by deprivation of freedom for a term not exceeding one year or by correctional tasks for the same term.

Article 236. *Limits of Operation of Chapter Eleven of the Present Code*
The operation of the present chapter shall extend to those autonomous republics, autonomous regions, and other localities of the RSFSR where the socially dangerous acts specified in the present chapter constitute survivals of local customs.

IN RE ZELENINA, Biulleten' Verkhovnogo Suda RSFSR, 1974, no. 9, pp. 11–12
Zelenina applied to the court for the establishment of the fact that she was in a state of *de facto* marital relations with Liakhovetskii, pointing out that establishment of the fact is necessary to receive an inheritance left after Liakhovetskii's death on May 19, 1972.
The Volgograd District People's Court of Moscow satisfied Zelenina's application. The file of the case was not considered by way of cassation.
The Presidium of the Moscow City Court left without satisfaction a protest of the RSFSR deputy procurator to vacate the court decision.
The Judicial Division for Civil Cases of the RSFSR Supreme Court on August 13, 1973, upon the protest of the deputy procurator of the RSFSR, vacated the decree in the case and sent the case for new consideration, indicating the following:
By Edict of the Presidium of the USSR Supreme Soviet of November 10, 1944, "On the Procedure for Recognizing *De Facto* Marital Relations in the Event of the Death or Disappearance without News on the Front of a Spouse" it is established that in those instances when *de facto* marital relations which existed prior to the promulgation of the Edict of the Presidium of the USSR Supreme Soviet of July 8, 1944, could not be registered according to Article 19 of the Edict, the subsequent death or subsequent disappearance without news on the front of a person who was in such relations, the other party shall have the right to petition a people's court to recognize the spouse of the deceased person or person who disappeared without news on the basis of previously existing legislation.
In justification of her application Zelenina referred to the fact that she was in *de facto* marital relations with Liakhovetskii from 1942 but the marriage was not registered because they had not attached proper significance to this.
In confirmation of the fact of being in *de facto* marital relations from 1942, the petitioner requested the interrogation of witnesses and submitted the power of attorney for receipt of a pension issued to her by Liakhovetskii.
However, the witnesses in the judicial session testified only that they knew the petitioner for thirty years and that she lived with her neighbor Liakhovetskii. The power of attorney issued to the petitioner regarding the right to receive a pension has no date. Despite the fact that the time of the petitioner's entering into *de facto* marital relations with Liakhovetskii was not established, the court held that the petitioner's *de facto* marital relations had been proved.
Establishing the time of the petitioner's entry into *de facto* marital relations has essential significance in the case since in accordance with point 6 of the decree of the Plenum of the USSR Supreme Court of February 25, 1966, "On Judicial Practice in Cases Concerning the Establishment of Facts Having Legal Significance",

the establishment of the fact of *de facto* marital relations may occur if such relations arose prior to the promulgation of the Edict of the Presidium of the USSR Supreme Soviet of July 8, 1944, and continued until the death of one of the spouses.

The court did not establish the time of the issuance by Liakhovetskii to the petitioner of the power of attorney for the right to receive a pension and did not elucidate why Zelenina and Likahovetskii did not take measures to combine the housing occupied by them at different addresses.

Moreover, the court considered the case in the absence of a representative of the district finance section, not having information concerning the reasons for his failure to appear at the judicial session, which violated the requirement of Article 157 of the RSFSR Code of Civil Procedure.

IN RE BULGUCHEV, Biulleten' Verkhovnogo Suda RSFSR, 1969, no. 8, pp. 5–6

By a judgment of the Suizhenskii District People's Court of the Checheno-Ingush ASSR of June 24, 1968, Bulguchev was sentenced to one year deprivation of freedom under Article 234, par. 1, of the RSFSR Criminal Code.

The judgment was left without change by a ruling of the Judicial Division for Criminal Cases of the Checheno-Ingush ASSR Supreme Court on July 11, 1968.

The Presidium of that court on December 18, 1968, left without satisfaction the protest of the deputy chairman of the RSFSR Supreme Court in which the question was raised of vacating the judgment and terminating the case because of the absence in the actions of Bulguchev of the constituent elements of a crime.

Bulgachev served the sentence in February 1969.

The deputy chairman of the RSFSR Supreme Court brought a protest to the Judicial Division for Criminal Cases of the RSFSR Supreme Court to vacate the judgment of the people's court, the cassational ruling, and the decree of the Presidium of the Checheno-Ingush ASSR Supreme Court regarding termination of the case.

The Judicial Division satisfied the protest, indicating the following in a ruling.

Bulguchev was found guilty in that on February 16, 1968, he concluded an agreement according to local customs regarding marriage with a minor, Galaeva Khanifa (born April 4, 1952).

In basing the guilt of Bulguchev on the fact that he concluded an agreement according to local customs regarding marriage with a person who had not attained marriageable age, the court referred to the testimony of Bulguchev himself, the victim Galaeva Sadikhat, and the mother of the convicted Bulguchev, Naskhat.

However, the testimony of all these persons does not give sufficient grounds for concluding that the constituent elements of a crime provided for by Article 234, par. 1, of the RSFSR Criminal Code were present in the actions of Bulguchev. Both Bulguchev and Galaeva testified that in February 1968 they, without informing their parents, agreed between themselves to enter into *de facto* marital relations without observing any local customs.

The parents of Bulguchev and Galaeva confirmed this testimony and declared that no one had previously discussed with them the questions linked with the entry of their children into marriage and that they learned of their intention to marry after Bulguchev and Galaeva were in *de facto* marital relations.

Under such circumstances, the conclusion of the court that the "guilt of the convicted Bulguchev is proved" cannot be deemed as well-founded, since it was not established that Bulguchev had concluded an agreement regarding marriage and that this agreement was concluded according to local customs.

The reference of the Presidium of the Checheno-Ingush ASSR Supreme Court in its decree to the fact that Bulguchev carried his bride to another populated locality as supporting the conclusion of an agreement regarding marriage as supposedly characteristic of local customs cannot be deemed convincing since Bulguchev explained this step by the fact that he "was afraid of the parents, since their consent to the marriage had not been sought". This explanation by Bulguchev is refuted by nothing in the case.

As regards the age of the victim, the following facts are established in the file of the case.

Galaeva asserted during the inquiry and at the medical examination that she was born on April 4, 1950, and her mother mistakenly registered her birth as April 4, 1952.

According to Bulguchev's testimony, Galaeva told him she was eighteen years old and had lost her birth certificate. Only through an inquiry of the Kustanziskii Region was it established that Galaeva was born in April 1952.

This fact demonstrates that Bulguchev might be deceived regarding the actual age of the victim and gives no grounds to conclude that an agreement regarding marriage was concluded with a person who had not attained marriageable age.

Taking this into account, it should be recognized that Bulguchev was convicted without sufficient grounds therefor.

IN RE BEREZHNAIA, Biulleten' Verkhovnogo Suda RSFSR, 1972, no. 6, pp. 4–5

Iu. A. Berezhnaia petitioned the court to recognize the lack of legal capacity of her father A. S. Berezhnyi and the invalidity of a marriage concluded on October 13, 1969, between A. S. Berezhnyi and M. P. Berezhnaia, since her father, born in 1894, suffered from vascular sclerosis of the brain with interruptions in the blood circulation of the brain and did not always correctly understand the significance of his actions. On October 13, 1969, he, without taking account of his actions, married the defendant, who in fact had no intention to create a family with him, and he died on February 13, 1970.

Berezhnaia opposed the suit and explained that she entered into marriage with the intention to create a family, and there was no doubt as to Berezhnyi's having full possession of his faculties.

The Rostov Regional Court satisfied the suit.

The Judicial Division for Civil Cases of the RSFSR Supreme Court, having considered the case by way of cassation, left the decision of the regional court without change and the appeal of Berezhnaia without satisfaction on the following grounds:

From the materials of the case it is clear that A. S. Berezhnyi had suffered since 1952 from vascular sclerosis of the brain and, in addition, since 1961, was ill with hypertension.

The witnesses questioned in the case, Garmash, N. S. Berezhnaia, Stepanenko, Basova, Medvedev, nurses Koparova, Voznichenko, and doctor of psychiatry Kovtun all confirmed that in the last years before death Berezhnyi was observed deviating from normal conduct and did not always correctly understand the situation around him.

Forensic psychiatric expertise gave an opinion that A. S. Berezhnyi during the period relating to the registration of the marriage with the defendant displayed signs of cerebral arteriosclerosis with effects on the psyche, and the change was reflected to the extent that it deprived him of the possibility to understand the significance of his actions and direct them.

Under these circumstances the court correctly came to the conclusion that Berezhnyi lacked legal capacity during the period of the registration of the marriage and deemed the marriage invalid for these reasons.

The reference of the defendant to the testimony of other witnesses questioned by the court, for whom Berezhnyi's full possession of his faculties was not in doubt, cannot serve as grounds to vacate the decision of the court. The court evaluated the testimony of the witnesses questioned in the case, taking into account all materials in the case, including the opinions of experts who were present at the judicial session, and gave a final opinion regarding the psychiatric state of Berezhnyi after having heard the testimony of witnesses called by both parties.

Thus, the decision was rendered by the court in accordance with Article 43 of the RSFSR Code on Marriage and the Family.

BOZIAKOVA vs. EVSEEV, Biulleten' Verkhovnogo Suda RSFSR, 1970, no. 4, pp. 4–5

Under a money-goods lottery ticket, the drawing of which was held on August 31, 1967, Evseev won a Moskvich-408 automobile, which he received on September 8, 1967. In July 1968 Boziakova brought suit against Evseev to recover 2256 rubles, half the value of the said motor vehicle, and 100 rubles, half the value of the garage, for a total of 2356 rubles.

As a basis for her claim, she indicated that from February 1967 to February 1968 she cohabited with Evseev and kept a common household with him. In July 1967 they jointly acquired seven money-goods lottery tickets.

On August 31, 1967, one of the said tickets received a prize: a Moskvich-408 automobile valued at 4512 rubles.

After receiving the vehicle, they jointly built a garage for it at a cost of 200 rubles. After the cohabitation terminated, Evseev refused to pay her half the value of the automobile and garage.

By decision of the Dzerzhinskii City People's Court, left without change by a ruling of the Gor'kii Regional Court, the suit of Boziakova was satisfied and 2299 rubles, 50 kopecks, recovered from Evseev for her benefit (taking account of 87 rubles spent on building the garage).

The protest of the procurator of the region to vacate the said judicial decisions was rejected by decree of the Presidium of the Gor'kii Regional Court.

The deputy chairman of the RSFSR Supreme Court brought a protest to the Judicial Division for Civil Cases of the R.S.F.S.R. Supreme Court to vacate the said decisions of the judicial agencies because they were contrary to the actual facts of the case and to reject Boziakova's suit.

The Judicial Division concurred with the protest on the following grounds.

In satisfying Boziakova's claim, the court proceeded from the fact that at the time the lottery ticket was acquired with which the Moskvich-408 was won, and also when the automobile was received, the parties lived as a single family, kept a common household, and Boziakova helped Evseev build a garage on which she spent 87 rubles.

The Judicial Division and presidium of the regional court, in concurring with the conclusions of the people's court, left the court decision without change, indicating that by virtue of Articles 116 and 121 of the RSFSR Civil Code Boziakova has the right to receive a share of the property in dispute.

However, the conclusions are contrary to the actual facts of the case.

The fact that the parties lived together during the period when the lottery tickets were acquired and the prize received under the lottery ticket in and of itself cannot in the present instance serve as adequate grounds for recognizing the plaintiff's right to a share in the property which is the object of dispute in the case.

Boziakova and Evseev were not in a registered marriage, and, therefore, their living together when the property in dispute was acquired had no legal significance. Article 10 of the 1926 RSFSR Code of Laws on Marriage, the Family, and Guardianship provides only for a community of property acquired by the spouses during marriage.

As regards the plaintiff's right to a share in the disputed property by virtue of Articles 116 and 121 of the RSFSR Civil Code, the conclusions of the judicial agencies in this part are not based on the materials of the case.

Boziakova did not present convincing evidence that the money-goods lottery ticket on which the prize of a Moskvich motor vehicle was won had been acquired with her personal participation, nor as regards her participation in building the garage.

Moreover, the basis for recognizing a person's right to a share in property as a participant in common ownership according to Articles 116 and 121 of the RSFSR Civil Code may be solely the actual participation of this person in the acquisition of the property.

The plaintiff's arguments concerning the joint purchase of the lottery tickets with Evseev, one of which won an automobile, are contradictory and are not confirmed during the repeated consideration of the case by judicial agencies.

She pointed out in the suit that these tickets were acquired in June 1967 and in the judicial session she declared that the tickets were bought in August. From a certificate of the Central Savings Bank of October 15, 1968, it seems tickets for the money-goods lottery issued in 1967 were on sale only from July 19, 1967.

Witnesses for the plaintiff gave no testimony regarding her participation in the acquisition of the lottery tickets by the defendant. She did not submit written or other evidence regarding this.

At the same time, the fact that Evseev personally acquired seven lottery tickets, including the winning ticket for the automobile, is confirmed by testimony of witness Faleev, who was an eye-witness of the purchase by the defendant of these tickets in August 1967. Moreover, the particular fact is objectively proved by documents submitted by Evseev concerning the submission by him in person of the winning lottery ticket for payment, the issuance of the automobile in his own name, and his being registered as owner of the automobile in dispute at the State Motor Vehicle Inspectorate.

Inasmuch as Evseev won the automobile on a lottery ticket acquired by him personally, this automobile was issued to him, and he alone was formalized as its owner at the State Motor Vehicle Inspectorate, the right of ownership in the motor vehicle belongs to him by virtue of Article 105 of the RSFSR Civil Code.

The plaintiff has submitted no claims relative to the fact that she is a co-owner of the motor vehicle when it was received from the store and registered at the State Motor Vehicle Inspectorate. She made no claim to half the value of the motor vehicle and garage also when terminating close relations with the defendant in January 1968. Her suit was filed only on July 18, 1968.

As is clear from the file of the case, there was no stable family life between parties. They cohabited for a short period (10–11 months). The garage for the motor vehicle, as is clear from the case, the defendant himself built.

Taking into account that the facts of the case are fully established and there is no need to gather additional evidence, the Judicial Division by a ruling of January 6, 1970, has vacated the decision of the Dzerzhinskii City People's Court, the ruling of the judicial division of the Gor'kii regional court, and the decree of the presidium of the regional court and rejected Boziakova's suit to recover 2356 rubles from Evseev for her benefit.

MIRZA-OSEPIAN vs. GAZHELOV, Biulleten' Verkhovnogo Suda SSSR, 1975, no. 5, pp. 46–47

The plaintiff M. Iu. Mirsa-Osepian and defendant P. A. Gazhelov were in a state of marriage from May 26, 1970, which was dissolved by decision of the Proletarian District People's Court in the city of Riga of March 1, 1974. The former spouses have no children of this marriage.

Since April 1968 Gazhelov has been a member of the Mezhtsiems Dacha Construction Cooperative, in connection with which he was allocated a plot of land to construct a dacha. At the time of the dissolution of the marriage Gazhelov and Mirza-Osepian had erected a dacha, the value of which was 7183 rubles.

Mirza-Osepian brought suit against Gazhelov for a division of the share in the cooperative, and for recognition of her right to one-half of the share and a determination of the procedure for using the dacha premises. In justification of these claims she referred to the fact that since 1967 she had lived with the defendant with registration of a marriage, and the dacha was built by them during the period of life together from common assets.

Gazhelov recognized the validity of the suit in part, asserting that the plaintiff did not participate in the construction of the dacha before marrying him, and her portion of the share-accumulation is equal to half the monies invested in the construction of the dacha during the marriage.

The Proletarian District People's Court in the city of Riga on June 27, 1974, satisfied the suit of Mirza-Osepian, recognizing her right to a one-half share, and, taking this into account, determined a procedure for the use of the dacha premises. This decision the court justified on the ground that the parties before registration of the marriage, beginning in 1967, had lived together and their contribution to the common budget was equal. Inasmuch as the dacha was erected during the period of their living together, the funds invested in the construction of the dacha belong to the former spouses equally.

The Judicial Division for Civil Cases of the Latvian Supreme Court deemed the decision of the people's court to be correct in that part dividing the share into equal portions, but vacated the decision in regard to the determination of the procedure for use of the dacha premises and sent the case for new consideration.

The chairman of the Latvian Supreme Court, considering the division of the share between the parties in equal portions to be not based on law, brought a protest to the presidium of the Latvian Supreme Court to vacate the decision of the people's court and the ruling of the judicial division; the case as a whole to be sent back for new consideration. The Presidium of the Latvian Supreme Court on October 28, 1974, left the protest without satisfaction, indicating that the people's court and Judicial Division in satisfying the suit had correctly proceeded from the fact that the dacha was built completely by the parties during their living together with common funds and labor. The fact that the parties' marriage was registered only on May 26, 1970, and that their living together and the construction of the dacha commenced earlier, cannot serve as a grounds for dividing only that part of the share which was acquired after registration of the marriage.

The deputy chairman of the USSR Supreme Court brought a protest to the Plenum of the Latvian Supreme Court in which the question was raised of vacating the judicial decrees in the case.

The Plenum of the Latvian Supreme Court satisfied the protest on the following rounds:

According to Article 12 of the Fundamental Principles of Legislation of the USSR and Union Republics on Marriage and the Family, property acquired during a marriage is the common joint ownership of spouses. The shares of the spouses in such property are, as a rule, deemed equal.

Inasmuch as by virtue of Article 9 of the same Fundamental Principles the rights and duties of the spouses arise only in a marriage registered in the procedure established by law, the norms of legislation on marriage and the family providing for common property of spouses and equality of shares cannot extend to property relations of persons living together without registering the marriage. The norms of civil legislation are to be applied to these relations.

As appears from the case, the construction of the dacha was carried out both before the parties were married and after registration of the marriage.

Consequently, their common joint property is only that part of the share which was formed from assets during the period of the marriage, and the portions of the spouses in this part of the share-accumulation should be deemed equal.

As regards the part of the share formed before registration of the parties' marriage, the plaintiff has no right to this part of the share and can only claim compensation as a cooperative member for funds and labor invested by her.

In resolving a dispute concerning the division of a share, neither the people's court nor the judicial division referred to the norms of material law. The people's court did not establish the size of the share formed during the marriage of the parties nor the extent of the plaintiff's participation in the construction of the dacha before registration of the marriage.

In connection with the foregoing, the plenum of the Latvian Supreme Court vacated the decision of the people's court and decrees adopted in regard to the particular case and transferred it for new consideration to the judicial division for civil cases of the Latvian Supreme Court at first instance.

MAN'KO vs. GOROKHOV, Biulleten' Verkhovnogo Suda RSFSR, 1974, no. 8, p. 5.

Man'ko and Gorokhov lived as one family since 1961 without registering a marriage. In September 1970 Man'ko brought suit against Gorokhov for a division of jointly acquired property in the amount of 826 rubles, as well as deposits in the savings bank in the amount of 1000 rubles in the name of the defendant and 180 rubles in her name.

The Iki-Burul'skii District People's Court of the Kalmytskii ASSR divided the deposits between the parties equally, recovering 410 rubles from Gorokhov to the benefit of Man'ko.

The Kalmytskii ASSR Supreme Court left the decision of the people's court without change.

[A protest of the deputy chairman of the RSFSR Supreme Court was satisfied by the Judicial Division for Civil Cases of that court on April 16, 1973, on the following grounds]:

As is clear from the materials of the case, the suit was filed for a division of property comprising the common ownership of the parties who were not spouses. In considering the case, the question was not resolved by the court of dividing the articles specified by the plaintiff in the amount of 821 rubles. The plaintiff declared at the judicial session that she did not object to a division of the articles and requested that monetary compensation be recovered for them if it was impossible for the defendant to return the articles in kind.

The court did not elucidate whether these articles existed and whether they were acquired jointly by the parties from their common assets. Depending on the extent of participation of the parties in creating the common property, the court should determine the share of the plaintiff on the basis of Article 121 of the RSFSR Civil Code and recover to her benefit property corresponding to this share or monetary compensation therefor.

The decision of the court in that part dividing the deposits of the parties is incorrect.

According to Article 395 of the Civil Code, a deposit may be divided only between spouses in a registered marriage.

Man'ko and Gorokhov were not in a registered marriage.

Consequently, the deposit of each is not subject to division.

In the present instance the people's court incorrectly applied Articles 20 and 21 of the Code on Marriage and the Family, whose norms extend only to the legal relations concerning the property of spouses living in registered marriage.

C. Abortion

CRIMINAL CODE, RSFSR (1960)
Article 116. *Illegal Performance of Abortion*

The illegal performance of an abortion by a doctor shall be punished by deprivation of freedom for a term not exceeding one year, or by correctional tasks for the same term, or by deprivation of the right to engage in medical activity.

The performance of an abortion by a person not having a higher medical education shall be punished by deprivation of freedom for a term not exceeding two years or by correctional tasks for a term not exceeding one year.

The actions provided for by paragraphs one and two of the present article, if committed repeatedly or if resulting in the death of the victim or any other grave consequences, shall be punished by deprivation of freedom for a term not exceeding eight years.

B. S. Nikiforov (ed.), NAUCHNO-PRAKTICHESKII KOMMENTARII UGOLOV-NOGO KODEKSA RSFSR [Scientific-Practical Commentary of the RSFSR Criminal Code] (Moscow, 1963), 275–276.

1. Abortion is the artificial termination of pregnancy. An Edict of the Presidium of the USSR Supreme Soviet of November 23, 1955, granted to women the right to decide themselves the question of motherhood and repealed punishment for the performance of an abortion. At the same time, protecting the life and health of a pregnant woman, the Edict allowed the performance of abortions only by a doctor in hospitals or other medical institutions, deeming other instances of the perfor-

mance of an abortion (except cases of urgent need) illegal and criminally punishable.

2. Proceeding from the Edict of the Presidium of the USSR Supreme Soviet of November 23, 1955, "On Repeal of the Prohibition of Abortion", one should consider the performance of an abortion by a doctor illegal first of all in those instances when this operation is performed outside a hospital or other medical institution. In such instances criminal liability of a doctor ensues irrespective of whether the abortion was done with the existence of or absence of medical evidence for an abortion, in a hygienic or non-hygienic situation, for compensation or without mercenary motives, etc. These facts should be taken into account in assigning punishment.

3. Liability of a doctor for performance of an abortion outside a hospital or other medical institution is excluded if the doctor acted in extreme urgency (for example, the pregnant woman cannot be moved to a hospital, and for medical reasons the abortion should be performed at once).

4. From a comparison of paragraphs 1 and 2 of [Article 116] it follows that a doctor is a person having a higher medical education. The medical specialization of such a person (*i.e.*, whether he is a surgeon, gynecologist, or therapist) has no significance, and any doctor having a higher education is liable for the performance of an abortion illegally under Article 116, par. 1.

5. The performance of an abortion by a person not having a higher medical education is an increased danger for the health of the woman and therefore under Article 116, par. 2, entails more severe punishment irrespective of whether the abortion was performed by surgical means or other means, in a hygienic or non-hygienic situation, for compensation or without mercenary motives, etc. The said facts should be taken into account in selecting measures of punishment. However, if a person not having a higher medical education performed an abortion under extreme urgency (for example, to eliminate danger of death threatening the pregnant woman), criminal liability is excluded (Art. 14).

6. According to Article 116, par. 3, specially classified types of abortion are first of all the repeated performance of an abortion, *i.e.*, performance by a doctor or person not having higher medical education of an illegal abortion two or more times irrespective of whether the guilty person was previously convicted of this crime or not.

7. Another classified abortion is the death of the pregnant woman or the ensuing of other grave consequences as a result of the illegal performance of an abortion by a doctor or the performance of an abortion by a person not having a higher medical education. In the latter instance, one has in mind the causing of serious harm to health; grave, incurable, or agonizing illness, sterility, significant persistent loss of capacity to work, etc.

The death of the woman or causing of harm to health as a result of a legal abortion may not entail liability under Article 116.

8. Article 116, par. 3, is applied on condition that there is a causal connection between the death of the pregnant woman and other grave consequences and the fact

of the performance of the illegal abortion is established. The psychological attitude of the guilty person toward such consequences of his actions may be reflected either in presumption of negligence or in direct intention (for example, a threat to the life of the woman arising as a result of an unsuccessful abortion, and the guilty person, endeavoring to avoid being unmasked, does not take necessary measures to save the victim, does not call a doctor, nor send her to the hospital, etc.).

D. Dissolution of Marriage

CODE OF MARRIAGE AND THE FAMILY, RSFSR (1969)

Article 30. *Termination of Marriage*

A marriage shall be terminated as a consequence of the death or the declaration of one of the spouses as deceased in a judicial proceeding.

During the life of the spouses, a marriage may be dissolved by a divorce upon the application of one or both spouses.

Article 31. *Inadmissibility of a Husband Filing a Claim for Dissolution of Marriage*

A husband shall not have the right to initiate a case concerning dissolution of a marriage without the consent of the wife during pregnancy of the wife nor within one year after the birth of a child.

Article 32. *Procedure for Dissolution of a Marriage*

A marriage shall be dissolved in a judicial proceeding, and in the instances provided for by Articles 38 and 39 of the present Code, at agencies for the registry of acts of civil status.

Article 33. *Dissolution of a Marriage by a Court*

Cases concerning dissolution of a marriage shall be considered by a court in the procedure of a suit established by the RSFSR Code of Civil Procedure.

The court shall take measures to reconcile the spouses and shall have the right to defer the examination of a case, designating for the spouses a period for reconciliation within the limits of six months.

The marriage shall be dissolved if it is established by a court that the further joint life of the spouses and preservation of the family has become impossible.

When rendering a decision concerning dissolution of a marriage, the court shall take measures when necessary to protect the interests of minor children and a spouse incapable of working.

Article 34. *Settlement of a Dispute Concerning Bringing Up Children*

If there is no agreement between the spouses as to with which of them the children will live after dissolution of the marriage and to what extent means for the support of the children will be paid, the court shall be obliged when rendering a decision concerning dissolution of the marriage to determine with which of the parents and which of the children shall remain, as well as from which of the parents and to what extent alimony shall be recovered for the maintenance of the children.

Article 35. *Recovery of Means for Support of a Spouse*

At the request of a spouse having the right to support from the other spouse, the court shall be obliged when rendering a decision concerning dissolution of a marriage to determine the amount of support subject to recovery from the other spouse.

Article 36. *Division of Common Joint Ownership of Spouses*

At the request of the spouses or one of them, the court shall be obliged when rendering a decision concerning dissolution of a marriage to divide the property in the common joint ownership of the spouses.

If such division affects the right of third persons, the dispute regarding division of property may not be settled simultaneously with the case concerning dissolution of a marriage.

Article 37. *State Duty Recovered Regarding a Court Decision When Issuing a Certificate Concerning Dissolution of a Marriage*

When rendering a decision concerning dissolution of a marriage, the court shall determine the amount subject to payment for issuance of a certificate concerning dissolution of a marriage by one or both spouses in an amount of from 50 up to 200 rubles. If the court deems it necessary to recover the state duty from both spouses, it shall determine the amount subject to payment by each.

Article 38. *Dissolution of Marriage by Mutual Consent of Spouses Not Having Minor Children*

With the mutual consent for dissolution of a marriage of spouses not having minor children, the marriage shall be dissolved in agencies for the registry of acts of civil status.

Formalization of the divorce and the issuance to the spouses of a certificate concerning dissolution of a marriage shall be upon the expiry of three months from the date the spouses file the application for divorce.

A state duty in the amount of 50 rubles shall be recovered for registration of the dissolution of marriage.

If there is a dispute between the spouses, the marriage shall be dissolved through a court.

Article 39. *Dissolution of a Marriage at Agencies for Registering Acts of Civil Status upon the Application of One of the Spouses*

A marriage shall be dissolved at agencies for the registration of acts of civil status upon the application of one of the spouses if the other spouse:

is deemed missing in accordance with the procedure established by law;

is deemed to lack legal capacity as a consequence of mental illness or feeble-mindedness in accordance with the procedure established by law;

is sentenced to deprivation of freedom for a term of not less than three years for the commission of a crime.

A state duty in the amount of 50 kopecks shall be recovered for registration of disolution of a marriage from the applicant spouse.

If a spouse under confinement or a guardian of a spouse lacking legal capacity initiates a dispute concerning children, division of property in the common joint ownership of spouses, or a dispute concerning payment of funds for the maintenance of a needy spouse incapable of working, the marriage shall be dissolved through a court.

Article 40. *Time of Termination of a Marriage in the Event of Divorce*

A marriage shall be considered terminated from the time of registration of a divorce in the book for the registration of acts of civil status.

Article 43. *Bases for Deeming a Marriage Invalid*

A marriage may be deemed invalid if the conditions established by Articles 15 and 16 of the present code are violated, as well as in instances of registration of a marriage without an intention to create a family (fictitious marriage).

A marriage may not be deemed fictitious if the persons who have registered this marriage have created a family *de facto* before consideration of the case by a court.

If at the moment the case is considered there are circumstances preventing the conclusion of the marriage, it may be deemed valid from the moment such circumstances disappear.

Article 45. *Deeming a Marriage Invalid in the Event of the Failure of a Spouse to Attain Marriageable Age*

A marriage concluded with a minor for whom the marriageable age has not been reduced (article 15 of the present Code) may be deemed invalid if the interests of the spouse who entered into marriage before attaining marriageable age require this.

A minor spouse, his parents or guardian (or curator), as well as agencies of guardianship and curatorship or the procurator, shall have the right to demand that a marriage be deemed invalid on these grounds.

An agency of guardianship or curatorship shall be enlisted in all instances to participate in the case.

If at the moment the case is considered the minor spouse has attained majority, the marriage may be deemed invalid at his demand or the demand of the procurator.

CHICHINSKAS vs. CHICHINSKENA, Biulleten' Verkhovnogo Suda SSSR, 1977, no. 1, pp. 28–29

In November 1974 B. Chichinskas brought suit against B. Chichinskena for dissolution of marriage. The plaintiff also requested a division of property, including a deposit made in the name of Chichinskena in a state labor savings bank.

The Lenin District People's Court in the city of Kaunas dissolved the marriage between Chichinskas and Chichinskena on October 29, 1975, and divided the property. From the deposit in the amount of 10,366 rubles it decreed that the plaintiff recover 4000 rubles.

[The Judicial Division for Civil Cases and the Presidium of the Latvian Supreme Court and the Plenum of that Court left the decision without change; the Plenum of the USSR Supreme Court satisfied a protest of the chairman of the USSR Supreme Court on the following grounds]:

According to Article 21, par. 3, of the Lithuanian Code on Marriage and the Family, a deposit made in the name of one spouse at a state labor savings bank is deemed the joint property of spouses if the court establishes that this deposit was made from funds acquired by the spouses during the marriage.

In recognizing the plaintiff's right to part of the deposit made in the defendant's name, the people's court and subsequent judicial instances proceeded from the fact that the deposit belongs to both spouses. However, no evidence was brought forward in confirmation of this conclusion.

The actual circumstances connected with the affiliation of the deposit were not elucidated, in violation of Article 16 of the Fundamental Principles of Civil Procedure of the USSR and Union Republics.

In objecting to the claim for a division of the deposit, the defendant referred to the fact, in the judicial session, that she and the plaintiff, receiving modest incomes, could not have significant savings. The amount of the deposit invested in her name in the savings bank was transferred to her for temporary keeping by her mother. The defendant filed in this connection at the judicial session a petition to demand and receive the necessary documents which could confirm the well-foundedness of her objections against the suit.

However, the court left this petition without satisfaction, and, despite the requirement of Article 18 of the Fundamental Principles of Civil Procedure, did not display initiative in demanding the evidence having significance for the proper resolution of the case, limiting itself only to the explanations of the parties. The defendant's mother, M. Val'mene, to whom according to Chichinskena's assertion, the amount in the savings bank belongs, was not questioned by the court.

Taking into account the foregoing, the Plenum of the USSR Supreme Court vacated the decision of the Lenin District People's Court in the city of Kaunas of October 29, 1975, and subsequent judicial decrees in that part dividing the deposit in the savings bank between B. Chichinskas and B. Chichinskena, and transferred the case for new consideration to the Lithuanian Supreme Court at first instance.

LENINGRAD PROCURATOR vs. KIRILLOVA, Biulleten' Verkhovnogo Suda RSFSR, 1975, no. 8, pp. 3–4

The Procurator of the city of Leningrad brought suit against Kirillova in accordance with the procedure of Article 4 of the RSFSR Code of Civil Procedure to recognize a marriage as invalid. He pointed out that Kirillova, who resided permanently in the city of Bel'sk, Archangel Region, arrived in Leningrad upon the summons of acquaintances to care for Revskii, ill and aged. Without having any intention of creating a family with him, Kirillova on November 30, 1973, registered a marriage with Revskii with a view to acquiring the right to his apartment and on December 10, 1973, left for the city of Bel'sk to return to her place of permanent residence. In her absence, on December 13, 1973, Revskii died, after which Kirillova, having returned to Leningrad, brought suit in court for recognition of her right to Revskii's dwelling premises; the suit, however, was rejected by decision of the people's court. Considering the marriage between Kirillova and Revskii to be fictitious, the procurator requested the court to deem it invalid on the grounds specified in Article 43 of the RSFSR Code on Marriage and the Family.

The Leningrad City Court satisifed the claim filed by the procurator.

In the cassational appeal Kirillova requested the decision of the court be vacated and the suit of the procurator be rejected. The defendant pointed out that she registered the marriage with Revskii upon his own initiative, not with a view to receiving the right to his apartment but with the intention to create a family.

The Judicial Division for Civil Cases of the RSFSR Supreme Court by a ruling of May 21, 1975, left the decision of the Leningrad City Court without change.

In accordance with Article 43 of the RSFSR Code and Marriage and the Family, marriage may be deemed invalid not only if the conditions exist which prevent an entry into marriage according to law, but also if the fact is proved that registration of a marriage occurred without an intention to create a family (fictitious marriage).

It seems from the materials of the case that Kirillova did not know Revskii before April 1973 and arrived in Leningrad not with a view to entering into a marriage with him but to care for him with the rights of a household worker, since Revskii after his wife's death, being 90 years old, required outside assistance.

Kirillova in essence does not deny that she agreed to render such services on condition of her being registered in Leningrad or its suburbs. As such efforts were not successful, she traveled from Leningrad while Revskii was in hospital to the place of her permanent residence in Bel'sk. She did not deny in court that before departing for Bel'sk in July 1973 Revskii was in a hospital and she lived in the apartment alone during May and June 1973.

From the contents of Revskii's letter of July 14, 1973, it seems that no arrangement in this period was reached concerning living jointly with Kirillova; he required outside care; the question of her being registered in the dwelling premises he occupied was not raised; but he only promised her his son's assistance to obtain registration in the city. Kirillova's arguments that she temporarily went to Bel'sk and returned to Leningrad, considering herself the spouse of the deceased, do not correspond to the actual circumstances of the case.

Using Revskii's need for care, Kirillova, as the son of the deceased testified in court, stipulated the condition that she be registered in Leningrad by formalizing a marriage with Revskii, intending otherwise to leave for Bel'sk. The said circumstances, *i.e.*, registration of a marriage with Revskii without the intention to create a family but with a view to being registered in Leningrad, is confirmed by the explanations of witnesses and the subsequent conduct of the defendant. Having registered a marriage with Revskii and filed the documents for being registered in his apartment, Kirillova, having left the gravely ill Revskii without supervision, went to Bel'sk, and having been notified that he died, was not interested either in his place of burial nor the circumstances in which he died, but immediately brought suit for recognition of her right to the dwelling space of the deceased.

Taking all of this into account the court had grounds for rendering a decision to satisfy the procurator's claim, and this decision is not contrary to law or the evidence gathered.

NAZAROVA vs. NAZAROV, Biulleten' Verkhovnogo Suda RSFSR, 1971, no. 3, p. 5

Nazarova brought suit against Nazarov for dissolution of marriage and eviction, basing the claim on the fact that he systematically comes home in a state of intoxication, swears, and beats her.

The Prokhladnenskii City People's Court combined the claims into one proceeding, dissolved the marriage between the Nazarovs and evicted Nazarov from the house belonging to the plaintiff by right of personal ownership.

[The decision was left without change by the Judicial Division for Civil Cases of the Kabardino-Balkarskii ASSR Supreme Court but returned for new consideration as regards the eviction by the Judicial Division for Civil Cases of the RSFSR Supreme Court on the following grounds]:

In accordance with Articles 34–36 of the RSFSR Code on Marriage and the Family, when rendering a decision on the dissolution of a marriage a court should determine with which of the parents and which of the children shall remain, from which of them and to what extent alimony for the children is to be recovered, recover at the request of the spouse having a right to maintenance from the other spouse the means for support, as well as at the request of the spouses or one of them divide property in the common joint ownership of the spouses.

Inasmuch as only the said claims may be combined into a single proceeding, the court was not right to combine Nazarova's claim for dissolution of the marriage and for eviction of the defendant.

ABRAMOVA vs. MAGIDSON, Biulleten' Verkhovnogo Suda RSFSR, 1971, no. 8, p. 4

In December 1969 Abramova brought suit against Magidson for dissolution of marriage, which was registered between them in 1960. She pointed out that they had two minor children, but quarrels frequently occurred in the family, and therefore in August 1969 she ceased cohabitation and did not intend to restore the family.

Magidson did not oppose the suit.

[The people's court satisfied the suit, the decision being confirmed by the judicial division of the Kabardino-Balkarskii ASSR Supreme Court. The Presidium of that Supreme Court vacated previous decisions and terminated the proceeding. The Judicial Division for Civil Cases of the RSFSR Supreme Court renewed the proceeding and returned it for new consideration on the following grounds]:

The people's court did not elucidate with sufficient care the interrelations of the parties; in violation of Article 33 of the RSFSR Code on Marriage and the Family did not take measures to reconcile the spouses; did not consider it necessary to defer consideration of the case in order to allow them the possibility of reconciliation, and several days after receiving the suit petition, decided the case in substance.

Consequently, on the fifth day after the decision was rendered, Abramova had appealed it by way of cassation, referring to the fact that the suit for divorce was filed thoughtlessly since their family could be restored.

Despite this petition, the Judicial Division of the Kabardino-Balkarskii ASSR Supreme Court left the decision of the people's court without change, indicating in the ruling that if spouses do not wish to be divorced they need not obtain a certificate of divorce.

In an appeal to the procurator of the Kabardino-Balkarskii ASSR, Abramova also confirmed the possibility of preserving the family with Magidson.

Under such circumstances, the presidium of the Kabardino-Balkarskii ASSR Supreme Court correctly vacated the decision of the people's court and the ruling of the Judicial Division of the Supreme Court but without sufficient grounds terminated the proceedings in the case.

The reference to Article 219, par. 4, of the RSFSR Code of Civil Procedure as a grounds for terminating the proceeding is correct; however, in the event of the refusal of the plaintiff to sue, the court before accepting the refusal, should, according to Article 165 of the Code of Civil Procedure, elucidate the reason for such refusal and explain the legal consequences of terminating the proceeding.

The presidium of the Kabardino-Balkarskii ASSR Supreme Court, having considered the case by way of supervision, did not explain to Abramova the consequences of terminating the proceeding. Therefore, it should not terminate the proceeding but send it for new consideration in the court of first instance.

E. Maintenance and Alimony

CODE ON MARRIAGE AND THE FAMILY, RSFSR (1969)
Article 67. *Duties of Parents Regarding Maintenance of Children*
Parents shall be obliged to maintain their minor children and children who have attained majority, are not capable of working, and require assistance.
Article 68. *Amount of Alimony Recovered from Parents for Minor Children*
Alimony for minor children shall be recovered from their parents in an amount: for one child, one quarter; for two children, one third; for three or more children, one-half of the earnings (or income) of the parents.

The amount of these shares may be reduced by a court if the parents obliged to pay alimony have other minor children who, if the amount of alimony established by the present Article were recovered, would be less provided for materially than the children receiving the alimony, as well as in those instances if the parent from whom alimony is recovered is a first or second group invalid or if the children work and have adequate earnings.

The court shall have the right to reduce the amount of alimony or to exempt it from being paid if the children are fully supported by the state or a social organization.
Article 70. *Types of Earnings (or Income) Subject to Reckoning in Withholding Alimony.*
The types of earnings (or income) subject to reckoning in withholding alimony

shall, in accordance with the Fundamental Principles of Legislation of the USSR and Union Republics on Marriage and the Family, be determined in the procedure established by the USSR Council of Ministers.

Article 74. *Provisional Recovery of Alimony Until Consideration of the Case by a Court*

In cases concerning the recovery from parents of funds for the maintenance of children in those instances when the defendant has been registered as the parent of a child in accordance with Articles 48 and 49 of the present Code, a court or judge shall have the right before consideration of the case to issue a ruling as to in what amount the defendant shall provisionally bear expenses for maintenance of the children.

The amount subject to provisional recovery may be determined as a share of the earnings (or income) of the defendant or as a fixed sum of money.

Article 77. *Duty of Children to Maintain Parents and to Care for Them*

Children who have attained majority shall be obliged to maintain parents who are not capable of working and require assistance and to care for them.

The extent of the participation of each of the children in the support of parents who are not capable of working and require assistance shall be determined by a court, proceeding from the financial and family situation of the parents and children, in a fixed sum of money to be paid monthly.

When determining this amount, the court shall take into account all children of the particular parent who have attained majority, irrespective of whether a claim was filed against all children or only against one or several of them.

Article 78. *Exempting Children from the Duty to Maintain Parents*

Children may be exempted from the duty to maintain their parents if it is established by a court that the parents have avoided the fulfillment of parental duties.

Article 79. *Modification of the Amount of Alimony Recovered from Parents for Children Who Have Attained Majority and from Children for their Parents*

If after the establishment by a court of the amount subject to recovery from parents for the maintenance of their children who have attained majority and are not capable of working and require assistance, or recovered from children for the maintenance of parents who are incapable of working and require assistance the financial or family situation of the parents or children has changed, the court shall have the right upon the suit of any of these to modify the amount of alimony established.

Article 89. *Payment of Alimony in a Voluntary Procedure*

Alimony shall be paid in a voluntary Procedure personally by the person obliged to pay the alimony or through the administration at the place of his work or the receipt by him of a pension or stipend.

The voluntary procedure for the payment of alimony shall not preclude the right of the person recovering the alimony to bring suit in court at any time regarding recovery of alimony.

Article 90. *Duty of the Administration of an Enterprise, Institution, or Organization to Withhold Alimony*

The administration of an enterprise, institution, or organization shall, on the basis of a written application of the person paying the alimony or a writ of execution, be obliged to withhold monthly the alimony from the earnings (or pension, benefits, stipends, or other) and to pay or transfer them within a three-week period from the date the earnings (or pension, benefit, stipend, or other) are paid to the person specified in the application or in the writ of execution.

In the event of the transfer of a citizen from whom alimony is withheld by application to other work or of a change of residence, the alimony shall be withheld on the basis of an application newly filed by him. Indebtedness during the time of non-payment of alimony in such instances may be withheld from the debtor upon his application or be recovered in a judicial proceeding.

Applications concerning the withholding of alimony, as well as modifying the amount or terminating the withholding of alimony, shall be kept by the administration of the enterprise, institution, or organization in the procedure established for keeping executory documents. A fine may be imposed in the procedure and in the amount established by Article 344 of the RSFSR Code of Civil Procedure on an official guilty of losing an application concerning the withholding of alimony.

Article 93. *Notation in Passports Concerning the Recovery of Alimony from Persons Who Maliciously Evade Payment*

Agencies of internal affairs shall make a notation (or entry) in the passports of persons convicted of malicious avoidance of payment of alimony, or investigative agencies of internal affairs in connection with the avoidance of payment of alimony, concerning the fact that such persons shall be obliged to pay alimony in accordance with a decision of a court.

Article 94. *Withholding of Alimony from the Earnings of Persons Who Avoid Payment*

In the event of the payment of wages, or other earnings, pension, or stipend to a person in whose passport there is a notation (or entry) of an agency of internal affairs that in accordance with a decision of a court this person is obliged to pay alimony, the administration of an enterprise, institution, or organization shall be obliged, until receiving a writ of execution, to withhold alimony in accordance with the notation (or entry) in the passport in the procedure established for withholding by writ of execution and to notify the sheriff of the people's court of the particular district (or city) thereof; if the address of the person to whose benefit the alimony is recovered is not known, the amounts withheld shall be transferred to the deposit account of the people's court. In the event of the failure to fulfill this duty, a fine may be imposed on the guilty officials in the procedure and in the amount established by Article 394 of the RSFSR Code of Civil Procedure.

IN RE KRASNOPEVTSEV, Biulleten' Verkhovnogo Suda RSFSR, 1971, no. 10, p. 5

Kransopevtsev, obliged by a decision of the Palkin District People's Court, Kostroma Region, of October 25, 1961, to pay Kranopevtseva alimony for his son Evgenii, born September 7, 1961, brought suit for a reduction of the amounts of alimony, since he had two children of another mother dependent on him.

By decision of the Antropov District People's Court the amount of alimony was reduced to one-fifth of all types of earnings.

[The Judicial Division for Civil Cases of the Kostroma Regional Court vacated the decision and returned the case for new consideration, but its Presidium reinstated the lower court decision. The Judicial Division for Civil Cases of the RSFSR Supreme Court vacated the ruling of the Presidium as being in violation of Article 68 of the RSFSR Code on Marriage and the Family in a ruling of June 10, 1971]:

The court based its decision on the fact that Krasnopevtseva's income, taking into account her earnings (60 rubles) and the alimony received by her, amount to 87 rubles for the two, the amount remaining for Krasnopevtsev after the withholding of taxes and alimony being 82 rubles for three.

Thus, the court determined the degree of material security for the child for which alimony was paid by taking into account the income of the recipient of the alimony.

Such a procedure does not correspond to point 18 of the decree of the Plenum of the USSR Supreme Court of December 4, 1969, according to which when deciding a suit concerning the reduction of the amount of alimony, a court shall take into account the income of the plaintiff (who is paying the alimony) as well as the existence of family members not capable of working to whom by law he should supply maintenance.

BUSAREVA vs. MITIN, Biulleten' Verkhovnogo Suda RSFSR, 1970, no. 10, p. 13

A. M. Busareva requested the court to recover alimony from V. A. Mitin for her daughter Svetlana, born December 12, 1968, referring to the fact that he does not give adequate financial assistance to the daughter.

[The Kuibyshev District People's Court of Moscow satisfied the suit, but its decision was vacated by the Presidium of the Moscow City Court for failure to investigate the materials of the file of the case]:

The people's court did not elucidate all the facts regarding the case and rendered a decision in violation of the requirements of Articles 14 and 50 of the RSFSR Code of Civil Procedure.

In his written explanations regarding the substance of the suit filed, Mitin deemed the claims of the plaintiff to be well-founded and indicated that he pays half of his earnings for the maintenance of children from a first marriage.

In an appeal by way of supervision, N. K. Mitina asserts that the plaintiff requested recovery of alimony for the sole purpose of endeavoring to reduce the amount of alimony recovered to her benefit for the three children from the first marriage.

The court considered the case in the absence of Mitin, and did not enlist his first wife, N.K. Mitina, to take part in the consideration of the case, and, therefore, the reasons for Busareva's filing the suit remained unelucidated.

Under such circumstances, the decision of the people's court is subject to be vacated.

In the new consideration of the case, the court should verify whether the defendant in fact does not fulfill his duties to maintain the daughter of the second marriage; whether the suit filed by Busareva serves as an attempt to evade the law so as to reduce the amount of alimony paid for the children of the first marriage; involve in the consideration of the case the mother of the defendant's children of the first marriage, N. K. Mitina; and resolve the dispute in accordance with the data obtained.

DAN'KO vs. DAN'KO, Biulleten' Verkhovnogo Suda RSFSR, 1970, no. 10, p. 14

R. I. Dan'ko brought suit against B. N. Dan'ko for the recovery of alimony for the maintenance of three children, having referred to the fact that the defendant during a business trip is not rendering financial assistance to the children.

The defendant was present at the judicial session and acknowledged the suit.

[The Leningrad District People's Court of Moscow awarded alimony to the plaintiff in the amount of half of all types of the defendant's earnings; The case was not considered by way of cassation. The Presidium of the Moscow City Court vacated the decision as contrary to the materials of the case in violation of Articles 14 and 50 of the RSFSR Code of Civil Procedure.]

As is obvious from the materials of the case, the marriage between the spouses Dan'ko is not dissolved, they live together in common dwelling premises, keep a common household, and bring up the children together. The defendant has not avoided rendering financial assistance to the family.

Given such facts, the court should have carefully verified the reasons for filing the suit, but did not do this. In the verification of the case by way of supervision it was established that pursuant to a judgment of the Minsk Regional Court of June 3, 1965, the sum of 8635 rubles was recovered from B. N. Dan'ko and other persons in a combined proceeding. In liquidation of the loss, 20% of B. N. Dan'ko's earnings were withheld.

After the decision of the court to recover alimony from B. N. Dan'ko for the maintenance of the children, the withholding of amounts for the revenue of the state was terminated.

The organization at B. N. Dan'ko's place of work confirmed that while traveling on an extended business trip the defendant had left a power of attorney for his wife to receive the earnings due to him.

In the new consideration, the court should carefully verify for what purpose the suit for recovery of alimony was filed and render a decision depending on the data obtained.

SOLOV'EV vs. SOLOV'EVA, Biulleten' Verkhovnogo Suda SSSR, 1973, no. 2, pp. 7–9

F. I. Solov'ev and S. A. Solov'eva have been in a registered marriage since 1935. During their life together S. A. Solov'eva purchased in April 1963 a 1/3 part of a house in the city of Kerson. In August 1963 the spouses terminated their cohabitation. Upon the suit of F. I. Solov'ev, the Kherson Regional Court dissolved their marriage on January 14, 1964. However, they did not formalize the dissolution of the marriage at a ZAGS agency and in July 1968 renewed their joint life. According to a notarially certified contract Solov'eva sold the said part of the house on November 13, 1968, and deposited the money in a savings account in her name.

In March 1969 the spouses again terminated family relations, and in April of the same year Solov'eva formalized the dissolution of the marriage at a ZAGS agency.

In July 1969 Solov'ev brought suit against Solov'eva for a division of the property, referring to the fact that 1/3 part of the house sold by her was acquired by them during their joint life and therefore he has the right to half of the amount received by the defendant. Although in the purchase-sale contract it was noted that the said part of the house was sold for 3000 rubles, the plaintiff asserted in his application that in reality the defendant received 9300 rubles from the buyer. In addition, Solov'ev requested a division be made of household belongings in the amount of 870 rubles acquired during the joint life with the defendant.

The People's Court of the Kalinin District in the city of Tallin, having considered the materials of the case, recognized that the 1/3 part of the house registered in the defendant's name was acquired by her during her cohabitation with the plaintiff and was sold for 3000 rubles, and not for 9300 rubles. In this connection on February 5, 1970, the court decreed that there be recovered from the defendant for the benefit of the plaintiff 1500 rubles for the part of the house sold, as well as half the value of the household belongings acquired by them, 435 rubles. In addition, by way of compensation for judicial expenses and amounts regarding payment of the state tax, and it was decreed that there be recovered from Solov'eva respectively 32 rubles and 116 rubles, 10 kopecks.

[This decision was left in force by the Judicial Division for Civil Cases and by the Presidium of the Estonian Supreme Court. The Plenum of the said Court rejected a protest of the Deputy USSR Procurator General urging the case be reconsidered in light of the fact that the plaintiff's son, a second group invalid, lived with Solov'eva and required daily assistance. The same consideration caused the Chairman of the USSR Supreme Court to bring a protest to the Plenum of that Court proposing that Solov'ev's share of the property be reduced to 300 rubles]:

The Plenum of the USSR Supreme Court satisfied the protest on the following grounds.

As already noted, the people's court established that during the cohabitation of the spouses, Solov'eva bought and then sold 1/3 part of a house for 3000 rubles in the city of Kherson. Living in the city of Kherson, the Solov'evs bought household belongings totaling 870 rubles. Proceeding from this, the court decreed that there be recovered from the defendant to the benefit of the plaintiff 1935 rubles, deeming the shares of the parties in the property subject to division to be equal.

However, when establishing the actual facts of the case the court had grounds to depart from the equality of the plaintiff's and defendant's shares of the property in their common joint ownership.

According to Article 12 of the Fundamental Principles of Legislation of the USSR and Union Republics on Marriage and the Family (Article 24 of the Estonian Code on Marriage and the Family), the court shall have the right to depart from the principle of equality of shares of spouses in common property if this is necessary, taking into account the interests of minor children or the interests of one of the spouses meriting attention.

Although at the time the case was considered by the court, the children of the plaintiff and defendant were of majority, the court when determining the shares of the parties in their joint property and proceeding from the actual facts established could not but take into account that one son of the former spouses, L. F. Solov'ev, living together with his mother, suffers psychiatric illness, has been deemed a second group invalid, and is dependent on the defendant. Her earnings are 70 rubles per month. The plaintiff also receives a pension, as a reserve officer, of 185 rubles and has earnings of 160 rubles per month.

By way of executing the judicial decision concerning recovery from the defendant to the benefit of the plaintiff of 1935 rubles, the sheriff has imposed arrest on the house bought by her after the formalization of the dissolution of marriage at a ZAGS agency. The defendant was warned by a letter of the people's court of April 19, 1972, that in the event of the failure to pay the said amount, the house will be sold at public auction. In the event of the sale of the house the defendant together with the ill son would be without housing.

The fact also deserves attention that the plaintiff previously did not claim the property in use by the defendant. Thus, in filing a suit in November 1963 for dissolution of the marriage, he wrote: "I do not claim the half-house purchased by her (the defendant) and renounce it." The fact that he did not intend to claim recognition of his rights to any part of the house was confirmed by the plaintiff in a written explanation for the cassational appeal of Solov'eva filed by her in the decision of the Suvorov District People's Court in the city of Kherson of April 14, 1966, in a case regarding the division of an apartment, as well as at judicial sessions of October 27, 1969, and February 5, 1970, during the consideration of the present case.

In leaving without satisfaction the protest of the deputy USSR Procurator General, the Plenum of the Estonian Supreme Court referred in the decree to the fact that the amount recovered from the defendant by decision of the people's court for the share of the house due to the plaintiff amounted to only 1/6 of the deposit of money in the savings bank in the defendant's name.

It is necessary to note in this connection that neither in the preparation of the case for judicial examination nor in the course of investigating the materials of the file of the case at the judicial session was evidence submitted to the court that the amount of the deposit in the amount of 9268 rubles, 70 kopecks, deposited by the defendant on several occasions was received by her from the sale in November 1968 of 1/3 of the house. As already indicated, the court of first instance came to the conclusion as a result of investigating and evaluating the evidence that Solov'eva sold 1/3 of the house for 3000 rubles. The deposit invested in the name of the defendant was received by her from the savings bank in April 1969, that is, more than three years ago. After this, the defendant purchased a house in the city of Kherson in which she lives with an ill son. According to the defendant's assertion, she now has no monetary savings.

Taking into account the specific facts of the case established by the court of first instance, and taking into consideration that recovery from Solov'eva, who has assumed the basis tasks of maintaining and caring for a son incapable of working, of 1935 rubles to the benefit of the plaintiff would create for her and the son great financial difficulties, the Plenum of the USSR Supreme Court found it possible to reduce the amount subject to recovery from her to 300 rubles.

In connection with the foregoing, the Plenum of the USSR Supreme Court has changed all judicial decisions rendered in the particular case, reducing the amount recovered from S. A. Solov'eva to the benefit of F. I. Solov'ev for the part of the property due him to 300 rubles, and the amount of state tax and other judicial expenses borne by the plaintiff subject to recovery from Solov'eva respectively to 6 rubles and 15 rubles.

DECREE ON TYPES OF EARNINGS TAKEN INTO ACCOUNT IN WITHHOLDING ALIMONY, Biulleten' Gosudarstvennogo Komiteta Soveta Ministrov SSSR po voprosam truda i zarabotnoi platy, 1969, no. 3

In accordance with the decree of the USSR Council of Ministers of December 9, 1968, "On the Procedure for Determining Types of Earnings (or Income) Subject to Being Taken into Account in Withholding Alimony", the State Committee of the USSR Council of Ministers for Labor and Wages and the Secretariat of the All-Union Central Council of Trade Unions adopted a decree of January 22, 1969, by which it was established:

1. Alimony from workers and employees shall be withheld from all types of earnings and supplementary compensation, both for basic and combined work for which under prevailing rules insurance contributions are calculated, including:

    (a) basic wages according to the basic salary scale, tariffs, piecework, etc.;

    (b) all types of additional payments for supplements to wages;

    (c) bonuses in cash or in kind;

    (d) payment for overtime work, as well as for holidays;

    (e) earnings retained during vacations, as well as compensation received in the event of dismissal for unused vacations in the event of vacations being combined for several years;

(f) earnings retained during the fulfillment of state and social duties, during a raising of qualifications, and in other instances of retaining average wages;

(g) supplements to wages for work in areas of the Far North and localities equated to areas of the Far North;

(h) lump-sum compensation (or percentage supplements) for years of service;

(i) compensation for the general annual results of the work of the enterprise or organization;

(j) compensation paid to regular literary workers of newspapers, journals, TASS, APN, radio and television, from the literary royalty fund, as well as to occasional literary workers subject to state social insurance;

(k) other types of earnings for which insurance contributions are calculated.

To withhold alimony from persons serving a sentence in places of deprivation of freedom or being treated in therapeutic labor dispensary, the amount of earnings shall be taken into account, less taxes, and alimony shall be recovered from the amount remaining after withholding from such earnings the cost of food, clothing allowance, special treatment, and transfer to the personal account of the minimum wages in accordance with the actual situation.

3. Alimony shall be withheld from collective farm members from the amounts received for work in the common husbandry of the collective farms (including the value of remittances in kind).

4. From writers, composers, artists, and other creative workers who are not workers and employees, alimony shall be withheld from the amounts of authors' royalties. From advocates, from all types of earnings received for work in legal consultation offices. From teachers giving lessons and doctors engaging in private practice, from their earnings.

5. Alimony also shall be withheld: (a) from state social insurance benefits, as well as from benefits for temporary inability to work established in collective farms; (b) from supplementary payments to state social insurance benefits made at the expense of enterprises, institutions, and organizations in areas of the Far North and in localities equated to the Far North; (c) from amounts paid in compensation of loss in connection with the loss of the capacity to work as a result of mutilation or other injury to health; (d) from pensions actually received; (e) from stipends paid during a period of study in higher and secondary special institutions of higher education and for courses; (f) from incomes from artisan trades and one-man farms; (g) from revenues emanating from the share of the person paying alimony in a personal plot or subsidiary husbandry.

6. Alimony shall not be withheld: (a) from gratuities in the event of dismissal and amounts of financial assistance; (b) from lump-sum bonuses for which insurance contributions are not computed; (c) from bonuses awarded for outstanding work in the domain of science, literature, and the arts; (d) from lump-sum compensation for

inventions and rationalization proposals; (e) from amounts of compensation for business trips and transfers to another locality; (f) from field allowances, supplements to wages, and other amounts paid in place of per diem and apartments; (g) from amounts of compensation paid for the depreciation of instruments and deterioration of clothing; (h) from the value of apartments and municipal services granted free of charge; (i) from compensation paid as an author's royalty (in addition to compensation paid to persons specified in point 1(j); (j) from the value of uniforms and clothing issued in kind (or monetary compensation).

7. Alimony shall be recovered from the amount of earnings (or income) due to a person paying the alimony after taxes are withheld from such earnings (or income).

F. Custody of Children

CODE ON MARRIAGE AND THE FAMILY, RSFSR (1969)
Article 52. *Duties of Parents in Bringing Up Children*

Parents should bring up their children in the spirit of the moral code of a builder of communism, concern for their physical development, and preparation for socially useful activity.

Parental rights may not be exercised contrary to the interests of children.

Article 53. *Duties of Parents to Protect the Rights and Interests of Children*

The protection of the rights and interests of minor children shall be the duty of their parents.

Parents shall be the legal representatives of their minor children and shall protect their rights and interests in all institutions, including judicial, without a special authorization.

Article 54. *Equality of Rights and Duties of Both Parents*

The father and mother shall have equal rights and duties with respect to their children.

Parents shall enjoy equal rights and bear equal duties with respect to their children also in instances when the marriage is dissolved.

All questions relating to the bringing up of children shall be decided by both parents by mutual consent.

In the absence of consent, a disputed question shall be settled by agencies of guardianship and curatorship with the participation of the parents.

Article 55. *Place of Residence of Children in the Event of Divided Residence of Parents*

If the parents as a consequence of dissolution of marriage or for other reasons do not reside together, then on their consent depends with whom the minor children should reside.

In the absence of agreement between the parents, the dispute shall be decided by a court, proceeding from the interests of the children.

Article 56. *Participation of Parents Residing Separately in Bringing Up Children*

A parent residing separately from children shall have the right to have contact with them and shall be obliged to take part in rearing them. A parent with whom the children reside shall not have the right to obstruct the other parent from having contact with the children and from participating in rearing them.

Agencies of guardianship and curatorship may for a specific period deprive a parent residing separately from a child of the right to have contact with him if this hinders the normal rearing of the child or has a harmful influence on him.

If the parents cannot reach an agreement on the procedure for the participation of the parent residing separately from the children in rearing them, this procedure shall be determined by the agencies of guardianship and curatorship with the participation of the parents.

In those instances when the parents do not subordinate themselves to the decision of an agency of guardianship and curatorship, the latter shall have the right to turn to a court for resolution of the dispute.

G. *Rules applicable to citizenship, foreign law, and international treaties*

CODE ON MARRIAGE AND THE FAMILY, RSFSR (1969)
Article 161. *Conclusion of Marriages of Soviet Citizens with Foreigners and of Foreigners Between Themselves in the RSFSR*

Marriages of Soviet citizens with foreigners, as well as marriages of foreigners between themselves, shall be concluded in the RSFSR in accordance with the general principles.

The entry into marriage of Soviet citizens with foreigners shall not in itself entail a change of citizenship.

Marriages between foreigners concluded in the USSR at embassies or consulates of foreign states shall be deemed valid in the RSFSR on the basis of reciprocity if such persons at the time of entering into marriage were citizens of the state represented by the said ambassador or consul.

Article 162. *Conclusion of Marriages of Soviet Citizens and Performance of Other Acts of Civil Status in Embassies and Consulates of the USSR. Recognition of Marriages Concluded Beyond the Limits of the USSR*

In accordance with the Fundamental Principles of Legislation of the USSR and Union Republics on Marriage and the Family, the marriages of Soviet citizens who are residing beyond the limits of the USSR shall be concluded at embassies or consulates of the USSR.

If the persons concerned are citizens of the RSFSR, the laws of the RSFSR shall be applied when concluding a marriage or performing other acts of civil status at embassies or consulates of the USSR abroad. If the persons concerned are citizens of different union republics or it is not established which republic they are a citizen of, then by their agreement the laws of one of the union republics shall be applied, and if there is disagreement, by decision of the official registering the act of civil status.

In those instances when marriages between Soviet citizens and marriages of Soviet citizens with foreigners are concluded beyond the limits of the USSR, observing the form of marriage established by the laws of the place where it was performed, such marriages shall be deemed valid in the RSFSR unless there are obstacles arising from Articles 15, 16, or 43 of the present Code.

Marriages of foreigners concluded beyond the limits of the USSR according to the laws of the respective states shall be deemed valid in the RSFSR.

Article 163. *Dissolution of Marriages of Soviet Citizens with Foreigners and Marriages of Foreigners Between Themselves in the RSFSR. Recognition of Divorces Performed Beyond the Limits of the USSR*

Marriages of Soviet citizens with foreigners, as well as marriages of foreigners between themselves, shall be dissolved in the RSFSR in accordance with the general grounds.

The dissolution of marriages between Soviet citizens and foreigners performed beyond the limits of the USSR according to the laws of the respective states shall be deemed valid in the RSFSR even if at the moment the marriage was dissolved one of the spouses resided beyond the limits of the USSR.

The dissolution of marriages between Soviet citizens performed beyond the limits of the USSR according to the laws of the respective states shall be deemed valid in the RSFSR if both spouses at the moment the marriage is dissolved resided beyond the limits of the USSR.

The dissolution of marriages between foreigners performed beyond the limits of the USSR according to the laws of the respective states shall be deemed valid in the RSFSR.

Cases concerning the dissolution of marriages between Soviet citizens permanently residing abroad may be considered by courts of the RSFSR upon the commission of the USSR Supreme Court.

Article 165. *Application of RSFSR Legislation on Marriage and the Family to Relations of Stateless Persons.*

Stateless persons residing in the RSFSR shall enter into marriage and dissolve marriage, shall enjoy the rights arising from RSFSR legislation on marriage and the family, and shall bear the duties provided for by such legislation on the general grounds with Soviet citizens.

Article 166. *Application in the RSFSR of Foreign Laws and of International Treaties and Agreements*

The application in the RSFSR of foreign laws on marriage and the family or the recognition of acts of civil status based on such laws may not occur if such application or recognition would be contrary to the bases of the Soviet system.

If other rules than those contained in RSFSR legislation on marriage and the family have been established by an international treaty or an international agreement in which the USSR or RSFSR participates, the rules of the international treaty or international agreement shall be applied on the territory of the RSFSR.

BAUER vs. BAUER, Biulleten' Verkhovnogo Suda RSFSR, 1970, no. 3, p. 7.

Bauer, a citizen of the USSR, brought suit against Mr. Bauer, a citizen of the German Democratic Republic, for dissolution of marriage, recovery of alimony for a son, and for division of property acquired during the marriage.

By a ruling of the Moscow City Court, Bauer's claim with regard to a division of property was rejected for lack of jurisdiction.

The Judicial Division for Civil Cases of the RSFSR Supreme Court, having considered the case upon the private appeal of Bauer, found that it was not subject to satisfaction, pointing out the following in its ruling of November 24, 1969:

It seems from the materials of the case that the property in dispute is situate at the defendant's place of residence in the German Democratic Republic where the parties lived together.

It is provided by Article 22, par. 2, of the Treaty between the Union of Soviet Socialist Republics and the German Democratic Republic on Legal Assistance in Civil, Family, and Criminal Cases that if one of the spouses is a citizen of one of the Contracting Parties and the second is a citizen of the other Contracting Party, their personal and property legal relations shall be determined by legislation of that Contracting Party on whose territory they reside or resided together.

Inasmuch as the parties resided together in the German Democratic Republic and the property in dispute is situate there, the dispute initiated by the plaintiff for division of the property is subject to consideration in accordance with the legislation of the German Democratic Republic.

Under such conditions the Moscow City Court in accordance with Article 129(7) of the RSFSR Code of Civil Procedure correctly refused to accept Bauer's claim in regard to the division of property for lack of jurisdiction of the Moscow City Court in the dispute.

CHAPTER XXIII

The Minor: His Rights and Responsibilities

As the future builders of communism, children have always occupied an important place in Soviet legal theory and practice. Since the early days of the postrevolutionary era, the law has reflected a zealous regard for the rights of minors and a deep concern with parental duties and their proper exercise. One aim of the 1918 family code was the elimination of any legal difference between children born in and out of wedlock. Illegitimacy was to be banished as a legal concept, and social stigma against bastardy was to be rooted out. In 1935 a Siberian court denounced such stigmatic thinking as a survival of capitalism in the mind of man.[1] Unwed mothers had the same rights as married mothers to claim maintenance from fathers under procedures designed to give the putative father an opportunity to contest paternity; there was to be no leniency toward such defendants, for the code permitted holding all members of a group liable for maintenance of a child where precise paternity could not be established. To avoid this absurdity, if there were several possibilities, the 1926 code required that the court select only one man as a father on the basis of the best obtainable evidence.[2]

The 1926 family code likewise eliminated the requirements for registration of marriages and abolished paternity suits. This sanctioning of casual family relations, without risks or legal consequences, when added to the elimination of bastardy, resulted in a weakening of the fabric of the Soviet family and gave the Soviet leadership some cause for concern.

Statistical studies in the mid-1930s showed that juvenile delinquency in the Soviet Union was mounting and that a major source of delinquents was the broken or inattentive home. Criminal statutes placed the burden upon parents to ensure that their children committed no crimes, for parents were required to pay damages[3] and even fines if they did.[4] Additional state homes for children, with varying degrees of disciplinary regimes, ranging from those of the ministries of health and of social security to the educational labor colonies of the Ministry of Internal Affairs,[5] were established at the same time. Campaigns were initiated to persuade the public that a

---

[1]Case of Krivozubova, Order of June 9, 1935, Sovetskaia iustitsiia, 1935, No. 22, p. 24.
[2]Art 32.
[3]Law of November 25, 1935, [1935] I Sob. Uzak, RSFSR, No. 1, item 1. s. 6.
[4]Ibid.
[5]Law of May 31, 1935, [1935]I Sob. Uzak, RSFSR, No. 32, item 252.

strong family was inspired by communism, and the local organs of the communist party were instructed to give special attention to supervision of influences brought to bear upon children.

This change in attitude led to the adoption of a sweeping revision of family law in 1944 which, *inter alia,* required once again that marriages be registered and declared without legal effect unregistered marriages contracted prior to that day. Under the 1944 enactment, children born out of wedlock were no longer to be a charge upon the father, but on the state, which assumed the obligation to pay the mother a stipend to cover some part of maintenance costs. Such children were to bear the surname of the mother.

Another factor exerting an influence upon the home was the development of boarding schools in increasing numbers after 1953, and the inclusion of large numbers of such schools has featured in plans since that time. Both orphans and children of working parents are placed in schools of this type.

The 1968 Fundamental Principles and union republic family codes have gone one step further in reinstating the paternity suit and holding parents to stricter accountability for support of children. Adoption procedures have been improved and divulging the secret of adoption made a criminal offense in several union republics. A scheme of child allowances was introduced in 1974 to assist low-income families. The incidence of juvenile crime continues to disturb Soviet authorities, and a number of measures have been initiated in recent years within state bodies and social organizations to guide and reform young offenders. Most juvenile offenses are dealt with in commissions for cases of minors attached to local soviets. These commissions have wide powers to hear and dispose of cases and to involve laymen as social educators or install guardianships as required. Institutions of this nature appear fated to assume greater responsibilities in the 1980s as part of increased emphasis on non-penal sactions and measures in coping with offenders, both juvenile and adult.

A. Children Born Out of Wedlock

CODE ON MARRIAGE AND THE FAMILY, RSFSR (1969)
Article 47. *Bases of Origin of Rights and Duties of Parents and Children*

The mutual rights and duties of parents and children shall be based on the parentage of the children certified in the procedure established by law.

The parentage of a child from parents who are married shall be certified by an entry concerning the marriage of the parents.

The parentage of a child from parents who are not married shall be established by means of the father and mother filing a joint application at state agencies for the registry of acts of civil status.

Article 48. *Establishing Paternity in a Judicial Procedure*

If a child is born of parents who are not married, in the absence of a joint application of the parents, paternity may be established in a judicial procedure upon the application of one of the parents or the guardian (or curator) of the child, of a person on whom the child is dependent, as well as of the child himself when he attains majority.

When establishing paternity, the court shall take into account the cohabitation and keeping of a common household of the child's mother and the defendant before the birth of the child or the joint upbringing or maintenance by them of the child, or evidence reliably confirming the acknowledgement of paternity by the defendant.

Article 49. *Entry of Parents in Birth Registry Books*

The father and mother who are married shall be entered as the parents of a child in the birth registry book upon the application of either of them.

If the parents are not married, the mother of the child shall be entered upon the application of the mother, and the entry concerning the father upon the joint application of the father and mother of the child, or the father shall be entered according to a decision of a court.

In the event of the mother's death, and also if it is impossible to establish her place of residence, the father of the child shall be entered upon the application of the father.

If a child is born of a mother who is not married, unless there is a joint application of the parents or a decision of a court concerning the establishment of paternity, the father of the child shall be entered in the birth registry book according to the surname of the mother; the name and patronymic of the father of the child shall be entered at her instruction.

A person entered as the father or mother of a child shall have the right to contest the entry made within a year from the time when it became known or should have become known to him that the entry was made. If at this time the person entered as a father or mother was a minor, the period of a year shall be computed from the time he attains eighteen years of age.

Article 50. *Rights and Duties of Children Born of Unmarried Persons in the Event Paternity is Established*

When paternity is established in the procedure provided for by Articles 47 and 48 of the present Code, the children shall have the same rights and duties in respect of parents and their relatives as children born of persons who were married.

ON THE PRACTICE OF APPLICATION IN THE RUSSIAN FEDERATION OF LEGISLATION ON MARRIAGE AND THE FAMILY, Decree of the Presidium of the RSFSR Supreme Soviet, February 19, 1972, [1972] Vedomosti Verkhovnogo Soveta RSFSR, no. 11, item 276

The new provisions of legislation concerning the establishment of paternity are widely applied with respect to children whose parents are not in a registered marriage. Paternity is acknowledged in the majority of instances not in a judicial, but in a voluntary, procedure upon the application of parents. Thus, according to the information of ŻAGS agencies, in 20 regions, territories, and autonomous republics in 1970 paternity was registered with respect to 62,330 children pursuant to applications concerning voluntary acknowledgement, and for nine months of 1971, with respect to 44,395 children.

A significant number of cases are considered by people's courts concerning the establishment of the fact of recognition of paternity in the event of the death of the person who maintained a child and who acknowledged himself as the father. When considering such cases, the courts involve as interested persons the social security agencies, financial agencies, and citizens who are family members of the deceased, as well as other relatives, which permits such cases to be considered objectively . . .

Some people's courts allow errors when considering cases concerning the establishment of paternity and the fact of recognizing paternity; do not always ensure the participation of social security agencies and interested persons in cases concerning the establishment of the fact of recognizing paternity; inadequately investigate the evidence necessary to establish paternity, in connection with which unfounded decisions are rendered (Karelian and Mordovian ASSR, Kalinin, Kursk, and a number of other regions).

A. I. Pergament and S. Ia. Palastina, DEVELOPMENT OF SOVIET LEGISLA-
   TION ON MARRIAGE AND THE FAMILY, Sovetskoe gosudarstvo i pravo,
   1975, no. 9, p. 51

Strengthening the Protection of Rights and Interests of Children Born Out of Wedlock. The fullest possible protection of the interests of mother and children and ensuring a happy childhood to each child is one of the principal tasks of Soviet legislation on marriage and the family. Numerous norms of the Fundamental Principles and codes on marriage and the family increasing the protection of the interests of mother and children have found extensive application in practice, for example, norms regulating the establishment of paternity with regard to children born out of wedlock. A study of the practice of their application by the USSR Ministry of Justice showed that the effectiveness of establishing paternity is rather great . . .

At the same time, the norms concerning establishment of paternity require improvement. It is advisable to reproduce Article 56 of the Estonian Code on Marriage and the Family permitting the filing of an application concerning the establishment of paternity during the mother's pregnancy in the codes on marriage and the family of all union republics. In the interests of children one should interpret the norms regulating the establishing of paternity in ZAGS agencies with respect to children born before October 1, 1968, if the mother of a child is dead, is deemed to lack legal capacity, is deprived of parental rights, or if it is impossible to establish her place of residence. A procedure for certifying the signature of an absent parent has not been established in all union republics, which complicates the voluntary acknowledgement of paternity. It is desirable in particular to regulate the contesting of paternity by persons who at the time of a voluntary acknowledgement of paternity knew of the child's parentage from another man.

When establishing paternity, a court takes into account the cohabitation and keeping of a common household by the child's mother and the defendant before the birth of the child or the joint bringing up or maintenance by them of a child or evidence reliably confirming the acknowledgement by the defendant of paternity (Article 16, par. 4, Fundamental Principles). Practice testifies to the unacceptability of an exhaustive list of facts to be taken into account by a court in cases of this category. For example, by a judgment of the Ludzen District People's Court of the Latvian SSR, E. was convicted under Article 122 of the Latvian Criminal Code for sexual relations with 15-year old Z., as a result of which a child was born. After the birth of the child, Z. brought suit for establishment of paternity. And although not one of the facts specified in Article 16, par. 4 of the Fundamental Principles was established, the court, having deemed the paternity of E. incontestable, satisfied the suit. There are frequently other instances in judicial practice when the parentage of a child from the defendant is incontestable despite the absence of facts provided by the Fundamental Principles.

Thus, to a significant extent objections regarding the complexity of proving the parentage of a child are refuted. The argument regarding the overloading of courts with cases concerning the establishment of paternity is not confirmed by practice. Despite a singificant increase in number, cases concerning the establishment of paternity in 1974 comprise 1.1% of civil suits and 6.1% of civil cases considered by courts in a special proceeding. In our view, it would be advisable to relieve the courts from considering uncontested cases, but not of suits concerning the establishment of paternity, which protect the interests of children born out of wedlock and their mothers.

A study of the materials concerning the establishment of paternity in ZAGS agencies of the Moscow Region showed that the majority of mothers of children out of wedlock were low-paid workers or employees. As a rule, the case concerns a youth who lives in communal housing of an enterprise or institution, and already by virtue of this the mother cannot refer to cohabitation and keeping a common household with the child's father. The exhaustive list of circumstances of Article 16, par. 4 of the Fundamental Principles essentially is applied not against casual alliances but against young workers and employees in complex financial and housing conditions.

The Soviet state bears great expenses in connection with the payment of benefits to unmarried and inadequately provided for mothers. Would it not be just to move the concern for maintenance of children out of wedlock to the shoulders of their fathers who avoid voluntary acknowledgement of paternity? With an average monthly wage for a worker and employee of 140.7 rubles per month, the amount of alimony significantly exceeds the amount of benefits paid. Consequently, limiting the establishment of paternity by a court does not correspond either to the interests of children nor to state interests.

Of course, we are talking of establishing paternity by a court only in those instances when the parentage of the child from the defendant may be reliably established. In the interests of the children it is advisable to grant the court the right to take into account any evidence confirming the parentage of a child out of wedlock in regard to paternal line. In our view, Article 16, par. 4 of the Fundamental Principles needs the following change: "When establishing paternity, the court shall take into account the cohabitation and keeping of a common household by the child's mother and the defendant before the birth of the child or the joint bringing up or maintenance by them of the child, or the acknowledgement by the defendant of paternity, as well as other circumstances reliably confirming the parentage of the child from the defendant."

SH. vs. O., Sotsialisticheskaia zakonnost', 1974, no. 4, p. 90.

The Spandarian District People's Court in the city of Erevan rejected a suit of Sh. against O. concerning the establishment of paternity and alimony. The Judicial Division for Civil Cases of the Armenian Supreme Court left this decision without change.

The Deputy USSR Procurator General brought a protest to the Presidium of the Armenian Supreme Court.

In concurring with the protest, the Presidium of the republic Supreme Court stated that Sh. and O.—students of the philological faculty at Erevan University—became acquainted in November 1970, and on November 29, 1971, filed an application for registration of marriage. Upon the petition of their parents, the ZAGS agencies did not register the marriage. Sh. and O. appealed the delay of registration of the marriage to the republic bureau of ZAGS and wrote about it to the editorial boards of newspapers. The defendant subsequently refused registration of the marriage. On August 29, 1972, Sh. gave birth to a daughter.

In refusing to satisfy the suit of Sh., the court justified this by the fact that Sh. and O. had not kept a common household, did not live together, the defendant did not care for the child, and did not extend it financial assistance. According to Article 16 of the Fundamental Principles of Legislation of the USSR and Union Republics on Marriage and the Family and point 3 of the decree of the Plenum of the USSR Supreme Court of December 4, 1969, "On the Practice of the Application by Courts of the Fundamental Principles of Legislation of the USSR and Union Republics on Marriage and the Family", when establishing paternity the court shall take into account evidence reliably confirming the acknowledgement by the defendant of paternity; such evidence may be letters, questionnaires, statements of the defendant, and other factual data. From the materials of the case, in particular the medical file of the plaintiff and applications of the parties concerning registration of the marriage, it is clear that they wished to create a family, that the conception of the child was toward the end of 1971, when the parties applied to the ZAGS bureau, that they appealed the actions of the ZAGS agencies which delayed registration of the marriage. The defendant did not deny at the judicial proceeding that he was at the ZAGS bureau with the plaintiff, appealed the actions of the ZAGS workers, wrote to the editor of the newspaper *Komsomol'skaia Pravda* that he had intimate relations with the plaintiff, and that he acknowledged in a letter to a comrade that the child was his. Witness S. Petrosian testified that O., learning of the plaintiff's pregnancy, did not authorize her to have an abortion and that they frequently met. Witness F. Pogosova testified that Sh. and O. came to her sister for advice in regard to pregnancy. Thus, the defendant knew about the plaintiff's pregnancy, met with her, and essentially did not deny his paternity. The plaintiff submitted a letter of the defendant from which it is clear that before the interference of their parents there were good mutual relations between them. The court did not give a proper evaluation to evidence submitted to the court and did not enlarge the group of witnesses who knew about the mutual relations of the parties to the case.

The Presidium of the republic Supreme Court, having vacated the judicial decrees in the case, sent it for new consideration at first instance in the Judicial Division for Civil Cases of the Armenian Supreme Court.

KRYLOV vs. KRYLOVA, Biulleten' Verkhovnogo Suda RSFSR, 1973, no. 8, p. 4

The Krylovs, in a registered marriage since June 1969, have a son born April 22, 1971. Krylov brought suit against Krylova to recognize as invalid the entry concerning the birth of the child in which he is indicated as the father.

In justification of his claim, the Plaintiff referred to the fact that on March 23, 1970, the marriage with the defendant was dissolved by the Kaliazin District People's Court, and on July 23, 1970, he received a certificate for dissolution of marriage at the ZAGS section; he is not the father of the child born April 22, 1971, since conjugal relations with Krylova had ceased even before March 1970.

The defendant did not acknowledge the suit and explained that after the decision concerning dissolution of the marriage she had a reconciliation with Krylov and began to continue conjugal relations with him, and on April 22, 1971, gave birth to his child, as the father of which he was entered in the birth certificate. At the same time, Krylova requested the recovery of alimony for the child.

The Kalinin Regional Court rejected the basic suit and satisfied the counter-suit.

The Judicial Division for Civil Cases of the RSFSR Supreme Court, having considered the case by way of cassation, left the decision without change by a ruling of January 15, 1973, indicating the following:

According to Article 149 of the RSFSR Code on Marriage and the Family, the registration of a child's birth conceived in a marriage but born after its dissolution, if not more than ten months have passed from the date of the dissolution of the marriage to the date of the birth of the child, shall be in the same procedure as the registration of a child's birth whose parents are married.

The marriage between the Krylovs actually was dissolved on March 23, 1970, the certificate of dissolution of marriage received at the ZAGS section by Krylov on July 23, 1970. Inasmuch as not more than ten months had passed from the time of receiving the certificate of dissolution of marriage and the birth of the child, the ZAGS agencies correctly entered Krylov as its father.

In accordance with Article 49 of the Code on Marriage and the Family, a person entered as the father or mother of a child shall have the right to contest the entry made within a year from the time when it became or should have become known to him that the entry was made.

If at the time the person entered as the father or mother was a minor, the year's period is computed from the time he attains eighteen years of age.

Krylova did not receive the certificate concerning termination of the marriage, and Krylov, having received it only on July 23, 1970, concealed this fact from Krylova.

From the opinion of a gynecologist it is clear that the conception of the child could occur in the second half of July or first half of August 1970.

Witnesses Abramova, Kolygina, Poterina, and others testified in court that the parties at this period of time, *e.g.*, after the decision concerning dissolution of the marriage, maintained conjugal relations and lived together.

With such data the court justifiably rejected Krylov's suit to deem the entry concerning paternity invalid.

By virtue of Article 67 of the Code on Marriage and the Family parents are obliged to maintain their minor children and children incapable of working who have attained majority and who require assistance. The amount of alimony recovered from parents for minor children is determined by Article 68 of the Code on Marriage and the Family. Therefore, the plaintiff's request for recovery of alimony for the son from the defendant is based on the law.

SURKOVA vs. BULKIN, Biulleten' Verkhovnogo Suda RSFSR, 1970, no. 4, pp. 4–5

Surkova brought suit against Bulkin for establishment of paternity.

In justification of her claims, she referred to the fact that in January 1968 she became acquainted with Bulkin, in April 1968 entered into intimate relations with him, in May 1968 their acquaintanceship was terminated, and on January 19, 1969, she gave birth to his child. Before the child's birth, Bulkin promised to register a marriage with her, but then refused to register a marriage and after the birth of the child does not wish voluntarily to formalize a paternity entry.

Bulkin did not acknowledge the suit and explained that he was an acquaintance of Surkova from January 1968; in August 1968 had the intention to register a marriage, but, learning about her pregnancy, did not register a marriage with her. He did not have intimate relations with her and is not the father of her child.

The Rostov Regional Court rejected the suit.

Having considered the case by cassational appeal of Surkova, the Judicial Division for Civil Cases of the RSFSR Supreme Court left the decision of the regional court without change and the cassational appeal without satisfaction indicating the following in a ruling of January 8, 1970:

The decision of the court was decreed in accordance with the materials of the case and the requirements of the law.

According to Article 16 of the Fundamental Principles of Legislation of the USSR and Union Republics on Marriage and the Family, when establishing paternity the court shall take into account the cohabitation and keeping of a common household by the child's mother and the defendant before the birth of the child or the joint rearing or maintenance by them of the child or evidence reliably confirming acknowledgement by the defendant of paternity.

From the explanations of the parties, testimony of witnesses, and other materials of the case it is clear that before the birth of the child Surkova and Bulkin did not live together, and did not keep a common household. After the birth of the child the parties did not rear it together nor maintain it.

The demand of Surkova for establishment of paternity is based on the fact that Bulkin recognized himself as the father of the child and thereafter refused to formalize a marriage and voluntarily register the child in his own name.

Establishment of paternity on these grounds may occur if evidence exists reliably confirming the acknowledgement by the defendant of paternity.

Surkova did not submit much evidence nor was such found by the court. Evidence confirming the other circumstances specified in the law also is lacking.

From Surkova's words, she became acquainted with Bulkin in January 1968 and at the end of April 1968 was intimate with him. The acquaintanceship between them ceased from May 1968. The gynecologist Lapin questioned as an expert in court explained that Surkova's pregnancy occurred between April 12 and 17, 1968, *i.e.*, in that period when according to her she did not have intimate relations with Bulkin. On the individual card of Surkova's pregnancy it is indicated that intimate life began in 1967, *i.e.*, before meeting Bulkin. Surkova declared in court that she learned about the pregnancy in June but told the defendant about it in August 1968 in order to resolve the question of registering a marriage. Bulkin contested this fact, stating that he wanted to register a marriage with Surkova, but after he learned about the pregnancy, took back the documents from ZAGS. The fact that Bulkin in August 1969 wanted to marry Surkova only characterizes the personal mutual relations of the parties and cannot serve a grounds to establish paternity.

B. The Right to Support

CODE ON MARRIAGE AND THE FAMILY (1969)
Article 67. *Duties of Parents to Maintain Children*
Parents shall be obliged to maintain their minor children and children who have attained majority, who are not capable of working, and who require assistance.
Article 69. *Recovery of Alimony for Children Placed in Children's Institutions*
Expenses for the maintenance of children placed in children's institutions may be recovered to the benefit of such institution from the parents of the children in amounts established by Article 68 of the present Code. In such instances funds for the maintenance of children shall be recovered from each of the parents unless they are exempted by law from making payments for the maintenance of children. The recovery of alimony awarded previously to one of the parents (or guardian, curator) in such instances shall be terminated.

A court may, taking into account the financial position of the parents, relieve them in full or in part from the payment of such funds.

Article 73. *Participation of Parents in Additional Expenses*

Parents who are paying alimony for minor children may be enlisted to participate in additional expenses arising out of exceptional circumstances (grave illness, mutilation of a child, etc.).

The extent of participation in such expenses shall be determined by a court, taking into account the financial and family position of the parents.

Article 76. *Amount of Alimony Recovered for Children Who Have Attained Majority and Who are Not Capable of Working.*

The amount of alimony recovered from parents for children who have attained majority, who are not capable of working, and who require assistance shall be determined by a court, proceeding from the financial and family situation of the parents and of the children requiring assistance, in a lump sum of money to be paid monthly.

CRIMINAL CODE, RSFSR (1960)

Article 122. *Malicious Avoidance of Payment of Alimony or Maintenance for Children*

The malicious avoidance by parents of payment, in accordance with a court decision, of funds for the maintenance of minor children, or of maintenance for children who have attained majority, are dependent on them, but are not capable of working shall be punished by deprivation of freedom for a term not exceeding one year, or by exile for a term not exceeding three years, or by correctional tasks for a term not exceeding one year.

Article 123. *Malicious Avoidance of Rendering Aid to Parents*

The malicious avoidance of payment, in accordance with a court decision, of funds for the maintenance of parents who are not capable of working shall be punished by correctional tasks for a term not exceeding one year or by social censure or shall entail application of measures of social pressure.

STATUTE ON THE PROCEDURE FOR ASSIGNING AND PAYING BENEFITS FOR CHILDREN OF LOW-INCOME FAMILIES, Confirmed by Decree of the USSR Council of Ministers, September 25, 1974, [1974] SP SSSR, No. 21, item 123

1. In accordance with the Edict of the Presidium of the USSR Supreme Soviet of September 25, 1974, "On Introducing Benefits for Children of Low-Income Families", benefits for children shall be assigned and paid to families according to the present Statute:

(a) of workers and employees of state, social, and cooperative enterprises, institutions, and organizations;

(b) of other citizens to whom state social insurance extends, except for persons performing work of a short-term or occasional character;

(c) of collective farm members;

(d) of persons who are members of creative unions (of writers, composers, artists, etc.);

(e) of persons engaged in work for individual citizens or collectives of citizens (domestic workers, guards, chauffeurs, etc.) on condition of the concluding of a labor contract with the employer and its registration at a trade union organization);

(f) of military servicemen, rank and file and officers of agencies of the USSR Ministry of Internal Affairs, workers of the militarized guard of ministries and departments not subject to state social insurance, rank and file and officers of the special communications service of the USSR Ministry of Communications and the union republic ministries of communications;

(g) of pensioners;

(h) of persons studying in higher and secondary specialized educational institutions, high schools, schools, and courses for the training of cadres, post-graduate students, and clinical house-surgeons.

2. Citizens having the right to a benefit for children may apply at any time to have it assigned after this right arises without limitation of time.

4. Benefits for children shall not be subject to imposition of taxes.

5. Families in which the average total income per family member does not exceed 50 rubles per month shall have the right to receive benefits for children.

6. A grant for children shall be assigned and paid for each child until he attains 8 years of age.

7. A grant for children shall be assigned in the amount of 12 rubles per month.

8. When determining the right to receive a benefit for children there shall be taken into account in the composition of the family: the husband, wife, the children dependent on them who have not attained 18 years of age or who are older and are receiving a benefit as I or II group invalids from childhood, as well as their parents living with the spouses who are not capable of working if they do not receive a pension and there are no other persons obliged by law to maintain them.

Military servicemen on active service, including those serving in military construction detachments, shall not be taken into account in the family composition.

DYSHENOV vs. DYSHENOVA, Biulleten' Verkhovnogo Suda RSFSR, 1972, no. 4, p. 6.

Dyshenov brought suit against Dyshenova to relieve him from payment of alimony for a son since, as from April 1970, the child has been in the Prokhladnensk Children's Boarding Home for mentally retarded children, and since 1971 Dyshenova has been relieved from paying for his maintenance at the boarding home.

[The people's court and Judicial Division for Civil Cases of the Kabardino-Balkarskii ASSR Supreme Court rejected the suit, but the Presidium of the latter court sent the case for new consideration. The Judicial Division for Civil Cases of the RSFSR Supreme Court reversed the presidium and by a ruling on November 25,

1971, reinstated the lower court decision on the following grounds]:

In vacating the decision and ruling, the presidium of the Kabardino-Balkarskii ASSR Supreme Court pointed out that in accordance with the requirements of Article 69 of the RSFSR Code on Marriage and the Family expenses for the maintenance of children placed in children's institutions may be recovered to the benefit of such institutions from each of the parents. The recovery of alimony awarded previously to one of the parents in such instances is terminated. Therefore, the presidium proposed during the new consideration to involve in the case the boarding home as an interested organization in order to recover to its benefit expenses for the maintenance of the child from both parents.

This instruction of the presidium can not be deemed correct.

According to Article 42 of the Fundamental Principles on Public Health, parents shall be relieved from paying funds for the maintenance of children in children's homes, a child's home, and other specialized children's institutions if placing a child in these institutions was caused by a defect in his physical or psychological development.

In accordance with Article 69 of the Code on Marriage and the Family, expenses for the maintenance of children placed in children's institutions may be recovered to the benefit of such institutions from each parent only if they are not relieved by law from making payments for the maintenance of children. Inasmuch as the child was placed in the children's institution in connection with a defect in his psychological and physical development, payment may not be recovered from the parents for his maintenance in the children's institution. As regards the plaintiff's claim to be relieved from paying alimony, this question should be resolved by the court in accordance with the instructions of Article 68 of the Code on Marriage and the Family, according to which the court shall have the right to reduce the amount of alimony or relieve him from paying it if the children are fully maintained by the state or a social organization.

Therefore the court during a new consideration of the case should elucidate whether the plaintiff's child is on complete state security and whether she has expenses' for the child and depending on the information obtained decide the question of the well-foundedness of the plaintiff's claim.

SUKRUTOVA vs. SUKRUTOVA AND ANIKINA, Biulleten' Verkhovnogo Suda RSFSR, 1971, no. 7, pp. 14–15

Sukrutova brought suit against her grandchildren, V. A. Sukrutova and Anikina for recovery of alimony respectively of 20 and 10 rubles per month on the grounds that she is too old to work and the pension assigned to her of 21 rubles is insufficient for existence. Her son, A. A. Sukrutov, is not in a position to render her financial assistance inasmuch as he himself is not capable of working and lives on a pension in the amount of 42 rubles, and his children, her grandchildren, do not voluntarily extend her financial aid although in a position to do so since they receive high earnings.

The Korsakovskii City People's Court joined as second defendants the children of Sukrutova—A. A. and K. A. Sukrutov and P. A. Proseniuk—and recovered to her benefit 10 rubles from K. A. Sukrutov, 5 rubles from P. A. Proseniuk, 10 rubles from V. A. Sukrutova, and 5 rubles from Anikina, monthly.

The Presidium of the Sakhalin Regional Court, having considered the case upon the protest of the chairman of that court to vacate the decision of the people's court and transfer the case for new consideration, satisfied the protest, pointing out the following:

Its decision to recover alimony from the grandchildren the people's court justified by the fact that they are financially well provided for and in a position to render assistance to a needy aged grandmother.

In reality, according to Article 84 of the RSFSR Code on Marriage and the Family, grandchildren possessing adequate means are obliged to maintain their grandfather and grandmother who are not capable of working and need assistance unless they receive maintenance from their own children and spouses.

It seems from the materials of the case that the plaintiff received a pension for the loss of a breadwinner in the amount of 21 rubles monthly and has four children. However, the people's court, in violation of the requirements of Articles 14 and 50 of the RSFSR Code of Civil Procedure, did not sufficiently investigate the financial position of all her children, but limited itself only to their explanations. As a consequence of this, the duty to maintain the grandmother was imposed on the grandchildren without sufficient grounds.

In a new consideration of the case, the people's court is to take into account the foregoing, to investigate fully the materials of the case, and to render a decision in strict accordance with the law, having in view that according to Article 77 of the RSFSR Code on Marriage and the Family the amount of participation of each of the children in maitaining parents not capable of working and needing assistance is determined by proceeding from the financial and family status of the parents and children in a lump-sum amount of money paid monthly. In determining this amount, all the children of the said parent who have attained majority shall be taken into account, irrespective of whether a claim has been filed against all the children or only against one or several of them.

KOVAL' vs. KOVAL', Biulleten' Verkhovnogo Suda RSFSR, 1971, no. 7, p. 14

Koval' brought suit against Koval' to recover alimony for a son, since being the father of the child he does not render financial assistance for his maintenance.

The Pronaiskii City People's Court satisfied the suit, recovering from Koval' for the benefit of Koval' 25 rubles monthly until the son attains majority.

The presidium of the Sakhalin Regional Court, having considered the case upon the protest of the chairman of that court to vacate the decision and transfer the case for new consideration, satisfied the protest on the following grounds.

The people's court did not justify its decision to recover the alimony on the basis of Article 68 of the RSFSR Code on Marriage and the Family in a fixed amount although the article to which it referred provides for the recovery of alimony from parents for minor children only in fractions of wages and not in a fixed amount. The amount of the fraction may be reduced by a court only in strictly limited instances. In particular, it may be reduced if a parent from whom alimony is recovered is a first or second group invalid.

In addition, a people's court in general has no grounds to reduce the fractional payment of alimony provided for by Article 68 of the Code on Marriage and the Family to one-quarter of the wages only because the defendant is a second group invalid inasmuch as he, as is clear from the materials of the case, works and receives a wage of 170 rubles, 30 kopecks per month.

Alimony for children in a fixed amount may be ordered paid only in instances provided for by Article 71 of the Code on Marriage and the Family; the presence of a parent obliged to pay alimony with irregular changing wages or receiving part of them in kind, as well as if children remain with each of the parents but one of them is less provided for. Such circumstances are lacking in the present case.

C Adoption

CODE ON MARRIAGE AND THE FAMILY, RSFSR (1969)
Article 98. *Children With Respect to Whom Adoption is Permitted*
Adoption shall be permitted only with respect to minor children and in their interests.

Adoption shall be by decision of the executive committee of the district (or city) soviet of working people's deputies at the request of the person wishing to adopt a child at the place of the adoptive parent's place of residence or the place of the residence of the adopted person.

Adoption shall arise from the time the executive committee of the district (or city) soviet of working people's deputies renders a decision concerning the adoption.
Article 99. *Citizens Having the Right to Be Adoptive Parents*
Citizens who have attained majority may be adoptive parents except for persons deprived of parental rights, as well as persons deemed in accordance with the procedure established by law to lack legal capacity or restricted in legal capacity.
Article 100. *Consent of Parents of a Child to Adoption*
The consent of the parents of a child not deprived of parental rights shall be required for adoption.

The consent of parents shall not be required if they have been deemed in accordance with the procedure established by law to lack legal capacity or to be missing without news.

Parents may give consent for the adoption of a child by a specific person (or persons) or, having given consent to adoption, grant to agencies of guardianship and curatorship the selection of adoptive parents.

The consent of parents to adoption should be expressed in writing.

Parents shall have the right to retract the consent given by them if a decision concerning adoption has not yet been rendered.

Article 101. *Adoption Without the Consent of Parents*

In instances when parents avoid participation in bringing up a child, adoption by way of exception may be without their consent if it is established that for more than a year they have not lived together with the child and, despite the warning of agencies of guardianship and curatorship, they do not take part in his upbringing or maintenance and do not manifest parental attention and concern with respect to the child.

Article 103. *Consent of the Adopted Person to Adoption*

The consent of the adopted person to an adoption is required if he has attained ten years of age.

If before filing an application for adoption a child has lived in the adoptive family and considers it his parents, adoption by way of exception may be without obtaining the consent of the adopted person.

The consent of the child to adoption shall be elicited by agencies of guardianship and curatorship.

Article 104. *Consent of the Spouse of an Adoptive Parent to Adoption*

When a person who is married adopted a child, if both spouses do not adopt the child, the consent of the other spouse to the adoption shall be required.

The consent of the spouse to adoption shall not be required if this spouse is deemed to lack legal capacity in accordance with the procedure established by law, as well as if the spouses have terminated family relations, do not live together for more than a year, and the residence of the other spouse is unknown.

Article 108. *Equating Adopted Persons to Relatives of the Adoptive Parent and Preservation of Legal Relations with One of the Parents*

Adopted persons and their descendants with respect to their adoptive parents and their relatives, and the adoptive parents and their relatives with respect to the adopted persons and their descendants, shall be equal in personal and property rights and duties to the relatives by descent.

Adopted persons shall lose personal and property rights and be relieved from duties with respect to their parents and their relatives.

In the event of the adoption of a child by one person, these rights and duties may be preserved at the wish of the mother, if the adoptive parent is a man, or of the father, if the adoptive parent is a woman.

If one of the parents is deceased, then at the request of the parents of the deceased (grandfather and grandmother of a child) the rights and duties may be preserved with respect to relatives of the deceased parent unless the adoptive parent objects thereto.

The preservation of legal relations with one of the parents or with relatives of a deceased parent should be specified in the decision concerning the adoption.

Article 110. *Ensuring the Secret of Adoption*

The secret of adoption shall be protected by law.

In order to ensure the secret of adoption, at the request of the adoptive parent the place of birth of an adopted child may be changed, as well as in exceptional instances the date of birth, but by not more than six months. Changes of place and date of birth should be specified in the decision concerning the adoption.

It shall be prohibited without the consent of the adoptive parents, and in the event of their death, without the consent of agencies of guardianship or curatorship, to communicate any information whatever about the adoption, as well as to issue extracts from registration books for acts of civil status from which it would be clear that the adoptive parents are not the blood parents of the adopted person.

Persons who have divulged the secret of adoption against the will of the adoptive parent may be brought to responsibility in accordance with the procedure established by law.

Article 112. *Grounds and Consequences of Deeming an Adoption Invalid*

An adoption may be deemed invalid in instances when it is established by a court that the decision concerning adoption was based on false documents or when a person deprived of parental rights or deemed to lack capacity in accordance with the procedure established by law or restricted in legal capacity was the adoptive parent, as well as in the event of a fictitious adoption.

Any person whose right was violated by the adoption, as well as agencies of guardianship and curatorship and the procurator, shall have the right to demand that an adoption be deemed invalid.

An adoption deemed invalid shall be considered invalid from the time the decision concerning the adoption was rendered. In such event no rights and duties deriving from the adoption shall arise between the adoptive parent, his relatives, and the adopted person.

In the event an adoption is deemed invalid, the rights and duties of a child with respect to his parents and their relatives shall be restored.

A child shall be transferred to the parents by a court decision, and if this does not correspond to the child's interests, to agencies of guardianship and curatorship.

Article 114. *Vacating an Adoption by Demand of the Parents*

An adoption made without the consent of the parents in those instances when such consent was required may be vacated by a court upon a suit of the parents if the court established that the return of the child to the parents corresponds to his interests.

Vacating an adoption at the request of parents in those instances when the adopted person has attained 10 years of age shall be permitted only with the consent of the adopted person.

In those instances when it is unknown to the parents who is the adoptive parent of their child, the demand to vacate the adoption shall be submitted to agencies of guardianship and curatorship at the place where the decision concerning the adoption was rendered.

In the event a suit is filed against an agency of guardianship or curatorship, the adoptive parent, who may take part in the consideration of the case in court, shall be notified thereof.

Article 164. *Adoption of Children Holding Soviet Citizenship and Residing Beyond the Limits of the USSR, Rules for Adoption of Children by Foreigners in the RSFSR*

In accordance with the Fundamental Principles of Legislation of the USSR and Union Republics on Marriage and the Family, the adoption of a child holding RSFSR citizenship and residing beyond the limits of the USSR shall be at an embassy or consulate of the USSR. If the adoptive person does not hold Soviet citizenship it is necessary to obtain the authorization of the RSFSR Ministry of Enlightenment for the adoption.

The adoption of a child holding RSFSR citizenship performed in agencies of the state on whose territory the child resides also shall be deemed valid on condition of obtaining in advance the authorization for such adoption from the RSFSR Ministry of Enlightenment.

The adoption of children holding Soviet citizenship by foreigners on the territory of the RSFSR shall be on the general bases established by Chapter 12 of the present Code, on condition of obtaining in each individual instance the authorization for such adoption of the Council of Ministers of the autonomous republic or of the executive committee of the territory, regional, Moscow, or Leningrad City Soviets of Working People's Deputies.

CRIMINAL CODE, RSFSR (1960)
Article 124-1. *Divulgence of Secret of Adoption*

The divulgence of a secret of adoption against the wish of the adoptive parent shall be punished by correctional tasks for a term not exceeding one year or by a fine not exceeding 50 rubles or by social censure.

CRIMINAL CODE, ARMENIAN SSR (1961)
Article 220-1. *Divulgence of Secret of Adoption*

The divulgence of a secret of adoption protected by law performed against the will of the adoptive parent shall be punished by correctional tasks for a term not exceeding one year or by a fine of 50 to 100 rubles.

The same act entailing grave consequences shall be punished by deprivation of freedom for a term of from one to three years.

CRIMINAL CODE, KAZAKH SSR (1961)
Article 184-1. *Divulgence of Secret of Adoption*

The divulgence of a secret of adoption by an official shall be punished by correctional tasks for a term not exceeding one year or by dismissal from office.

The divulgence of a secret of adoption by a private individual committed for mercenary or other base motives and entailing grave consequences shall be punished by correctional tasks for a term not exceeding one year or by a fine of up to 100 rubles.

STATUTE ON THE PROCEDURE FOR ASSIGNING AND PAYING BENEFITS FOR CHILDREN OF LOW-INCOME FAMILIES, Confirmed by Decree of the USSR Council of Ministers, September 25, 1974. [1974] SP SSSR, No. 21, item 123

9. For adopted children residing with the adoptive parent, a benefit shall be assigned and paid to their adoptive parents on the same basis as natural children.

Children adopted by one person, if the rights and duties of one of the parents with respect to such children are preserved at the wish of the mother (if the adoptive parent is a man) or of the father (if the adoptive parent is a woman), shall, when determining the right to receive a grant, be taken into account according to their actual residence in the family of the adoptive parent or of the mother (or father).

K. vs. EXECUTIVE COMMITTEE OF TIRASPOL' CITY SOVIET, Sotsialisticheskaia zaknnost', 1971, no. 8, p. 86

The Tiraspol' People's Court on March 23, 1970, rejected a suit of K. against the executive committee of the Tiraspol' City Soviet of Working People's Deputies to vacate an adoption.

[The people's court decision was confirmed by the Judicial Division for Civil Cases of the Moldavian Supreme Court and protests of the Moldavian procurator to the presidium and the plenum of the Moldavian Supreme Court were rejected. Upon the protest of the USSR Procurator General, the Plenum of the USSR Supreme Court vacated all judicial decrees in the case and transferred it for a new hearing to the Moldavian Supreme Court with the participation of the procurator on the following grounds:]

The plaintiff, a student of the IV course of the pedagogical institute, after being discharged from a maternity home with a child born to her on December 24, 1969, was in a grave situation: she was not married, living in a student dormitory with a child was forbidden, and her relatives would not take the child for her. The maternity home accepted the child on condition that the child's mother give written consent to its adoption by other persons. Such consent the plaintiff was obliged to give on January 12, 1970, as a consequence of a confluence of grave personal and family circumstances. However, the plaintiff had no intention to renounce her child. On the same day she appealed to the dean's office of the institute with a request for assistance. She was granted academic leave and allotted a room in the student dormitory to live with the child. On the following day, January 13, 1970, she went to the maternity home for the child, but her child already had been transferred to adoptive parents without a decision of the executive committee of the city soviet of working people's deputies concerning the adoption. Such a decision was rendered only on January 14, 1970—after the plaintiff declared her wish to take back the child from the maternity home. Having transferred the said application of the mother regarding consent to adoption to the agencies of guardianship and curatorship, the administration of the maternity home did not notify these agencies that the plaintiff had changed her decision. Thus, the adoption of the child was in fact made without the consent of the mother. In the given instance a violation of Article 24 of the Fundamental Principles of Legislation of the USSR and Union Republics on Marriage and the Family was permitted, which established that the consent of the parents is required for an adoption. In addition, the requirements of Article 102 of the Moldavian Code on Marriage and the Family were not observed, which provided that the parents have the right to retract the consent given by them if the decision concerning adoption has not yet been rendered.

[At the new consideration of the case the adoption was vacated and the child transferred to its mother].

KUZ'MINOVA vs. NAZAROVA AND DIBIZHEVA, Biulleten' Verkhovnogo Suda RSFSR, 1971, no. 9, p. 14

Kuz'minova brought suit against her daughters Nazarova and Dibizheva for the recovery of alimony, pointing out that she is aged and not capable of working and requires assistance since she does not receive a pension and the daughters do not voluntarily supply her with funds for maintenance.

By a decision of the Pervomaiskii District People's Court in the city of Krasnodar, left without change by a ruling of the Krasnodar Territory Court, ten rubles were recovered from Nazarova and seven rubles from Dibizheva monthly for the benefit of the plaintiff.

[The presidium of the Krasnodar Territory Court satisfied a protest to vacate the earlier decision and send the case for new consideration]:

The judicial decrees in the case with regard to the recovery of alimony from Dibizheva are subject to being vacated since they were rendered pursuant to inadequately researched materials of the case in violation of the requirements of Articles 14 and 50 of the RSFSR Code of Civil Procedure.

According to Article 77 of the RSFSR Code on Marriage and the Family, children who have reached majority are obliged to maintain parents who are not capable of working and require assistance and to care for them. However, if the child was adopted, then by virtue of Article 108 of the Code on Marriage and the Family the adopted person loses personal and financial rights and is relieved from duties with respect to its parents and their relatives.

In confirmation of Dibizheva's adoption a copy of the birth certificate issued on January 5, 1950, was submitted in which her parents were specified as V. G. Dibizhev and S. G. Dibizheva, as well as a certificate of the rural Soviet of July 21, 1930, confirming that she was a dependent of her mother Dibizheva.

The court, having established that Dibizheva was in fact adopted by her grandfather and grandmother, did not advance arguments why the defendant's objections to the suit could not be taken into account.

The Division of the Territory Court noted in the ruling that the court correctly did not take into account the said objections of the defendant inasmuch as she lived at her grandfather's with the grandmother together with her mother. The judicial decrees in the case can not be deemed legal and well-founded since they contain contradictory reasons.

If the certification of the fact of the adoption of the defendant did not raise doubts for the court, then the court should discuss the question of the well-foundedness of Kuz'minova's claim for the recovery of alimony from Dibizheva.

In the new consideration of the case the court should verify the facts of the case and, depending on the information obtained, render an appropriate decision.

IN RE OLEG VOITIUL', Biulleten' Verkhovnogo Suda RSFSR, 1974, no. 1, pp. 5–6

By decision of the executive committee of the Apatit City Soviet of Working People's Deputies of August 22, 1972, at the request of Bonadrenko the adoption of Oleg Voitiul', born June 6, 1958, was carried out with conferment on him of the adoptive parent's surname

In January 1973 the mother of the adopted person, Luk'ianskiaia, brought suit to vacate the adoption, pointing out that it was done without her knowledge and consent. Bondarenko lived as one family with her brother Voitiul' and took the boy from the mother of Voitiul' in 1970 in the absence of the plaintiff. Having received a regular vacation at the end of 1970, the plaintiff came for her son to the city of Apatit, but the brother and Bondarenko persuaded her to leave the boy with them until the end of the academic year since the school was nearby and not 18 kilometers away, as at the place of his residence in Belorussia. After terminating cohabitation with Voitiul', Bondarenko adopted the boy, concealing from the agencies of guardianship the address of the natural mother of the child.

The procurator of the Murmansk Region joined in the suit. The Judicial Division for Civil Cases of the Murmansk Regional Court satisifed the suit and obliged Bondarenko to transfer the child to the mother.

The Judicial Division for Civil Cases of the RSFSR Supreme Court, having considered the case by way of cassation, left the decision without change by a ruling of June 28, 1973, on the following grounds:

In accordance with Article 114 of the RSFSR Code on Marriage and the Family, an adoption made without the consent of the parents in those instances in which such consent is required may be vacated by a court upon the suit of the parents if the court establishes that the return to the parents of the child corresponds to his interests. If the adopted person has attained 10 years of age, vacating the adoption is permitted with the consent of the adopted person.

Sufficient evidence was presented to the court that the adoption of Oleg Voitiul' was without the consent of the mother, who until this irreproachably brought up her son.

Bondarenko acknowledged that she deliberately did not name the place of residence of the natural mother of the child since she believes that the residence of a child for more than a year without the mother formally gave a right not to require the consent of the mother for adoption.

The court properly verified all the facts relating to the transfer of the boy to the upbringing of the mother, who in 1971 entered into a registered marriage with Luk'ianskii and verified the conditions in which the boy would live were the adoption vacated.

According to the opinion of the agencies of guardianship and curatorship of the Murmansk Regional Public Education Section, it is necessary to transfer Oleg Voitiul' when he finishes the 8th class for further upbringing to his mother. It is pointed out in the opinion that Oleg loves the mother, regrets the misunderstanding which occurred, and considers it necessary to correct the situation which has been created.

Under such circumstances the conclusion of the court that the return of Oleg to his natural mother corresponds to his interests is correct.

D. Parental rights and guardianship

CODE ON MARRIAGE AND THE FAMILY, RSFSR (1969)
Article 119. *Purposes of Guardianship and Curatorship*

Guardianship and curatorship shall be established to bring up minor children who as a consequence of the death of parents, the deprivation of parents of parental rights, illness of parents, or for other reasons were left without parental care, as well as for the protection of the personal and property rights and interests of such children.

Guardianship and curatorship shall be established also for the protection of the personal and property interests of persons who have attained majority and who by the state of their health cannot independently exercise their rights and fulfill their duties.

Article 120. *Agencies of Guardianship and Curatorship*

The executive committees of district (or city), settlement, or rural soviets of working people's deputies shall be agencies of guardianship and curatorship.

Guardianship and curatorship shall be established by the executive committee of a district, city, settlement, or rural soviet of working people's deputies at the place of residence of a person subject to guardianship or curatorship or at the place of residence of the guardian (or curator).

Implementation of the functions relating to guardianship and curatorship shall be entrusted to the public education sections with regard to minors, to public health sections with regard to persons deemed by a court to lack legal capacity or restricted in legal capacity, and to social security sections with regard to persons having legal capacity who need a curatorship for reasons of health.

Article 121. *Persons Over Whom a Guardianship or Curatorship is Established*

A guardianship shall be established over children who have not attained fifteen years of age, as well as over persons deemed by a court to lack legal capacity as a consequence of mental illness or feeble-mindedness (Article 15 of the RSFSR Civil Code).

A curatorship shall be established over minors from fifteen to eighteen years of age.

A curatorship shall be established over persons having legal capacity who have attained majority if they by reason of their health can not independently exercise their rights and fulfill their duties, as well as over persons limited by a court in legal capacity as a consequence of the abuse of alcoholic beverages or narcotics (Article 16, RSFSR Civil Code).

Article 123. *Establishment of a Guardianship or Curatorship Over a Minor Whose Parents Avoid Rearing Him.*

In instances when a child does not live together with parents and the latter avoid the duties relating to his upbringing, a guardianship or curatorship shall be established over the child. Agencies of guardianship and curatorship shall have the right in this event to demand in court the deprivation of the parents' parental rights.

Article 129. *Duties of Guardians and Curators to Rear Minors and Protect Their Rights and Interests*

Guardians and curators of minors shall be obliged to rear those under curatorship in the spirit of the moral code of a builder of communism, of concern for their physical development, study and training for a socially useful activity, and to protect their rights and interests.

Guardians and curators shall be obliged to live together with their minor wards.

In individual instances agencies of guardianship and curatorship may give authorization for the separate residence of the curator and his ward who has attained sixteen years of age if separate residence does not reflect unfavorably on the upbringing and protection of the rights and interests of the ward.

Guardians and curators shall be obliged to notify agencies of guardianship and curatorship about any change of place of residence.

Article 130. *Right of Guardians and Curators to Demand the Return of Children to Them from Persons Illegally Detaining Children with Themselves*

Guardians and curators shall have the right to demand the return to them of children who are under guardianship or curatorship with them from any persons detaining the children without legal grounds.

STATUTE ON THE PROCEDURE FOR ASSIGNING AND PAYING BENEFITS FOR CHILDREN OF LOW-INCOME FAMILIES, Confirmed by Decree of the USSR Council of Ministers, September 25, 1974, [1974] SP SSSR, No. 21, item 123

11. Their guardians shall have the right to receive a benefit for children under guardianship. When determining the right to a benefit in such instances there shall be taken into account not the income of the guardians but the pensions, benefits, and alimony received for such children and the income of parents not paying alimony.

13. Children with regard to whom the parents have been deprived of parental rights shall not be taken into account when determining the right to receive benefits as members of the family of these parents (or parent).

When the parents reside separately, the children shall be taken into account according to their actual residence in the family of the mother or father.

CRIMINAL CODE, RSFSR (1960)
Article 124. *Abuse of Duties of Guardianship*
The abuse of a guardianship for mercenary purposes or leaving a ward without supervision and necessary assistance shall be punished by deprivation of freedom for a term not exceeding two years or by correctional tasks for a term not exceeding one year.

MEILAKH vs. ZAGS AND FREIDINA, Sotsialisticheskaia zakonnost', 1972, no. 8, p. 91

The spouses Meilakh were married and on November 30, 1961, a son was born, upon whom was conferred the surname Meilakh. After dissolution of the marriage, the son remained with his mother for upbringing. In October 1967 R. Meilakh married Freidin and when registering took the surname of her husband. In 1969 she petitioned for a change of surname for the son from Meilakh to Freidin. By a decree of the public education section of the executive committee of the Tallin City Soviet of Working People's Deputies of October 17, 1969, the surname Freidin was conferred on the minor E. Meilakh. On the basis of this decree the ZAGS agencies changed the surname of the child in the act regarding his birth.

A. Meilakh brought suit against the section for the registry of acts of civil status and R. Freidina and, referring to the fact that his son's surname was changed without his consent, requested the surname Meilakh be restored to the child. The Central District People's Court of Tallin by a decision of March 11, 1971, satisfied the suit and restored the surname Meilakh to the minor child. The Judicial Division for Civil Cases of the Estonian Supreme Court by a ruling of May 4, 1971, vacated the decision of the people's court and rejected Meilakh's suit.

The deputy USSR Procurator General brought a protest against the judicial decrees in the case on the grounds that the case was not within the jurisdiction of a court.

The Presidium of the Estonian Supreme Court, concurring with the protest, vacated the judicial decrees and terminated the case, indicating in the decree that "according to Article 63, par. 1, of the Estonian Code on Marriage and the Family if the parents have different surnames, the surname of the father or mother shall be conferred on the child by the mutual agreement of the parents, and in the absence of agreement by a determination of agencies of guardianship and curatorship. If a parent with whom a child has been left for upbringing after dissolution of a marriage wishes to confer her surname on the child, then according to Article 65, par. 2, of the Estonian Code on Marriage and the Family, the agencies of guardianship and curatorship shall decide this depending on the interests of the child. The decision of the agencies of guardianship and curatorship is final, and disputes on this matter are not subject to consideration in a court."

FROM THE PRACTICE OF ZAGS, Sovetskaia iustitsiia, 1973, no. 8, cover.

Citizens turn to ZAGS agencies with the request that their names be expunged from records of birth after they have been deprived of parental rights. Have ZAGS agencies the right to satisfy such requests?

According to Article 47 of the RSFSR Code on Marriage and the Family, the parentage of the child (blood parentage) certified in accordance with law is the basis for the origin of mutual rights and duties of parents and children. The procedure for the entry of information concerning parents in the book for birth entries is established by Article 49 of the Code on Marriage and the Family. The entry made by ZAGS agencies in the registration book for acts concerning births serves as evidence of the parentage of a child from the parents specified therein. A person specified in an entry of an act concerning a birth as the father or mother of a child has the right to contest the entry made in the procedure established by law.

In the event of the deprivation of parental rights, the parents lose all rights based on the fact of birth of a child with regard to which they have been deprived of parental rights. However, deprivation of parental rights does not relieve parents from the duty to maintain children, and if the conditions provided for by Article 63 of the Code on Marriage and the Family are present, restoration of parental rights also is permitted. Therefore, a court decision concerning deprivation of a person of parental rights may not serve as a basis for excluding information concerning him from an entry of an act regarding the birth of a child.

ON THE PROCURATOR'S PROTEST, Chelovek i zakon, 1973, no. 2, p. 58

The guardianship council of the public health section of the executive committee of the Smol'ninsk District Soviet of Working People's Deputies of Leningrad by a decree of June 8, 1972, appointed Citizen R. as guardian over her son, deemed by a court to lack legal capacity.

The district procurator protested this decree on the following grounds. According to Article 120 of the RSFSR Code on Marriage and the family, a guardianship and curatorship shall be established by executive committees of district, city, settlement, or rural Soviet of working people's deputies at the place of residence of the person subject to guardianship or curatorship or the place of residence of the guardian (or curator). Questions concerning the appointment of a guardianship or curatorship shall be considered at a session of the executive committee, which also shall adopt an appropriate decision. The guardianship council of a public health section is not allocated the right to establish a guardianship or curatorship. In adopting the aforesaid decision, it exceeded its powers.

The procurator's protest was satisfied by the executive committee of the Smol'ninsk district Soviet; the decree of the guardianship council was vacated and a decision on the essence of the question was adopted which corresponded to the requirements of the law.

E. *The Minor as Employee*

CODE OF LAWS ON LABOR, RSFSR (1972)
Article 173. *Age from Which Hiring is Permitted*

Persons younger than sixteen years of age shall not be permitted to be hired.

In exceptional instances, by agreement with the factory, plant, and local trade union committee, persons who have attained fifteen years of age may be hired for work.

Article 174. *Rights of Minors in Labor Legal Relations*

Minors (persons who have not attained eighteen years of age) shall in labor legal relations be equated in rights to persons who have reached majority, and in the domain of labor protection, work hours, vacations, and certain other labor conditions shall enjoy exemptions established by the Fundamental Principles of Legislation of the USSR and Union Republics on Labor, by the present Code, and by other acts of labor legislation.

Article 175. *Work for Which the Use of Labor of Persons Younger than Eighteen Years is Prohibited*

The use of labor of persons younger than eighteen years of age for heavy work and for work with harmful or dangerous labor conditions, as well as underground work, shall be prohibited.

A list of heavy work and work with harmful or dangerous labor conditions for which the use of labor of persons younger than eighteen years of age is prohibited shall be confirmed in the procedure established by legislation.

The carrying and movement of heavy objects by minors exceeding the maximum norms established for them shall be prohibited.

Article 176. *Medical Examinations of Persons Younger than Eighteen Years of Age*

All persons younger than eighteen years of age shall be hired only after a preliminary medical examination and thereafter, until attaining eighteen years of age, annually shall be subject to a compulsory medical examination.

Article 177. *Prohibition Against Enlisting Workers and Employees Younger than Eighteen Years of Age for Night and Overtime Work*

It shall be prohibited to enlist workers and employees younger than eighteen years of age for night and overtime work and for work on days off.

Article 178. *Vacation for Workers and Employees Younger than Eighteen Years of Age*

Annual vacations for workers and employees younger than eighteen years of age (Article 67, par. 2) shall be granted in the summertime or, at their wish, at any time of the year.

Article 182. *Providing Young Workers and Specialists Who Have Completed Educational Institutions with Work According to their Specialty and Qualification*
Young workers who have finished professional-technical and technical high schools and young specialists who have finished higher and secondary specialized educational institutions shall be provided with work in accordance with the specialty and qualification received.

Article 183. *Limitation on the Dismissal of Workers and Employees Younger than Eighteen Years*
The dismissal of workers and employees younger than eighteen years of age at the initiative of the administration shall be permitted, besides the observance of the general procedure for dismissal, only with the consent of the district (or city) commission for cases of minors. Dismissal on the grounds specified in Article 33, points 1, 2, and 6 of the present Code shall be only in exceptional instances and shall not be permitted without arranging employment.

ON GENERAL SUPERVISION, Sotsialisticheskaia zakonnost', 1969, no. 1, p. 89
The director of the Novokozul'skii Timber Industry Enterprise of the Krasnoiarsk Territory hired a young specialist, Ignatov, who after finishing the Siberian Technological Institute was sent under job assignment to the Fudzinskii Timber Industry Enterprise of the Primorskii Territory.

The order to hire Ignatov is illegal on the following grounds. By decree of the Central Committee of the CPSU and the USSR Council of Ministers "On the Periods for the Preparation and for Improving the Use of Specialists with a Higher and Secondary Specialised Education" it was established that specialists with a higher and secondary specialized education shall be obliged to work after completing study for not less than three years in accordance with an assignment of a commission for personnel distribution of young specialists. By this decree directors of enterprises and institutions were prohibited from hiring young specialists who had not worked three years after finishing the educational institution without an authorization sending him for work at the particular enterprise (or institution) or documents granting the possibility to find work independently. It was proposed to ministries and departments to bring to strict responsibility officials hiring young specialists in violation of this procedure.

Upon the protest of the procurator of the Krasnoiarsk Territory the order of the director of the Novokozul'skii Timber Industry Enterprise was repealed. The director of the timber industry enterprise was brought to disciplinary responsibility.

ASSIGNMENT TO JOB, Chelovek i zakon, 1972, no. 11, p. 62.
The head of the Vitebsk Branch of the Belorussian Institute "Sel'khoztekhproekt" formalized by an order the hiring of engineer L., who theretofore worked in another place where he was sent after finishing an institution of higher

education by the state commission for the distribution of graduates of higher educational institutions.

The Procurator of the Belorussian SSR protested this order on the basis that by prevailing legislation directors of enterprises, institutions, and organizations were prohibited from hiring young specialists who had not worked three years after finishing the educational institution without an authorization sending for work or documents granting the right to come for work without job assignment.

The protest was satisfied. Engineer L. was dismissed and sent to his previous work.

F. Legal Capacity and Civil Liability of Minors

CIVIL CODE, RSFSR (1964)

Article 13. *Legal Capacity of Minors from Fifteen to Eighteen Years of Age*

Minors from fifteen to eighteen years of age shall perform legal transactions with the consent of parents, adoptive parents, or curators.

They shall, however, have the right independently to perform small everyday legal transactions, dispose of their earnings or stipend, and exercise their copyright or invention rights.

If there are sufficient grounds, an agency of guardianship and curatorship may, at its own initiative or on the petition of a social organizations or other interested persons, restrict or deprive a minor from fifteen to eighteen years of age of the right to dispose independently of his earnings or stipend.

The right of minors from fifteen to eighteen years of age to make deposits in credit institutions and to dispose of them shall be determined by legislation of the USSR.

Article 14. *Legal Capacity of Minors up to Fifteen Years of Age*

For minors who have not attained fifteen years of age, legal transactions shall be performed in the name of their parents, adoptive parents, or guardians.

Minors up to fifteen years of age shall have the right to perform independently small everyday legal transactions.

The right of minors up to fifteen years of age to make deposits in credit institutions and to dispose of them shall be determined by USSR legislation.

Article 51. *Invalidity of Legal Transaction Performed by a Minor Who has not Attained Fifteen Years of Age*

A legal transaction performed by a minor who has not attained fifteen years of age shall be void, except for legal transactions provided for by Article 14, paragraphs two and three, of the present Code.

Each of the parties to such a legal transaction shall be obliged to return to the other party everything received under the legal transaction, and if it is impossible to return that received in kind, to compensate its value in money.

The party having legal capacity shall be obliged, in addition, to compensate the other party for expenses incurred, loss, or damage of its property if the other party knew or should have known about the lack of legal capacity of the other party.

Article 54. *Invalidity of a Legal Transaction Performed by a Minor from Fifteen to Eighteen Years of Age*

A legal transaction performed by a minor from fifteen to eighteen years of age without the consent of his parents, adoptive parents, or curator shall be deemed void by a court upon the suit of the parents, adoptive parents, or curator.

If such a legal transaction is deemed void, the rules provided for by Article 51 of the present Code shall be applied.

The rules of the present article shall not extend to a legal transaction of minors from fifteen to eighteen years of age concluded in accordance with Article 13, paragraphs two and four, of the present Code.

Article 450. *Liability for Harm Caused by a Minor Who has not Attained Fifteen Years of Age*

For harm caused by a minor who has not attained fifteen years of age his parents or curator shall be liable unless they prove that the harm did not arise by their fault.

If a minor who has not attained fifteen years of age caused harm at the time when he was under the supervision of an educational institution or an educational or medical institution, they shall be liable for such harm unless they prove that the harm arose not by their fault

Article 451. *Liability for Harm Caused by a Minor from Fifteen to Eighteen Years of Age*

A minor from fifteen to eighteen years of age shall be liable for harm caused by him on the general bases (Articles 444, 449, and 454).

In instances when a minor from fifteen to eighteen years of age has no property or earnings sufficient to compensate the harm, the harm should be compensated in respective part by his parents or curator unless they prove that the harm arose not by their fault. This duty ceases when the person who caused the harm attains majority, as well as in the event that before attaining majority he has property or earnings sufficient to compensate the harm.

GINOSIAN vs. MUSIKIAN, Sotsialisticheskaia zakonnost', 1969, no. 10, p. 89.

The Lenin District People's Court of Tbilisi by a decision of June 21, 1968, satisfied a suit of Ginosian against Musikian concerning quartering and alimony. By a ruling of a cassational instance of July 24, 1968, the decision of the court in respect to the quartering of Ginosian was left without change and in respect of the recovery of alimony was vacated and transferred for new judicial consideration.

The deputy USSR procurator general protested the judicial decrees in the case as not based on law.

The plaintiff Ginosian, born in 1952, was taken by Musikian and his spouse when four years old from a children's home; reared by them for eleven years; studied at school. In September 1967 the mother searched for and found her, took her from the Musikian family, and carried her to her place of residence in Leninakan, where the daughter continued her studies. At the beginning of 1968, Ginosian returned to Tbilisi and upon the expiration of six months from the day of departure brought suit against Musikian for quartering and alimony, although she studied at a professional-technical school where she lived and was on full state security.

According to Article 32 of the Georgian Code of Civil Procedure, civil procedural legal capacity appertains to citizens who have attained majority. Minors from fifteen to eighteen years of age have the right to take part independently in a proceeding and personally to protect their rights in court only in instances provided for by law, in cases arising from labor, family, marriage, and collective farm legal relations and from legal transactions connected with the disposition of earnings received by them. The independent protection by minors of their housing rights without the participation of legal representatives (parents, adoptive parents, curators) is not provided by the Code of Civil Procedure.

Ginosian is a minor, and a case regarding quartering and recovery of alimony could be considered only by a suit brought by her parents or curator. Moreover, her mother did not file suit, was not questioned in regard to the case, and her attitude toward the daughter's claims is unknown. A curatorship over Ginosian was not formalized, therefore the indication in the court decision to joining as plaintiff a representative of the children's room of the district police section has no legal significance. The substance of the case was not investigated by the court. It was not elucidated whether Ginosian has permanently or temporarily left her mother, how long she has been absent, and whether she lost a right to the housing space in dispute in accordance with Article 300 of the Georgian Civil Code.

NOTARIAL PRACTICE, Sovetskaia iustitsiia, 1973, no. 16, cover.

Minor S. applied to one of the RSFSR notarial offices for certification of a will, which was refused to him. The notary justified the refusal by the fact that according to Article 41 of the Statute on the State Notariat of the RSFSR the wills of citizens having legal capacity are certified, and S. had not attained eighteen years of age at the time of certification of the will.

In refusing to certify the will, the notary did not take into account that the executive committee of the district soviet of working people's deputies, being guided by Article 15 of the RSFSR Code on Marriage and the Family, lowered the marriage age for minor S., in connection with which he already for nearly a year was in a marriage with V. registered at ZAGS agencies, and he wished to certify a will to the benefit of V. But in accorance with Article 11, par. 2, of the RSFSR Civil Code, when entry into marriage is permitted by law before attainment of eighteen years of age, a citizen who has not attained eighteen years of age acquires legal capacity in full measure from the time of entry into marriage. Therefore the notary does not have the right to refuse to certify the will of a person who has not attained eighteen years of age if at the time of certification of the will this person is in a marriage registered at ZAGS agencies.

IN RE SARAEV, Biulleten' Verkhovnogo Suda RSFSR, 1972, no. 11, p. 16

By judgment of the Novosibirsk District People's Court, Novosibirsk Region, Saraev was convicted under Article 89, par. 1, of the RSFSR Criminal Code with recovery from Saraeva, the grandmother of the convicted person, of compensation for harm caused to the benefit of the Novolugovinskii State Farm Workers' Cooperative of 293 rubles, 62 kopecks.

The case was not considered by way of cassation.

The presidium of the Novosibirsk Regional Court, having considered the case upon the protest of the regional procurator, by a decree of July 14, 1972, vacated the judgment in respect of the recovery from Saraeva of 293 rubles, 62 kopecks, and rejected the suit of the State Farm Workers' Cooperative on the following grounds:

Saraev was deemed guilty in that he on the night of August 9, 1971, committed a theft of money and other valuables from the store of the Novolugovinskii State Farm Workers' Cooperative totaling 644 rubles. Part of the property stolen was seized and returned to the store, but 293 rubles, 62 kopecks, remained uncompensated.

His guilt was established by the materials of the case, and his actions properly classified. However, the civil suit was incorrectly permitted by the people's court.

In accordance with Article 450 of the RSFSR Civil Code, for harm caused by a minor who has not attained fifteen years of age, his parents or guardians shall be liable unless they prove that the harm arose not by their fault.

As is obvious from the materials of the case, at the time of committing the crime the convicted person had not attained fifteen years of age, he has no father, and does not live with his mother since the latter was deprived of parental rights. Before committing the crime, he lived with his grandmother Saraeva and was dependent on her. Since Saraeva had not been appointed a guardian of the convicted person in the procedure established by law, she can not bear financial liability for harm caused by her grandchild.

G. Treatment of the Youthful Offender

CRIMINAL CODE, RSFSR (1960)
Article 10. *Responsibility of Minors*

Persons who have attained the age of sixteen years before the commission of a crime shall be subject to criminal responsibility.

Persons from fourteen to sixteen years of age who commit crimes shall be subject to criminal responsibility only for homicide (Articles 102–106), intentionally inflicting bodily injuries causing an impairment of health (Articles 108–111, 112, par. one), rape (Article 117), assault with intent to rob (Articles 91 and 146), theft (Articles 89 and 144), robbery (Articles 90 and 145), malicious hooliganism (Article 206, paragraphs two and three), intentionally destroying or damaging state or social property or the personal property of citizens, with grave consequences (Articles 98, par. two, and 149, par. two) or intentionally committing actions that can cause a train wreck (Article 86).

If a court finds that a person who, while under the age of eighteen years, has committed a crime not constituting a great social danger can be reformed without application of criminal punishment, it may apply to such person compulsory measures of an educational character which do not constitute a criminal punishment (Article 63).

Under the conditions specified in paragraph three of the present article, a minor may be relieved of criminal responsibility and punishment and sent to a commission for cases of minors for consideration of the question of applying to him compulsory measures of an educational character.

Article 38. *Circumstances Mitigating Responsibility*

In assigning punishment the following shall be deemed circumstances mitigating responsibility: . . .

(7) commission of the crime by a minor;

STATUTE ON COMMISSIONS FOR CASES OF MINORS, Confirmed by Edict of the Presidium of the USSR Supreme Soviet, June 3, 1967. [1967] Ved. Verkh. Sov. RSFSR, No. 23, item 536, as amended to March 11, 1977

Article 1. The principal tasks of commissions for cases of minors shall be to organize work in regard to preventing the neglect of, and violations of law by, minors, to settle the affairs of minors and protect their rights, to coordinate the efforts of state agencies and social organizations in regard to the said questions; to consider cases concerning violations of law by minors; and to effectuate control over the conditions for the maintenance and conduct of educational work with minors in institutions of the Ministry of Internal Affairs and special educational institutions.

Article 2. Commissions for cases of minors shall be created attached to executive committees of district, city, national area, region, and t rritory soviets of working people's deputies, attached to autonomous republic councils of ministers, and attached to the RSFSR Council of Ministers.

By way of exception commissions for cases of minors may be created attached to executive committees of settlement soviets of working people's deputies located a significant distance from district centers. The question of forming such commissions shall be decided by the executive committee of the region or territory soviet of working people's deputies or by the Presidium of the autonomous republic supreme soviet.

Commissions for cases of minors attached to executive committees of settlement soviets of working people's deputies shall have the rights and duties of district, city (without district division) commissions for cases of minors.

Article 6. The activity of commissions for cases of minors shall be carried out with the broad participation of the Soviet public.

Representatives of factory, plant, and local trade union committees, Komsomol committees, parents' committees attached to schools, guardian councils of children's homes and boarding schools, voluntary people's guard detachments, block and house committees, and other representatives of the public shall be enlisted for the commission's work.

From among the *aktiv* enlisted for work, the commissions shall designate social inspectors and social educators for work among minors.

Commissions for cases of minors shall interact, in regard to all questions relegated to their competence, with the standing commissions of soviets of working people's deputies.

Article 8. District (or city) commissions for cases of minors shall unify and coordinate the efforts of agencies and institutions of public education, public health, social security, culture, internal affairs, and other institutions, enterprises, and organizations in the district (or city), as well as of teachers and organizers regarding the carrying out of work with children and adolescents at their place of residence and of social agencies entrusted with the duty to rear children and adolescents, settle their affairs, strengthen their health, prevent neglect and violations of law by minors, and protect their rights.

District (or city) commissions for cases of minors shall work out and effectuate measures, both directly and through the respective state agencies and social organizations, for the prevention of neglect and of violations of law by minors, for settling their affairs and organizing cultural spare time of children and adolescents, as well as rendering assistance in rearing minors.

Article 13. District (or city) commissions for cases of minors shall, jointly with agencies of internal affairs, effectuate observance over the conduct of minors subjected to measures of educational or administrative pressure, sentenced to punishment not connected with deprivation of freedom, conditionally sentenced or conditionally released early from serving a punishment, and over the conduct of minors who have returned from special educational or therapeutic-educational institutions or who have served a sentence in educational labor colonies, and shall supervise the conduct of convicted persons with regard to whom the execution of a judgment for deprivation of freedom is delayed, as well as register these minors.

When necessary, commissions shall take measures to find employment for minors or send them to educational institutions.

Article 14. District (or city) commissions for cases of minors shall have the right to:

(h) initiate petitions concerning a pardon for minors; submit proposals to a court concerning the nonapplication of punishment or the application of a ligher punishment, concerning conditional conviction, early quashing of the conviction of minors; submit to a court jointly with an agency executing a punishment proposals for conditional early release of minors from punishment or replacement of the unserved part of a punishment with a lighter punishment in instances provided for by Article 55 of the RSFSR Criminal Code; petition a court jointly with an agency of internal affairs regarding the relieving from punishment of a convicted person who has been granted a delay in execution of punishment, as well as submit jointly with an agency of internal affairs to a court a proposal concerning the vacating of such a delay and sending the convicted person to serve deprivation of freedom assigned by the judgment (Article 46-1 of the RSFSR Criminal Code); give consent to the administration of an educational labor colony to submit to a court proposals regarding changes of conditions for the maintenance of persons sentenced to deprivation of freedom while serving a punishment (Article 364 of the RSFSR Code of Criminal Procedure).

Article 17. District (or city) commissions for cases of minors shall be entrusted with consideration of cases concerning minors who have:

(a) commited, at an age of up to 14 years, socially dangerous acts;

(b) committed, at an age of 14 to 16 years, socially dangerous acts not provided for by Article 10 of the RSFSR Criminal Code;

(c) committed crimes, at an age of from 14 to 18 years, with respect to which the initiation of a criminal case has been refused or a criminal case has been terminated in the procedure provided by Articles 8 and 10 of the RSFSR Code of Criminal Procedure;

(d) committed, at an age of up to 16 years, petty hooliganism or, at an age up to 18 years, petty speculation or other administrative violations, responsibility for which is provided directly by acts of supreme agencies of state authority and state administration of the USSR, RSFSR, and autonomous republics, as well as by decisions of local soviets of working people's deputies.

committed, at an age from 16 to 18 years, petty hooliganism, if the head of a police agency or a people's judge, taking into account the personality of the offender and the character of the offense committed, finds it advisable to transfer the materials for the consideration of a commission;

(e) committed other antisocial offenses;

(f) avoided study or work.

Article 18. District (or city) commissions for cases of minors may, in the instances provided for by Article 17 of the present statute, apply the following measures of pressure to minors:

(a) oblige them to make a public or other form of apology to the victim;

(b) issue a warning;

(c) announce a reprimand or severe reprimand;

(d) impose on a minor who has attained 15 years of age the duty to compensate for material damage caused if the minor has independent earnings and the amount of damage does not exceed 20 rubles, or impose the duty to eradicate by his own labor material damage caused which does not exceed 20 rubles;

(e) impose a fine on a minor who has attained 16 years of age and who has independent earnings in the instances and in the amounts provided for by acts of higher agencies of state authority or state administration of the USSR, RSFSR, autonomous republics, or by decisions of local soviets of working peoples deputies and their executive committees;

(f) hand over a minor to the supervision of parents or persons replacing them or to social educators, as well as to the observation of a collective of working people or social organization with their consent;

(g) hand over a minor on probation to a collective of working people or a social organization upon their petitions;

(h) send a minor to a special therapeutic-educational institution;

(i) place a minor who has committed socially dangerous actions or maliciously and systematically violated rules of social conduct in a special educational institution. A minor from 11 to 14 years of age may be sent to a special school, and from 14 to 18 years of age, to a special professional-technical school. The said measures of pressure may be established also conditionally for a year's experimental period by a commission for cases of minors.

District (or city) commissions for cases of minors shall have the right to propose to an agency of guardianship and curatorship that the right of a minor from 15 to 18 years of age to dispose independently of his earnings or stipend be restricted or deprived.

Article 21. When applying the measures of pressure provided for by Article 18 of the present Statute, a district (or city) commission should take into account the character and causes of the violation of law, the age of the minor and conditions of his life, the degree of his participation in the violation of law, as well as his conduct at home, in school, or at work.

The decree of a commission for cases of minors concerning the announcement of a warning, reprimand, or severe reprimand shall be in effect for one year. A measure of pressure shall be considered cancelled if the minor to whom it was applied during this period has not committed a new violation of law. The commission for cases of minors which has applied the measure of pressure may, by its own decree, repeal it before the expiry of the year in the event of the exemplary conduct of the minor with respect to whom this measure of pressure was applied.

The effect of a decree of a commission for cases of minors on handing over a minor to the supervision of parents, persons replacing them, social educators, or to the observation of a collective of working people or social organization may be terminated at any time by the commission itself upon the petition of those persons or organizations if the minor has proved his reform by exemplary conduct and a conscientious attitude toward work and study.

When the selected measure of educational pressure with regard to a minor has proved to be unsuccessful, the commission shall have the right to apply a more severe measure to this minor from among those specified in Article 18 of the present Statute.

STATUTE CONCERNING SOCIAL EDUCATORS OF MINORS, Confirmed by Edict of the Presidium of the RSFSR Supreme Soviet, December 13, 1967 [1967] Ved. Verkh. Sov. RSFSR, 51, item 1239

1. The institution of social educators was founded with a view to increasing the role of the public in nurturing minors who have committed a violation of law.

The basic task of social educators is to render assistance to parents or to persons replacing them in the re-education of minor offenders in a spirit of respect for and observance of the laws and rules of socialist community life.

2. Workers, employees, collective farmers, representatives of the intelligentsia, military servicemen, students, pensioners, and other citizens who take an active part in social life and who have the necessary general educational preparation, experience in living, and work experience with children may be social educators, on condition that they agree to assume the duties of a social educator.

Persons recommended as social educators shall be put forward by the general meeting of the collective of working people or social organization of which they are members or by residents of the house of their place of residence. Lists of recommended persons shall be transferred to the commission for cases of minors attached to the executive committee of the district (or city) soviet of working people's deputies. These persons shall become members of the *aktiv* of the commission.

3. A social educator shall be appointed when this is deemed necessary in order to prevent the neglect and violations of law by a minor:

(a) who has committed a violation of law but has been relieved of criminal responsibility by virtue of age or in connection with the inadvisability of applying measures of criminal punishment to him, if it would be premature to place him in a special educational institution;

(b) who has been conditionally sentenced or sentenced to a measure of punishment not connected with deprivation of freedom;

(c) who has served a sentence or who has been conditionally released from punishment;

(d) who has returned from a special school, special professional-technical school, or therapeutic educational institution, children's home, or boarding school.

When a social educator is appointed, the parents or persons replacing them shall not be relieved from the duty to bring up the minor or from responsibility for his conduct.

4. A minor shall be transferred to the supervision of a social educator by the district (or city) commission for cases of minors on the basis of a ruling, judgment, or decree of a court which deems it necessary to appoint a social educator or at its own personal initiative, or the inititative of state agencies, social organizations, and citizens.

A commission for cases of minors shall, within five days after adopting the decision to appoint a social educator, notify the court, state agencies, social organizations, and citizens at whose initiative the case was considered, as well as the parents of the minor or persons replacing them, of the surname, forename, patronymic, place of work, and residence of the social educator.

11. A social educator shall be obliged to:

(a) render assistance to parents or persons replacing them in nurturing the minor; make every effort to correct the minor, eliminating harmful or amoral habits or notions which he has; prepare him for conscious, socially useful activity; nurture the minor in a spirit of revolutionary, labor, and fighting traditions of our people, respect for the aged, love for the Motherland; inculcate in him a feeling of responsibility to society and the state;

(b) watch over the punctual attendance of the minor at lessons, his progress, fulfillment of domestic tasks, conduct in school, at work, in the family, on the street, in public places; involve him in the work of extracurricular children's institutions and circles; take measures to create proper conditions for the correct organizations of study, labor, and leisure of the minor;

(c) render assistance, when necessary, in enlisting the minor in socially useful labor, in settling him in an educational institution or a sport, technical, or other circle or section.

In the process of his work the social educator should, taking into account the personality of the minor, use the most effective forms and means of educational work, having recourse when necessary to the assistance of the district (or city) commission for cases of minors, social organizations, police workers, teachers, doctors, and other specialists.

12. A social educator shall have the right to:

(a) visit the minor at the place of residence, study, or work, control his expenditures, give necessary advice with regard to observance of rules of conduct; in the event of the repeated failure to fulfill his demands or of the absence of positive results in re-educating the minor, to bring the question for discussion to the commission for cases of minors in order to apply the necessary measures of pressure to him;

(b) call the attention of parents or persons replacing them to their improper fulfillment of parental duties and to explain the responsibility for bringing up and for the conduct of the minor; to raise before the commission for cases of minors the question of notifying the place of work of the parents about their unsatisfactory fulfillment of duties to bring up children, about the discussion of their conduct at the commission session, and about other measures of pressure taken;

(c) demand from administrations and social organizations at the place of study, work, or residence of the minor the elimination of shortcomings in educational work and the creation of more favorable conditions for his study or work.

FUNDAMENTAL PRINCIPLES OF CORRECTIONAL LABOR LEGISLATION OF THE USSR AND UNION REPUBLICS. Entered into force November 1, 1969. [1969] Vedomosti Verkhovnogo Soveta SSSR, No. 29, item 247
Article 16. *Educational Labor Colonies*

Educational labor colonies shall be divided into general regime and strict regime colonies.

A male minor sentenced for the first time to deprivation of freedom for a crime which is not grave and sentenced for the first time for a term not exceeding three years for grave crimes, as well as all convicted female minors, shall serve sentences in general regime educational labor colonies; male minors who have previously served a sentence in the form of deprivation of freedom, as well as those sentenced to deprivation of freedom for a term exceeding three years for grave crimes, in strict regime colonies.

CRIMINAL CODE, RSFSR (1960)
Article 46-1. *Deferment of Execution of Judgment for a Minor*

When assigning punishment of a minor sentenced for the first time to deprivation of freedom for a term not exceeding three years, the execution of the judgment for deprivation of freedom with respect to this person may be deferred for a period of from six months to two years by a court, taking into account the character and degree of social danger of the crime committed, the personality of the guilty person, and other circumstances of the case, as well as the possibility of reforming and re-educating him without isolation from society. In such instances a court may defer also the execution of additional punishments.

When deferring the execution of a judgment for a minor, a court may oblige him to take up work or study for a specific period and to eradicate harm caused. A court also may impose on a particular collective of working people or a person, with their consent, the duty to watch over the convicted person and carry on educational work with him.

Control over the conduct of convicted persons with respect to whom the execution of a judgment for deprivation of freedom has been deferred shall be effectuated by commissions for cases of minors attached to the executive committees of district (or city) soviets of working people's deputies and by agencies of internal affairs in accordance with legislation of the USSR and RSFSR.

If within the period established by a court for deferment of execution of judgment the convicted person by model conduct and an honorable attitude toward labor and study proves his reform, then upon the petition of a commission for cases of minors attached to the executive committee of a district (or city) soviet of working people's deputies or an agency of internal affairs, a court may relieve him from punishment.

If a convicted person with respect to whom the execution of judgment for deprivation of freedom has been deferred does not fulfill the duties placed upon him by a court or permits violations of public order entailing the application of measures of administrative pressure, then upon the representation of a commission for cases of minors attached to an executive committee of a district (or city) soviet of working people's deputies or an agency of internal affairs, a court may issue a ruling vacating the deferment of execution of judgment for deprivation of freedom and sending the convicted person to serve the deprivation of freedom assigned by the judgment.

In the event the convicted person with respect to whom the execution of a judgment was deferred commits a new crime, a court shall join to the new punishment that previously assigned according to the rules provided for by Article 41 of the present Code.

ON THE BASIC DUTIES AND RIGHTS OF INSPECTORATES FOR CASES OF MINORS, RECEPTION-DISTRIBUTION CENTERS FOR MINORS, AND SPECIAL EDUCATIONAL INSTITUTIONS FOR THE PREVENTION OF THE NEGLECT OF AND OF LAW VIOLATIONS BY MINORS, Edict of the Presidium of the USSR Supreme Soviet, February 15, 1977, [1977] Vedomosti Verkhovnogo Soveta SSSR, No. 8, item 138

1. Inspectorates for cases of minors of agencies of internal affairs, reception-distribution centers for minors of agencies of internal affairs, special schools of general education for children and adolescents needing special conditions for education, and special professional-technical higher schools shall be called upon to resolve in accordance with the present Edict the tasks relating to the prevention of the neglect of and of law violations by minors, to rendering them necessary educational influence, and to ensuring proper conditions for study.

6. Inspectorates for Cases of Minors of Agencies of Internal Affairs shall:

(a) carry on work relating to the prevention of law violations among minors:

—released from places of deprivation of freedom;

—sentenced conditionally or to measures of punishment not connected with deprivation of freedom;

—who have committed crimes but were relieved from criminal responsibility in connection with the application of measures of social pressure or as a consequence of an act of amnesty, as well as who have committed socially dangerous acts before attaining the age for which criminal responsibility ensues;

—have returned from special educational institutions;

—have committed a violation of law entailing measures of social or administrative pressure;

—have abused alcoholic beverages, narcotics, or psychotropes;

—systematically and deliberately left their family before attaining 16 years of age or deliberately left special educational institutions;

—maliciously avoided study or work;

—systematically engaged in gambling, as well as led another antisocial way of life;

(b) take part in carrying on educational work with minors and take measures to prevent violations of law and other antisocial offenses of minors;

(c) uncover parents and persons replacing them who maliciously do not fulfill duties relating to the upbringing of children and by their antisocial conduct promote the commission by them of violations of law; . . .

8. Reception-Distribution Centers for Minors of Agencies of Internal Affairs shall:

(a) provisionally maintain, take measures to settle the affairs of, and return to their family, children's institution, or educational institution children and adolescents from three to 18 years of age who require assistance from the state and society, as well as minor violators of law;

(b) establish the reasons and conditions furthering the neglect of and law violations by minors who are delivered to reception-distribution centers and send information to state agencies and social organizations with proposals to eliminate such reasons and conditions;

(c) ensure conditions for the maintenance of minors excluding the possibility of deliberately running away and of law violations.

11. Special schools of general education for children and adolescents and special professional-technical higher schools in the system of public education agencies shall have as their purpose the study and preparation for choosing a profession or the professional training, re-education, and correction of minors and developing their moral qualities in a spirit of the requirements of communist morality and their physical, labor, esthetic, and legal upbringing.

12. To special schools shall be sent minor offenders from 11 to 14 years of age on the basis of decrees of commissions for cases of minors attached to executive committees of district or city soviets of working people's deputies.

To special professional-technical higher schools shall be sent minor offenders from 14 to 18 years of age on the basis of decrees of commissions for cases of minors attached to the executive committees of district or city soviets of working people's deputies or by a ruling of a court.

A minor may be maintained in special schools until attaining 15 years of age, and in special professional-technical higher schools until 18 years of age.

In exceptional instances the stay of pupils in special schools may be extended until they attain 16 years of age.

A minor shall be in special educational institutions until correction, but not more than three years.

A commission for cases of minors at the place where special educational institutions are located may authorize a pupil to remain in the special school or special professional-technical higher school also upon the expiration of the three year period until finishing the respective class of the school of general education or professional study in the current academic year.

In partial compensation of expenses for the maintenance of pupils in special educational institutions, payment shall be recovered from parents in the procedure determined by legislation of the USSR and union republics.

IN RE SHCHERBAKOV, Biulleten' Verkhovnogo Suda RSFSR, 1974, no. 2, p. 6

By judgment of the Moscow City Court of June 19, 1973, Shcherbakov was sentenced under Article 117, par. 3, of the RSFSR Criminal Code to eight years deprivation of freedom in an educational labor colony of strict regime.

By the same judgment Fadeev, Kuprasov, and Dontsov were convicted.

Shcherbakov, Fadeev, and Dontsov admitted their guilt in the group rape of M. Fadeev, in addition, of the theft of personal property of citizens committed by preliminary agreement with a group of persons, robbery committed repeatedly, and the petty stealing of state property committed repeatedly.

Kuprasov was convicted for theft of personal property of citizens committed by preliminary agreement with a group of persons.

The Judicial Division for Criminal Cases of the RSFSR Supreme Court, having considered the case on June 19, 1973, upon cassational appeals of the convicted persons and lawyers, lowered the punishment for Shcherbakov and indicated the following:

The conclusion of the court regarding the guilt of Shcherbakov in the rape of M. is justified and the classification of his actions is correct. However, the court did not take account of a number of important circumstances mitigating the guilt of this convicted person. At the moment the crime was committed, Shcherbakov was only 14 years old and, as the court established, he was not the initiator of the rape of M. The role of Shcherbakov in the crime was less active and the degree of his guilt significantly less than certain other participants in the crime.

All this and other circumstances in the case and the data as a whole were not taken into account by the court when determining punishment for Shcherbakov, which led to the assignment of an exceedingly severe punishment to a person who has only just attained the age of criminal responsibility.

The Judicial Division of the RSFSR Supreme Court, taking into account the specific circumstances of the case and information on Shcherbakov's personality, applied Article 43 of the RSFSR Criminal Code to Shcherbakov and determined a punishment lower than the lowest limit provided for by law.

IN RE NAUMOV, Biulleten' Verkhovnogo Suda RSFSR, 1968, no. 7, pp. 10–11

By judgment of the Kaliningrad Regional Court M. Naumov, born March 27, 1953, was sentenced under Article 144, par. 2, Article 89, par. 2, and Article 102 (e) and (f) of the RSFSR Criminal Code.

M. Naumov was convicted of systematically committing the stealing of state and personal property, for attempted murder of Osipov, and for the murder of Ermakov, which was carried out at his order by the young Martsenkiavichus under the following circumstances.

On October 7, 1967, the brothers Naumov and Martsenkiavichus, having discovered a tractor and a motor vehicle standing in a forest, committed the theft of products belonging to workers from them and the ignition key of the motor vehicle.

The workers Osipov, Ermakov, and Khitrin, having discovered the theft, began to search for the guilty persons, who at this time sat in a field.

Seeing the workers, Naumov approached Osipov and gave back the ignition key stolen from the motor vehicle. Osipov suggested the convicted person and Martsenkiavichus follow him. In reply, M. Naumov, for the purpose of murder, aimed a double-barrled shotgun at Osipov, pulled the trigger, and twice attempted to shoot. But as a result of the safety catch there were no shots.

After this, the Naumov brothers and Martsenkiavichus began to flee. Supposing that the shotgun which the youths had was not loaded, Osipov and other workers ran after them. This time M. Naumov gave the shotgun to the young Martsenkiavichus and ordered him to shoot the following workers. Martsenkiavichus aimed the shotgun at Osipov, pulled the trigger, but there were no shots since it was not cocked. Having stopped, Martsenkiavichus cocked the weapon and shot toward Ermakov and Khitrin, who were running in close proximity to one another. The blast hit Ermakov, who died immediately. Khitrin did not suffer. When Ermakov already was killed, M. Naumov cried to Martsenkiavichus to shoot the other worker, but the latter did not do this.

In the cassational appeal the convicted M. Naumov requested the case be reconsidered, taking into account his age and the fact that he was not the direct murderer of Ermakov.

Having considered the case with regard to M. Naumov by way of cassation, the Judicial Division for Criminal Cases of the RSFSR Supreme Court pointed out that, although the victim Ermakov was killed directly by Martsenkiavichus, according to Article 8 (b) of the decree of the Plenum of the USSR Supreme Court of July 3, 1963, "On Judicial Practice in Cases of Crimes of Minors", responsibility for the execution of this crime must be borne by M. Naumov inasmuch as to carry out his criminal intention he used the youth who by virtue of his age is not a subject of a crime.

The fact that M. Naumov himself is a minor can not affect the legal classification of his actions since he has attained the age from which criminal liability for intentional homicide ensues.

Proceeding from the foregoing, the Judicial Division of the RSFSR Supreme Court by a ruling of April 4, 1968, left the judgment with respect to M. Naumov without change, and his appeal without satisfaction.

ion
APPENDIX
LEGAL FORMS*

Contract for the Sale by an enterprise of a newly constructed house

Contract

City of Lipetsk.   1968 January 20

The "Tsentrolit" plant, in the person of the deputy director, Sidorov Nikolai Alekseevich, acting on the basis of a power of attorney issued by the plant director, Lavrov, Ivan Vasil'evich, on January 1, 1968, No. 46, hereinafter the "Seller", on one side, and Petrov, Nikolai Ivanovich, hereinafter the "Buyer", on the other, have concluded the purchase-sale contract below:

1. The "Seller" has sold, and the "Buyer" has bought, a wooden, one-story, three-room dwelling house (design No. 3), situate on Lenin Street No. 5, on a land parcel of 500 (five hundred) square meters.

Note. The plan of the land parcel allocated for the said house showing the structure thereon is attached to the present contract.

2. The said dwelling house is sold for one thousand five hundred (1500) rubles, which sum is paid by the "Buyer" to the "Seller" in cash money when concluding the contract.

3. Within one year from the day of concluding the purchase-sale contract for the house built by the enterprise, the "Buyer" may file claims regarding unfinished parts discovered and poor-quality construction materials. If the correctness of such claims are confirmed by a commission composed of a representative of the "Seller", of the local municipal (housing) agency, and of the "Buyer", the "Seller" shall be obliged to eliminate defects uncovered at its expense and by its means within a period established by the said commission.

4. The landscaping and the services and utilities of the parcel, the building of fences and sidewalks within the limits of the parcel, the care and maintenance in proper order of both the parcel and the sidewalks and pathways adjacent thereto, as well as of the water pipes connecting with the street network, drain pipes, electric wires, gas, and other networks shall be conducted by the "Buyer" at his expense.

5. The "Buyer" shall be obliged to:

(a) carry out necessary house repair;

---

*Documents selected from *Spravochnik gosudarstvennogo notariusa; sbornik ofitsial'nykh materialov* [Handbook of a State Notary: Collection of Official Materials] (2d ed.; Moscow, 1972).

(b) fulfill all technical, sanitary, fire prevention, and other rules for the maintenance of house ownership;

(c) preserve on the personal plot and along the facade of the plot all green plantings, except for those subject to being transplanted or cut down on the basis of the written authorization of the appropriate agencies of the local soviet of working people's deputies, as well as to plant trees and shrubs on the parcel according to the plan established by the local Soviet;

(d) make payments for compulsory insurance and pay all taxes and fees relating to the house and personal plot;

(e) not rebuild the house nor erect on the personal plot new structures without the authorization of the "Seller" and the respective agencies of the local soviet of working people's deputies.

6. In the event of the death of the "Buyer", all rights and duties under the present contract shall transfer to his heirs.

7. Expenses relating to the performance of the present contract shall be on the account of the "Buyer".

8. The contract shall be subject to compulsory certification in a notarial procedure and registration at the executive committee of the local soviet of working people's deputies.

9. The present contract shall be drawn up in triplicate, one copy of which shall remain in the files of the notarial office, the second shall be issued to the "Buyer", and the third to the "Seller".

10. The legal addresses of the parties:
"Seller": Lipetsk, Lenin Street, House No. 4.
"Buyer": Lipetsk, Lenin Street, House No. 5.
Signatures:

Contract of gift for share of dwelling house
Contract

City of Liuberts, 26 March 1969

We, the undersigned, Vetrov Viktor Petrovich residing in the city of Moscow, Kirov Street, House No. 15, Apartment No. 10, and Krasnikov Vasilii Timofeevich residing in the city of Liuberts, Moscow Region, Lenin Street, House No. 6, have concluded the present contract regarding the following:

1. I, Vetrov Viktor Petrovich, have given to Krasnikov Vasilii Timofeevich one-twelfth share of a brick dwelling house with common-use premises of 86 square meters, including living space; of 58.5 square meters of auxiliary structures and installations located on a land parcel of 400 square meters in the city of Liuberts, Lenin Street, No. 6.

2. The said 1/12 share of the dwelling house belongs to me, Vetrov V. P., on the basis of a purchase-sale contract certified by the Liuberts State Notarial Office on 15 February 1960, Register No. 1565, and certificates of the technical inventory

bureau of the executive committee of the Liuberts city soviet of working people's deputies of 20 March 1969, Nos. 156/158.

3. I, Krasnikov V. T., accept the gift from Vetrov V. P. of 1/12 share of the dwelling house.

4. The 1/12 share of the dwelling house being given is valued by the parties according to the inventory valuation in the amount of 600 (six hundred) rubles.

5. Before the present contract the 1/12 share of the dwelling house being given has not been sold to anyone, mortgaged, disputed, nor is it under a prohibition (or arrest).

6. The content of Article 107 of the RSFSR Civil Code has been explained to the donee by the notary.

7. Expenses relating to the conclusion of the present contract shall be paid by Krasnikov V. T.

8. A copy of the present contract shall be kept at the Liuberts State Notarial Office (Komsomol'skaia Street, House No. 15) and a copy shall be issued to the donee, Krasnikov V. T.

Signatures:

Agreement concerning dissolution of a contract
City of Moscow, 3 February 1967

We, the undersigned, Konev Ivan Dmitrievich, residing in Moscow, Donskoi pereulok, House No. 12, Apartment No. 7, and Sitnikova Mariia Kuz'minichna, residing there, Apartment No. 2, have concluded the present agreement on the following:

1. The purchase-sale contract certified by the First Moscow State Notarial Office on 15 September 1966, Register No. 1c-785 and registered at the technical inventory bureau of the Kuibyshev District of the City of Moscow, according to which I, Konev I. D., sold, and I, Sitnikova M. K., bought 1/2 share of a dwelling house located in the city of Moscow, Donskoi pereulok, No. 12, is dissolved by the present agreement.

2. Expenses relating to the concluding of the agreement of the parties shall be paid in equal shares.

Signatures:

Contract of gift for Motor Car

Contract

City of Moscow, 10 March 1968

We, Ivanov Viktor Petrovich, residing in the city of Moscow, Serafimovich Street, House No. 15, Apartment No. 16, and Sitnikov Vasilii Ivanovich, residing in the city of Moscow, Kolodeznaia Street, House No. 26, Apartment No. 22, have concluded the present contract concerning the following:

1. I, Ivanov V. P., have given to Sitnikov V. I. a motor car belonging to me,

Volga make, 1960, Chassis No. 13555, Engine No. 8158, State License No. ME-16-38.

2. The said motor car belongs to me, Ivanov V. P., on the basis of a technical passport issued by the State Motor Vehicle Inspectorate, Kiubyshev District, of the City of Moscow, 18 December 1960, No. 5K-007535.

3. I, Sitnikov V. I., accept the gift from Ivanov V. P. of the said motor car.

4. The said motor car is valued by the parties at four thousand (4000) rubles.

5. Before the present contract the motor car being given has not been sold to anyone, pledged, disputed, nor is it under a prohibition (or arrest).

6. Expenses relating to the concluding of the present contract shall be paid by Sitnikov V. I.

7. One copy of the present contract shall be kept at the First Moscow State Notarial Office (Kirov Street, House No. 8), and the second issued to Sitnikov V. I.

Signatures:

Loan contract
Contract
City of Moscow, 15 February 1968

We, Semenov Mikhail Sergeevich, residing in Moscow, Kirov Street, House No. 48, Apartment No. 12, and Sergeev Semen Ivanovich, residing at Moscow, prospekt Mira, House No. 86, Apartment No. 45, have concluded the present contract regarding the following:

1. I, Semenov Mikhail Sergeevich, have borrowed from Sergeev Semen Ivanovich, one thousand five hundred (1500) rubles for a period until the first of October 1969 without additional sums of interest.

2. Payment should be made in the city of Moscow.

3. I, Sergeev S. I., shall have the right to pay the borrowed money, and I, Semenov M. S., shall be obliged to accept payment earlier than the said period.

4. If I, Sergeev S. I., do not pay the money borrowed by me within the aforesaid period, then Semenov M. S. shall have the right to submit the present contract for recovery.

5. Expenses relating to the concluding of the present contract shall be paid by Sergeev Semen Ivanovich.

6. The first copy of the present contract shall be kept at the Sixth Moscow State Notarial Office, and the second copy shall be issued to Semenov Mikhail Sergeevich.

Signatures:

Power of attorney for the administration of property (general)
Power of Attorney
City of Nal'chik, 5 February 1967

I, the undersigned, Aksenov Petr Nikolaevich, residing in the city of Nal'chik, Lenin Street, House No. 88, Apartment No. 46, by the present power of attorney empower Sinitsina Mariia Petrovna, residing in the city of Ordzhonikidze, Pushkin Street, House No. 28, to administer and dispose of all my property, of whatever it consists and wherever located, to conclude all legal transactions authorized by law relating to the administration and disposition of property; to buy, sell, give, accept a gift, exchange, pledge, and accept on pledge structures and other property and keep accounts relating to the legal transactions concluded; accept an inheritance or refuse it; receive property, money (or deposits), securities, as well as documents due me from all persons, institutions, enterprises, and organizations, including from branches of the State Bank and savings banks, postal branches, and telegraph on all grounds; to dispose of accounts at the State Bank and Foreign Trade Bank, receive postal, telegraph, and any kind of correspondence, including money and packages, to conduct in my name affairs in all state institutions, cooperative and social organizations, as well as conduct my affairs in all judicial institutions with all the rights which are granted by law to a plaintiff, defendant, third person, or victim, including the right of complete or partial rejection of suits, acknowledgement of a suit, change of the subject of a suit, concluding a settlement agreement, appealing a court decision, submitting a writ of execution for recovery, and receiving property or money awarded.

The power of attorney is issued for a period of three years.

Signature

Power of attorney to receive a certificate of the right to inheritance
Power of Attorney
City of Moscow, 2 January 1967

I, Ovanesova Lora Vitol'dovna, residing in the city of Moscow, Trubnaia Street, House No. 10, Apartment 12, trust Leonidov Matvei Ivanovich, residing in the city of Moscow, Zhdanov Street, House No. 15, Apartment No. 1, to receive at the First Kursk State Notarial Office a certificate of the right to inheritance for property left after the deceased father, Alekseev Vitol'd Borisovich, consisting of household articles and a dwelling house located in the city of Kursk, Nekrasov Street No. 3 for the right to receive the estate property.

I commission Leonidov M. I. to register the said dwelling house in my name at the technical inventory bureau of the Lenin District of the city of Kursk.

To perform the said actions, I empower him to file in my name an application, receive certificates and documents, and to sign for me.

The power of attorney is issued for a period of two years.

Signature.

Last will and testament

Will

City of Moscow, 15 December 1967

I, Vishnevskii Viktor Mihailovich, residing in the city of Moscow, Tsvetnoi Bul'var, House No. 16, Apartment No. 30, by the present will make the following disposition:

1. All my property which on the day of my death appertains to me, of whatever it consists or wherever located, including a dwelling house located in the city of Lipetsk, Timiriazev Street No. 5, and a deposit in the state labor savings bank No. 2525/35 in the city of Moscow, I bequeath in equal shares to my son Vishnevskii Anatoliia Viktorovich and to my daughter Vinokurova Liudmila Viktorovna.

2. The content of Article 535 of the RSFSR Civil Code has been explained to me by the notary.

3. The present will has been drawn up and signed in two copies, one of which is kept at the First Moscow State Notarial Office at the address: Moscow, Kirov Street, House No. 8; the other is issued to the testator Vishnevskii Viktor Mikhailovich.

Signature

Application for issuance of certificate of right to inheritance
To the First Krasnoiarsk State Notarial Office
                Krasnobaev Iurii Mikhailovich,
                Merkulov Ivan Mikhailovich, residing
                in the city of Serpukhov, Osipenko
                Street, House 15

Application

On 13 February 1970 died Citizen Krasnobaev Mikhail Ivanovich, permanently residing in the city of Krasnoiarsk, Chekistov Street, House No. 26.

Son Krasnobaev Iurii Mikhailovich and grandson Merkulov Ivan Mikhailovich, whose father died 25 January 1968, residing at the said address, are the heirs.

The estate property consists of a dwelling house located in the city of Krasnoiarsk, Chekistov Street, No. 25, a Moskvich 408 motor car, and a deposit in the state labor savings bank No. 1526/325 in the city of Krasnoiarsk.

I request the issuance of a certificate of the right of inheritance; there are no other heirs provided for by Article 532 of the RSFSR Civil Code except the aforesaid.

15 May 1970

Signatures: Krasnobaev Iurii Mikhailovich and Merkulov Ivan Mikhailovich

Certificate of right to inheritance

Certificate

... February 1970, I (surname and initials), state notary of the (name) state notarial office, certify that on the basis of Article 532 of the RSFSR Civil Code the heir to the property of Citizen Sobolev Vasilii Ivanovich, who died 2 August 1969 having accepted an inheritance but not having formalized his inheritance rights to the property of his father, Sobolev Ivan Petrovich, who died 3 January 1968, is his wife Soboleva Elana Pavlovna, residing at . . .

The estate property for which the present certificate is issued consists of: (specify the property for which the certificate of the right to inheritance is issued).

Registered in Register No. . . .

Recovered state tax . . . . . . rubles . . . . kopecks.

State notary (signature)

Seal

BIBLIOGRAPHY OF BOOKS AND JOURNALS IN ENGLISH ON THE SOVIET LEGAL SYSTEM

The listing below contains the principal works published in the English language on the Soviet legal system and the principal journals devoted exclusively or primarily to Soviet law in the English language. Basic postwar materials are emphasized, and only books are recorded. No particular attention is given to dissent literature, although some items are included, and recent materials on East-West commerce are incorporated if they dwell on the legal structure of trade in the USSR.

Many important Eastern European journals appear in the French language, e.g., *Droit polonais contemporain; Le droit bulgare; Revue roumaine des sciences sociales;* and others. The *Revue de l'est* and *Annuaire de L'URSS et des pays socialistes europeens* are equally significant publications which should not be overlooked, the latter sometimes carrying contributions in English.

A. REFERENCE WORKS

Butler, W. E., ed.   Russian and Soviet Law: An Annotated Catalogue of Reference Works, Legislation, Court Reports, Serials and Monographs on Russian and Soviet Law (including International Law). Zug, IDC, 1976. xvi, 122 pp.

Butler, W. E., ed.   Writings on Soviet Law and Soviet International Law. Cambridge, Harvard Law School Library, 1966. 165 pp.

Feldbrugge, F.J.M., ed.   Encyclopedia of Soviet Law. Leiden, A. W. Sijthoff, 1973, 2 vols.

Klesment, J., et. al.   Legal Sources and Bibliography of the Baltic States. New York, Praeger, 1963. 197 pp.

Lew, J.D., Rathkopf, Jr. C.A., Starr, R.   Selected Bibliography on East-West Trade and Investment, New York, Oceana, 1976. 151 pp.

Mostecky, V., Butler, W.E., eds.   Soviet Legal Bibliography. Cambridge, Harvard Law School Library, 1965. 288 pp.

Prischepenko, N.P. Russian-English Law Dictionary. New York, Praeger, 1969. 146 pp.

Pushkarev, S., comp. Dictionary of Russian Historical Terms from the Eleventh Century to 1917. New Haven, Yale University Press, 1970. 199 pp.

Romashkin, P.S. ed. Literature on Soviet Law; Bibliographic Index. Moscow, Foreign Languages, Publishing House, 1960. 279 pp.

Szladits, C., ed. A Bibliography of Foreign and Comparative Law; Books and Articles in English. New York, Oceana Publications, 1955. 3 vols. and supp.

Telberg, I. Soviet-English Dictionary of Legal Terms and Concepts. New York, Telberg Publishing Company, 1961. 111 pp.

B. CASEBOOKS

Hazard, J.N., Shapiro, I. The Soviet Legal System: Post-Stalin Documentation and Historical Commentary. New York, Oceana Publications, 1962, 2nd ed., 1969 (with *P. B. Maggs*). 667 pp.

Hazard, J.N., Weisberg, M.J. Cases and Readings in Soviet Law. New York, Columbia School, 1950. mimeo.

Zile, Z. L. Ideas and Forces in Soviet Legal History. Madison, College Printing Company, 1967. 2nd ed. 1970. 456 pp.

C. LEGISLATION AND COURT REPORTS

Ablin, F., ed. 'Decision-Making in Soviet Higher Education (A Documentary History)', Soviet Education, Vol. XII, No. 9-11, 1970. 287 pp.

Akhapkin, Yu., ed. First Decrees of Soviet Power. London, Lawrence & Wishart, 1970. 186 pp.

Berman, H.J. Kerner, M., ed. & trans. Documents on Soviet Military Law and Administration. Cambridge, Harvard University Press, 1955. 164 pp.

Berman, H.J.,
Konstantinovksy, B.A. Soviet Law in Action. The Recollected Cases of a Soviet Lawyer. Cambridge, Harvard University Press, 1953. 77 pp.

Berman, H.J.,
Quigley, J.B.
ed. & trans. Basic Laws on the Structure of the Soviet State. Cambridge, Harvard University Press. 1969, 325 pp.

Berman, H.J.,
Spindler, J.W.,
ed. & trans. Soviet Criminal Law and Procedure: The RSFSR Codes. 2nd ed. Cambridge, Harvard University Press, 1972. Introduction by H.J. Berman. 396 pp.

Browne, M., ed. Ferment in the Ukraine. London, Macmillan, 1971. 267 pp.

Butler, W.E.,
trans. & ed. Customs Code of the USSR. Washington, D.C., Hazen Publications, 1966. 55 pp.

Butler, W.E., trans. Russian Family Code. Cambridge, Hazen Publications, 1965. 35 pp.

Butler, W.E.,
Quigley, J.B.
ed. & trans. The Merchant Shipping Code of the Soviet Union, 1968. Baltimore, The Johns Hopkins Press, 1970. 169 pp.

Cooper, D., trans. The Air Code of the USSR. Charlottesville, Michie Publications, 1965. 298 pp.

Feldbrugge, F. J.,
trans. The Federal Criminal Law of the Soviet Union. Leiden, A. W. Sijthoff, 1959. 157 pp. (Law in Eastern Europe Series No. 3.)

Hanna, G.H., trans. Fundamentals of Soviet Criminal Legislation, the Judicial System and Criminal Court Procedure. Moscow, Foreign Languages Publishing House, 1960. 103 pp.

Gray, W.
Stults, R., ed. & trans. Civil Code of the Russian Soviet Federated Socialist Republic: An English Translation. Ann Arbor, University of Michigan Press, 1965. 150 [54] pp.

Hayward, M. ed.	On Trial: The Soviet State versus 'Abram Tertz' and 'Nikolai Arzhak'. Rev. ed. New York, Harper and Row, 1967. 284 pp.
Kiralfy, A. K. R., trans.	The Civil Code and the Code of Civil Procedure of the RSFSR, 1964. Leiden. A. W. Sijthoff, 1966. 312 pp. (Law in Eastern Europe Series No. 11.)
Litvinov, P. M.	The Demonstration in Pushkin Square, Boston, Gambit, 1969, 128 pp.
Litvinov, P. M.	The Trial of the Four. London, Longmans, 1972. 432 pp.
Matthews, M.	Soviet Government. A Selection of Official Documents on Internal Policies, London, Jonathan Cape, 1974. 472 pp.
Meisel, J., Kozera, E. S.	Materials for the Study of the Soviet System: State and Party Constitutions. Laws, Decrees, Decisions and Official Statements of the Leaders in Translation. 2nd ed. Ann Arbor, University of Michigan Press, 1953. 495 pp.
Reddaway, P., ed.	Uncensored Russia: The Human Rights Movement. London, Jonathan Cape, 1972. 499 pp.
Saifulin, M., Sdobnikov, E., trans.	Fundamentals of Legislation of the USSR and the Union Republics. Moscow, Progress Publishers, 1974, 387 pp.
Sdobnikov, E. trans.	Soviet Civil Legislation and Procedure. Moscow, Foreign Languages Publishing House, n.d. 175 pp.
Shpektorow, A.I., Comp.	Collected Arbitration Cases. Moscow, USSR Chamber of Commerce, 1972. 3 vols.
Szirmai, Z. et al., trans.	The Merchant Shipping Code of the Soviet Union. Leiden, A. W. Sijthoff, 1960. 151 pp. (Law in Eastern Europe Series No. 4.)
	Trial of the U-2. Chicago, Translation World Publishers, 1960. Introduction by H. J. Berman. 375 pp.
Tucker, R.C., Cohen, S., ed. & trans.	The Great Purge Trial. New York, Grossett and Dunlap, 1965. 725 pp.

Van Het Reve, K., ed. Dear Comrade: Pavel Litvinov and the Voices of Soviet Citizens in Dissent. New York, Pitman Publishing Co., 1969. 199 pp.

D. MONOGRAPHS

Aleksandrov, N.G. Soviet Labour Law. New Delhi, University Book House, 1961. 454 pp.

Archer, P. Communism and the Law. London, Bodley Head, 1963. 112 pp.

Babb, H., trans. Soviet Legal Philosophy. Cambridge, Harvard University Press, 1951. 465 pp.

Barou, N. Cooperatives in the Soviet Union. London, Fabian Society, 1946. 123 pp.

Barry, D., Butler, W.E. Ginsburgs, G., eds. Contemporary Soviet Law: Essays in honor of John N. Hazard. The Hague, Nijhoff, 1974. 242 pp.

Batygin, K.S., ed. Soviet Labor Law and Principles of Civil Law: A Textbook. Jerusalem, Israel Program for Scientific Translations, 1972. 354 pp.

Beck, F., Godin, W. Russian Purge and Extraction of Confession. New York, 1951. 277 pp.

Berger, J. Shipwreck of a Generation: The Memoirs of Joseph Berger. London, Harvill Press, 1971. 286 pp.

Berman, H.J. Justice in the USSR. Rev. ed. Cambridge, Harvard University Press, 1963. 450 pp.

Berman, H. J., Maggs, P. B. Disarmament Inspection Under Soviet Law. New York, Oceana Publications, 1967. 154 pp.

Berman, H.J., Kerner, M. Soviet Military Law and Administration. Cambridge, Harvard University Press, 1955. 208 pp.

Bezuglov, A.	Soviet Deputy (Legal Status). Moscow, Progress Publishers, 1972. 155 pp.
Björk, I.	Wages, Prices and Social Legislation in the Soviet Union. London, Dobson, 1953. 199 pp.
Boguslavsky, M. M., Rubanov, A.A.	The Legal Status of Foreigners in the USSR. 2nd ed. Moscow, Foreign Languages Publishing House, 1963. 123 pp.
Boim, L., et al.	Legal Controls in the Soviet Union. Leiden, A. W. Sijthoff, 1966. 360 pp. (Law in Eastern Europe Series No. 13.)
Brown, E. D.	Soviet Trade Unions and Labor Relations. Cambridge, Harvard Univeristy Press, 1966. 394 pp.
Bunyan, J.	The Origin of Forced Labor in the Soviet State. 1917–1921. Baltimore The John Hopkins Press, 1967. 276 pp.
Callcott, M.S.	Russian Justice. New York, Macmillan, 1935. 265 pp.
Carson, G. B.	Electoral Practice in the USSR. New York, Praeger. 1955. 160 pp.
Chkhikvadze, V. M., ed.	The Soviet Form of Popular Government. Moscow, Progress Publishers, 1972. 254 pp.
Chkhikvadze, V. M., ed.	The Soviet State and Law. Moscow, Progress Publishers, 1969, 333 pp.
Chkhikvadze, V. M.	The State, Democracy, and Legality in the USSR: Lenin's Ideas Today. Moscow, Progress Publishers, 1972. 371 pp.
Connor, W. D.	Deviance in Soviet Society: Crime, Delinquency and Alcoholism. New York, Columbia U. P. 1972. 327 pp.
Conquest, R., ed.	Justice and the Legal System in the USSR. London, The Bodley Head, 1968. 152 pp.
Conquest, R., ed.	The Soviet Police System. London, The Bodley Head, 1968. 103 pp.
Conquest, R., ed.	The Soviet Political System. London, The Bodley Head, 1968. 144 pp.

Daiches, L.	Russians at Law. London, M. Joseph, 1960. 208 pp.
Dallin, D. J., Nikolaevksy, B. I.	Forced Labor in Soviet Russia. New Haven, Yale University Press, 1947. English ed. Hollis & Carter, 1948. 331 pp.
David, R., Brierly, J. E. C.	Major Legal Systems in the World Today: An Introduction to the Comparative Study of Law. London, Stevens & Sons, 1968. 528 pp.
Denisov, A. I., Kirichenko, M. G.	Soviet State Law. Moscow, Foreign Languages Publishing House, 1960. 459 pp.
Eissenstat, B. W., ed.	Lenin and Leninism: State, Law & Society. London, Lexington Books, 1971. 322 pp.
Fainsod, M.	Smolensk Under Soviet Rule. Cambridge. Harvard University Press, 1958. 484 pp.
Feifer, G.	Justice in Moscow. New York, Simon and Schuster. 1964, 353 pp.
Feldbrugge, F. J. M.,	Codification in the Communist World. Leiden, A. W. Sijthoff, 1975. 350 pp. (Law in Eastern Europe Series No. 19.)
Feldbrugge, F.J.M.	Samizdat and Political Dissent in the Soviet Union. Leiden. A. W. Sijthoff, 1975. 250 pp.
Feldbrugge, F.J.M.	Soviet Criminal Law: General Part. Leiden, A. W. Sijthoff, 1964, 291 pp. (Law in Eastern Europe Series No. 9.)
Fleishits, Ye., Makovsky, A.	The Civil Codes of the Soviet Republics. Moscow. Progress Publishers, 1976. 288 pp.
Fox, I. K., ed.	Water Resources Law and Policy in the Soviet Union. London, American University Publishers Group, 1971. 256 pp.
Gallik, D., et al.	The Soviet Financial System: Structure, Operation, and Statistics. Washington, D. C., GPO 1968, 416 pp.

Garnefsky, A.	Public Policy in Soviet Private International Law. 2nd ed. The Hague, M. Nijhoff, 1970. 186 pp.
Giffen, J. H.	The Legal and Practical Aspects of Trade with the Soviet Union. Rev. ed. New York, Praeger, 1971. 354 pp.
Ginsburgs, G.	Soviet Citizenship Law. Leiden, A. W. Sijthoff, 1968. 270 pp. (Law in Eastern Europe Series No. 15.)
Golyakov, I. T.	The Role of the Soviet Court. Washington, D.C., Public Affairs Press, 1948. 20 pp.
Gorodissky, M. L.	Licenses in USSR Trade. Springfield, Va., NTIS, 1972. 144 pp.
Grigoryan, L., Dolgopolov, Yu.	Fundamentals of Soviet State Law. Moscow, Progress Publishers, 1971. 328 pp.
Grzybowski, K.	Soviet Legal Institutions. Ann Arbor, University of Michigan Press, 1962. 285 pp.
Grzybowski, K.	Soviet Private International Law. Leiden, A. W. Sijthoff, 1965. 179 pp. (Law in Eastern Europe Series No. 10.)
Gsovski, V.	Soviet Civil Law. Ann Arbor, University of Michigan Law School, 1948–49. 2 vols.
Guins, G. C.	Soviet Law and Society. The Hague, Martinus Nijhoff, 1954. 457 pp.
Hazard, J. N.	Law and Social Change in the USSR. London, Stevens & Sons, 1953. 310 pp.
Hazard, J. N.	Settling Disputes in Soviet Society. New York, Columbia University Press, 1960. 534 pp.
Hazard, J. N.	Soviet Housing Law. New Haven, Yale University Press, 1939. 178 pp.
Hildebrand, J. L.	The Sociology of Soviet Law. Buffalo, N.Y., W. S. Hein & Co., 1972. 227 pp.

Ivanov, G.	Notes of a People's Judge. Moscow, Foreign Languages Publishing House, 1950. 78 pp.
Jaworskj, M.	Soviet Political Thought. Baltimore, The John Hopkins Press, 1967, 621 pp.
Johnson, E.L.	An Introduction to the Soviet Legal System. London, Methuen, 1969. 248 pp.
Karpinsky, V.	The Social and State Structure of the USSR. Moscow, Foreign Languages Publishing House, 1950. 239 pp.
Kelsen. H.	The Communist Theory of Law. New York, Praeger, 1955. 203 pp.
Kucherov, S.	The Organs of Soviet Administration of Justice: Their History and Operation. Leiden, E. J. Brill, 1970. 754 pp.
LaFave, W., ed	Law in the Soviet Society. Champaign, University of Illinois Press, 1965. 297 pp.
Lapenna, I.	Soviet Penal Policy. London, Bodley Head, 1968. 148 pp.
Lapenna, I.	State and Law: Soviet and Yugoslav Theory. New Haven, Yale University Press, 1964. 135 pp.
Levitsky, S. L.	Introduction to Soviet Copyright Law. Leiden, A. W. Sijthoff, 1964. 303 pp. (Law in Eastern Europe Series No. 8.)
Lipetsker, M. S.	Property Rights of Soviet Citizens. London, Soviet News, 1946. 45 pp.
McAuley, M.	Labour Disputes in Soviet Russia: 1957–1965. Oxford, Clarendon Press, 1969. 269 pp.
Medvedev, Zh.A.	The Medvedev Papers. London, Macmillan, 1971. 471 pp.
Morgan, G. G.	Soviet Administrative Legality. Stanford, University Press, 1962. 281 pp.
Morozov, G. V. *Kalashnik, Ya. M.* ed.	Forensic Psychiatry. New York, International Arts & Sciences Press, 1970. 499 pp.

Mote, M. E.	Soviet Local and Republic Elections. Stanford, Hoover Institution, 1965. 123 pp.
Pisar, S.	Coexistence & Commerce. London, Penguin Press, 1970. 558 pp.
Quigley, Jr., J. B.	The Soviet Foreign Trade Monopoly: Institutions and Laws. Columbus, Ohio State University Press, 1974. 256 pp.
Riasanovsky, V. A.	Customary Law of the Nomadic Tribes of Siberia. Bloomington, Indiana University Press, 1965. 151 pp.
Romashkin, P. S. ed.	Fundamentals of Soviet Law. Moscow, Foreign Languages Publishing House, 1962. 517 pp.
Rudden, B.	Soviet Insurance Law. Leiden, A. W. Sijthoff, 1966. 219 pp. (Law in Eastern Europe Series No. 12.)
Schlesinger, R. ed.	The Family in the USSR: Documents and Readings. London, Routledge and Kegan Paul, 1949. 408 pp.
Schlesinger, R.	Soviet Legal Theory. Rev. ed. New York, Oxford University Press, 1951. 299 pp.
Sheinin, L. R.	People's Courts in the USSR. Moscow, Foreign Languages Publishing House, 1957. 111 pp.
Shevtsov, V. S.	National Sovereignty and the Soviet State. Moscow, Progress Publishers, 1974. 175 pp.
Skilling, H.G., Griffiths, F., ed.	Interest Groups in Soviet Politics. Toronto, University of Toronto Press, 1971. 433 pp.
Smith, G. A.	Soviet Foreign Trade: Organization, Operation and Policy, 1918–1971. New York, Praeger, 1973. 370 pp.
Sprudzs, A, Rusis, A., eds.	Res Baltica. Leiden, A. W. Sijthoff, 1968. 303 pp.
Strong, J.W.	The Soviet Union under Brezhnev and Kosygin. New York, Van Nostrand, 1971. 277 pp.

Sverdlov, G.M.	Legal Rights of the Soviet Family: Marriage, Motherhood, and the Family in Soviet Law. London, Soviet News, 1945. 55 pp.
Sverdlov, G.M.	Marriage and Family in the USSR. Moscow, Foreign Languages Publishing House, 1956. 56 pp.
Syrodoyev, N.	Soviet Land Legislation. Moscow, Progress Publishers, 1975. 147 pp.
Terebilov, V. I.	The Soviet Court. Moscow, Progress Publishers, 1973. 182 pp.
Trusov, A. I.	An Introduction to the Theory of Evidence. Moscow, Foreign Languages Publishing House, n.d. 262 pp.
Tumanov, V. A.	Contemporary Bourgeois Legal Thought: A Marxist Evaluation of the Basic Concepts. Moscow, Progress Publishers, 1974, 311 pp.
Volkov, A. A.	Maritime Law. Jerusalem, US Department of Commerce National Technical Information Service, 1971. 162 pp.
Vyshinsky, A. Ya.	The Law of the Soviet State. New York, Macmillan, 1948. 749 pp.
Zaitsev, E., Poltorak, A.	The Soviet Bar. Moscow, Foreign Languages Publishing House, 1959. 255 pp.
Zelitch, J.	Soviet Administration of Criminal Law. Philadelphia, University of Pennsylvania Press, 1931. 418 pp.
Zile, Z., et al.	The Soviet Legal System and Arms Inspection: A Case Study in Policy Implementation. London, Praeger, 1972. 394 pp.
Zlatopolsky, D.	State System of the USSR. Moscow, Foreign Languages Publishing House, n.d. 199 pp.

SERIALS

ABSEES: Soviet and East European Abstract Series, a quarterly journal summarizing important books, journal articles, and daily press published in the USSR and Eastern Europe. Invaluable in general, but particularly the law section. Publication ceased in 1976.

ACTA JURIDICA ACADEMIAE SCIENTIARUM HUNGARICAE, a semi-annual journal containing articles in English, French, German, and Russian, issued by the Hungarian Academy of Sciences.

BULLETIN OF CZECHOSLOVAK LAW, a quarterly publication of the Union of Lawyers of the Czechoslovak Socialist Republic in Prague.

COLLECTION OF YUGOSLAV LAWS, a series issued irregularly by the Yugoslav Institute of Comparative Law in Belgrade since 1962 containing translations of Yugoslav legislation. 20 volumes have so far appeared.

CURRENT DIGEST OF THE SOVIET PRESS, a weekly journal of translations from the Soviet press and, occasionally, learned journals. Current legal materials appear with some frequency.

HUNGARIAN LAW REVIEW, issued twice yearly by the Hungarian Lawyers' Association in Budapest.

INTERNATIONAL BULLETIN FOR RESEARCH ON LAW IN EASTERN EUROPE, a semi-annual publication containing brief articles, documentation notes, and news items supplied by specialists in Soviet and East European comparative legal studies, published in Cologne by the Deutsche Gesellschaft für Osteuropakunde.

LAW AND LEGISLATION IN THE GERMAN DEMOCRATIC REPUBLIC, published twice yearly by the Lawyers' Association of the GDR.

LAW IN EASTERN EUROPE SERIES, a collection of monographs issued by the Documentation Office for East European Law, University of Leiden, since 1958. Volumes 1, 2, 7, and 14 contain miscellanous articles and texts treating both the Soviet and East European legal systems. Other titles in the series are listed above under the names of the individual authors or editors.

OSTEUROPA-RECHT, a quarterly journal devoted exclusively to the law of communist-ruled states. Contributions frequently are published in the English language.

REVIEW OF CONTEMPORARY LAW, issued semi-annually in Brussels by the International Association of Democratic Lawyers.

REVIEW OF SOCIALIST LAW, a quarterly issued under the auspices of the Documentation Office for East European Law, Leiden University, and devoted to the legal systems of all communist-ruled states.

SOVIET LAW AND GOVERNMENT, a quarterly journal of translations from Soviet sources, much of which relates to law, published by M. E. Sharpe, Inc. in New York (formerly International Arts and Sciences Press).

SOVIET STATUTES AND DECISIONS, a quarterly journal of translations of Soviet legislation and judicial materials, published in New York by M. E. Sharpe, Inc. (formerly International Arts and Sciences Press). Editors to present: Harold J. Berman (1964–69); William E. Butler (1969–76); Peter B. Maggs (1976–   ). Each volume is devoted to a particular theme, and contents to the present include:

Vol. I	No. 1	Criminal Code of the RSFSR
	No. 2—3	Code of Criminal Procedure of the RSFSR
	No. 4	Cases on Criminal Law and Procedure
Vol. II	No. 1	Soviet Economic Law: Arbitrazh
	No. 2	Soviet Economic Law: Contracts of Delivery
	No. 3	Soviet Economic Law—Contracts of Delivery (continued)
	No. 4	Soviet Economic Law: contracts of construction
Vol. III	No. 1	Soviet International Law: Legal Status of Foreigners in the USSR
	No. 2—3	Diplomatic and Consular Law of the USSR
	No. 4	Soviet Public International Law
Vol. IV	No. 1—2	Civil Law and Procedure: Compensation for Harm
	No. 3	Soviet Civil Law and Procedure: Property Contracts, Inheritance
	No. 4	Family Law
Vol. V	No. 1	Soviet Administrative Law: Administrative Penalties
	No. 2	Soviet Administrative Law: Administration of Retail Trade
	No. 3—4	Soviet Administrative Law: Administration of Public Health
Vol. VI	No. 1—4	Soviet Maritime Law
Vol. VII	No. 1—4	Soviet Citizenship Law
Vol. VIII	No. 1—2	Soviet State Symbolism: Arms and Flags of the USSR and the Union Republics
	No. 3—4	Soviet State Symbolism: Medals, Honorary, Titles, Awards, and Prizes

Vol. IX   No. 1—4   Soviet Conservation Law: Land; Water, and Forestry
Vol. X   No. 1—4   Soviet Administration of Legality
Vol. XI   No. 1—4   Socialist International Organizations
Vol. XII   No. 1—4   Techniques and Law Reform in the Soviet Union
Vol. XIII   No. 1—4   Soviet Patent Law

SOVIET UNION, a quarterly journal published by the University of Pittsbirgh Center for International Studies in conjunction with Temple University which contains a regular section on Soviet law and occasional special issues devoted exclusively to law.

CHECKLIST OF SOVIET NORMATIVE ACTS AVAILABLE IN ENGLISH TRANSLATION

This checklist is a selective compilation: the principal codification acts are included, as are some noteworthy examples of subordinate legislation. All items listed are believed to be in force as of 1 July 1977.

Most items contain a reference to a Russian language source, the official gazette whenever possible. Citations to amendments are not given, although acts known to have been amended are asterisked. With only a very few exceptions, the sources given for English language translations contain the complete text of the act (although not necessarily as amended). At least two translations of each text are cited whenever possible, but beyond this, comprehensive listings have not been attempted. The 1977 Constitution of the USSR, replacing that of 1936, is reproduced in full in Volume II of the present work.

Volume II (cited as SLS) also contains up-to-date translations of many of the enactments, and the USSR and RSFSR codes will appear in a forthcoming volume of the Law in Eastern Europe Series. Abbreviations used below are indicated at the end of the checklist.

Constitutional Law

1. Constitution (Basic Law) of the Union of Soviet Socialist Republics, confirmed December 5, 1936*
    R: Sbornik, pp. 3–24
    E: Berman & Quigley, pp. 3–28
        Constitution (Fundamental Law) of the Union of Soviet Socialist Republics (Moscow, 1967). 107 p. (Soviet Legislation Series)
        SLS
        Triska, J.F. (ed.), *Constitutions of the Communist Party-States* (Standord, 1968), pp. 37–36
2. Constitution (Basic Law) of the Russian Soviet Federated Socialist Republic, confirmed January 21, 1937*
    R: *Konstitutsiia (osnovnoi zakon) RSFSR . . .* [i] *konstitutsii . . . avtonomnikh sovetskikh sotsialisticheskikh respublik vkhodiashchikh v sostav RSFSR* (Moscow, 1972). 420 p.

E: Berman & Quigley, pp. 32-57
3. Statute on the Commission for Legislative Proposals of the Council of the Union of the USSR Supreme Soviet, adopted February 25, 1947
    R: *Vedomosti SSSR* (1947), No. 8
    E: Denisov, pp. 435-437
4. Edict on the Procedure for the Publication and Entry into Force of Laws of the USSR, Decrees of the USSR Supreme Soviet, and Edicts and Decrees of the Presidium of the USSR Supreme Soviet, adopted June 19, 1958*
    R: *Vedomosti SSSR* (1958), no. 14, item 275
    E: Berman & Maggs, pp. 108-109
    SS&D, XII (1975-76), 111-113.
5. Edict on the Procedure for the Publication and Entry into Force of Decrees and Regulations of the USSR Government, adopted March 30, 1959.
    R: *SP SSSR* (1959) no. 6, item 37
    E: Berman Maggs, pp. 110-111, III, no. 4, pp. 60-61 SS&D
6. Statute on Standing Committees of the Council of the Union and the Council of Nationalities of the USSR Supreme Soviet, adopted October 12, 1967
    R: *Vedomosti SSSR* (1967), no. 42, item 536
    E: Berman & Quigley, pp. 121-131
    CDSP, XIX, no. 44 (1967), pp. 22-25
    SL&G, VI, No. 2 (1967), pp. 13-19
7. Statute on Elections to the USSR Supreme Soviet, adopted January 9, 1950
    R: *Vedomosti SSSR* (1950), no. 2
    E: Berman & Quigley, pp. 100-118; Denisov, pp. 413-434
    Regulations for Election to the Supreme Soviet of the U.S.S.R. (Moscow, 1967). 38 p. (Soviet Legislation Series)
8. General Statute on Ministries of the USSR, adopted July 10, 1967
    R: *Ekonomicheskaia gazeta*, no. 34 (1967), pp. 7-9
    E: Berman & Quigley, pp. 83-97
    CDSP, XIX, no. 37 (1967), pp. 3-8
    SL&G, VI, no. 2 (1967), pp. 3-12
    SLS
9. Statute on State Planning Committee of the USSR, adopted September 9, 1968
    R: *SP SSSR* (1968), no. 17, item 94
    E: SLS
10. Statute on State Committee of USSR Council of Ministers for Science and Technology, confirmed October 1, 1966
    R: *SP SSSR* (1966), no. 21, item 193
    E: SLS
11. Statute on State Committee of USSR Council of Ministers for Labor and Wages, confirmed August 25, 1955
    R: *Tööõiguslikud Aktid* (Tallin, 1969), pp. 13-17
    E: *Review of Socialist Law,* I (1975), 309-314

12. USSR Edict on the Basic Rights and Duties of Rural and Settlement Soviets of Working People's Deputies, adopted April 8, 1968
    R: *Vedomosti SSSR* (1968), No. 16, item 131
    E: Berman & Quigley, pp. 133–140
13. USSR Edict on the Basic Rights and Duties of City and District (in City) Soviets of Working People's Deputies, adopted March 19, 1971
    R: *Vedomosti SSSR* (1971), no. 12, item 133
    E: CDSP, XXIII, no. 13 (1971), pp. 27–30, 38
    SLS
14. Statute on the City Soviet of Working People's Deputies of the Azerbaidzhan SSR, adopted December 29, 1958
    R: *Sbornik zakonov Azerbaidzhanskoi SSR i ukazov prezidiuma verkhovnogo soveta Azerbaidzhanskoi SSR* (Baku, 1967), I, p. 185
    E: Berman & Quigley, pp. 142–164
15. Law on the Status of Deputies of Soviets in the USSR, adopted September 20, 1972
    R: *Vedomosti SSSR* (1972), no. 39, item 347
    E: *CDSP,* XXIV, no. 39 (1972), pp. 9–13
    SLS
16. Statute on Permanent Commissions of Local Soviets of Working People's Deputies of the Ukrainian SSR, adopted May 31, 1957
    E: Berman & Quigley, pp. 116–171
17. Statute on the State Flag of the Union of Soviet Socialist Republics, adopted August 19, 1955
    R: *Vedomosti SSSR* (1955), no. 15, item 304
    E: *SS&D,* VII (1971/72), 58–61
18. Instruction concerning the Application of the Statute on the state Flag of the Latvian SSR, confirmed May 30, 1967
    R: *Spravochnik po zakonodatel'stvu dlia ispolnitel'nykh komitetov sovetov deputatov trudiashchikhsia* (Riga, 1970–), I, p. 66
    E: *SS&D,* VII (1971/72), 143–145
19. Instruction concerning the Application of the Statute on the State Flag of the RSFSR, confirmed January 31, 1956
    R: *SS RSFSR,* II, p. 467
    E: *SS&D,* VIII (1971/72), 173–174
20. Law of the Tuva Autonomous Soviet Socialist Republic on the Arms, Flag, and Capital of the Tuva ASSR, adopted January 10, 1962
    R: *SS RSFSR,* II, p. 230
    E: *SS&D,* VIII (1971/72), 193–95

21. Edict on the Procedure for Flying the State Flag of the Uzbek SSR, adopted October 31, 1955
    R: *Sbornik zakonov Uzbekskoi SSR i ukazov prezidiuma verkhovnogo soveta Uzbekskoi SSR* (Tashkent, 1964), p. 185
    E: *SS&D*, VII (1971/72), 208–212

Administrative Law

22. USSR Edict on the Further Limitation of the Application of Fines Imposed by Administrative Procedure, adopted June 21, 1961*
    R: *Vedomosti SSSR* (1961), no. 35, item 368
    E: *SS&D*, V, No. 1 (1967), pp. 7–14
    SLS
23. RSFSR Edict on the Further Limitation of the Application of Fines Imposed by Administrative Procedure, adopted March 3, 1962*
    R: *Vedomosti RSFSR* (1962), no. 9, item 121
    E: *SS&D*, V, no. 1 (1967), pp. 18–28
24. RSFSR Statute on Administrative Commissions of Executive Committees of District and City Soviets of Working People's Deputies, adopted March 30, 1962
    R: *Vedomosti RSFSR* (1962), no. 13, item 166
    E: Berman & Quigley, pp. 277–285
    SS&D, V. no. 1 (1967), pp. 29–38; X (1974), 280–289
    SLS
25. RSFSR Statute on Commissions for the Struggle Against Drunkenness, confirmed August 21, 1972
    R: *Vedomosti RSFSR* (1972), no. 34, item 845
    E: *SS&D*, X (1974), 313–321
    SLS
26. USSR Edict on the Procedure for Considering Proposals, Applications, and Appeals of Citizens, adopted April 12, 1968
    R: *Vedomosti SSSR* (1968), no. 17, item 144
    E: *CDSP*, XX, no. 17 (1968), pp. 7–8
    SS&D, X (1974), 357–364
    SLS
27. USSR Law on Universal Military Service, adopted October 12, 1967
    R: *Vedomosti SSSR* (1967), no. 42, item 552
    E: *CDSP*, XIX, no. 45 (1967), pp. 4–10
28. Statute on People's Control Agencies in the USSR, adopted December 19, 1968
    R: *SP SSSR* (1969), no. 1, item 2
    E: *SS&D*, V, no. 2 (1968/69), pp. 107–120
    SLS

29. RSFSR Statute on the State Inspectorate for the Quality of Goods and Trade of the RSFSR, confirmed March 13, 1959
    R: *SP RSFSR* (1959), no. 2, item 20
    E: *SS&D*, V, no. 2 (1968/69), pp. 32–41
30. Edict on the Procedure for the Award of Orders and Medals of the USSR, adopted February 11, 1958
    R: *Vedomosti SSSR* (1958), no. 4, item 87
    E: *SS&D*, VIII (1972), 349–368
31. Instruction on the Procedure for the Presentation of Orders and Medals of the USSR. . . . , adopted April 1, 1958
    R: *Sbornik zakonov SSSR i ukazov prezidiuma verkhovnogo soveta SSSR v dvukh tomakh* (Moscow, 1968), II, p. 115
    E: *SS&D*, VIII (1972), 368–376
32. USSR Statute on the Passport System, confirmed August 28, 1974
    R: *SP SSSR* (1974), no. 19, item 109
    E: *Review of Socialist Law*, II (1976), 47–56

Economic Law and Arbitrazh

33. Statute on the State Production Combine, confirmed March 27, 1974
    R: *SP SSSR* (1974), no. 8, item 38
    E: SLS
34. Statute on the Socialist State Production Enterprise, adopted October 4, 1965
    R: *SP SSSR* (1965), no. 19–20, item 155
    CDSP, XVII, no. 42 (1965), pp. 3–10
    E: *SS&D*, II, no. 3 (1966), pp. 52–84
    SLS
35. Statute on the Fund for Material Incentives and Socio-Cultural Measures of State Farms and Other State Agricultural Enterprises, adopted December 23, 1968
    R: *Ekonomicheskaia gazeta*, no. 14 (1969), p. 15
    E: *CDSP*, XXI, no. 21 (1969), pp. 7, 14
36. Statute on State Arbitrazh attached to the USSR Council of Ministers, adopted January 17, 1974
    R: *SP SSSR* (1974), no. 4, item 19
    E: *SS&D*, X (1974), 247–260
    SLS
37. Statute on Arbitrazh of the USSR Ministry of Fisheries, confirmed April 8, 1967
    R: Ivanchenko, N.S. (comp.), *Sbornik rukovodiashchikh materialov po rybnomu khoziaistvu* (Leningrad, 1970), I (Part 2), p. 362
    E: *SS&D*, X (1974), 262–268

Associations

38. RSFSR Decree on Religious Associations, adopted April 8, 1929*
    R: SU RSFSR (1929), no. 35, item 353
    E: *Review of Socialist Law,* I (1975), 223–234
    SLS

Public Health

39. Fundamental Principles of Public Health Legislation of the USSR and Union Republics, adopted December 19, 1969
    R: *Vedomosti SSSR* (1969), no. 52, item 466
    E: *CDSP,* XXII, no. 1 (1970), pp. 7–13
       Saifulin, pp. 62–86
       SL&G, IX, no. 1 (1970), pp. 28–56
       SLS
40. Statute on the USSR Ministry of Public Health, adopted July 17, 1968
    E: *SS&D,* V, no. 4 (1969), pp. 11–20
41. Decree on the Sanitary Protection of USSR Boundaries, adopted August 23, 1931
    R: *SZ SSSR* (1931), no. 55, item 355
    E: *SS&D,* VI (1969), 100–103
42. Statute on State Sanitary Supervision in the USSR, adopted October 29, 1963
    R: *Resheniia partii i pravitel'stva po khoziaistvennym voprosam* (Moscow, 1967–), V, 421–427
    E: *SS&D,* V, no. 4 (1969), pp. 109–117
43. Statute on the RSFSR Ministry of Public Health, adopted March 8, 1960
    R: *SP RSFSR* (1960), no. 11, item 46
    E: *SS&D,* V, No. 4 (1969), pp. 21–28

Public Education

44. Fundamental Principles of Legislation of the USSR and the Union Republics on Public Education, adopted July 19, 1973
    R: *Vedomosti SSSR* (1973), no. 30, item 392
    E: *CDSP,* XXV, no. 31 (1973), pp. 10–19
       Saifulin, pp. 359–385
       SLS
45. Statute on the Ministry of Higher and Secondary Specialized Education of the USSR, confirmed May 12, 1968
    R: *Biulleten' MVSSO SSSR,* no. 8 (1968)
    E: *Soviet Education,* XII, nos. 9–11, (1970), pp. 216–226

46. Statute on Higher Educational Institutions of the USSR, confirmed January 22, 1969
    R: *Biulleten' MVSSO SSSR,* no. 5 (1969)
    E: *Soviet Education,* XII, nos. 9–11 (1970), pp. 227–253
47. USSR Statute on the Secondary General-Education School, adopted September 8, 1970
    R: *Uchitel'skaia gazeta,* September 15, 1970, pp. 1–2
    E: *CDSP,* XXII, No. 37 (1970), pp. 1–6
48. Decree on Compensation of State Expenditure for Training by Citizens of the USSR Exiting for Permanent Residence Abroad, adopted August 3, 1972
    R: *SP SSSR* (1973), no. 1, item 4
    E: *ILM,* XII (1973), 427-430

Financial Law

49. Law on Budgetary Rights of the USSR and Union Republics, adopted October 30, 1959
    R: *Vedomosti SSSR* (1959), no. 44, item 221
    E: *Budgetary Powers of the U.S.S.R. and the Union Republics* (Moscow, 1967), pp. 5–24 (Soviet Legislation Series)
    SLS
50. USSR Decree on the Taxation of Income Derived from Royalties, adopted September 4, 1973*
    R: *Vedomosti SSSR* (1973), no. 37, item 497
    E: *ILM,* IX (1973), 1517–1520

Civil Law

51. Fundamental Principles of Civil Legislation of the USSR and Union Republics, adopted December 8, 1961*
    R: *Vedomosti SSSR* (1961), no. 50, item 525
    E: *CDSP,* XIV, no. 4 (1962), pp. 3–13, 20
    Cooper, pp. 157–235
    Fundamentals of Soviet Civil Legislation and Civil Procedure (Official Texts) (Moscow, 1968), pp. 7–87 (Soviet Legislation Series)
    LEE, VII, pp. 268–298, 318–330 (1960 draft; LEE, V. pp. 271–294)
    Saifulin, pp. 150–203
    Sdobnikov, pp. 55–114
    SLS
52. Civil Code of the Russian Soviet Federated Socialist Republic, adopted June 11, 1964*
    R: *Sovetskaia iustitsiia,* no. 13–14 (1964), pp. 4–63

E: Gray, W. (transl.), *Soviet Civil Legislation* (Ann Arbor, 1965), pp. 1–150 (also reproduces Russian text)
LEE, XI, pp. 11–154
SLS

53. RSFSR Statute on Registry for Acts of Civil Status, confirmed June 19, 1974
R: *SP RSFSR* (1974), no. 17, item 94
E: Simons

54. Decree on Transfers Abroad of Funds in Estates, adopted April 21, 1955
R: *Sbornik postanovlenii, prikazov i instruktsii po finansovo-khoziaistvennym voprosam*, no. 11 (1959), p. 31
E: *SS&D*, II, no. 1 (1966), p. 40

55. Statute on Discoveries, Inventions, and Rationalization Proposals, confirmed August 21, 1973
R: *SP SSSR* (1973), no. 19, item 103
E: *Industrial Property*, no. 7 (1971), 298

56. Instruction on State Scientific and Technical Expert Examination of Inventions, confirmed December 13, 1973
R: *Voprosy izobretatel'stva*, no. 8 (1974), p. 29
E: *SS&D*, XIII (1976), 5–96

57. Statute on Trademarks, adopted June 23, 1962*
R: *Sbornik zakonodatel'nykh aktov i postanovlenii po izobretatel'stvu i ratsionalizatsii* (3d ed.; Moscow, 1965), pp. 290–294
E: *Idea*, XII (1968), 812–817
Industrial Property, VI (1967), 133–136; IV (1965), 252–255
Patent and Trademark Review, LXVI (1968), 97–103
Trademark Reporter, LVIII (1968), 911–919

Family Law

58. Fundamental Principles of Legislation of the USSR and Union Republics on Marriage and the Family, adopted June 27, 1968
R: *Vedomosti SSSR* (1969), no. 27, item 241
E: *CDSP*, XX, no. 39 (1968) pp. 14–18
International & Comparative Law Quarterly, XVIII (1969), 410–423
Saifulin, pp. 337–354
SS&D, IV, no. 4 (1968), pp. 109–126
SLS

59. Code of Laws of the Russian Soviet Federated Socialist Republic on Marriage and the Family, adopted July 30, 1969
R: *Vedomosti RSFSR* (1969), no. 32, item 1086
E: *SL&G*, IX, no. 2 (1970), pp. 103–158
Simons

Land Law

60. Fundamental Principles of Land Legislation of the USSR and Union Republics, adopted December 13, 1968
    R: *Vedomosti SSSR* (1968), no. 51, item 485
    E: *CDSP,* XXI, no. 1 (1969), pp. 14–20
    Saifulin, pp. 10–34
    SL&G, VII, no. 4 (1969), pp. 13–26
    SLS
61. USSR Statute concerning State Control of Land Use, adopted May 14, 1970
    R: *SP SSSR* (1970), no. 9, item 71
    E: *SS&D,* IX (1972), 60–68
62. Land Code of the Russian Soviet Federated Socialist Republic, adopted July 1, 1970
    R: *Vedomosti RSFSR* (1970), no. 28, item 581
    E: *SS&D,* IX (1972), 37–59 (excerpts)
    Simons
63. RSFSR Decree on the Procedure for Granting Plots for Land Use, adopted March 23, 1971
    R: *SP RSFSR* (1971), no. 8, item 53
    E: *SS&D*, IX (1972), 68–83

Forestry Law

64. Fundamental Principles of the USSR and Union Republics on Forestry Legislation, distributed for comments, February 8, 1977. Adoption expected in 1977.
    R: Vedomosti SSSR (1977), no. 7. item 123
    E: SLS

Minerals Law

65. Fundamental Principles of Legislation of the USSR and Union Republics on Minerals, adopted July 9, 1975
    R: Vedomosti SSSR (1975), no. 29, item 435
    E: SLS

Water Law

66. Fundamental Principles of Water Legislation of the USSR and Union Republics, adopted December 10, 1970
    R: *Vedomosti SSSR* (1970), no. 50, item 566

E: *CDSP*, XXII, no. 52 (1970), pp. 7–12

Fox, I. K. (ed.), *Water Resources Law and Policy in the Soviet Union* (Madison, 1971), pp. 221–239

Saifulin, pp. 39–60

SLS

67. Water Code of the Russian Soviet Federated Socialist Republic, adopted June 30, 1972

    R: *Vedomosti RSFSR* (1972), no. 27, item 692

    E: *SS&D*, IX (1972/73), 129–165

    Simons

68. USSR Rules for the Protection of Surface Water from Pollution by Liquid Waste, confirmed July 15, 1961

    R: Blinov, B.M. (ed.), *Okhrana prirody: sbornik normativnykh aktov* (Moscow, 1971), p. 302

    E: *SS&D*, IX (1972/72), 112–125

69. USSR Decree on Measures Relating to the Prevention of Pollution of the Caspian Sea, adopted September 23, 1968

    R: *SP SSSR* (1968), no. 19, item 134

    E: *SS&D*, VI (1969/70), 197–206

Nature Conservation

70. USSR Decree on Measures for the Further Improvement of Nature Conservation and the Rational Utilization of Natural Resources, adopted September 20, 1972

    R: *Vedomosti SSSR* (1972), no. 39, item 346

    E: *CDSP*, XXIV, no. 38 (1972), pp. 18–19

    SS&D, IX (1973), 300–306

71. USSR Decree on the Intensification of Nature Conservation and the Improved Utilization of Natural Resources, adopted December 29, 1972

    R: *SP SSSR* (1973), no. 2, item 6

    E: *SS&D*, IX (1973), 306–345

72. RSFSR Law on Nature Conservation, adopted October 27, 1960

    R: *Vedomosti RSFSR* (1960), no. 40, item 586

    E: *SS&D*, IX (1972), 11–23

73. USSR Law on the Protection and Use of Monuments of History and Culture, adopted October 29, 1976

    R: *Vedomosti SSSR* (1976), no. 44, item 628

    E: SLS

Collective Farm Law

74. Model Collective Farm Charter, adopted November 28, 1969
    R: *Izvestia,* November 29, 1969, p. 1
    E: SLS
75. USSR Basic Statute on the Procedure for the Conclusion and Performance of State Contracts for the Procurement of Agricultural Produce, confirmed October 22, 1970
    E: *Review of Socialist Law,* I (1975), 53–65

Maritime Law

76. Merchant Shipping Code of the Union of Soviet Socialist Republics, adopted September 17, 1968*
    R: *Vedomosti SSSR* (1968), no. 39, item 351
    E: Andrianov, S.N. (transl.), *The Merchant Shipping Code of the USSR* (Moscow, 1971), pp. 3–56
    Butler, W.E., Quigley, J.B. Jr., *The Merchant Shipping Code of the USSR (1968)* (Baltimore-London, 1970), pp. 39–120
    CDSP, XXI, no. 6 (1969), pp. 10–29, 45
    Simons
77. Statute on the Administration of the Northern Sea Route, adopted September 16, 1971
    R: *SP SSSR* (1971), no. 17, item 124
    E: *ILM,* XI (1972), 645–646
    Lay, S.H. Churchill, R., & Nordquist, M. (comps.), *New Directions in the Law of the Sea* (Dobbs Ferry, 1973), II, 710–711
    The Polar Record, XVI (1972), 420–421
78. Statute on the Maritime Arbitration Commission attached to the All-Union Chamber of Commerce and Industry, adopted December 13, 1930
    R: *SZ SSSR* (1930), no. 60, item 637
    E: Butler and Quigley, pp. 123–125
    Gsovski, II, pp. 641–644
    Kos, pp. 219–220
    USSR Chamber of Commerce, *Maritime Arbitration Commission* (Moscow, 1968), pp. 17–19 (also reproduces Russian text)
79. Rules of Procedure for Cases in the Maritime Arbitration Commission attached to the All-Union Chamber of Commerce and Industry, confirmed January 21, 1949
    R: USSR Chamber of Commerce, *Maritime Arbitration Commission,* pp. 6–12

E: Butler and Quigley, pp. 126–131
Gsovski, II, pp. 645–650
Kos, pp. 221–225
USSR Chamber of Commerce, *Maritime Arbitration Commission*, pp. 20–26

Air Law

80. Air Code of the Union of Soviet Socialist Republics, adopted December 26, 1961*
    R: *Vedomosti SSSR* (1961), no. 52, item 538
    E: *Air Law of the USSR* (Moscow, 1967), 63 p.
       Cooper, pp. 35–155
       LEE, XIV, pp. 86–116
       Simons

Labor Law

81. Fundamental Principles of Labor Legislation of the USSR and Union Republics, adopted July 15, 1970
    R: *Vedomosti SSSR* (1970), no. 29, item 265
    E: *CDSP*, XXII, no. 34 (1970), pp. 1–11
       ILO Legislative Series, 1970 USSR-1, pp. 1–30
       Saifulin, pp. 90–131
       SLS
82. Labor Code of the Russian Soviet Federated Socialist Republic, adopted December 9, 1971
    R: *Vedomosti RSFSR* (1971), no. 50, item 1007
    E: ILO Legislative Series, 1971 USSR-1, pp. 1–69
       Simons
83. USSR Statute on Rights of Factory, Plant, and Local Trade Union Committees, adopted September 27, 1971
    R: *Vedomosti SSSR* (1971), no. 39, item 382
    E: *CDSP*, XXIII, no. 39 (1971), pp. 15–18
       SLS

Social Security

84. Law on State Pensions of the Union of Soviet Socialist Republics, adopted July 14, 1956*
    R: *Vedomosti SSSR* (1956), no. 15, item 313

E: ILO Legislative Series, 1956 USSR-4, pp. 1–17
   LEE, I, pp. 58–69
   Pension Laws (Moscow, 1967), pp. 6–38 (Soviet Legislation Series)
85. USSR Law on Pensions and Allowances for Collective Farm Members, adopted July 15, 1964*
    R: *Vedomosti SSSR* (1964), no. 29, item 340
    E: *CDSP*, XVI, no. 29 (1964), pp. 23–25
       ILO Legislative Series, 1964 USSR-1, pp. 1–6
       Pension Laws (Moscow, 1967), pp. 40–49 (Soviet Legislation Series)

Minors

86. Statute on Labor Colonies for Minors of the USSR Ministry of Internal Affairs, adopted June 3, 1968
    R: *Vedomosti SSSR* (1968), no. 23, item 189
    E: *CDSP*, XX, no. 24 (1968), pp. 3–7
       SL&G, VII, no. 1 (1968), pp. 27–36
       SLS
87. Latvian SSR Statute on Commissions for Cases of Minors, adopted March 18, 1967*
    R: *Vedomosti Latviiskoi SSR* (1967), no. 14, p. 881
    E: *SS&D*, X (1974), 290–308
88. RSFSR Statute on Commissions for Cases of Minors, adopted June 3, 1967*
    R: *Vedomosti RSFSR* (1967), no. 23, item 536
    E: *CDSP*, XIX, no. 38 (1967), pp. 15–19
       SL&G, VII, no. 1 (1968), pp. 37–46
       SLS
89. RSFSR Statute on Social Educators of Minors, adopted December 13, 1967
    R: *Vedomosti RSFSR* (1967), no. 51, item 1239
    E: *SS&D*, X (1974), 308–313
       SLS

Criminal Law

90. Fundamental Principles of Criminal Legislation of the USSR and Union Republics, adopted December 25, 1958*
    R: *Vedomosti SSSR* (1959), no. 1, item 6
    E: *Burma Law Institute Journal*, I (1959), 257–267
       CDSP, XI, no. 4 (1959), pp. 3–7
       FLPH, pp. 5–27
       Highlights, VII (1959), 19–35
       LEE, III, pp. 31–71
       Saifulin, pp. 238–266
       SLS

91. Criminal Code of the Russian Soviet Federated Socialist Republic, adopted October 27, 1960*
    R: *Vedomosti RSFSR* (1960), no. 40, item 591
    E: Berman & Spindler (2d), pp. 125–202; (1st), pp. 141–245
      Criminal Code of the RSFSR (Washington D.C., 1961) mimeo.
      SS&D, I, no. 1 (1964), pp. 3–111
      Simons
92. RSFSR Decree on Making Arrests on Foreign Merchant Vessels, adopted May 24, 1927
    R: *SU RSFSR* (1927), no. 52, item 348
    E: *SS&D,* VI (1969), 79
93. USSR Law on the Defense of Peace, adopted March 12, 1951
    R: *Vedomosti SSSR* (1951), no. 5
    E: *American Journal of International Law, Supplement,* XLVI (1952), 34
      SS&D, III, No. 4 (1967), 84–85
94. USSR Law on Criminal Responsibility for Crimes Against the State, adopted December 25, 1958*
    R: *Vedomosti SSSR* (1959), no. 1, item 8
    E: *CDSP,* XI, no. 5 (1959), pp. 3–4
      LEE, III, pp. 72–85
      U.S. Library of Congress, *Law Concerning Criminal Responsibility for Crimes Against the State* (Washington D.C., 1959). 9 p. mimeo
95. USSR Law on Criminal Responsibility for Military Crimes, adopted December 25, 1958*
    R: *Vedomosti SSSR* (1959), no. 1, item 10
    E: *CDSP,* XI, no. 5 (1959), pp. 4–7
      Highlights, VII (1959), 58–67
      LEE, III, pp. 86–109

Penology

96. Fundamental Principles of Correctional Labor Legislation of the USSR and Union, adopted July 11, 1969
    R: *Vedomosti SSSR* (1969), no. 29, item 247
    E: *CDSP*, XXI, no. 29 (1969), pp. 3–10
      Saifulin, pp. 301–330
      SL&G, VIII, no. 1 (1969), pp. 36–68
      Soviet Review, XI, no. 2 (1970), pp. 176–208
      SLS
97. USSR Statute on Preliminary Confinement Under Guard, adopted July 11, 1969
    R: *Vedomosti SSSR* (1969), no. 29, item 248

E: *CDSP*, XXI, no. 29 (1969), pp. 11-13
SLS
98. RSFSR Statute on Supervisory Commissions attached to Executive Committees of District and City Soviets of Working People's Deputies, adopted September 30, 1965
R: *Vedomosti RSFSR* (1965), no. 40, item 990
E: *CDSP,* XVII, No. 46 (1965), pp. 6-7

Judiciary

99. Fundamental Principles of Legislation on Court Organization of the USSR and Union Republics, adopted December 25, 1958*
R: *Vedomosti SSSR* (1959), no. 1, item 12
E: *CDSP,* XI, no. 4 (1959), p. 8
FLPH, pp. 40-51
Highlights, VI (1959), 89-97
SS&D, X (1973/74), 102-111
Saifulin, pp. 137-148
SLS

100. Statute on the USSR Supreme Court, adopted February 12, 1957*
R: *Vedomosti SSSR* (1957), no. 4, item 84
E: Berman & Quigley, pp. 199-204
Denisov, pp. 438-443
SS&D, X (1973/74), 111-117
SLS
101. USSR Statute on Military Tribunals, adopted December 25, 1958*
R: *Vedomosti SSSR* (1959), no. 1, item 14
E: Berman & Quigley, pp. 206-213
Highlights, VII (1959), 99-102
SS&D, X (1973/74), 120-127
SLS
102. Law on Court Organization of the Russian Soviet Federated Socialist Republic, adopted October 27, 1960*
R: *Vedomosti RSFSR* (1960), no. 40 item 588
E: Berman & Quigley, pp. 216-234
Berman & Spindler (2d), pp. 335-150; (1st), pp. 425-449
Simons
103. Law on Court Organization of the Tadzhik Soviet Socialist Republic, adopted January 5, 1961*
R: *Sbornik zakonov Tadzhikskoi SSR i ukazov prezidiuma verkhovnogo soveta Tadzhikskoi SSR 1938-1968* (Dushanbe, 1970), pp. 505-521
E: *SS&D*, X (1973/74), 127-144

104. Law on Court Organization of the Uzbek Soviet Socialist Republic, adopted May 21, 1959*
    R: *Sbornik zakonov Uzbekskoi SSR i ukazov prezidiuma verkhovnogo soveta Uzbekskoi SSR 1938–1964 gg.* (Tashkent, 1964), pp. 391–441
    E: *Highlithst,* VII (1959), 319–338
105. Statute on Elections of District (or City) People's Courts of the RSFSR, confirmed October 28, 1960*
    R: *Vedomosti RSFSR* (1960), no. 41, item 608
    E: *SS&D*, X (1973/74), 144–164
106. Statute on Elections of District (or City) People's Courts of the Ukrainian SSR, adopted November 2, 1960
    E: Berman & Quigley, pp. 237–248
107. Statute on the Procedure for Early Recall of Judges and People's Assessors of RSFSR Courts, confirmed October 5, 1961
    R. *Vedomosti RSFSR* (1961), no. 40, item 558
    E: *SS&D*, X (1973/64), 174–180
108. Statute on an Arbitration Court (Annex 3 to RSFSR Code of Civil Procedure), adopted June 11, 1964
    R: *SS RSFSR,* XIII, p. 300
    E: *SS&D*, X (1974), 269–272

Procuracy

109. Statute on Procuracy Supervision in the USSR, adopted May 24, 1955*
    R: *Vedomosti SSSR* (1955), no. 9, item 222
    E: Berman & Quigley, pp. 183–196
       Denisov, pp. 444–459
       SS&D, X (1974), 192–207
       SLS
110. USSR Statute on the Military Procuracy, adopted December 14, 1966
    R: *Vedomosti SSSR* (1966), no. 50, item 1021
    E: *CDSP,* XIX, no. 2 (1967), pp. 11–13
       SS&D, X (1974), 207–216
111. Statute on Incentives for and Disciplinary Responsibility of Procurators and Investigative Agencies of the USSR Procuracy, adopted February 24, 1964
    R: *Vedomosti SSR* (1964), no. 10, item 123
    E: *SS&D* X (1974), 220–225

Notariat

112. USSR Law on the State Notariat, adopted July 19, 1973
    R: *Vedomosti SSSR* (1973), no. 30, item 393
    E: *CDSP,* XXV, no. 30 (1973), pp. 23–27
    SS&D, X (1974), 231–247
    SLS

Legal Profession

113. Statute on the USSR Ministry of Justice, confirmed March 21, 1972*
    R: *SP SSSR* (1972), no. 6, item 32
    E: *SS&D,* X (1973), 6–15
    SLS
114. Statute on the RSFSR Ministry of Justice, confirmed June 21, 1972
    R: *Sovetskaia iustitsiia,* no. 16 (1972), pp. 3–6
    E: *SS&D* (1973), 15–26
115. RSFSR Statute on the Advocates, adopted July 25, 1962
    R: *Vedomosti RSFSR* (1972), no. 29, item 450
    E: Berman & Quigley, pp. 309–321
    Friedman, L.M., Zile, Z., "Soviet Legal Profession: Recent Developments in Law and Practice," *Wisconsin Law Review* (1964), pp. 32–77
    SLS
116. Instruction on the Procedure for Payment of Legal Assistance Rendered by Advocates to Citizens, Enterprises, Institutions, State and Collective Farms, and Other Organizations, approved February 14, 1966
    R: *SP RSFSR* (1966), no. 3, item 22
    E: *SS&D,* X (1973), 38–47
117. Methods Instructions concerning the Work of Advocates in Rendering Legal Assistance to Enterprises, Institutions, and Organizations (except Collective Farms), approved August 31, 1973
    R: *Biulleten',* no. 1 (1974), pp. 43–48
    E: *SS&D,* X (1974), 370–381
118. USSR General Statute on the Legal Section (or Office), Chief (or Senior) Jurisconsult, and Jurisconsult of a Ministry, Department, Executive Committee of Soviet of Working People's Deputies, Enterprise, Organization, or Institution, approved June 22, 1972
    R: *Biulleten',* no. 3 (1972), pp. 3–10
    E: *SS&D,* X (1973), 70–81
    SLS

119. USSR Model Statute on a Social Legal Consultation Office, confirmed August 20, 1973
    R: *Biulleten'*, no. 12 (1973), pp. 39–40
    E: *SS&D*, X (1973/74), 93–95

Social Organizations Administering Legality

120. RSFSR Statute on Comrades' Courts, confirmed March 11, 1977
    R: *Vedomosti RSFSR* (1977), no. 12, item 254
    E: SLS
121. RSFSR Statute on Social Councils for Work of Comrades' Courts, confirmed March 11, 1977
    R: *Vedomosti RSFSR* (1977), no. 12, item 254
    E: SLS
122. USSR Model Statute on Voluntary People's Guard Detachments for the Protection of Public Order, approved May 20, 1974
    R: *SP SSSR* (1974), no. 12, item 67
    E: *SS&D*, X (1974), 339–357
      SLS

Civil Procedure

123. Fundamental Principles of Civil Procedure of the USSR and Union Republics, adopted December 8, 1961*
    R: *Vedomosti SSSR* (1961), no. 50, item 525
    E: *CDSP*, XIV, no. 5 (1962), pp. 3–9
      Fundamentals of Soviet Civil Legislation and Civil Procedure (Official Texts) (Moscow, 1968), pp. 91–131. (Soviet Legislation Series)
      LEE VII, pp. 299–320
      Saifulin, pp. 205–231
      Sdobnikov, pp. 146–175
      SLS
124. Code of Civil Procedure of the Russian Soviet Federated Socialist Republic, adopted June 11, 1964*
    R: *Grazhdanskii protsessual'nyi kodeks RSFSR* (Moscow, 1968), 231 p.
    E: *LEE*, XI, pp. 157–280
      Simons

Criminal Procedure

125. Fundamental Principles of Criminal Procedure of the USSR and Union Republics, adopted December 25, 1958*
    R: *Vedomosti SSSR* (1959), no. 1, item 15
    E: *Burma Law Institute Journal*, I (1959), 267–277
    CDSP, XI, no. 4 (1959), 7–11, 25
    FLPH, pp. 61–87
    Highlights, VII (195), 69–87
    LEE, III, pp. 111–151
    Saifulin, pp. 272–295
    SLS
126. Code of Criminal Procedure of the Russian Soviet Federated Socialist Republic, adopted October 27, 1960*
    R: *Vedomosti RSFSR* (1960), no. 40, item 592
    E: Berman & Spindler (2d), pp. 203–333; (1st), pp. 247–424
    SS&D, I, nos. 2–3 (1965), pp. 5–183
    Simons

Foreign Relations Law

127. Law on Citizenship of the Union of Soviet Socialist Republics, adopted August 19, 1938*
    R: *Vedomosti* SSSR (1938), no. 11, p.1
    E: Gsovski, II, pp. 293–294
    SS&D, III, no. 1 (1966), pp. 1–2; VII (1971), 256–258
128. Decree on the Nationalisation of Foreign Trade, adopted April 22, 1918
    R: *SU RSFSR* (1918), no. 32, item 432
    E: Akhapkin, pp. 124–126
    Giffen, pp. 306–307
129. Statute on Trade Representations and Trade Agencies of the USSR Abroad, adopted September 13, 1933
    R: *SZ SSSR* (1933), no. 59, item 354
    E: Gsovski, II, pp. 347–352
    SS&D, III, nos. 2–3 (1967), pp. 21–26
130. Customs Code of the Union of Soviet Socialist Republics, adopted May 5, 1964*
    R: *Vedomosti SSSR* (1964), no. 20, item 242
    E: Butler, W.E. (transl.), *Customs Code of the USSR* (Washington D.C., 1966), pp. 7–36
        Customs Law of the USSR (Moscow, 1967). 48 p. (Soviet Legislation Series)
        Simons

131. Statute on the Foreign Trade Arbitration Commission attached to the USSR Chamber of Commerce and Industry, adopted April 16, 1975
    R: *Vedomosti SSSR* (1975), no. 17, item 269
    E: *ILM*, XIV (1975), 1035–1036.
132. Rules of Procedure of the Foreign Trade Arbitration Commission attached to the USSR Chamber of Commerce and Industry, adopted January 21, 1949*
    R: *Sbornik normativnykh materialov po voprosam vneshnei torgovli SSSR* (Moscow, 1970), I, pp. 383–389
    E: Gsvoski, II, pp. 654–659
    Kos, pp. 215–218
133. Decree on the Proclamation of Lands and Islands Located in the Northern Arctic Ocean as Territory of the USSR, adopted April 16, 1926
    R: *SZ SSSR* (1926), no. 32, item 203
    E: Butler, p. 97
    SS&D, III, no. 4 (1967), p. 9
    Taracouzio, T.A., *Soviets in the Arctic* (New York, 1938), p. 381
134. Decree on the Use of Wireless Radio Equipment by Foreign Vessels While in USSR Waters, adopted July 24, 1928
    R: *SZ SSSR* (1928), no. 48, item 341
    E: Barabolia, pp. 58–60
    Butler, pp. 97–100
135. Statute on the Protection of the USSR State Boundaries, adopted August 5, 1960*
    R: *Vedomosti SSSR* (1960), no. 34, item 324
    E: Butler, pp. 111–125
    SS&D, III, no. 4 (1967), pp. 10–24
136. USSR Edict on the Continental Shelf, adopted February 6, 1968
    R: *Vedomosti SSSR* (1968), no. 6, item 40
    E: *CDSP*, XX, no. 8 (1968), pp. 22–23
    ILM, VII (1968), 392–394
    SS&D, VI (1970), 258–261
137. USSR Decree on the Procedure for Conducting Work on the Continental Shelf of the USSR and the Protection of its Natural Resources, adopted July 18, 1969
    R: *SP SSSR* (1969), no. 18, item 103
    E: *ILM*, IX (1970), 975–977
    SS&D, VI (1970), 409–414
138. USSR Edict on Provisional Measures for Preservation of Living Resources and Regulation of Fishing in Marine Areas Adjacent to the USSR Coast, adopted December 10, 1976
    R: *Izvestia*, December 11, 1976, p. 2
    E: *CDSP*, XXVIII, no. 50 (1977), p. 3

ILM, XV (1976),
Review of Socialist Law, III (1977),
139. Rules for Visits by Foreign Warships to Territorial Waters and Ports of the USSR, adopted June 6, 1960
R: *Izveshcheniia moreplavateliam* (1966), no. 14
E: Barabolia, pp. 63–69
Butler, pp. 126–132
SS&D, III, no. 4 (1967), pp. 24–30; VI (1969), 65–71
140. Statute on the People's Commissariat for Foreign Affairs of the USSR, November 12, 1923*
R: *SU RSFSR* (1923), no. 107, item 1033
E: *SS&D*, III, Nos. 2–3 (1967), pp. 11–19
141. USSR Edict on the Establishment of Ranks for Diplomatic Representatives of the USSR Abroad, adopted May 9, 1941
R: *Vedomosti SSSR* (1941), no. 21
E: *SS&D*, III, nos 2–3 (1967) pp 9–10
142. USSR Edict on Establishment of Ranks for Diplomatic Workers of the People's Commissariat for Foreign Affairs, Embassies, and Missions Abroad, adopted May 28, 1943
R: *Vedomosti SSSR* (1943), no. 22
E: *SS&D*, III, nos. 2–3 (1967), pp. 10–11
143. Consular Statute on the Union of Soviet Socialist Republics, confirmed June 25, 1976
R: *Vedomosti SSSR* (1976), no. 27, item 404
E: *ILM*, XV (1976), 1178–1190
Review of Socialist Law, II (1976), 233–249
144. USSR Edict on the Procedure for Relations of USSR State Institutions and Their Officials with the Institutions and Officials of Foreign States, adopted December 16, 1947
R: *Vedomosti SSSR* (1948), no. 5, p. 2
E: Berman & Maggs, pp. 114–115
SS&D, III, nos. 2–3 (1967), pp. 36–39
145. Statute on Diplomatic and Consular Representations of Foreign States on the Territory of the USSR, adopted May 23, 1966
R: *Vedomosti SSSR* (1966), no. 22, item 387
E: Berman & Maggs, pp. 116–121
ILM, V (1966), 801–813
SS&D, III, nos. 2–3 (1967), pp. 40–50
146. Decree on the Procedure for Submission of International Treaties and Agreements Concluded in the Name of the USSR for Approval, Confirmation, and Ratification of the USSR Government, adopted October 2, 1925*
R: *SZ SSSR* (1925), no. 68, item 503
E: *SS&D*, III, no. 4 (1967), pp. 54–56

147. Law on the Procedure for the Ratification and Denunciation of International Treaties of the USSR, adopted August 20, 1938
R: *Vedomosti SSSR* (1938), no. 11
E: *SS&D*, III, no. 4 (1967), pp. 56–57

Abbreviations

Akhapkin	Akhapkin, Y. (ed.), *First Decrees of Soviet Power* (London, 1970)
Barabolia	Barabolia, P.D., et al., *Naval International Law Manual* (Washington, D.C., 1968)
Berman & Maggs	Berman, H.J., Maggs, P.B., *Disarmament Inspection Under Soviet Law* (New York, 1967)
Berman & Quigley	Berman, H.J., Quigley, J.B., Jr., *Basic Laws on the Structure of the Soviet State* (Cambridge, 1969)
Berman & Spindler	Berman, H.J., Spindler, J.W. (transl.), *Soviet Criminal Law and Procedure: The RSFSR Codes* (2d ed., Cambridge, 1972; 1st ed., 1966)
Biulleten'	*Biulleten' normativnykh aktov ministerstv i vedomstv* (Bulletin of Normative Acts of Ministries and Departments of the USSR) (Moscow, 1972–). Published monthly
Biulleten' MVSSO SSSR	*Biulleten' Ministerstva vysshego i srednego spetsial'nogo obrazovaniia SSSR* (Bulletin of the Ministry of Higher and Secondary Specialized Education of the USSR) (Moscow). Published monthly
Butler	Butler, W.E., *The Law of Soviet Territorial Waters* (New York, 1967)
CDSP	*Current Digest of the Soviet Press* (Columbus, 1949–). Published weekly
Cooper	Cooper, D. (transl.), *The Air Code of the U.S.S.R.* (Charlottesville, 1965)
Denisov	Denisov, A., Kirichenko, M., *Soviet State Law* (Moscow, 1960)
FLPH	*Fundamentals of Soviet Criminal Legislation; the Judicial System and Criminal Court Procedure* (Moscow, 1960)
Giffen	Giffen, J.H., *The Legal and Practical Aspects of Trade with the Soviet Union* (rev. ed.; New York, 1971)
Gsovski	Gsovski, V., *Soviet Civil Law* (Ann Arbor, 1948–49). 2 vols
Highlights	U.S. Library of Congress, *Highlights of Current Legislation and Activities in Eastern Europe*

ILM	*International Legal Materials* (Washington D.C., 1962–). Published bi-monthly
ILO	International Labor Office Legislative Series
Kos	Kos-Rabcewicz-Zubkowski, L., *East European Rules on the Validity of International Commercial Arbitration Agreements* (New York, 1970)
LEE	Sxirmai, Z., (ed.), *Law in Eastern Europe Series* (Leiden, 1958–)
Saifulin	Saifulin, M., Sdobnikov, Y. (transl.), *Fundamentals of Legislation of the USSR and the Union Republics* (Moscow, 1974)
Sbornik	*Sbornik zakonov SSSR i ukazov prezidiuma verkhovnogo soveta SSSR 1938–1975* (Moscow, 1975). 4 vols.
Sdobnikov	Sdobnikov, Y. (transl.), *Soviet Civil Legislation and Procedure* (Moscow, ca 1963)
Simons	Simons, W. (ed.). *Soviet Codes* (Leiden, 1978)
SL&G	*Soviet Law and Government* (New York, 196-). Published quarterly
SLS	Hazard, J.N., Butler, W.E., Maggs, P.B., *The Soviet Legal System* (3d rev. ed.; New York, 1977–78); Vol. 2
SP RSFSR	*Sobranie postanovlenii pravitel'stva RSFSR* (Collected Decrees of the Government of the RSFSR) (Moscow). Published irregularly
SP SSSR	*Sobranie postanovlenii pravitel'stva SSSR* (Collected Decrees of the Government of the USSR) (Moscow). Published irregularly
SS&D	*Soviet Statutes and Decisions* (New York, 1964–) Published quarterly
SS RSFSR	*Sistematicheskoe sobranie zakonov RSFSR, ukazov prezidiuma verkhovnogo soveta RSFAR i reshenii pravitel'stva RSFSR* (Systematic Collection of RSFSR Laws, Edicts of the Presidium of the RSFSR Supreme Soviet, and Decisions of the RSFSR Government((Moscow, 1967–70). 15 vols.
SU RSFSR	*Sobranie uzakonenii i rasporiazhenii Raboche-Krest'ianskogo pravitel'stva RSFSR* (Collected Decrees and Regulations of the Workers'-Peasants' Government of the RSFSR) (Moscow), Published irregularly

SZ SSSR	*Sobranie zakonov i rasporaizhenii Raboche-Krest'ianskogo pravitel'stva SSSR* (Collected Laws and Regulations of the Workers'-Peasants' Government of the USSR) (Moscow) Published irregularly
Vedmosti RSFSR	*Vedomosti verkhovnogo soveta RSFSR* (Gazette of the RSFSR Supreme Soviet((Moscow, 1957–). Published weekly
Vedomosti SSSR	*Vedomosti verkhovnogo soveta SSSR* (Gazette of the USSR Supreme Soviet) (Moscow, 1938–). Published weekly

Appendix

ANNOTATION TO 1977 DRAFT CONSTITUTION OF THE U.S.S.R.

A third federal constitution for the U.S.S.R. was published in draft form for national discussion on June 4, 1977. The text in English translation provided by the Soviet news agency TASS is published in full in Volume II of this work, but to facilitate systematic comparison with the materials included in Volume I selected articles are set forth below. They are keyed to the chapters to which they are relevant.

PART I

Chapter I (A)

Preamble (excerpt)

The supreme purpose of the Soviet state is to build a classless communist society. The principal tasks of the state are: to build the material and technical basis of communism, to perfect socialist social relations and transform them into communist relations, to mold the citizen of communist society, to raise the living standard and cultural level of the working people, to ensure the country's security, to help strengthen peace and to promote international cooperation.

Article 4: The Soviet state, all its organs, shall function on the basis of socialist legality and assure the protection of law and order, the interests of society and the rights of citizens. State institutions, public organizations and officials shall observe the constitution of the U.S.S.R. and Soviet laws.

Article 6: The Communist Party of the Soviet Union is the leading and guiding force of Soviet society and the nucleus of its political system, of all state and public organizations. The C.P.S.U. exists for the people and serves the people.

Armed with the Marxist-Leninist teaching, the Communist Party shall determine the general perspective of society's development, and the guideline of the internal and external policy of the U.S.S.R., give guidance to the great creative endeavor of the Soviet people and place their struggle for the triumph of communism on a planned, scientific basis.

Chapter II (A)

Article 7: In accordance with their statutory purposes, the trade unions, the All-union Leninist Young Communist League, the co-operatives and other mass public organizations shall participate in the administration of state and public affairs, in the solution of political, economic, social and cultural questions.

Article 8: The principal orientation of the development of Soviet society's political system shall be the further unfolding of socialist democracy: increasingly broader participation of the working people in the administration of the affairs of society and the state, continuous improvement of the state apparatus, enhancement of the activity of public organizations, intensification of control by the people, strengthening of the legal foundations of state and social life, extension of publicity, and constant account of public opinion.

Chapter III (A)

Article 19: The Soviet state shall create the conditions for enhancing society's social homogeniety, erasing the essential distinctions between town and countryside and between labor by brain and by hand, and further developing and drawing together all the nations and nationalities of the U.S.S.R.

(B)

Article 69: The Union of Soviet Socialist Republics is an integral federal multinational state formed on the basis of the free self-determination of nations and the voluntary union of equal Soviet Socialist Republics.

The U.S.S.R. embodies the state unity of the Soviet people and brings all the nations and nationalities together for the joint building of communism.

Article 70: In the Union of Soviet Socialist Republics there shall be united:

[There is no change in the list of Union Republics, as they appeared in Article 13 of the 1936 Constitution]

Article 71: Every Union Republic shall retain the right freely to secede from the U.S.S.R.

Article 72: The jurisdiction of the Union of Soviet Socialist Republics, as represented by its higher organs of state power and administration, shall extend to:

(III) Definition of general principles of the organization and functioning of Republican and local organs of state power and administration;

(IV) Establishment of uniformity of legislative regulation throughout the territory of the U.S.S.R. and definition of the principles of legislation of the Union of Soviet Socialist Republics and the Union Republics;

(V) Pursuance of an integral social and economic policy, and administration of the country's economy; determination of the main directions of scientific and technical progress; drafting and approval of plans of economic, social and cultural development of the U.S.S.R., and approval of reports of their fulfilment;

(XI) Control over the observance of the Constitution of the U.S.S.R., and conformity of the Constitutions of the Union Republics with the Constitution of the U.S.S.R.;

Article 73: The laws of the U.S.S.R. shall have the same force on the territory of all the Union Republics. In the event of discrepancy between a law of a Union Republic and an All-union law, the law of the U.S.S.R. shall prevail.

Article 75: A Union Republic is a Soviet Socialist State that has united with other Soviet republics in the Union of Soviet Socialist Republics.

Outside of the spheres defined in Article 72 of the Constitution of the U.S.S.R., a Union Republic shall exercise state authority independently in its territory.

A Union Republic shall have its own Constitution drawn up in conformity with the Constitution of the U.S.S.R. with due account for the specific features of the Republic.

Article 79: A Union Republic shall have the right to enter into relations with foreign states, conclude treaties with them, exchange diplomatic and consular representatives, and participate in the work of international organizations.

Article 80: The sovereign rights of the Union Republic shall be safeguarded by the Union of Soviet Socialist Republics.

Chapter IV (C)

Article 173: Amendment of the Constitution of the U.S.S.R. shall be by decision of the Supreme Soviet of the U.S.S.R. adopted by a majority of not less than two-thirds of the total number of deputies of each of its chambers.

(D) and (E)

[There is no basic change in the structure of the legislative organs from that established by the 1936 Constitution, but the draft introduces some steps in the legislative process not previously stated in the Constitution although developed in practice during the post-Stalin years]

Article 111: The right to initiate legislation in the Supreme Soviet of the U.S.S.R. shall be exercised by the Soviet of the Union and the Soviet of Nationalitities, the Presidium of the Supreme Soviet of the U.S.S.R., the Council of Ministers of the U.S.S.R., the Union Republics represented by their higher organs of state power, the commissions of the Supreme Soviet of the U.S.S.R. and the standing commissions of its chambers, deputies of the Supreme Soviet of the U.S.S.R., the Supreme Court of the U.S.S.R., and the Procurator-General of the U.S.S.R.

The right to initiate legislation shall be enjoyed also by mass public organizations represented by their All-union organs.

Article 112: After a draft law has been debated at sittings of the chambers it may be referred for examination to one or several commissions. The chambers shall also have the right to debate and vote for a draft without referring it to a commission.

Laws of the U.S.S.R., decisions and other acts of the Supreme Soviet of the U.S.S.R. shall be adopted at separate or joint sittings of the chambers.

A law of the U.S.S.R. shall be deemed enacted if passed by both chambers of the Supreme Soviet of the U.S.S.R. by a simple majority vote in each.

By decision of the Supreme Soviet of the U.S.S.R. or the Presidium of the Supreme Soviet of the U.S.S.R. adopted on their initiative or on the recommendation of a Union Republic draft laws of the U.S.S.R. may be submitted for discussion by the whole people, and likewise put to a vote (referendum) by the whole people.

Chapter V: (E)

Article 163: Supreme supervisory power over the precise and uniform execution of laws by all ministries, state committees and departments, enterprises, institutions and organizations, executive and administrative organs of local soviets of people's deputies, collective farms, co-operative and other public organizations, officials and citizens, shall be exercised by the Procurator-General of the U.S.S.R. and procurators subordinate to him.

Chapter VI (A)

Article 34: Citizens of the U.S.S.R. shall be equal before the law, irrespective of origin, social and property status, nationality, or race, sex, education, language, attitude to religion, type or character of occupation, domicile, or other particulars.

Equality of rights of citizens of the U.S.S.R. shall be ensured in all fields of economic, political, social, and cultural life.

Article 36: Soviet citizens of different nationalities and races shall have equal rights.

The exercise of these rights shall be ensured by the policy of all-round development and drawing together of all nations and nationalities of the U.S.S.R., education of citizens in the spirit of Soviet patriotism and socialist internationalism, and the opportunity for using the mother tongue and languages of the other peoples of the U.S.S.R.

Any and all direct or indirect restriction of the rights of, or the establishment of direct or indirect privileges for citizens on grounds of race or nationality, and likewise any advocacy of racial or national exclusiveness, hositility or contempt, shall be punishable by law.

Article 39: Citizens of the U.S.S.R. shall possess in their entirety the social, economic, political and personal rights and freedoms proclaimed and guaranteed by the Constitution of the U.S.S.R. and Soviet laws. The socialist system shall ensure the extension of rights and freedoms and unintermittent improvement of the conditions of life of citizens relative to the fulfillment of programs of social, economic and cultural development.

Exercise by citizens of rights and freedoms must not injure the interests of society and the state, and the rights of other citizens.

Article 44: Citizens of the U.S.S.R. shall have the right to housing.

This right shall be ensured by the development and protection of state and public housing, assistance to co-operative and individual house building, fair distribution under public control of housing, allotted with reference to the implementation of the housing program and likewise by low rent.

Article 45: Citizens of the U.S.S.R. shall have the right to education.

This right shall be ensured by free education at all levels, universal compulsory secondary education of the youth, extensive development of vocational, secondary specialized and higher education linked to life and production; by development of education by correspondence and evening education; provision by the state of scholarship grants and other benefits to pupils and students; free issue of school textbooks; the opportunity for instruction in schools in the mother tongue; by development of the system of professional orientation and provision of conditions for the self-education of working people.

Article 46: Citizens of the U.S.S.R. shall have the right to use the achievements of culture.

This right shall be ensured by public access to the values of home and world culture preserved in state and public repositories, by development and balanced distribution of cultural institutions in the country, and by expanding cultural exchanges with other countries.

Article 50: In conformity with the interests of the working people and for the purpose of strengthening the socialist system, citizens of the U.S.S.R. shall be guaranteed freedom of speech, press, assembly, meetings, street processions and demonstrations. Exercise of these political freedoms shall be ensured by putting at the disposal of the working people and their organizations of public buildings, streets and squares, by broad dissemination of information, and the opportunity for using the press, television and radio.

Article 51: In conformity with the aims of building communism, citizens of the U.S.S.R. shall have the right to unite in public organizations facilitating the development of their political activity and initiating, and satisfaction of their diverse interests.

Public organizations shall be guaranteed conditions for the successful performance of their statutory functions.

Article 52: Freedom of conscience, that is, the right to to profess any religion and freedom to perform religious rites or not profess any religion, and to conduct atheistic propaganda, shall be recognized for all citizens of the U.S.S.R. Incitement of hostility and hatred on religious grounds shall be prohibited.

The church in the U.S.S.R. shall be separated from the state, and the school from the church.

Article 56: The privacy of citizens, of correspondence, telephone conversations and telegraphic messages shall be protected by law.

Article 59: Exercise of rights and freedoms shall be inseparable from performance by citizens of their duties.

Citizens of the U.S.S.R. shall be obliged to observe the Constitution of the U.S.S.R., Soviet laws, to respect the rules of socialist behavior, to bear with dignity the high calling of citizens of the U.S.S.R.

Chapter VIII (A)

Article 54: Citizens of the U.S.S.R. shall be guaranteed inviolability of the person. No person shall be subjected to arrest other than by decision of a court of law, or with the sanction of a procurator.

Article 55: Citizens of the U.S.S.R. shall be guaranteed inviolability of the home. No person shall without lawful grounds enter a home against the will of the persons residing in it.

Article 57: Respect for the individual, protection of the rights and freedoms of Soviet citizens shall be the duty of all state organs, public organizations and officials.

Citizens of the U.S.S.R. shall have the right to legal protection against attempts on their life and impingements on their health, property and personal freedom, honor and dignity.

Article 153: Examination of civil and criminal cases in all courts shall be collegial, and in courts of the first instance with the participation of people's assessors. In the administration of justice people's assesors shall have all the rights of a judge.

Article 154: Judges and people's assessors shall be independent and subject only to the law.

Article 155: Justice in the U.S.S.R. shall be administered on the principle of the equality of citizens before the law and court.

Article 156: Legal proceedings in all courts shall be public. The hearing of cases in camera shall be allowed solely in cases defined by law with the observance of all rules of judicial procedure.

Article 157: The defendant shall be guaranteed the right of defence.

Article 158: Judicial proceedings shall be conducted in the language of the Union or Autonomous Republic, Autonomous Region or Autonomous Area, or in the language spoken by the majority of the population in the locality. Persons participating in the proceedings not conversant with the language in which they are conducted shall have the right fully to acquaint themselves with the materials of the case, to participate in court proceedings through an interpreter, and to address the court of law in their own language.

Article 159: No person shall be considered guilty of commission of a crime and subjected to criminal punishment other than by a verdict of the court and in conformity with criminal law.

Article 160: There shall be collegiums of lawyers for the purpose of rendering legal counsel to citizens and organizations. In cases provided for by law legal counsel to citizens shall be free of charge.

Article 161: Representatives of public organizations and work collectives shall be allowed to take part in civil and criminal proceedings.

Chapter VIII

Article 153: Examination of civil and criminal cases in all courts shall be collegial, and in courts of the first instance with the participation of people's assessors. In the administration of justice people's assessors shall have the rights of a judge.

Chapter IX (A)

Article 62: The citizen of the U.S.S.R. shall be obliged to safeguard the interests of the Soviet state, to contribute to the strengthening of its might and prestige.

Defence of the socialist motherland shall be a sacred duty of every citizen of the U.S.S.R.

High treason shall be the gravest crime against the people.

PART II

Chapter X (A)

Article 9: Socialist ownership of the means of production shall be the foundation of the economic system of the U.S.S.R. Socialist ownership shall comprise: state property (belonging to the whole people), property of collective farms and other co-operative organizations (collective farm co-operative property), and property of trade unions and other public organizations.

The state shall protect socialist property and create the conditions for its enlargement.

Nobody shall have the right to use socialist property for personal gain.

Article 10: State property, i.e. property belonging to the whole people, shall be the principal form of socialist ownership.

The land, its minerals, waters, and forests shall be the exclusive property of the state. The state shall be in possession of the basic means of production: industrial, building and agricultural enterprises, means of transport and communication, and also the banks, distributive enterprises and community services and the bulk of urban housing.

Article 11: The property of the collective farms and other co-operative organizations, and of their associations, shall be the means of production and other property serving the attainment of their statutory purposes. The land held by collective farms shall be allocated to them for their free use for an unlimited time.

The state shall facilitate the development of collective farm co-operative ownership and its approximation to state ownership.

The property of the trade unions and other public organizations shall be the properties they require to perform their statutory functions.

Article 15: The economy of the U.S.S.R. shall be an integral economic complex embracing all the elements of social production, distribution and exchange on the territory of the U.S.S.R.

The economy shall be managed on the basis of state plans for economic, social and cultural development with due account for the branch and territorial principles, and combining centralized leadership with the economic independence and initiative of enterprises, associations and other organizations. Here active use shall be made of cost accounting, profit and production costs.

Article 17: Individual occupation in handicrafts, agriculture and everyday services for the population, and likewise other forms of occupation based exclusively on the individual labor of citizens and members of their families shall be permitted in the U.S.S.R. in accordance with the law.

Chapter XIV

Article 162: Settlement of economic disputes between organizations, institutions and enterprises shall be entrusted to state organs of arbitration. The organization of and conduct of business by state organs of arbitration shall be defined by law.

Guidance and supervision of the activity of all organs of arbitration shall be exercised by the State Court of Arbitration of the U.S.S.R. The Chief Arbiter of the State Court of Arbitration of the U.S.S.R. shall be appointed by the Supreme Soviet of the U.S.S.R. for a term of five years.

Chapter XVI (A)

Article 35: In the U.S.S.R. women shall have equal rights with men.

Exercise of these rights shall be ensured by according to women equal opportunities for education and professional training, for employment, remuneration and promotion, for social, political and cultural activity, and likewise by special measures for the protection of the labor and health of women; by legal protection, material and moral support of mother and child, including paid leaves and other benefits to mothers and expectant mothers, and state aid to unmarried mothers.

Article 40: Citizens of the U.S.S.R. shall have the right to work, that is, to guaranteed employment and remuneration for their work in accordance with its quantity and quality, including the right to choice of profession, type of occupation and employment in accordance with their vocation, abilities, training, education, and with due account for the needs of society.

This right shall be ensured by the socialist economic system, steady growth of the productive forces of society, free vocational training, improvement of skills, and training in new trades.

Article 41: Citizens of the U.S.S.R. shall have the right to rest and leisure.

This right shall be ensured by the 41 hour working week for industrial, office and professional workers and a reduced working day for a number of trades and occupations and reduced working hours at night time; provision of annual paid leaves, weekly days of rest, and likewise by extension of the network of cultural, educational and health-building institutions, and development of sports, physical education and tourism on a mass scale; provision on the residential principle of favorable opportunities for rest and of other conditions for the rational use of free time.

Duration of working time and of rest and leisure for collective farmers shall be regulated by the rules of collective farms.

Article 42: Citizens of the U.S.S.R. shall have the right to health protection.

This right shall be ensured by free competent medical care rendered by state health institutions, development and improvement of safety techniques and sanitation in production, extension of the network of medical and health building institutions; by broad preventive measures and measures of environmental improvement; special care for the health of the rising generation, prohibition of child labor; furtherance of scientific research directed to preventing and reducing the incidence of diseases and to ensuring a long active life for citizens.

Article 43: Citizens of the U.S.S.R. shall have the right to maintenance in old age, in the event of sickness, and likewise in the event of complete or partial disability or loss of breadwinner.

This right shall be guaranteed by social insurance of industrial, office and professional workers and collective farmers; old age and disability pensions for loss of breadwinner, and allowances for temporary disability; employment of partly disabled citizens; care for kithless elderly and disabled citizens.

Article 60: It shall be the duty of, and a matter of honor for every able-bodied citizen of the U.S.S.R. to work conscientiously in his chosen socially useful occupation and strictly to observe labor and production discipline.

Chapter XVII

Article 14: The supreme purpose of social production under socialism shall be the fullest possible satisfaction of the people's growing material and spiritual requirements.

Relying on the creative initiative of the working people, the socialist emulation movement and the achievements of scientific and technical progress, the state shall ensure the growth of labor productivity, the enhancement of efficiency in production, and the improvement of the quality of work, and the dynamic and proportionate development of the national economy.

PART III

Chapter XVIII (A)

Article 12: In their personal possession citizens of the U.S.S.R. may have earned income and savings, a house, a subsidiary husbandry, and articles of everyday use and personal consumption and convenience. The right of citizens to personal property and also the right of citizens to inherit personal property shall be protected by law.

Citizens may have the use of plots of land allocated by the state or collective farms under the procedure defined by the law for a subsidiary husbandry (including the maintenance of livestock and poultry), gardening and vegetable growing, and also for the building of individual houses.

Property in the personal ownership or use of citizens shall not be a means of deriving non-earned incomes or damaging society.

Chapter XXI (A)

Article 61: The citizen of the U.S.S.R. shall be obliged to safeguard and fortify socialist property. It shall be the duty of the citizen of the U.S.S.R. to combat theft and dissipation of state and public property.

Persons impinging on socialist property shall be punishable by law.

(D)

Article 57: Respect for the individual, protection of the rights and freedoms of Soviet citizens shall be the duty of all state organs, public organizations and officials.

Citizens of the U.S.S.R. shall have the right to legal protection against attempts on their life and impingements on their health, property and personal freedom, honor and dignity.

Article 58: Citizens of the U.S.S.R. shall have the right to lodge complaints against actions of officials in state organs and public organizations. These complaints shall be examined in the manner and within the terms defined by law.

Actions of officials performed in violation of the law, over and above the powers vested in them, impinging on the rights of citizens, may be referred to a court of law in the manner defined by law.

Citizens of the U.S.S.R. shall have the right to compensation for damage inflicted by unlawful actions of state institutions and public organizations, and likewise by officials in the performance of their duties, in the manner and within the limits defined by law.

Chapter XXII (A)

Article 53: The family shall be under the protection of the state.

Marriage shall be entered into with the free consent of the intending spouses; spouses shall be completely equal in their matrimonial relations.

The state shall aid the family by ensuring and developing an extensive network of child-care institutions, organizing and improving the community services and public catering, and by provision of allowances and benefits to families with many children, and by paying allowances for the birth of a child.

Chapter XXIII:

Article 66: Citizens of the U.S.S.R. shall be obliged to devote themselves to the upbringing of their children, to prepare them for socially useful labor, to raise worthy members of the socialist society.

INDEX TO PRINCIPAL TEXTS

USSR Constitution (1936)

Art.	Page
4, 5, 6, 7, 9, 10	186
11	247
12	324
13	41
14, 15, 16, 17, 19, 20	42
64, 65, 66, 67	212
74, 75, 76, 79	212
80, 84, 86, 87, 88	212
94, 95, 96, 97	43
103	110
104	55
110, 111	110
112	55
122, 123, 124, 125	87
126	88
127, 128, 134, 135	110
146	54

USSR Constitution (1977) [Draft]

Preamble (excerpt)	599
4, 6, 7, 8	599
9, 10, 11	605
12, 14	607
15, 17	605
19	600
34	602
35	606
36, 39	602
40, 41, 42	606
43	607
44, 45	602
46, 50, 51, 52	603
53	608
54, 55, 56	603
57	604, 608
58	608
59	603
60, 61	607
62	604
66	608
69, 70, 71, 72, 73, 75	600
79, 80, 111, 112	601
153, 154, 155, 156, 157, 158, 159, 160, 161	604
162	606
163, 173	601

Air Code, USSR (1961)

101	450

Civil Law, USSR Fundamentals (1961)

18	44
21	186
25	187
44	248
96, 97, 98	330
99, 100, 101, 102, 103	331
104, 105	332
107, 110	343
111, 112, 113, 114, 115, 116	344
117, 118	392
119, 120, 121, 127	393

Civil Procedure, USSR Fundamentals (1961)

5, 6, 16, 17	137
18, 19, 21, 24	138
28, 29, 30, 33, 35	139
37	140

Correctional Labor Law, USSR Fundamentals (1969)

16	548

Criminal Law, USSR Fundamentals (1958)

1	14
4	45
21	151
22, 23, 24, 25	152
23 (amendment)	153

Criminal Procedure, USSR Fundamentals (1958)

32	110

Judicial System, USSR Fundamentals (1958)

1, 8, 16, 17, 18, 19	62
20, 21, 24, 25, 26	63
27, 29, 30, 31, 33, 35, 37, 38	64

Labor Law, USSR Fundamentals (1970)

1	15

Land Law, USSR Fundamentals (1968)

Preamble	195
1, 2, 3, 4	196
7, 8	197
16	206
18, 19	207
24, 25	197
26	198

Marriage and the Family, USSR Fundamentals (1968)

1	14
8	45

Civil Code, RSFSR (1964)

1	14
13, 14	538
41, 42, 43, 44, 45	417
46	421
47	418
48, 49, 50, 51, 52	421
53, 54, 55, 56	422
57, 58	423
92	365
105	365
106	366
107	375
108	376
111	379
112	376
126, 127	369
129, 130, 131, 132, 133	370
134	371
137	374
141, 142	382
143, 149, 150	383
151, 152, 156	366
157	367
158, 160	418
186, 187, 189	430
191, 218, 219, 220, 221, 222	431
444	440
445	459
448	440
449	441
450, 451	539
452, 453	441
454	450
455, 457, 458	441
460	459
461	460
472	466
496	413
528, 529	408
532, 533	402
534, 535	397
536, 537, 539, 540	398
541, 542	399
544, 545, 546	408
547, 548, 549, 550	409
554	410
560	405

Correctional Labor, RSFSR (1972)

1	153

Criminal Code, RSFSR (1960)

10	541
38	542
46-1	548
116	491
118	300
122, 123	521
124	534
124-1	528
132, 133	88
137, 138, 139, 140	300
141	345
154	380
176, 177	111
178, 179, 180	112
190-1, 190-3	97
198	94
232, 233, 234, 235	482
236	483

Criminal Procedure, RSFSR (1960)

1	45
11	110
13	111
35, 36, 37, 38, 40	66
96	111
122	111

Labor Law, RSFSR (1972)

15, 17, 31, 33	308
35	309
159	460
173, 174, 175, 176, 177, 178	536
182, 183	537
236, 237, 243	460

INDEX TO PRINCIPAL TEXTS

Marriage, Family and Guardianship, RSFSR (1969)

Preamble	472
1, 2	473
3, 4, 5, 6, 7	474
8	475
13, 14	480
15, 16, 17, 20, 21	481
22	482
30, 31, 32, 33, 34, 35	493
36, 37, 38, 39	495
40, 43, 45	485
47, 48	513
49, 50	514
52, 53, 54, 55	508
56	509
67, 68	499
69	520
70	499
73	521
74	459
76	521
77, 78, 79, 89	499
90, 93, 94	501
98, 99, 100	525
101, 103, 104, 108, 110	526
112, 114	527
119, 120, 121	532
123, 129, 130	533
161, 162	509
163, 165, 166	510

INDEX

A

Abandonment of property,
code provision on, 383; what constitutes, 386

Abortion,
legal status of, 491

Academic degree,
certification of diploma copy, 70; depriving of as penalty, 158

Adoption,
consent of child over 10 to return to natural parent is required before vacating adoption, 531; crime of divulging secrecy of adoption, 528; equality with natural children for State benefits, 529; no duty of adopted child to support adopting parents, 530; suit to vacate adoption in absence of mother's consent, 529, 531

Alcoholism,
decree of measures to reduce, 162; procedures for compelling cure for, 130

Alimony,
computation of shall not consider recipient's wages, 502; decree of types of earnings to be taken into account, 506; determination of amount due permitted only after all interested parties are joined in suit, 502; in computation a court may depart from principle of equality of shares of spouses in community property if necessary, 504; judgment must indicate fraction of wages payable, not specific monthly amount, 524; reduction permitted when child is on full maintenance by State or social organization, 522

Amnesty,
inapplicable to persons of great social danger, 135; procedural problems of, 131

Analogy (in civil law),
recognized as appropriate when civil code has gap, 468

Analogy (in criminal law),
currently inadmissible, 468; prior Soviet practice, 148-49

Arbitration,
as agency of production quality control, 26; compulsion to conclude contract, 249, 251, 263; history of, 243; restriction on transfer to private arbitration, 245; statute of 1974 on, 244

Arrest,
code on, 110; illegal arrest, 112

Artisans,
constitutional guarantee (1936) of, 186; *ibid* (1977), Appendix; statute of 1976 on, 101, 187; taxation of, 192; test cases, 189-90

Assembly: *see* **Civil rights**
Association: *see* **Civil rights**
Author's certificate: *see* **Patent**

B

Banks,
nationalization of (1917), 184; property of small depositors, 361

Bar: *see* **Legal profession**

Brezhnev, L.I.,
on civil rights, 86; on federation, 40; on goal of law, 9-10

Budgetary procedures,
generally, 210-11

C

Censorship,
as security measure, 85-6; law on, 101; supervision of printers and booksellers, 102

Child,
aged grandmother has right to support from grandchildren if investigation proves children's inability to pay, 523; change of surname after divorce is not subject to court's jurisdiction, 534; civil liability of, 539; conditions of employment, 536; custody of, 508; education labor colonies for male offenders, 548; establishing paternity, 514-15; evidence suitable to establish paternity, 534; gynecologist's testimony necessary to resolution of paternity dispute, 519; inspectorate created to prevent law violations by minors, 549; juvenile delinquency, 542; responsibility for rape, 551; lacks capacity to execute will unless married, 540; lacks capacity to sue, 539; legal capacity generally, 538; liability for harm caused by does not extend to grandmother not appointed guardian, 541; names of parents may not be expunged from birth records on loss of parental rights, 535; responsibility of nearly adult child for murder committed at his command by irresponsible minor, 551; right to support, 520; rights and responsibilities, history of, 512; State benefits to children of low-income

families, 521, 529, 533; status when born
out of wedlock, 513; statute of "social educators," 546; suit after divorce to invalidate paternity notation on birth certificate
of child born after divorce, 518; suspension
of sentence for a minor, 548; *see* also Adoption, Alimony, Crime, Guardianship, Labor
law

Civil law,
function of, 14

Civil procedure,
absence of necessary party, 143, 144; absence of necessary witness, 145; class approach, 134; contrast to social procedures,
136; fair trial, 143-45; history of, 132-36;
judgment signed by improper judge, 145;
procurator's participation in, 145; res judicata, 142; USSR Fundamental Principles
on, 137-40

Civil rights,
absence of bill of rights in 1923 USSR
Constitution, 83; bill of rights (1936) 86,
ibid. (1977) Appendix; class approach,
82-3; deprivation of citizenship: Allilueva,
153; Solzhenitsyn, 99; due process of civil
law, 132-46; due process of criminal law,
107-32; emigration, 104-06; expression,
96-104; history of in USSR, 81-6; manifesting indignation at collective farm general
meeting is not hooliganism, 284; movement, 94-6; religion, 90-4; representation,
88-90; trial of authors, 1966, 97; United
Nations covenants ratified, 85

Codes of law,
introduced in 1922, 6, 47; simplification
plans, 1927, 6; Stalin attacks simplification, 1930, 7

Collective bargaining,
history of, 298

Collective farm,
admission to membership: not automatic,
282, not conditional, 282; auxiliary plots
of members: size to be determined only by
general meeting, 283; civil code on household's personal ownership, 365; claim for
damages in event of reservoir flooding,
239; communist party decree on future
(1976) 288; constitution on land use, 197;
distinction between collective farm and
worker's household, 406; expulsion from,
283; history of, 194; inheritance in, 405;
model charter, 281, 371; statute on delivery
contract (1966) 285; suit for division of
member's dwelling and orchard, 372-73;
wage disputes of non-member employees,
284

Communes,
history of, 194

Communist Manifesto (1948),
on inheritance, 389; on property ownership, 183

Communist Party
Constitutional status of: (1936) 88, *ibid.*
(1977) Appendix; influence on judiciary,
67; on future of collective farm, 288; party
discipline does not release member from
responsibility, 266

Communist Party Congress,
XXII (1961) 11; XXIV (1971) 18; XXV
(1976) 9, 40; as guide to Soviet press on
law and order, 130

Comrade's court,
origin of, 1917, 16; proceedings in, 25-7;
relation to people's court, 27; statute of
1961, 22

Conflict of laws,
application of foreign law on marriage and
family, 510-11; code provisions on, 44-5;
law applicable to inheritance by foreigner,
400; practice of, 45; signature on application for right to inheritance to be certified
by Notary at applicant's domicile or place
of work, 410

Constitution of USSR (1936),
amendment of, 54; constitutional review
proposal, 53; distinctive characteristics,
54; supremacy of, 53

Constitution of USSR (1977) [Draft]
relevant provisions of, Appendix (full text
in vol. II)

Contract,
capacity of minors to contract, 538; computation of maximum permitted rental
for dwelling lease, 419; consequences of
failure to notarize dwelling sale, 420; criticism of contracts under capitalism, 415;
forfeiture under contract terms to be exacted with thought to delinquent's financial
situation, 434; forms, 553-56; gift contract,
423; history of, 414-15; illegality, 420; invalidity for mistake, 429; invalidity generally, 420; notarial function in certification of, 69-71, 418; purpose under socialism, 426; recovery of cost of defective goods,
432; remedies for breach, 430; recovery of
money for state as punishment for conclusion knowingly contrary to State's interests,
424; revocation of sale when dwelling purchaser fails to perform obligation to support seller for life, 433; suit for repayment
of loan, 418; suit to invalidate fictitious
contract, 426

INDEX

Contract of adhesion,
assignment of plot of land, 198; repair of private dwelling, 271

Contract, Collective farm,
delivery contract, 285

Contract, labor,
collective agreement, 304-05; personal employment, 308-10

Contract of Supply,
alteration of terms, 251; damages, 269; fault as necessary to liability for non-performance, 262-63; force majeure as defense to suit for breach, 257; impossibility, 252, 253, 255, 257; measure of damages, 253, 266, 267; model contract, 248; obligation to conclude enforced by State Arbitration, 249-51; philosophy of, 241-44; role in plan performance, 242, 264; sanctions for non-performance, 250, 252, 253, 256, 257, 258, 263

Cooperatives,
expulsion from, 204; garage coops, 297; gardening coops, 291-3; housing construction coops, 288-296; history of, 278-81; individual builders' coops, 294; philosophical base for, 278; prohibition of surcharge to enter historical coop restaurant, 224. *see* also Collective farms

Copyright,
criminal penalty for plagiarism, 345; fundamental principles of civil law on, 330; history of, 327-30; improper royalty payments, 333; inheritance of, 413; plagiarism, 333, 345; royalty for accepted but unused manuscript, 337; royalty for composite moving picture film incorporating previously produced film, 340; royalty for revision of dictionary, 338; royalty for work produced under employment plan, 340, 342; suit for prize money on dolls raising question of independent status of items conceived in single artistic style, 354; violation by publisher of integrity of author's manuscript, 335

Counsel,
refusal of, 121, 123; representation of conflicting interests by, 115, 121-24; right to choose specific person, 123; right to timely notice of trial, 123

Courts,
federal Supreme Court statute, 55,65; first decree of 1917, 56, 106; judges of 55, 63, 67, 68; People's Court Act of 1918, 107; second decree on of 1918, 106; structure and jurisdiction, 59; military, 66; third decree on of 1918, 107

Crime,
abuse of duties of guardianship, 534; anti-soviet libel, 97; appointment of "Soviet Educator" to perform parole function over minor, 546; assault with intent to rob, 97, 114; bribe taking, 21, 158; causes of, 159-60; criminally negligent storage of agricultural equipment, 237; divulging secret of adoption, 528; education labor colonies for minors, 554; exceeding authority, 20; falsification of reports on plan fulfillment, 213; forbidden trade, 101-02, 187-91; hooliganism, 155, 156; intentional homicide, 156, 164, 170, 171; intentional infliction of grave bodily harm causing death, 162-65; issuing fictitious invoices, 286; intentional infliction of light bodily injury, 175; juvenile delinquents, 541; malicious hooliganism, 171; marriage concluded under customary law, 484; negligent homicide, 165; private enterprising, 189, 190; racial slurs, 99; rape, 120, 121, 124, 125; resisting arrest, 112; speculation, 173, 190; swindling, 21; theft of personal property, 28; theft of socialist property, 131, 154, 156, 174; vagrancy, 95, 167, 325; violation of passport rules, 325; violation of transport operating rules resulting in death, 157, 166

Criminal law,
basic aid of 1919, 147; code of 1922, 147; code of 1926, 148; conflict of laws, 44-45; commitment to psychiatric hospital, 171; deprivation of citizenship, 99, 153; effect of aggravating circumstances, 154, 173; effect of mitigating circumstances, 153, 174, 257; effect of statute of limitations, 156, 166; federal fundamental principles, 149, 151; function of, 14; history of, 146-50; immunity of deputy to soviet, 176; insanity, generally, 171-73; intent, generally, 162-68; negligence, generally, 169-71; philosophical base of, 150; punishment, types of, 151-52; self-defense, 175-76

Criminal procedure,
absence of accused, 125; absence of key witness, 126; amnesty as bar to prosecution, 131; arrest, 110, 112; codification of in 1922, 108; confrontation of witnesses, 117; constitutional provisions on: (1936) 110, (1977) Appendix; departure from indictment, 124; discovery of new circumstances on appeal, 128; disqualification of judge, 127; elements of fair trial, 124-27; expert opinion, 118; history of, 106-09; increase in penalty on appeal, 127, 128;

judicial incompetence to set term of cure for alcoholism, 130; misjoinder of issues, 124; preliminary investigation, 76, 114-18; inquest, 110; presumption of innocence, 119-20; relation to social procedures, 129; right to counsel, 115, 121-24; right to interpreter, 115; right to notice of trial, 131; use of preliminary investigation's testimony at trial, 126

Culture,
confiscation of neglected cultural objects, 382; constitutional provision (1977) on, Appendix; regulation on protection of historical and cultural monuments, 377

Customary law,
attitudes toward, 47; conformity to customary law of marriage is crime, 484

Cybernetics (computers)
as planning aid, 211

D

Decedent's estate,
notarial administration of, 70

Defense attorney, *see* **Legal profession**

Definition of law,
by Lenin, 5; by A.Y. Vyshinsky, 7

Dictatorship of proletariat,
end of, 1961, 8

Detention, *see* **Arrest**

Dissent,
L.I. Brezhnev's assessment of, 86; Daniel and Siniavskii case, 97; Solzhenitsyn decree, 99; Soviet reaction to foreign comment on, 98

Divorce,
action for may not join suit for eviction from common home, 498; bank deposit in name of one spouse, 495; involving foreigners, 450; must be delayed until efforts at reconciliation have failed, 498

Drug abuse,
statute of 1974 on, 177

Dwelling,
authority of enterprise director to purchase from individual, 225; confiscation of for excessive rent, 381; confiscation for neglect, 202, 382; confiscation for use to gain non-labor income, 379; confiscation for violation of approved architectural plans, 385; eviction of tenant from, 380; illegal rental, 205; limitation on frequency of sale, 378; limitation on rent, 419; model contract for assignment of land use 198; ownership includes use of plot, 367; payment for demolished structures, 207; numerical limitation on ownership of, 378; right of released convict to regain when occupied by another, 385; right to ventilation cut off by neighbor, 368

E

Easement,
right to ventilation, 368

Economic law,
dispute over its existence, 243-44, 274-77

Edinolichniki,
as private homesteads, 194

Elections,
constitution on (1936), 88; nominating procedure, 89; results of, 90; statute on, 88

Emigration,
fees for, 104-05

Eminent domain, *see* **Land**

Evidence,
absense of necessary witnesses, 145; confiscation of material evidence, 156; confrontation of witnesses, 117; inadequate clarification of testimony, 114; to establish paternity, 517

Expert opinion,
requirement for, 118

Expression, *see* **Civil rights**

F

Family law,
bank deposit is not under community property regime unless marriage is registered, 490; community property regime applies to that part of dwelling built after marriage, but not to part built earlier, 488; constitutional provisions on: (1936) 472, (1977) Appendix; function of, 14, 472; history of, 469-72; philosophy of, 475; *see* also Child, Divorce, Guardianship, Marriage

Fault,
as necessary to civil liability, 252-63

Federation,
competency of, 40, 42; conflict of laws in, 44; constitutional provisions on, 41-2; history of, 35-8; Soviet as distinctive type of, 38-9

Force majeure,
as element of breach of contract, 257

Fraud,
in reporting of plan fulfillment, 231, 232

Freedom of movement,
criminal code on, 94; statute on domestic passports, 95; violation of passport regulations, 94-5

Function of law,
statutory definition of, 14-5

INDEX

G

Gift,
contract of, 423; form of, 555

Guarianship,
crime of abuse of duties of guardianship, 534; established only by Soviet's executive committee, 535; qualification of wards for state benefits, 533

H

Handicrafts, *see* **Artisans**

Hierarchy of law, *see* **Sources of law**

History,
of Soviet law, 5-8

I

Industry,
authority of enterprise director to appoint subordinate, 230; autonomy over enterprise housing for employees, 229; civil liability to creditors on liquidation, 239; civil liability for overdelivery by enterprise manager of perishable product to overfulfill plan and obtain bonuses, 236; constitutional provisions on administration: (1936) 212, *ibid.* (1977) Appendix; independence of enterprise director from local soviet influence on hiring policies, 224; general outline for administration, 221; managerial authority to purchase employee housing from individuals, 225; managerial "triangle," 220, 240; model charaters: for production combine, 222, for production enterprise, 224, for importexport combine, 226; nationalization of in 1920, 184; operating forms, history of, 218-21; partial denationalization in 1921, 219; penalty for fraudulent reporting, 231, 232; role of profit in stimulating production, 228; state production standards are not subject to reduction by local soviet, 231; statute on permanent production conference, 240

Inheritance,
adopted child loses right to inherit from natural parent, 403; by operation of law, 402-05; by will, 397; certification of foreigner's will, 400; collective farm household system, 405; creditor of decedent has right against heir of mortgaged dwelling, 411; denied to son who murdered father, 395; determination of "dependency" to qualify as heir, 402; forced heirship overcomes will's provisions, 400; form of application for, 558; heir must submit notarized certification of his signature on acceptance of inheritance, 410; heir who has not used decedent's dacha in dacha coop has no right to it, only to its value, 395; history of, 389; limitation on use of bequeathed property is not recognized, 399; of copyright, 413; probate and estate administration, 408; right of unregistered spouse, prior to 1944, 404; right to life insurance proceeds in event of simultaneous death of insured and beneficiary, 397; significance of, to socialism, 394; will of member of collective farm household is invalid as to common dwelling, 406; USSR fundamental principles on, 392

Insanity,
distinguished from severe mental agitation, 172; procedure for commitment to psychiatric hopsital, 171; release from criminal responsibility, 171

Inspection, *see* **People's control**

Insurance,
Ministerial order on property insurance of vehicles, 446; *see* also Social insurance

Interpretation of law,
role of Supreme Court, 55

Interpreter,
refusal of by defendant, 116; right to, 116

Intoxication,
as bar to driver's suit based on strict liability of automobile owner, 458; as basis for dismissal from job, 167, 321; as cause of crime, 162, 166, 176

J

Judge,
disciplining of, 68; election of, 63; independence of, 55, 67, 68; influence on, 67

Judicial decision,
as source of law, 48

Judicial function,
interpretation of law, 55

Judicial system,
fundamental principles on, 62-64

K

K.G.B.,
role as security police and investigators, 75 *see* also Special Boards

Khrushchev, N.S.,
on "withering away" of law, 16; proclaims end of dictatorship of the proletariat, 8

L

Labor law,
Church is subject to, 316; collective agree-

ment, 304; collective bargaining, history of, 297-298; constitutional provisions on: (1936) 299-300, (1977) Appendix; discharge: for systematic non-fulfillment of labor obligations, 323, for damage to truck while driving intoxicated, 321, for lack of suitability as educator, 320, on reduction of staff, 317, without labor union consent, 315, 318; duty of specialist to serve 3 years on assigned job after graduation, 537; duty to work, 324-27; employee responsible for store inventory bears burden of proof of no fault if goods are spoiled, 315; employment contract, 308-10; enforcement of constitutional right to work, 300-02; function of, 14; grievance procedure, 296, 310-11; model individual state employment contract, 309; permanent production conference, 240; philosophy of, 298; private employment, 310; protection of rights under, 310-12; liability of manager for failure to reinstate employee on court order, 238; right to job-connected housing is not lost on voluntary severance following failure of manager to provide appropriate job, 319; recovery of wages during period labor book was withheld after discharge, 323; statutory regulation of hours and wages, 296; transfer without worker's consent, 322; vacations: no court jurisdiction unless vacation was scheduled properly, 313; voluntary severance after employer financed study, 313; withholding cost of public baths from State farmers' pay is illegal, 322

Land ownership,
abolished in 1917-18, 193

Land use,
allocation of, 198-205, 208; by collective farm, 194; by individuals 197, 198, 201, 202, 203; by state enterprise, 197, 208; by state farms, 197; deprivation of, 203, 204, 208; fundamental principles of, 195; history of, 193-5; misuse, 198, 204; model contract for assignment of, 198; prohibition of allocation for private dwelling in urban communities (1963), 380; recovery of value of installations on arable land when flooded for reservoir, 239; relation to ownership of dwelling, 367; rent, 205; taking for state use (eminent domain) 206-07; notarial certification of, 70

Legal education,
as aspect of general education, 34

Legal profession,
activities of, 81; disciplining of, 73-4; ethics of, 73-4, 79; fees, 80; statute on advocates, 77; supervision of by Ministry of Justice, 77; utility of, 80

Legislative process,
agencies of, 55; constitutions on: (1936), 55, *ibid.* (1977), Appendix

Lenin, V.I.,
definition of law, 5; introduces New Economic Policy, 185; on absence of "private law" under socialism, 359; on civil rights, 84; on cooperatives, 278; on motive for federation, 35-6; on nature of law, 5; on "private" property, 361

Life estate,
illegal, but substitution permitted in form of contract of sale of dwelling on condition of lifetime support of seller, 433

Livestock,
limitations on personal ownership, 376; on feeding bread, 378

M

Marine insurance,
principles governing liability of insurance carrier, 259

Marriage,
action to invalidate, 145; claim of *de facto* marriage is inadequate to support demand for share in property acquired during relationship, 486; code provisions on, 480-83; conforming to customary law on is criminal, 482; *de facto* is recognized only if commenced before 1944 edict on registration and proved adequately, 483; invalid if entered into without intention to create family (fictitious) 496; invalid if participant lacked capacity to understand portent of act, 485; with foreigners, 509

Meetings,
licensing of, 102

Military tribunals,
statute on, 66

Ministries (industrial),
history of reorganizations, 210-11

Ministry of Justice,
statute on, 68

Mistake,
invalidity of contract because of, 429

Model contract,
for assignment of land use, 198; for repair of private dwelling, 271; of supply, 248

Mortgage,
mortgagee has right against heir of mortgagor to recover loan from dwelling, 411

INDEX

N

New Economic Policy (NEP),
expectation of draftsmen that law codes drafted for it were temporary, 6; denationalization of factories for, 185; impact on codification, 57; impact on administration of state industry, 241; phased out in 1928, 185; reasons for introduction of, 185; revision of Marxist property theory caused by, 362

Notary,
certification of minor's will permitted only if minor is married, 540; certification of foreigner's will, 400; mandamus unavailable to compel registration by if land use contract relates to use in urban community, 380; practice of, 70-1, 225; statute on, 69

O

Ownership: *see* **Property**

P

Parasites,
measures of control, 324-27

Passports,
statute on, 95; violations of regulations on, 94, 325

Patent,
criminal prosecution for infringement of, 345; dispute over co-authorship of invention, 346; dispute over priority of invention, 345, 347, 349; fundamental principles on, 343; history of, 327-30; stimulus under socialism, 328; suit for infringement, 349; suit for compensation for use of invention, 350, 351; *ibid.*, for rationalizing proposal, 352; suit for recognition of priority to rationalizing proposal, 353

People's control,
Order on (1968) 31

Periodical press,
extra-legal review of court decisions, 129

Philosophy of law,
contemporary, 8-15; early, 5-8; future prospects, 15-18

Planning,
agencies for, 209-12; constitutions on: (1936), 247, *ibid.* (1977), Appendix; civil liability for over-delivery of perishable goods to overfulfill plan, 236; introduction of, 185; prerequisites for, 184; procurator as auditor of violation of plan discipline, 215; production quality control, 216; profit as stimulation for performance of, 228; prosecution for falsification of reports on performance of, 213; philosophical basis for, 181; "plan as law," 242; role of contract in performance of, 242, 247-69

Political base of law,
basis for, 5, 7

Power of attorney,
forms for, 557

Preliminary investigation,
as stage of criminal procedure, 114; by public order agencies, 76

Press,
role in correcting judicial and procuratorial error, 129

Presumption of innocence,
principle and practice of, 119-20

Printing,
constitutional provision on, 87; prohibition of by private persons, 101

Private enterprise,
constitutions on: (1936), 87, 186, *ibid.* (1977), Appendix; handicraftsmen, 87, 101, 186-190

Private law,
declared by Lenin not to exist under socialism, 359

Private ownership,
history of restraints on, 183-85; of artisans' tools, 87, 101, 187; recognition of "personal" property, 187; theoretical basis for restraints on, 183

Probate: *see* **Inheritance**

Procuracy,
constitutional protection of: (1936), 72-4; *ibid.* (1977), Appendix; statute on, 72

Procurator,
as auditor for violation of planning discipline, 215, 231; as initiator of suit for harm to collective farm, 239; disavowal of civil suit by procurator does not keep citizen from continuing action, 145; protest against: adoption without mother's consent, 529; automatic admission of collective farmer's children to collective farm membership, 282; classification of shouts of indignation at collective farm meeting as hooliganism, 284; conditional admission to collective farm, 283; conviction in view of amnesty, 155; demanding fire-safety training as prerequisite to employment, 302; discrimination in employment, 300; error in classification of crime, 162, 165; excessive judgment against civil defendant because of judicial misinterpretation of facts, 424; exclusion of mortgagee's claim against heir because of delay in filing claim, 411; extension of work week, 303; fee for entering historic restaurant, 224; guardianship decree issued by improper authority, 535; hiring young specialist prior to expiration of 3 year work assignment, 537; holding

responsible for theft by minor a grandmother not appointed guardian, 541; illegal assignment of land, 202; illegal decision of collective farm general meeting, 198; illegal deduction from wages, 303; illegal disciplinary action, 313; illegal expulsion from collective farm, 283; illegal sale of dacha, 201; illegal withholding from state farmer's pay of public bath costs, 322; judicial assumption of jurisdiction over change of child's name after parent's divorce, 534; judicial deprivation of academic degree, 158; judicial error in determination of fictitiousness of contract, 426; judgment upholding claim based on community property regime when alleged marriage was not registered, 486; lengthening work day, 303; lenient sentence, 157; limitation on hiring, 301; local soviet intervention in enterprise employment policy, 224; order prohibiting export of household furnishings and motorcycles from Leningrad, 388; recognition of publishing contract when author plagiarized, 333; reduction in sentence on appeal, 173; reduction of auxiliary plots of collective farm members improperly, 283; refusal of court to hear paternity suit, 517; release of enterprise manager from civil liability, 236; suit brought by minor without parental participation, 539; violation by Ministry of enterprise director's right to appoint subordinates, 230; violation of legislation on production standards, 231; withdrawal by plaintiff of civil complaint, 74-5; suit for damage caused by negligently ignited fire in school, 442; suit for divorce on behalf of deceased husband on ground of fraud in marriage, 496; suit to void gift contrat, 423

Profit,
role in stimulating enterprise production, 228
Property,
confiscation for neglect, 202; compensation for appropriation of, 238; constitutional provisions on: (1936), 186, *ibid.* (1977), Appendix; fundamental principles of, 181-85
Property, community,
bank deposit in name of one spouse is declared property of both or of depositor depending on source of funds, 495; regime of is created only if persons living together register marriage, 490
Property, cooperative: *see* **Cooperatives**
Property, in land: *see* **Land**

Property, personal,
articles prohibited to ownership without special authorization, 374; confiscation of when acquired by criminal means, 384; constitutional provisions on: (1936), 365; *ibid.* (1977) Appendix; determination of "abandonment," 385; disposition of when abandoned, 383; firearms, 383; history of attitudes toward, 362; limitations by non-statutory means on ownership of, 399; livestock ownership, 376; protection against theft of, 28; regulation on protection of historical and cultural monuments, 376; requisition and confiscation, 383; socialist theory of, 363; use of to consume and to produce, 87, 101, 187; *see also* Dwelling, Inheritance
Property, State: *see* **Industry**
Public opinion,
influence on judges, 68
Public order agencies (police)
functions of, 76
Public self-administration,
aims of, 17-18; comrades' courts: statute on, 22, proceedings in, 25, relation to people's courts, 27; education for, 34; People's control as phase of, 31; social prosecutors and defenders as phase of, 32-3; third party umpires, 30; voluntary people's guards, 16-17, 19-22

R

Radio transmission,
licensing of, 103
Rape,
prosecution for, 120-25, 166; responsibility of minor for, 551
Recidivism,
prosecution of, 156; statistics on, 160
Regional Economic Councils (Sovnarkhoz),
Khrushchev's experiment with, 211
Religious worship,
constitutions on: (1936) 87, *ibid.* (1977) Appendix; criminal provisions on, 90-91; prosecution of clergy, 93; registration of religious associations, 91; State agencies of control, 92
Rent,
computation of maximum rental permitted on lease of dwelling, 419; desirability of as aid to land use planning, 195, 205; fear of rent as reawakening capitalist tendencies, 194; no rent from collective farms or State enterprises, 197

S

Security agencies,
structure and function of, 75

INDEX   621

Social insurance,
labor code on, 460; subrogation of agencies of to victim's claim against tort feasor, 461

Social prosecutors and defenders,
participants as, 32-33; purpose of, 32

Sources of law,
collective farm charter, 51; collective farm agreements, 51; constitution, 51; custom, 47; legislation, 53; judicial decisions, 48; labor unions, 51; legal precedent (when code has gap), 466; social consciousness, 5; theoretical approach to, 50

Soviet law,
as unique legal system, Preface; Brezhnev on, 9-10; goals set in fundamental principles, 14-15; history of, 5-8; Lenin's definition of, 5; philosophy of, 5-18

Soviets,
prohibition: against interference in state enterprise decisions on employment policies and employee housing, 224, 229; against relaxation of state production standards for goods supplied local consumers, 231; *see also* Arbitration, Elections

Special Boards,
abolished, 1953, 58; created, 1934, 57; role of, 84

Speech: *see* **Civil rights**

Stalin, J.V.,
attacks simplifiers of law, 16; denunciation of, 4; on civil rights, 84; on cooperatives, 278; on federation, 36

Statute of limitations,
effect of in expunging prior conviction, 156, 166; no bar to mortgagee's claim against heir of mortgaged dwelling, 411

T

Taxation,
copyright value and royalties are excluded from value of estate subject to tax, 414; on income, 192-3

Telephone,
loss of when misused, 103

Third party umpire,
role of, 30

Torts,
claims for supplemental medical expenses exceeding state free care, 446; code provision for strict liability of owner of source of increased danger applies also to operator under lease or Ministerial regulation, 453; comparative negligence, 442; employment related injuries, 459; fault may include failure of public transit enterprise to reroute buses around damaged street, 463; formula for determining value of damaged motor vehicle, 446; history of, 436-40; impact of social insurance on claims for, 459; insured plaintiff's recovery from thief, 444; judgment must consider financial status of tort feasor, 442, 450; liability for injury to rescuers, 466; liability of minor, 539; measure of damages is wages lost, 444; owner of motor vehicle is strictly liable, 450; philosophy of, 438; plaintiff bears burden of proof of causation, 457; released prisoner's right to damages for injury in prison, 461; rules for administrative procedures for satisfaction of employee's claims, 465; strict liability, 450-59; strict liability is avoided if victim is grossly negligent, 456; strict liability is mitigated if victim is grossly negligent, 454; strict liability is not avoided when car driver swerves to avoid negligent motorcycle driver and injures bystander, 455; strict liability of owner of vehicle driven by unauthorized driver, 451; strict liability of owner of vehicle when driver is intoxicated, 458

TOZ,
an early form of agricultural organization, 194

Vital statistics,
no right to expunge from birth records names of parents deprived of parental rights, 535; registration by ZAGS, 71; right to change child's surname, 534; social duties of ZAGS, 71

Voluntary people's guards,
organization and responsibility of, 16-17, 19-22

Vyshinsky, A.Y.,
interpretation of Lenin's definition of Soviet law, 7

Will,
Forms for, 558; minor lacks capacity to make will unless married, 540; notarial certification of, 70; suit to void for mental incompetence of testator, 143; *see also* Inheritance

ZAGS: *see* **Vital statistics**